THE
SEVEN STARS
COOKBOOK

HARRAH'S ENTERTAINMENT

PRESENTS

✦

THE
SEVEN STARS
COOKBOOK

RECIPES FROM WORLD-CLASS CASINO RESTAURANTS

EDITED AND INTRODUCED BY JOHN SCHLIMM
FOREWORD BY PAULA DEEN
PREFACE BY GARY W. LOVEMAN
PHOTOGRAPHS BY FRANKIE FRANKENY

CHRONICLE BOOKS
SAN FRANCISCO

ISBN: 978-0-8118- 7476-2

Library of Congress Cataloging-in-Publication Data
available under ISBN 978-0-8118-7475-5.

Manufactured in China.

Design by Public .

This book has been set in Akzidenz Grotesk and Vendetta.

10 9 8 7 6 5 4 3 2 1

For more information about
Harrah's Entertainment, Inc.,
visit www.harrahs.com

Chronicle Books LLC
680 Second Street
San Francisco, California 94107

www.chroniclebooks.com/custom

TO ALL THOSE WHO LOVE
TO EAT, LAUGH, AND LIVE LIFE TO THE FULLEST,
THIS BOOK IS FOR YOU.

FOREWORD
by Paula Deen 15

PREFACE
by Gary W. Loveman 18

INTRODUCTION
by John Schlimm 20

1
APPETIZERS

✦

Colors of Caviar   32
Restaurant Guy Savoy at Caesars Palace Las Vegas / Chef Guy Savoy

Peel & Eat Shrimp   35
Jimmy Buffett's Margaritaville at Flamingo Las Vegas / Chef Phil Klinkenberg

Besh Steak Oysters Casino   35
Besh Steak at Harrah's New Orleans / Chef John Besh

Baja Blue Black Bean Dip   36
Baja Blue Restaurant & Cantina at Harrah's Laughlin /
Executive Sous-Chef Jeremy Hughes

Bruschetta Pomodoro   36
Andreotti at Harrah's Reno / Chef Jason Harris

Fried Portobello Mushrooms   39
The Range Steakhouse & Bar at Tunica Roadhouse Casino & Hotel /
Chef de Cuisine Raymond Carter

Range Crab Cocktail   40
The Range Steakhouse at Harrah's St. Louis / Executive Chef Ray Leung

Jumbo Lump Crab Cakes   43
'37 at Harrah's Tunica / Executive Chef Steve Pairolero

Jack Binion's Premium Crab Cakes   44
Jack Binion's Steak House at Horseshoe Council Bluffs /
Executive Chef James Reber

Goat Cheese Truffled Baklava   46
BOA Steakhouse at The Forum Shops at Caesars Palace Las Vegas /
Chef Jose Aleman

Japanese Yellowtail Sashimi with Diced Chiles   47
Sushi Roku at The Forum Shops at Caesars Palace Las Vegas /
Chef Vernon Cardenas

Avocado Spring Rolls   48
Augustus Café at Caesars Windsor / Executive Chef Patrick McClary

Seared Scallops with Tempura Ramps & Roasted Corn Custard   50
Búzios Seafood Restaurant at Rio All-Suite Hotel & Casino /
Chef de Cuisine Trang Tran

CONTENTS

Seared Beef Tenderloin & Goat Cheese Salad   54
Augustus Café at Caesars Windsor / Executive Chef Patrick McClary

Tennessee Prosciutto & Warm Goat Cheese Salad with   57
Honey-Walnut Truffle Dressing
Magnolia, A Delta Grille at Horseshoe Tunica

Cucumber & Mint Salad   58
Harrah's Lake Tahoe & Harveys Lake Tahoe / Executive Chef Joe Wells

Fresh Market Potato Salad   58
Fresh Market Square Buffet at Harrah's Cherokee /
Executive Chef Keith Andreasen

Apple & Blood Orange Vinaigrette over Bibb   60
Lettuce & Watercress
Harrah's Joliet / Chef Peter Jeschke

Pecan Herbed Orzo Salad   62
Harrah's North Kansas City / Chef Roy Askren

Fennel, Endive & Arugula Salad   65
with a Citrus-Basil Vinaigrette & Parmesan Cheese Twists
Reflections Café at Harrah's Resort Atlantic City / Chef James Coombs

Garden Basket-Weave Salad   67
with Heirloom Tomatoes & Fresh Mozzarella
Harrah's Metropolis / Executive Chef Jon M. Kell

Fried Green Tomatoes   68
The Range Steakhouse & Bar at Tunica Roadhouse Casino & Hotel /
Executive Chef & Director of Food & Beverage Christopher J. Hencyk

Roasted Pepper Antipasto   72
Caesars Atlantic City / Chef de Cuisine John Mejlak

Fiore Tomato Caprese   74
Fiore at Harrah's Rincon Casino & Resort / Executive Chef Vesa Leppala

Leek, Sun-Dried Tomato, Shiitake Mushroom   79
& Champagne Soup
K-Paul's Louisiana Kitchen / Chef Paul Prudhomme

Grilled Shrimp Gazpacho   80
Reserve at Harrah's Joliet / Chef de Cuisine Tye Nielsen

Harrah's Steak House Creamy Five-Onion Soup   82
Harrah's Steak House at Harrah's Reno / Executive Chef Klaus Feyersinger

Wild Mushroom Chowder   84
Caesars Windsor / Executive Chef Patrick McClary

Pickles' Famous Mushroom-Barley Soup   87
Pickles at Bally's Atlantic City / Chef Rolf Bechtold

Seven Stars Split Pea Soup   87
Fresh Market Buffet at Harrah's North Kansas City / Chef Jeff Craig

Classic Gumbo   88
Harrah's Louisiana Downs / Executive Chef J. Ryan Gillespie

Gumbo   89
The Range Steakhouse & Bar at Tunica Roadhouse Casino & Hotel /
Executive Chef & Director of Food & Beverage Christopher J. Hencyk

New Orleans Gumbo   90
The Buffet at Harrah's at Harrah's New Orleans / Chef Hoyce Oatis

Beef & Onion Soup with Short Rib Croutons &   92
Five-Onion Salad
The Steakhouse at Harrah's Resort Atlantic City / Chef Richard Leadbetter

Chicken & Shrimp Jambalaya   93
French Quarter Buffet at Showboat Atlantic City /
Chef Todd Bannan & Chef Armando Cortes

Roasted Eggplant Soup   94
Waterfront Buffet at Harrah's Resort Atlantic City / Chef David Suscavage

Selu Turkey & Roasted Corn Soup   96
Selu Garden Café at Harrah's Cherokee / Executive Chef Keith Andreasen

Italian Meatball & Sausage Chili   98
Breakaway Café at Bally's Atlantic City /
Food Service Director Rolf J. Weithofer

4
SIDE DISHES

✦✦✦✦

Bradley Ogden's Blue Corn Muffins   103
Bradley Ogden at Caesars Palace Las Vegas / Chef Bradley Ogden

Paula Deen's Hoecakes   105
Paula Deen Buffet at Harrah's Tunica / Paula Deen &
Executive Sous-Chef Tammy Williams-Hansen

Mashed Sweet Potatoes   106
The Range Steakhouse at Harrah's North Kansas City /
Chef William Dworzan

Cauliflower Purée   106
Neros Steakhouse at Caesars Windsor / Chef Deron Lepore

Potatoes au Gratin   109
The Range Steakhouse at Harrah's North Kansas City / Chef Hugh Reno

Parmesan & Garlic Potato Chips   109
Bally's Steakhouse at Bally's Las Vegas / Chef Joshua Siergey

Tomato Confit Chips   110
Arturo's at Bally's Atlantic City / Chef Maurizio Dimarco

Crispy Fried Green Beans   110
Ah Sin at Paris Las Vegas / Chef Thierry Mai-Thanh

Buttermilk Potatoes   112
Harrah's Louisiana Downs / Executive Chef J. Ryan Gillespie

Sweet Iowa Creamed Corn   112
360 Steakhouse at Harrah's Council Bluffs /
Executive Chef Christopher Colello

Cauliflower Gratin   115
Le Village Buffet at Paris Las Vegas / Chef Steven Kisner

Patate Arrostite (Roasted Potatoes with Speck)   116
Polistina's Italian Ristorante at Harrah's Resort Atlantic City /
Chef Mike Laurenza

Garlic Bread Fingers   116
Mosaic at Harrah's Joliet / Chef Matthew E. Secko

Paula Deen's Cheese Biscuits   119
Paula Deen Buffet at Harrah's Tunica / Paula Deen &
Executive Sous-Chef Tammy Williams-Hansen

Sweet Potato & Raisin Pancakes   119
Harrah's Joliet / Executive Chef Scott D. LeCompte

5
BEEF + PORK

✦✦✦✦✦

Sage Steak   127
Sage Room Steak House at Harveys Lake Tahoe /
Executive Chef Joe Wells

The Best Steak in Kansas City   128
The Range Steakhouse at Harrah's North Kansas City /
Chefs Hugh Reno, Andy Sparks, Jeff Craig & William Dworzan

Grilled Citrus-Marinated Skirt Steak   130
with Saffron–Heirloom Tomato Salad
Rib & Chophouse at Showboat Atlantic City /
Restaurant Chef Edward Ledwon

Pan-Roasted Dry-Aged Rib-Eye Steak   132
with Fingerling Potatoes & Asparagus-Morel Ragout
VooDoo Steak & Lounge at Rio All-Suite Hotel & Casino /
Chef de Cuisine Honorio Mecinas

Steak au Poivre   134
Jack Binion's Steak House at Horseshoe Bossier City /
Executive Sous-Chef Robert Brooks

Grilled Bourbon Pork Chops   137
The Range Steakhouse at Harrah's Metropolis / Executive Chef Jon M. Kell

Veal Chops Portobello   139
Murano's at Harrah's Tunica / Executive Chef Steve Pairolero

Braised Short Rib Sliders   141
with Goat Cheese, Ricotta & Horseradish Gremolata
Preview Bar at Bally's Atlantic City /
Food Service Director Rolf J. Weithofer

Cajun Skillet Filets   143
360 Steakhouse at Harrah's Council Bluffs /
Executive Chef Christopher Colello

Applewood-Smoked Molasses & Five Peppercorn–Crusted   146
Pork Loin
Forest Buffet at Harrah's Lake Tahoe / Executive Chef Joe Wells

Ming's Glazed Chinese Pork Spareribs   148
Ming's Table at Harrah's Las Vegas / Chef Winston Chung

Black Forest Ham & Gruyère Cheese Feuilletées   151
Harrah's Lake Tahoe & Harveys Lake Tahoe / Executive Chef Joe Wells

Monte Cristo Sandwich   152
Bally's Atlantic City / Executive Sous-Chef Ron Ulczak

Smoked Baby Back Ribs   155
Toby Keith's I Love This Bar & Grill & The Range Steak House at Harrah's
North Kansas City / Toby Keith & Chef William Dworzan

6
POULTRY
✦✦✦✦✦✦

Chanterelle & Parmesan-Crusted Chicken   159
with Lemon-Basil Cream Sauce
Harrah's Steak House at Harrah's Reno / Chef Jeffrey Galick

Portobello Chicken Chardonnay   160
Harrah's Joliet / Executive Chef Scott D. LeCompte

Chicken Romano   163
Carvings Buffet at Harrah's Reno / Executive Chef Klaus Feyersinger

Toby Keith's Who's Your Daddy? Chicken Wings   164
Toby Keith's I Love This Bar & Grill at Harrah's North Kansas City /
Toby Keith & Chef William Dworzan

Cream of Cilantro Chicken   166
Caesars Atlantic City / Sous-Chef Steve Ortiz

Mediterranean Artichoke Chicken   168
The Range Steakhouse at Harrah's Laughlin /
Executive Sous-Chef Jeremy Hughes

Deep-Fried Turkey   173
Harrah's Louisiana Downs / Executive Chef J. Ryan Gillespie

Smoked Turkey & White Bean Casserole   174
with Herbed Crumb Topping
The Seven Stars Club at Harrah's Resort Atlantic City /
Chef William Scaffidi

7
PASTA
✦✦✦✦✦✦✦

Pennette alla Vodka   179
Rao's at Caesars Palace Las Vegas / Chef de Cuisine Carla Pellegrino

Black Pepper Fettuccine with Wild Mushrooms   180
Sage Room Steak House at Harveys Lake Tahoe /
Executive Chef Joe Wells

Steak & Blue Cheese Macaroni   182
Les Artistes Steakhouse at Paris Las Vegas /
Assistant Executive Chef Kurtess Mortensen

Mac & Cheese   185
Nero's at Caesars Palace Las Vegas / Executive Chef Eric Damidot

Ricotta Ravioli   186
Casa di Napoli at Showboat Atlantic City / Chef Georgeann Leaming

Signature Lasagna   187
Al Dente at Bally's Las Vegas / Chef Benoit Chobert

Ricotta Gnocchi   189
Grand Biloxi Casino, Hotel & Spa / Executive Chef Jason Carlisle

Cajun Seafood Pasta   190
Harrah's North Kansas City / Chef Roy Askren

8
FISH + SEAFOOD
✦✦✦✦✦✦✦✦

Blue Corn–Crusted Red Snapper with Warm Tomato Relish   196
Bobby Flay's Mesa Grill at Caesars Palace Las Vegas / Chef Bobby Flay

Peanut-Crusted Trout   198
Sycamores on the Creek at Harrah's Cherokee /
Executive Chef Keith Andreasen

Bronzed Fish with Jalapeño Tartar Sauce   200
K-Paul's Louisiana Kitchen / Chef Paul Prudhomme

Red Grouper with Stewed Tomatoes, Okra & Crawfish   203
Magnolia, A Delta Grille at Horseshoe Tunica

Pan-Roasted Halibut with Salsa Provençal   204
Fiore at Harrah's Rincon Casino & Resort / Executive Chef Vesa Leppala

Lemon Sole–Wrapped Asparagus with Orange-Citrus   205
Beurre Blanc
Sycamores on the Creek at Harrah's Cherokee / Sous-Chef Kevin Conrad

Blackened Mahi Mahi with Butternut Squash Polenta &   207
Grilled Asparagus
Oyster Bar at Penazzi at Harrah's Las Vegas / Chef Brian Fairhurst

Pacific Shutome Swordfish Chops   208
with Port Wine & Cherry Reduction
Reserve at Bally's Atlantic City / Chef Brian Annapolen

Parmesan-Crusted Orange Roughy   210
Embers at Imperial Palace / Chef Matthew Heppner

Phillips Clam Bake for Two   211
Phillips Seafood at The Pier Shops at Caesars Atlantic City /
Executive Chef Paul Drew

Barbecued Shrimp   213
Magnolia Buffet at Harrah's New Orleans / Chef Hoyce Oatis

Seared Scallops, Asparagus & Crabmeat   214
with Hollandaise Sauce & Potato Cakes
Voga at Flamingo Las Vegas / Executive Chef Christophe Doumergue

Seafood Risotto   217
Mosaic at Harrah's Joliet / Chef Matthew E. Secko

Crab & Eggplant Lasagna   219
Casa di Napoli at Showboat Atlantic City / Chef Georgeann Leaming

Lobster Mac Casserole   220
Jack Binion's Steakhouse at Horseshoe Southern Indiana /
Executive Sous-Chef Joshua Miragliotta

Grilled Shrimp Skewers   223
Eat Up! Buffet at Harrah's St. Louis / Executive Chef Ray Leung

P.E.I. Mussels in Magners Cider   223
Trinity Pub & Carvery at The Pier Shops at Caesars Atlantic City /
Chef Brian Perry

9
BREAKFAST BUFFET
✦✦✦✦✦✦✦✦✦

Boursin Cheese, Lobster & Cognac Omelet   227
Sterling Brunch at Bally's Steakhouse at Bally's Las Vegas /
Chef Eric Piston

Poached Eggs with Bacon-Potato Hash & Hollandaise Sauce   229
Harrah's Chester Casino & Racetrack / Executive Chef Sean Kinoshita

Bacon & Cream Cheese Frittata   230
with Roasted Red Pepper Hollandaise
The Rivercrest at Harrah's Metropolis / Executive Chef Jon M. Kell

Hazelnut Pancakes   232
Harrah's Joliet / Executive Chef Scott D. LeCompte

Coconut Crêpes with Caramelized Cinnamon Apples,   234
Chocolate Whipped Cream & Caramel Sauce
Harrah's Chester Casino & Racetrack / Executive Chef Sean Kinoshita

Flavor's Buffet Lemon Squares   236
Flavor's Buffet & The Range Steakhouse at Harrah's Las Vegas /
Executive Pastry Chef Amy Byro

10
VIP LUNCHEON
✦✦✦✦✦✦✦✦✦

APPETIZERS

Artisanal Cheese Platter   241
Nero's at Caesars Palace Las Vegas / Executive Chef Eric Damidot

Roast Beef with Creamy Horseradish & Blue Cheese Spread   242
Seven Sisters Lounge at Harrah's Cherokee / Chef Randy Phillips

Smoked Scallops with Cucumber–Red Pepper Salsa   244
Diamond Lounge at Harrah's Reno / Chef Stephen Tucker

Chef Rolf's VIP Finger Sandwiches   246
Bally's Atlantic City / Food Service Director Rolf J. Weithofer

Escargots Provençal   246
Le Provençal at Paris Las Vegas / Chef Robert Derwinski

Lobster & Crab Tarts   249
Banquet Kitchen at Harrah's Lake Tahoe & Harveys Lake Tahoe /
Chef Rick Maricle

Duck with Porcini Mushrooms   250
Penazzi at Harrah's Las Vegas / Chef George Alberto Tapia

MAIN DISHES

Pistachio-Encrusted Loin of Lamb   252
with Mint-Infused Rice & Port Wine Reduction
Harrah's Ak-Chin / Chef James Shewmake

Mahi Mahi & Grilled Shrimp with Black Beans & Mango   253
Seven Stars Lounge at Horseshoe Hammond / Chef Chris Basil

Mao Pao Tofu   254
Ah Sin at Paris Las Vegas / Chef Thierry Mai-Thanh

Crab-Stuffed Salmon Fillets   256
Harrah's North Kansas City / Sous-Chef Jerry Roxas

DESSERTS

Crème Brûlée in Tuile Cups   259
Grand Biloxi Casino, Hotel & Spa / Executive Chef Jason Carlisle

Chocolate-Coconut Cake   261
Payard Pâtisserie & Bistro at Caesars Palace Las Vegas /
Chef François Payard

11
DESSERTS

✦ ✦ ✦ ✦ ✦ ✦ ✦ ✦ ✦ ✦ ✦

Berry Napoleon 266
Andreotti at Harrah's Reno / Executive Pastry Chef Cathy Haynes

Paula Deen's Gooey Butter Cake 269
Paula Deen Buffet at Harrah's Tunica / Paula Deen &
Executive Sous-Chef Tammy Williams-Hansen

Pecan Praline Cheesecake 270
Fresh Market Buffet at Harrah's North Kansas City / Chef Anthony Galate

Friday's Peanut Butter Mousse Cups 272
Friday's Station Steak & Seafood Grill at Harrah's Lake Tahoe /
Executive Pastry Chef Christine Baird

Prosecco Gelée 273
Caesars Atlantic City / Executive Chef Keith Mitchell

Passion Fruit Crème Brûlée 273
Red Pearl at Bally's Atlantic City / Executive Pastry Chef Michael D'Angelo

Oreo Cookie Macaroons 274
Voga at Flamingo Las Vegas / Executive Pastry Chef Olivier Carlos

Chocolate Fun-Do 277
Voga at Flamingo Las Vegas / Executive Pastry Chef Olivier Carlos

Coconut Panna Cotta with Rum-Flamed Berries 278
The Pool at Harrah's Resort Atlantic City / Executive Chef Edward Daggers,
Atlantic City Country Club

Tiramisù 281
Jack Binion's Steak House at Horseshoe Hammond /
Assistant Pastry Chef Mary Therese Priesol

Seven Sisters Lounge Orange Cake 283
Seven Sisters Lounge at Harrah's Cherokee /
Executive Chef Keith Andreasen

Eiffel Tower Raspberry Soufflés 284
Eiffel Tower Restaurant at Paris Las Vegas / Chef Jean Joho

12
HIGH ROLLERS' BAR

✦ ✦ ✦ ✦ ✦ ✦ ✦ ✦ ✦ ✦ ✦

Absinthe Sazerac 289
Besh Steak at Harrah's New Orleans / Chef John Besh

German Chocolate Cake 289
VIP Lounges & High Limit Bar at Harrah's Lake Tahoe &
Harveys Lake Tahoe / Beverage Manager Charlotte Rogers

Sex in the Biggest Little City 290
Sapphire at Harrah's Reno / Assistant Beverage Manager Michael Bays

Oasis Tropical Treat 290
Harrah's Ak-Chin / Beverage Supervisor Joseph Caruso

Mint Julep 293
The Range Steakhouse at Harrah's Metropolis /
Executive Chef Jon M. Kell

Parrothead-Chef Margarita 293
Harrah's Cherokee / Executive Chef Keith Andreasen

Cucumber-Mint Splash 297
The Steakhouse at Harrah's Resort Atlantic City /
Beverage Operations Manager Joseph Crilley

Jewel of the Desert 297
Harrah's Ak-Chin / Beverage Supervisor Joseph Caruso

Goodnight Kiss Martini 298
Toby Keith's I Love This Bar & Grill at Harrah's Las Vegas / Toby Keith &
Entertainment Flair Bartender Rob Vergara

Invisible Hombre 298
Baja Blue Restaurant & Cantina at Harrah's Laughlin /
Beverage Manager Deborah Oram

Gulf Coast Bloody Mary 301
Grand Biloxi Casino, Hotel & Spa / Executive Chef Jason Carlisle

Harrahcane 302
Masquerade at Harrah's New Orleans /
Beverage Supervisor Rickie Deano

Cloud Nine 302
VooDoo Lounge at Harrah's North Kansas City / Manager Aaron Lund

Raspberry Lemonade 305
Carnaval Court Bar & Grill at Harrah's Las Vegas /
Entertainment Flair Bartender Joshua A. Nemerow

Tahoe Wabo: Lake Tahoe's Trademark Margarita 305
Sammy Hagar's The Cabo Wabo Cantina at Harveys Lake Tahoe /
Restaurant Manager Kevin McGirk

HARRAH'S ENTERTAINMENT
PROPERTIES 310

INDEX 312

REGISTERED TRADEMARKS 317

DESTINATION PHOTO INDEX 317

TABLE OF EQUIVALENTS 319

ACKNOWLEDGMENTS 320

Machine Pays Up To $1,200.⁰⁰ ALL OTHER WINS PAID BY ATTENDANT

Play 180 Credi

1¢
INSERT TICKET OR BILLS

est Dishes   Hey

Jackpot

PAULA DEEN

FOREWORD

by Paula Deen

I was delighted when my friends at Harrah's Entertainment asked me to write a foreword for *The Seven Stars Cookbook*. This is an area I know well. After all, between my husband, Michael, and me, we must have dined at nearly every restaurant they have.

I had the pleasure of partnering with this fine company when Harrah's approached me a couple years ago about opening a restaurant with them. I mean, we're talking about my two absolute favorite passions: food and casinos! Within a short time of working with the Harrah's team, I realized that these folks are the ultimate pros and the best in the industry. More importantly, they share my vision when it comes to our customers, and that's to provide people with entertainment and great food at a good value.

Together, in May 2008, we launched the Paula Deen Buffet at Harrah's Tunica. That was one of the proudest days of my life. After years of turning down offers to open more restaurants with other investors, I realized that I had waited for the perfect partner. These folks are the best of the best.

What impresses me most about Harrah's is their approach to business. Unlike most companies, they challenge their people to think outside the box. Take my restaurant, for instance. The inspired result of our collaboration, the Paula Deen Buffet Tunica, is a series of rooms that are exact replicas of my home in Savannah. Not only can folks taste my delicious Southern Fried Chicken and Biscuits, they can experience what it's like to visit my home. The setting is so real I have to stop myself from reaching into the cupboards to search for my things!

I love the Harrah's folks, and I know you will, too. It doesn't matter which location you visit, you can be sure that you will have the best in dining and entertainment. Whether you're looking for a casual quick bite or the ultimate in fine dining, Harrah's will bring it to the table.

That's where *The Seven Stars Cookbook* comes in. This is a beautiful collection of recipes created by Harrah's many talented chefs. This compilation not only allows you to bring your Seven Stars dining experience home, but it is also full of great entertaining ideas and tips from the pros. Y'all, take it from me—you will hit the jackpot with this book!

I know you will enjoy every delicious recipe. In the meantime, I hope I bump into you the next time I drop by a Harrah's.

Best dishes,

—Paula Deen

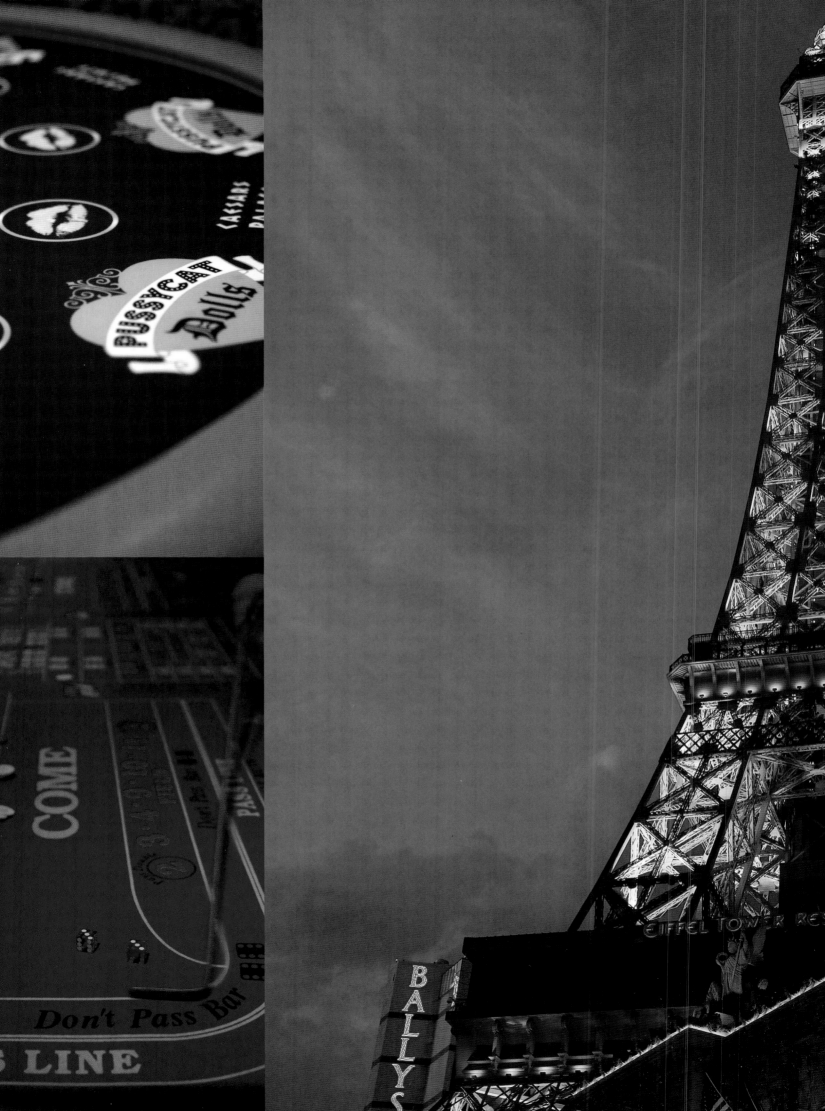

PREFACE

by Gary W. Loveman
CEO, Harrah's Entertainment, Inc.

Great food and first-class service have been hallmarks and sources of pride at Harrah's Entertainment for more than seventy-one years. Our founder, William F. Harrah, was a firm believer in rolling out the red carpet and offering wonderful amenities to augment the excitement of gaming and enhance the customer experience. It was his way of saying, "We're delighted to have you as our guest."

From a humble beginning in 1937 in Reno, Nevada, Harrah's has grown into the world's largest gaming-entertainment company, with fifty-three locations in seven countries. Our owned or managed facilities include thirty-six properties in the United States operating primarily under the Harrah's, Caesars, and Horseshoe brand names, as well as casinos in Canada, Uruguay, the United Kingdom, Egypt, and South Africa and a world-class golf course in Macau. Yet we still approach our business one guest at a time, offering personal touches to our loyal customers in a spirit Bill Harrah would admire.

One of Mr. Harrah's earliest efforts in the culinary realm was The Summit, a restaurant offering spectacular views of Lake Tahoe and its surrounding snow-capped mountains from atop Harrah's Tahoe, Nevada's first five-star resort. From the table settings to the menus to the quality of the food served, The Summit epitomized Bill Harrah's commitment to offering guests the best experience possible. That's still what we strive to do every day.

In 1992, a time when casino food service generally centered on all-you-can-eat buffets for $1.99, Caesars Palace invited celebrity chef Wolfgang Puck to open a branch of his famed Los Angeles restaurant, Spago, in The Forum Shops in Las Vegas. The guests loved his fresh, bold flavors. That was followed by the opening of Napa at the Rio Las Vegas, with vaunted French chef Jean-Louis Palladin at the helm. It, too, was a smash hit.

The larger result was an industry trend at casinos worldwide. Celebrity chefs became the next best thing since foie gras. Closer to home, for Harrah's customers, food took on a meaning greater than its traditional role as fuel for gaming. For all levels of Harrah's customers, dining blossomed into a source of pleasure all its own, one more way that friends and family could gather at our casinos and resorts to relax in the spirit of celebration.

That's what *The Seven Stars Cookbook* is all about. More than a memento of great times at Harrah's, it is a book to take home and use in your own kitchen. The recipes have been scaled for the home cook, and make it easy to bring the touch of Harrah's style to any gathering.

Glitz and glamour have always been part of the fun at Harrah's. Our guests have been thrilled by the vast array of celebrity entertainers who've performed in years past at our supper clubs and now in our concert venues. Frank Sinatra, Bill Cosby, Sammy Davis Jr., Cher, Elton John, Bette Midler, and Celine Dion are among the headliners who have and do grace our stages.

The corollary in the culinary world is our partnership with celebrity chefs who bring bold entertainment to the dining table. Among them are American icons Paula Deen, Bobby Flay, and Bradley Ogden, along with renowned French chef Guy Savoy and pastry chef François Payard. They've weighed in here with delicious dishes served in their establishments.

Among the recipes, you'll find treats from their acclaimed venues at Caesars Palace in Las Vegas, including Blue Corn–Crusted Red Snapper with Warm Tomato Relish from Bobby Flay's Mesa Grill, Colors of Caviar from Restaurant Guy Savoy, Blue Corn Muffins from Bradley Ogden, and a decadent Chocolate-Coconut Cake from Payard Pâtisserie & Bistro.

Southern cooking maven and Food Network star Paula Deen is represented by her down-home Cheese Biscuits, Gooey Butter Cake, and Hoecakes as served at Harrah's Tunica. And there are crowd-pleasing offerings from Sammy Hagar's The Cabo Wabo Cantina at Harveys Lake Tahoe, Toby Keith's I Love This Bar & Grill at Harrah's Las Vegas and Harrah's North Kansas City, and more.

But the heart and soul of restaurant experiences at our properties reside in the many chefs who have worked their way up through the ranks of our own kitchens. Growing such talent from within and making sure they have the support and inspiration required to do their best work is essential to the Harrah's Code of Commitment.

The Harrah's Code governs how we do business. It expresses our respect for Harrah's employees and our pledge to provide them with opportunities to build satisfying careers. It speaks to our commitment to our guests to promote responsible gaming. And it details our desire to help make every community in which we do business a vibrant place to live and work. In that spirit, across the Harrah's brand, our kitchens are manned by men and women who hold Bill Harrah's core principle of pleasing customers close to heart. They take their work very seriously. And, as you might expect, these folks play to win.

A great example is Michael D'Angelo, executive pastry chef at Bally's Atlantic City. He was awarded Pastry Chef of the Year 2009 by the Professional Chefs Association of South Jersey. In this cookbook, you'll find his recipe for Passion Fruit Crème Brûlée. Another is Tammy Williams-Hansen, executive sous-chef at Harrah's Tunica, who was awarded Chef of the Year 2008 by the American Culinary Federation, Greater Memphis Chapter. Her recipes in collaboration with Paula Deen from the Paula Deen Buffet throughout this book include Paula Deen's Hoecakes, Paula Deen's Cheese Biscuits, and Paula Deen's Gooey Butter Cake.

William Becker, vice president of food & beverage at Rio All-Suite Hotel & Casino, was the team captain for Team Las Vegas at the 2004 Culinary Olympics in Erfurt, Germany, where he won three silver medals. Be sure to check out his Top 10 List for the pots and pans every kitchen should have. And Carnaval Court at Harrah's Las Vegas employs more champion entertainment flair bartenders than any other place on the Las Vegas Strip.

Many of the recipes in *The Seven Stars Cookbook* are for the dishes our guests love best. Peel & Eat Shrimp from Jimmy Buffett's Margaritaville, Crab Cakes from Jack Binion's Steak House at Horseshoe Council Bluffs, Wild Mushroom Chowder from Caesars Windsor, and Pecan Praline Cheescake from Fresh Market Buffet at Harrah's North Kansas City give you a glimpse of the pleasures that await you at every Harrah's property.

You'll also find a chapter on cocktails, with exemplars drawn from our casinos across the United States. Any one of them is sure to liven up your next party. From haute cuisine to down-home cooking, Harrah's has something for everyone.

We're very proud of this cookbook. It is a wonderful testament to the talent and dedication of our culinary professionals. A sincere thank-you is due every member of Harrah's kitchen brigades around the world and all who contributed to the book. It is a great pleasure to work with you every day.

To our guests, we're happy to share the secrets of our kitchens with you and to help you bring the fun of Harrah's home with you. Enjoy! Even more, we look forward to seeing you on your next visit with us. Now, if you'll excuse me, I'm off to whip up a batch of P.E.I. Mussels in Magners Cider from Trinity Pub & Carvery at The Pier Shops at Caesars Atlantic City. Care to join me?

—Gary W. Loveman

INTRODUCTION

by John Schlimm

The first time I saw a casino was at age twelve, when my mother and grandparents took me to Atlantic City. I remember chewing taffy amidst the salty breeze and crashing waves of the ocean as the iconic wind-battered boardwalk ran off ahead of me. I was flanked on one side by the hot sand and waving grass, while flashy, towering edifices touched the blue sky on the other side of me. It was like a surreal landscape straight out of some fantastic fairy tale.

Although I wasn't allowed on the casino floor, my mother and I walked into the grand lobby of one casino to wait there for my grandparents, great aunts, and cousins, who were inside trying their hand at courting Lady Luck. I can still see the plush staircase rising up in front of me while my mother and I sat on a nearby bench. We were surrounded by a kaleidoscope of rich reds, purples, silvers, and golds. There were ornate chandeliers and shards of mirrors that sparkled like a million captured stars, all igniting my wide-eyed imagination. I can still hear the jovial *ching-ching-ching-clang-clang-clang-ding-ding-ding-ding* followed by laughter and cheers that echoed from inside the cavernous casino floor, heralding the latest jackpot winner.

As a little kid from a small rural town, I had, indeed, just walked into a bona fide fantasyland. And what I walked away with that day so long ago was something I've always carried in my heart. It was a taste of the authentic glamour and excitement that only a casino can induce; an indoctrination into true fabulousness that dates back to the era of the Rat Pack and other Old Hollywood types, and even a few swanky gangsters, who interjected their imitable sophistication and star power up and down the Vegas Strip.

Every casino, whether on the two coasts or tucked away in the heartland and desert, is an allusion to all those legendary luminaries. Their colorful sense of style and zest for life provide the true, underlying prologue to our story herein, reminding us what it really means to possess elegance and to live life to the absolute fullest with laughter and adventure. Little did I know back then that my first visit to that casino was a mere prologue to my life and this book as well.

The next time I found myself inside a casino, it was on a warm spring evening, and I was standing alone quietly in a back hallway just off the large commercial kitchen at Harrah's North Kansas City. Chefs and waiters buzzed around me, carrying trays of Blue Cheese Dip and crackers, Blazing Hot Chicken Wings, Onion Rings, and Beach Party Punch. A thin head mike hugged my head and cheek, coming to rest comfortably near my mouth. It was connected to a sound crew I'd never see.

When I peeked out through a crack in the door, I could watch the large banquet hall on the other side without being seen myself. At the front was an enormous stage, erected just for the occasion and filled with lush greenery as a backdrop and a well-prepped stainless-steel table. On either side were cinema-size movie screens. At the back of the room on a dais, there was a film crew with a large camera, and another camera was suspended above the main stage for aerial closeup shots. The cameras would record what was about to happen and project the images onto the screens so the guests in the back could see it all, larger than life.

The middle of the room was filled with hundreds of people, talking, laughing, and eating. Long buffet tables, set with shiny platters and elaborate chafing dishes, ran alongside the walls, framing the room.

After several minutes, I heard my name introduced from onstage by the emcee. The door was opened, and I strode through, smiling and waving, and hoping I wouldn't stumble up the five or so steps onto the stage. Applause thundered from the guests, now shadowed as the bright lights exploded in front of me, bathing both me and the stage. For a moment in time, I got to play rock star. I was once more walking into that fairy tale I had glimpsed many years earlier, only this time it was the culmination of many years of hard work and dreaming combined with the pure adrenaline rush that only Harrah's Entertainment can provide.

Almost three decades after I sat in awe with my mother on a bench in that Atlantic City casino, I was now launching the national Harrah's Entertainment tour for my latest book at the time, *The Ultimate Beer Lover's Cookbook.* From that stage in North Kansas City, I would go on to crisscross the country, visiting Harrah's Entertainment properties on what seemed akin to a magic carpet ride. And the best part is, I was able to take everyone with me.

Along the way, I met thousands of my fellow food (and beer) lovers, and I got to feast on some of the best dishes prepared by some of the world's top chefs, all in residence at the Harrah's Entertainment properties. In North Kansas City, I savored the award-winning Best Steak in Kansas City and Toby Keith's Who's Your Daddy? Chicken Wings. At Harrah's Tunica near Memphis, I enjoyed Jumbo Lump Crab Cakes from '37, and Veal Chops Portobello from Murano's, and I went absolutely crazy for Paula Deen Buffet, which is a replica of Paula's home in Savannah. One night I ate in her pantry, another night in her dining room, and I devoured her Gooey Butter Cake (which can even do its own Elvis impersonation—see page 269) on her screened-in porch on my third night at the property. In Lake Tahoe, the chefs at Harrah's and Harveys introduced me to their delicious Cucumber & Mint Salad and the Forest Buffet's Applewood-Smoked Molasses & Five Peppercorn–Crusted Pork Loin.

At Harrah's Joliet outside Chicago, I dined on Grilled Shrimp Gazpacho at Reserve. My stop at Harrah's Rincon Casino & Resort, north of San Diego, gave me the chance to dive into the decadence of Fiore Tomato Caprese and many other outstanding dishes. Finally, at Bally's in Atlantic City, where my journey had begun as a child, I had Pickles' Famous Mushroom-Barley Soup and Braised Short Rib Sliders with Goat Cheese, Ricotta & Horseradish Gremolata. And this was all just for starters.

At each Harrah's Entertainment property I visited, I made a point of exploring every restaurant on-site, from the wonderful cafés, delis, and endless signature buffets just off the casino floors to the higher-end restaurants that have become regular hangouts among Seven Stars guests, celebrities, and other discerning foodies. After doing a show and visiting with the hundreds of new friends who were in the audience, I would often saunter alone through the rows of slot machines and game tables and then dine, savoring every moment and slowly digesting the marvelous spectacle going on around me.

My private tour of all these culinary gems from coast to coast quickly sparked the inspiration for *The Seven Stars Cookbook.* With each bite, I realized more and more that I had discovered an untapped gold mine of talent unparalleled anywhere else on the planet. While Harrah's Entertainment is the largest gaming company in the world, I soon came to appreciate what others had known for years, that it has now also become a mecca for food connoisseurs, who are as interested in hitting a jackpot on their plates as they are striking it rich at the slots. Indeed, today, this company started by the visionary William F. Harrah in 1937 is the ultimate purveyor of entertainment and luxury in all its many forms, not least of which is fine dining. I became determined to give the many new friends I had met on my *Ultimate Beer Lover's* book tour as well as the millions of other Harrah's Entertainment guests and food lovers everywhere the opportunity to bring this same eloquence and artful dining into their own homes and parties.

During the two years I compiled and edited this cookbook, I had the honor of working with the executive chefs at each Harrah's Entertainment property across the United States and in Canada, and the dozens of other chefs and staff members who make sure every bite their guests take is a memorable experience. Consummate professionals and artisans, these men and women know full well how to rock the kitchen!

What has emerged from this unprecedented partnership between an author and a dream team of chefs is a collection of recipes that not only promises to satisfy your hunger for the good life, but that also encapsulates the vibe and culinary heritage of who we are as a people. These recipes are pure poetry for the palate and the spirit.

On the following pages, you will find food and drinks that celebrate and unite our regional diversity in one glowing tapestry. You'll revel in the classic gumbos from Harrah's Louisiana Downs and Harrah's New Orleans; Fried Green Tomatoes from Tunica Roadhouse Casino & Hotel; Sweet Iowa Creamed Corn from Harrah's Council Bluffs; Peanut-Crusted Trout from Harrah's Cherokee; Clam Bake for Two from Phillips Seafood at The Pier Shops at Caesars Atlantic City; Red Grouper with Stewed Tomatoes, Okra & Crawfish from Horseshoe Tunica; and cocktails such as Sex in the Biggest Little City from Harrah's Reno, Mint Julep from Harrah's Metropolis, Gulf Coast Bloody Mary from Grand Biloxi Casino, Hotel & Spa, and Jewel of the Desert from Harrah's Ak-Chin.

I also sought to transform *The Seven Stars Cookbook* into every host's and hostess's secret weapon. Using this book as your new entertaining bible, you can now bring a Seven Stars flair to any meal or event, big or small, outside or inside, all to resounding effect.

Imagine your guests discovering your dinner or buffet table filled with an opulent Vegas smorgasbord: Colors of Caviar from Restaurant Guy Savoy at Caesars Palace Las Vegas; Peel & Eat Shrimp from Jimmy Buffett's Margaritaville at Flamingo Las Vegas; Blue Corn Muffins from Bradley Ogden at Caesars Palace Las Vegas; Seared Scallops with Tempura Ramps & Roasted Corn Custard from Búzios Seafood Restaurant at Rio All-Suite Hotel & Casino; Blue Corn–Crusted Red Snapper with Warm Tomato Relish from Bobby Flay's Mesa Grill at Caesars Palace Las Vegas; Parmesan-Crusted Orange Roughy from Embers at Imperial Palace; Eiffel Tower Raspberry Soufflés from the Eiffel Tower Restaurant at Paris Las Vegas; and Chocolate-Coconut Cake from Payard Pâtisserie & Bistro, also at Caesars Palace Las Vegas.

Or, how about dazzling your weekend guests with a first-class breakfast spread, boasting Boursin Cheese, Lobster & Cognac Omelets from Sterling Brunch at Bally's Steakhouse at Bally's Las Vegas; Poached Eggs with Bacon-Potato Hash & Hollandaise Sauce from Harrah's Chester Casino & Racetrack; and other selections from the Breakfast Buffet chapter? And nothing makes a more powerful statement, whether for business or for ladies and gentlemen who lunch, than selections from the VIP Luncheon menu, such as Duck with Porcini Mushrooms from Penazzi at Harrah's Las Vegas and Mahi Mahi & Grilled Shrimp with Black Beans & Mango from Seven Stars Lounge at Horseshoe Hammond.

However, if you're more the stay-at-home type, *The Seven Stars Cookbook* has the ultimate comfort food just for you. After all, at its core, this collection is all about treating you and your guests to the absolute best this life has to offer. Therefore, never hesitate to pamper yourself with Baja Blue Black Bean Dip from Baja Blue Restaurant & Cantina at Harrah's Laughlin; Leek, Sun-Dried Tomato, Shiitake Mushroom & Champagne Soup from Chef Paul Prudhomme's K-Paul's Louisiana Kitchen; the Range Crab Cocktail from The Range Steakhouse at Harrah's St. Louis; Premium Crab Cakes from Jack Binion's Steak House at Horseshoe Council Bluffs; Wild Mushroom Chowder from Caesars Windsor; Lobster Mac Casserole from Jack Binion's Steakhouse at Horseshoe Southern Indiana; Besh Steak Oysters Casino from Besh Steak at Harrah's New Orleans; Steak au Poivre from Jack Binion's Steak House at Horseshoe Bossier City; Ricotta Ravioli from Casa di

Napoli at Showboat Atlantic City; and Coconut Panna Cotta with Rum-Flamed Berries from The Pool at Harrah's Resort Atlantic City; topping it all off with an irresistible cocktail from the High Roller's Bar chapter, such as the star-studded Tahoe Wabo: Lake Tahoe's Trademark Margarita from Sammy Hagar's The Cabo Wabo Cantina at Harveys Lake Tahoe. You deserve every bite and sip of it.

There is also practicality amidst the scrumptious treasures in *The Seven Stars Cookbook.* More than thirty-five of Harrah's Entertainment's top chefs share their expertise in a series of Top 10 lists woven throughout the book. They advise, muse, and educate us on topics ranging from the ingredients and utensils every kitchen should always have on hand to choosing the best meat, fish, seafood, fruits, and vegetables and incorporating color, seasonality, and regional flair into your meals. And one of Harrah's Entertainment's premiere sommeliers serves as your private guide to pairing both wine and beer with food.

While epic in its creation and breadth, to say this book has been a labor of love for myself and the hundreds of chefs and other employees who have worked tirelessly to bring Harrah's Entertainment's unique brand of Seven Stars entertaining and dining into your kitchen would be a gross understatement. It has been that and so much more. For me, *The Seven Stars Cookbook* has been another opportunity to reach out my hand and take hold of yours and those of our fellow foodies who long for the perfect meal, exhilarating adventure, and laughter and to take you all along on that magic carpet ride with me once more.

So please join me now for this unforgettable journey that will allow your palate to crisscross the country and encounter some of the most visionary chefs and some of the most enlightened culinary masterpieces of our time. In doing so, I hope you will find your way through this book time and again over the years with the same starry-eyed enthusiasm you experienced when you, too, stepped into a casino for the first time and discovered a whole new world of possibilities awaiting your arrival.

Rock the kitchen!

—John Schlimm

TOP 10 TIPS
FOR PLANNING A CREATIVE MENU

BALLY'S ATLANTIC CITY

Use the following tips to prepare for your next dinner party:

1 Food:

Choose the freshest foods available, from local farms, butchers, fish markets, or produce and gourmet markets. Look for those that are seasonal, unique, original, and have a story line, such as fresh-picked blueberries, sweet corn from New Jersey, vine-ripened tomatoes.

To decide on what to cook, ask yourself the following questions:

+ Who are my guests?

+ Where do they come from?

+ Are they into trying new foods?

+ Are they willing to have their food horizons broadened? (If the answer to this one is yes, then that's when it gets fun!)

2 Wording:

For the menu cards on your table, what you write is what you should eat. It's that simple! I love text that is clean and gives information on the food, such as origin, breed, season, age, etc. Your words should entice the palate and give a sense of comfort.

I am a firm believer that when you go to a restaurant and read through the menu, there should be at least one description there that will have you salivating. That's good writing.

3 Wine pairings:

There are no more rules! Wines are so complex these days that they have the character to stand up to any food combination, including those with flavors that are not dominant, such as tomatoes and sweet potatoes, and those with intense flavors, such as yuzu fruit or porcini mushrooms.

When pairing, be imaginative and be daring! California red table wine with sea urchin—why not?! Wine research is much easier with the Internet. Searching online will help you to find out what type of grape is used in a particular wine, which, in turn, will help you decide how daring you can be with flavors.

4 Creativity:

One of the most difficult things to teach anyone is creativity. In cooking, that means taking certain ingredients and seeing what evolves.

Flavor profiles play a large part in culinary creativity. Think about the ingredients you are using for your menu. However, the bottom line is Try! Try! Try! You may be surprised. I always am!

5 *Mise en place*:

French for "putting in place," *mise en place* refers to preparing and assembling all the necessary ingredients and equipment for cooking a dish before you begin. It includes not just physical objects, but also a knowledge of your ingredients and how to use them. This is a key tool to success in menu creativity.

6 Texture:

Food textures can be described as silky, crunchy, slimy, crispy, clean, spicy, soft, chewy, and so on. Your mouth seeks texture before it begins to define taste. Combining textures is one of the secrets to cooking interesting food.

7   Aroma and taste:

Like texture, aroma and taste are both very important. Aroma, of course, is the fragrance of the food, while taste is the mixture of flavors from all the ingredients used in a dish.

8   Contrast:

Contrast is the best way to achieve a sense of balance in a dish. A balance of tastes and textures is necessary to create memorable food.

9   Seasonality/origin:

In the culinary world, every season brings new gifts for the kitchen. For example, you can enjoy white asparagus in spring, Jersey tomatoes and corn during the summer, fall's abundance of root vegetables and wild mushrooms, and blood oranges in winter. And don't forget great oysters in all months ending in *r*.

Although many foods can be found in the markets year-round, sourced from different parts of the world, it's the foods you find in the backyards, farmers' markets, and local grocery stores that are best. Chef Alfred Portale says chefs have a twelve-season year, not a four-season one.

10   Guests:

Your table should be surrounded by family, friends, and colleagues who appreciate your passion for food and fun, because at the end of the day that is what it is all about!

++

Love, food, and wine—who needs more?
Guten appetit.

1

APPETIZERS

COLORS OF CAVIAR

RESTAURANT GUY SAVOY AT CAESARS PALACE LAS VEGAS
CHEF GUY SAVOY

Restaurant Guy Savoy at Caesars Palace Las Vegas has garnered numerous accolades, including two Michelin stars and the AAA Five Diamond Award. In doing so, famed French chef Guy Savoy's U.S. endeavor has set new standards for a fine-dining atmosphere. Now you can bring a little of Guy Savoy to your kitchen with his indulgent Colors of Caviar, a layered dish that will make you and your guests feel instantly transported to the City of Light.

CAVIAR VINAIGRETTE

½ sheet plain gelatin

1 cup very cold water

1 cup Sherry Vinaigrette
(see recipe facing page)

⅓ cup hackleback
(American sturgeon) caviar

Sea salt

CAVIAR CRÈME FRAÎCHE

½ sheet gelatin

1 cup very cold water

1¾ cups crème fraîche

⅓ cup hackleback caviar

Sea salt

CAVIAR SABAYON

1¼ cups haricots verts
(French green beans), trimmed

6 egg yolks

⅓ cup water

Salt

¼ cup golden osetra caviar

15 tablespoons golden osetra
caviar for garnish

SERVES 15

For the caviar vinaigrette: In a medium stainless-steel bowl, soak the gelatin in the cold water until it has softened, about 5 minutes. Drain the gelatin and add the Sherry Vinaigrette. Set the vinaigrette mixture over a saucepan with 2 inches of warm water. Stir until the gelatin dissolves and then remove from the heat. Add the caviar and blend with an immersion blender until most of the individual eggs are broken up and the mixture has turned a light gray color. Season with sea salt.

Spoon 2 tablespoons of the mixture into each *verrine* glass (a clear, cylindrical glass for layered desserts) or drinking glass. Gently tap each glass on a towel set on the work surface until the vinaigrette is evenly distributed. Refrigerate the glasses for at least 20 minutes in order to set.

For the caviar crème fraîche: In a medium stainless-steel bowl, soak the gelatin in the cold water until softened, about 5 minutes. Drain the gelatin and add the crème fraîche. Set the bowl over a saucepan with 2 inches of barely simmering water. Stir until the gelatin dissolves; remove from the heat. Gently fold in the caviar, season with sea salt, and transfer to a clean bowl.

Put 2 tablespoons caviar crème fraîche on top of the caviar vinaigrette in each glass and gently tap until it is evenly distributed. Refrigerate the glasses for at least 20 minutes to set.

For the caviar sabayon: In a large pot of salted boiling water, cook the beans until very tender, about 6 minutes. Transfer to a bowl of ice water to cool. Drain and coarsely chop the beans. In a blender, purée the beans until smooth. Transfer the purée to a pastry bag and set aside.

In a medium bowl set over a saucepan of 2 inches of barely simmering water, combine the egg yolks and water. Whisk vigorously, incorporating as much air as possible, until the mixture increases by at least 4 times the original volume. Continue to whisk until the sabayon is warm and forms a thick ribbon on the surface when the spoon is lifted. Season lightly with salt and carefully fold in the ¼ cup caviar.

To finish the dish, remove the glasses from the refrigerator and bring to room temperature. Carefully squeeze 2 tablespoons of the haricot vert purée into each glass. Gently tap the glasses until the purée is evenly distributed. Spread 1 tablespoon of the golden osetra caviar on top of the purée in each glass. Top each glass with a dollop of the sabayon. Serve with a small mother-of-pearl caviar spoon.

SHERRY VINAIGRETTE

¼ cup Dijon mustard
¼ cup sherry vinegar
1 egg yolk
2½ cups grapeseed oil
Salt and freshly ground white pepper

In a small bowl, whisk together the mustard, vinegar, and egg yolk. Gradually whisk in the oil in a thin stream to create an emulsion. Season with salt and white pepper.

MAKES ABOUT 3 CUPS

PEEL & EAT SHRIMP

JIMMY BUFFETT'S MARGARITAVILLE AT FLAMINGO LAS VEGAS
CHEF PHIL KLINKENBERG

Iconic singer Jimmy Buffett brings his island-hopping adventures and spirited rhythm for life to his Island-themed restaurant, Jimmy Buffett's Margaritaville, at Flamingo Las Vegas. Chef Phil Klinkenberg explains, "Jimmy Buffett's Peel & Eat Shrimp is an original Margaritaville recipe dating back to our first menu. For twenty-plus years it has been a favorite." In this recipe, everyone's favorite beverage, beer, is matched with everyone's favorite seafood, shrimp, in a delicious love fest that will turn you and your guests into the ultimate beach bums. Sand not included.

6 bottles Land Shark lager beer

2 teaspoons salt

¼ cup Old Bay Seasoning

12 lemons, halved

3½ pounds medium shrimp in the shell, preferably Key West pink shrimp

Cocktail sauce for serving

SERVES 8 TO 10

Fill a large pan half full with ice and set aside. In a large saucepan, combine the beer, salt, and Old Bay Seasoning. Squeeze the lemons into the pan and then add the lemon halves. Bring the beer mixture to a boil, add the shrimp, and cook for 1 minute. Turn off the heat and let the shrimp steep for 3 minutes. Drain the shrimp and empty them onto the ice; let cool, then drain again. Serve at once or cover and refrigerate. Serve with a favorite cocktail sauce.

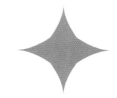

BESH STEAK
OYSTERS CASINO

BESH STEAK AT HARRAH'S NEW ORLEANS
CHEF JOHN BESH

From one of the most celebrated chefs in America, John Besh, comes one of the favorite appetizers, a brilliant reimagining of the popular oysters Rockefeller, at his signature Besh Steak restaurant at Harrah's New Orleans. As is evidenced by Besh Steak Oysters Casino, the former U.S. Marine turned award-winning chef is dedicated to the "culinary riches of Louisiana, preserving and promoting ingredients, techniques, and heritage one mouth-watering dish at a time." Serve these on a bed of rock salt to hold the oysters in place.

1 cup (2 sticks) unsalted butter

1½ cups diced bacon

1½ cups minced shallots

¼ cup minced garlic

Pinch cayenne pepper

1 cup all-purpose flour

2 cups oyster liquor or water

½ cup grated Parmesan cheese

1 cup minced fresh flat-leaf parsley

8 ounces fresh lump crabmeat, picked over for shell

1 dozen oysters on the half shell

Kosher salt

Dry bread crumbs for sprinkling

SERVES 2

Preheat the oven to 350°F. In a heavy, medium saucepan, melt the butter over medium heat. Add the bacon, shallots, garlic, and cayenne and sauté for 5 minutes. Stir in the flour and cook, stirring, for 3 minutes; do not brown. Add the oyster liquor and cheese and cook, stirring occasionally, for 10 minutes. Remove from heat and stir in the parsley. Gently fold in the crab-meat. Remove from the heat, spread the mixture out on a baking sheet, and let cool. Place the oysters on a small jellyroll pan. Spoon 2 tablespoons of the crab mixture onto each oyster and spread the mixture evenly over the oyster. Sprinkle lightly with salt and bread crumbs. Bake at 400°F for 10 to 15 minutes, or until golden brown and bubbling around the edges.

APPETIZERS

BAJA BLUE BLACK BEAN DIP

BAJA BLUE RESTAURANT & CANTINA AT HARRAH'S LAUGHLIN
EXECUTIVE SOUS-CHEF JEREMY HUGHES

This dip has been a staple for years at Baja Blue Restaurant & Cantina, where it is an accompaniment to chips and salsa. Chef Jeremy Hughes explains, "We have had numerous customers over the years inquire about this recipe, and that is why I think it is a great addition to the Harrah's Laughlin collection in this cookbook."

4 slices bacon, chopped
½ yellow onion, diced
1 tablespoon minced garlic
1 pound (2 cups) dried black beans, rinsed and picked over
1 jalapeño chile, halved lengthwise and seeded
3 cups water
2 tablespoons chili powder
1 cup shredded Monterey jack cheese
Tortilla chips for serving
Salsa (optional)

MAKES 6 TO 8 CUPS

In a medium skillet, cook the bacon over medium heat until crisp. Transfer to paper towels to drain. Cook the onions in the bacon fat until translucent, about 3 minutes. Add the garlic and cook for 30 seconds. Add the beans, jalapeño, and water. Bring to a boil, reduce heat to a simmer, and cook until the beans are tender, about 1½ hours. Stir in the chili powder and cheese.

In a food processor, purée the beans (with their broth), in batches if necessary, until smooth. Serve with tortilla chips and top with your favorite salsa, if desired.

BRUSCHETTA POMODORO

ANDREOTTI AT HARRAH'S RENO
CHEF JASON HARRIS

This dish will allow you to experience the tastes of northern Italy, just like the guests who enjoy the bistro atmosphere of Andreotti at Harrah's Reno. Bruschetta Pomodoro is a classic Italian hors d'oeuvre. Its light combination of Roma tomatoes, garlic, and extra-virgin olive oil makes a great pairing with a glass of white wine. Chef Jason Harris notes, "Andreotti's guests like to start off with this appetizer because it's not too filling nor does it lack in flavor. I'm sure you will enjoy making this dish as well as eating it."

POMODORO SAUCE
1½ pounds Roma tomatoes, finely diced
5 tablespoons olive oil
1½ teaspoons salt
1½ tablespoons minced garlic
12 large fresh basil leaves, thinly sliced

Sixteen ¼-inch-thick sourdough baguette slices
Olive oil for brushing
4 slices prosciutto
8 ounces fresh mozzarella, finely diced

SERVES 4

For the pomodora sauce: In a small bowl, mix together all the ingredients.

Preheat the oven to 425°F. Put the baguette slices on a baking sheet and brush the tops with olive oil. Bake for about 5 minutes, or until golden brown. Remove and let cool on wire racks. Cut each slice of prosciutto into 4 pieces. Place a piece of prosciutto on top of each crostini and spoon the sauce on top. Finish with the mozzarella.

FRIED PORTOBELLO MUSHROOMS

Bite-sized pieces of portobello mushrooms will beckon you and your guests to dip them to your heart's content in your favorite ranch dressing or other sauce. This crisp and subtle dish is the most frequently ordered appetizer on the menu at The Range Steakhouse & Bar. Chef Raymond Carter explains, "Although there are more variations, we take pride in the decision to embellish the flavor of nature with the bold flavor of our vinegary marinade and perfectly seasoned batter to bring such a gentle yet elegant expression to our menu."

Note: The mushrooms need to be marinated the night before cooking.

BALSAMIC DRESSING

3 tablespoons balsamic vinegar

2 tablespoons fresh lemon juice

½ tablespoon Dijon mustard

1 garlic clove, minced

1 tablespoon minced shallot

½ cup olive oil

Salt and freshly ground pepper

3 portobello mushrooms, stemmed and cut into ¼-inch-thick slices

4 cups all-purpose flour

1 tablespoon kosher salt

2 teaspoons freshly ground pepper

2 teaspoons granulated garlic

Peanut oil for deep-frying

Buttermilk Dressing (recipe follows) or other dipping sauce for serving

SERVES 2

For the dressing: In a medium bowl, whisk together the vinegar, lemon juice, mustard, garlic, and shallot. Gradually whisk in the oil. Season with salt and pepper.

In a small bowl, soak the mushroom pieces in the balsamic dressing overnight and then drain. In a medium bowl, combine the flour, salt, pepper, and granulated garlic. Stir with a whisk to blend. Add the mushrooms and toss until well coated.

In a Dutch oven or large, heavy pot, heat 2 inches of the peanut oil to 375°F on a deep-fat thermometer. Add the mushroom pieces and cook until golden brown, 5 to 6 minutes. Using a wire skimmer, transfer to paper towels to drain. Serve hot, with buttermilk dressing or other dipping sauce of choice.

BUTTERMILK DRESSING

½ cup well-shaken buttermilk

2 tablespoons mayonnaise

2 tablespoons cider vinegar

2 tablespoons minced shallots

1 tablespoon sugar

½ teaspoon salt

¼ teaspoon freshly ground pepper

3 tablespoons minced fresh chives

In a large bowl, whisk together the buttermilk, mayonnaise, vinegar, shallots, sugar, salt, and pepper until the sugar is dissolved, then whisk in the chives.

MAKES ABOUT 1 CUP

RANGE CRAB COCKTAIL

THE RANGE STEAKHOUSE AT HARRAH'S ST. LOUIS
EXECUTIVE CHEF RAY LEUNG

Instead of serving the traditional shrimp cocktail, mix it up with this unique award-winning twist on a classic from Hawaii that combines crab salad, salsa, and microgreens, topped off with a garnish of star fruit. This dish will provide a colorful and memorable launch to your meal with what chef Ray Leung calls a "refreshing touch of aloha!"

Note: To make this dish, you will need four 3-inch ring molds.

CRAB COCKTAIL SALAD

1½ teaspoons minced shallot

1½ teaspoons minced fresh basil

4½ tablespoons crème fraîche

1½ teaspoons minced fresh mint

¼ teaspoon hazelnut oil

¼ teaspoon salt

¼ teaspoon minced garlic

¼ teaspoon freshly ground pepper

12 ounces fresh lump crabmeat, picked over for shell

SALSA

6 tablespoons finely chopped fresh pineapple

6 tablespoons finely chopped mango

3 tablespoons finely chopped red bell pepper

1½ teaspoons minced fresh chives

MICROGREEN SALAD

½ cup microgreens

1 teaspoon fresh lemon juice

2 teaspoons fresh mandarin orange juice

Salt and freshly ground pepper

Thirty-two ⅛-inch-thick half-moon slices cucumber

Eight ¼-inch-thick slices star fruit

SERVES 4

For the crab cocktail salad: In a medium bowl, combine all the ingredients except the crabmeat, stirring to blend. Add the crabmeat and toss gently to coat. Cover and refrigerate for at least 15 minutes or up to 30 minutes.

For the salsa: In a small bowl, combine all the ingredients and stir to blend. Cover and refrigerate for at least 15 minutes or up to 30 minutes.

For the microgreen salad: In a medium bowl, combine all the ingredients, tossing to combine.

In a 3-inch ring mold, evenly space 8 cucumber slices, standing upright, against the inside walls of the mold. Fill the mold with 2 tablespoons of the salsa and then spoon in the crab salad. Unmold gently by holding down the crab cocktail with your left index finger while pulling the mold up with your right hand. Repeat to make 4 servings. Top each serving with the microgreen salad and 2 star fruit slices. Serve immediately.

ACCORDING TO A 2006 SURVEY CONDUCTED BY HARRAH'S ENTERTAINMENT, TABLE GAMES ARE MORE THAN TWICE AS POPULAR AMONG MEN THAN WOMEN.

TOP 10 TIPS
FOR SETTING A CREATIVE TABLE

HARRAH'S AK-CHIN

1   Use colorful linen napkins and experiment with different napkin folds. Books and online instructions are available to help you with these topics.

2   Learn proper silverware etiquette so you will know where and how to place the silverware.

3   Polish everything, from china to the flatware to the glassware, before using it.

4   Set the table with all the silverware and glassware needed for the meal so your guests will know what to expect.

5   There is a flower for every occasion, so use them whenever possible. Consult your local florist if you are not familiar with floral arrangements.

6   Lighting is key. It should be bright and sunny for breakfast and lunch, more subtle at dinner, and don't forget unscented candles for those romantic nights.

7   Use the elements of fire, air, and water whenever possible:

    ✦   Air: Open a window or door for fresh air, turn on a ceiling fan, or eat outside, depending on the weather.

    ✦   Fire: Light unscented candles or a fire in a fireplace.

    ✦   Water: Use a clear water pitcher or a floating candle in a bowl of water.

8   Let the food aromas be the essence of your meal. Don't complicate aromas with incense and scented candles.

9   For multiple-course meals, choose adequately padded chairs for your guests' comfort.

10 Never forget that every meal is a gift. Enjoy it with friends and family. Cherish every meal with friends and family as though it were your last.

JUMBO LUMP CRAB CAKES

'37 AT HARRAH'S TUNICA / EXECUTIVE CHEF STEVE PAIROLERO

Chefs from every region of the country have their special recipe for the great American crab cake. This one from Harrah's Tunica, outside Memphis, is full of bright flavors. These are favorites at '37, which is named in tribute to the opening of the first Harrah's casino on October 30, 1937.

8 sea scallops

4 large egg yolks

2 tablespoons mayonnaise

1 teaspoon Dijon mustard

1½ pounds fresh lump crabmeat, picked over for shell

¼ cup finely chopped red bell pepper

½ teaspoon Old Bay Seasoning

1 tablespoon minced fresh flat-leaf parsley

1 teaspoon minced fresh dill

1 cup panko (Japanese bread crumbs)

½ cup clarified butter (recipe follows)

Cajun Rémoulade (recipe follows) or lemon vinaigrette for serving

MAKES 16 CRAB CAKES;
SERVES 6 TO 8

In a food processor, purée the scallops to a pastelike consistency. In a large bowl, mix together the scallops, egg yolks, mayonnaise, and mustard. In a medium bowl, combine the crabmeat, red bell pepper, Old Bay Seasoning, and herbs; toss to coat. Add the crabmeat mixture to the scallop mixture and gently stir to blend. Shape into 16 crab cakes and dredge each in the bread crumbs. Cook now, or place on a plate, cover in plastic wrap, and refrigerate for up to 1 hour.

In a large sauté pan or skillet, heat the clarified butter over medium-high heat and cook the crab cakes for 3 minutes on each side, or until golden brown. Serve immediately, with the rémoulade or vinaigrette.

CAJUN RÉMOULADE

2 cups mayonnaise

1 tablespoon chopped capers

1 teaspoon minced garlic

1 teaspoon minced fresh flat-leaf parsley

2 tablespoons fresh lemon juice

½ jalapeño chile, seeded and minced

2 tablespoons ketchup

1 teaspoon Dijon mustard

1 teaspoon anchovy paste

¼ teaspoon cayenne pepper

1 teaspoon Tabasco sauce

1 teaspoon Worcestershire sauce

½ teaspoon freshly ground pepper

1 teaspoon Cajun seasoning

In a food processor, combine all the ingredients and process until smooth.
MAKES 2½ CUPS

Clarifying butter: In a heavy saucepan, melt 1 cup (2 sticks) unsalted butter over low heat. Remove from the heat and skim the foam from the surface. Pour the clear yellow liquid into a glass container, leaving the milky residue behind (this can be added to soups and sauces). Cover and refrigerate indefinitely. Makes about ⅔ cup.

JACK BINION'S PREMIUM CRAB CAKES

JACK BINION'S STEAK HOUSE AT HORSESHOE COUNCIL BLUFFS
EXECUTIVE CHEF JAMES REBER

These classic crab cakes are one of Jack Binion's Steak House's original recipes. Chef James Reber and his team use sweet jumbo lump crabmeat, a touch of mayonnaise, and a secret blend of seasonings to make these tender golden cakes.

2 tablespoons mayonnaise

1 teaspoon dry mustard

2 teaspoons minced fresh flat-leaf parsley

½ teaspoon cayenne pepper

½ tablespoon minced garlic

2 dashes Worcestershire sauce

1 tablespoon fresh lemon juice

1 teaspoon kosher salt

1 teaspoon freshly ground black pepper

3 tablespoons panko (Japanese bread crumbs)

1 pound fresh lump crabmeat, picked over for shell

2 tablespoons extra-virgin olive oil

4 lemon wedges for garnish

Aioli Sauce for dipping (see recipe facing page)

SERVES 4

Preheat the oven to 350°F. In a medium bowl, whisk together the mayonnaise, mustard, parsley, cayenne, garlic, Worcestershire sauce, lemon juice, salt, and pepper. Add the panko and crabmeat. Using a rubber spatula, fold the mixture together gently to prevent breaking up the crabmeat too much. Mold the mixture into 4 cakes. In a large sauté pan or skillet, heat the oil over medium heat. Sauté the crab cakes for 3 minutes on each side, or until brown and crusty. Serve with the lemon wedges and aioli sauce.

WHEN IT'S TIME TO CUT LOOSE,
WHISKEY ROADHOUSE AT HORSESHOE CASINO COUNCIL BLUFFS
IS THE PLACE TO HEAR YOUR FAVORITE MUSIC UP CLOSE AND UNTAMED.
BO DIDDLEY PLAYED HIS LAST PERFORMANCE HERE
BEFORE HE DIED IN JUNE 2008. ERIC CHURCH, BETTER THAN EZRA,
AND GAVIN ROSSDALE
HAVE ALSO ALL PLAYED THE ROADHOUSE.

AIOLI SAUCE

1 cup mayonnaise

2 tablespoons fresh lemon juice

¼ teaspoon powdered garlic

1 teaspoon Worcestershire sauce

¼ teaspoon kosher salt

¼ teaspoon freshly ground pepper

In a medium bowl, combine all the ingredients and stir to blend.

MAKES ABOUT 1 CUP

GOAT CHEESE TRUFFLED BAKLAVA

BOA STEAKHOUSE AT THE FORUM SHOPS AT CAESARS PALACE LAS VEGAS
CHEF JOSE ALEMAN

Chef Jose Aleman at BOA Steakhouse has transformed the classic Greek dessert into an intriguing starter layered with goat cheese and flavored with truffles. Served on a bed of frisée tossed with a grapefruit dressing, it is an intriguing mixture of sweet and savory, crisp and creamy.

1 pound thawed frozen filo dough

1 cup (2 sticks) unsalted butter, melted

¼ cup honey

2 tablespoons truffle peelings

½ cup ground pistachios

16 ounces fresh white goat cheese

2 tablespoons truffle oil

SALAD

Leaves from 2 heads frisée lettuce

2 tablespoons grated grapefruit zest

2 tablespoons grapefruit juice

2 tablespoons extra-virgin olive oil

SERVES 12

Preheat the oven to 400°F. Line a baking sheet with parchment paper.

Cover the stack of filo dough with a cloth to keep it moist. Layer 1 sheet of filo dough on the prepared pan and brush it with butter. Repeat to layer 8 sheets of dough.

In a medium bowl, mix together the honey and truffle peelings. Drizzle the layered dough with 4 tablespoons of the honey mixture, followed by 6 table-spoons of the pistachios. Place another sheet of filo dough on top and brush it with melted butter. Repeat to layer 16 more sheets of dough, for a total of 24 sheets. Drizzle the top layer with 2 tablespoons of the remaining honey mixture and then sprinkle with the remaining pistachios. Bake for 45 minutes, or until golden brown.

Remove from the oven and let cool for 30 minutes on the pan. Drizzle with the remaining honey mixture. Let cool completely. Cut into twelve pieces.

In a medium bowl, combine the goat cheese and truffle oil. Stir to blend well. Transfer the mixture to a piping bag fitted with a ½-inch round tip. Lift off the top three-fourths of each pastry and pipe the goat cheese mousse into 3 rows along the length of the filo. Replace the tops.

For the salad: In a medium bowl, combine all the ingredients and toss to coat.

To serve, place each pastry on a salad plate and serve a mound of salad alongside.

JAPANESE YELLOWTAIL SASHIMI
WITH DICED CHILES

SUSHI ROKU AT THE FORUM SHOPS AT CAESARS PALACE LAS VEGAS
CHEF VERNON CARDENAS

In this appetizer, raw yellowtail is served with a ponzu sauce made with the juice of the yuzu, a sour citrus fruit. Ponzu sauce, a popular combination of sweet and sour flavors, is often used in Japanese cuisine. Here, it makes a tangy counterpoint to the tender, buttery fish.

4 ounces yellowtail fish fillet, cut into twelve 1/16-inch-thick diagonal slices

1/4 teaspoon minced garlic

1 tablespoon shredded fresh ginger

1 tablespoon finely chopped green onion (white part only)

1 teaspoon minced red jalapeño chile

1 teaspoon minced green jalapeño chile

YUZU PONZU SAUCE

4 teaspoons ponzu sauce

1 teaspoon soy sauce

1/8 teaspoon yuzu juice

1/2 teaspoon olive oil

1/4 teaspoon shredded daikon radish

Lemon slices for garnish

SERVES 2 TO 4

On a large serving dish, place the yellowtail slices in one layer. Brush the garlic over each slice. Evenly scatter the ginger, green onion, and red and green jalapeños on each slice of the yellowtail.

For the sauce: In a medium bowl, combine all ingredients and stir well. Drizzle the sauce over the yellowtail.

Just before serving, heat the oil in a small skillet over medium heat until shimmering. Pour it over the fish. Place the daikon radish on the center of the plate and garnish with the lemon slices.

AVOCADO SPRING ROLLS

AUGUSTUS CAFÉ AT CAESARS WINDSOR
EXECUTIVE CHEF PATRICK MCCLARY

These Asian-inspired spring rolls combine the best of East and West. Avocado, garlic, ginger, sun-dried tomatoes, and lime juice are the filling for crunchy morsels that will surprise your guests. Chef Patrick McClary comments, "This dish contains a great contrast of textures and just enough lime to enliven the senses. Spice it up with a Szechuan dip to complete the experience."

3 avocados, peeled and pitted

1 tablespoon roasted garlic
(see note)

½ tablespoon minced fresh ginger

3 tablespoons finely chopped
red onion

1 tablespoon finely chopped
oil-packed sun-dried tomato

2 tablespoons fresh lime juice

Salt and freshly ground pepper

Sixteen 4-inch-square
spring roll wrappers

1 large egg yolk beaten with
1 tablespoon water

Canola or peanut oil for deep-frying

Bottled spiced plum or
Szechuan sauce for serving

MAKES 16 PIECES

In a large bowl, combine the avocados, garlic, ginger, onion, and tomato and mash them coarsely with a fork. Add the lime juice and salt and pepper, mixing well.

Put the wrappers on a work surface and brush each with the egg mixture on two adjoining edges of the wrapper. Place 2 tablespoons of the mixture in the center of each wrapper and fold corner to corner to form a triangle. Press the edges together to form a seal. Brush one corner of the triangle with the egg mixture. Bring the opposite corners together and press to form a seal.

In a Dutch oven or large, heavy pot, heat 2 inches of the oil to 365°F on a deep-fat thermometer. Cook the spring rolls in batches for 4 minutes, or until golden brown. Using a wire skimmer, transfer to paper towels to drain. Serve hot, with plum or Szechuan sauce.

✦

Roasted garlic cloves: Cut a bulb of garlic in half and brush cut sides with olive oil. Roast in a preheated 400°F oven until tender and golden brown, about 20 minutes. Let cool. Press out the individual garlic cloves and chop.

SEARED SCALLOPS
WITH TEMPURA RAMPS & ROASTED CORN CUSTARD

BÚZIOS SEAFOOD RESTAURANT AT RIO ALL-SUITE HOTEL & CASINO
CHEF DE CUISINE TRANG TRAN

Although this appetizer is not on the regular menu at Búzios Seafood Restaurant, it often makes its appearance on the chef's tasting menu in some version. This dish is sure to impress your dinner guests with its vibrant colors and fresh combinations of flavors. Chef Trang Tran suggests, "A great wine pairing would be a Sauvignon Blanc or a Sancerre."

CITRUS VINAIGRETTE

Grated zest of 1 orange

2 tablespoons orange juice

½ teaspoon minced shallot

¼ teaspoon Dijon mustard

2 to 3 tablespoons canola oil

1 tablespoon chopped fresh chives

Salt and freshly ground pepper

ROASTED CORN CUSTARD

1 ear corn, shucked and roasted (see note)

1 large egg, lightly beaten

4 tablespoons heavy cream

1 shallot, minced

1 garlic clove, minced

2 tablespoons cornmeal

1 tablespoon flour

½ teaspoon salt

Freshly ground pepper

TEMPURA RAMPS

¼ cup cornstarch

¼ cup all-purpose flour, plus more for coating

1 teaspoon salt, plus more to taste

½ teaspoon freshly ground pepper, plus more to taste

½ cup soda water

3 tablespoons canola oil, plus more for frying

4 ramps (wild onions), trimmed to 4 inches

4 sea scallops

1 tablespoon fresh lemon juice

1 blood orange, cut into 12 segments (see note)

1 handful microgreens or mixed baby greens for garnish

For the vinaigrette: In a medium bowl, combine the orange zest and juice, shallot, and mustard. Gradually whisk in the oil to emulsify. Stir in the chives and season with salt and pepper.

For the corn custard: Preheat the oven to 325°F. In a medium bowl, stir all the custard ingredients together. Pour the mixture into a buttered 10-ounce ramekin. Set the ramekin in a baking dish and add hot water to come halfway up the sides of the ramekin. Bake until the custard is set and lightly brown, about 20 minutes. Transfer to a wire rack.

For the ramps: In a medium bowl, combine the cornstarch, the ¼ cup flour, the 1 teaspoon salt, and the ½ teaspoon pepper; stir well. Whisk in the soda water. The batter should be thin. Set aside to rest for 1 hour.

In a Dutch oven or large, heavy pot, heat 2 inches of the oil to 365°F. Coat the ramps in flour, and then dip them into the batter. Fry the ramps for 1 minute, or until golden. Using a wire skimmer, transfer to a paper towel to drain. Sprinkle with salt and pepper. Keep warm in a low oven.

Pat the scallops dry with paper towels and season them lightly with salt and pepper. In a medium sauté pan or skillet, heat the 3 tablespoons oil over high heat until smoking. Add the scallops and sear on one side for 2 minutes, or until golden brown. Turn and cook until golden brown on the second side, 1 minute. Transfer to a plate and sprinkle with the lemon juice.

To serve, drizzle 1 tablespoon of the vinaigrette on each plate. Place a large spoonful of the corn custard in the center. Nestle a scallop on top of the custard. Set a tempura ramp on top, leaning on the scallop. Place 3 blood orange segments on the scallop. Garnish with the greens and serve at once.

SERVES 4

Roasting corn: Brush the ear lightly with canola oil and season with salt and pepper. Under a preheated broiler, on a hot grill, or in a hot grill pan, roast the corn, turning as needed, until browned on all sides. Let cool. Using a large knife, cut the kernels from the cob.

✦

Segmenting citrus: Using a large knife, cut the peel off each end down to the flesh. Set the fruit, one end down, on a cutting board. Cut off the peel down to the flesh, following the curvature of the fruit. Hold the fruit over a bowl and cut on each side of each membrane to release the segments. Squeeze the empty fruit to release the juice.

ON A DAILY BASIS,
THE AWARD-WINNING CARNIVAL WORLD BUFFET
AT RIO ALL-SUITE HOTEL & CASINO:

✦ EMPLOYS MORE THAN FIFTY COOKS ✦

✦ OPERATES NINE COOKING STATIONS
IN A SERVICE LINE AS LONG AS A FOOTBALL FIELD ✦

✦ MAINTAINS TWELVE DIFFERENT
FOOD STATIONS SERVING A VARIETY OF FOODS
FROM AROUND THE WORLD ✦

✦ MAKES EVERYTHING FROM SCRATCH
IN THE RIO'S PASTRY SHOP,
INCLUDING NINE TYPES OF GELATO ✦

✦ CHANGES MENU ITEMS THREE TIMES A DAY,
SEVEN DAYS A WEEK ✦

2

SALADS

SEARED BEEF TENDERLOIN & GOAT CHEESE SALAD

AUGUSTUS CAFÉ AT CAESARS WINDSOR
EXECUTIVE CHEF PATRICK MCCLARY

Whether served as a first-course salad or a light lunch, this layered dish is both easy and elegant. Chef Patrick McClary notes, "This salad has all it takes to make a great meal. It's well-balanced with the sharpness of the goat cheese, a sassy dressing, and the beef tenderloin. It's especially enjoyed by our guests on hot summer days."

2 teaspoons canola oil

1 pound beef tenderloin

1 teaspoon minced fresh rosemary

1½ teaspoons minced garlic

Salt and freshly ground pepper

4 Roma tomatoes, halved lengthwise

½ cup fresh white goat cheese

SPICY TOMATO DRESSING

1 cup plus ½ tablespoon canola oil

1 tablespoon coarsely chopped onion

½ ripe tomato, coarsely chopped

Grated zest of ½ lemon

½ teaspoon fresh lemon juice

¼ teaspoon Kashmiri mirchi chili powder or cayenne pepper

¼ cup tomato juice

Salt and freshly ground pepper

3 cups mixed baby greens

Twelve 4-inch squares focaccia bread, lightly toasted and cut into ¼-inch-thick slices

SERVES 4 AS A
MAIN-COURSE LUNCHEON
SALAD, 6 TO 8 AS A FIRST COURSE

Preheat the oven to 400°F. In a large sauté pan, heat the oil over medium-high heat and sear the beef on all sides. Season the beef with rosemary, garlic, and salt and pepper. Put on a rack in a roasting pan and roast for about 25 minutes for medium-rare. Remove from the oven, transfer to a carving board, and let cool to room temperature. Cut into 16 thin slices.

Preheat the broiler. Place the tomato halves on a broiler pan. Place 1 table-spoon of the goat cheese on each tomato half and broil 8 inches from the heat source until the cheese is melted and lightly browned, about 1 minute. Remove from the broiler and sprinkle with pepper.

For the dressing: In a medium skil-let, heat ½ tablespoon of the oil over medium heat. Add the onion and sauté until golden brown, about 5 minutes. Add the tomato and sauté for 3 to 4 minutes. Add the lemon zest, juice, chili powder, and tomato juice. Pour the mixture into a blender and purée. Transfer the mixture to a medium bowl and gradually whisk in the remaining 1 cup oil. Add salt and pepper to taste.

To serve, toss the greens in just enough of the dressing to coat; there will be leftover dressing. On each plate, layer the ingredients as follows: Place ¼ cup of the greens in the cen-ter, followed by 2 focaccia slices and 2 beef slices. Repeat with a second layer of greens, bread, and beef, then top with a layer of ¼ cup greens. Place a tomato half on either side of the salad.

IN ONE YEAR, THE MARKET BUFFET AT CAESARS WINDSOR USES ALMOST 150,000 POUNDS OF PRIME RIB AND 50,000 POUNDS OF INSIDE ROUND.

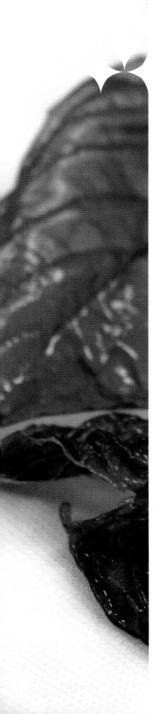

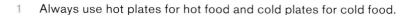
1. Always use hot plates for hot food and cold plates for cold food.

2. Never forget that people eat with their eyes first: Food should always be visually appealing. The use of color and height can catch a guest's eye, and lead to the success of the dish. If you create a dish that is beautiful, no matter what the ingredients, guests will probably enjoy it.

3. Think of the serving plate as a picture frame or blank canvas: Consider your food as art on the plate. Be sure to keep the rim of the plate clean to nicely frame your masterpiece.

4. Always use edible garnishes: Nothing should go on the plate that can't be eaten.

5. The use of nontraditional serving dishes can add excitement and flair to your dish: For example, when serving a cheese course, use a cheese box as a cheese plate. When serving seafood, use shells as vessels, or choose dishes with whimsical shapes and designs. Use one of the ingredients in the dish, such as a bell pepper or an orange shell, for serving the dish. Large leaves, such as fig leaves and sections of banana leaves, can be used in place of plates.

6. Fresh herbs can accent a dish as well as make it visually appealing: They add an alluring aroma that will capture your guests' attention and imagination. For example, fried basil looks like glass, has a clean, refreshing aroma, and will add a stylish touch to your dish.

7. Positioning is key: How you place the food on the serving plate is important because it brings the whole dish together. For example, if you're serving a dish like pan-seared halibut with root vegetable ragù, poached prawns, and a pepper fumet, you could position the ragù in the center of the plate and the fish on top. Then, you could place the prawns to the right of the fish and pool the fumet on the plate. This gives the dish a unified look, adds a dazzling visual appeal, and shows the love that was put into the dish.

8. Never use unnatural colors in a dish: Unnatural colors are those that invoke the wrong response from the guest. For example, one of my fellow chefs made a blueberry risotto, and many of our guests found the bright purple rice unappetizing.

9. Always highlight the key element of your dish: Place the main ingredient on the plate so that it becomes the central focus and is complemented by the side dishes.

10. KISS (Keep It Super Simple).

TENNESSEE PROSCIUTTO & WARM GOAT CHEESE SALAD

WITH HONEY-WALNUT TRUFFLE DRESSING

MAGNOLIA, A DELTA GRILLE AT HORSESHOE TUNICA

This tantalizing fall salad of warm goat cheese and prosciutto was inspired by an American-made version of prosciutto. The addition of fresh honey, walnut oil, and that slight hint of truffle provide the perfect balance to the salty prosciutto. To order Tennessee prosciutto, go to www.bentonshams.com.

DRESSING

5 tablespoons clover honey

¼ teaspoon white truffle oil

2 tablespoons walnut oil

Pinch of minced fresh lavender blossoms

Pinch of minced fresh rosemary

Juice of ½ lemon

Salt and freshly ground pepper

FRIED GOAT CHEESE

5 ounces fresh white goat cheese at room temperature

½ tablespoon minced fresh rosemary

½ tablespoon minced fresh thyme

½ tablespoon freshly ground pepper

1 large egg

4 large eggs, beaten

4 cups all-purpose flour

4 cups panko (Japanese bread crumbs)

Peanut oil for deep-frying

Herb flowers or edible flowers, such as pansies, violas, and nasturtiums

6 cups mixed baby greens

6 thin slices prosciutto, preferably Benton's

SERVES 6

For the dressing: In a small bowl, combine all the ingredients and whisk to emulsify. Taste and adjust the seasoning.

For the goat cheese: In a small bowl, combine the goat cheese, rosemary, thyme, pepper, and the 1 egg. Stir well to blend. Shape the mixture into six ½-inch-thick disks.

Put the 4 beaten eggs, the flour, and the panko in each of 3 separate shallow bowls. Dip a goat cheese disk first into the eggs, coating evenly all over, then in the flour, and back into the eggs again, coating evenly all over with each layer. Coat the disk evenly all over with the panko. Repeat with the remaining disks.

In a Dutch oven or heavy pot, heat 2 inches of the oil to 350°F on a deep-fat thermometer. Gently add the goat cheese and cook until golden brown, 2 to 3 minutes. Using a wire skimmer, transfer to paper towels to drain. Set aside and keep warm.

Soak the flowers in ice water for 2 to 3 minutes; drain and dry on paper towels.

Reserve 1 tablespoon of the dressing. In a medium bowl, toss the greens with the remaining dressing to coat. On a work surface, lay out the prosciutto slices. Place one-sixth of the greens on one end of each slice and roll up. Pool a small amount of dressing on each plate. Place a goat cheese disk on top, then top the cheese with the prosciutto roll. With a soup spoon, drizzle more of the dressing around the stack. Garnish with the flowers.

MAGNOLIA, A DELTA GRILLE FEATURES LOCALLY SOURCED FOODS, INCLUDING ALLEN BENTON'S TENNESSEE BACON AND HAM.

CUCUMBER & MINT SALAD

HARRAH'S LAKE TAHOE & HARVEYS LAKE TAHOE
EXECUTIVE CHEF JOE WELLS

This refreshing dish is derived from the famous Thai cucumber salad. At Harrah's Lake Tahoe and Harveys Lake Tahoe, it is served as a side dish for some of their Hawaiian fish specials. Chef Joe Wells advises how to vary the dish: "Sometimes, for a change, we mix it up and add julienned carrots and daikon."

4 cucumbers, peeled every other pass with a vegetable peeler, halved lengthwise, and seeded

1 white onion, halved and thinly sliced

10 radishes, thinly sliced

30 fresh mint leaves, coarsely chopped

20 fresh cilantro leaves, coarsely chopped

2 teaspoons red pepper flakes

1½ cups seasoned rice vinegar

8 butter leaf lettuce cups

Cut the cucumbers into diagonal slices. In a medium bowl, mix together all the ingredients except the leaf lettuce cups. Divide the mixture equally among the leaf lettuce cups and serve at once.

SERVES 8

HARRAH'S LAKE TAHOE WAS THE FIRST HOTEL IN THE WORLD TO FEATURE TWO FULL BATHROOMS IN EVERY ROOM.

FRESH MARKET POTATO SALAD

FRESH MARKET SQUARE BUFFET AT HARRAH'S CHEROKEE
EXECUTIVE CHEF KEITH ANDREASEN

When you visit the Fresh Market Square Buffet, you will encounter three things: great food, a friendly staff, and their famous potato salad. Chef Keith Andreasen says, "The chefs at Fresh Market Square Buffet have been making this salad since the day the buffet opened, and for more than ten years the guests have loved every bite of it."

1 pound Yukon gold potatoes, peeled and diced

¼ cup finely diced celery

¼ cup finely diced yellow onion

3 large eggs, hard-cooked and cut into ½-inch dice

½ cup sweet pickle relish

¾ cup mayonnaise

2 teaspoons salt

2 teaspoons ground white pepper

1 tablespoon diced pimiento

2 teaspoons minced fresh flat-leaf parsley

Put the potatoes in a medium saucepan of salted cold water. Bring to a boil and cook for 8 to 10 minutes, or until just tender. Drain.

In a large bowl, combine the potatoes, celery, onion, and eggs. Stir gently to mix. Gently stir in the sweet relish and mayonnaise, then the salt and pepper, pimientos, and parsley, mixing well. Cover and refrigerate for 1 hour before serving.

SERVES 4 TO 6

APPLE & BLOOD ORANGE VINAIGRETTE OVER BIBB LETTUCE & WATERCRESS

HARRAH'S JOLIET
CHEF PETER JESCHKE

This is a lovely vinaigrette to use in late fall and winter when blood oranges are in season. The apple balances the acidity of the vinaigrette and complements the sliced apples, Gorgonzola, and walnuts in this satisfying salad.

APPLE & BLOOD ORANGE VINAIGRETTE

Juice of 1 blood orange

1 tablespoon Dijon mustard

½ Granny Smith apple, peeled, cored, and chopped

1 teaspoon minced fresh thyme

⅓ cup apple cider vinegar

⅔ cup extra-virgin olive oil

Salt and freshly ground pepper

Leaves from 2 heads Bibb lettuce

2 bunches watercress, stemmed

1 cup crumbled Gorgonzola cheese

1 Granny Smith apple, peeled, cored, and sliced

½ cup walnuts, toasted (see note)

SERVES 4

For the vinaigrette: In a blender or food processor, combine the orange juice, mustard, apple, and thyme and pulse for 15 seconds. Add the vinegar and pulse quickly. With the machine running, gradually add the oil in a thin stream to emulsify. Season with salt and pepper. Use now, or cover and refrigerate for up to 24 hours.

In a medium bowl, combine the lettuce and watercress. Use ½ cup of vinaigrette to toss and serve the remainder on the side. The vinaigrette may be kept refrigerated for up to 1 week. Divide the Gorgonzola, sliced apples, and toasted walnuts among the salads.

✦✦

Toasting nuts: Spread the nuts in a pie pan and toast in a preheated 350°F oven until fragrant, 5 to 8 minutes. Remove from the oven and pour into a bowl to let cool.

TOP 10 KNIVES
EVERY KITCHEN SHOULD HAVE

HARRAH'S ATLANTIC CITY

No chef, at home or in a professional kitchen, can execute even the most basic of tasks without the correct tools. And of all the tools used in the kitchen, knives are a hallmark of our profession. It is imperative to have a small arsenal of knives that will cover the many requirements of chopping, dicing, and slicing. A good knife essentially becomes an extension of your own hands.

The following is my dream team of knives that will be the foundation to your success in the kitchen.

1 A 10-inch chef's knife (also called a French knife): If you were only able to have one knife in your kitchen, this all-purpose culinary tool would be it.

2 A 3½-inch paring knife: This short knife is used for trimming and paring vegetables and fruits.

3 A 5- to 7-inch utility knife: This is a smaller, lighter chef's knife that is used for light cutting chores.

4 A 6-inch boning knife: As the name suggests, this rigid knife is used to separate raw meat from bones.

5 A 9-inch fillet knife: This flexible knife is perfect for filleting fish, both round and flat, and for steak cuts.

6 A 10- to 14-inch carving/scimitar knife: This knife usually has a long blade with a rounded tip and a fluted edge with hollow-ground ovals for easier slicing of cooked meats.

7 An 8½-inch bread knife: This serrated knife cuts soft and hard breads without damaging their structure.

8 A 7-inch santoku knife: The extremely sharp blade of this Japanese-style knife is tapered and looks similar to a cleaver. It is used for sushi cookery and precise slicing.

9 A 10- to 12-inch cleaver: This is a bone-breaking chopper.

10 A 12- to 16-inch sharpening steel: Although this is not a knife, it is a necessity. Sharp knives are the safest and easiest to use.

TOP 10 UTENSILS
EVERY KITCHEN SHOULD HAVE

BALLY'S LAS VEGAS AND PARIS LAS VEGAS

1 Paring knife: The most versatile knife in a chef's kitchen. It can be used to cut almost anything.

2 French knife: Also called a chef's knife, the French knife has a broad, tapered shape and fine edge and is perfect for chopping all types of food.

3 Digital scale: A digital scale is more accurate when weighing smaller amounts, and accuracy is everything in cooking.

4 Wooden spoon: The handle of a wooden spoon stays cool so you won't burn yourself as you could with a metal spoon.

5 Wire whisk: This hand whip can be used for everything from whipping egg whites to smoothing out sauces.

6 Kitchen tongs: Tongs are gentle on your food and will never pierce your steaks the way a fork will.

7 Corkscrew: This one is pretty self-explanatory: No corkscrew, no wine.

8 Vegetable peeler: Choose a swivel-head peeler, which cuts on both downward and upward strokes and gets the job done in half the time.

9 Offset spatula: An offset spatula is identical to the palette knife except that the blade is bent at a 90-degree angle from the handle. It is great for spreading, flipping, and lifting all types of foods.

10 Rolling pin: Every baker needs a good, sturdy rolling pin. Some of the best and most cherished are those handed down through the generations.

PECAN HERBED ORZO SALAD

HARRAH'S NORTH KANSAS CITY
CHEF ROY ASKREN

Guests at Harrah's North Kansas City come back multiple times to savor this pasta salad made with fresh orange juice, cranberries, and mint. Chef Roy Askren comments, "Our guests always ask how to make this salad at home for their families and parties."

3 quarts chicken stock

2 cups (14 ounces) orzo pasta

2 cups chopped pecans

1 shallot, minced

1 tablespoon minced garlic

1 orange, scrubbed and quartered

1 cup dried cranberries

2 tablespoons minced fresh chives

DRESSING

½ cup white wine vinegar

½ cup extra-virgin olive oil

½ cup fresh orange juice

¼ cup sugar

1 tablespoon Dijon mustard

Salt and freshly ground pepper

1 tablespoon minced fresh flat-leaf parsley

1 tablespoon minced fresh mint

2 tablespoons finely diced red bell pepper

SERVES 4 TO 6

In a large stockpot, bring the chicken stock to a boil. Reduce the heat to a low boil and add the orzo, stirring constantly to prevent the pasta from sticking. Add the pecans, shallot, garlic, and orange, continuing to stir the pasta to prevent sticking. Cook until al dente, 10 to 12 minutes. Drain and transfer to a bowl of ice water to cool for 1 to 2 minutes. Drain again for 10 minutes. Remove and discard the orange. Empty into a medium bowl and add the cranberries and chives, lightly tossing until blended. Set aside.

For the dressing: In a medium bowl, combine all the ingredients and whisk until thoroughly blended.

Add the dressing to the pasta mixture and toss to coat well. Garnish with the parsley, mint, and bell pepper. Let stand at room temperature for 1 to 2 hours before serving.

FENNEL, ENDIVE & ARUGULA SALAD
WITH A CITRUS-BASIL VINAIGRETTE & PARMESAN CHEESE TWISTS

REFLECTIONS CAFÉ AT HARRAH'S RESORT ATLANTIC CITY
CHEF JAMES COOMBS

Reflections Café is regarded by guests as one of the best eateries in Atlantic City, and this salad's sophisticated blend of flavors and textures is one of the reasons. Chef James Coombs explains, "Our guests would always request this salad after we offered it as a special. The fresh fennel with its licorice flavor balances the sharpness of the endive and arugula greens. This salad can be a great starter for an Italian dinner or be served as a luncheon meal."

PARMESAN CHEESE TWISTS

½ sheet thawed frozen puff pastry dough

1 large egg, beaten

½ cup grated Parmesan cheese

¼ cup minced fresh flat-leaf parsley

Coarsely ground pepper

1 fennel bulb, cored and thinly sliced

Leaves from 2 heads Belgium endive, thinly sliced

4 cups arugula leaves

CITRUS-BASIL VINAIGRETTE

¼ cup fresh orange juice

¼ cup fresh lime juice

¼ cup fresh lemon juice

1 tablespoon Dijon mustard

¼ bunch basil, stemmed

2 tablespoons honey

½ cup extra-virgin olive oil

1 cup canola oil

Salt and freshly ground pepper

8 thin slices prosciutto

8 thin slices Manchego cheese

SERVES 4

For the cheese twists: Preheat the oven to 375°F. Lay the puff pastry dough on a work surface and lightly roll it out with a rolling pin. Using a fork, dock the dough all over. Brush the dough with the egg. Sprinkle the Parmesan cheese, parsley, and pepper over it. Fold the dough in half and roll it lightly with the rolling pin. Cut the dough into 8-inch crosswise strips about ¾ inch thick and twist each one into a spiral. Place the twists 2 inches apart on a baking sheet. Bake for 12 minutes, or until golden brown. Remove from the oven and transfer the twists to a wire rack.

In a large bowl, combine the fennel, endive, and arugula.

For the vinaigrette: In a blender, combine all three juices, the mustard, basil, and honey and blend. With the machine running, gradually add the olive oil and canola oil until emulsified. Stir in salt and pepper.

To serve, alternately lay 2 slices each of prosciutto and Manchego cheese on each plate. Add 2 cups of the vinaigrette to the salad greens and toss lightly. Place 1½ to 2 cups of the salad over each serving of prosciutto and Manchego cheese. Garnish with cheese twists.

REFLECTIONS CAFÉ HAS BEEN VOTED THE BEST CAFÉ IN ATLANTIC CITY FOR THE PAST THREE YEARS BY *CASINO PLAYER* MAGAZINE.

GARDEN BASKET-WEAVE SALAD

WITH HEIRLOOM TOMATOES & FRESH MOZZARELLA

HARRAH'S METROPOLIS
EXECUTIVE CHEF JON M. KELL

Woven thin slices of carrot, squash, and cucumber make a cunning presentation for this salad, which will allow each of your guests to have his or her own edible favor.

4 yellow squash

4 zucchini

2 cucumbers

2 carrots, peeled

4 cups arugula

4 heirloom tomatoes, quartered

Four 3-ounce fresh mozzarella balls, sliced and halved

½ cup finely sliced fresh basil

4 tablespoons extra-virgin olive oil

4 tablespoons balsamic vinegar

SERVES 4

Using a mandoline or a large sharp knife, cut the squash, zucchini, cucumber, and carrots into paper-thin lengthwise slices. Cut the squash and zucchini strips in half lengthwise. Lay 4 yellow squash slices next to each other on a cutting board with the short ends facing you and the skin sides facing left. Take a slice of zucchini with the long side facing you and the skin side facing away from you. Weave the zucchini into the squash as if you were making a woven lattice pie pastry top by lifting the first slice of yellow squash and placing the zucchini beneath it. Lay the zucchini on top of the second slice of yellow squash. Lift the third slice of yellow squash and lay the zucchini under it. Repeat until the zucchini has gone over, then under, each of the yellow squash slices. Repeat with slices of zucchini until a woven sheet is formed.

Next, place one cucumber slice in the center of the sheet. Place 2 carrot slices in the center of the sheet on top of the cucumber. Place some arugula on the sheet. Roll up the sheet and place it seam side down. Cut each end on the diagonal and transfer the roll to a salad plate. Repeat with the remaining sliced vegetables and arugula.

Place 4 tomato quarters and 2 cheese slices on each plate. Sprinkle with the basil. Drizzle each serving with 1 tablespoon oil and 1 tablespoon balsamic vinegar.

FRIED GREEN TOMATOES

THE RANGE STEAKHOUSE & BAR AT TUNICA ROADHOUSE CASINO & HOTEL
EXECUTIVE CHEF & DIRECTOR OF FOOD & BEVERAGE CHRISTOPHER J. HENCYK

In this fabled Southern dish from Tunica Roadhouse Casino & Hotel in the heart of Mississippi, fried tomatoes are accented with mustard vinaigrette and onion jam. Chef Christopher J. Hencyk sums up this treat, "Fix ya up some of mama's sweet tea, fry ya up some tomatoes, and watch the sunset. What more can you ask for?"

MUSTARD VINAIGRETTE

½ tablespoon coarse-grain mustard

1 tablespoon minced shallot

½ teaspoon sugar

⅛ teaspoon salt

Pinch of freshly ground pepper

2 tablespoons white wine vinegar

3 tablespoons extra-virgin olive oil

---

4 firm green (unripe) tomatoes, cut into crosswise slices

Salt and freshly ground pepper

1 cup finely ground cornmeal

1 teaspoon sweet paprika

2 large eggs

Canola oil, as needed

1 cup spinach leaves

1 slice applewood-smoked bacon, cooked and crumbled

¼ cup Onion Jam
(see recipe facing page)

SERVES 4

For the vinaigrette: In a small bowl, whisk together the mustard, shallot, sugar, salt, pepper, and vinegar. Gradually whisk in the oil until emulsified.

Sprinkle the tomato slices with salt and pepper and set aside. In a shallow bowl, combine the cornmeal and paprika. In another shallow bowl, beat the eggs.

In a large, heavy skillet, heat ½ inch of the oil over medium-high heat. Coat the tomato slices in the egg, then dredge them in the cornmeal mixture. Fry the tomatoes in batches until nicely browned, about 2 minutes per side. Using a slotted spatula, transfer to paper towels to drain.

In a large bowl, toss the spinach in 2 tablespoons of the vinaigrette. Arrange the tomatoes on a plate and put the tossed spinach on top of them. Sprinkle some of the bacon pieces over the spinach and dot the spinach with spoonfuls of Onion Jam. Pass the remaining vinaigrette alongside. Serve at once.

THE SHERATON HOTEL & CASINO, NOW TUNICA ROADHOUSE CASINO & HOTEL, WAS AMONG THE FIRST CASINOS TO ADOPT THE DOCKSIDE ARCHITECTURAL APPROACH PREVALENT AMONG MISSISSIPPI CASINOS TODAY. EARLY MISSISSIPPI CASINOS WERE ACTUAL WORKING RIVERBOATS.

SALADS

68   69

ONION JAM

8 ounces red onions, very thinly sliced

2 cups dry red wine

2 tablespoons honey

1 tablespoon chopped fresh thyme

2 tablespoons red wine vinegar

1 tablespoon water (optional)

Salt and pepper

In a large skillet, combine the onions, wine, honey, and thyme. Bring to a boil over medium-high heat. Reduce the heat to medium-low and simmer, stirring occasionally, until the wine is almost absorbed, about 55 minutes. Mix in the red wine vinegar. Simmer, stirring frequently, for 10 minutes to blend the flavors, adding water as needed and stirring often (the onions will still be slightly crunchy). Season with salt and pepper. Remove from the heat. Use now, or cover and refrigerate for up to 3 days.

Before using, rewarm over medium heat until just warm, adding more water by tablespoonfuls if the jam is dry.

TOP 10 TIPS
FOR PREPARING MEMORABLE, FAST, AND EASY MEALS

TUNICA ROADHOUSE CASINO & HOTEL

1   Involve the entire family in the preparation of the meal. You'll have more fun and share quality time with loved ones while cutting down on the preparation time.

2   Use your slow cooker.

3   Keep the total number of ingredients in each dish to six or fewer.

4   Create or use recipes that can be prepared in one pot or pan.

5   Plan your menu for the entire week and utilize leftovers for lunch or breakfast.

6   Make use of pantry foods, such as pasta and rice, as a base and vary the sauce, vegetable, or protein.

7   Use leftover fresh vegetables and meats to create an awesome salad.

8   Chop vegetables or meats in the morning or the day before your meal.

9   Use high-quality canned, frozen, or packaged vegetables or fruits to save preparation time.

10   Simply adding a single fresh herb or glaze of butter can bring a whole new dimension to a meal without a lot of additional work.

TOP 10 TIPS
FOR CREATING A BALANCED DISH
THAT YOUR GUESTS WILL LOVE

HORSESHOE HAMMOND

1   Budget: First, consider what you are willing to spend on food.

2   Know your guests: Ask yourself such questions as: What are my guests' likes and dislikes? Do any of my guests have allergies? Are any of my guests vegetarians?

3   Menu planning: Creating a dish can be fun and challenging at the same time. Many factors should be considered first. For example: What is the occasion? What season of the year is it? What foods are now in season?

4   Variety: Because we all have different tastes, you need to ensure that you have a good variety of dishes on your menu.

5   Freshness: The freshness of your ingredients is the key to a quality and memorable meal.

6   Spices: Choose the correct spices to complement your ingredients.

7   Cooking equipment: Make sure you have the right equipment to cook the meal you have in mind.

8   Wine selection: This could make or break your dinner. The flavor profiles of the wine and the food should complement each other.

9   Timing: Timing when your food is ready to be served is a vital part of preparing a great meal, especially if the menu includes dishes that need to be served at once.

10 Presentation! Presentation! Presentation! Always remember, people eat with their eyes first. If the food looks great, it will taste great.

ROASTED PEPPER ANTIPASTO

CAESARS ATLANTIC CITY
CHEF DE CUISINE JOHN MEJLAK

An antipasto (Italian for "before the meal") is a first course that traditionally combines several colorful ingredients. For your next dinner party, dazzle your guests with this vibrant array of red, yellow, and green bell peppers. Chef John Mejlak comments, "This is a nice, easy salad that I like to make for my family."

3 red bell peppers

2 yellow bell peppers

2 green bell peppers

2 tablespoons balsamic vinegar

5 tablespoons extra-virgin olive oil

Tabasco sauce

Kosher salt and freshly ground pepper

Four 12-ounce cans artichoke hearts, drained and quartered

½ cup oil-packed sun-dried tomatoes, drained and julienned

1 garlic clove, thinly sliced

8 basil leaves, stemmed and coarsely chopped

SERVES 6

Preheat the oven to 400°F. Line a baking sheet with aluminum foil and oil the foil. Place the peppers on the prepared pan and roast for 45 minutes, or until blackened. Put the peppers in a medium bowl, cover, and let cool for 15 minutes.

Meanwhile, in a small bowl, whisk together the balsamic vinegar, oil, and Tabasco sauce to taste. Season with salt and pepper.

Peel, seed, and devein the peppers. Cut them into strips about 1 inch wide. In a large bowl, combine the peppers with the artichokes, tomatoes, and garlic. Pour the dressing over and toss gently to coat. Serve garnished with the basil.

FIORE TOMATO CAPRESE

FIORE AT HARRAH'S RINCON CASINO & RESORT
EXECUTIVE CHEF VESA LEPPALA

Fiore Tomato Caprese is Fiore's variation of a classic salad from the island of Capri. Serve this at the height of summer, when tomatoes are at their most flavorful, with the best mozzarella you can find.

BALSAMIC REDUCTION

1 cup balsamic vinegar

¼ cup ruby port

**4 ripe tomatoes, cut into
¼-inch-thick slices**

Salt and freshly cracked peppercorns

12 fresh basil leaves

**10 ounces fresh mozzarella,
cut into ¼-inch-thick slices**

3 tablespoons extra-virgin olive oil

SERVES 4

For the balsamic reduction: In a small nonreactive saucepan, combine the vinegar and port. Bring to a boil over medium heat, reduce to a simmer, and cook until reduced by half. Remove from the heat and let cool. The mixture will thicken as it cools. Pour into a squeeze bottle and set aside at room temperature.

To serve, place 1 slice of tomato on a plate and sprinkle with a little salt and pepper. Layer the tomato slice with a basil leaf, then a slice of mozzarella. Repeat the process to make three layers. Sprinkle the top layer with salt and pepper and drizzle with the balsamic reduction, then the olive oil. Repeat to make 4 servings. Serve at once.

3
SOUPS

LEEK, SUN-DRIED TOMATO, SHIITAKE MUSHROOM & CHAMPAGNE SOUP

K-PAUL'S LOUISIANA KITCHEN
CHEF PAUL PRUDHOMME

This is a unique recipe of flavors, which in concert create a rich and mouthwatering soup suitable for the chilly fall and winter months. The splash of Champagne adds a festive touch!

Note: Chef Prudhomme's sauces and seasonings are available at www.ChefPaul.com.

½ cup dry-packed sun-dried tomatoes

2 pounds leeks

3 tablespoons unsalted butter

1 cup chopped onions

1½ tablespoons Chef Paul Prudhomme's Vegetable Magic (see note)

4 cups shiitake mushrooms, sliced

¾ cup Champagne or dry sparkling wine (optional)

2 cups unsalted chicken stock

2 cups heavy cream

1 cup shredded Gouda cheese

SERVES 8

Soak the sun-dried tomatoes in warm water for 30 minutes. Drain and julienne. Trim off the dark green leaves (leaving the white and light green parts) and the root ends of the leeks and discard. Split the remaining leeks in half lengthwise and wash thoroughly under running water, making sure that all the dirt is removed from between the sections. Slice the leek halves crosswise into very thin half-rounds. You should have about 3 cups.

In a medium saucepan, melt the butter over medium-high heat. Add the leeks and onions and cook, stirring frequently, until the onions are wilted and soft, about 8 minutes. Add the Vegetable Magic and stir well. Continue to cook until the seasoning begins to darken slightly, about 2 minutes. Add the shiitake mushrooms and the sun-dried tomatoes. Cook, stirring frequently, until the mushrooms begin to darken, about 4 minutes. Add ¼ cup of the Champagne, if using, and stir to scrape up the browned bits from the bottom of the pan. Add the chicken stock. Bring to a boil, then reduce the heat to medium-low and simmer for 20 minutes. Add the cream, stir well, and return to a boil. Reduce heat and simmer until the soup has reduced slightly, about 10 minutes. Gradually stir in the cheese and continue stirring until it has melted. Add the remaining ½ cup of the Champagne and stir briefly. Remove from the heat and serve.

GRILLED SHRIMP GAZPACHO

RESERVE AT HARRAH'S JOLIET
CHEF DE CUISINE TYE NIELSEN

Gazpacho, that hot-weather standby, is here made more substantial with the addition of grilled shrimp. The simple flavors blend together to create a harmony of vegetables and cool broth, leaving you fulfilled and invigorated. Look for the best vine-ripened tomatoes to make this refreshing dish.

Note: The gazpacho needs to be prepared the day before serving.

GAZPACHO

1 small to medium red onion, diced

2 small celery stalks, diced

3 small to medium tomatoes, diced

15 red grapes

Grated zest and juice of 1 lime

Juice of 1 lemon

3 fresh basil leaves, chopped

½ bunch cilantro, stemmed and chopped

½ cup sweet white wine

4 cups water

Salt and freshly ground pepper

2 garlic cloves, crushed

3 tablespoons canola oil

8 to 12 jumbo shrimp, shelled and deveined

5 cilantro sprigs for garnish

SERVES 4 TO 6

For the gazpacho: In a large glass or ceramic bowl, combine the vegetables, grapes, lime zest, lime and lemon juices, basil, chopped cilantro, wine, water, and a pinch of salt. Cover and refrigerate overnight. Season with salt and pepper.

Soak 2 wooden skewers in water to cover for 30 minutes. Prepare a hot fire in a charcoal grill, preheat a gas grill to high, or heat a grill pan over high heat. In a medium bowl, combine the garlic and oil. Add the shrimp and toss to coat. Thread the shrimp on the skewers and grill them for 2 to 3 minutes on each side, or until evenly pink.

To serve, ladle the gazpacho into martini glasses or bowls and top each serving with 2 to 3 shrimp. Garnish with the sprigs of cilantro.

THE RESERVE AND MOSAIC RESTAURANTS
AT HARRAH'S JOLIET
SUPPORT CHARITIES SUCH AS BIG BROTHERS
BIG SISTERS AND MARCH OF DIMES.

HARRAH'S STEAK HOUSE CREAMY FIVE-ONION SOUP

HARRAH'S STEAK HOUSE AT HARRAH'S RENO
EXECUTIVE CHEF KLAUS FEYERSINGER

Voted Reno's No. 1 Steak House, Harrah's is not only legendary for its steaks, but also for its side dishes and soups. Five different members of the onion family go into this soup, which is complemented with sweet basil and Burgundy wine and served in a dramatic presentation. Chef Klaus Feyersinger explains, "This longtime favorite will start your dining experience off right. The creamy, hot soup is ladled into a hollowed-out colossal onion and crowned with a golden brown Swiss cheese crust. This is Harrah's Steak House's most requested menu item. One taste and you'll know why."

1 cup (2 sticks) unsalted butter

1 large white onion, julienned

1 red onion, julienned

4 shallots, finely diced

1½ cups chopped green onions, white and light green parts only

1 small leek, white part only, cut into crosswise slices and washed well

1 tablespoon dried basil

½ teaspoon freshly ground pepper

1 cup all-purpose flour

1 cup Burgundy or other dry red wine

8 cups beef consommé

2 cups heavy cream

8 large onions, hollowed out (optional)

8 large round croutons, 2 inches in diameter

8 slices Swiss cheese

8 slices Gruyère cheese

SERVES 8

Preheat the oven to 450°F. In a large stockpot, melt the butter over medium heat and sauté the white onion, red onion, shallots, ½ cup of the green onions, the leek, basil, and pepper until the onions are tender, about 5 minutes. Stir in the flour and cook, stirring constantly, for 1 minute. Add the wine, consommé, and cream. Bring to a boil, then reduce the heat to a simmer and cook, stirring frequently, for 10 minutes.

Ladle the soup into the onions or ovenproof soup bowls. Top each with a crouton and 1 slice of each cheese. Bake for 10 minutes, or until the cheese is melted and browned. Remove from the oven, sprinkle with the remaining green onions, and serve.

HARRAH'S STEAK HOUSE HAS HELD
THE FOUR-DIAMOND RATING FROM
THE AMERICAN AUTOMOBILE ASSOCIATION (AAA)
LONGER THAN ANY OTHER RESTAURANT IN RENO.

WILD MUSHROOM CHOWDER

CAESARS WINDSOR
EXECUTIVE CHEF PATRICK MCCLARY

Add a woodsy aura to your entertaining with this hearty chowder, which will have mushroom lovers coming back again and again. Don't let the long list of ingredients intimidate you; the preparation is minimal and the result is an intensely flavorful, satisfying dish.

¼ cup dried morels

¾ cup dried porcini mushrooms, or 2 tablespoons porcini powder

8 cups chicken stock

⅓ cup unsalted butter

4 shallots, minced

2 garlic cloves, chopped

½ cup all-purpose flour

¼ cup canola oil

1½ ounces oyster mushrooms, sliced

1½ ounces shiitake mushrooms, stemmed and sliced

1½ ounces chanterelle mushrooms, sliced

¾ cup dry white wine

¼ cup cooked wild rice

½ cup diced cooked potatoes

¼ cup cooked black beans

¼ cup cooked white beans

3 tablespoons honey

1 tablespoon minced fresh rosemary

2 cups heavy cream

Salt and cracked pepper

SERVES 10

Soak the morels in warm water to cover for 30 minutes, then drain and slice. In a blender, grind the dried porcini to a powder. Bring the chicken stock to a boil, reduce the heat, and maintain at a simmer.

In a large soup pot, melt the butter over medium heat and sauté the shallots and garlic until the shallots are translucent, about 3 minutes. Stir in the flour and cook, stirring constantly, for about 3 minutes; do not brown.

Gradually whisk the hot chicken stock into the flour mixture. Reduce the heat to medium-low and stir in the porcini powder. Let the soup simmer.

In a large skillet, heat the oil over medium-high heat and sauté the oyster, shiitake, and chanterelle mushrooms for 5 to 7 minutes, or until tender. Stir in the morels, then add the wine, stirring to scrape up the browned bits from the bottom of the pan. Cook for 10 minutes.

Add the mushrooms and wine mixture to the simmering soup base, reduce the heat to a simmer, and cook for 45 minutes. Add the rice, potatoes, beans, honey, rosemary, and cream. Cook for 15 minutes. Season with salt and pepper. Serve in deep soup bowls.

1   Thyme: My favorite herb, thyme, is used in a wide range of dishes, including stews, meats, poultry, and seafood. Thyme adds a savory touch to every dish and is a standard ingredient in bouquet garnis. It can be added to hot teas to help get rid of a cough and bronchitis, or to various cocktails to bring out savory notes. Buy a plant and keep it on your back porch or in a sunny window.

2   Basil: Basil adds a fresh note to every dish made with it. The leaves can be stacked, rolled, and cut into fine shreds, or used whole or minced. Add it to food just before serving, as basil is pungent and delicate. Basil can also be used as a garnish and is even added to many drinks in Asian cultures, where it's noted for its medicinal properties.

3   Chives: Fresh and delicate, chives instantly remind me of springtime on the farm. This herb will add a light touch of onion flavor to your cooking. Minced chives are added to sauces, soups, potatoes, and seafood just before serving and are very often used as a garnish.

4   Cilantro: Also known as fresh coriander, cilantro adds an undeniable energy to every dish it's used in, and perhaps most famously to many salsas. I have a cilantro plant in my yard and use it for fruit salsas, seafood, and my favorite spicy Vietnamese soup, pho. When the plant flowers and seeds, I collect the seeds and dry them. I then grind the seeds and use the coriander to flavor seafood and sauces.

5   Flat-leaf, or Italian, parsley: I love this herb for its deep color and palate-cleansing notes. My mother used this herb in her salads. Flat-leaf parsley has more flavor than the more common curly-leaf parsley.

6   Bay leaf: Bay leaves come from California, from the California laurel tree, or from Turkey. The ones from California have a stronger flavor. Although the prized, distinct flavor develops after several weeks of drying, I like to buy this herb fresh and freeze it. I use bay leaves daily, in stocks, étouffée, gumbos, jambalaya, red beans, and much more. This hardy leaf should be added early in the cooking process to develop its flavor. Be sure to remove it before serving the dish.

7   Rosemary: Use this highly aromatic herb with assertively flavored foods like lamb and game. Rosemary can be overpowering, so use it lightly. I like to keep the branches and use them for flavorful skewers in grilling and roasting.

8   Thai basil: This basil has small leaves, purple stems, and flavors of licorice and mint. It is used in Thai dishes and is a refreshing addition to the Vietnamese soup pho; it also adds a fresh note to fried rice and stir-fried noodles.

9   Chervil: Also known as gourmet's parsley and garden chervil, this delicate herb adds a faint licorice flavor to seafood, omelets, soups, salads, and vegetables.

10   Spearmint: Spearmint has serrated, wrinkly leaves and a milder flavor than peppermint. Use it in cooking, to garnish desserts, and to make the perfect mojito.

PICKLES' FAMOUS MUSHROOM-BARLEY SOUP

PICKLES AT BALLY'S ATLANTIC CITY
CHEF ROLF BECHTOLD

Straight from Atlantic City's favorite deli, this hearty soup is one of the town's favorite indulgences. A rustic mixture of garden vegetables and comforting grain, it's somehow right at home among the bright lights of the big city.

5 tablespoons unsalted butter

2 cups pearl barley

1½ cups finely diced onions

1½ cups finely diced celery

1½ cups finely diced carrots

1 pound white mushrooms, cleaned and sliced

1 bay leaf

1 tablespoon dried thyme

8 cups chicken stock

Salt and freshly ground pepper

SERVES 8 TO 10

In a large soup pot, melt the butter over medium heat. Add the barley and sauté for 5 minutes. Add the onions, celery, and carrots and sauté until tender, 4 to 5 minutes. Add the mushrooms, bay leaf, thyme, and stock. Bring the mixture to a boil, then reduce the heat to a simmer. Cook until the barley is tender, 20 to 25 minutes. Season with salt and pepper.

SEVEN STARS SPLIT PEA SOUP

FRESH MARKET BUFFET AT HARRAH'S NORTH KANSAS CITY
CHEF JEFF CRAIG

This mouthwatering take on a classic soup is a favorite at Harrah's North Kansas City. Chef Jeff Craig says, "Our Seven Stars Split Pea Soup is not only fast to make and tastes great, but it's a great recipe for cold weather."

1 tablespoon olive oil

2 cups chopped yellow onions

Salt and freshly ground black pepper

Red pepper flakes

1 tablespoon minced garlic

1 bay leaf

1 pound green split peas, picked over and rinsed

8 cups chicken stock

1 cup milk

SERVES 6 TO 8

In a large soup pot, heat the oil over medium heat. Add the onions and salt, black pepper, and red pepper flakes to taste. Sauté for 2 minutes. Add the garlic, bay leaf, and split peas and cook, stirring, for 1 minute. Add the stock and bring to a boil, then reduce the heat to a simmer and cook, stirring occasionally until the peas are tender, about 45 minutes. Remove from the heat and let cool slightly. Remove the bay leaf and discard. Add the milk. Working in batches, purée in a blender until smooth. Taste and adjust the seasoning. Serve hot.

CLASSIC GUMBO

HARRAH'S LOUISIANA DOWNS
EXECUTIVE CHEF J. RYAN GILLESPIE

Gumbo is eaten year-round in Louisiana. Chef J. Ryan Gillespie explains, "This is an item that we offer every day. We couldn't pull it off the menu even if we wanted to. This recipe isn't considered a traditional gumbo due to the fact that it has both okra and filé. Normally, it is one or the other, but we have such die-hard gumbo connoisseurs here that we like to keep them all happy—no matter their preference." He also warns, "Be careful not to burn the roux, as a large part of this classic dish's flavor comes from it."

¾ cup canola oil or ¾ cup (1½ sticks) unsalted butter

¾ cup all-purpose flour

3 bell peppers, seeded, deveined, and diced

1 large tomato, seeded and diced

½ cup diced onion

½ cup diced celery

1 tablespoon plus 2 teaspoons filé powder, preferably Cajun Chef brand

4 bay leaves

1 tablespoon crawfish boil, preferably LaDon's brand

1 tablespoon Durkee Hot Sauce or other hot sauce

1 tablespoon Worcestershire sauce

½ tablespoon minced garlic

2 teaspoons red pepper flakes

2 teaspoons onion powder

7 cups chicken stock

8 ounces medium shrimp, shelled and deveined

8 ounces smoked sausage, cooked and sliced

8 ounces okra, sliced

8 ounces diced cooked chicken meat, diced

Steamed white rice for serving

SERVES 10 TO 12

In a heavy, medium saucepan, heat the oil or melt the butter over medium heat and stir in the flour until blended. Cook, stirring frequently, until the roux has turned a dark brownish red and has a nutty fragrance, about 25 minutes; take care not to burn. Remove from the heat and set aside.

In a large soup pot, combine the bell peppers, tomato, onion, celery, seasonings, and stock. Bring to a low boil and cook until the vegetables are very tender, about 20 minutes. Stir in the roux until thoroughly blended. Reduce the heat to a simmer and cook for about 30 minutes, or until thickened and flavorful.

Stir in the shrimp, sausage, and okra; cook for about 3 minutes, or until the shrimp is evenly pink. Stir in the chicken and cook another minute or two until heated through.

Serve in deep bowls, spooned over the rice.

FOOD USAGE PER YEAR AT
HARRAH'S LOUISIANA DOWNS:
8,875 GALLONS OF MILK,
2,184 GALLONS OF VANILLA ICE CREAM,
2,063 GALLONS OF KETCHUP,
1,208 GALLONS OF MAYONNAISE,
AND 75,420 EGGS.

GUMBO

THE RANGE STEAKHOUSE & BAR AT TUNICA ROADHOUSE CASINO & HOTEL
EXECUTIVE CHEF & DIRECTOR OF FOOD & BEVERAGE CHRISTOPHER J. HENCYK

Chef Christopher J. Hencyk's version of Southern gumbo earned a top award at the 2008 Porter-Leath Rajun Cajun Crawfish Festival in Memphis. One taste, and you'll know why this distinctive blending of flavors is a winner.

¾ cup canola oil

¾ cup all-purpose flour

½ cup (1 stick) unsalted butter

1 green bell pepper, seeded, deveined, and diced

1 white onion, diced

2 celery stalks, diced

5 garlic cloves, chopped

1 teaspoon dried basil

1 teaspoon dried thyme

1 teaspoon dried oregano

1 bay leaf

1 teaspoon cayenne pepper

1 tablespoon Tabasco sauce

2 teaspoons Worcestershire sauce

2 tablespoons seafood base

2 tablespoons chicken base

1 teaspoon crab boil (liquid)

1 teaspoon filé powder

¼ pound shredded cooked chicken

¾ pound andouille sausage

¼ pound crawfish tail meat

1¼ pounds shrimp meat (bay shrimp)

½ pound lump crabmeat, picked over for shell

2 dozen oysters, shucked

One 14-ounce can crushed tomatoes

1 pound frozen okra

3 quarts water

Salt and freshly ground pepper

Steamed white rice for serving

SERVES 12 AS A MAIN COURSE

In a medium saucepan, heat the oil over medium heat and gradually stir in the flour. Cook, stirring frequently, until well browned, about 20 minutes; the roux should have a rich, nutty aroma. Remove from the heat and set aside.

In a large soup pot, melt the butter over medium heat and sauté the pepper, onion, and celery until the onion is translucent, about 3 minutes. Add the garlic, herbs, cayenne, Tabasco, Worcestershire, bases, crab boil, filé powder, chicken, sausage, seafood, tomatoes, and okra and cook for 10 minutes. Add the water and bring to a boil. Stir in the roux until smooth. Season with salt and pepper. Reduce the heat to a simmer and cook for 30 minutes.

Serve in deep bowls, spooned over the rice.

OF THE NINE CASINO BRANDS CURRENTLY OPERATING IN TUNICA, TUNICA ROADHOUSE CASINO & HOTEL WAS THE FIFTH TO OPEN ITS DOORS, IN 1994, AS THE SHERATON HOTEL & CASINO.

NEW ORLEANS GUMBO

THE BUFFET AT HARRAH'S AT HARRAH'S NEW ORLEANS
CHEF HOYCE OATIS

Chef Hoyce Oatis says, "When you talk about Southern cuisine, gumbo is usually the theme. This recipe is one of our most famous and tastiest delights, and can be served as a first, second, or third course. Gumbo is on every menu of all New Orleans restaurants and is truly the favorite meal of many local households."

½ cup canola oil for frying

2 fresh or frozen blue crabs

¾ cup (1½ sticks) unsalted butter

1¼ cups all-purpose flour

1 small onion, diced

½ large bell pepper, seeded, deveined, and diced

2 celery stalks, diced

⅓ cup tomato paste

1 cup canned crushed tomatoes

1 bay leaf

½ tablespoon dried thyme

8 cups shrimp stock (page 202)

4 ounces chicken gizzards, halved

¼ cup diced pickle meat (pickled pork) or tasso, sliced

4 ounces smoked sausage

1 cup sliced okra

½ cup filé powder

¼ cup water

8 ounces medium shrimp, shelled and deveined

Salt and freshly ground pepper

Steamed white rice for serving

SERVES 8

In a large sauté pan, heat the oil over low heat and fry the crabs until golden brown, about 2 minutes on each side. Remove from the heat and set aside.

In a large soup pot, melt the butter over low heat. Gradually stir in the flour and continue to cook the roux, stirring constantly, until it becomes the color of peanut butter. Stir in the onion, bell pepper, and celery, mixing well, then the tomato paste, tomatoes, bay leaf, thyme, and shrimp stock. Add the crabs, then the chicken gizzards and pickle meat. Stir very well and let simmer for 30 minutes. Add the smoked sausage and okra. Increase the heat to medium-high and bring to a rolling boil. Mix the filé powder with the water and pour it into the boiling pot. Add the shrimp. Stir for 2 minutes, then season with salt and pepper.

Serve in deep bowls spooned over the rice.

LOCATED IN THE HEART OF THE CRESCENT CITY, STEPS FROM THE HISTORIC FRENCH QUARTER, HARRAH'S NEW ORLEANS CASINO RIVALS THE GRANDEUR OF A VEGAS-STYLE CASINO. THE SOLE LAND-BASED CASINO IN DOWNTOWN NEW ORLEANS, WITH MORE THAN 2,100 OF THE NEWEST SLOTS, IT HOSTS ACTION-PACKED TABLE GAMES TWENTY-FOUR HOURS A DAY EVERY DAY OF THE WEEK.

BEEF & ONION SOUP

WITH SHORT RIB CROUTONS & FIVE-ONION SALAD

THE STEAKHOUSE AT HARRAH'S RESORT ATLANTIC CITY
CHEF RICHARD LEADBETTER

Chef Richard Leadbetter says, "One of my favorite cuts of beef is the short rib. The rich baritone flavors that are derived from the short ribs make for robust stocks and tender beef. The combination of a deconstructed onion soup of hearty broth, crispy crostini, pulled short rib meat, and onion salad takes the traditional French onion soup to the next level. Served as a soup and salad course or as a meal, this combination will always satisfy."

2 pounds bone-in beef short ribs

Kosher salt and
freshly ground pepper

2 cups all-purpose flour

1 cup olive oil

1 cup diced celery

2 pounds sweet white onions,
such as Vidalia, sliced,
plus 1 cup diced white sweet onion

1 cup diced carrots

6 garlic cloves

3 cups dry red wine

2 cups tomato juice

8 cups beef stock

8 thyme sprigs

1 rosemary sprig

2 cups dry sherry

FIVE-ONION SALAD

2 shallots, finely shaved

1 small bunch chives, minced

1 tablespoon finely chopped red onion

2 green onions, green parts only,
julienned

1 tablespoon finely chopped sweet
white onion, such as Vidalia

1 tablespoon minced fresh flat-leaf
parsley

1 tablespoon extra-virgin olive oil

Salt and freshly ground black pepper

SERVES 8

CROUTONS

1 loaf French or Italian bread

Olive oil for brushing

2 cups shredded
white Cheddar cheese

Preheat the oven to 300°F. Prepare the short ribs by cutting between each bone to separate them. Season with salt and pepper. Dredge each piece of short ribs in the flour and set aside.

In a large, heavy sauté pan, heat ½ cup of the olive oil over medium-high heat until shimmering. Sear the short ribs on all sides until well browned. Transfer the short ribs to a small roasting pan.

Immediately add the celery, the 1 cup diced onions, the carrots, and garlic to the sauté pan that the short ribs were seared in. Sauté the mixture over medium heat for 10 minutes, or until caramelized. Add 2 cups of the red wine and cook to reduce by half. Add the tomato juice and 3 cups of the beef stock. Simmer the mixture for about 5 minutes. Add 4 sprigs of the thyme and the rosemary.

Pour the braising liquid over the seared short ribs in the roasting pan. Cover the pan with aluminum foil and braise in the oven for at least 4 hours, or until the meat falls off the bone. Remove the short ribs from the braising liquid and let cool to the touch.

Pull the meat from the ribs, being careful not to pull the gristly part close to the bone. Add some of the braising liquid to the pulled meat. Strain the braising liquid and set aside.

In a large, heavy soup pot, heat the remaining ½ cup olive oil over high heat and sauté the 2 pounds sliced onions, stirring occasionally, until caramelized, about 10 minutes. Add the remaining 1 cup red wine and the sherry, and cook to reduce by half. Add the remaining beef stock and the reserved braising liquid. Let the mixture simmer for about 30 minutes. Add the remaining thyme sprigs. Taste and adjust the seasoning.

For the salad: In a medium bowl, combine all the ingredients and toss to coat.

For the croutons: Preheat the oven to 325°F. Cut the bread into eight to ten ¼-inch-thick slices. Brush the slices with the olive oil and season with salt and pepper. Place on a baking sheet and bake for 15 minutes, or until crisp. Remove from the oven.

Increase the oven temperature to 375°F. Top each crouton with some pulled short rib and Cheddar cheese. Bake at 375°F for 20 minutes, or until golden brown.

To serve, ladle the soup into deep soup bowls. Place a crouton on top of each. Garnish the croutons with the salad and serve at once.

CHICKEN & SHRIMP JAMBALAYA

FRENCH QUARTER BUFFET AT SHOWBOAT ATLANTIC CITY
CHEF TODD BANNAN & CHEF ARMANDO CORTES

Like gumbo, jambalaya is one of Louisiana's culinary superstars. The co-creator of this one, chef Todd Bannan, explains, "It is believed that the word 'jambalaya' comes from the French word *jambon*, meaning 'ham'; the Acadian language, where everything is *à la*; and the African *ya*, meaning 'rice.' Most purists believe that a jambalaya should be brown in color." In this recipe, the color is achieved by browning the sausage and the chicken in a cast-iron Dutch oven.

2 boneless, skinless chicken thighs, diced

1 teaspoon dried oregano

1 teaspoon dried thyme

1 teaspoon onion powder

½ teaspoon ground cumin

¼ teaspoon cayenne pepper, or to taste

2 tablespoons olive oil

8 ounces andouille sausage, sliced

½ cup sliced onion

½ cup diced green bell pepper

¼ cup diced celery

2 tablespoons minced garlic

½ cup chopped tomatoes

3 bay leaves

1 teaspoon Louisiana hot sauce

¾ cup rice

3 cups chicken stock

12 extra-large shrimp, shelled and deveined

Salt and freshly ground pepper

Warm French bread for serving

SERVES 4

In a medium bowl, combine the chicken, herbs, and spices. Coat the chicken well. In a large cast-iron Dutch oven, heat the oil over medium-high heat. Add the sausage and chicken and cook until seared on all sides, about 2 minutes per side. Add the onion, bell pepper, and celery, and sauté for about 3 minutes. Add the garlic, tomatoes, bay leaves, and hot sauce. Stir in the rice and then gradually stir in the stock. Reduce the heat to medium and cook until the rice absorbs the liquid and becomes tender, about 15 minutes. Add the shrimp about 3 minutes before the rice is done and cook until evenly pink. Season with salt and pepper. Serve with warm French bread.

TO SATISFY THE MEAT-AND-POTATO CROWD THAT IS SHOWBOAT ATLANTIC CITY'S RIB AND CHOPHOUSE CUSTOMER BASE, MORE THAN 4,200 POUNDS OF PRIME RIB WERE SERVED IN 2008. ACCOMPANYING THE RIBS WERE 7,800 ORDERS OF POTATOES, VARYING FROM TRUFFLE PARMESAN FRIES TO FORK-SMASHED AND THE EVER-CLASSIC BAKED.

ROASTED EGGPLANT SOUP

WATERFRONT BUFFET AT HARRAH'S RESORT ATLANTIC CITY
CHEF DAVID SUSCAVAGE

Eggplant stars in this class act of a soup with a supporting cast of flavorful ingredients, such as celery, onion, garlic, and white wine. Chef David Suscavage comments, "Roasted eggplant soup is a family favorite and a great summer soup. The firmness and earthy flavors of the eggplant make for a versatile ingredient in the kitchen. This soup can be served piping hot or finished with fresh cream and served chilled."

¾ cup olive oil

4 cups diced celery

1 pound onions, diced

3 pounds eggplant, diced

1 pound potatoes, peeled and diced

3 garlic cloves

¾ cup dry white wine

1 cup tomato purée

1 cup cooked kidney beans

4 cups low-salt chicken broth or vegetable stock

Salt and freshly ground pepper

Red pepper flakes

1 bunch basil, stemmed and chopped

SERVES 4 TO 6

In a soup pot, heat the oil over medium heat. Add all the vegetables and garlic and sauté until the vegetables turn golden brown, about 12 minutes. Add the white wine and cook to reduce by half. Add the tomato purée and kidney beans and simmer for 10 minutes. Add the chicken broth and simmer until the vegetables are tender, about 15 minutes. Working in batches, purée the soup in a blender. Return to the pan and season with salt, black pepper, and red pepper flakes to taste. Reheat for a minute or two, then pour into shallow bowls and garnish with the basil.

THE WATERFRONT BUFFET FEATURES ELEVEN FOOD STATIONS: BRAZILIAN, AMERICAN, ITALIAN, ASIAN, MONGOLIAN, SUSHI, CRÊPES, DESSERT, DIM SUM, SALAD, AND GELATO, AND HAS BEEN *CASINO PLAYER* MAGAZINE'S PICK AS THE NO. 1 BUFFET IN ATLANTIC CITY FOR THE PAST THREE YEARS.

SELU TURKEY & ROASTED CORN SOUP

SELU GARDEN CAFÉ AT HARRAH'S CHEROKEE
EXECUTIVE CHEF KEITH ANDREASEN

Chef Keith Andreasen explains the Native American inspiration for his soup: "Selu is known as the mother of corn and Kanati as the great hunter. They were married, and their story is the basis of many Cherokee legends. In the Cherokee language, *selu* means 'corn.' Corn is held in high regard among Native peoples and continues to occupy a special place in Cherokee traditions. Native Americans have indeed given the world the most precious of our blessings, corn."

¾ cup corn kernels (about 1½ ears)

½ tablespoon canola oil

8 cups water

⅓ cup diced carrot

1½ cups diced raw turkey breast

6 tablespoons chicken base or
2 chicken bouillon cubes

⅓ cup diced onion

⅓ cup diced celery

¼ cup diced red bell pepper

¼ teaspoon granulated onion

¼ teaspoon ground white pepper

¼ teaspoon dried thyme

SERVES 6 TO 8

Preheat the oven to 350°F. In a cast-iron skillet, toss the corn in the oil to coat and roast in the oven for 20 minutes, or until lightly browned. Remove from the oven and set aside.

In a large soup pot, combine the water and carrot and bring to a boil over medium-high heat. Add the turkey and return to a boil. Add the chicken base, onion, celery, bell pepper, granulated onion, white pepper, thyme, and corn. Return to a boil, reduce to a simmer, and cook for 30 minutes. Serve in deep soup bowls.

ITALIAN MEATBALL & SAUSAGE CHILI

BREAKAWAY CAFÉ AT BALLY'S ATLANTIC CITY
FOOD SERVICE DIRECTOR ROLF J. WEITHOFER

Until now, employees of Bally's Atlantic City have enjoyed this Italian version of chili all to themselves in the employee dining room they've named Breakaway Café. Hot and sweet Italian sausages are matched with such Mediterranean favorites as cannellini beans, cremini mushrooms, and roasted garlic to make a hearty, spicy stew to enjoy year-round.

½ cup extra-virgin olive oil

2 pounds cremini mushrooms, quartered

4 red bell peppers, seeded, deveined, and diced

4 white onions, finely diced

3 pounds ground beef

2 pounds hot Italian sausage, casings removed

2 pounds sweet Italian sausage, casings removed

One 4-ounce can tomato paste

1 tablespoon red pepper flakes

4 cups canned diced Italian tomatoes

2 cups cooked cannellini beans

1 cup dry red wine

2 bunches flat-leaf parsley, stemmed and minced

1 cup fresh basil, cut into fine shreds

½ cup minced fresh oregano

2 cups roasted garlic cloves (see page 48)

Salt and freshly ground pepper

Toasted or grilled Italian bread slices, rubbed with garlic

Grated Parmesan cheese for serving

SERVES 20

In a medium sauté pan, heat the oil over medium heat and sauté the mushrooms, bell peppers, and onions until tender and lightly browned, about 8 minutes. Using a slotted spoon, transfer to a large soup pot. Add the beef and sausage to the pan and sauté over medium heat, cooking meat until cooked through, about 10 minutes, and then skim off excess grease. Stir in the tomato paste and red pepper flakes, then the tomatoes, beans, red wine, herbs, and garlic. Reduce the heat to low and simmer for about 1 hour. Season with salt and pepper. Serve with the garlic bread and Parmesan cheese alongside.

THE DENNIS HOTEL WAS
ONE OF THE MOST MAGNIFICENT HOTELS
IN THE COUNTRY WHEN CONSTRUCTED IN 1921.
CURRENTLY, IT IS PART OF BALLY'S ATLANTIC CITY
AND IS STILL IN USE AS A HOTEL.

4

SIDE
DISHES

BRADLEY OGDEN'S
BLUE CORN MUFFINS

BRADLEY OGDEN AT CAESARS PALACE LAS VEGAS
CHEF BRADLEY OGDEN

Celebrated San Francisco Bay Area chef Bradley Ogden has earned numerous awards and other national accolades for his version of American cuisine. Bradley Ogden at Caesars Palace Las Vegas is his first restaurant outside of California. These muffins will bring the memory of simpler times and country cooking into your kitchen, whether you live down on the farm or in the city. This recipe makes enough for a large gathering or for extras that your guests can take home with them.

6¼ cups all-purpose flour

3 cups sugar

3 tablespoons baking powder

5 tablespoons baking soda

4 cups blue corn flour

3 bunches dill, stemmed and minced

4 cups corn kernels (from 8 ears corn)

4 tablespoons salt

Pinch of ground pepper

2 pounds unsalted butter at room temperature

8 cups sour cream

6 cups buttermilk

1 cup heavy cream

20 large eggs, beaten

MAKES 30 MUFFINS

Preheat the oven to 350°F. Butter 30 muffin cups.

In a large bowl, combine the dry ingredients and stir with a whisk to blend. Add the dill, corn, salt, and pepper. Cut in the butter. In another large bowl, mix together the sour cream, buttermilk, heavy cream, and eggs and fold into the dry mixture until just mixed. Fill the prepared muffin cups three-fourths full. Bake for 6 minutes, then rotate them, and bake for 6 more minutes, or until golden brown. Remove from the oven and unmold onto wire racks. Serve warm or at room temperature.

PAULA DEEN'S HOECAKES

PAULA DEEN BUFFET AT HARRAH'S TUNICA
PAULA DEEN & EXECUTIVE SOUS-CHEF TAMMY WILLIAMS-HANSEN

A classic from Paula Deen's famed Savannah restaurant, The Lady & Sons, as well as Paula Deen Buffet at Harrah's Tunica, her Hoecakes prove to be a perfect Southern side for incorporating a yummy touch of Paula's unique charm into your next party or family dinner. A type of cornbread, Paula Deen's Hoecakes are irresistible when served hot off the griddle with some maple syrup.

1 cup self-rising flour

1 cup self-rising cornmeal or corn bread mix, such as Aunt Jemima's

1 tablespoon sugar

2 large eggs

¾ cup buttermilk

⅓ cup plus 1 tablespoon water

¼ cup canola oil or bacon grease

Canola oil, clarified butter (see page 43), or unsalted butter for frying (enough to generously cover the entire cooking surface)

MAKES 16 HOECAKES

In a medium bowl, combine the flour, cornmeal, and sugar. Stir with a whisk to blend. In a small bowl, whisk the eggs, buttermilk, water, and canola oil together until blended. Stir the wet ingredients into the dry ingredients until blended.

In a large skillet, heat the oil or clarified butter or melt the butter over medium heat. Drop 2 tablespoons batter per hoecake 1 to 2 inches apart into the skillet and fry until golden brown and crisp on both sides, 3 to 5 minutes per side. Using a slotted metal spatula, transfer to paper towels to drain. Keep warm in a low oven while cooking the remaining hoecakes. Serve hot.

Note: The batter can be covered and refrigerated for up to 2 days.

PAULA DEEN BUFFET'S SOUTHERN CUISINE NATURALLY CALLS FOR GREAT ICED TEA. SINCE OPENING IN MAY 2008, THE BUFFET HAS SERVED MORE THAN 40,000 GALLONS OF LUZIANNE ICED TEA, PAULA'S FAVORITE, WHICH IS SERVED WITH FRESH MINT.

MASHED SWEET POTATOES

THE RANGE STEAKHOUSE AT HARRAH'S NORTH KANSAS CITY
CHEF WILLIAM DWORZAN

Chef William Dworzan says, "These sweet potatoes garner a lot of compliments at the Steakhouse. But then, how in the world can you go wrong with ingredients like brown sugar, cinnamon, and butter? This side dish is especially popular during the holiday season."

2 pounds sweet potatoes
½ cup packed brown sugar
2 tablespoons mascarpone cheese
1 tablespoon unsalted butter
2 tablespoons maple syrup
Dash of ground cinnamon
Salt and ground white pepper

SERVES 4 TO 6

In a large pot of boiling water, cook the sweet potatoes until they are tender when pierced with a knife. Transfer to a platter and let cool to the touch. Peel and put the potatoes in a large bowl. Beat in all the remaining ingredients until smooth. Serve hot.

> HARRAH'S NORTH KANSAS CITY
> WON THE *KANSAS CITY BUSINESS JOURNAL*'S
> BEST PLACE TO WORK AWARD IN 2007 AND 2008.

CAULIFLOWER PURÉE

NEROS STEAKHOUSE AT CAESARS WINDSOR
CHEF DERON LEPORE

A high-quality white truffle oil brings out the robust flavor of cauliflower in this dish, which is equally at home with fish, lamb, and game fowl such as partridge. Chef Deron Lepore comments, "Our guests love its velvety texture, and its unique flavor is surprising because of its impressive white color, making this a favorite of mine given the lack of natural white produce found in nature."

1 cup chicken stock
1 cauliflower, cored and chopped (about 2 cups)
½ cup heavy cream
2 tablespoons unsalted butter
Sea salt and cracked pepper
½ teaspoon white truffle oil

SERVES 4

In a medium saucepan, bring the chicken stock to a boil and add the cauliflower. Reduce the heat to a simmer and cook until tender, about 10 minutes. Drain the cauliflower, reserving the stock.

In a blender, purée the cauliflower and ¼ cup of the reserved stock. Return to the pan over low heat. Add the heavy cream and butter and heat until the butter melts. Stir in salt and pepper. Divide among serving plates and drizzle each serving with a few drops of the white truffle oil.

TOP 10 TIPS
FOR CHOOSING FRUITS AND VEGETABLES

HARRAH'S METROPOLIS

1　Grow your own: There is nothing better than homegrown fruits and vegetables. You have complete control of the growing process, including how to fertilize. Gardening is also a fun activity that can save a lot of money. At Harrah's Metropolis, we're working on a rooftop garden to help supply our kitchen.

2　Buy from a farmers' market that sells local produce: When you support local growers, you're not only helping the farmers, but you are most likely getting produce that is much fresher than what is available at the grocery store.

3　Buy produce that is in season: While nearly every kind of produce is available year-round these days, fruits and vegetables that are in season will have the best quality and will usually be more affordable. For example: In spring, buy apricots, artichokes, asparagus, avocados, beets, cauliflower, cherries, radishes, rhubarb, and spinach. In summer, buy berries, corn, cucumbers, eggplant, garlic, and tomatoes. In fall, buy apples, broccoli, Brussels sprouts, squash, pears, sweet peppers, and sweet potatoes.

4　Look closely, smell, and touch: In other words, use your senses to choose the best fruits and vegetables.

Following are some tips for selecting my six favorite kinds of produce:

5　Asparagus: Asparagus should be firm and bright green, with purple-tinted buds. The thinner asparagus stalks are more tender and flavorful than thicker ones.

6　Avocados: Avocados should be slightly soft and squeezable, but not mushy. If you buy hard avocados, let them sit on a kitchen windowsill for a few days to ripen, or put them in a closed brown paper bag to expedite the process.

7　Corn: Look for tightly wrapped, grass green, slightly damp husks. Many grocery stores will allow you to partially open the husks to check for rotten kernels.

8　Tomatoes: These should be bright red, firm, and free of bruises.

9　Berries: Look for those with a bright, vivid color and a fruity aroma. Check the berries in the bottom of the container for signs of mold. Blueberries, one of my favorites, should be plump, firm, and uniform in color, with a silvery frost.

10　Mushrooms: All types of mushrooms should be smooth and even in color, without blemishes or brown spots. Avoid presliced, slimy, or wrinkled mushrooms.

POTATOES AU GRATIN

THE RANGE STEAKHOUSE AT HARRAH'S NORTH KANSAS CITY
CHEF HUGH RENO

This recipe from chef Hugh Reno takes comfort food to a new level. The many layers of flavors work together to create a warm, soothing richness. Serve with your favorite steak or, perhaps, smoked chicken.

3 tablespoons softened unsalted butter

2 pounds russet potatoes, peeled and cut into ⅛-inch-thick slices

8 ounces Swiss cheese, sliced

½ cup heavy cream

1 teaspoon minced garlic

Salt and freshly ground pepper

SERVES 4 TO 6

Preheat the oven to 325°F. Rub the sides and bottom of a 12-cup gratin dish with the butter. Alternately layer with the potatoes and Swiss cheese, ending with the Swiss cheese on top. In a medium bowl, mix together all the other ingredients and pour the mixture over the layers. Cover with aluminum foil and bake for 45 minutes. Remove the foil and bake for 25 minutes, or until the potatoes are tender and the cheese is browned. Remove from the oven and let stand for 10 minutes. Cut into squares or spoon out sections to serve.

PARMESAN & GARLIC POTATO CHIPS

BALLY'S STEAKHOUSE AT BALLY'S LAS VEGAS
CHEF JOSHUA SIERGEY

Serve these addictive chips with any steak or burger, or alone in a bowl for almost any occasion. Chef Joshua Siergey says, "This recipe has been a fixture at Bally's Steakhouse for many years for one reason: It is as timeless and classic as Bally's Steakhouse itself. Although basic, the complexity of flavors and textures is remarkable. The natural sweetness of the potato is concentrated with slow frying. The combination of the flavorful garlic and cheese with the salty crunch of kosher salt provides a contrast to the potato."

Canola oil for deep-frying

2 large russet potatoes, peeled and cut paper thin

½ cup grated Parmesan cheese

6 minced roasted garlic cloves (see page 48)

2 tablespoons minced fresh flat-leaf parsley

Kosher salt for sprinkling

SERVES 4

In a Dutch oven or large, heavy pot, heat 4 inches of the oil to 325°F on a deep-fat thermometer. Meanwhile, rinse the potato slices to remove the excess starch. Drain well and dry on paper towels to remove as much water as possible.

Add the potato slices to the hot oil in 2 batches. Fry, stirring constantly to ensure even cooking, until golden brown, 6 to 8 minutes. Using a wire skimmer, transfer to dry paper towels to drain. Transfer to a large bowl and sprinkle with the Parmesan cheese, garlic, parsley, and salt. Toss to coat and serve at once.

TOMATO CONFIT CHIPS

ARTURO'S AT BALLY'S ATLANTIC CITY
CHEF MAURIZIO DIMARCO

Bring a touch of Italy to your table with these chips from Arturo's at Bally's Atlantic City. Their deep, rich color will add a spark to your meal, and their flavor will complement other foods. Chef Maurizio Dimarco says, "Tomato confit chips are a great garnish for salads, entrées, and appetizers."

1 teaspoon olive oil

One large tomato (about 5 inches in diameter), cut into ⅛-inch-thick slices

1 teaspoon sugar

MAKES ABOUT 10 CHIPS

Preheat the oven to 250°F. Line a small baking sheet with parchment paper or a Silpat baking mat. Brush the paper or mat with the oil. Add the tomato slices in one layer. Lightly sprinkle the sugar on top of the tomato slices. Wait for 10 seconds, then turn them over. Bake for 45 minutes to 1 hour, or until caramelized and semi-crisp. Remove from the oven and, using a metal spatula, transfer to a plate lined with paper towels and let cool completely.

Serve now, or store the chips in an airtight container for up to 1 week, placing a paper towel between the layers.

CRISPY FRIED GREEN BEANS

AH SIN AT PARIS LAS VEGAS
CHEF THIERRY MAI-THANH

These crisp green beans are served at Ah Sin with the guest's sauce of choice, such as sweet chile, Thai peanut, or hoisin. Serve as a side dish or a crunchy anytime treat.

2 pounds green beans, trimmed

1 cup plus 2 tablespoons cornstarch

2 large eggs

1 cup ice water

1 cup all-purpose flour

About 1 cup chilled soda water

Canola oil or peanut oil for deep-frying

Salt and freshly ground pepper

SERVES 4 TO 6

In a large bowl, toss the green beans lightly in the 2 tablespoons cornstarch. In a shallow bowl, beat the eggs with the ice water. In a medium bowl, combine the flour and the 1 cup cornstarch. Stir the egg mixture into the dry ingredients just until blended. Gradually whisk in the soda water to the consistency of heavy cream.

In a wok, Dutch oven, or large, heavy pot, heat 2 inches of the oil to 350°F on a deep-fat thermometer. Dip the beans in the batter, one at a time, coating evenly. In batches, deep-fry the coated beans for 4 minutes, or until golden. Using a wire skimmer, transfer to paper towels to drain. Put all the beans in a bowl and toss with salt and pepper. Serve at once.

BUTTERMILK POTATOES

HARRAH'S LOUISIANA DOWNS
EXECUTIVE CHEF J. RYAN GILLESPIE

These deep-fried potato wedges are a wonderful alternative to French fries, and go well with almost any chicken, beef, or pork dish. The buttermilk and flour batter makes a crunchy contrast to the tender potatoes.

12 cups buttermilk

1 tablespoon cayenne pepper

½ cup minced fresh rosemary

¼ cup kosher salt

5 Idaho potatoes, scrubbed, dried, and cut into wedges

Canola oil for deep-frying

3 cups all-purpose flour

In a large saucepan, combine 8 cups of the buttermilk, the cayenne, rosemary, salt, and potatoes and bring to a simmer over medium heat. Cook until the potatoes are almost tender, 30 to 40 minutes. Using a wire skimmer, transfer to baking sheets to cool completely.

In a Dutch oven or large, heavy pot, heat 2 inches of the oil to 350°F on a deep-fat thermometer. Pour the remaining 4 cups of buttermilk into a medium bowl and put the flour in another medium bowl. Dip the potato wedges in the buttermilk first and then the flour. Add the wedges to the oil in batches and fry until golden brown, 3 to 5 minutes. Using a wire skimmer, transfer to paper towels to drain. Serve at once.

SERVES 10 TO 12

TELEVISION PERSONALITY LARRY KING WAS THE DIRECTOR OF PUBLIC RELATIONS AT HARRAH'S LOUISIANA DOWNS IN THE 1970S.

SWEET IOWA CREAMED CORN

360 STEAKHOUSE AT HARRAH'S COUNCIL BLUFFS
EXECUTIVE CHEF CHRISTOPHER COLELLO

The state of Iowa produces some of the heartland's best sweet corn. This spin-off of a classic Iowa dish is the perfect blend of savory, creamy, and sweet. Chef Christopher Colello advises, "Always taste the corn before cooking, as its sweetness varies. If the corn is very sweet, you may want to reduce the amount of sugar."

15 ears sweet Iowa corn, shucked

3½ cups heavy cream

2 bay leaves

¾ cup sugar

2 tablespoons kosher salt

8 tablespoons (1 stick) unsalted butter at room temperature

2 tablespoons minced fresh chives

Cut the corn kernels from the cobs and reserve the kernels and 5 of the cobs. In a large, heavy saucepan, combine the reserved cobs, the cream, bay leaves, sugar, and salt. Place over medium heat, bring to a simmer, and cook for 45 minutes.

Drain the corn, reserving the cream, and return the reserved cream to the pan. Add one-third of the corn kernels and cook for 12 minutes, or until tender. In batches, purée the corn mixture until smooth. With the machine running, add the butter, 2 tablespoons at a time. Strain the mixture through a fine-mesh sieve, pressing on the solids with the back of a large spoon. Return the mixture to the pan, add the remaining corn kernels, and cook until tender, about 12 minutes. Taste and adjust the seasoning. Remove from the heat and sprinkle the chives on top of each serving. Serve at once, in shallow soup bowls.

SERVES 6

SIDE DISHES

HARRAH'S COUNCIL BLUFFS'
STIR CONCERT COVE, THE MIDWEST'S
PREMIERE OUTDOOR CONCERT VENUE,
WAS RANKED ONE OF THE TOP 100 AMPHITHEATERS
IN THE WORLD BY *POLLSTAR* MAGAZINE.

CAULIFLOWER GRATIN

LE VILLAGE BUFFET AT PARIS LAS VEGAS
CHEF STEVEN KISNER

Walking into Le Village Buffet in Paris Las Vegas is like entering a quaint French village. The cuisine stations are housed in country-style homes, and each one represents a different French culinary region. Chef Steven Kisner says, "On the Brittany station, we offer this rich and luxurious gratin. With subtle horseradish and yellow curry highlights, the natural flavors of cauliflower, aged cheese, and fresh cream marry together beautifully. Few things are more enticing than pulling a browned and bubbling gratin dish out of a hot oven on a cool day."

2 cauliflowers (about ½ pound each)

5 tablespoons unsalted butter

2 garlic cloves, smashed

Salt and freshly ground pepper

1 teaspoon grated fresh horseradish

¼ cup milk

3 thyme sprigs

1 sage sprig

1 cup heavy cream

Freshly grated nutmeg

¼ teaspoon curry powder

⅓ cup grated Parmesan cheese

⅔ cup shredded Swiss cheese

¼ cup fresh bread crumbs

SERVES 4 TO 6

Trim the leaves and stems from the cauliflowers. Cut the cauliflowers into ½-inch-long florets. Reserve all the trimmings. Finely chop all the trimmings, including the leaves.

In a medium sauté pan, melt 2 tablespoons of the butter over medium heat and sauté the garlic until the butter starts to foam. Add the florets and toss to coat. Sprinkle with salt and pepper and cook until tender, 8 to 10 minutes. Using a slotted spoon, transfer to a baking sheet and let cool. Transfer to the refrigerator.

In a medium saucepan, melt the remaining 3 tablespoons butter over medium heat. Add the horseradish and a little salt. Sauté for 1 minute. Add the chopped cauliflower trimmings, the milk, thyme, and sage. Simmer over very low heat until the cauliflower is very soft and the milk has mostly evaporated, 5 to 6 minutes. Add the cream, nutmeg to taste, and curry powder and simmer for 2 more minutes. Remove and discard the thyme and sage. In batches, purée the mixture until smooth. Taste and adjust the seasoning. Fold in the florets and Parmesan cheese.

Preheat the oven to 400°F. Butter a 6-cup gratin dish. Pour the mixture into the prepared dish and top with the Swiss cheese, then the bread crumbs. Bake for 20 to 30 minutes, or until browned and bubbling hot.

PATATE ARROSTITE
(ROASTED POTATOES WITH SPECK)

POLISTINA'S ITALIAN RISTORANTE AT HARRAH'S RESORT ATLANTIC CITY
CHEF MIKE LAURENZA

Polistina's is a celebration of the foods from Venice, Florence, and Rome, right in the heart of Atlantic City. The main attraction of this authentic potato dish is the speck. Chef Mike Laurenza explains, "Speck is a juniper-flavored ham that originated in the Tyrol region, which lies in both Austria and Italy. Speck's distinctive flavor comes from a time-honored combination of salt-curing and smoking."

2 pounds Yukon gold potatoes, unpeeled and quartered

½ cup olive oil

2 rosemary sprigs

1 garlic clove, chopped

Kosher salt and cracked black pepper

4 ounces speck or prosciutto, sliced

1 bunch flat-leaf parsley, stemmed and minced

1 cup grated Parmigiano-Reggiano cheese

Preheat the oven to 350°F. In a roasting pan, combine the potatoes, oil, rosemary, garlic, and salt and pepper. Toss well to coat. Roast for 30 minutes, then stir in the speck. Return to the oven for 4 minutes. Remove from the oven and transfer to a large bowl. Add the parsley and cheese and toss well to mix. Serve at once.

SERVES 4 TO 6

POLISTINA'S ITALIAN RISTORANTE SERVES OVER EIGHT THOUSAND POUNDS OF CALAMARI ANNUALLY.

GARLIC BREAD FINGERS

MOSAIC AT HARRAH'S JOLIET
CHEF MATTHEW E. SECKO

Serve these treats with your favorite pasta dish or on their own. Chef Matthew E. Secko comments, "As a variation, the bread fingers can be transformed into a nice appetizer by spreading the garlic and butter on top and toasting them in the oven. Serve the tomato mixture alongside as a dipping sauce."

1 large garlic clove, coarsely chopped

¼ teaspoon salt

5 tablespoons unsalted butter at room temperature

2 tablespoons minced fresh flat-leaf parsley

2 tablespoons finely chopped green onion, white part only

2 tablespoons finely chopped pitted kalamata olives

2 tablespoons finely chopped oil-packed sun-dried tomatoes

12 slices firm white bread, crusts trimmed

Preheat the broiler. In a food processor, combine all the ingredients, except the bread, and process until a smooth paste forms. Spread the tomato mixture on top of the bread slices. Cut each bread slice into 3 pieces and put them on a broiler pan 6 to 8 inches from the heat source. Toast for 45 seconds to 1 minute, or until the mixture starts to bubble and melt into the bread and is golden brown. Serve immediately.

SERVES 6

SIDE DISHES

PAULA DEEN'S CHEESE BISCUITS

PAULA DEEN BUFFET AT HARRAH'S TUNICA
PAULA DEEN & EXECUTIVE SOUS-CHEF TAMMY WILLIAMS-HANSEN

Paula Deen takes a beloved Southern treat to a new level with her cheese biscuits, a favorite at the Paula Deen Buffet. Chef Tammy Williams-Hansen says, "The secret of these biscuits is that you must brush them with butter and serve them right out of the oven. We scoop over three thousand a day in the Paula Deen Buffet! Hey, y'all, I think you will agree these are a great accompaniment to any Southern meal."

2 cups self-rising flour

1 teaspoon baking powder

1 teaspoon sugar

½ teaspoon salt

⅓ cup vegetable shortening

¾ cup shredded sharp Cheddar cheese

1 cup buttermilk

4 tablespoons unsalted butter, melted

MAKES 16 TO 20 BISCUITS

Preheat the oven to 350°F. Grease a baking sheet.

In a medium bowl, mix together the flour, baking powder, sugar, and salt using a fork. Cut in the shortening with a pastry cutter or your fingers until it resembles cornmeal. Add the cheese. Stir in the buttermilk all at once, just until blended. Do not overstir. Drop by tablespoonfuls, or use an ice cream scoop, onto the prepared pan. Brush the dough with the butter. Bake for 12 to 15 minutes, or until golden brown. Transfer to wire racks to cool slightly. Serve warm.

SWEET POTATO & RAISIN PANCAKES

HARRAH'S JOLIET
EXECUTIVE CHEF SCOTT D. LECOMPTE

Potato pancakes have been one of chef Scott D. LeCompte's favorite morning indulgences for as long as he can remember. He credits his grandmother with making some of the best he has ever eaten. In this recipe, the chef has created a variation on potato pancakes to pair with his version of pork chops and applesauce.

1 Idaho potato, peeled and shredded

1 sweet potato, peeled and shredded

½ small red onion, thinly sliced

1 large egg

Pinch of dried thyme

¼ cup golden raisins

Salt and freshly ground pepper

1 tablespoon all-purpose flour

2 tablespoons canola oil

Apple compote and crème fraîche or sour cream and minced fresh chives for serving

MAKES 10 PANCAKES;
SERVES 2 TO 3

In a medium bowl, combine the Idaho and sweet potatoes, onion, egg, thyme, raisins, and salt and pepper. Add the flour and toss to coat.

In a large sauté pan or skillet, heat the oil over medium heat. Form ¼ cupfuls of the potato mixture into pancakes about 2½ inches in diameter. Put the pancakes into the heated pan and brown on both sides for a total of 3 to 4 minutes. Serve with apple compote and crème fraîche, or sour cream and chives.

TOP 10 TIPS
FOR COOKING SEASONALLY

1   Spring means new vegetables, but it also brings some of the best fish, including wild salmon, scallops, and brown crabs. When purchasing seafood, check for firmness and aroma. Fish should spring back when pressed and have a fresh aroma.

2   Visit a local farmers' market and build your menu around the vegetables that you find in season. For example, during spring, you may find some beautiful watercress that can be used with a seared salmon and drizzled with blood orange vinaigrette.

3   Like vegetables, meats are seasonal; visit your local butcher to see what is available. Lamb is a spring meat and can be served in a hearty dish or a light one. For example, marinate lamb with rosemary, mint, and garlic, roast it to perfection, and serve sliced with roasted spring potatoes.

4   Summer brings berries and stone fruits to add to sauces and salads. Think about pairing meats with the kinds of food the animal eats, such as accompanying venison dishes with currants and loganberries.

5   Spring and summer are the times for light, refreshing foods, such as lettuces, citrus fruits, berries, fish, tomatoes, and peppers. Season them with light oils, vinegars, and citrus juices.

6   Tomatoes are one of the most versatile summer foods. Look for firm vine-ripened fruit with no blisters or bruises, especially heirloom tomatoes, which come in a wide variety of colors, shapes, and sizes.

7   Fresh corn, available in summer and fall, can be used grilled or roasted or cut from the cobs in dishes from a Southwestern black bean and corn relish to corn pudding.

8   Fall and winter bring long-cooked dishes that use such seasonal ingredients as mushrooms, salsify, turnips, chestnuts, apples, and pears. Many of these foods complement not only pork, but also duck and pheasant.

9   The hearty foods of fall and winter make us feel warm inside when it is cold outside. Squashes, root vegetables, greens, apples, pears, and nuts are great additions to roasted and braised meats. Warm spices like cinnamon, nutmeg, and cardamom complement many cold-weather dishes.

10 The seasonality of dishes can be enhanced with the addition of special drinks to complement foods. During spring and summer, choose fruit drinks, citrus fruit juices, ice teas, and lemonades. During fall and winter, choose coffees, hot chocolates, hot tea, and hot apple cider.

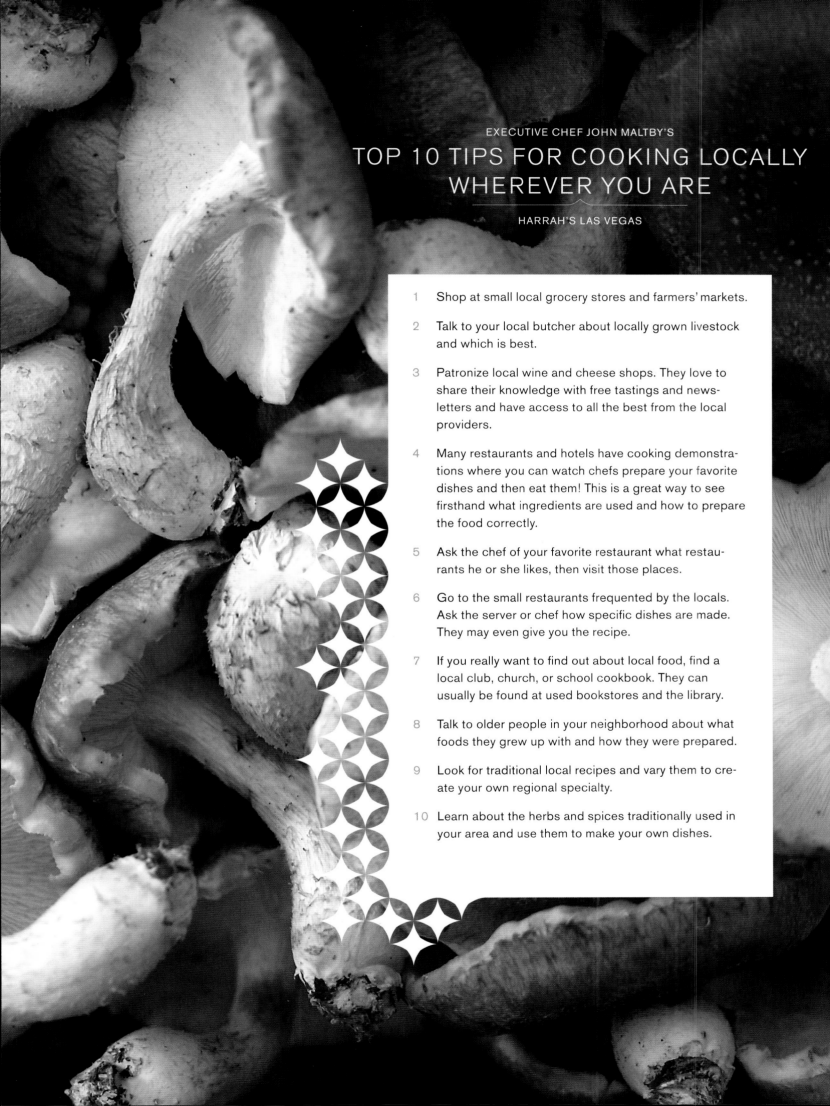

TOP 10 TIPS FOR COOKING LOCALLY WHEREVER YOU ARE

1   Shop at small local grocery stores and farmers' markets.

2   Talk to your local butcher about locally grown livestock and which is best.

3   Patronize local wine and cheese shops. They love to share their knowledge with free tastings and newsletters and have access to all the best from the local providers.

4   Many restaurants and hotels have cooking demonstrations where you can watch chefs prepare your favorite dishes and then eat them! This is a great way to see firsthand what ingredients are used and how to prepare the food correctly.

5   Ask the chef of your favorite restaurant what restaurants he or she likes, then visit those places.

6   Go to the small restaurants frequented by the locals. Ask the server or chef how specific dishes are made. They may even give you the recipe.

7   If you really want to find out about local food, find a local club, church, or school cookbook. They can usually be found at used bookstores and the library.

8   Talk to older people in your neighborhood about what foods they grew up with and how they were prepared.

9   Look for traditional local recipes and vary them to create your own regional specialty.

10 Learn about the herbs and spices traditionally used in your area and use them to make your own dishes.

"The Greenbacks"
Created by
Hanerraño & Chiodo

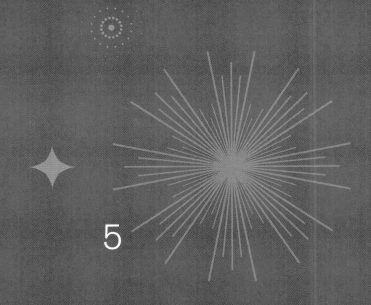

5

BEEF + PORK

1   Build a friendly relationship with your local butcher:

Ask your butcher questions, respect his or her opinions, see what the specials are, and find out when new shipments of meat are coming in. Following are some questions to ask your butcher:

+   How fresh is the meat? Was it just put out in the case that day?

+   Was the meat previously frozen? If so, for how long?

+   Explain what you intend to use the meat for and ask if it is the best choice or what the butcher would recommend.

+   Why is the meat at a reduced price? Is it old?

+   Where does the butcher get his or her meat from?

2   Inspect the meat:

Always check to make sure the label on beef, poultry, ham, veal, and other meats says that the meat was inspected by the United States Department of Agriculture (USDA). If this is not noted on the label, ask the butcher why.

Also, look for bruising, blood clots, and irregular discolorations, such as freezer burn, which is a grayish color, and dark spots on red meat, which may indicate it is a few days old. All these signs may mean the meat was mishandled in production or transportation.

Check the label for an expiration date.

3   Color:

If the meat looks discolored in any way, ask the butcher why. The color could be perfectly natural or a sign the meat is old. For example, fresh beef should be ruby red with no bruising or brownish or dark spots.

4   Cut:

The basic cuts of meat are called primal cuts. Each cut lends itself to various cooking techniques. Always use the proper cut for your specific preparation.

Primal cuts and their uses include:

+   Chuck: Pot roast and hamburgers

+   Rib: Ribs, rib-eye steak, and prime rib loin for strip steaks, T-bone, porterhouse, and tenderloin

+   Round: Roast beef

+   Brisket: Barbecued brisket, corned beef, pot roast

+   Plate: Short ribs for braising cuts, such as the outside skirt steak for fajitas and hanger steak (this is typically a cheap, tough, and fatty meat)

+   Shank for broth, stews, and soup (this is the toughest of the cuts)

+   Flank: Ground meat, flank steak

5   Marbling:

The white, speckled fat found in meat. The more marbling in beef, the higher the grade of the beef and the more tender it will be.

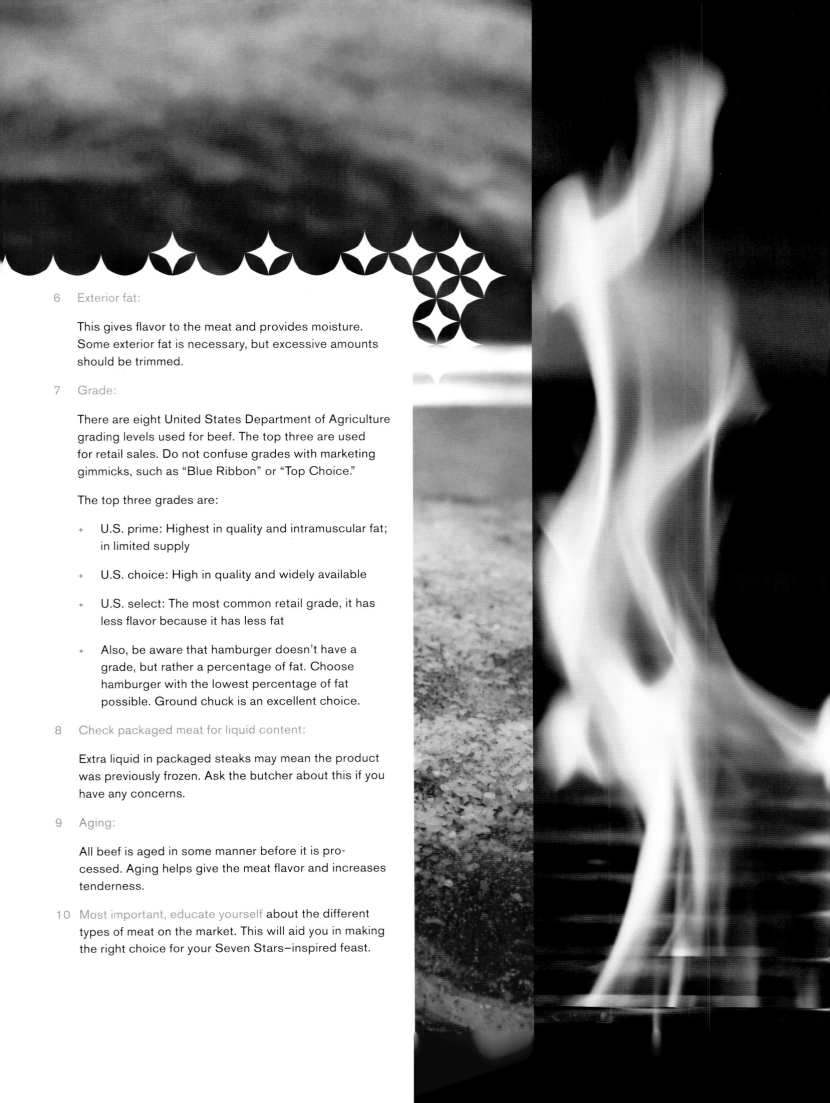

6   Exterior fat:

This gives flavor to the meat and provides moisture. Some exterior fat is necessary, but excessive amounts should be trimmed.

7   Grade:

There are eight United States Department of Agriculture grading levels used for beef. The top three are used for retail sales. Do not confuse grades with marketing gimmicks, such as "Blue Ribbon" or "Top Choice."

The top three grades are:

+   U.S. prime: Highest in quality and intramuscular fat; in limited supply

+   U.S. choice: High in quality and widely available

+   U.S. select: The most common retail grade, it has less flavor because it has less fat

+   Also, be aware that hamburger doesn't have a grade, but rather a percentage of fat. Choose hamburger with the lowest percentage of fat possible. Ground chuck is an excellent choice.

8   Check packaged meat for liquid content:

Extra liquid in packaged steaks may mean the product was previously frozen. Ask the butcher about this if you have any concerns.

9   Aging:

All beef is aged in some manner before it is processed. Aging helps give the meat flavor and increases tenderness.

10   Most important, educate yourself about the different types of meat on the market. This will aid you in making the right choice for your Seven Stars–inspired feast.

SAGE STEAK

SAGE ROOM STEAK HOUSE AT HARVEYS LAKE TAHOE
EXECUTIVE CHEF JOE WELLS

This signature steak is one of the most popular dishes on the menu at the Sage Room. Poblano chiles and Gorgonzola are surprising partners in this intensely flavorful sauce. Chef Joe Wells advises, "roasted-shallot mashed potatoes are a very good side with this dish."

Four 12-ounce New York steaks, trimmed and lightly pounded

Salt and freshly ground pepper

1½ cups clarified butter (see page 43)

1 cup julienned red onion

2 teaspoons minced garlic

1 cup julienned red bell pepper

2 large poblano chiles, roasted, peeled, and julienned (1 cup; see page 196)

¾ cup dry red wine

1 cup veal demi-glace

½ cup crumbled Gorgonzola cheese

4 watercress sprigs for garnish (optional)

SERVES 4

Season both sides of the steaks with salt and pepper. Heat 2 large sauté pans or skillets over high heat. Add ½ cup clarified butter to each pan. Add 2 steaks to each pan and reduce the heat to medium. Cook the steaks for 3 to 4 minutes on each side for medium-rare. Transfer the steaks to a platter and keep warm.

Pour off the fat from one of the pans. Add the remaining ½ cup clarified butter and melt over medium heat. Add the red onion to the pan and sauté for 2 to 3 minutes. Add the garlic, bell pepper, and chiles and sauté for 2 to 3 minutes. Season the vegetable mixture with salt and pepper. Transfer the vegetables to a bowl and keep warm.

Add the red wine to the pan and stir over medium heat to scrape up the browned bits from the bottom of the pan. Cook to reduce the wine to about ½ cup. Add the demi-glace and cook for 2 to 3 minutes. Taste and adjust the seasoning.

To serve, preheat the broiler to 550°F. Top each steak with one-fourth of the vegetable mixture, then the cheese. Place under the broiler about 6 inches from the heat source for 2 minutes, or until the cheese is melted. Pool ¼ cup of the sauce on each plate and place a steak on top. Garnish with the watercress sprigs, if desired, and serve at once.

SINCE 1947, THE SAGE ROOM STEAK HOUSE HAS BEEN WORLD RENOWNED FOR ITS OLD WEST AMBIANCE AND ITS FINE CUISINE. HERE, DINERS CAN PERUSE ARTWORKS BY RUSSELL AND REMINGTON WHILE ENJOYING TRADITIONAL STEAK HOUSE DINING WITH TABLESIDE SERVICE.

THE BEST STEAK IN KANSAS CITY

THE RANGE STEAKHOUSE AT HARRAH'S NORTH KANSAS CITY
CHEFS HUGH RENO, ANDY SPARKS, JEFF CRAIG & WILLIAM DWORZAN

In 2008 chefs Hugh Reno, Andy Sparks, Jeff Craig, and William Dworzan joined forces as Team Harrah's and entered this dish in the prestigious Great American Barbecue Contest in Kansas City. When the smoke cleared, this dynamic team was the grand-prize winner for the Best Steak in Kansas City, and a new Kansas City legend was born. Follow the recipe below to re-create it in your own kitchen.

MARINADE

2 cups Jack Daniel's Black Label whiskey

1 cup (2 sticks) unsalted butter

2 teaspoons beef base

3 shallots, minced

8 garlic cloves, minced

2 teaspoons kosher salt

2 teaspoons freshly ground pepper

Six 12-ounce Kansas City strip steaks or
New York strip steaks
(depending on what part of
the country you are in)

COMPOUND BUTTER

1 cup (2 sticks) unsalted butter
at room temperature

2 tablespoons dry white wine

2 tablespoons white truffle oil

6 shallots, julienned

1 teaspoon minced fresh
flat-leaf parsley

1 teaspoon minced fresh basil

1 teaspoon minced fresh rosemary

1 teaspoon minced fresh thyme

SERVES 6

For the marinade: Add the whiskey to a medium saucepan and warm over medium heat. Turn off the heat, stand back from the stove, and light the whiskey with a long match or long-handled lighter. Once the alcohol is lit, do not stir or shake the saucepan. Let the flame burn itself out naturally. Stir in the butter, beef base, shallots, garlic, salt, and pepper. Let the mixture cool to room temperature.

Put the steaks in a nonreactive bowl or heavy self-sealing plastic bag and add the marinade. Cover the bowl or close the bag and refrigerate for 24 hours.

Remove the steaks from the refrigerator about 30 minutes to 1 hour before cooking. Light a very hot fire in a charcoal grill, or preheat a gas grill to high.

Meanwhile, make the compound butter: Put the butter in a medium bowl. In a medium sauté pan or skillet, heat the white wine and truffle oil over medium heat. Add the shallots and sauté, stirring constantly, until well browned, 2 to 3 minutes. Pour the mixture into a bowl and let cool, then cover and refrigerate for at least 30 minutes. Mince the shallots and stir into the butter. Stir in the herbs until well blended.

Grill the steaks for about 5 minutes on each side for medium-rare. Transfer to plates and let rest for 5 minutes. Place a dollop of the compound butter on each steak and serve at once.

GRILLED CITRUS-MARINATED SKIRT STEAK

WITH SAFFRON–HEIRLOOM TOMATO SALAD

RIB & CHOPHOUSE AT SHOWBOAT ATLANTIC CITY
RESTAURANT CHEF EDWARD LEDWON

This feast for your eyes and palate starts with marinating skirt steaks in a mixture of fresh orange and lime juice, garlic, shallots, and cilantro. It's crowned with a tomato salad that could also be served on its own as a side dish for many other main courses. Chef Edward Ledwon says, "The skirt steak is an amazing cut of beef. Its tenderness and light gaminess allow you to play with bold flavors and textures. The marriage of saffron and coffee would overpower any other steak. Our guests are always surprised and delighted by this dish. In fact, there is no other item on our menu that brings me out to the table more often."

Note: The steak must be marinated overnight before cooking.

MARINADE

Juice of 3 oranges

Juice of 4 limes

1 tablespoon minced garlic

2 tablespoons minced shallots or red onion

1 bunch cilantro, stemmed and coarsely chopped

3 cups extra-virgin olive oil

Four 8-ounce skirt steaks, trimmed

TOMATO SALAD

6 heirloom tomatoes, each cut into 6 wedges

2 red onions, thinly sliced

1 bunch basil, stemmed and leaves torn

2 tablespoons minced fresh chives

Pinch of powdered saffron

½ cup extra-virgin olive oil

Juice of 1 lemon

Salt and freshly ground pepper

½ cup extra-virgin olive oil

1 cup finely ground coffee

Salt

SERVES 4

For the marinade: In a medium bowl, combine all the marinade ingredients and stir to blend. Put the steaks in a nonreactive bowl or heavy self-sealing plastic bag and add the marinade. Cover the bowl or close the bag and refrigerate overnight.

For the salad: In a large ceramic or glass bowl, combine all the ingredients. Toss well. Cover and refrigerate overnight.

Remove the steaks from the marinade 30 minutes to 1 hour before cooking. Light a very hot fire in a charcoal grill, or preheat a gas grill to 500°F. (Since the steaks are thin, they need to be grilled over a high flame.)

Rub the steaks with the olive oil, coffee, and salt. Grill the steaks for 1 to 2 minutes on each side for medium-rare. Transfer to a carving board and let rest for about 5 minutes.

To serve, cut the steaks into thin diagonal slices and top with the tomato salad and some of its dressing.

CONDIMENTS ARE A HUGE PART OF THE STEAK HOUSE APPEAL, ALLOWING CUSTOMERS TO PERSONALLY CRAFT THEIR DINING EXPERIENCE. OVER THE YEARS, THE RIB & CHOPHOUSE HAS DOLED OUT EVERYTHING FROM 1,100 BOTTLES OF WORCESTERSHIRE SAUCE, 600 BOTTLES OF TABASCO SAUCE, 4,000 POUNDS OF BUTTER IN VARIOUS FLAVORED FORMS, 200 POUNDS OF BLUE CHEESE, AND AN ASTOUNDING 400 GALLONS OF THE CLASSIC BORDELAISE SAUCE.

EXECUTIVE CHEF KEITH MITCHELL'S

TOP 10 TIPS FOR MAINTAINING AN ORGANIZED KITCHEN

CAESARS ATLANTIC CITY

1   Keep cabinets and pantries well stocked and clutter-free.

2   Stock your pantry with your favorite staples and must-haves.

3   Keep knives sharp and hand tools where you can find them when you need them.

4   Keep your refrigerator well stocked with fresh fruits, vegetables, and herbs.

5   Buy spices in small amounts and replace them frequently.

6   Get rid of kitchen clutter, such as old pans and containers, and tools that don't work.

7   Clean up as you go.

8   Make cooking a family affair; get the kids into the kitchen to help.

9   Think green and recycle.

10 Plan your meals and events, then stick to your plan!

PAN-ROASTED DRY-AGED RIB-EYE STEAK

WITH FINGERLING POTATOES & ASPARAGUS-MOREL RAGOUT

VOODOO STEAK & LOUNGE AT RIO ALL-SUITE HOTEL & CASINO
CHEF DE CUISINE HONORIO MECINAS

VooDoo Steak & Lounge guests always rave about their steaks. Chef Honorio Mecinas's dry-aging process gives the meat superior tenderness and flavor. The chef advises, "Currently, you can find dry-aged beef in gourmet stores. Always look for center cuts and marbling." In this recipe, fingerling potatoes and a spring ragout of morels and white asparagus complement the rich beef.

ROASTED POTATOES

1 pound fingerling potatoes, halved

10 garlic cloves, sliced

3 thyme sprigs

2 slices bacon, cut into bite-sized pieces

¼ cup canola oil

Salt and freshly ground pepper

Four 18-ounce dry-aged bone-in
rib-eye steaks

Sea salt and cracked pepper

Canola oil for brushing

ASPARAGUS AND MOREL RAGOUT

1 cup (2 sticks) unsalted butter

2 shallots, sliced

16 morel mushrooms, rinsed

8 stalks white asparagus, trimmed,
peeled, and cut into matchsticks

1 cup dry sherry

SERVES 4

For the potatoes: Preheat the oven to 350°F. Combine the potatoes, garlic, thyme, and bacon in a medium bowl. Add the oil and salt and pepper to taste; toss to coat. Put the mixture in a roasting pan and roast for about 20 minutes, or until tender. Remove from the oven and keep warm.

While the potatoes are cooking, season the steaks with sea salt and cracked pepper. Heat a large cast-iron pan over high heat and brush with a little oil. Sear the steaks until well browned, about 3 minutes on each side. Transfer the pan to the oven and roast for 6 minutes for medium-rare. Transfer the steaks to a carving board and let rest for about 5 minutes.

For the ragout: In a medium saucepan, melt half of the butter over low heat. Add the shallots and morels and cook for about 4 minutes. Add the asparagus and cook for 2 minutes, or until tender. Add the sherry and stir well. Remove from the heat and stir in the remaining ½ cup butter.

To serve, divide the potatoes and ragout among 4 plates. Add the steaks. Drizzle the pan juices over the steaks and sprinkle with a little more sea salt. Serve at once.

THE AWARD-WINNING VILLAGE SEAFOOD BUFFET
AT RIO ALL-SUITE HOTEL & CASINO:

• OPERATES 5 COOKING STATIONS •

• MAKES EVERYTHING FROM SCRATCH IN THE RIO'S PASTRY SHOP,
INCLUDING 12 FLAVORS OF GELATO •

• HOSTS A FULL SUSHI BAR,
WHICH PRODUCES 3,000 PIECES OF SUSHI ROLLS,
NIGIRI SUSHI, AND SASHIMI •

• PREPARES MORE THAN 2,100 POUNDS OF
PEEL AND EAT SHRIMP AND 5,000 POUNDS OF
CRAB LEGS PER WEEK •

• PREPARES MORE THAN 2,000 POUNDS OF BEEF RIBS AND
1,250 POUNDS OF PRIME RIB PER WEEK •

STEAK AU POIVRE

JACK BINION'S STEAK HOUSE AT HORSESHOE BOSSIER CITY
EXECUTIVE SOUS-CHEF ROBERT BROOKS

This classic French dish has become a staple at Jack Binion's Steak House. The magical combination of a rich brandy cream sauce, fresh-cracked pepper, and tender, buttery filet proves that some things never go out of style.

Four 7-ounce filet mignons

Kosher salt and crushed pepper

3 tablespoons extra-virgin olive oil

1 teaspoon minced shallot

¼ cup brandy

1 cup veal demi-glace or your favorite brown gravy

1 tablespoon Dijon mustard

½ cup heavy cream

4 tablespoons unsalted butter

SERVES 4

Season the filets on both sides with salt and pepper. In a medium sauté pan or skillet, heat the oil over medium-high heat until it begins to smoke. Add the filets and sear for 4 to 5 minutes. Turn and cook on the second side for 4 minutes for medium-rare. Transfer to 4 plates and keep warm.

Drain the excess oil from the pan and add the shallot. Remove the pan from the heat and add the brandy. Standing back from the stove, light the brandy with a long match or long-handled lighter. Once the alcohol is lit, do not stir or shake the pan. Let the flames subside, then add the demi-glace, mustard, and heavy cream. Cook over medium heat for 1 to 2 minutes, stirring well. Add the butter and swirl until melted.

To serve, pour the sauce over the filet mignons and serve at once.

GARY W. LOVEMAN BECAME
CHIEF EXECUTIVE OFFICER OF HARRAH'S
ENTERTAINMENT IN 2003.
SINCE THEN, *INSTITUTIONAL INVESTOR* MAGAZINE
4 TIMES NAMED HIM "BEST CEO"
IN THE GAMING AND LODGING INDUSTRY.

TOP 10 SPICES
THAT SHOULD BE IN EVERY KITCHEN

FLAMINGO LAS VEGAS

Each of the following spices can be used in a variety of different dishes. Having this collection in your spice rack means you have the flavors of the world right at your fingertips.

1   Curry powder

2   Chili powder

3   Paprika

4   Cumin

5   Sesame seeds

6   Fennel seeds

7   Black peppercorns

8   Szechuan pepper

9   Red pepper flakes

10 Coriander

GRILLED BOURBON PORK CHOPS

THE RANGE STEAKHOUSE AT HARRAH'S METROPOLIS
EXECUTIVE CHEF JON M. KELL

The thick pork chops at The Range Steakhouse receive a stellar treatment: First they're grilled over charcoal, then dipped in a mixture of maple syrup, molasses, bourbon, and mango-chili sauce and grilled again. Juicy inside, dark and flavorful outside— that is the essence of these unparalleled chops, which are one of the restaurant's most popular specials.

BOURBON SAUCE

1 cup pure maple syrup

1 cup molasses

1 cup bourbon

¼ cup bottled mango-chili sauce (available in specialty foods stores)

Four 12-ounce bone-in pork chops

Salt and freshly ground pepper

SERVES 4

Prepare a medium fire in a charcoal grill, or preheat a gas grill to 400°F.

For the sauce: In a medium saucepan, combine all the ingredients. Heat over low heat, stirring well. Pour half of the mixture into a shallow dish. Cover the remaining sauce; set aside and keep warm.

Season the chops on both sides with salt and pepper. Grill the pork chops for 5 to 7 minutes on each side. Dip the chops in the pan of sauce to coat both sides. Move the chops to the edge of the fire, not over direct heat, and cook for 15 to 20 minutes, or until an instant-read thermometer inserted in the center of a chop registers 160°F.

Transfer to plates and serve with the remaining sauce alongside.

THE REAL CITY OF METROPOLIS IN ILLINOIS SHARES ITS NAME WITH THE FICTIONAL CITY (ORIGINALLY MODELED AFTER TORONTO) THAT IS THE HOME OF THE MAN OF STEEL— SUPERMAN! JUST A FEW BLOCKS FROM THE CASINO, THE FAMED BRONZE STATUE OF SUPERMAN STANDS IN THE TOWN SQUARE.

VEAL CHOPS PORTOBELLO

MURANO'S AT HARRAH'S TUNICA
EXECUTIVE CHEF STEVE PAIROLERO

This dish of portobello mushrooms, veal loin chops, and asparagus tips will transport you and your guests to Tuscany. Chef Steve Pairolero says, "This is definitely one of my favorite flavor combinations. The heartiness from the portobello mushrooms and the mild flavor of the veal make for a fantastic meal. To further enhance this dish, serve it with a really nice glass of Pinot Noir."

4 portobello mushrooms, stemmed

4 tablespoons extra-virgin olive oil

½ teaspoon salt

½ teaspoon freshly ground pepper

Four 10-ounce veal loin chops

2 teaspoons minced garlic

4 ounces sliced porcini mushrooms

1 bunch asparagus, cut into tips

1 cup dry red wine

¼ cup veal demi-glace

1 cup diced tomatoes for garnish

4 rosemary sprigs for garnish

SERVES 4

Preheat the oven to 350°F. Using a spoon, scrape the underside of the portobello mushroom caps to remove the gills. Rub the caps with 2 tablespoons of the olive oil and sprinkle with ¼ teaspoon of the salt and ¼ teaspoon of the pepper. Place the mushrooms on a baking sheet and roast for about 10 minutes, or until tender. Remove from the oven and set aside.

Light a charcoal or wood fire in a charcoal grill, or preheat a gas grill to 400°F. Season the veal chops with the remaining ¼ teaspoon salt and ¼ teaspoon pepper. Grill the chops 6 to 8 minutes on each side for medium-rare. Remove from the heat and keep warm.

In a medium sauté pan or skillet, heat the remaining 2 tablespoons oil. Add the garlic, porcini mushrooms, and asparagus tips and sauté for 4 to 6 minutes, or until the asparagus turns bright green and you can pierce it with a fork. Add the red wine and stir to scrape up the browned bits on the bottom of the pan. Stir in the demi-glace and cook for 3 to 5 minutes, or until slightly thickened.

To serve, place a roasted portobello mushroom in the center of each plate and top with a veal chop. Ladle the sauce over the chop. Garnish with the tomatoes and rosemary.

BRAISED SHORT RIB SLIDERS

WITH GOAT CHEESE, RICOTTA & HORSERADISH GREMOLATA

PREVIEW BAR AT BALLY'S ATLANTIC CITY
FOOD SERVICE DIRECTOR ROLF J. WEITHOFER

Preview Bar at Bally's Atlantic City is known for both its outstanding cocktails and its great bar food, like these sliders. For your next picnic or casual get-together, kick it up a notch with short ribs topped with goat cheese and horseradish gremolata.

BRAISED SHORT RIBS

10 boneless beef short ribs, cut into about 3-inch pieces

1 tablespoon salt

1 ½ teaspoons freshly ground pepper

¼ cup canola oil

4 ounces pancetta, diced

2 cups diced mixed onions, carrots, and celery

¼ cup tomato paste

½ cup plus ⅓ cup dry red wine

1 cup brown veal stock

2 cups veal demi-glace

2 bay leaves

Pinch of minced fresh thyme

GOAT CHEESE, RICOTTA & HORSERADISH GREMOLATA

1 cup crumbled fresh white goat cheese

½ cup ricotta cheese

1 teaspoon grated lemon zest

1 teaspoon minced fresh oregano

1 teaspoon grated fresh horseradish

Salt and freshly ground pepper

2 tablespoons extra-virgin olive oil

2 tablespoons minced fresh chives

10 mini-hamburger buns, toasted

SERVES 10

For the short ribs: Preheat the oven to 275°F. Season the short ribs with the salt and pepper. In a large ovenproof sauté pan, heat the oil over medium-high heat until shimmering. Sear the short ribs on all sides until a deep golden brown. Transfer the short ribs to a plate.

Add the pancetta and chopped vegetables to the pan and sauté until golden brown, 8 to 10 minutes. Add the tomato paste and cook for 3 to 5 minutes, or until it turns a deeper color and gives off a sweet aroma; do not burn. Stir in the ½ cup wine and cook to reduce by one-fourth.

Return the short ribs and any juices to the pan. Add the stock and demi-glace. Bring to a gentle simmer, cover, and braise in the oven for 45 minutes. Spoon the fat from the top of the liquid and add the bay leaves and thyme. Return to the oven and braise for another 45 minutes, or until fork-tender.

Using a wire skimmer, transfer the short ribs to a plate. Spoon off the fat from the top of the pan liquid, stir in the remaining ⅓ cup wine, and bring to a simmer. Taste and adjust the seasoning. Strain the sauce into a bowl and add the short ribs; set aside and keep warm.

For the gremolata: In a small bowl, combine all the ingredients and stir to blend.

To serve, toast the buns and place a short rib on top of the bottom half of each bun and dollop with the gremolata. Drizzle a little of the sauce over the gremolata. Close the buns and serve at once.

BLACKENING SPICE

2 tablespoons red pepper flakes

3 tablespoons garlic powder

3 tablespoons onion powder

2 tablespoons dark chili powder

3 tablespoons sweet paprika

1 tablespoon salt

1 teaspoon dried parsley

1 teaspoon dried thyme

1 teaspoon celery powder

Pinch of cayenne pepper

In a medium bowl, combine all the ingredients, mixing well. Store in an airtight container.

MAKES ABOUT 1 CUP

CAJUN SKILLET FILETS

360 STEAKHOUSE AT HARRAH'S COUNCIL BLUFFS
EXECUTIVE CHEF CHRISTOPHER COLELLO

The ultimate taste of this dish comes from its many layers of flavor. The wave of flavor starts with the bacon fat and the blackening spice and ends at the tiger shrimp with just a splash of cream to blend everything together. Serve with a favorite side dish.

Four 8-ounce center-cut beef filets

**¾ cup blackening spice
(see recipe facing page)**

6 tablespoons bacon fat

12 jumbo shrimp, shelled and deveined

6 tablespoons unsalted butter

**¾ cup lobster stock or shrimp stock
(page 202)**

¼ cup heavy cream

SERVES 4

Season the filets with all but 1 tablespoon of the blackening spice, making sure to completely cover the meat on all sides. Reserve the 1 tablespoon blackening spice for the shrimp. In a large sauté pan or skillet, melt the bacon fat over medium-high heat. Cook the filets for 9 minutes on each side for medium-rare. Transfer to a plate and keep warm. Discard the bacon fat.

Season the shrimp with the reserved blackening spice. In the same pan used to cook the meat, melt 4 tablespoons of the butter over medium heat until lightly browned. Immediately add the shrimp and cook for about 1½ minutes on each side, or until evenly pink. Using a slotted spoon, transfer to a plate and keep warm.

Using the same pan, add the lobster stock to the butter in the pan and cook over medium heat to reduce to about ½ cup. Add the cream and cook to reduce slightly. Add the remaining 2 tablespoons butter and simmer until the sauce is thick.

To serve, place each filet on a plate with 3 shrimp on top. Evenly drizzle the sauce among the 4 plates.

THE GREEN AND BLUE FAÇADE OF
HARRAH'S COUNCIL BLUFFS HOTEL REPRESENTS ITS
LOCATION NEAR THE MIGHTY MISSOURI RIVER AND
THE RIVERBANKS OF OMAHA, NEBRASKA,
AND COUNCIL BLUFFS, IOWA.

1 TurboChef Oven: This oven rapidly and evenly browns the outside of food while evenly cooking the inside without compromising food quality. In laymen's terms, it cooks really fast and kicks . . . well, you know. Especially important in high-volume restaurants.

2 Beurre mixer: Also known as the stick blender, hand blender, or, as some chefs affectionately refer to it, "the happy stick." And why not? It has 750 watts of power that spins at 18,000 RPMs. For anyone who needs to purée about fifty gallons of soup, this immersion blender is the right tool for that job.

3 Jade Infrared Broiler: Its four 26,000-BTU burners will perfectly char a magmalike crust on a twenty-eight-ounce porterhouse and cook it to medium-rare in seven minutes flat. It's like standing next to the sun. However, it's not for beginners; experienced riders only, please!

4 Rational Combi Oven: This oven allows you to roast, steam, bake, oven-poach, reheat, or execute a combination of the aforementioned. You can auto-program it to cook specific foods with specific settings, times, and various methods of cooking. You may even be able to program it to wake you up and make coffee, I just haven't found that button yet.

5 Cleveland Tilting Skillet: Also known as the braiser. It's very versatile. You can sauté, braise, poach, and sear meat in it. It will handle almost any task. Make sure you get the manual hand-crank model; it will last for centuries. The electric tilt models are junk.

6 Commercial smoker: Nothing to do for twelve hours or so? What's better than a smoker full of cured pork bellies going low and slow?

7 Vertical chopper and mixer (VCM): It's like a Cuisinart on steroids. If the Cuisinart had a big brother, this would be it. As a young aspiring saucier, I was amazed at the sight of my first one. If you ever need to purée a brick, this could probably handle it.

8 Cryovac machine: This machine is great for storing any perishable food. We mostly use it for portion-cut meat, as it creates an airtight environment. It's also great for marinating meat, as it penetrates the protein faster, giving a consistent flavor throughout.

9 Treif Puma industrial meat slicer: I strongly suggest that if you have 45K laying around, you get one of these slicers. We produce deli meat for two large properties, and it blows through a day's worth of work in about two hours. At four hundred cuts per minute, this thing will pay for itself. When you are slicing lunch meat in thousand-pound increments, it beats the conventional slicing method.

10 iPod docking station with Bose speakers: Okay, technically this is not a kitchen appliance, but I do consider it a necessity during prep times. Nothing like a little Disturbed, Metallica, or if you are having "one of those days," "Break Stuff" by Limp Bizkit to get you through some rather monotonous tasks. Prepping for four-thousand customers a day in the buffet requires much caffeine and heavy metal music.

TOP 10 POTS AND PANS
EVERY KITCHEN SHOULD HAVE AND WHY

1   Teflon omelet pan: A great omelet screams for an unscratched Teflon pan. Unless you're from the generation that grew up without Teflon, you probably have never had to cope without it, which is a good thing. Teflon allows easy-in and easy-out for crêpes, eggs, meats, and so on, without sticking.

2   Half-sheet pan, also known as a baking sheet: One of my favorite pans in the kitchen is the half-sheet pan, mostly because it fits in home ovens and refrigerators. It is nice for baking and for roasting lightweight meats and fish.

3   Roasting pan: For larger cuts of meat, the roasting pan is very durable and able to withstand the weight of larger cuts of meat and fish. The roasting pan also allows for added vegetables and liquid for making great pan gravy.

4   Saucepans: You will need these in small, medium, and large sizes. Small saucepans are perfect for reductions and blanching small quantities of vegetables or garnishes, and for small amounts of soup and sauce.

5   Stockpot: For making large quantities of soups and stocks, these range in size from small to large. A stockpot is also great for cooking pasta.

6   Sauce pot, also known as a soup pot: For larger quantities of soups and sauces, the sauce pot is the next gradation up from the saucepan. This pot is also used for cooking pasta and blanching vegetables.

7   Sautoir, also known as a sauté pan: A great pot for panfrying. It has straight sides and is versatile for both stove-top and oven cooking. Covered with a lid, it can be used for braising in the oven or on the stove top.

8   Sauteuse: Like a sauté pan, but with two short side handles instead of one long handle, which allows for easier storage. Curved sides allow the food in the pan to be tossed back and forth with small amounts of oil. This pan is very versatile; it comes in various sizes and has a place in every kitchen.

9   Wok: There are many different types of woks made of different materials. I prefer a thin-gauge steel wok that can fit on a home burner. A wok heats quickly and maintains heat so that food can be cooked quickly. There are two ways to manage the wok on the stove top: (1) Use wok utensils and stir the food; (2) Use the wok handles and flip the food from back to front. Both are effective, but the flipping method takes a bit of time to master.

10 Paella pan: One of my favorite dishes is a great paella. This type of pan is typically made of thin-gauge steel and is meant to be used on the stove top and in the oven.

APPLEWOOD-SMOKED MOLASSES & FIVE PEPPERCORN–CRUSTED PORK LOIN

FOREST BUFFET AT HARRAH'S LAKE TAHOE
EXECUTIVE CHEF JOE WELLS

Year after year, the Forest Buffet is voted Best Buffet in the annual Best of Tahoe readers' poll conducted by the *Tahoe Daily Tribune*. *Casino Player* magazine readers have also selected the restaurant as Lake Tahoe's Best Buffet. One reason for these glowing accolades is the following dish: boneless pork loin, brined in a sweet and salty mixture to keep it juicy, then smoked lightly over applewood, is brushed with molasses and spiced with peppercorns before being roasted to perfection and finished with more warmed molasses.

Notes: You will need ¾ cup applewood chips to make this recipe. The pork must be brined 48 hours and refrigerated overnight prior to cooking.

BRINE

8 cups cold water

¾ cup molasses

½ cup brown sugar

3 garlic cloves, crushed

½ cup kosher salt

¼ cup five-peppercorn blend

One 5- to 6-pound boneless pork loin roast

½ cup molasses

¾ tablespoon coarsely ground pepper mixed with 3 pinches onion powder

SERVES 15

For the brine: In a large pot, combine all the ingredients and bring to a boil. Remove from the heat and let cool.

Add the pork loin to the pot; it should be submerged in the liquid. Cover and refrigerate for 48 hours. Remove from the brine. Rinse and dry the pork well with paper towels. Refrigerate, uncovered, overnight. Remove from the refrigerator 30 minutes before cooking.

Soak ¾ cup applewood chips in water for 30 minutes. Drain.

Open the kitchen windows and turn on the exhaust fan. Add the drained chips to a pan smoker and place a wire rack over the chips. Or, to use a wok, line the wok with aluminum foil first, then add the drained chips and wire rack. Turn on the burner to medium heat. When the chips begin to smoke, reduce the heat to low, add the pork to the pan, and cover. Smoke for 1 hour and check, being sure not to go over 155°F.

Preheat the oven to 350°F. In a small saucepan, warm the molasses over low heat. Brush the warm molasses over the top of the pork loin, then sprinkle with the cracked pepper and onion powder mixture. Transfer the pork to a rack set in a roasting pan and roast 30 minutes, or until an instant-read thermometer inserted in the center of the meat registers 155°F. Transfer to a carving board, tent with aluminum foil, and let rest for 15 minutes. Cut into slices to serve.

HARRAH'S/HARVEYS LAKE TAHOE IS THE HOME OF THE *TAHOE STAR* (PICTURED ON PAGE 307), A 54-FOOT YACHT THAT WAS CUSTOM BUILT FOR WILLIAM F. HARRAH IN 1978, JUST BEFORE HE DIED. SPECIFICALLY DESIGNED FOR MR. HARRAH TO TAKE GUESTS OUT ON THE LAKE DURING THE SUMMER MONTHS, IT IS STILL USED FOR THIS PURPOSE TODAY.

MING'S GLAZED CHINESE PORK SPARERIBS

MING'S TABLE AT HARRAH'S LAS VEGAS
CHEF WINSTON CHUNG

Ming's Table boasts some of the finest Asian cuisine in Las Vegas. Chef Winston Chung is especially known for his pork spareribs, marinated in a mixture that includes soy sauce, hoisin sauce, and ginger.

Notes: The ribs need to be marinated for at least 8 hours before cooking. You can find ground bean sauce and malt sugar in most Asian markets.

2 pounds pork spareribs

MARINADE

¼ cup soy sauce

3 tablespoons hoisin sauce

3 tablespoons Shaoxing wine

2 garlic cloves, minced

¼ teaspoon five-spice powder

1 teaspoon minced fresh ginger

6 tablespoons sugar

3 pieces fermented bean curd, chopped

4 large eggs, beaten

1 tablespoon red food coloring

½ cup ground bean sauce (see notes)

GLAZE

1 teaspoon malt sugar (see notes)

1 tablespoon soy sauce

1 teaspoon Shaoxing wine

½ cup malt sugar for brushing the ribs
Sesame seeds for sprinkling (optional)

SERVES 4

Separate the ribs and trim off the excess fat. Put the ribs in a large baking dish.

For the marinade: In a medium bowl, combine all the ingredients and stir well. Pour the marinade over the ribs, cover, and refrigerate for at least 8 hours or overnight, turning occasionally. Remove from the refrigerator 30 minutes before cooking. Remove the ribs from the marinade and discard the marinade. Preheat the oven to 350°F.

For the glaze: In a small bowl, combine all the glaze ingredients, mixing well. Brush half of the glaze on the ribs.

Line a large roasting pan with aluminum foil. Put a wire rack in the pan and place the ribs on the rack. Roast for 30 minutes, then turn the ribs, brush with the remaining glaze, and roast for about 40 minutes more, or until tender when pierced. Remove from the oven.

To serve, brush the ribs with the malt sugar and sprinkle with sesame seeds, if you like.

BLACK FOREST HAM
& GRUYÈRE CHEESE FEUILLETÉES

HARRAH'S LAKE TAHOE & HARVEYS LAKE TAHOE
EXECUTIVE CHEF JOE WELLS

A spectacular brunch dish: savory ham and cheese enclosed in crisp, golden puff pastry packets. A refreshing mesclun salad is just the right counterpoint. Chef Joe Wells and his team serve this as a special dish at Harrah's Lake Tahoe and Harveys Lake Tahoe.

3 sheets thawed frozen puff pastry

12 thin slices Black Forest ham (18 ounces total)

12 tablespoons (¾ cup) German mustard

2 cups shredded Gruyère cheese

5 large egg yolks beaten with 3 tablespoons heavy cream or water

9 ounces mesclun lettuce

1 apple, peeled, cored, and cut into thin slices

1 pear, peeled, cored, and cut into thin slices

12 walnut halves

¾ cup vinaigrette of choice

SERVES 6

Preheat the oven to 375°F. Line a baking sheet with parchment paper.

Lay a sheet of puff pastry on a work surface. Using a 6-inch round pastry cutter, cut out 12 rounds of pastry (4 per sheet). Place 1 slice of the ham on the puff pastry and brush with 1 tablespoon of the German mustard. Place ⅓ cup of the Gruyère cheese on the ham and top with another slice of ham and 1 tablespoon of the mustard. Brush another piece of puff pastry with the egg wash around the edge to use as a seal and place it on top. Press gently with a fork to seal the top pastry to the bottom pastry. Repeat this process to create 6 stacks. Brush the top of each with the egg wash and prick with a fork. Using a metal spatula, transfer to the prepared pan and bake for 10 minutes, or until puffed and golden. Remove from the oven and keep warm.

Divide the mesclun among 6 plates and top with the apple and pear slices. Sprinkle with the walnuts and drizzle with the vinaigrette. Place 1 pastry on each plate next to the salad and serve at once.

MOST OF THE 740 ROOMS AND SUITES
AT HARVEYS LAKE TAHOE OFFER STRIKING VIEWS OF
EITHER LAKE TAHOE OR
THE MAJESTIC SIERRA NEVADA MOUNTAINS.

MONTE CRISTO SANDWICH

BALLY'S ATLANTIC CITY
EXECUTIVE SOUS-CHEF RON ULCZAK

A variation on the croque monsieur, the traditional Monte Cristo is a ham or turkey sandwich that is battered and fried. Chef Ron Ulczak's version hews close to the original while adding refinements that make all the difference: He uses both ham and turkey; he adds beer, soda water, and baking powder to the batter to make it extra light; he uses rich and delicate challah for the bread; and he adds a little raspberry jam and confectioners' sugar for the perfect touch of sweetness.

BATTER

2 cups all-purpose flour

1 cup cornstarch

1 tablespoon baking powder

¼ teaspoon cayenne pepper

1 teaspoon salt

One 12-ounce bottle beer, preferably Heineken

1 cup club soda

4 tablespoons raspberry jam

8 slices challah bread

4 slices Swiss cheese

4 slices ham

4 slices turkey

¾ cup canola oil for frying

Confectioners' sugar for dusting

SERVES 4

For the batter: In a large bowl, combine all the dry ingredients and stir with a whisk. Gradually whisk in the beer and club soda until smooth. Set aside.

For each sandwich, spread ½ tablespoon of the jam on 2 slices of bread. Cut the sliced cheese, ham, and turkey to the same dimensions as the bread slices. Top a slice of bread with 1 slice of cheese, then ham, and then turkey and a second slice of bread. Cut each sandwich in half.

In a large skillet, heat the oil over medium heat. Dip 2 sandwich halves in the batter to coat completely. Drop a little of the batter in the oil to see that it begins to cook. Once ready, add the sandwich and fry until golden brown, about 2 minutes on each side. Transfer to a low oven to keep warm. Repeat to fry the remaining sandwiches. Dust sandwiches with confectioners' sugar and serve.

SMOKED BABY BACK RIBS

TOBY KEITH'S I LOVE THIS BAR & GRILL & THE RANGE STEAKHOUSE AT HARRAH'S NORTH KANSAS CITY
TOBY KEITH & CHEF WILLIAM DWORZAN

These back ribs are a big seller at both of the Harrah's North Kansas City restaurants: A versatile dish, they can be ordered as appetizers, half slabs, and full slabs. They're also a favorite among Harrah's North Kansas City employees, who often enjoy them as a take-home meal. As chef William Dworzan says, "Everyone likes smoked ribs in Kansas City!"

Notes: The barbecue sauce needs to be prepared the day before the ribs are cooked. You will need 2 pounds hickory chips for this recipe. You can purchase Toby Keith's signature sauces and seasonings at his restaurant and at www.tobykeith.com.

MUSTARD-STYLE BARBECUE SAUCE

1 cup yellow mustard

½ cup sugar

¼ cup packed brown sugar

½ cup apple cider vinegar

¼ cup water

2 tablespoons chili powder

¾ teaspoon ground black pepper

¾ teaspoon ground white pepper

½ teaspoon soy sauce

2 tablespoons unsalted butter

1½ teaspoons liquid smoke

PORK DRY RUB

¼ cup ground black pepper

¼ cup sweet paprika

2 tablespoons sugar

1 teaspoon salt

½ tablespoon chili powder

1½ teaspoons garlic powder

1½ teaspoons onion powder

4 slabs pork baby back ribs

For the sauce: In a medium saucepan, mix together the mustard, sugar, brown sugar, apple cider vinegar, water, chili powder, black pepper, and white pepper. Bring to a simmer over medium-low heat and cook for 30 minutes. Stir in the soy sauce, butter, and liquid smoke and simmer for 10 more minutes. Remove from the heat and let cool. Cover and refrigerate overnight to allow the flavors to blend.

For the rub: In a small bowl, combine all the ingredients and stir to blend.

To cook the ribs, soak 2 pounds of hickory wood chips in water to cover for 1 hour. Score the back side of the ribs with a sharp knife moving across the bones. Rub the ribs completely and liberally with the dry rub on both sides.

Light a low fire in a charcoal grill. Move the coals to opposite sides of the grill for indirect heat. Place a disposable aluminum pan in the center of the fuel bed of the grill to catch drips. Drain the wood chips and sprinkle half of them over the coals. Place the ribs, bone side up, on the grill grids. Cover the grill and cook for 1 hour. Replenish the coals with live coals lighted in a charcoal chimney starter. Sprinkle the remaining wood chips over the coals and cook the ribs for 1 more hour. Replenish the coals again. Wrap the ribs completely with aluminum foil and cook them for 2 more hours, moving the coals together or replenishing them to maintain low heat as necessary.

Take the ribs out of the aluminum foil and baste them with the barbecue sauce. Serve immediately.

SERVES 4 TO 6

6

POULTRY

CHANTERELLE & PARMESAN–CRUSTED CHICKEN

WITH LEMON-BASIL CREAM SAUCE

HARRAH'S STEAK HOUSE AT HARRAH'S RENO
CHEF JEFFREY GALICK

Leave it to an award-winning steakhouse to serve the best chicken dish in town. If you're looking for a new way to serve chicken, chef Jeffrey Galick at Harrah's Steak House in Reno has the solution: Coat it in an intensely flavorful mixture of dried mushrooms and Parmesan, pan-roast it, and serve on a bed of sautéed spinach, topped with a tangy and velvety sauce.

1 cup all-purpose flour

Salt and freshly ground pepper

2 large eggs

½ cup heavy cream

2 cups grated Parmesan cheese

½ cup finely chopped dried black or golden chanterelle mushrooms

4 skinless, boneless chicken breast halves

5 tablespoons canola oil

LEMON-BASIL CREAM SAUCE

4 cups heavy cream

¼ cup water

2 tablespoons cornstarch

Juice of 3 lemons

Salt and freshly ground pepper

5 fresh basil leaves, julienned

1 tablespoon olive oil

2 cups spinach leaves, rinsed

SERVES 4

Preheat the oven to 400°F. In a shallow bowl, combine the flour and salt and pepper to taste and stir with a whisk to blend. In a second shallow bowl, whisk the eggs and heavy cream until blended. In a third shallow bowl, stir the Parmesan and mushrooms together.

Coat the chicken in the seasoned flour and shake off the excess. Next, dip the chicken in the egg mixture and let the excess run off. Lastly, coat the chicken well in the Parmesan and chanterelle mixture. In a large ovenproof sauté pan or skillet, heat the canola oil over medium heat and cook the chicken for 1 minute on each side. Transfer to the oven and bake for 12 minutes, or until opaque throughout.

For the sauce: In a small, heavy saucepan, simmer the cream over medium heat to reduce by half. In a small bowl, stir the water and cornstarch together until the cornstarch is dissolved. Gradually whisk the cornstarch mixture into the simmering cream until it thickens. Whisk in the lemon juice until smooth. Cook for 2 more minutes and season with salt and pepper. Remove from the heat. Stir in the basil just before serving.

In a small sauté pan, heat the olive oil over medium heat and sauté the spinach until wilted. Season with salt and pepper.

To serve, divide the spinach among 4 plates and place a chicken breast on each serving. Top with the cream sauce and serve at once.

PORTOBELLO CHICKEN CHARDONNAY

HARRAH'S JOLIET
EXECUTIVE CHEF SCOTT D. LeCOMPTE

This is one of those appealing dishes that looks complicated but is really quite simple to prepare. Chef Scott D. LeCompte says, "While some preparations can be done ahead of time, you will be able to cook and finish this dish while still hosting your guests around the kitchen counter. The end result is a harmonious balance of quality fresh ingredients, which complement each other very well."

2 portobello mushrooms, stemmed

1 bunch asparagus, trimmed

1 teaspoon balsamic vinegar

Salt and freshly ground pepper

Four 10-ounce boneless chicken breasts, skin on and wing bone attached

4 ounces buffalo mozzarella, sliced

4 tablespoons olive oil

2 teaspoons minced garlic

2 teaspoons minced shallot

¼ cup Chardonnay or Pinot Grigio wine

¼ cup chicken stock

½ cup diced tomatoes

1 pound angel hair pasta, cooked

2 teaspoons sliced green onion

2 tablespoons cold unsalted butter, cut into bits

2 tablespoons grated Parmesan cheese

SERVES 4

Heat a grill pan over medium-high heat; oil the pan. Rub the mushrooms and asparagus with the balsamic vinegar and season them with salt and pepper. Grill the mushrooms for 4 to 5 minutes on each side and transfer to a plate; grill the asparagus for 3 to 4 minutes on each side and transfer to a plate. Let the mushrooms cool and cut them into thin slices.

Preheat the oven to 350°F. Using your fingers, make a pocket under the skin of each chicken breast. Stuff the mushrooms and mozzarella equally under the skin of each breast. Season the chicken with salt and pepper.

In a large ovenproof sauté pan or skillet, heat 2 tablespoons of the oil over medium-high heat and sauté the chicken, skin side down, for 3 to 4 minutes. Using tongs, transfer the chicken to a plate.

In the same pan, sauté the garlic and shallot until golden, about 4 minutes. Add the wine and chicken stock and stir to scrape up the browned bits from the bottom of the pan. Return the chicken to the pan and transfer the pan to the oven. Roast for 15 minutes, or until opaque throughout. Remove from the oven; transfer the chicken to a cutting board and keep warm.

Place the pan on the stove top over medium heat and cook to reduce by half. Add the tomatoes, asparagus, and pasta and cook for 2 minutes. Add the green onions. Taste and adjust the seasoning. Using a wire skimmer, transfer the pasta and vegetables to a platter and keep warm. Gradually whisk the butter into the sauce a few pieces at a time over low heat. Stir in the Parmesan cheese until melted. Cut the chicken into diagonal slices, place it on top of the pasta, pour the sauce over, and serve.

THE RESERVE RESTAURANT AT HARRAH'S JOLIET HAS RECEIVED *WINE SPECTATOR* AWARDS TWO YEARS IN A ROW FOR ITS DIVERSE MENU AND GRAND SELECTION OF WINES.

TOP 10 STAPLES THAT SHOULD BE IN EVERY KITCHEN AND WHY

1   Kosher salt or sea salt: **You need to season your food. It doesn't come to you already seasoned.**

2   Pepper mill with peppercorns: **You will need this to properly season your food.**

3   Coffee beans and a French coffee press: **This produces the best coffee ever.**

4   Soy sauce: **A staple in every Asian kitchen.**

5   Tabasco sauce: **What else are you going to put on your eggs at 4 A.M.?**

6   Instant noodles: **When you don't know what to eat, you eat instant noodles.**

7   Nishiki rice: **This is a great short-grain rice. I eat this every day.**

8   Rice wine vinegar: **You need this when eating pot stickers, lumpia, or dumplings.**

9   Instant brown gravy: **This is necessary for loco moco: a large bed of rice, hamburger on top of that, gravy on top of that, and an over-easy egg on that. It's a Hawaiian delicacy that you can have right in your own kitchen whenever you want it!**

10   Scotch: **In case your recipes don't work out so well.**

CHICKEN ROMANO

CARVINGS BUFFET AT HARRAH'S RENO
EXECUTIVE CHEF KLAUS FEYERSINGER

Chicken breasts, breaded and sautéed until golden brown, are topped with a long-cooked tomato sauce and served on buttered pasta for a satisfying dish. Carvings Buffet's time-tested version of the classic marinara sauce is equally good with seafood, pasta, and red meats.

MARINARA SAUCE

5 tomatoes

1½ cups olive oil, plus 3 tablespoons

2 teaspoons kosher salt

10 roasted garlic cloves (see page 48)

10 raw garlic cloves, peeled

½ cup finely chopped carrot

1 cup finely chopped celery

1½ cups finely chopped onions

1½ cups dry Marsala wine

4 cups canned San Marzano tomatoes

¼ cup sugar

2 teaspoons whole fresh thyme leaves

1 tablespoon minced fresh rosemary

2 tablespoons minced fresh oregano

3 tablespoons minced fresh basil

2 cups water

½ cup shredded fresh basil leaves

1 cup panko (Japanese bread crumbs), seasoned with a little salt and pepper

1 cup grated Romano cheese

1 cup all-purpose flour

Salt and freshly ground pepper

1 large egg

Four 6-ounce boneless, skinless chicken breast halves

2 tablespoons canola oil

Buttered cooked pasta for serving

Grated Parmesan cheese for garnish

SERVES 4

For the sauce: Preheat the oven to 400°F. Put the tomatoes in a small roasting pan. Coat with the 3 tablespoons olive oil and sprinkle with 1 teaspoon of the salt. Roast for 25 minutes, or until soft. Remove from the oven, let cool to the touch, and pull off the skins. Purée the tomatoes in a blender and set aside.

In a large, heavy saucepan, heat the 1½ cups olive oil over medium heat and sauté the roasted garlic, raw garlic, carrot, celery, and onions for about 8 minutes, or until the vegetables are tender. Add the wine and stir to scrape up the browned bits from the bottom of the pan. Add the canned tomatoes, roasted-tomato purée, sugar, thyme, rosemary, oregano, minced basil, remaining 1 teaspoon salt, and water. Bring to a boil over high heat, then reduce the heat to a simmer and cook for 1 hour. Working in batches, purée in a blender until smooth. Return to the pan and fold in the basil leaves.

In a shallow bowl, stir the panko and Romano cheese together. In a second shallow bowl, combine the flour with salt and pepper to taste; stir to blend. In a third shallow bowl, whisk the egg until blended. Dredge each chicken breast in the seasoned flour, then the egg, then the panko mixture.

In a large sauté pan or skillet, heat the oil over medium-high heat and sauté the chicken for 2 to 3 minutes on each side, or until golden brown on the outside and opaque throughout.

To serve, place some buttered pasta on each serving plate. Top with some of the sauce, then a chicken breast. Sprinkle with Parmesan cheese and serve at once.

WILLIAM F. HARRAH OPENED HIS FIRST BINGO PARLOR IN RENO IN 1937.

TOBY KEITH'S
WHO'S YOUR DADDY?
CHICKEN WINGS

TOBY KEITH'S I LOVE THIS BAR & GRILL AT HARRAH'S NORTH KANSAS CITY
TOBY KEITH & CHEF WILLIAM DWORZAN

At country music star Toby Keith's restaurant, these fiery classics can be purchased by the dozen or by the hundreds. Now, you can enjoy them at home for any occasion, from football games to backyard parties.

Note: You can purchase Toby Keith's signature sauces and seasonings at his restaurant and at www.tobykeith.com.

1 teaspoon cayenne pepper

½ cup hot pepper sauce

2½ pounds chicken wings, tips removed, halved at the joint

Canola oil for deep-frying

SERVES 4 TO 6

In a small bowl, mix the cayenne pepper with the hot sauce. In a large pot of boiling water, cook the chicken wings for 10 minutes. Drain and let cool.

In a large, shallow ceramic or glass bowl, combine the chicken with half of the hot sauce and toss well to combine. Cover and refrigerate for at least 1 hour or up to 3 hours.

In a Dutch oven or large heavy pot, heat 3 inches of the oil to 360°F on a deep-fat thermometer. In two batches, add the chicken and cook, turning occasionally, for 3 to 4 minutes, or until brown on all sides. Using a wire skimmer, transfer to paper towels to drain. Toss the chicken wings with the remaining hot sauce and serve immediately.

NEXT TIME YOU'RE AT TOBY KEITH'S RESTAURANT AT HARRAH'S NORTH KANSAS CITY OR HARRAH'S LAS VEGAS, DON'T BE SURPRISED TO SEE TOBY HIMSELF THERE SOME NIGHT. TOBY USUALLY STOPS BY THE RESTAURANT WHENEVER HE IS IN TOWN AND HAS ALSO BEEN KNOWN TO SING A SONG OR TWO FOR THE CROWD.

CREAM OF CILANTRO CHICKEN

CAESARS ATLANTIC CITY
SOUS-CHEF STEVE ORTIZ

Cilantro shines brightly in this dish, adding zip to the creamy sauce that dresses up the grilled chicken breasts. Chef Steve Ortiz says, "I created this recipe at home, and it was such a big hit that I decided to use it for my demo when I came to Caesars to work as a chef. We've been using it ever since."

6 boneless, skinless chicken breast halves

1 bunch cilantro, stemmed

¾ cup heavy cream

1 cup water

1 teaspoon chicken base

3 tablespoons unsalted butter

3 tablespoons all-purpose flour

Salt and freshly ground pepper

SERVES 6

Butterfly the chicken breasts by cutting them in half horizontally almost to the end; open them flat like a book. Heat a grill pan over medium-high heat and oil the pan. Cook the chicken breasts for 5 minutes on each side, then transfer to a plate and keep warm.

In a blender, combine the cilantro, cream, water, and chicken base, blending well; set aside.

In a medium saucepan, melt the butter over medium heat. Stir in the flour and cook, stirring constantly, for 3 minutes; do not brown. Whisk in the cilantro mixture and cook over medium heat, stirring frequently, until the mixture boils and thickens slightly. Season with salt and pepper.

Divide the chicken among plates and serve with the sauce poured over.

TOP 10 FOODS
THAT SHOULD BE IN EVERY FREEZER AND WHY

CAESARS WINDSOR

Although we all prefer to use fresh ingredients, high-quality processed frozen foods as well as food you've prepared and frozen are very helpful. Frozen foods can be highly nutritious and convenient, and they can allow the cook to create new and exciting dishes.

This list is in no particular order as it depends on personal needs and preference. You may have a butcher just around the corner or grow your own herbs year-round.

To begin with, here are a few important points:

+ For processed items, follow the manufacturer's directions for cooking and thawing.

+ Look for individually quick frozen (IQF) foods: Foods that are individually frozen before being packaged make thawing quicker and allow you to use just what you need. You can do this as well. For example, buy fresh chicken breasts in bulk and freeze them on a tray (keep the pieces from touching one another and use parchment paper between the layers). Once frozen, individually wrap the chicken breasts and place them into doubled freezer bags.

+ When processing or repackaging foods, properly label and date them.

+ Thaw frozen food in the refrigerator or under cold running water.

Always keep these foods in your freezer:

1   Meat: Freeze your own chicken breasts, satays, fish, seafood, and steaks, all of which can be thawed quickly in case of unexpected guests.

2   Hors d'oeuvres: Shrimp, meatballs, puff pastry shells, and tart shells for mini quiches.

3   Frozen fruits and berries: These are great for quick desserts, pancakes, or waffle toppings.

4   Vegetables: In most cases, frozen vegetables are picked when perfectly ripe and blanched before freezing. These processes preserve vitamins, color, and texture very effectively. In some cases, fresh vegetables can spend up to a week in transport and are not always better. Take care not to overcook frozen vegetables, as they are already partially cooked due to being blanched.

5   Stocks: Whether you make your own or buy a low-sodium stock, keep it on hand in small quantities, such as frozen into ice cubes. For larger amounts, make sure to use containers that will not burst and leave room for the liquid to expand when frozen. This week's chicken bones from a roasted chicken can be turned into a stock to use in next week's soup.

6   Base sauces: With frozen stock, make extra gravy the next time you have a pot roast. Freeze it and you will have a base for a peppercorn sauce for steak, and so on. A tomato sauce can be turned into a tomato-vegetable sauce, a bolognese, or even a quick tomato soup.

7   Fresh herbs: This is a great way to preserve fresh herbs: Wash, dry, and chop, then freeze covered on a tray, immediately crumble, and store in a bag. They are then ready to use as you would fresh.

8   Shredded potatoes: These are very helpful to have on hand. They can be used for hash browns, potato pancakes, potato-based frittatas, and more.

9   Partially cooked beans: Dried beans too often are avoided because of the cooking time they require. Partially cooking and then freezing them or purchasing them frozen opens up many possibilities for using these great sources of fiber and protein.

10 Breads and doughs: Keep frozen bread dough on hand for pizza, sweet rolls, dinner rolls, and loaves.

MEDITERRANEAN ARTICHOKE CHICKEN

THE RANGE STEAKHOUSE AT HARRAH'S LAUGHLIN
EXECUTIVE SOUS-CHEF JEREMY HUGHES

Of this popular dish, chef Jeremy Hughes remarks, "It was first introduced as a seasonal offering to complement our Mediterranean-themed menu. However, because of the popular demand for the dish, the restaurant has kept it through three menu changes."

3 tablespoons olive oil

1 cup all-purpose flour

Salt and freshly ground white pepper

Four 4-ounce boneless, skinless chicken breast halves

16 white mushrooms, each cut into fourths

4 teaspoons minced garlic

1 tomato, diced

20 artichoke hearts, each cut into fourths

4 teaspoons cracked black pepper

4 teaspoons dried oregano

½ cup fresh lemon juice

1½ cups sweet sherry

¾ cup whipped butter

12 mushroom ravioli

8 ounces feta cheese, crumbled (optional)

SERVES 4

Preheat the oven to 350°F. In a large ovenproof sauté pan or skillet, heat 1 tablespoon of the oil over medium-high heat. Put the flour in a shallow bowl and add salt and white pepper to taste. Coat the chicken in the flour on all sides. Cook the chicken for 2 to 3 minutes on each side. Transfer the pan to the oven and roast for 15 to 20 minutes, or until opaque throughout.

In a medium sauté pan, heat 1 tablespoon of the oil over medium heat and sauté the mushrooms for 1 minute. Add the garlic, tomato, artichokes, black pepper, oregano, and salt and white pepper and sauté for 3 minutes. Add the lemon juice and sherry and simmer for 1 minute. Add the butter, stirring until it is completely melted. Remove from the heat and keep warm.

In a large pot of salted boiling water, cook the ravioli for 5 minutes; drain. Add the ravioli to the vegetable and sherry mixture.

To serve, divide the ravioli among the plates. Spoon some of the vegetables on top of the ravioli, then place a chicken breast on top of each serving. Top with another spoonful of vegetables and some of the pan liquid. Sprinkle the feta cheese on top, if desired.

TOP 10 INGREDIENTS
EVERY KITCHEN SHOULD HAVE AND WHY

HARRAH'S LAKE TAHOE & HARVEYS LAKE TAHOE

1   Unsalted butter: Use unsalted butter to finish a sauce or any dish that's already perfectly seasoned.

2   Extra-virgin and virgin olive oil: Extra-virgin oils are not refined, which means that each one has its own unique character; virgin oils have a little more acidity. I use extra-virgin for vinaigrettes and to drizzle over vegetables. I combine virgin and butter for sautéing.

3   Kosher salt and fleur de sel: Kosher salt has no iodine and has a cleaner taste than regular table salt. Fleur de sel is an unrefined sea salt from France that is also worth having in your pantry.

4   White and black peppercorns, pepper blends, and pepper mills: Pungent, fiery flavor and aroma are the traits that pepper gives so many of the dishes we all love. Many times, this is the ingredient that awakens your taste buds.

5   Good white and red table wines for drinking and cooking: A good rule of thumb where wine and cooking are concerned is if you don't drink it, don't cook with it. Every variety of grape has certain foods that it belongs with.

6   Chicken and beef stock, fresh or from a can: Stock is a base for soups, sauces, and many other preparations. If making your own, cool the stock when finished and put it in ice cube trays to freeze. Seal the frozen cubes in airtight bags for quick pan sauces. Stock made from scratch provides a clean and fresh flavor to food. And the aroma of a stock cooking is as good as it gets.

7   Garlic and shallots: These are the building blocks for many savory recipes. Any haute cuisine recipe for sauce or soup will call for these members of the lily family.

8   A variety of vinegars: Made from wine, fruit juices, and similar acidic liquids, different vinegars have different levels of tartness. Some must-have vinegars include balsamic, Champagne, red and white wine, cider, sherry, and rice vinegar.

9   Herbes de Provence: I use this famous dried herb mixture for roast lamb, chicken, pork, and beef. It's a must in your kitchen, especially when fresh herbs aren't available.

10 Different varieties of rice: I can never get enough risotto, which is made with Arborio or Carnaroli rice. Other kinds of rice to keep on hand include jasmine and basmati.

(Can I sneak in pasta?)

11 A variety of good-quality dried pasta: This is a must for every kitchen. I have orzo, pappardelle, spaghetti, linguine, and conchiglie in my kitchen at home at all times. There are so many to choose from. If you prefer fresh pasta and have the time to make it, go for it.

Always remember, cook with your heart and buy in season.

TOP 10 FOODS
EVERY KITCHEN SHOULD HAVE AND WHY

CAESARS PALACE LAS VEGAS

1   Butter: The best fat, with multiple uses, including searing, emulsion, and more.

2   Heavy cream: The perfect finishing ingredient for such dishes as scrambled eggs, sauces, stews, and so on.

3   Garlic: Chopped, fried, or whole, garlic perfumes all dishes and is very healthy.

4   Shallots or onions: Raw or cooked, these staples will enhance most of the dishes you prepare, including salads, steaks, and fish.

5   Fresh herbs: Always keep some fresh herbs in your refrigerator crisper. Thyme, rosemary, basil, parsley, and others are perfect for all stages of preparation and for final touches and garnishes.

6   Wines: White, red, and sparkling wines are great for cooking, reducing, seasoning, and other uses. Often, wine is a must-have ingredient to create the desired marriage of flavors in a dish.

7   Eggs: When you have eggs in the refrigerator, you always have the makings of a meal. Cook them baked, poached, fried, or sunny side up, or make a cake, French toast—and the list goes on.

8   Cheeses: Cheese, from domestic shredded to fancy artisan ones, is a must-have for gratins, melting, spreading, and so on.

9   Yukon gold potatoes: Potatoes are a cheap, healthy vegetable that can be used to make hot appetizers such as potatoes soufflé, or side dishes like whipped potatoes or potato gratin. And everyone likes these sweet golden potatoes.

10 Tomatoes: A healthy accompaniment to many dishes. Preferably, you should use vine-ripened tomatoes, because they are so sweet and flavorful.

DEEP-FRIED TURKEY

HARRAH'S LOUISIANA DOWNS
EXECUTIVE CHEF J. RYAN GILLESPIE

Deep-fried turkey, which is injected with flavored melted butter before cooking, is moist and delicious. Chef J. Ryan Gillespie adds, "A word of caution: A common problem is that people misjudge the amount of oil needed, not allowing room for the turkey. But even when the oil is at the right level, a partially frozen turkey can also cause hot oil to spew a jet of fire." Use a fresh turkey for this recipe, or thaw a frozen turkey in the refrigerator for about twenty-four hours for every five pounds of turkey.

Note: This dish is best made out of doors, on grass, using the following equipment:

A turkey injection needle

A heavy-duty portable propane burner

A turkey-frying pot or a 40- to 60-quart stockpot

A deep-fat thermometer

A turkey hanger (which has a hook that is attached deep inside the turkey, through the neck cavity) or a frying basket (which comes with a turkey-frying pot and fits inside it)

To figure how much oil to add to the pot: Put the turkey in the pot and add water to come to 3 to 5 inches from the top of the pot. Lift out the turkey and drain it well. Measure the water level in the pot with a ruler, then drain the pot. Dry the pot well. Dry the turkey inside and out as thoroughly as possible. Add oil to the correct level and heat. Keep children and pets away from the pot when it is filled with oil. Let the oil cool completely before draining it from the pot.

1 cup (2 sticks) unsalted butter

2 tablespoons iodized salt (do not use kosher salt, as it will clog the injector)

2 teaspoons garlic powder

2 teaspoons finely ground white pepper (do not use black pepper, as it will clog the injector)

2 teaspoons cayenne pepper

½ teaspoon onion powder

One 10- to 14-pound turkey, giblets and excess fat removed

3½ to 5 gallons of peanut oil for deep-frying

SERVES 10 TO 12

In a medium saucepan, melt the butter over low heat. Stir in the seasonings. Pour the mixture into a jar with a lid; close the lid tightly and shake the jar vigorously. Using a turkey injection needle, inject half of the mixture deeply into the two sides of the breast, half of the remaining mixture into the two legs/ thighs, and the rest into the two meaty wing sections. Let the turkey sit for 1 hour before deep-frying it.

Fill the pot with oil to the previously measured mark. Heat the oil to 325°F to 350°F. Using the frying basket or the turkey hanger, gradually lower the turkey into the hot oil; it should be completely covered with oil. Cook the turkey for 3½ minutes per pound, 35 to 50 minutes. Carefully remove the turkey from the oil. Insert a meat thermometer into the thickest part of the thigh but not touching bone; the internal temperature should be 165°F to 170°F.

Transfer the turkey to a platter lined with paper towels to drain. Let rest for at least 15 minutes. Transfer to a carving board and carve the turkey.

HARRAH'S LOUISIANA DOWNS' SIGNATURE RACE IS THE SUPER DERBY. IT IS TOUTED AS A PREPARATORY RACE FOR PROSPECTIVE PARTICIPANTS TO THE BREEDERS' CUP CLASSIC. THE RACE TESTS THE NATION'S BEST THREE-YEAR-OLD THOROUGHBREDS AT A DISTANCE OF 1⅛ MILES. IT IS THE HIGHLIGHT OF HARRAH'S LOUISIANA DOWNS' DISTINGUISHED STAKES SCHEDULES.

SMOKED TURKEY & WHITE BEAN CASSEROLE

WITH HERBED CRUMB TOPPING

THE SEVEN STARS CLUB AT HARRAH'S RESORT ATLANTIC CITY
CHEF WILLIAM SCAFFIDI

This recipe takes the humble casserole to an entirely new level with a combination of smoky flavors, Cajun seasoning, and Parmesan cheese. Chef William Scaffidi comments, "This hearty casserole is a seasonal favorite with guests at our Seven Stars lounge and bar. Whether served as a side dish or as an entrée, this dish is always well received."

Note: Dried beans must be soaked overnight before cooking.

2 pounds smoked turkey breast
or smoked duck breast,
finely diced

8 cups chicken stock

¼ cup olive oil, plus 3 tablespoons

2 cups finely chopped onions

1 cup finely chopped celery

½ cup finely chopped bell pepper

2 tablespoons minced garlic

4 teaspoons minced fresh thyme

¼ teaspoon cayenne pepper

1½ teaspoons Cajun seasoning

2 bay leaves

1 pound dried white beans
(navy or cannellini),
soaked overnight and drained

Salt and freshly ground pepper

1¼ cups Italian bread crumbs

½ cup finely grated Parmesan cheese

2 tablespoons minced fresh flat-leaf
parsley leaves

1 tablespoon minced fresh chives

1 tablespoon minced fresh basil

SERVES 6 TO 8

In a medium bowl, combine the diced meat and 2 cups of the chicken stock.

In a large Dutch oven or heavy pot, heat the 3 tablespoons oil over medium heat and sauté the onions, celery, and bell pepper until the vegetables are tender, 4 to 6 minutes. Add the garlic, 2 teaspoons of the thyme, the cayenne pepper, Cajun seasoning, and bay leaves and cook for 1 minute. Add the beans and the remaining 6 cups stock and return to a boil. Reduce the heat to a simmer and cook, partially covered, until the beans are tender but still firm enough to hold their shape, about 1½ hours. The beans should be moist but not soupy. Stir the turkey and stock mixture into the beans and season with salt and pepper. Transfer to a large ovenproof casserole dish.

Preheat the oven to 375°F. In a small bowl, combine the remaining thyme, the bread crumbs, cheese, parsley, chives, and basil. Add the remaining ¼ cup oil and stir with a fork until well blended. Season with salt and pepper. Sprinkle the bread-crumb mixture evenly over the beans. Bake for 25 to 30 minutes, or until the topping is golden brown and the beans are bubbly around the edges.

7

PASTA

PENNETTE ALLA VODKA

RAO'S AT CAESARS PALACE LAS VEGAS
CHEF DE CUISINE CARLA PELLEGRINO

Rao's has been a family affair for more than 110 years: Ron Straci and Frank Pellegrino are the powers behind the restaurant today, which began in New York and now is also featured at Caesars Palace in Las Vegas. Here, chef Carla Pellegrino prepares the same kind of simple, honest, Italian food that made the restaurant famous on the East Coast, like this classic pasta dish. The chef explains, "It's possible to find this dish in any Italian region. It's originally from the city of Parma, the ham and Parmesan cheese land. The Parmeggiani (people who were born in Parma) always came up with great recipes to use those two ingredients. This specific one from Rao's is easy, delicious, and memorable when served at any kind of party."

4 cups heavy cream

2 tablespoons unsalted butter

2 tablespoons olive oil

1½ large white onions, finely chopped

8 ounces Italian cooked ham, finely diced

5⅓ cups tomato sauce or blended canned peeled Italian tomatoes

3 tablespoons minced fresh flat-leaf parsley

¾ bottle vodka, preferably Absolut

Salt and freshly ground pepper

2 pounds imported Italian penne pasta, preferably De Cecco

SERVES 8

In a medium, heavy saucepan, bring the cream to a simmer and cook until reduced by half. Set aside.

In a large, heavy sauté pan or skillet, melt the butter with the oil over medium-high heat until the butter foams. Add the onions and sauté for 5 minutes, or until golden. Stir in the ham, reduce the heat to medium-low, and cook for about 15 minutes, stirring occasionally. Stir in the tomato sauce and simmer for 20 minutes. Add the parsley and simmer for 3 minutes. Add the reduced cream. Remove from the heat and stir in the vodka, mixing well. Return to medium-low heat and simmer for 20 minutes, or until thick enough to coat the back of a spoon. Season with salt and pepper. Set aside and keep warm.

Add the penne to a large pot of salted boiling water; stir well, reduce the heat to medium, partially cover the pot, and cook, stirring occasionally, until al dente, about 11 minutes; drain.

Add the cooked penne to the sauce. Simmer for 2 minutes and serve hot.

BLACK PEPPER FETTUCCINE
WITH WILD MUSHROOMS

SAGE ROOM STEAK HOUSE AT HARVEYS LAKE TAHOE
EXECUTIVE CHEF JOE WELLS

The Sage Room Steak House's famous Black Pepper Fettuccine with Wild Mushrooms is the perfect pasta dish on a cold night. Chef Joe Wells comments, "This dish is a little heavier pasta because of the cream sauce, while the peppercorns add spice and warmth, which I enjoy when it is a cold evening outside." It can also be served as an appetizer or a side dish for roasted chicken.

24 ounces black pepper pasta

1 teaspoon olive oil

2 ounces finely chopped pancetta

4 tablespoons whole butter

2 ounces morel mushrooms

2 ounces shiitake mushrooms, stemmed

2 ounces porcini mushrooms, chopped

2 teaspoons minced garlic

2 teaspoons minced shallot

4 artichoke bottoms, sliced

2 tablespoons Madeira wine

1 cup heavy cream

½ cup veal demi-glace

2 teaspoons finely chopped green onions, white part only

2 tablespoons cold unsalted butter

Salt

2 tablespoons crumbled fresh white goat cheese

SERVES 4

In a large pot of salted boiling water, cook the pasta until al dente, 8 to 9 minutes. Drain.

Meanwhile, in a medium sauté pan or skillet over medium heat, heat the oil and sauté the pancetta for 4 to 5 minutes, or until the fat is rendered. Add the 4 tablespoons of butter and the mushrooms and sauté until the mushrooms are tender, 3 to 4 minutes. Add the garlic, shallot, and artichoke bottoms and sauté for 1 minute. Add the wine and stir to scrape up the browned bits from the bottom of the pan. Add the heavy cream, demi-glace, and green onions. Whisk in the 2 tablespoons of unsalted butter, 1 tablespoon at a time. Season with salt.

In a pasta bowl, combine the drained pasta and hot sauce; stir to coat. Serve topped with goat cheese.

HARVEYS LAKE TAHOE WAS OPENED BY HARVEY GROSS IN 1947 AND WAS ACQUIRED BY HARRAH'S ENTERTAINMENT IN 2001.

PASTA

STEAK & BLUE CHEESE MACARONI

LES ARTISTES STEAKHOUSE AT PARIS LAS VEGAS
ASSISTANT EXECUTIVE CHEF KURTESS MORTENSEN

Guests at Les Artistes enjoy this grown-up version of mac and cheese with its sophisticated combination of steak and blue cheese. Chef Kurtess Mortensen comments, "Beef and blue cheese are a classic pairing in French cuisine, almost as much as macaroni and cheese are for most Americans. We have found that bringing these two together elevates them both to a new level. The fact that the orders keep coming in tells us we are right!" This recipe redefines the concept of comfort food.

MORNAY SAUCE

5 tablespoons unsalted butter

½ cup all-purpose flour

4 cups milk

1 cup shredded Swiss cheese

¼ cup grated Parmesan cheese

Salt and freshly ground pepper

8 ounces elbow macaroni

2 tablespoons unsalted butter

8 ounces top sirloin, cubed

1 cup (5 ounces)
crumbled Roquefort cheese

¼ cup panko
(Japanese bread crumbs)

¼ cup grated Parmesan cheese

Salt and freshly ground pepper

SERVES 4 TO 6

For the sauce: In a large saucepan, melt the butter over medium-low heat. Stir in the flour and cook, stirring constantly, for 2 to 3 minutes. Do not let the mixture brown. Gradually whisk in the milk, continuing to stir as the sauce thickens. Bring to a boil, reduce the heat, and simmer for 4 to 5 minutes. Gradually stir in the cheeses and continue cooking until they are completely melted. Season with salt and pepper. Remove from the heat; set aside and keep warm.

In a large pot of salted boiling water, cook the macaroni until al dente, about 9 minutes. Drain and set aside.

In a large sauté pan or skillet, melt the butter over medium heat; add the sirloin and sauté for 5 minutes, or until medium-rare. Using a slotted spoon, transfer to paper towels to drain.

Preheat the oven to 325°F. In a large bowl, combine the macaroni, beef, and the Mornay sauce; stir well. Put the mixture in a 6-cup baking dish, cover with aluminum foil, and bake for 22 minutes. Remove the foil and top with the Roquefort cheese, panko, and Parmesan cheese. Season with salt and pepper. Return to the oven and bake for 10 minutes, or until golden brown. Remove from the oven and let cool for 5 minutes before serving.

TOP 10 TIPS
FOR HOME COOKS

HARRAH'S CHEROKEE

1   Always play with your food. When creating dishes, think of it as playtime. Are you cooking just to satisfy hunger, or are you trying to create something new?

2   Cook and serve others first, and hopefully a little will be left for you to enjoy. This is the best way to find out if the people you are feeding are enjoying your food. A lot of leftovers means you either cooked too much or they did not like it.

3   Cook like it's your last meal. When creating new dishes, savor the flavors.

4   Some maintain that belching is an option to show appreciation for great food. Use your discretion!

5   A way to a woman's heart is to clean up the kitchen after you have cooked for her. Hey, let's face it, no one likes to clean up after someone else.

6   With your meal, drink the wine you like, not the one "they" tell you to like. Everyone has an opinion of wine. The bottom line is: Who is drinking it?

7   Cook with your heart and soul, and others will follow with knives and forks. If you're a good cook, you'll always have lots of friends.

8   Always cook with passion. If you love to do something, you will always succeed. I cannot stress this enough: Cook with your heart and soul.

9   The best ribs are the ones that leave sauce all over your face. Have you ever seen a two-year-old eat? They have food all over their face, and did you ever notice how happy they look when they're done?

10 The best meals are the ones you eat with the ones you love. Even if the meat loaf is burnt, you are still with the ones you love, so what does it matter?

TOP 10 RULES
FOR HOME COOKS

HORSESHOE TUNICA

1   Start with quality ingredients.

2   Use quality knives.

3   Measure and weigh out ingredients before you start.

4   Have everything handy when cooking.

5   Clean as you go.

6   Enjoy what you are doing.

7   Research ingredients before you use them.

8   Use heavy saucepans to prevent burning or scorching.

9   Taste as you go.

10 Cook with good friends.

MAC & CHEESE

NERO'S AT CAESARS PALACE LAS VEGAS
EXECUTIVE CHEF ERIC DAMIDOT

Chef Eric Damidot explains his version of this classic comfort food: "M&C, the most popular, simple-for-anyone dish—you eat it when you are a kid, you eat it after a nightclub 'extravaganza' night, you eat it when you are in a famous steakhouse making a huge business deal . . ." One thing for sure, the mac and cheese that follows is not the kind you ate as a kid.

WHITE CHEDDAR CHEESE SAUCE

½ cup (1 stick) unsalted butter

¼ cup minced garlic

1 bay leaf

2 shallots, minced

3 cups heavy cream

2 cups shredded
white Cheddar cheese

¼ cup grated Parmesan cheese

Salt and freshly ground white pepper

6 ounces pipette pasta

1½ ounces sliced prosciutto, julienned

Toasted bread crumbs for garnish

SERVES 2

For the sauce: In a large, heavy sauté pan or skillet, melt the butter over medium heat and sauté the garlic, bay leaf, and shallots until the shallots are translucent, about 3 minutes. Add the cream and simmer for 10 minutes. Remove from the heat and remove the bay leaf. Stir in the white Cheddar and Parmesan cheeses until melted. Season with salt and pepper. Set aside and keep warm.

In a large pot of salted boiling water, cook the pasta until al dente. Do not overcook. Drain.

Add the drained pasta to the sauce. Add the prosciutto and cook over low heat until slightly thickened. Divide among serving bowls and garnish with the bread crumbs.

RICOTTA RAVIOLI

CASA DI NAPOLI AT SHOWBOAT ATLANTIC CITY
CHEF GEORGEANN LEAMING

The chefs at Casa di Napoli believe that Italian food should be fun, fresh, and uncomplicated. This recipe for cheese ravioli, topped with a creamy tomato, shrimp, and crab sauce, meets that criterion. Chef Georgeann Leaming notes, "This pasta dish is a popular item with our guests. Typically, Italians do not serve cheese with their seafood, but that's the fun thing about cooking—if something tastes good, enjoy it and forget the rules."

1 tablespoon olive oil

8 ounces medium shrimp, shelled and deveined

1 cup diced tomatoes

2 cups marinara sauce

2 cups heavy cream

8 ounces fresh lump crabmeat, picked over for shell

Salt

⅛ teaspoon red pepper flakes

2 tablespoons thinly sliced fresh basil

2 pounds ricotta cheese ravioli

2 tablespoons minced fresh flat-leaf parsley

SERVES 4

In a large sauté pan or skillet, heat the oil over medium-high heat. Add the shrimp and sauté until they curl, about 1½ minutes. Turn the shrimp over and sauté on the other side, about 2 minutes. Reduce the heat to medium and add the tomatoes and marinara. Bring to a simmer, then add the heavy cream. Simmer for 5 minutes, then add the crabmeat, salt to taste, and red pepper flakes. Continue to simmer for another 5 minutes. Add the basil.

Meanwhile, in a large pot of salted boiling water, cook the ravioli until they rise to the surface, 10 to 12 minutes. Drain.

To serve, place the ravioli on a serving platter and pour the sauce over. Lightly toss the ravioli to coat. Garnish with the parsley.

SHOWBOAT CHEFS PURCHASE FRESH PRODUCE FROM THE LOCAL FARMERS' MARKET TO SHOWCASE THEIR RECIPES AND SUPPORT AREA FARMERS.

SIGNATURE LASAGNA

AL DENTE AT BALLY'S LAS VEGAS
CHEF BENOIT CHOBERT

Al Dente prides itself on blending the robust flavors of the Old World with contemporary flair. The secret to this lasagna's success is the ragù napolitano that masterfully blends sausage, beef, and pork for a rich, savory sauce. Chef Benoit Chobert says, "For more than a decade, al Dente has been at the heart of the Las Vegas Italian food scene. Using the best ingredients, we simmer the sauce for many hours, bringing out the boldness of the flavors. This is an everyday challenge, but an exciting one. We hope that you will enjoy this recipe at home and visit us at al Dente in the future."

RAGÙ NAPOLITANO

¼ cup olive oil

8 ounces sweet Italian sausage with fennel, removed from casing

8 ounces ground beef

8 ounces ground pork

1 onion, finely chopped

¾ cup dry red wine

Two 28-ounce cans Italian plum tomatoes with juice, passed through a food mill

Pinch of red pepper flakes

Salt and freshly ground pepper (optional)

2½ pounds lasagna noodles

4 cups fresh whole-milk ricotta cheese

1 teaspoon freshly ground black pepper

1 tablespoon minced fresh flat-leaf parsley

1 teaspoon minced fresh thyme

1 teaspoon dried oregano

1 tablespoon minced fresh basil

1 cup grated Parmesan cheese

1 pound fresh mozzarella cheese, shredded

SERVES 10 TO 12

For the ragù: In a large, heavy saucepan, heat the oil over medium heat and separately sear the sausage, beef, and pork until golden brown, transferring each to a plate with a slotted spoon as it is cooked. Add the onion and stir to scrape up the browned bits from the bottom of the pan. Add the wine, browned meats, tomatoes, and pepper flakes to the pot and bring to a boil. Reduce the heat to a simmer and cook, stirring occasionally and skimming the excess fat when necessary, for 3 hours. Taste and adjust the seasoning, if necessary. Set aside and keep warm.

Preheat the oven to 325°F. In a large pot of salted boiling water, cook the pasta until al dente. Do not overcook. Drain. In a medium bowl, combine the ricotta and the black pepper, parsley, thyme, oregano, and basil. Stir to blend.

Using a 12-by-20-inch lasagna pan, spread ½ cup of the ragù in the bottom of the pan. Top with a layer of lasagna, followed by a layer of ragù, ricotta, Parmesan, and mozzarella. Repeat the process to make 3 to 4 layers. Bake for 45 minutes, or until the top is browned and the lasagna is bubbling at the edges. Remove from the oven and let stand for 10 minutes prior to cutting and serving.

TOP 10 WAYS
TO ADD COLOR TO A PLATE

1   Emulsions: A mixture of two or more ingredients that are normally unblendable. Culinary emulsions are usually liquids suspended in a fat, such as vinegar and oil in a vinaigrette, or egg yolks and oil in mayonnaise.

2   Reductions: Boiling a liquid (usually stock, wine, or a sauce mixture) rapidly until the volume is reduced by evaporation will thicken the liquid and intensify its color and flavor.

3   Infusions: Flavor and color can be extracted from an ingredient, such as tea leaves, herbs, or fruit, by steeping it in a liquid (usually hot), such as water or even olive oil.

4   Blanching: Plunging food (usually fruits and vegetables) briefly into boiling water, then into cold water to stop the cooking process, firms flesh, loosens skins, and heightens and sets color and flavor.

5   Purées: A purée is any food (usually a fruit or vegetable) that is finely mashed or ground to a smooth, thick consistency, which intensifies the color of the food.

6   Spices and powders: Spices, such as saffron and cumin, and powders, such as wasabi, can be added to foods to give both color and flavor.

7   Searing: Cooking foods over high heat on the stove top, under a broiler or on a grill, or in a very hot oven will give them a browned surface.

8   Caramelizing: Sugar can be cooked until it liquefies and darkens in color from golden to dark brown. The natural sugars in fruits and vegetables will also caramelize when the food is roasted, sautéed, grilled, or broiled.

9   Garnishes: These edible decorations can add color and interest to finished dishes from appetizers to desserts. Garnishes can be placed under, around, or on food, depending on the dish. They vary from simple sprigs of parsley to exotically carved vegetables. Garnishes should not only be appealing to the eye, but should also echo or complement the flavors of the dish.

10   Sauces: A wide variety of thickened, flavored liquids can enhance foods by adding both color and flavor.

RICOTTA GNOCCHI

GRAND BILOXI CASINO, HOTEL & SPA
EXECUTIVE CHEF JASON CARLISLE

These light cheese dumplings are easier to make than potato gnocchi and can be served with any number of sauces. Chef Jason Carlisle comments, "I love gnocchi, but hate potato gnocchi. My fellow chef and brother, Justin Carlisle, gave me this recipe several years ago, and I still use it to this day. It is a very simple all-cheese dumpling with minimal starch."

1 pound whole-milk ricotta
Salt and freshly ground white pepper
Pinch of grated nutmeg
1 large egg
1 cup all-purpose flour
Sauce of choice for serving

SERVES 6 TO 8 AS A FIRST COURSE
OR SIDE DISH

In a large bowl, combine the ricotta, salt and white pepper to taste, nutmeg, and egg. Stir well to mix. Fold in the flour, 1/3 cup at a time, until you can form a ball. Wrap the ball in plastic wrap and refrigerate for at least 30 minutes or up to 24 hours.

Divide the dough into 6 pieces. Roll each piece into a thick log. Cut the logs into teaspoon-size chunks. Roll the chunks into balls and press them onto the back of a fork.

In a large pot of salted boiling water, cook the gnocchi until they rise to the surface, 3 to 4 minutes. Toss with your favorite sauce and serve at once.

CAJUN SEAFOOD PASTA

HARRAH'S NORTH KANSAS CITY
CHEF ROY ASKREN

This hearty pasta dish makes a great main course, and you can also serve it in smaller portions as an appetizer to get your taste buds bubbling for more. It has a bounty of different flavors that is tantalizing to anyone's taste buds. The total combination of different meats, vegetables, and the blending of herbs increases the flavor of the seafood in the dish. And the bacon also adds a new and exciting flavor to this pasta. Chef Roy Askren warns, "Once they taste it, your guests will want more, so make plenty!"

1 pound large sea scallops

Salt and freshly ground pepper

¼ cup olive oil

1½ pounds penne pasta

8 strips bacon, cut into ½-inch pieces

2 ounces andouille sausage, thinly sliced

1 tablespoon finely diced red bell pepper

3 tablespoons mixed finely diced carrot, celery, and onion

1 tablespoon sliced garlic cloves

½ tablespoon minced fresh thyme

6 bay leaves

2½ tablespoons Zatarain's Blackened Seasoning

8 ounces extra-large shrimp, shelled and deveined

2½ cups lobster stock (page 202)

2¼ cups heavy cream

2 finely diced fresh tomatoes

4 ounces fresh lump crabmeat, picked over for shell (optional)

2 tablespoons grated Parmesan cheese

1 tablespoon minced fresh chives

Fried leeks for garnish (optional)

SERVES 6 AS A MAIN COURSE, OR 10 AS A FIRST COURSE

Pat the scallops dry with paper towels and season with salt and pepper. In a large sauté pan or skillet, heat the oil over high heat and sear the scallops until golden, about 4 minutes on each side. Using a slotted spoon, transfer to a plate and keep warm.

In a large pot of salted boiling water, cook the pasta until al dente, about 12 minutes. Drain.

Add the bacon and sausage to the pan used to cook the scallops and cook until lightly browned, about 7 minutes. Add the vegetables, garlic, thyme, bay leaves, seasoning, and shrimp and sauté for 2 or 3 minutes. Remove the shrimp and set aside to keep warm. Add the lobster stock and heavy cream, bring to a simmer, and then add the pasta and tomatoes. Cook to reduce the sauce to about 2 cups. Add the crabmeat, if using, and Parmesan cheese. Toss together and divide among the plates. Divide the scallops and shrimp among the servings, sprinkle with the chives, and the leeks, if you like, and serve at once.

8

FISH + SEAFOOD

TOP 10 TIPS
FOR CHOOSING FISH

HARRAH'S LAUGHLIN

Knowing how to choose fresh fish is a vital skill for a seafood cook. Unless you have caught the fish yourself, you have no way of knowing exactly how fresh it is. But buying fresh fish is easy if you know what to look for.

WHOLE FISH

1   Look for bright, clear eyes: The eyes are the window to a truly fresh fish, for they fade quickly into gray dullness. Dull-eyed fish may be safe to eat, but they are past their prime.

2   Look at the fish: Does it shine? Does it look metallic and clean? Or has it dulled or have discolored patches on it? If so, it is marginal.

3   Smell the fish: A fresh fish should smell like clean water, or a touch briny or even like cucumbers. Under no circumstances should you buy a nasty-smelling fish. Cooking won't improve it.

4   Look at the gills: The gills should be a rich red. When a fish is old, they will be the color of faded brick.

FISH FILLETS

5   Look for vibrant flesh: All fish fade as they age. If a fillet has skin, that skin should look as pristine as the skin on an equally good whole fish (shiny and metallic).

6   Smell them: The smell test is especially important with fillets. They should have no pungent aroma.

7   Is there liquid on the meat? If so, that liquid should be clear, not milky. Milky liquid on a fillet is the first stage of rot.

8   Press the meat with your finger: It should be resilient enough so that your indentation disappears. If your fingerprint remains, move on.

9   If you can, buy your fish at a fish market: These are the places where turnover is so rapid, you can be assured of fresh fish. Make friends with your fish supplier: Find out when a fresh supply comes in and be there to buy that day.

10 When buying live fish, look for "life": When picking live fish, choose one that is swimming around with energy, not just staying in one corner of the tank.

TOP 10 TIPS
FOR PURCHASING SEAFOOD

HARRAH'S LOUISIANA DOWNS

1   Smell the air in the store before you buy anything and notice how busy the seafood department is. You want to find a place that sells a lot of fish, not one that keeps its fish on ice until it starts to get that strong fishy odor.

2   Buy whole fish if you see that the scales are even and attached to moist, glistening skin. If the gills are still attached, skip it if they are brownish or slimy instead of bright red. Also, the eyes should be clear, not cloudy.

3   Select fillets that have an even, appropriate color for that kind of fish (translucent white to deep red, depending on the variety). They should be neatly trimmed, not ragged or torn. You should see no signs of freezer burn, and the flesh should be firm.

4   Reject any smoked fish that feels sticky, has skin and eyes that do not look glossy, or that smells like anything besides smoke.

5   Choose only frozen fish that have no evidence of thawing, freezer burn, or damaged packaging. The flesh should be frozen hard, not mushy or squishy.

6   Buy fresh fish fillets whenever possible. Frozen fish can end up soggy and tasting watery. Check that the fillet is more or less the same thickness throughout. If it is not, the thinner parts will overcook. You can always trim the fillets to remove the thinner sections and cook them separately, starting with the thicker piece first.

7   Look over shellfish carefully. Shells should not be broken, cracked, or damaged in any way. Opened oyster and mussel shells should close when tapped. Lobsters, crabs, and shrimp should feel heavy for their size and not be missing any legs. Live crabs and lobsters should show some signs of movement.

8   When buying mollusks, ask to see shellfish tags. These tags allow you to see when and where the mollusks were harvested.

9   If fish at the store is on sale, ask yourself why and go back through the previous eight steps.

10 Only purchase what you plan on cooking and eating within the next two to three days. Fish will keep better when stored packed in ice in a self-draining container in the refrigerator.

BLUE CORN–CRUSTED RED SNAPPER

WITH WARM TOMATO RELISH

BOBBY FLAY'S MESA GRILL AT CAESARS PALACE LAS VEGAS
CHEF BOBBY FLAY

Famed chef Bobby Flay comments, "This warm, fresh tomato relish is my take on the traditional Mexican recipe, sauce Veracruz. As the tomatoes, olive oil, and capers are also Mediterranean ingredients, the addition of basil and picholine olives is a natural choice. The relish is great with the red snapper or halibut in a crisp blue corn coating." The smoked red pepper sauce, one of the workhorses of the chef's Mesa Grill kitchen, adds a deep color and flavor to this dish and can be used with many others.

WARM TOMATO RELISH

2 tablespoons olive oil

1½ cups halved red cherry or grape tomatoes

2 garlic cloves, minced

2 serrano chiles, thinly sliced

1 cup V8 juice

2 teaspoons honey

½ cup pitted picholine olives

2 tablespoons drained capers

2 tablespoons chopped fresh basil

2 teaspoons chopped fresh oregano

Kosher salt and freshly ground black pepper

BLUE CORN-CRUSTED SNAPPER

1 cup all-purpose flour

3 large eggs

2 tablespoons water

2 cups coarsely crushed blue corn chips

Kosher salt and freshly ground pepper

Four 8-ounce skinless red snapper or halibut fillets

¼ cup canola oil

Smoked Red Pepper Sauce (see recipe facing page)

Fresh oregano leaves, sliced green onion, and microgreens for garnish (optional)

SERVES 4

For the relish: In a medium sauté pan or skillet, heat the oil over high heat. Add the tomatoes, garlic, and chiles and sauté for 1 minute. Add the vegetable juice and honey, bring to a simmer, and cook for 2 to 3 minutes. Add the olives, capers, basil, and oregano and cook for 1 minute more. Season with salt and pepper. Use now, or let cool, cover, and refrigerate for up to 24 hours. Reheat before serving.

For the snapper: Put the flour in a medium, shallow bowl. In another shallow bowl, whisk the eggs with the water. Put the blue corn chips in a third shallow bowl. Season the flour and eggs with salt and pepper.

Season each fillet on both sides with salt and pepper. Dredge one side of each fillet first in the flour, tapping off any excess flour, then in the egg, and finally in the crushed blue corn chips. In a large nonstick sauté pan or skillet, heat the oil over medium-high heat. Put the fish in the pan, coated side down, and cook until a crust forms, 2 to 3 minutes. Flip the fish over and continue cooking for 4 to 5 minutes, or until just opaque throughout.

To serve, spoon some of the relish in each of 4 large shallow bowls. Place the fillets on top, garnish with more of the relish, and drizzle with the Smoked Red Pepper Sauce. Garnish with oregano leaves, green onion, and microgreens, if desired.

✦ ✦ ✦ ✦ ✦ ✦ ✦

Roasting and peeling bell peppers: Brush the peppers with olive oil and season them with salt and pepper. Place on a rimmed baking sheet and roast in a preheated 375°F oven, rotating them until they are charred on all sides, 15 to 17 minutes. Remove from the oven, place in a bowl, and cover with plastic wrap. Let stand for 15 minutes to allow the skin to loosen. Peel and seed. Roasted red peppers can be covered and stored for up to 5 days in the refrigerator.

SMOKED
RED PEPPER SAUCE

4 red bell peppers, roasted, peeled, and chopped (see note facing page)

½ small red onion, coarsely chopped

4 cloves roasted garlic (see page 48)

¼ cup red wine vinegar

1 tablespoon honey

1 tablespoon Dijon mustard

1 tablespoon puréed chipotle chiles en adobo

½ cup canola oil

Kosher salt and freshly ground black pepper

In a blender, combine the bell peppers, onion, garlic, vinegar, honey, mustard, and chipotle purée and blend until smooth. With the machine running, gradually add the oil and blend until emulsified. Empty the sauce into a bowl and add salt and pepper. Use now, or cover and refrigerate for up to 24 hours.

MAKES ABOUT 2½ CUPS

PEANUT-CRUSTED TROUT

SYCAMORES ON THE CREEK AT HARRAH'S CHEROKEE
EXECUTIVE CHEF KEITH ANDREASEN

One of the renowned trout-fishing areas in this country is in Cherokee, North Carolina. Chef Keith Andreasen says, "When we opened Sycamores on the Creek, we had to create a great trout dish. We did that with this recipe. Everyone was in agreement that this dish was going to be a favorite of our guests, and it didn't disappoint us. This has turned out to be one of our most popular dishes."

Two 8-ounce skin-on trout fillets

2 tablespoons crushed peanuts

½ cup plus 2 tablespoons canola oil

6 extra-large shrimp, shelled and deveined

1 tablespoon corn kernels

1 tablespoon diced tomato

½ cup baby spinach leaves

½ cup heavy cream

Salt and freshly ground pepper

Mashed potatoes for serving

2 tablespoons minced fresh flat-leaf parsley for garnish

2 lemon wedges for garnish

SERVES 2

Preheat the oven to 350°F. Encrust the flesh-side of the trout with the peanuts. In a large ovenproof sauté pan or skillet, heat the ½ cup oil over medium-high heat and sear the trout, crusted side down, until golden brown, about 4 minutes. Turn the trout over and transfer the pan to the oven. Roast for 5 minutes, or until opaque throughout. Remove from the oven and keep warm.

In a medium sauté pan or skillet, heat the 2 tablespoons oil over high heat. Add the shrimp and cook for 1½ minutes on each side, or until evenly pink. Add the corn, tomato, and spinach and cook until the spinach is lightly wilted. Add the heavy cream and season with salt and pepper. Cook until the sauce has thickened enough to coat the back of a spoon.

To serve, place a scoop of mashed potatoes off-center toward twelve o'clock on a plate. Lean the trout, tail-side up, on the mashed potatoes. Pour the sauce over the trout and place the shrimp on top of the trout. Garnish each plate with parsley and a lemon wedge.

BRONZED FISH
WITH JALAPEÑO TARTAR SAUCE

K-PAUL'S LOUISIANA KITCHEN
CHEF PAUL PRUDHOMME

Chef Prudhomme says: "Bronzing is a wonderful cooking technique for meat or fish—and it's so simple. You roast one side of the meat or fish at a time on a heavy griddle or in a large, heavy aluminum skillet or an electric skillet heated to 350°F. (You can purchase a surface thermometer, or pyrometer, to measure dry temperature of a griddle or aluminum skillet.) If you omit the butter or oil, bronzing produces delicious reduced-fat meat and fish dishes. Just spray the fish or meat surfaces with nonstick cooking spray before seasoning."

Note: Chef Prudhomme's sauces and seasonings are available at www.ChefPaul.com.

JALAPEÑO TARTAR SAUCE

1 cup mayonnaise, preferably Hellman's or Best Foods

1 tablespoon minced green jalapeño chile

2 teaspoons minced red jalapeño chile

½ teaspoon fresh lemon juice

2 tablespoons prepared horseradish sauce

2 tablespoons minced red onion

2 tablespoons minced green bell pepper

¼ cup sweet pickle relish

1 teaspoon minced garlic

2 hard-boiled eggs, shelled and finely diced

1 teaspoon Chef Paul Prudhomme's Vegetable Magic

1 teaspoon Chef Paul Prudhomme's Barbecue Magic

1 teaspoon Chef Paul Prudhomme's Magic Pepper Sauce

Four 4½-ounce fish fillets, each about ½ to ¾ inch thick at thickest part

3 tablespoons unsalted butter, melted, or canola oil

About 4 teaspoons Chef Paul Prudhomme's Seafood Magic

SERVES 4

For the jalapeño tartar sauce:
Combine all the sauce ingredients in a food processor and pulse until well blended. Cover and refrigerate.

Place a nonstick aluminum skillet over medium-high heat until very hot, about 7 minutes. Lightly coat both sides of each fillet with the butter or oil, then sprinkle one side with ½ teaspoon of Seafood Magic. Place the fish in the skillet, seasoned-side down, and sprinkle the top of all the fillets evenly with the remaining seasoning. Cook until the undersides of the fillets are bronzed, about 2½ minutes. Watch as the fish cooks and you'll see a white line coming up the side of each fillet as it turns from translucent to opaque; when the bottom half of the fillet is opaque, the fish is ready to be turned.

Turn the fish and cook about 2½ minutes longer. To test for doneness, simply touch the fish in the center; it should be lightly firm. You also can use a fork to flake the fish at its thickest part—if it flakes easily, it is done. You can turn the fish more than once until cooked to the desired doneness. Do not overcook, as the fish will continue to cook even after you remove it from the heat.

Serve immediately with the jalapeño tartar sauce as a garnish or dipping sauce.

EXECUTIVE CHEF VESA LEPPALA'S

TOP 10 MISTAKES
TO AVOID IN THE KITCHEN

HARRAH'S RINCON CASINO & RESORT

1   Using dull knives.

2   Sautéing food in a sauté pan or skillet that is not hot enough, unless you like a boiled dinner.

3   Overloading food in a sauté pan or skillet.

4   Using salt for sugar (except on a margarita).

5   Using a wet rag or kitchen towel to grab a hot pan.

6   Running in the kitchen.

7   Not tasting what you cook or tasting too much of what you cook.

8   Overcooking pasta.

9   Undercooking egg yolks for hollandaise sauce.

10   Invoking the three-second rule. Don't believe in it!

TOP 10 THINGS
FOR THE NOVICE CHEF
NOT TO DO
IN THE KITCHEN

(BASED ON ONE CHEF'S EXPERIENCES)

1   If you burn your hand on a hot pan, do not bend down in agony and then burn your forehead on the stove.

2   When having two people lift a full twenty-gallon, boiling-hot soup pot from the floor onto the steam table, please make sure that the person on one side is not six feet five and the other five feet two.

3   If you answer the wall phone in the kitchen, do not place the handset and cord in or on a mixer while you go looking for the chef, because when you can't find the chef (again) and you return to the mixer and turn it on, this will rip a hole in the wall. The health department does not like holes.

4   Flambéing is not the best way to remove eyebrows, but it may be the fastest.

5   Be careful when ordering sweetbreads for your function as you may receive Mexican pan dulce (sweet rolls) instead. This happens all the time in southern California.

6   When a recipe calls for whole eggs, make sure the shell is removed.

7   Do not taste boiling caramel sauce with your finger (even if it looks good) and especially do not (as a reflex) put the burning finger in your mouth. That's a double whammy.

8   You do not need a huge flatbed truck to go and pick up one horse . . . radish.

9   Don't plate next Wednesday's banquet for 150 people on Wednesday of the current week.

10   Never cook osso buco medium-rare.

Here is one more for good measure:

Never answer your cell phone while standing over a full two-hundred-gallon stock kettle!

SHRIMP STOCK

3 cups shrimp shells

1 gallon water

1 large leek, cut into 1-inch pieces

1 pound carrots, cut into 1-inch pieces

1 pound onions, cut into 1-inch pieces

1 pound celery stalks, cut into 1-inch pieces

1½ tablespoons tomato paste

5 or 6 thyme sprigs

½ bunch flat-leaf parsley sprigs

1 bay leaf

½ teaspoon peppercorns

In a stockpot, combine all the ingredients. Bring to a boil, then reduce the heat to a simmer. Cook for 2 to 3 hours, or until flavorful. Strain. Cover and refrigerate for up to 2 days, or freeze for up to 3 months in a plastic container with a lid.

Lobster Stock: Replace the shrimp shells with lobster shells in the above recipe.

MAKES ABOUT 14 CUPS

RED GROUPER
WITH STEWED TOMATOES, OKRA & CRAWFISH

MAGNOLIA, A DELTA GRILLE AT HORSESHOE TUNICA

The Mississippi Delta, some say, starts in Memphis and ends in New Orleans. This is the area the chefs focus on in the restaurant. Everyone in the South has had stewed tomatoes and okra at some point in their stay there. These foods are homey and local. In this dish, a Cajun/Creole flair is added, making them even better.

CAJUN SEASONING

1 tablespoon paprika

2 teaspoons ground black pepper

1½ teaspoons salt

1 teaspoon garlic powder

1 teaspoon cayenne pepper

½ teaspoon dried oregano

½ teaspoon dried thyme

4 cups shrimp stock
(see recipe facing page)

6 to 8 tomatoes, peeled and quartered

1 to 2 cups fresh or frozen okra

6 ounces cooked and peeled
crawfish tails

Salt and freshly ground pepper

Four 6- to 8-ounce red grouper fillets

3 tablespoons mild-flavored oil or
clarified butter (see page 43)

Minced fresh chives for garnish

SERVES 4

For the seasoning: In a small bowl, combine all the ingredients and stir to blend.

In a medium saucepan, bring the shrimp stock to a simmer. Add the tomatoes and cook for 3 minutes. Add the okra and cook for 2 to 3 minutes. Add the crawfish, salt and pepper to taste, and 1 tablespoon of the Cajun seasoning. Cook for 1 minute. Remove from the heat and keep warm.

Preheat the oven to 500°F. Season the fish with salt, pepper, and Cajun seasoning.

In a large ovenproof sauté pan or skillet, heat the oil or clarified butter over medium-high heat until almost smoking. Add the fish, being careful not to overload the pan, and cook for 1 to 2 minutes on each side, until golden. If cooking in batches, add all the fish to the pan and transfer to the oven for about 5 minutes, or until opaque throughout.

To serve, using a slotted spoon, place some of the tomato mixture in each of 4 large shallow bowls and place the fish on top. Ladle some of the liquid from the tomato mixture into the bowls. Garnish with the chives and serve at once.

BLUESVILLE, HORSESHOE TUNICA'S ENTERTAINMENT VENUE,
IS ONE OF THE BEST IN THE AREA.
GUESTS CAN WATCH HEADLINE ENTERTAINMENT IN AN INTIMATE,
FIFTEEN-HUNDRED-SEAT PERFORMANCE SPACE.
STARS SUCH AS VINCE GILL, CHICAGO, JOE COCKER, FAITH HILL,
ROGER DALTREY, AND RAY CHARLES, TO NAME A FEW,
HAVE PERFORMED ON THE BLUESVILLE STAGE.

PAN-ROASTED HALIBUT
WITH SALSA PROVENÇAL

FIORE AT HARRAH'S RINCON CASINO & RESORT
EXECUTIVE CHEF VESA LEPPALA

Chef Vesa Leppala sums up the appeal of this dish, the most popular seafood offering at Fiore: "It's light, healthy, and full of Mediterranean flavor." The combination of roasted fingerling potatoes, pan-roasted halibut, and a fresh salsa of cherry tomatoes and kalamata olives makes for a satisfying and savory meal.

SALSA PROVENÇAL

⅓ cup extra-virgin olive oil
¼ cup halved cherry tomatoes
¼ cup pitted kalamata olives
1 tablespoon sliced garlic
1 tablespoon minced fresh basil
1 tablespoon capers
Salt

1½ pounds fingerling potatoes
3 tablespoons canola oil
1 tablespoon minced fresh thyme
Salt and freshly ground pepper
2 tablespoons extra-virgin olive oil
Four 8-ounce halibut fillets

SERVES 4

For the salsa: In a medium bowl, combine all the ingredients and stir to blend. Cover and refrigerate for 3 hours.

Preheat the oven to 375°F. In a large bowl, combine the potatoes, canola oil, thyme, and salt and pepper to taste; toss well to coat. Place on a sided baking sheet and roast until tender, about 20 minutes. Remove from the oven, leaving the oven on; set aside and keep warm.

In a large ovenproof sauté pan or skillet, heat the olive oil over medium-high heat until shimmering. Add the halibut and sauté for 3 minutes on each side. Transfer to the oven and roast for 10 minutes, or until the fish is opaque throughout. Transfer to a plate and let stand for 5 minutes. The fish will continue to cook.

To serve, divide the potatoes among the plates, place the halibut on top, and spoon 2 to 3 tablespoons of salsa over each serving of fish. Serve at once.

FIORE WON *WINE SPECTATOR* MAGAZINE'S AWARD OF EXCELLENCE FOR THREE CONSECUTIVE YEARS, 2007, 2008, AND 2009.

LEMON SOLE–WRAPPED ASPARAGUS

WITH ORANGE-CITRUS BEURRE BLANC

SYCAMORES ON THE CREEK AT HARRAH'S CHEROKEE
SOUS-CHEF KEVIN CONRAD

In this beautiful presentation, lemon sole fillets are wrapped around asparagus spears and baked, then served topped with a tangy cloud of beurre blanc. It's a favorite at Sycamores on the Creek and a perfect choice for a special-occasion dinner at home.

Four 6-ounce lemon sole fillets

Salt and freshly ground pepper

20 to 24 asparagus spears, trimmed

1½ tablespoons unsalted butter, melted

2 tablespoons minced shallots

2 tablespoons grated orange zest

½ cup water

BEURRE BLANC

½ cup fresh orange juice

1 tablespoon minced shallot

½ cup (1 stick) cold unsalted butter, cut into 8 pieces

¼ teaspoon salt

Pinch of cayenne pepper

½ teaspoon dry white wine

SERVES 4

Preheat the oven to 450°F. Season the fish with salt and pepper. Lay 5 or 6 asparagus spears across each fillet. Wrap the fish around the asparagus to form a bundle. Using the melted butter, grease a 9-by-13-inch roasting pan and sprinkle the shallots and orange zest in the pan. Add the fish, then the water. Cover the pan with aluminum foil and bake for 20 minutes. Remove from the oven and keep warm.

For the beurre blanc: In a small, heavy saucepan, combine the orange juice and shallot. Bring to a boil over medium-high heat and cook for 4 to 5 minutes, until the shallots are translucent. Reduce the heat to low and whisk in the butter, 1 tablespoon at a time, whisking constantly to make a thick sauce. Remove from the heat and add the remaining ingredients. Drain the juice from the cooked fish into a small, heavy saucepan. Bring to a boil and cook for 2 minutes. Gradually whisk the juice into the beurre blanc.

Serve at once, with the beurre blanc poured over the fish and asparagus.

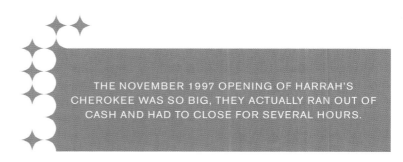

THE NOVEMBER 1997 OPENING OF HARRAH'S CHEROKEE WAS SO BIG, THEY ACTUALLY RAN OUT OF CASH AND HAD TO CLOSE FOR SEVERAL HOURS.

BLACKENED MAHI MAHI
WITH BUTTERNUT SQUASH POLENTA & GRILLED ASPARAGUS

OYSTER BAR AT PENAZZI AT HARRAH'S LAS VEGAS
CHEF BRIAN FAIRHURST

This sophisticated dish from the Oyster Bar at Penazzi can also be a special-occasion feast for the home cook. For family-style serving, spread the butternut squash polenta down the center of a large platter. Place the asparagus on top in a line, then place the blackened mahi mahi on top. Drizzle the sun-dried tomato vinaigrette over the fish.

BUTTERNUT SQUASH POLENTA

2 cups diced butternut squash

3 cups milk

1½ cups quick white grits

1 teaspoon ground nutmeg

3 tablespoons packed brown sugar

Salt and freshly ground pepper

SUN-DRIED TOMATO VINAIGRETTE

1 cup drained oil-packed sun-dried tomatoes

¼ cup pine nuts

½ cup balsamic vinegar

1 cup extra-virgin olive oil

Salt and freshly ground pepper

BLACKENED MAHI MAHI

¼ cup olive oil

Six 5- to 6-ounce mahi mahi fillets

¾ cup blackening spice (page 142)

2 bunches asparagus, trimmed

SERVES 6

For the polenta: In a medium saucepan of salted boiling water, cook the squash until just tender, 8 to 10 minutes. Drain. In another medium saucepan, bring the milk to a boil and gradually stir in the grits. Reduce the heat to low and cook, stirring occasionally, until thickened, about 5 minutes. Stir in the squash, nutmeg, brown sugar, and salt and pepper to taste. Set aside and keep warm.

For the vinaigrette: In a food processor, combine the tomatoes, pine nuts, and balsamic vinegar and purée until smooth. With the machine running, gradually drizzle in the oil until emulsified. Transfer to a bowl and season with salt and pepper. Set aside.

For the mahi mahi: In a large sauté pan or skillet, heat the oil over high heat. Dust one side of each fillet with the blackening spice. Add the fish to the pan, spice side down, and cook for 4 minutes without touching the fish. After 4 minutes, flip the fish and cook on the other side for 3 minutes. Using a slotted metal spatula, transfer the fish to a baking sheet. Add the asparagus to the sauté pan and cook, turning to cook evenly, for 3 minutes, or until crisp-tender.

To serve, spread the polenta in the center of each plate and top with asparagus. Place a fillet on top, drizzle with the vinaigrette, and serve. Or, serve family-style on a large platter, as in the introduction to the recipe.

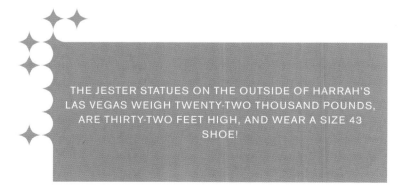

THE JESTER STATUES ON THE OUTSIDE OF HARRAH'S LAS VEGAS WEIGH TWENTY-TWO THOUSAND POUNDS, ARE THIRTY-TWO FEET HIGH, AND WEAR A SIZE 43 SHOE!

PACIFIC SHUTOME SWORDFISH CHOPS

WITH PORT WINE & CHERRY REDUCTION

RESERVE AT BALLY'S ATLANTIC CITY
CHEF BRIAN ANNAPOLEN

Pacific shutome swordfish, generally available from Hawaii, has a much more buttery texture than regular swordfish. Chef Brian Annapolen explains, "I can only describe the flavor as being the way swordfish tasted when I was a kid: rich and meaty, with a slightly gamy note and porklike consistency." The savory braised greens and the sweet port wine and cherries round out the flavor notes of this dish, which is served over creamy risotto.

MARINADE

3 thyme sprigs, chopped

3 oregano sprigs, chopped

3 basil sprigs, chopped

4 garlic cloves, crushed

1 cup olive oil

Four 12-ounce swordfish chops or steaks (see note)

RISOTTO

3 to 4 tablespoons olive oil

3 shallots, minced

2 garlic cloves, minced

2 thyme sprigs

1 cup Arborio rice

½ cup dry white wine

3 to 5 cups chicken stock, simmering

½ cup grated Parmesan cheese

⅓ cup unsalted butter

Salt and freshly ground pepper

✦ ✦ ✦ ✦ ✦ ✦ ✦

Note: Swordfish chops are bone-in, cut from the pectoral fins of the fish. Boneless swordfish steaks can be substituted.

BRAISED GREENS

2 tablespoons olive oil

8 ounces pancetta slices, cut into bite-size pieces

1 red onion, thinly sliced

1 garlic clove, sliced

1 pound mixed braising greens, such as chicory, mustard greens, kale, and collard greens

¼ cup dry white wine

Salt and freshly ground pepper

SAUCE

One 750-ml bottle port wine

1 cup sweet cherry purée (found in specialty foods stores)

2 bay leaves

2 to 3 tablespoons veal demi-glace

4 tablespoons cold unsalted butter, cut into 4 pieces

For the marinade: In a large bowl, combine all the marinade ingredients, mixing well. Add the swordfish chops and refrigerate for 1 to 2 hours.

For the risotto: In a large sauté pan or skillet, heat the oil over medium heat and sauté the shallots, garlic, and thyme for 2 to 3 minutes. Add the rice and stir to coat with the oil. Add the wine and cook, stirring, until almost dry. Add the chicken stock in 3 equal increments, stirring constantly, until al dente, about 25 minutes. Add the cheese and butter, stirring to incorporate. Season with salt and pepper and let stand for 2 minutes before serving.

For the braised greens: Just before the risotto is done, in a large sauté pan or skillet, heat the oil over medium heat and sauté the pancetta until crisp. Add the onion and cook until translucent, about 3 minutes. Using a slotted spoon, transfer the pancetta mixture to a saucer. Reduce the heat to low; add the garlic and sauté until golden brown. Return the pancetta mixture to the pan. Increase the heat to medium and add the greens; sauté until wilted. Stir in the wine and cook until evaporated. Season with salt and pepper. Set aside and keep warm.

For the sauce: Just before cooking the fish, cook the wine in a medium non-reactive saucepan over medium heat to reduce to about 1 cup. Add the cherry purée and bay leaves and cook for 2 or 3 minutes. Add the demi-glace and cook until the mixture is slightly thickened. Gradually whisk in the butter, one piece at a time, to make a thick sauce. Keep warm over tepid water.

Heat a grill pan over medium-high heat and oil the pan. Remove the chops from the marinade and season with salt and pepper. Grill the chops for about 5 minutes on each side, or until opaque throughout.

To serve, divide the risotto among the plates and top with the braised greens. Place a swordfish chop on each serving and drizzle with the sauce.

SERVES 4

THE RESERVE AT BALLY'S ATLANTIC CITY IS THE AREA'S HOT SPOT
FOR MODERN SEAFOOD AND HAND-SELECTED STEAK PREPARATIONS.
THE RESTAURANT BOASTS SEASONAL MENUS WITH A STRONG
FOCUS ON LOCAL, FRESH, AND MODERN CUISINE.

PARMESAN-CRUSTED ORANGE ROUGHY

EMBERS AT IMPERIAL PALACE
CHEF MATTHEW HEPPNER

Orange roughy, a fish caught off the shores of New Zealand, is prized for the mild flavor of its flaky white flesh. The crisp, flavorful coating contrasts with the tender fish, which is served topped with a delicate beurre blanc sauce.

BEURRE BLANC

1 cup dry white wine

¼ cup white wine vinegar

2 tablespoons minced shallots

1½ cups heavy cream

4 tablespoons cold unsalted butter, cut into 10 pieces

Kosher salt and white pepper

BREADING

4 large eggs, beaten

¾ cup whole milk

2 cups all-purpose flour

1 teaspoon kosher salt

1 teaspoon freshly ground black pepper

3 cups panko (Japanese bread crumbs)

¾ cup grated Parmigiano-Reggiano cheese

2 tablespoons minced fresh flat-leaf parsley

Four 6-ounce orange roughy fillets

2 tablespoons clarified butter (see page 43)

¼ cup diced red bell pepper for garnish

SERVES 4

For the beurre blanc: In a small, heavy saucepan, combine the wine, vinegar, and shallots. Place over medium heat, bring to a boil, and cook to reduce to ¼ cup. Add the cream and cook to reduce to ¾ cup. Turn the heat to very low and whisk in a piece of butter until melted; repeat to whisk in the remaining butter, 1 piece at a time, to make a thick sauce. Season with salt and white pepper. Strain into a bowl and keep warm over tepid water.

For the breading: In a shallow bowl, whisk the eggs and milk together until blended. In another shallow bowl, combine the flour, salt, and black pepper; stir to blend. In a third shallow bowl, stir the panko, grated cheese, and 1 tablespoon of the parsley (leaving the rest for garnish) together to blend (you will work this together to smash up the larger pieces of panko).

Dredge a fish fillet in the seasoned flour and shake off the excess flour. Next, dip the fillet in the egg mixture to coat evenly and let the excess egg mixture drip off. Finally, coat the fillet in the panko mixture to cover evenly, pressing the crumbs to adhere. Remove any excess breading. Place aside and repeat to coat the remaining fillets.

In a large sauté pan or skillet, heat the clarified butter over medium-high heat until shimmering. Add the fish and cook until firm and golden brown, about 4 minutes on each side.

Serve with the beurre blanc ladled over the top, garnished with the remaining 1 tablespoon of parsley and the bell pepper.

PHILLIPS CLAM BAKE FOR TWO

PHILLIPS SEAFOOD AT THE PIER SHOPS AT CAESARS ATLANTIC CITY
EXECUTIVE CHEF PAUL DREW

In 1956 the Phillips family opened a small carryout restaurant called Phillips Crab House in Ocean City, Maryland. This endeavor grew quickly into a two-story establishment seating fourteen hundred guests. Today, the empire has expanded to include Phillips Seafood at The Pier Shops. All along, the family has held true to a few simple rules: serve the freshest and finest seafood available, provide outstanding service, and create a memorable dining experience, like the following seafood bonanza, for their guests. While the restaurant serves this dish for two people, it can be easily multiplied to serve many more.

Note: Phillips Seafood Seasoning is available at www.phillipsfoods.com.

6 Red Bliss potatoes

2 ears corn, shucked

1 gallon water

2 teaspoons seafood seasoning blend such as Phillips Seafood Seasoning (see note), plus more for sprinkling

4 bay leaves

1 cup dry white wine

3 lemons, 2 halved and 1 cut into 6 wedges

1 teaspoon pickling spice

¼ bunch flat-leaf parsley, stemmed (reserve stems)

Salt and freshly ground pepper

Two 1¼-pound live lobsters

9 extra-large shrimp in the shell

6 littleneck clams, scrubbed

8 Prince Edward Island (P.E.I.) mussels, scrubbed

8 ounces king crab legs

3 romaine or leaf lettuce leaves

¾ cup (1½ sticks) unsalted butter, melted

SERVES 2

Put the potatoes in a medium saucepan of salted cold water; bring to a boil and cook until almost tender, 10 to 12 minutes. Drain and set aside. In a large saucepan of salted boiling water, cook the corn for about 3 minutes, or until almost tender; drain and set aside.

In the bottom of a large (2-gallon) steamer, add the water, the 2 teaspoons seafood seasoning, the bay leaves, wine, the 4 lemon halves, the pickling spice, the reserved parsley stems, and salt and pepper to taste. Cover and bring to a boil. Place the lobsters in the steamer basket, add to the pot, and cover. Cook until the lobster is beginning to turn pink. Add the shrimp, clams, and mussels to the basket, cover, and steam for 5 minutes.

Add hot water to the pot if the level is running low. Add the potatoes, corn, and king crab legs to the steamer basket. Cover, bring to a boil, and cook for about 5 minutes, or until the potatoes are tender and the clams have opened.

To serve, discard any clams or mussels that haven't opened. Arrange the lettuce on a platter. Transfer the lobsters to a cutting board. Split the tail down the back (don't cut all the way through) and, with the back of your knife, crack the claws. Transfer the shrimp, clams, mussels, crab legs, corn, and potatoes to the serving plate. Place the lobsters on top. Sprinkle some of the Phillips Seafood Seasoning over the steamed seafood. Garnish with the parsley leaves and lemon wedges. Pour the melted butter into a small bowl and serve on the side.

BARBECUED SHRIMP

MAGNOLIA BUFFET AT HARRAH'S NEW ORLEANS
CHEF HOYCE OATIS

A simple dish straight from the heart of New Orleans. Chef Hoyce Oatis says, "This recipe represents the unique style of Cajun and Creole cuisine, which is noted for its spices and seasonings. One of the authentic ways of eating this dish is to dip small portions of French bread into the sauce, which many consider to be the best part of this dish. It can be served as a main course or appetizer."

½ cup canola oil

1 small onion, diced

6 garlic cloves

1 bay leaf

1 teaspoon minced fresh thyme

1 teaspoon minced fresh rosemary

1 teaspoon minced fresh oregano

1 teaspoon sweet paprika

1 teaspoon minced fresh flat-leaf parsley

1 pound 16/20 shrimp with shells and heads

¼ cup brandy

¼ cup dry white wine

½ cup water

½ cup (1 stick) unsalted butter at room temperature

SERVES 4

In a large sauté pan or skillet, heat the oil over medium-high heat until shimmering. Add the onion and sauté until lightly browned, about 5 minutes. Add the garlic cloves and sauté until golden, about 2 minutes. Add the herbs and spices and sauté for 1 minute. Add the shrimp and sauté for 2 minutes.

Turn off the heat and pour in the brandy. Standing back from the stove, light the brandy with a long match or long-handled lighter. Using caution, shake the pan until the flames subside. Add the wine and return to medium heat. Cook for 1 minute and then add the water.

To finish, add the butter and stir until melted. Serve divided among shallow bowls.

POKER WAS INVENTED IN NEW ORLEANS ON CANAL STREET IN THE EIGHTEENTH CENTURY.

SEARED SCALLOPS, ASPARAGUS & CRABMEAT

WITH HOLLANDAISE SAUCE & POTATO CAKES

VOGA AT FLAMINGO LAS VEGAS
EXECUTIVE CHEF CHRISTOPHE DOUMERGUE

This fusion of Old World culinary technique and New World culinary flair is a fitting dish for Voga, a mixture of city chic and Neapolitan gusto. Chef Christophe Doumergue comments, "This dish is our best portrayal of what Voga is all about."

YUKON POTATO CAKES

2 cups chopped peeled Yukon gold potatoes

2 tablespoons heavy cream

1 teaspoon minced garlic

1 teaspoon unsalted butter

Salt and freshly ground pepper

1 tablespoon all-purpose flour

1 egg beaten with 1 teaspoon water

1 cup dried bread crumbs

1 tablespoon olive oil

1 cup asparagus tips

8 sea scallops

Salt and freshly ground pepper

¼ cup extra-virgin olive oil, plus more for drizzling

4 ounces fresh lump crabmeat, picked over for shell

Hollandaise Sauce
(see recipe facing page)

SERVES 2

For the potato cakes: Add the potatoes to a small saucepan of salted cold water; bring to a boil and cook for 30 minutes, or until tender. Drain. Add the cream, garlic, butter, and salt and pepper to taste. Using a whisk or an electric mixer, beat until smooth. Spread the mixture into a ½-inch-thick round on a baking sheet. Refrigerate for 1 hour, or until firm. Cut into cakes with a 2-inch round biscuit cutter.

Put the flour, egg mixture, and bread crumbs in three separate shallow bowls. Season the flour with salt and pepper. Coat each potato cake first in the flour, then the egg mixture, then the crumbs.

In a large sauté pan or skillet, heat the oil over medium heat and fry the potato cakes until golden brown, about 2 minutes on each side. Transfer to a low oven to keep warm.

In a medium saucepan of salted boiling water, cook the asparagus tips for 4 minutes, or until crisp-tender. Drain. Set aside and keep warm.

Season the scallops with salt and pepper. In a large sauté pan or skillet, heat the ¼ cup oil over medium-high heat until shimmering and sauté the sea scallops for 3 minutes on each side, or until opaque throughout. Transfer to a plate and keep warm.

To serve, preheat the broiler. Divide the asparagus, potato cakes, and scallops between 2 ovenproof plates. Top each scallop with the crabmeat and then the Hollandaise Sauce. Place under the broiler about 3 inches from the heat source until lightly browned, about 2 minutes. Remove from the broiler, drizzle with extra-virgin olive oil, and serve at once.

VOGA,
MEANING "FASHION"
IN ITALIAN, OPENED IN JANUARY
2008 AND WAS VOTED
ONE OF THE BEST
NEW RESTAURANTS
IN LAS VEGAS.

HOLLANDAISE SAUCE

1 cup clarified butter (see page 43)
3 large egg yolks
2 tablespoons fresh lemon juice
2 pinches salt
Cayenne pepper or Tabasco sauce

In a small saucepan, heat the butter until hot. In a blender, combine the egg yolks, lemon juice, and salt and blend at high speed for 2 minutes. With the machine running, gradually add the butter in a very thin stream to make a thick sauce. Stir in the cayenne to taste. Keep warm over tepid water.

MAKES 1 CUP

SEAFOOD RISOTTO

MOSAIC AT HARRAH'S JOLIET
CHEF MATTHEW E. SECKO

Chef Matthew E. Secko explains the romantic history behind his seafood risotto: "This is a great dish to prepare and serve to someone you want to impress to make an everlasting first impression. I first served this dish when asked to make a special meal for someone, who fell in love with it. And to this day, almost three years later, that person talks about how amazing it was. It is a well-balanced dish that is very bold and flavorful, but will not leave you feeling weighed down and uncomfortable. All the flavors complement each other, and the lemon and lime zest provide a very refreshing citrus taste to accent the seafood as well as the risotto. Enjoy, and I hope that your luck with this dish is as good as mine."

6 cups chicken stock

1 cup (2 sticks) unsalted butter

1 cup Arborio rice

1 teaspoon Boursin cheese

Salt and freshly ground pepper

1 teaspoon minced garlic

1 teaspoon minced shallot

6 sea scallops

6 large shrimp, shelled and deveined

1 lobster tail, halved lengthwise

Grated zest of ½ lemon

Grated zest of ½ lime

½ cup citron vodka

Asparagus tips, basil sprigs, and microgreens for garnish (optional)

SERVES 2

In a large saucepan, bring the chicken stock to a low simmer. In a large sauté pan or skillet, melt 4 tablespoons of the butter over medium heat, add the rice, and stir until opaque, 2 to 3 minutes. Stir in just enough stock to cover the rice and cook, stirring constantly, until almost all the stock is absorbed. Repeat this process until the rice is al dente, about 25 minutes. Stir in the Boursin and season with salt and pepper.

Halfway through cooking the risotto, melt 4 more tablespoons of the butter over medium heat in a large sauté pan or skillet. Add the garlic and shallot and sauté for 3 minutes. Add the scallops and sauté until golden brown on the bottom, about 1½ minutes. Turn the scallops over and add the shrimp. Sauté until the shrimp curl. Season with salt and pepper. Add the lobster and lemon and lime zests. Turn off the heat and add the vodka. Return to medium heat and stir to scrape up the browned bits on the bottom of the pan. Cook until the liquid is reduced to about ¼ cup. Add the remaining ½ cup butter, remove from the heat, and swirl the pan to combine all the ingredients.

To serve, mound the risotto in the center of a large serving plate and space the scallops around the outside of the risotto. Place the shrimp in between the scallops and place the lobster on top of the risotto. Pour the sauce over the scallops and shrimp. Garnish with asparagus tips, basil sprigs, and microgreens, if desired.

CELEBRITY CHEF RICK BAYLESS WAS ON HAND FOR THE GRAND OPENING OF MOSAIC IN 2006.

CRAB & EGGPLANT LASAGNA

CASA DI NAPOLI AT SHOWBOAT ATLANTIC CITY
CHEF GEORGEANN LEAMING

In this no-pasta lasagna, eggplant slices are marinated in herb oil, then coated in flour and fried until golden brown. Sandwiched with a creamy crabmeat filling and topped with a crumb crust flavored with sun-dried tomatoes, the slices are baked to yield a dish that combines textures, flavors, and colors. Serve with a glass of wine and a green salad for a satisfying, luxurious meal.

HERB OIL

1 cup olive oil

¼ cup fresh whole basil leaves

¼ cup fresh flat-leaf parsley leaves, chopped

1 teaspoon fresh lemon juice

1 teaspoon kosher salt

½ teaspoon freshly ground pepper

Eight ¼-inch-thick globe eggplant slices

SUN-DRIED TOMATO CRUST

2 cups fresh bread crumbs

½ cup julienned oil-packed sun-dried tomatoes

2 tablespoons minced fresh basil

1 teaspoon kosher salt

½ teaspoon freshly ground pepper

CRAB FILLING

1 pound fresh lump crabmeat, picked over for shell

1 tablespoon finely diced red bell pepper

1 tablespoon finely diced onion

1 teaspoon Dijon mustard

1 cup mayonnaise

½ cup fresh bread crumbs

Olive oil for sautéing

All-purpose flour for dredging

Balsamic glaze (see notes)

SERVES 4

For the herb oil: Combine all the ingredients in a blender and purée until smooth.

Pour half of the herb oil into a large baking dish and add the eggplant slices. Let stand at room temperature for 15 minutes, turning the slices halfway through. Remove from the marinade and shake off the excess.

For the crust: Combine the ingredients in a food processor and pulse until finely ground. Set aside.

For the filling: In a large bowl, combine the ingredients; stir to blend and set aside.

Preheat the oven to 400°F. In a large sauté pan or skillet, heat ¼ inch oil over medium-high heat until shimmering. Dredge 2 eggplant slices in the flour, shaking off the excess. Add to the pan and sauté until golden brown, about 5 minutes on each side. Using a slotted metal spatula, transfer to paper towels to drain. Repeat with the remaining slices. Put 4 eggplant slices on a baking sheet and spread each slice with one-fourth of the crab filling. Top with the remaining eggplant slices. Spread about ¼ cup of the sun-dried tomato mixture on each top slice. Bake for 15 to 20 minutes, or until the crusts are browned and the filling is hot.

To serve, place the lasagnas on a platter and drizzle with some of the remaining herb oil and the balsamic glaze.

✦ ✦ ✦ ✦ ✦ ✦ ✦

Balsamic glaze: In a small, heavy saucepan, bring 1 cup balsamic vinegar to a simmer over medium heat and cook until reduced to a syrup. Remove from the heat, let cool, and transfer to a squeeze bottle.

Note: Balsamic glaze is also available in specialty foods markets.

THE WATERFRONT BUFFET AT HARRAH'S RESORT ATLANTIC CITY GOES THROUGH 22,360 CASES OF CRAB LEGS A YEAR. IF YOU'RE WONDERING, THAT'S 670,800 POUNDS!

LOBSTER MAC CASSEROLE

JACK BINION'S STEAKHOUSE AT HORSESHOE SOUTHERN INDIANA
EXECUTIVE SOUS-CHEF JOSHUA MIRAGLIOTTA

Lobster Mac Casserole was created especially for Jack Binion's Steakhouse guests who love seafood. Chef Joshua Miragliotta comments, "This dish combines succulent lobster, shell pasta, a creamy, bubbling white Cheddar béchamel scented with white truffle oil, and a topping of toasted bread crumbs. It is one of our most popular dishes."

CHEDDAR BÉCHAMEL SAUCE

2 tablespoons unsalted butter

2 tablespoons all-purpose flour

3 cups heavy cream

3 cups half-and-half

4 bay leaves

1 yellow onion, cut into fourths

Pinch of ground nutmeg

2½ cups shredded
white Cheddar cheese

2 teaspoons kosher salt

2 teaspoons freshly ground
white pepper

2¼ pounds shell pasta

4 tablespoons unsalted butter, melted

1¼ pounds uncooked lobster meat, cut
into 1-inch cubes

1½ cups panko
(Japanese bread crumbs)

1½ cups clarified butter
(see page 43)

1½ cups shredded Gruyère cheese

White truffle oil for drizzling

SERVES 6

For the sauce: In a small saucepan, melt the butter over low heat and whisk in the flour; stir constantly for 2 to 3 minutes; do not let brown. Remove from the heat and set aside.

In a medium saucepan, combine the heavy cream and half-and-half. Add the bay leaves, onion, and nutmeg. Bring the mixture to a simmer over medium-low heat and cook for 10 minutes. Strain, discarding the solids, and return the cream mixture to the pan. Return to a simmer over medium-low heat. Gently whisk in the white Cheddar cheese, 1 cup at a time, until melted. Cook, whisking constantly, for a few minutes until thickened slightly; remove from the heat as necessary to keep from scorching. Whisk in the butter and flour mixture and cook, whisking, for several minutes. Whisk in the salt and pepper. Remove from the heat and let cool.

Preheat the oven to 400°F. In a large pot of salted boiling water, cook the pasta until al dente, 10 to 12 minutes; drain and set aside.

In a medium sauté pan or skillet, heat the butter over medium heat and sauté the lobster meat for 2 or 3 minutes. Add the béchamel and cook for about 2 minutes, stirring constantly. Stir in the pasta.

In a small bowl, combine the bread crumbs and clarified butter and stir to moisten evenly. Butter six 8-ounce casserole dishes or ramekins. Fill each prepared dish with the pasta mixture. Top each serving with ¼ cup Gruyère and ¼ cup bread crumbs. Place on a baking sheet and bake for 7 to 8 minutes, or until the bread crumbs are golden brown and the cheese has completely melted. Remove from the oven and drizzle each serving with white truffle oil.

SINCE OPENING IN 2004,
THE BUFFET AT HARRAH'S LOUISIANA DOWNS
HAS FED 1.5 MILLION PEOPLE.
IT SERVES MORE THAN 1,800 POUNDS
OF CATFISH AND 1,000 POUNDS OF
PEEL AND EAT SHRIMP EVERY WEEK.

GRILLED SHRIMP SKEWERS

EAT UP! BUFFET AT HARRAH'S ST. LOUIS
EXECUTIVE CHEF RAY LEUNG

This light dish of skewered shrimp and cherry tomatoes is quick and easy to prepare, but will dazzle any palate. The orange-Champagne vinaigrette adds a zesty flavor and a touch of glamour to the shrimp, and the rosemary-stalk skewers add their own pungent taste and make for a beautiful presentation. Chef Ray Leung promises that this dish will be sure to "impress at your next barbecue."

2 tablespoons Champagne vinegar

2 tablespoons grated orange zest

1 cup fresh orange juice

1 tablespoon olive oil

1 tablespoon Italian dressing mix

20 large shrimp, shelled and deveined

Twenty 5-inch rosemary stalks

20 cherry tomatoes

SERVES 4

Prepare a medium fire in a charcoal grill or preheat a gas grill to 350°F. In a medium bowl, combine the vinegar, orange zest and juice, oil, and Italian dressing mix. Whisk to blend. Add the shrimp and toss to coat. Set aside.

Strip off all the leaves from the rosemary stalks except the top few. Skewer 1 shrimp and 1 cherry tomato on each rosemary skewer. Wrap the leafy end of each rosemary skewer in a 2-inch aluminum foil square to prevent burning during grilling. Grill for about 2 minutes per side, or until the shrimp turn pink. Remove the foil from the ends of the skewers and serve.

P.E.I. MUSSELS IN MAGNERS CIDER

TRINITY PUB & CARVERY AT THE PIER SHOPS AT CAESARS ATLANTIC CITY
CHEF BRIAN PERRY

This mussel dish was designed to showcase the seafood side of Trinity Pub & Carvery's Irish menu. Chef Brian Perry comments on one of the dish's standout ingredients: "We use Magners Irish Cider not only because of the Irish theme but because it matches really well with seafood like mussels."

2 tablespoons canola oil

½ cup minced shallots

½ cup minced garlic

½ cup diced plum tomatoes

2 pounds Prince Edward Island (P.E.I.) mussels, scrubbed

½ cup dry white wine

¾ cup Magners Irish Cider

2 teaspoons minced fresh thyme

2 teaspoons minced fresh tarragon

2 teaspoons minced fresh flat-leaf parsley

Salt and freshly ground pepper

2 tablespoons cold butter

4 thick slices grilled crusty white bread

¼ cup sliced green onions, including some green parts

SERVES 2

In a large sauté pan or skillet, heat the oil over medium-high heat. Add the shallots and garlic and sauté until the shallots are translucent, about 2 minutes. Add the tomatoes and sauté for 30 seconds. Add the mussels, tossing them in the pan. Add the wine. Cook to reduce the wine by one-half, then add the cider and herbs and season with salt and pepper. Toss the mussels, then cover and cook for 1½ minutes, or until the mussels have opened. Turn off the heat and add the butter, swirling the pan until it is incorporated. Discard any mussels that have not opened.

To serve, divide the mussels and broth between two bowls. Cut the grilled bread in half lengthwise and arrange it with the points touching in the center of the bowl. Garnish with the green onions.

9

BREAKFAST
BUFFET

BOURSIN CHEESE, LOBSTER & COGNAC OMELET

STERLING BRUNCH AT BALLY'S STEAKHOUSE AT BALLY'S LAS VEGAS
CHEF ERIC PISTON

Start your day in luxury with this Sterling Brunch signature omelet. A mixture of rich ingredients makes it perfect for that special breakfast or brunch. Chef Eric Piston says, "Flavor-wise, the lobster meat and Cognac work very well together, and the Boursin cheese adds a smoothness to the omelet as well as a very light garlic flavor." Even if you're planning to serve more than one person, make one omelet at a time; once you have all your ingredients in place, each one takes just a few minutes.

2 large eggs

1 tablespoon clarified butter
(see page 43)

1 teaspoon finely chopped onion

1 ounce cooked lobster meat, chopped

2 tablespoons Cognac

1 tablespoon Boursin cheese

2 tablespoons shredded
white Cheddar cheese

SERVES 1

In a small bowl, whisk the eggs until blended. In a nonstick 6-inch pan, heat the clarified butter over medium heat and sauté the onion until golden, about 5 minutes. Add the lobster and Cognac and cook for 30 seconds. Add the eggs and let set for a few seconds, then cook for 1 minute, pushing in the sides to let the uncooked egg flow under. Sprinkle with the cheeses and fold the omelet in half. Cook for 1 more minute and serve.

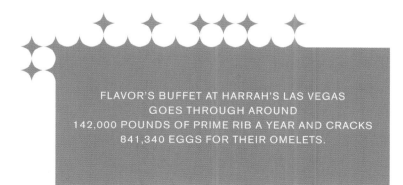

FLAVOR'S BUFFET AT HARRAH'S LAS VEGAS
GOES THROUGH AROUND
142,000 POUNDS OF PRIME RIB A YEAR AND CRACKS
841,340 EGGS FOR THEIR OMELETS.

HOLLANDAISE SAUCE

2 large egg yolks
2 cups unsalted butter, melted
Juice of 2 lemons
Pinch of cayenne pepper
Salt and freshly ground pepper

Put the egg yolks in a stainless-steel bowl and set the bowl over a sauce-pan filled with 2 inches of simmering water. Cook, whisking constantly, until thick enough that you can see the bottom of the bowl when the whisk makes a path through the mixture. Gradually whisk in the butter, beginning with a few drops and progressing to a very thin stream as the mixture thickens. Season with the lemon juice, cayenne, and salt and pepper. Keep warm over tepid water if necessary.

MAKES 2 CUPS

POACHED EGGS

WITH BACON-POTATO HASH & HOLLANDAISE SAUCE

HARRAH'S CHESTER CASINO & RACETRACK
EXECUTIVE CHEF SEAN KINOSHITA

Chef Sean Kinoshita explains how he created this brunch specialty: "One of my all time-favorite brunch dishes is the classic eggs Benedict. For this recipe, I added more of my favorite foods, like bacon, potatoes, and biscuits. With this recipe, you get my version of the best of all breakfast items."

CORNMEAL–BROWN BUTTER BISCUITS

5 tablespoons unsalted butter

1¼ cups all-purpose flour

¼ cup cornmeal

2 tablespoons sugar

2 teaspoons baking powder

¼ teaspoon salt

½ cup heavy cream

2 teaspoons vanilla extract

2 large egg yolks, beaten

BACON-POTATO HASH

1 cup chopped bacon

1 onion, diced

1 red bell pepper, seeded, deveined, and diced

1 green bell pepper, seeded, deveined, and diced

Canola oil for deep-frying

2 russet potatoes, peeled and diced

⅓ cup chicken stock

4 tablespoons butter

Salt and freshly ground pepper

3 tablespoons minced fresh flat-leaf parsley

1 tablespoon salt

1 tablespoon white vinegar

4 large eggs

Hollandaise Sauce (see recipe facing page)

SERVES 4

For the biscuits: Preheat the oven to 375°F. In a small, heavy saucepan, cook the butter over medium-low heat until browned, about 5 minutes. Pour into a small bowl and freeze for 1 hour until hard.

In a large bowl, combine the flour, cornmeal, sugar, baking powder, and salt. Stir with a whisk to blend. Cube the hard butter and add. Using a pastry cutter, cut in the butter until the mixture resembles coarse meal. Using a fork, mix in the cream, vanilla, and egg yolks. Turn the dough out onto a floured work surface. Lightly knead. Roll out to a ½-inch thickness. Using a 2-inch round biscuit cutter, cut out 8 biscuits. Place on a small baking sheet and refrigerate until firm, about 1 hour. Transfer the pan to the oven and bake the biscuits for 15 minutes, or until golden brown. Remove from the oven and transfer the biscuits to wire racks.

For the hash: In a medium sauté pan or skillet, cook the bacon over medium heat until crisp, about 3 minutes. Using a slotted spoon, transfer to paper towels to drain. In another medium sauté pan or skillet, heat the bacon fat over medium heat and cook the onion and bell peppers separately until tender. Transfer the vegetables to a pie pan and add the bacon.

In a Dutch oven or heavy casserole, heat 2 inches of the oil to 350°F on a deep-frying thermometer and cook the potatoes in two batches until golden, about 6 minutes; using a slotted spoon, transfer to a bowl. Return all the ingredients including the chicken stock and butter to one of the sauté pans or skillets and heat through over low heat. Season with salt and pepper. Add the parsley and toss just before serving.

Meanwhile, poach the eggs: In a large sauté pan, bring 2 inches of water to a bare simmer. Add the salt and white vinegar. Crack the eggs, one at a time, into a saucer and slide into the water. Cook until the egg whites are firm but the yolks are soft, 4 to 5 minutes. Using a slotted metal spatula, transfer to a plate.

To serve, place 2 biscuits on each plate and top with ¼ cup hash, then a poached egg. Pour some of the Hollandaise Sauce over each serving.

BACON & CREAM CHEESE FRITTATA

WITH ROASTED RED PEPPER HOLLANDAISE

THE RIVERCREST AT HARRAH'S METROPOLIS
EXECUTIVE CHEF JON M. KELL

In this brunch buffet staple from The Rivercrest at Harrah's Metropolis, smoky bacon and mellow cream cheese are complemented by the robust flavor of a hollandaise flavored with roasted red peppers. A versatile dish, the frittata can be served either hot or at room temperature, making it perfect for a buffet or picnic.

4 russet potatoes, peeled and shredded

½ cup (1 stick) unsalted butter, melted

1 pound bacon, cooked, drained, and crumbled

1 pound cream cheese, cubed

12 large eggs

6 egg whites (save yolks for hollandaise, below)

¼ teaspoon salt

¼ teaspoon freshly ground pepper

ROASTED RED PEPPER HOLLANDAISE

6 large egg yolks (reserved from above)

2 teaspoons water

½ teaspoon sugar

¾ cup (1½ sticks) cold unsalted butter, cut into 24 pieces

1 teaspoon kosher salt

4 teaspoons fresh lemon juice

¼ teaspoon cayenne pepper

One 10.6-ounce can roasted red peppers, drained and finely chopped

1 bunch asparagus, trimmed and steamed for 2 to 3 minutes

SERVES 6

Preheat the oven to 350°F. Coat a large baking dish with nonstick cooking spray. Spread the potatoes evenly in the dish. Pour the butter over the potatoes as evenly as possible. Bake for 20 minutes, or until lightly browned. Sprinkle the bacon crumbles and cream cheese cubes evenly over the potatoes. Set aside, leaving the oven on.

In a large bowl, whisk the eggs and egg whites until blended, then whisk in the salt and pepper. Pour the egg mixture over the potatoes in the baking dish. Return to the oven and cook for 20 to 30 minutes, or until the eggs are firm. Remove from the oven and keep warm.

For the hollandaise: In a medium stainless-steel bowl, combine the egg yolks and water and whisk until the mixture lightens in color, 1 to 2 minutes. Add the sugar and whisk for another 30 seconds. Set the bowl over a saucepan with 2 inches of barely simmering water and whisk constantly for 3 to 5 minutes, or until a path is drawn in the mixture when you pull your whisk through. Remove the bowl from the pan and gradually whisk in the butter, 1 piece at a time, until all the butter is incorporated. Put the bowl back over the simmering water occasionally if necessary so that it will be warm enough to melt the butter. Add the salt, lemon juice, and cayenne pepper. Fold in the peppers. Keep warm over tepid water or in a thermos.

To serve, cut the frittata into squares and serve on a pool of hollandaise. Garnish with the asparagus.

EACH DAY, 1,464 EGGS ARE CRACKED AND NINETY-NINE POUNDS OF BACON ARE FRIED FOR BREAKFAST AT HARRAH'S CHEROKEE.

HAZELNUT PANCAKES

HARRAH'S JOLIET
EXECUTIVE CHEF SCOTT D. LECOMPTE

Impress your family by making a great American breakfast with a twist. Serve these pancakes, fragrant with hazelnuts, as a special treat on Saturday morning with some chocolate chips, pure maple syrup, whipped butter, and whipped cream.

¾ cup all-purpose flour

¼ cup hazelnut flour (found in specialty foods stores)

½ teaspoon baking powder

¼ teaspoon baking soda

Pinch of salt

⅞ cup milk

1 teaspoon maple syrup

3 large eggs

1½ teaspoons vanilla extract

1 teaspoon honey

¾ cup (1½ sticks) unsalted butter, melted

Toppings of choice for serving

SERVES 4

In a large bowl, combine the dry ingredients and stir with a whisk to blend. In a medium bowl, whisk together the milk, maple syrup, eggs, vanilla, and honey until smooth. Add to the dry ingredients and stir to blend. Fold in the butter just until blended.

Heat a lightly oiled griddle or skillet over medium-high heat. Pour the batter onto the griddle, using about 1 tablespoon for small pancakes or ¼ cup for larger ones. Cook for 2 to 3 minutes, or until bubbles have stopped coming to the surface; turn and cook on the second side until golden brown. Serve at once, with your favorite toppings.

COCONUT CRÊPES
WITH CARAMELIZED CINNAMON APPLES,
CHOCOLATE WHIPPED CREAM & CARAMEL SAUCE

HARRAH'S CHESTER CASINO & RACETRACK
EXECUTIVE CHEF SEAN KINOSHITA

This might just be the most delicious dish you will ever have in the morning. Coconut, whipped cream, chocolate, and caramel! Together they will make an awesome start to your day.

COCONUT CRÊPES

2 cups all-purpose flour

4 large eggs, beaten

1 cup well-stirred or shaken canned coconut milk

1 cup water

½ teaspoon salt

¼ cup melted unsalted butter

Canola oil for brushing

CARAMELIZED CINNAMON APPLES

2 cups sugar

Pinch of salt

¼ teaspoon ground cinnamon

½ cup (1 stick) unsalted butter

8 Fuji apples, peeled, cored, and each cut into 8 wedges

CHOCOLATE WHIPPED CREAM

½ cup heavy cream

1 tablespoon sugar

⅛ teaspoon sifted unsweetened cocoa powder

Caramel Sauce (see recipe facing page)

4 mint sprigs

SERVES 4

For the crepes: In a large bowl, whisk together the flour and eggs. Gradually whisk in the coconut milk and water. Add the salt and butter, beating until smooth. Heat a 6-inch crêpe pan or skillet over medium-high heat and brush with oil. Pour a scant ¼ cup batter into the pan and tilt the pan with a circular motion so that the batter coats the surface evenly. Cook for about 1 minute, or until the bottom is light brown. Loosen with a spatula, and then turn and cook the other side. Place the crêpe on a plate and cover to keep warm. Repeat to cook the remaining batter, stacking the finished crêpes as you go.

For the apples: In a large bowl, mix together the sugar, salt, and cinnamon. In a large nonstick sauté pan or skillet, melt the butter over medium heat. Toss the apples in the cinnamon sugar mixture and add to the pan. Sauté until tender, about 5 minutes. Remove from the heat and keep warm.

For the whipped cream: In a medium bowl, combine all the ingredients. Using an electric mixer, beat the cream until stiff peaks form.

Preheat the oven to 350°F. Place a crêpe on a work surface and place ⅓ cup of the apples in the center. Fold the crêpe over the filling like an envelope. Place, seam-side down, on a baking sheet. Repeat to use the remaining crêpes and apples, making 12 filled crêpes. Place in the oven until heated through, about 7 minutes.

To serve, place 3 crêpes on each plate. Place a dollop of chocolate whipped cream on top of each serving and drizzle with Caramel Sauce. Top with a mint sprig and serve at once.

CARAMEL SAUCE

1 cup sugar

¼ cup water

½ cup heavy cream

4 tablespoons unsalted butter, melted

In a large, heavy saucepan, combine the sugar and water and cook over medium heat, tilting the pan occasionally but not stirring, until the mixture turns a deep amber. Brush the sides of the pan with a wet pastry brush if sugar crystals form. Remove from the heat and carefully whisk in the cream; take care, as it will spatter. Whisk in the butter. Serve warm.

MAKES 2 CUPS

FLAVOR'S BUFFET LEMON SQUARES

FLAVOR'S BUFFET & THE RANGE STEAKHOUSE AT HARRAH'S LAS VEGAS
EXECUTIVE PASTRY CHEF AMY BYRO

Everybody loves lemon squares, including the guests at Flavor's Buffet. Chef Amy Byro explains just how popular this dessert is: "On average, we go through about five hundred each day in the Flavor's Buffet. They are light and creamy, and not too tart, making them very addictive! They are so easy to make, and many of our guests tell us they remind them of home. We have even shipped them all over the United States. Often requested specifically by our Seven Stars guests, these lemon squares are a must-try!" While they are popular throughout the day, these lemon squares are a particular hit with the brunch crowd.

CRUST

1 cup (2 sticks) unsalted butter at room temperature

½ cup sifted confectioners' sugar

2 cups all-purpose flour

1 cup chopped pecans (optional)

Pinch of salt

FILLING

4 large eggs

2 cups granulated sugar

¼ cup all-purpose flour

1 teaspoon lemon extract

⅓ cup fresh lemon juice

Confectioners' sugar for dusting

MAKES 24 SQUARES

For the crust: Preheat the oven to 350°F. Lightly spray a 9-by-13-inch baking pan with nonstick cooking spray. In a large bowl, combine all the ingredients and stir to blend well. Pat the mixture evenly into the bottom of the prepared pan. Bake for 15 to 18 minutes, or until set and lightly golden. Transfer to a wire rack and let cool in the pan, leaving the oven on.

For the filling: In a large bowl, combine all the ingredients and stir well to blend. Spread over the cooled crust. Return to the oven and bake for 15 minutes, or until the filling is set, rotating the pan halfway through the cooking time to bake evenly.

Transfer the pan to a wire rack and let cool completely. Dust with confectioners' sugar. Cut into 24 squares.

TOP 10 TIPS FOR CREATING AN UNFORGETTABLE SEVEN STARS BUFFET AT HOME

HARRAH'S NORTH KANSAS CITY

1   To create a dramatic raised centerpiece for your buffet, find a sturdy container, place it upside down in the center of the buffet table, and cover it with a decorative tablecloth. Place a vase filled with seasonal flowers on top of it.

2   Always use the freshest, most vibrant produce, herbs, and extra-virgin or virgin olive oil for all of your cooking.

3   When creating your menu, think of color coordination and eye appeal. We all know that people eat with their eyes first.

4   Timing is a key to quality and freshness. Do not make your buffet food too far in advance. The longer it stands before your guests arrive, the more the quality and freshness will diminish.

5   Look for interesting decorations for your buffet, including fresh flowers. If you can find them, ivy runners are nice to use.

6   Use a small backlight behind your centerpiece to show how beautiful the piece is on your buffet.

7   Use different sizes of elevation on your buffet table to break up an otherwise flat look. Start from the centerpiece and work your way toward each end of the table.

8   For displaying foods, use different sizes of dishes, platters, soup cups, bowls, and so on, and mix and match patterns for an artistic effect.

9   Use only edible decorations for your buffet dishes, such as tomato roses, lemon roses, radish flowers, and carrot cups. There are numerous books that will show you how to create these decorations. Here are two of my favorite books on the subject: *Food Art: Garnishing Made Easy* by John Gargone, and *Garnishing: A Feast for Your Eyes* by Francis T. Lynch. These books will be your secret weapon to impress your guests.

10 When choosing seafood, poultry, beef, pork, or lamb, ask your butcher to give you the freshest available. The meats should be free of any discoloration.

10

VIP
LUNCHEON

ARTISANAL CHEESE PLATTER

NERO'S AT CAESARS PALACE LAS VEGAS
EXECUTIVE CHEF ERIC DAMIDOT

Everyone loves cheese, especially when accompanied with a good bottle of wine. Chef Eric Damidot's beautiful cheese platter will add an elegant touch to your next dinner party. Choose the specific cheeses listed below, or your own favorite selection, varying the textures and flavors. Serve this as a first course, as for the VIP luncheon, or preceding, or in place of dessert for a dinner party.

RED WINE PEAR PURÉE

1 pear, peeled, cored, and quartered

1 cup dry red wine

1 wedge blue Benedictin cheese

1 square Old Chatham Hudson Valley Camembert cheese

1 wedge Tourmalet cheese

1 wedge tomme de Savoie cheese

1 disk cabecou feuille cheese

HERBED APPLES

1½ tablespoons unsalted butter

1 rosemary sprig

2 Fuji apples, peeled, cored, and quartered

1 wedge guava paste

Fig Chutney (recipe follows)

2 handfuls mâche, dressed with a vinaigrette, for garnish

Baguette slices for serving

SERVES 4

For the pear purée: In a medium bowl, combine the pear and red wine. Cover and refrigerate for 48 hours. Pour off the wine and save for another use. Purée the pear in a blender or food processor until smooth.

Take the cheeses from the refrigerator at least 30 minutes before serving, removing any wrappings. Place on a large serving plate.

For the apples: In a small sauté pan or skillet, combine the butter and rosemary. Melt the butter over medium heat and cook until lightly browned. Add the apples and toss several times to coat well in the butter. Remove from the heat when you can insert the tip of a small paring knife inside each apple and the center feels tender.

Serve the pear purée, apples, guava paste, and Fig Chutney in small spoonfuls on the same plate as the cheese. Garnish the plate with the dressed mâche. Serve with slices of baguette.

FIG CHUTNEY

½ cup port wine

1½ cups dry red wine

3 star anise pods

2 tablespoons sugar

1 pound Black Mission figs, stemmed and quartered

1½ tablespoons fresh lemon juice

In a heavy, medium nonreactive saucepan, combine the port wine, red wine, star anise, sugar, and figs. Bring to a boil; reduce the heat to a simmer and cook until thickened, about 1 ½ hours. Remove from the heat and stir in the lemon juice. Use now, or spoon into sterilized jars, close tightly, and refrigerate for up to 2 weeks.

MAKES ABOUT 2 CUPS

THE BAND BARENAKED LADIES, WHILE PERFORMING IN TOWN, ALSO PLAYED SEVERAL HANDS OF BLACKJACK IN THE WHISKEY PIT AT HORSEHOE COUNCIL BLUFFS.

ROAST BEEF
WITH CREAMY HORSERADISH & BLUE CHEESE SPREAD

SEVEN SISTERS LOUNGE AT HARRAH'S CHEROKEE
CHEF RANDY PHILLIPS

Don't wait for a party! Fix these tasty little morsels any time you want to indulge yourself with a Seven Stars snack. The classic flavor duo of roast beef and horseradish harmonizes well with blue cheese. Add a little depth and balance with some red onion and capers, and you have an appetizer that is a hit with any crowd.

CREAMY HORSERADISH & BLUE CHEESE SPREAD

½ cup whipped cream cheese at room temperature

⅓ cup crumbled Danish blue cheese

¼ cup sour cream

1 tablespoon mayonnaise

2 teaspoons prepared horseradish sauce

1 tablespoon minced onion

1 tablespoon Italian seasoning

Dash of hot pepper sauce

4 slices peppered bacon, cooked until crisp and crumbled

2 loaves cocktail pumpernickel bread (32 slices)

32 slices deli roast beef (2 pounds)

½ cup diced red onion

One 3½-ounce jar small capers, drained

MAKES 32 APPETIZERS

For the spread: In a food processor, combine the cream cheese, blue cheese, sour cream, mayonnaise, horseradish, onion, Italian seasoning, and pepper sauce. Pulse the mixture until it is very smooth. Add the bacon and pulse until just blended. Transfer to a bowl, cover, and refrigerate until the flavors are well integrated, for at least 1 hour or overnight.

Preheat the oven to 325°F. On a baking sheet, arrange the bread slices. Bake in the preheated oven for 10 minutes, or until lightly toasted, turning the slices over halfway through. Remove from the oven and transfer to wire racks.

Pat the roast beef dry with paper towels. Fold each slice of beef into a triangle and place one on each slice of toast. Top with a small amount of the spread. Garnish with a few pieces of the red onion and several capers.

TOP 10 TIPS FOR PREPARING A MULTICOURSE MEAL

1   Write out your menu and have it in front of you when you are cooking and preparing.

2   Have all your food preparation done way in advance so you don't have to stop and prep anything. That way, the actual cooking will go more smoothly and you will have more time to enjoy your company.

3   Prepare any cold dishes, such as salads or desserts, earlier in the day.

4   Know how long each dish takes to cook so you can time them properly. Make a schedule of when to start each dish.

5   Make sure to preheat the oven at least 30 minutes before baking or roasting.

6   Allow enough time for meats to rest before carving.

7   Keep foods warm in a low oven if needed.

8   Set your table with all the silverware and glassware needed for the meal.

9   Pick out your food vessels and serving utensils in advance and have them handy for serving the finished dishes.

10 If serving meat, be sure to ask your guests how well done they would like it.

SMOKED SCALLOPS
WITH CUCUMBER-RED PEPPER SALSA

DIAMOND LOUNGE AT HARRAH'S RENO
CHEF STEPHEN TUCKER

The deep flavors of smoke and balsamic vinegar in this dish are balanced by the fresh salsa. Chef Stephen Tucker suggests, "If you'd like to serve this dish as a salad, simply chop the scallops and add them to the salsa. Also, remember to smoke the scallops lightly—don't overcook them."

SMOKED SCALLOPS

20 sea scallops

2 tablespoons Old Bay Seasoning

¼ cup dry white wine

CUCUMBER-RED PEPPER SALSA

2 cucumbers, peeled, seeded, and finely diced

1 red bell pepper, roasted, peeled, and finely diced (see page 196)

1 green onion, chopped (including some green parts)

2 tablespoons fresh lemon juice

2 tablespoons chopped fresh cilantro

1 tablespoon chile-garlic paste

Kosher salt and freshly ground white pepper

PEPPERED TOAST POINTS

10 slices firm sandwich bread, such as pullman bread, crusts removed

4 tablespoons unsalted butter, melted

½ cup grated Parmesan cheese

Ground black pepper

Balsamic Reduction (recipe follows)

MAKES 40 APPETIZERS

For the smoked scallops: Heat a smoker to 300°F following the manufacturer's instructions. Or, use a wok to smoke the scallops (see page 146). In a large bowl, toss the scallops with the Old Bay Seasoning and wine to coat. Place the scallops in a small baking pan in a single layer. Put the scallops in the smoker and smoke until just cooked through, 10 to 15 minutes. They will be opaque and firm with a slight give to the touch. Remove the scallops from the smoker and let cool in the pan.

For the salsa: In a medium bowl, combine all the ingredients and stir to blend.

For the toast points: Preheat the oven to 350°F. Brush the bread with the butter. Sprinkle the cheese evenly over the bread. Dust the cheese with the pepper. Place on a baking sheet and bake until the cheese is melted and golden brown, about 10 minutes. Remove from the oven and transfer to a cutting board. Cut each slice of bread into 4 triangles. Transfer to wire racks to cool.

To serve, place 1 tablespoon salsa on each toast point. Cut the scallops in half horizontally. Place a halved scallop on the salsa on each toast point. Drizzle the scallops with the Balsamic Reduction.

BALSAMIC REDUCTION

1 cup balsamic vinegar
1 cup dry white wine
¼ cup sugar
Salt and freshly ground white pepper

In a small, heavy saucepan, combine the balsamic vinegar and wine and heat to a simmer. Cook to reduce to 1 cup. Add the sugar and cook until thickened to a syrup. Season with salt and pepper. Use now, or pour into a bottle, seal, and refrigerate for up to 1 month.

MAKES ABOUT 1 CUP

CHEF ROLF'S VIP FINGER SANDWICHES

BALLY'S ATLANTIC CITY
FOOD SERVICE DIRECTOR ROLF J. WEITHOFER

No cocktail party is complete without classic finger sandwiches. Chef Rolf J. Weithofer creates these signature appetizers by layering two types of bread with smoked salmon, cucumbers, Swiss cheese, ham, and more. Served in a checkerboard pattern on a beautiful silver tray, these appetizers will make your guests feel like very important people indeed at your gathering.

6 slices white sandwich bread

6 slices whole-wheat sandwich bread

4 tablespoons whipped cream cheese

1 English cucumber, cut into thin diagonal slices

4 slices smoked salmon

2 tablespoons mustard mixed with 2 tablespoons mayonnaise

8 slices Swiss cheese

8 slices ham

16 pitted olives or cherry tomatoes for garnish (optional)

MAKES 16 APPETIZERS

Lay a slice of white bread and a slice of wheat bread on a work surface. Spread each with 1 tablespoon of the cream cheese, an overlapping layer of cucumber slices, then a slice of salmon. Top the white bread with a slice of wheat bread and the wheat bread with a slice of white. Spread each slice with 1 tablespoon of the mustard mixture. Top each with 2 thin slices of cheese and 2 thin slices of ham. Top each with the same kind of bread used for the first layer. Using a large knife, cut the crusts off the bread and cut each sandwich into 4 crosswise pieces. Repeat to make 8 more finger sandwiches. Pierce an olive or cherry tomato, if using, with a food pick and insert it in the center of each sandwich to hold it together. Arrange the sandwiches in a checkerboard pattern on a tray and serve immediately, or cover and chill until needed.

✦✦✦✦✦✦✦✦✦✦

ESCARGOTS PROVENÇAL

LE PROVENÇAL AT PARIS LAS VEGAS
CHEF ROBERT DERWINSKI

Le Provençal at Paris Las Vegas proudly serves traditional French-Italian cuisine, including this Provence-style dish. Chef Robert Derwinski sautés escargots with shallots, garlic, artichokes, and white wine to craft an unforgettable appetizer. Chef Robert explains, "The salty escargots and sweet artichokes complement each other well, while the white wine butter sauce helps bring it all together."

Eight or twelve ¼-inch-thick diagonal baguette slices

¼ cup olive oil, plus extra for brushing

Salt and freshly ground pepper

12 ounces canned escargots, rinsed and drained

2 tablespoons julienned shallot

2 teaspoons minced garlic

1 cup quartered artichoke hearts

½ cup dry white wine

1 cup (2 sticks) cold unsalted butter, cut into 8 pieces

½ cup diced peeled tomatoes

¼ bunch flat-leaf parsley, stemmed and minced

SERVES 4 TO 6 AS AN APPETIZER

Preheat the oven to 350°F. Brush the bread with olive oil on one side and season with salt and pepper. Place on a baking sheet and toast for about 5 minutes, or until beginning to brown. Remove from the oven and transfer the toasts to wire racks.

In a medium sauté pan or skillet, heat the ¼ cup olive oil over medium heat. Add the escargots and sauté for 1 minute. Add the shallot and garlic and sauté until the shallot is translucent, about 3 minutes. Add the artichokes and sauté for 30 seconds. Add the wine and cook to reduce by half. Reduce the heat to low and stir in the butter, 1 piece at a time, until all the butter is incorporated. Add the tomatoes and parsley and season with salt and pepper.

To serve, divide among serving bowls and top each bowl with 2 toasts.

LOBSTER & CRAB TARTS

BANQUET KITCHEN AT HARRAH'S LAKE TAHOE & HARVEYS LAKE TAHOE
CHEF RICK MARICLE

Created for New Year's Eve dinner at Harrah's Lake Tahoe and Harveys Lake Tahoe several years ago, this appetizer is perfect for any festive occasion. Chef Rick Maricle suggests, "A variation to the dish would be to substitute the shellfish with wild mushrooms sautéed in butter and flamed with brandy, and add chopped fresh chives for garnish."

2 slices bacon, minced

¼ cup finely chopped onion

¼ cup finely diced cooked lobster

¼ cup fresh lump crabmeat, picked over for shell and flaked

3 large eggs, beaten

⅔ cup heavy cream

1 cup grated Parmesan cheese

Kosher salt and freshly ground white pepper

Four 4-inch tart shells, partially baked

SERVES 4 AS AN APPETIZER

Preheat the oven to 350°F. In a medium skillet over medium-high heat, sauté the bacon and onion until the bacon is crisp, about 5 minutes. Using a slotted spoon, transfer to paper towels to drain.

In a medium bowl, combine the lobster and crabmeat; stir in the bacon and onion. In another medium bowl, combine the eggs, cream, cheese, and salt and pepper to taste. Whisk to blend well.

Evenly divide the lobster mixture among the tart shells. Fill each tart shell to the rim with the egg mixture. Place the tarts on a baking sheet. Bake for 15 to 20 minutes, or until the custard is set (a toothpick inserted in the center will come out clean). Remove from the oven and let cool slightly on wire racks. Serve warm.

HARRAH'S LAKE TAHOE'S SOUTH SHORE ROOM CELEBRATED ITS FIFTIETH ANNIVERSARY IN 2009. IT OPENED IN DECEMBER 1959 IN ADVANCE OF THE 1960 WINTER OLYMPIC GAMES AT LAKE TAHOE. SOME OF THE MANY STARS WHO HAVE PERFORMED AT THE SOUTH SHORE ROOM INCLUDE BILL COSBY, DON RICKLES, JIMMY DURANTE, RED SKELTON, DEAN MARTIN, FRANK SINATRA, LIZA MINNELLI, JUDY GARLAND, AND SAMMY DAVIS JR.

VIP LUNCHEON

DUCK WITH PORCINI MUSHROOMS

PENAZZI AT HARRAH'S LAS VEGAS
CHEF GEORGE ALBERTO TAPIA

The recipe for this traditional Tuscan appetizer was brought to Penazzi from Italy by chef George Alberto Tapia. It soon became as popular at the restaurant as it is in its home region.

8 thin slices prosciutto

4 Muscovy duck breast halves, cut into 8 pieces

Salt and freshly ground pepper

2 tablespoons olive oil

2 tablespoons unsalted butter

1 tablespoon minced shallot

½ teaspoon minced garlic

2 ounces porcini mushrooms, sliced

2 tablespoons brandy

Pinch of minced fresh rosemary

1 teaspoon truffle oil

1 cup chicken stock

SERVES 4 AS AN APPETIZER,
OR 1 TO 2 AS A MAIN COURSE

Wrap a slice of prosciutto around each piece of duck and season with salt and pepper. In a large sauté pan or skillet, heat the oil over medium heat and sear the packets until lightly browned, about 2 minutes on each side. Transfer to a plate and keep warm in a low oven.

In the same pan, melt the butter over medium heat and sauté the shallot, garlic, and mushrooms for 2 minutes. Remove from the heat and add the brandy, stirring to scrape up the browned bits from the bottom of the pan. Return to medium heat and add the rosemary, truffle oil, and chicken stock. Cook to reduce the liquid for about 5 minutes.

To serve, place the duck packets on a platter and pour the pan sauce over them. Serve immediately with a seasonal salad of choice.

THE ORIGINAL HARRAH'S LAS VEGAS, BUILT IN 1973, HAD A FAÇADE WITH A STEAMBOAT MOTIF AND WAS NAMED THE HOLIDAY CASINO. IT WAS RENAMED HARRAH'S LAS VEGAS IN 1992.

PISTACHIO-ENCRUSTED LOIN OF LAMB

WITH MINT-INFUSED RICE & PORT WINE REDUCTION

HARRAH'S AK-CHIN
CHEF JAMES SHEWMAKE

Lamb has a natural affinity for both pistachios and mint, and here a loin is rolled in a mixture of the bright green nuts and served with a mint-flavored pilaf. This is a simple but elegant dish that really warms the heart and soul. Great for all seasons, this dish has wonderful diversity; it is sweet and savory and really hits your palate with unique flavor combinations.

MINT-INFUSED RICE

3 tablespoons unsalted butter

¼ cup diced celery

¼ cup diced onion

2 garlic cloves, minced

Salt and freshly ground pepper

2 cups lamb stock or chicken stock

1 cup long-grain rice

Leaves from 4 mint sprigs, chopped

PORT WINE REDUCTION

1½ cups tawny port wine

1 to 2 tablespoons unsalted butter

PISTACHIO-ENCRUSTED LOIN OF LAMB

½ cup pistachios (see note)

2 tablespoons olive oil

One 8- to 10-ounce lamb loin, trimmed of fat and silver skin

¼ teaspoon salt

½ teaspoon freshly ground pepper

SERVES 2 AS A MAIN COURSE

For the rice: In a large, heavy saucepan, melt the butter over medium heat. Add the celery, onion, and garlic. Sauté for 2 to 3 minutes, until the onion is translucent, then season with salt and pepper. Add the lamb stock and bring to a boil. Add the rice and mint, and then return to a boil. Cover and reduce the heat to a simmer. Simmer for 15 to 20 minutes, or until the rice is tender. Remove from the heat and fluff with a fork. Cover and keep warm.

For the port wine reduction: In a heavy, small saucepan, bring the port wine to a boil over high heat. Reduce to a simmer and cook until reduced to ½ cup. Remove from the heat and whisk in the butter. Set aside and keep warm.

For the lamb: Preheat the oven to 350°F. In a food processor, chop the pistachios until coarsely ground. In an ovenproof medium sauté pan or skillet, heat the oil over medium heat. Season the lamb with the salt and pepper and roll it in the pistachios. Sear the lamb on all sides until golden brown, about 1 minute per side. Transfer the pan to the oven and roast the lamb for 10 minutes for medium-rare. Remove from the oven, transfer the lamb to a cutting board, and tent with aluminum foil for about 5 minutes.

To serve, cut the lamb into medallions. Portion the rice in the center of each plate, place the lamb on the rice, and spoon ¼ cup of the port wine reduction over each serving.

++++++++++

Skinning pistachios: If your pistachios still have their brown skin, blanch them in boiling water for 2 minutes, then drain, wrap in a towel, and rub to remove the skins. Put them in a colander and shake well to remove any leftover skins.

MAHI MAHI & GRILLED SHRIMP
WITH BLACK BEANS & MANGO

SEVEN STARS LOUNGE AT HORSESHOE HAMMOND
CHEF CHRIS BASIL

Mahi mahi, also called dolphinfish, is found in warm waters around the world. For this Seven Stars favorite, chef Chris Basil pairs it with grilled shrimp. Black beans, mango, and a vanilla-flavored sauce add their tropical flavors. Chef Chris advises, "I like serving this dish in either the spring or summertime. It works best with a Pinot Grigio."

SHRIMP

¼ teaspoon minced garlic

½ teaspoon red pepper flakes

¼ teaspoon ground ginger

¼ cup canola oil

8 extra-large shrimp, shelled and deveined

BLACK BEANS AND MANGO

2 cups cooked black beans, drained (and rinsed, if canned)

1 mango, peeled, cut from pit, and cut into ⅜-inch dice

½ cup ⅜-inch-diced sweet white onions, such as Vidalia or Walla Walla

VANILLA SAUCE

½ cup sugar

⅓ cup distilled white vinegar

1 vanilla bean, split lengthwise, or 1 teaspoon vanilla extract

1 tablespoon finely chopped onion

½ teaspoon dry mustard

1¼ cups canola oil

Fresh lemon juice as needed

Salt and freshly ground pepper

MAHI MAHI

Eight 4-ounce mahi mahi steaks

Salt and freshly ground pepper

½ cup macadamia nuts, finely ground in a food processor

1 cup clarified butter (see page 43)

For the shrimp: In a medium bowl, combine the garlic, red pepper flakes, and ginger. Stir in the oil. Add the shrimp and stir to coat.

Cover and refrigerate for 2 hours, stirring the shrimp every 30 minutes. Remove from the refrigerator 30 minutes before cooking. Heat a medium sauté pan or skillet over medium heat and sauté the shrimp for 1 minute on each side. Remove from the heat and empty onto a plate.

For the black beans and mango: In a large bowl, combine all the ingredients, gently tossing together. Set aside.

For the vanilla sauce: In a blender, combine the sugar and vinegar. Scrape the seeds from the vanilla bean into the blender (reserve the pod for another use) or add the vanilla extract. Add the onion and mustard. With the machine running, gradually add the oil in a thin stream. Add the lemon juice if the sauce is too thick. Stir in salt and pepper to taste.

For the mahi mahi: Preheat the oven to 400°F. Season the fish with salt and pepper, then dredge in the macadamia nuts. In a large ovenproof sauté pan or skillet, heat the clarified butter over medium-high heat and sauté the fish for 2 minutes on each side. Remove from the heat, add the shrimp to the pan, and transfer the pan to the oven. Roast for 5 minutes, or until the mahi mahi is opaque throughout. Remove from the oven.

To serve, overlap 2 pieces of fish on each plate. Spoon some of the black bean mixture in the center and divide the shrimp on each side of the plate. Drizzle the fish with the vanilla sauce.

SERVES 4 AS A MAIN COURSE

MAO PAO TOFU

Chef Thierry Mai-Thanh says this traditional dish, an Ah Sin favorite, is supposedly named after the woman who created it. In this dish, tofu takes on the spirited flavors of stir-fried jalapeños, garlic, green onions, chile paste, and hoisin sauce. To serve this to your favorite vegetarians, replace the chicken broth with vegetable stock.

1½ pounds soft tofu, cut into 1-inch cubes

¼ cup canola oil

2 jalapeño chiles, seeded and sliced

3 tablespoons minced garlic

1 cup canned straw mushrooms, drained and halved

¼ cup finely chopped green onion, including some green parts

1 teaspoon sambal oelek chile paste, or more to taste

2 cups chicken broth

2 tablespoons soy sauce

½ cup hoisin sauce

Steamed jasmine rice for serving

SERVES 4 TO 6 AS A MAIN COURSE

Pat the tofu dry with paper towels and set aside. In a wok, heat the oil over medium-high heat and stir-fry the jalapeños, garlic, mushrooms, green onions, and chile paste for 40 seconds. Add the chicken broth and cook to reduce to ½ cup. Add the soy sauce and bring to a boil. Add the hoisin sauce and cook to reduce to a demi-glace consistency. Add the tofu, gently tossing so as not to break it up, and cook until it absorbs the flavor from the sauce, about 1 minute. Remove from the heat. Serve over rice in deep bowls.

CRAB-STUFFED SALMON FILLETS

HARRAH'S NORTH KANSAS CITY
SOUS-CHEF JERRY ROXAS

After enjoying this sumptuous dish at Harrah's North Kansas City, guests often ask chef Jerry Roxas, "How can I cook this at home?" Here is the recipe for a dish to impress and honor your guests with.

Six 8-ounce salmon fillets, skin and pin bones removed

Salt and freshly ground pepper

CRABMEAT STUFFING

8 cups panko (Japanese bread crumbs)

1 pound fresh lump crabmeat, picked over for shell, or canned crabmeat, drained

2 garlic cloves, minced

½ teaspoon dry mustard

1 tablespoon Worcestershire sauce

2 large eggs, beaten

¾ cup finely diced red bell pepper

¼ cup olive oil

6 lemon slices

GARNISH

1 cup finely diced fresh pineapple

1 cup finely diced English cucumber

¼ cup finely diced red bell pepper

¼ cup minced fresh cilantro

1½ tablespoons minced fresh thyme

1½ tablespoons minced fresh basil

SERVES 6 AS A MAIN COURSE

Preheat the oven to 400°F. With a sharp knife, cut a pocket in the side of each fillet. Be careful to not cut through the fillets. Season the fillets with salt and pepper.

For the stuffing: In a large bowl, combine all the ingredients. Stir to blend. Spoon ⅓ cup of the stuffing into the pocket in each fillet.

In a large ovenproof sauté pan or skillet, heat the olive oil over medium-high heat and cook the salmon for 4 minutes on each side to achieve a golden brown color on the fish. Put the lemon slices on top of the salmon. Transfer the pan to the oven and roast the salmon for 6 to 7 minutes, or until still slightly translucent in the center. Remove from the oven and keep warm.

For the garnish: In a medium bowl, combine the pineapple, cucumber, bell pepper, and cilantro. Stir to blend. Portion the mixture on top of each fillet and sprinkle with the thyme and basil. Serve at once.

HARRAH'S WAS FIRST LISTED ON THE AMERICAN STOCK EXCHANGE IN 1972.

TOP 10 ALCOHOLIC BEVERAGES
EVERY HOME BAR SHOULD HAVE

HARRAH'S ST. LOUIS

1   Jack Daniel's whiskey

2   Kahlúa

3   Baileys Irish Cream

4   Stoli (Stolichnaya) vodka (Russian vodka), chilled

5   Malibu rum, chilled

6   VSOP (Very Superior Old Pale) Cognac, chilled

7   Otokoyama sake, chilled

8   Nigori sake, chilled

9   Don Julio tequila, chilled

10   Negra Modelo (Mexican dark beer), chilled

CRÈME BRÛLÉE IN TUILE CUPS

GRAND BILOXI CASINO, HOTEL & SPA
EXECUTIVE CHEF JASON CARLISLE

A fabulous meal deserves an extraordinary dessert. Chef Jason Carlisle comments, "I love using this recipe at home, for dinner parties and special occasions. It takes guests by surprise, as the entire dish is edible. The crème brûlée with its thin caramel crust sits in a thin cookie cup called a tuile cup. It takes a little time and a disciplined hand, but the outcome is unforgettable."

TUILE CUPS

1 cup (2 sticks) unsalted butter, melted and cooled

2 cups confectioners' sugar, sifted

1⅓ cups all-purpose flour, sifted

12 large egg whites

CRÈME BRÛLÉE CUSTARD

2 cups heavy cream

½ vanilla bean, split lengthwise

12 large egg yolks

½ cup plus 2 tablespoons granulated sugar

6 tablespoons granulated sugar

Fresh berries, whipped cream, and mint sprigs for garnish

SERVES 6

For the tuile cups: Preheat the oven to 400°F. Put the butter in the bowl of a stand mixer fitted with the paddle attachment and gradually beat in the confectioners' sugar on low speed until smooth. Add the flour in the same fashion and beat until smooth. Add the egg whites, one at a time, beating just until smooth so as not to incorporate air in the mixture. Strain the mixture through a fine-mesh sieve into a bowl. Let rest for 30 minutes.

Spray a nonstick baking sheet with nonstick cooking spray. Pour a tablespoonful of batter on the prepared pan. In a circular motion, spread the batter to form a very thin round about 6 inches in diameter.

Place a custard cup upside down on the counter near the oven. You will use this to shape the tuile. Have a pot holder and a metal spatula ready. Bake the tuile for 5 minutes, or until browned around the edges and lightly colored in the center. Remove from the oven. Using the metal spatula, immediately transfer the tuile to the custard cup, centering it so that it drapes down to form a scalloped cup. Let cool, then carefully transfer the delicate cup to a work surface. Repeat to make a total of 6 cups.

For the custard: In a heavy, medium saucepan, combine the cream and vanilla bean. Cook over medium-low heat until bubbles form around the edges of the pan. In a large bowl, whisk the egg yolks and sugar together until smooth. Gradually whisk ½ cup of the hot cream into the egg mixture. Return to the saucepan, turn the heat to low, and cook, whisking constantly, until the custard is very thick. Remove from the heat and strain through a fine-mesh sieve into a bowl, pushing the last part through with the back of a large spoon; let cool. Cover and refrigerate for at least 30 minutes or up to 2 days.

To assemble, just before serving place about ½ teaspoon custard in the center of a dessert plate. Place a tuile cup on top of the custard; this will keep the cup from sliding on the plate. Fill the cup three-fourths full with custard. Repeat with the remaining cups and custard.

In a small, heavy saucepan, cook the 6 tablespoons sugar over medium-low heat; do not stir, just move the pan in a circular motion. The sugar will begin to liquefy and caramelize. When the color is a dark amber, remove from the heat and bring the pan to the work surface, holding it over a custard-filled cup. Dip a fork into the caramel and drizzle it over the custard to cover it in a thin layer. Repeat to top the remaining custards. Garnish each plate with berries, whipped cream, and mint. Serve at once.

VIP LUNCHEON

CHOCOLATE-COCONUT CAKE

PAYARD PÂTISSERIE & BISTRO AT CAESARS PALACE LAS VEGAS
CHEF FRANÇOIS PAYARD

Celebrated pastry chef François Payard tells this story: "A chef visiting my kitchen happened to see our recipe for this cake, and his immediate response was, 'There is something missing here!' But there is not. I had been experimenting with variations of sponge cake and devised this one, which is like a macaroon layer. A serving of this cake is like popping a coconut macaroon into your mouth. It is so simple that you may not believe how delicious it is until you actually try it. I suggest serving it with vanilla ice cream or chocolate sorbet." For a shimmery effect, edible gold leaf can be used as a garnish.

COCONUT SPONGE CAKE

4 large eggs

1½ cups sugar

3⅔ cups unsweetened shredded dried coconut

GANACHE

10½ ounces bittersweet chocolate, finely chopped

3½ ounces milk chocolate, finely chopped

1⅔ cups heavy cream

1 cup unsweetened shredded dried coconut, toasted (see note)

MAKES ONE 5-BY-10-INCH CAKE;
SERVES 6 TO 8

For the cake: Preheat the oven to 350°F. Spray a 12½-by-17½-inch jelly roll pan with nonstick cooking spray. Line the bottom of the pan with parchment paper.

Fill a medium saucepan one-third full with water and bring to a simmer. Whisk together the eggs and sugar until blended. Place the bowl over the pan of simmering water and whisk constantly until the egg mixture is warm to the touch. Transfer the bowl to a stand mixer and beat on high speed until it has tripled in volume, about 5 minutes. Using a rubber spatula, fold in the coconut just until blended. Pour the batter onto the prepared pan and spread it evenly in the pan with a rubber spatula.

Bake the cake for 20 to 25 minutes, or until the top is a light golden brown and a toothpick inserted in the center comes out clean. Remove from the oven and let cool in the pan on a wire rack for 15 minutes. Run a small sharp knife around the sides of the pan to loosen the cake. Place a wire rack over the cake and invert. Carefully peel off the parchment paper (the cake is extremely delicate). Let cool completely.

For the ganache: In a large bowl, combine the bittersweet and milk chocolates. In a medium saucepan, bring the cream to a boil. Immediately pour the hot cream over the chocolate and whisk until the chocolate is completely melted and smooth. Cover with plastic wrap, pressing it directly onto the surface of the ganache. Let cool, then refrigerate until firm enough to pipe, about 4 hours.

To assemble, trim off any uneven edges of the cake and cut it crosswise into three equal rectangles, each measuring about 5 by 10 inches. Place one of the rectangles on a serving platter. Using a small metal offset spatula, spread a generous layer of the ganache over the top of the cake layer. Cover with another cake layer and spread a layer of the ganache over it. Top with the third cake layer and spread a layer of the ganache over the top and sides of the cake. Sprinkle the toasted coconut over the tops and sides of the cake. If not serving immediately, refrigerate the cake. The cake can be made up to 1 day ahead. Bring to room temperature before serving.

✦ ✦ ✦ ✦ ✦ ✦ ✦ ✦ ✦

Toasting coconut: Spread the coconut on a sided baking sheet and toast in a preheated 350°F oven until golden, 6 to 10 minutes, shaking the pan 2 or 3 times as the coconut toasts. Empty onto a plate and let cool completely.

TOP 10 SERVING TIPS
FOR THE HOST OR HOSTESS

1   Let time work for you, not against you: This means allowing adequate time to plan for the party or event you are throwing. Give yourself time to shop for supplies, create any party favors, organize activities, and clean your house.

2   Choose food wisely: If you aren't a real whiz in the kitchen, pick easy, make-ahead recipes. Even if you are a French-trained chef, it's still a good idea to select dishes that can be prepped ahead of time. That way, all you're doing the day of your event is putting on the finishing touches, not creating something from start to finish.

3   Set the mood: People's moods are very affected by their environment. Choose appropriate lighting (low light for a cocktail party, ample lighting for a kids' party with arts and crafts, etc.). Use music to help you set the mood as well.

4   Have an emergency supply of foods: Keep snacks in the pantry that you can serve to guests in case you run low on food or burn one of your dishes. Also, keep plenty of beverages on hand in case you run low.

5   The glass should always be at least half full: Keep an eye on guests' beverages. Offer to fill them up before they are completely drained. That will keep people from having to leave conversations or activities they might be enjoying.

6   Introduce your guests: A good host or hostess makes sure guests are introduced with a tip on what they have in common for a conversation starter. Happy guests make for a successful party.

7   Choose your attitude: If you're having a bad day, don't let that affect your guests. Put your happy face on and enjoy the evening. If you're laughing, talking to people, and having a good time, chances are greater your guests will be, too.

8   Do your homework: Know who your guests are and think about what you can do to help them feel comfortable. For example, if many of your guests are elderly, have enough places for them to sit.

9   Establish a "last call": Determine the hour when no more alcoholic drinks are served and coffee and tea become the beverages of choice. Remember, though, that coffee and tea do not make you sober.

10   Make sure your guests get home safely: Find out who needs a ride, a taxi, or a designated driver.

EXECUTIVE CHEF KLAUS FEYERSINGER'S

TOP 10 GIFTS
FOR YOUR HOST OR HOSTESS

HARRAH'S RENO

1   A set of crystal wineglasses or Champagne glasses

2   A crystal bowl

3   Signed cookbooks by celebrity chefs: Have cookbooks autographed and personally inscribed at book signings, or by sending the book to the author in care of their publisher

4   A knife set, such as one by J.A. Henckels or Wüsthof

5   Bottled sauces and seasonings

6   Gift cards from kitchenware stores

7   Gift baskets filled with foods and/or kitchen utensils: For example, imported Italian pasta, pasta sauces, wooden spoons or other kitchen utensils, assorted nuts and dried fruits

8   Chocolate truffles or cookies

9   A gift certificate for a local wine and/or food tasting at a local winery

10 A great bottle of Napa Valley wine

11

DESSERTS

BERRY NAPOLEON

ANDREOTTI AT HARRAH'S RENO
EXECUTIVE PASTRY CHEF CATHY HAYNES

At Andreotti, guests are entertained by both the northern Italian food and the singing restaurateur Pier Perotti, who performs operatic arias while musician Corky Bennett accompanies him. Serve this favorite Andreotti dessert for your next dinner party, and play some Pavarotti in the background, unless, of course, you have an opera singer at your beck and call.

6 thawed frozen filo pastry sheets

4 tablespoons unsalted butter, melted

Granulated sugar for sprinkling

2 cups heavy cream

¼ cup confectioners' sugar, sifted

2 tablespoons Grand Marnier

2 cups mixed fresh berries

SERVES 6

Preheat the oven to 350°F. Keeping the filo covered with a cloth, transfer one sheet to a work surface and brush with butter. Top with a second sheet, brush with butter, and repeat until all sheets have been stacked and brushed. Sprinkle the top lightly with granulated sugar. Place the stack with a long side toward you. Using a large knife, cut the stack into thirds lengthwise and into sixths crosswise to make 18 pieces. Bake for 12 to 15 minutes, or until golden. Remove from the oven and place the pan on a wire rack to cool.

In a medium bowl, beat the cream until soft peaks form. Fold in the confectioners' sugar and Grand Marnier until blended.

To assemble the dessert, place 1 piece of filo on a dessert plate and top with a dollop of cream, then some berries. Repeat with 1 more layer of filo, then cream and berries. Top with another layer of filo. Repeat to use the remaining filo, cream, and berries, making a total of 6 desserts. Garnish the plates with additional berries and serve.

SAMMY'S SHOWROOM WAS NAMED FOR LEGENDARY PERFORMER SAMMY DAVIS, JR., WHO STARTED HIS CAREER AT HARRAH'S RENO.

TOP 10 TIPS FOR
SERVING UNFORGETTABLE DESSERTS

HARRAH'S LAKE TAHOE

1   Plan your dessert in relation to the main course. For example, if your menu features a robust dish, the dessert should be a lighter one, such as a delicate mousse.

2   Offering a sampler plate with a variety of textures and tastes will help the most discriminating palates enjoy the end of the meal.

3   Having a "theme" for your dinner will help you choose the last course. For instance, a fall dinner that features harvest-type vegetables and venison might end with a dessert using figs or apples.

4   Always remember: "The eyes eat first!" The best-tasting dessert will lose appeal if it is not presented well.

5   Revamping classical desserts by using unexpected ingredients and interesting presentations can turn a simple meal into a lasting memory.

6   Turn the day upside down, for a change: For example, serve a breakfast waffle topped with ice cream and an exciting sauce for dessert.

7   Use the best ingredients available to make unforgettable finales to your meals.

8   Healthy choices that look rich and inviting can greatly contribute to a wonderful dining experience.

9   A meal should be a harmonious blend of ingredients, and the dessert should complement the courses that precede it.

10 Most of all, keep it simple; don't overdo the different kinds of ingredients and garnishes for your dessert. The last course should be a beautiful end to a memorable occasion.

PAULA DEEN'S
GOOEY BUTTER CAKE

PAULA DEEN BUFFET AT HARRAH'S TUNICA
PAULA DEEN & EXECUTIVE SOUS-CHEF TAMMY WILLIAMS-HANSEN

When butter, vanilla, and a culinary superstar join forces, you have a Southern dessert that is a favorite at the Paula Deen Buffet. Chef Tammy Williams-Hansen explains, "Paula's Gooey Butter Cake is a melt-in-your-mouth Southern treat that can be enhanced with many flavors. One of Paula's favorite variations is the Elvis-inspired cake, which is made with peanut butter and banana and is a perfect ending to any great meal." To transform this cake into Paula Deen's Elvis Presley Gooey Butter Cake, incorporate ½ cup peanut butter and 1 puréed banana into the filling.

CAKE

One 18¼-ounce package yellow cake mix

1 large egg

½ cup (1 stick) unsalted butter, melted

FILLING

One 8-ounce package cream cheese at room temperature

2 large eggs

1 teaspoon vanilla extract

½ cup (1 stick) unsalted butter, melted

One 16-ounce box confectioners' sugar, sifted

Ice cream for serving (optional)

MAKES ONE 9-BY-13-INCH CAKE;
SERVES 15 TO 20

For the cake: Preheat the oven to 350°F. Lightly grease a 9-by-13-inch baking pan.

In the bowl of an electric mixer, combine the cake mix, egg, and butter. Mix well. Pat the mixture evenly into the bottom of the prepared pan.

For the filling: In a large bowl, beat the cream cheese until smooth. Add the eggs, vanilla, and butter and beat until blended. Gradually beat in the confectioners' sugar until blended.

Spread the filling evenly over the cake and bake for 40 to 50 minutes, or until the edges are set but a toothpick inserted in the center comes out wet. Remove from the oven and let cool in the pan on a wire rack. Let the cake set for 1 hour after coming out of the oven. To serve, cut into squares and top with ice cream, if desired.

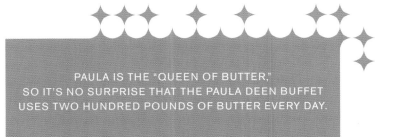

PAULA IS THE "QUEEN OF BUTTER,"
SO IT'S NO SURPRISE THAT THE PAULA DEEN BUFFET
USES TWO HUNDRED POUNDS OF BUTTER EVERY DAY.

PECAN PRALINE CHEESECAKE

FRESH MARKET BUFFET AT HARRAH'S NORTH KANSAS CITY
CHEF ANTHONY GALATE

A match made in culinary heaven: crunchy pecans and brown sugar blended with velvety cream cheese, eggs, and vanilla. Chef Anthony Galate comments, "This recipe is such a particular favorite of our Seven Stars guests that it has become a signature item at Harrah's North Kansas City. Guests also order this cheesecake to take home for the holidays to their families to enjoy."

1 cup sweetened condensed milk

½ cup finely chopped pecans

¼ cup packed brown sugar

¼ cup unsalted butter, melted

¾ cup graham cracker crumbs

16 ounces cream cheese at room temperature

3 large eggs, beaten

2 tablespoons vanilla extract

PECAN PRALINE TOPPING

⅓ cup heavy cream

⅓ cup packed brown sugar

⅓ cup chopped pecans

MAKES ONE 9-INCH CAKE;
SERVES 10 TO 12

Preheat the oven to 300°F. In a medium saucepan, combine the condensed milk, pecans, brown sugar, and butter, mixing well. Cook over medium-low heat, stirring frequently, for about 5 minutes, or until slightly thickened. Remove from the heat and let cool to room temperature.

Press the graham cracker crumbs firmly into the bottom of a 9-inch springform pan.

In a large bowl, beat the cream cheese until fluffy. Gradually stir the cooled pecan mixture into the cream cheese until blended. Stir in the eggs and vanilla, mixing well to blend. Pour the filling into the crust. Bake for 55 to 60 minutes, or until the center is set.

For the topping: In a medium saucepan, combine the heavy cream and brown sugar. Bring to a simmer over medium-low heat and cook, stirring constantly, for 5 to 10 minutes, until the mixture thickens slightly. Remove from the heat and let cool to room temperature. Stir in the pecans.

Remove the cheesecake from the oven and let cool for 10 minutes on a wire rack. Run a dinner knife around the inside of the pan to loosen the cheesecake. Lift off the sides of the pan. Let cool completely. Top the cheesecake evenly with the topping.

FRIDAY'S PEANUT BUTTER MOUSSE CUPS

FRIDAY'S STATION STEAK & SEAFOOD GRILL AT HARRAH'S LAKE TAHOE
EXECUTIVE PASTRY CHEF CHRISTINE BAIRD

This irresistible dessert was developed by chef Christine Baird especially for Friday's and is available by special request at the restaurant. The chocolate cups can also be used to serve fresh berries, chocolate mousse, strawberries Romanoff, strawberry Bavarian cream, and many other delectable fillers.

Note: You will need 4 small balloons to make the cups.

8 ounces semisweet chocolate, chopped

½ cup cream cheese at room temperature

2 tablespoons sugar

½ cup smooth peanut butter

1 tablespoon unsalted butter at room temperature

½ teaspoon pure vanilla extract

1¼ cups heavy cream

CHOCOLATE GANACHE

4 ounces semisweet chocolate, chopped

½ cup heavy cream

1½ teaspoons light or dark corn syrup

Whipped cream for garnish

SERVES 4

In a medium stainless-steel bowl set over a saucepan with 2 inches of barely simmering water, melt the chocolate and stir until smooth. Remove from the heat and let cool to room temperature.

Meanwhile, inflate 4 small balloons to a diameter of about 3 inches, stretching the top until smooth and tying the end of each balloon securely into a knot. Line a baking sheet with parchment paper or waxed paper.

Dip a balloon halfway into the chocolate to coat. Shake it gently to let the excess chocolate drip off. Transfer the balloon to the prepared pan and hold it in place upside down for a few moments until it can stand on its own. Repeat to coat a total of 4 balloons. With the remaining chocolate, make handles for the bowls, if you like, by piping them from a small parchment paper cone.

In the large bowl of an electric mixer, combine the cream cheese and sugar. Beat on low speed to blend. Add the peanut butter and butter, beating on medium speed until light and fluffy. Stop the mixer and scrape down the sides and bottom of the bowl, as well as the paddle or beaters. Add the vanilla and mix to blend.

In a medium bowl, whisk ¼ cup of the cream until soft peaks form. Gently fold it into the peanut butter mixture, making sure there are no white streaks in the mix. Cover and refrigerate the filling for at least 4 hours or up to 24 hours.

In a deep bowl, whisk the remaining 1 cup cream until soft peaks form. With the whisk, stir the peanut butter mousse until smooth. Fold in one-third of the whipped cream at a time.

Remove the balloons from the chocolate cups by piercing them with a small knife. Remove all balloon residue from the chocolate, then fill each cup with peanut butter mousse. Refrigerate while preparing the ganache.

For the ganache: Put the chocolate in a medium bowl. In a small, heavy saucepan, combine the cream and corn syrup. Bring to a boil over medium heat and immediately pour over the chocolate, stirring until melted and smooth. Let cool to room temperature; take care that it is not warm.

To serve, top the peanut butter cups with the cooled ganache. Garnish each serving with a dollop of whipped cream.

PROSECCO GELÉE

CAESARS ATLANTIC CITY
EXECUTIVE CHEF KEITH MITCHELL

A perfect warm-weather treat: vanilla-flavored sparkling-wine gelatin, molded in martini glasses and served with fresh peaches and cream. Serve this grown-up gelatin dessert after a cookout for the perfect end to a summer day. Chef Keith Mitchell suggests this variation: "Use a sparkling rosé or a still red wine in place of the Prosecco, and fresh berries in place of the peaches."

1¼ **cups water**

1 **package unflavored gelatin**

1 **cup sugar**

1 **vanilla bean, split lengthwise**

2½ **cups Prosecco or other sparkling wine**

3 **peaches, peeled, pitted, and sliced**

Sweetened whipped cream for garnish

SERVES 6

Put ¼ cup of the water in a small bowl and sprinkle the gelatin over; let stand until softened. Put the sugar in a small bowl. Scrape the seeds from the vanilla bean into the sugar and stir to blend.

In a large saucepan, combine the remaining 1 cup water and the vanilla-sugar mixture. Cook over medium heat until simmering. Stir in the gelatin mixture until dissolved. Add the wine and stir gently. Divide the liquid among 6 extra-large martini glasses. Place on a baking sheet and refrigerate until set, about 2 hours.

To serve, divide the peach slices among the glasses and top with dollops of whipped cream.

PASSION FRUIT CRÈME BRÛLÉE

RED PEARL AT BALLY'S ATLANTIC CITY
EXECUTIVE PASTRY CHEF MICHAEL D'ANGELO

Everyone loves the play of textures in crème brûlée: rich, smooth custard with a crackling caramelized sugar topping. Here, chef Michael D'Angelo dresses up the classic by adding the sweet tropical flavor of passion fruit.

3 **cups heavy cream**

½ **vanilla bean, split lengthwise**

10 **large egg yolks**

⅓ **cup sugar, plus 6 tablespoons for topping**

½ **cup passion fruit purée (not juice)**

Florentine cookie sticks with sliced almonds or other cookies for garnish

SERVES 6

Preheat the oven to 325°F. In a large, heavy saucepan, combine the cream and vanilla bean. Cook over medium-low heat until bubbles form around the edges of the pan. In a large bowl, whisk together the egg yolks and the ⅓ cup sugar. Remove the vanilla pods from the hot cream and gradually whisk the cream into the egg mixture. Stir in the passion fruit purée.

Divide the mixture among 6 shallow ramekins. Place them in a baking pan and add water to the pan to come halfway up the sides of the ramekins. Bake for 35 to 40 minutes, or until the center is set. Remove from the oven and the water bath. Let cool for 30 minutes, then refrigerate for at least 2 hours or up to 24 hours.

To serve, evenly sprinkle 1 tablespoon sugar over the surface of each custard. Caramelize with a torch, or place under a preheated broiler for about 2 minutes, or until the sugar melts to a golden brown caramel on top. Remove from the oven and let cool for at least 10 minutes. Garnish with cookies of your choice.

OREO COOKIE MACAROONS

VOGA AT FLAMINGO LAS VEGAS
EXECUTIVE PASTRY CHEF OLIVIER CARLOS

Chef Olivier Carlos explains the inspiration behind these cunning treats: "Everyone likes Oreos! My grandmother used to give me Oreo cookies so I could dunk them in a glass of milk. My childhood came into play when I created this recipe. The outcome was a reinvention of the famous Oreo with a hint of French flair that brought it all to perfection. The taste will surprise you and make you wonder what else you can do with an Oreo cookie." Here, the all-American cookies are combined with French macaroons and brownies for a sophisticated treat.

FRENCH MACAROONS

2 cups blanched almonds

2 cups granulated sugar

4 large egg whites, lightly beaten

1 teaspoon vanilla extract

2 tablespoons crushed Oreo cookies

¼ cup confectioners' sugar

EASY SAUCEPAN BROWNIES

6 tablespoons unsalted butter

2 ounces unsweetened dark chocolate

½ teaspoon vanilla extract

1 cup granulated sugar

2 large eggs

¾ cup all-purpose flour

¼ teaspoon baking powder

¼ teaspoon salt

½ cup chopped pecans or walnuts

OREO COOKIE SANDWICH MOUSSE

2 teaspoons unflavored gelatin

2½ tablespoons water

⅓ stick unsalted butter at room temperature

½ cup cream cheese at room temperature

1 drop vanilla extract

½ tablespoon granulated sugar

1½ tablespoons sour cream

1 cup heavy cream

⅓ cup chopped Oreo cookies

½ cup semisweet chocolate, chopped

MAKES 10 COOKIES

For the macaroons: Preheat the oven to 400°F. Line a baking sheet with parchment paper.

In a food processor, combine the almonds, sugar, egg whites, and vanilla extract and pulse to a very coarse paste. Turn the food processor on high speed and blend the paste for 2 minutes, or until it is very smooth and thick. Add the Oreo pieces and continue to blend at high speed until well incorporated. Spoon the batter into a pastry bag fitted with a wide plain tip and pipe the batter into uniform 1-inch mounds on the prepared pan. Let rest, uncovered, for 15 minutes. Bake the macaroons for 12 minutes, or until slightly golden brown. Remove from the oven and transfer the macaroons from the pan to a wire rack. Let cool to room temperature. Dust with the confectioners' sugar before serving.

For the brownies: Preheat the oven to 325°F. Grease and flour a 12-inch square baking pan; knock out the excess flour. In a large, heavy saucepan, melt the butter and dark chocolate over low heat, stirring constantly until smooth. Remove from the heat and let cool. With a whisk, beat in the vanilla and sugar. Whisk in the eggs, one at a time, beating well after each addition.

In a small bowl, combine the flour, baking powder, and salt. Stir with a whisk to blend. Stir the flour mixture into the chocolate mixture. Stir in the nuts, blending well. Spoon the mixture into the prepared pan and spread evenly.

Bake for about 25 minutes, or until a toothpick comes out clean when inserted. Remove from the oven and transfer the pan to a wire rack. Let cool completely. Unmold the cake onto a cutting board. Using a 2-inch biscuit cutter, cut the brownies into 10 rounds.

For the sandwich mousse: In a small bowl, sprinkle the gelatin over the water and let stand for 5 minutes to soften. In a large bowl, cream the butter, cream cheese, vanilla, and granulated sugar together until light and fluffy, stopping once or twice to scrape down the sides and bottom of the bowl. Melt the gelatin in a microwave for 10 seconds and then mix with the sour cream. Stir the sour cream mixture into the cream cheese mixture. Whip the heavy cream to soft peaks, then fold it into the previous mixture. Fold in the Oreo pieces until just incorporated.

To assemble, pipe sandwich mousse on top of half of the macaroons. Place another macaroon on top of each to form a sandwich. Refrigerate for about 2 hours to set the mousse.

In a double boiler over barely simmering water, melt the chocolate. Remove from the heat and stir until smooth. Dip the sandwiched macaroons vertically halfway into the chocolate to coat. Place a macaroon sandwich on top of each brownie. Refrigerate for 30 minutes to set the chocolate.

TOP 10 TIPS FOR HOSTING A SEVEN STARS DINNER PARTY AT HOME

With a little creativity and the tips below, anyone can throw a Seven Stars–inspired dinner party.

1   Fun: The ultimate rule for any dinner or event is to make sure everyone has a good time and enjoys themselves.

Always remember, your guests come first. They should be enthralled by the entertainment (even if it is not live but rather a playlist you created), impressed by the decorations, absolutely captivated by the other guests (always invite an interesting group of people with many different interests and professions), and, of course, your guests should enjoy every bite of the food you serve.

2   Expenses: It's not essential to spend a lot of money on your dinner, but the ingredients should be the best available and the setting should be comfortable and memorable for your guests.

3   Day of the week: Choose a day that will work for all the guests you want to attend. A cocktail party or fund-raising dinner may work well during the week when people can attend after work, but larger gala-type dinners and relaxing dinner parties with friends should be reserved for Friday and Saturday nights when no one has to get up early the next day.

4   Time: The starting time for your dinner is just as important as what day you choose. The best time to start is usually between 6 and 8 P.M.—early enough for after-work cocktails on weeknights, and not so early that guests will feel rushed on weekends.

5   Weather: The season and local weather forecast will help you decide if your dinner should be indoors or outdoors. The goal is to make sure your guests are comfortable, and not too hot or too cold. If you are planning an outdoor dinner, make sure you have back-up plans in case Mother Nature decides to throw you a curveball.

6   Décor: Place settings and centerpieces can enchant your guests and give them an experience they'll never forget. Draw your inspiration for décor from nature, specific occasions, and your own imagination.

7   Music: The right music will always enhance your dining event. Know your guests, and play music they will enjoy and appreciate; also make sure the music suits the occasion.

8   Help: If you can, hire someone to assist you with your event, either in the kitchen or serving. This will give you more time to enjoy yourself with your guests.

9   Menu: Give your menu great thought and attention, use the freshest products you can find, and make sure the food for your event is the best it can possibly be.

10 Plan, plan, plan: To ensure the best results for your event, you need to think ahead. Make the guest list and shopping lists for food, drinks, and decorations; schedule when you will clean the house and decorate it for the event; decide when and how to send out invitations; create a music playlist; plan your wardrobe; and make a schedule of when to start and finish each dish on the menu so that all the food can be served at the right time.

CHOCOLATE FUN-DO

VOGA AT FLAMINGO LAS VEGAS
EXECUTIVE PASTRY CHEF OLIVIER CARLOS

Chocolate Fun-Do takes chocolate fondue to a new level: In place of fruit, mini cheesecakes in a variety of flavors are dipped into warm chocolate sauce. Chef Olivier Carlos comments, "This dish was created to give you and your guests the feeling of being at a party right in your own backyard." Serve this dish as a fun ending to any dinner party.

CHEESECAKES

Four 8-ounce packages cream cheese at room temperature

1 cup sugar

⅓ cup unsalted butter, melted

1 teaspoon vanilla extract

4 large eggs

½ cup mango purée

½ cup raspberry purée

3 ounces bittersweet chocolate, melted

2 tablespoons coffee powder

1 tablespoon pistachio paste (found in specialty foods stores)

HOT CHOCOLATE SAUCE

6 tablespoons unsalted butter

1 cup water

1¼ cups heavy cream

3½ tablespoons honey

14 ounces bittersweet chocolate, chopped

3½ tablespoons dark rum

SERVES 8

For the cheesecakes: Preheat the oven to 300°F. Oil two 12-cup muffin pans. In an electric mixer, beat the cream cheese, sugar, butter, and vanilla on medium speed until the mixture is well blended. Add the eggs, one at a time, mixing on low speed after each addition just until blended.

Divide the batter equally among 5 small bowls. Add the mango purée to one bowl, the raspberry purée to a second bowl, the chocolate to a third, the coffee powder to a fourth, and the pistachio paste to the fifth bowl. Stir each to blend. Divide among the prepared muffin cups and bake until set, 30 minutes. Remove from the oven and let cool completely. Unmold onto a baking sheet and refrigerate for 1 hour.

For the chocolate sauce: In a heavy, medium saucepan, melt the butter over medium-low heat. Add the water, cream, and honey, and bring to a simmer over medium-high heat. Put the chocolate in a medium bowl and pour the hot cream over. Let stand for 1 minute, then stir until smooth. Stir in the rum.

To serve, cut the cheesecakes in half. Pour the chocolate sauce into a fondue bowl or other heavy bowl. Using fondue forks, dip the cheesecake pieces into the sauce.

NUMBER OF CUPCAKES SOLD ANNUALLY
IN THE EAT UP! BUFFET AT HARRAH'S ST. LOUIS:

BOSTON CREAM • 21,000

CUPCAKE OF THE MONTH • 3,000

GERMAN CHOCOLATE • 22,500

CARROT • 22,000

OREO • 17,000

TOTAL • 85,500

COCONUT PANNA COTTA

WITH RUM-FLAMED BERRIES

THE POOL AT HARRAH'S RESORT ATLANTIC CITY
EXECUTIVE CHEF EDWARD DAGGERS, ATLANTIC CITY COUNTRY CLUB

The exquisite Italian gelled dessert is given a tropical accent here with coconut milk and rum in place of the usual milk and cream. The rum-flamed berries provide just the right finishing touch. Chef Edward Daggers suggests, "This panna cotta works well as a dessert or a side dish with fruit or salad, or it could be served with a fruit purée." At The Pool at Harrah's, it's sometimes served with a tropical fruit salad.

PANNA COTTA

2 cups well-shaken canned coconut milk

1½ cups sugar

2 envelopes unflavored gelatin

1 cup whole milk

½ cup dark rum

1 teaspoon vanilla extract

RUM-FLAMED BERRIES

3 tablespoons unsalted butter

2 cups mixed fresh strawberries, blackberries, and raspberries

1 tablespoon brown sugar

¼ cup dark rum

2 tablespoons coconut, toasted (optional; see page 261)

4 to 6 mint sprigs (optional)

SERVES 4 TO 6

For the panna cotta: In a large, heavy saucepan, combine the coconut milk and sugar. Bring to a low simmer over medium heat.

In a medium saucepan, sprinkle the gelatin into the whole milk and bring to a low simmer over medium heat. Stir in the rum. Add this mixture to the coconut milk mixture, return to a simmer, and cook for 5 minutes. Remove from the heat and pour into a serving bowl or glass. Stir in the vanilla. Let cool for 20 minutes, then cover and refrigerate until set, about 4 hours.

For the berries: In a medium sauté pan or skillet, melt 2 tablespoons of the butter over medium heat until foaming. Add the berries and brown sugar and sauté for 1 minute. Turn off the heat and add the rum, stirring well. Standing back from the stove, light the rum with a long match or long-handled lighter. Using caution, shake the pan until the flames subside. Return to medium heat and cook to reduce for 2 minutes. Stir in the remaining 1 tablespoon butter.

To serve, spoon the panna cotta into bowls and top with the berries. Garnish with the coconut and mint sprigs, if desired.

POLISTINA'S AT HARRAH'S RESORT ATLANTIC CITY REPORTS TIRAMISÙ AS THE MOST POPULAR DESSERT ON THE MENU.

TIRAMISÙ

JACK BINION'S STEAK HOUSE AT HORSESHOE HAMMOND
ASSISTANT PASTRY CHEF MARY THERESE PRIESOL

In chef Mary Therese Priesol's version of this famous Italian sweet, ladyfingers are dipped in a mixture of espresso and Kahlúa instead of Marsala, and the mascarpone cream is flavored with rum. Chef Mary Therese says, "This layered Italian dessert is a classic and has been for many years here at the Horseshoe. The creamy texture, with the slight taste of rum, combined with the espresso and Kahlúa—soaked cookies is a timeless dessert that is sure to leave a lasting impression on your dining experience."

MASCARPONE CREAM

4 cups heavy cream

5 large egg yolks

¾ cup sugar

1 pound mascarpone cheese at room temperature

⅓ cup light rum

4 cups cold brewed espresso

½ cup Kahlúa

70 to 90 ladyfingers

4 ounces bittersweet chocolate, cut into shavings

Unsweetened cocoa powder for dusting

SERVES 8

For the mascarpone cream: In a large bowl, whip the cream to stiff peaks. In another large bowl, combine the egg yolks, sugar, and mascarpone cheese and beat until light in color. Add the rum to the mascarpone mixture and beat until combined. Fold the whipped cream into the mascarpone mixture until blended.

In a shallow bowl, combine the espresso and Kahlúa. Line an 8-by-10-inch baking pan with plastic wrap, allowing extra plastic wrap to hang over two sides of the pan. Dip 2 or 3 ladyfingers in the espresso mixture and place in the bottom of the prepared pan, making sure all the ladyfingers are pointing in the same direction. Repeat to line the entire bottom of the pan in one layer.

Spread half of the mascarpone cream evenly on top of the soaked ladyfingers. Make another layer of ladyfingers on top of the cream, soaking 2 or 3 at a time and pointing them in the same direction as the bottom layer. In the same fashion, make a third layer, placing the ladyfingers at right angles to the ones in the second layer. Add the remaining mascarpone cream and smooth the top. Sprinkle with the chocolate shavings. Cover in plastic wrap and refrigerate for 12 hours.

Remove from the refrigerator 30 minutes before serving. Unmold by lifting the two sides of the plastic wrap to remove the dessert. Remove the plastic wrap. Cut the tiramisù into slices and serve on dessert plates; dust edges of plates with cocoa powder.

VARIATION

To prepare tiramisùs as in the photo, use eight 2½-inch-wide by 3-inch-tall ring molds. Line the outside of each ring mold with plastic wrap to come halfway up the sides. Dip the ladyfingers into the espresso mixture and line the bottom of each mold with one layer, breaking them as needed to make them fit. Spread about ¼ cup mascarpone mixture evenly on top of the ladyfingers. Repeat to make three layers of cookies and mascarpone mixture in each mold. Freeze for 4 hours. To unmold, dip a plastic-wrapped mold into a bowl of hot water for about 5 seconds; remove immediately. Remove the plastic wrap and let the tiramisù slide out of the mold onto a plate. Beat about 2 cups heavy cream until soft peaks form. Pipe a little whipped cream on the flat side of a ladyfinger and press it vertically against the side of the tiramisù. Repeat to line the desserts. Omit the chocolate shavings and finish with sifted cocoa.

SEVEN SISTERS LOUNGE
ORANGE CAKE

SEVEN SISTERS LOUNGE AT HARRAH'S CHEROKEE
EXECUTIVE CHEF KEITH ANDREASEN

Vibrant in both color and taste, this orange cake is welcome year-round, but especially in winter when oranges are at their peak of flavor. Chef Keith Andreasen notes, "This cake is great with many dishes."

CAKE

1½ cups cake flour

¾ cup granulated sugar

1½ teaspoons baking powder

½ teaspoon salt

¼ teaspoon cream of tartar

¼ cup water

¼ cup canola oil

3 large eggs, separated

3 tablespoons fresh orange juice

½ teaspoon grated lemon zest

ORANGE CREAM CHEESE FROSTING

1½ cups (12 ounces) cream cheese at room temperature

1 teaspoon grated orange zest

2 tablespoons plus 2 teaspoons fresh orange juice

¾ cup sifted confectioners' sugar

3 drops yellow food coloring

3 drops red food coloring

2 oranges, segmented (see page 51)

MAKES ONE 10-INCH CAKE;
SERVES 6 TO 8

For the cake: Preheat the oven to 350°F. In a large bowl, sift together the flour, sugar, baking powder, salt, and cream of tartar. Make a well in the center of the dry ingredients. Add the water, oil, egg yolks, orange juice, and lemon zest. Beat until smooth. In a large bowl, beat the egg whites until soft peaks form. Gradually fold the egg whites into the cake batter with a rubber spatula until blended. Pour the batter into an ungreased 10-by-2-inch round cake pan and smooth the top. Bake for 25 to 30 minutes or until golden and a toothpick inserted in the center comes out clean.

Remove the cake from the oven and let cool completely in the pan on a wire rack. To unmold, run a knife around the edges of the pan and invert on a plate. With a long serrated knife, cut the cake into 2 horizontal layers.

For the frosting: In a large bowl, beat the cream cheese until fluffy. Add the orange zest and juice. Gradually blend in the confectioners' sugar until well blended. Add the yellow and red food coloring and blend well. Put ½ cup of the frosting in a separate bowl. Reserve 6 to 8 orange segments and drain them in a colander. Coarsely chop the remaining orange segments and stir them into the ½ cup frosting. Spread this filling on one layer of the cake. Top with the second layer of cake and frost the top and sides with the remaining frosting.

To serve, garnish each portion with an orange segment.

EIFFEL TOWER RASPBERRY SOUFFLÉS

EIFFEL TOWER RESTAURANT AT PARIS LAS VEGAS
CHEF JEAN JOHO

Chef Jean Joho says: "The Eiffel Tower Restaurant is famous for its soufflés, and we serve thousands of them every year. We always have at least ten different flavors at the restaurant, depending on the season. Guests love watching these being made at the dessert station in the kitchen." Although this recipe is for raspberry soufflés, perfect for spring and summer, it can be varied to reflect the season or your whim, such as pumpkin in the fall or mandarin orange in the winter, or chocolate, Grand Marnier, and pistachio any time of the year.

Note: The soufflé base needs to be refrigerated at least 4 hours or overnight before cooking.

SOUFFLÉ BASE

4 cups whole milk

2 large eggs

18 large egg yolks

3 tablespoons plus 1 teaspoon sugar

1½ cups all-purpose flour

6 tablespoons cornstarch

3½ tablespoons cold unsalted butter, cut into cubes

8 large egg whites

2 tablespoons sugar

½ teaspoon cream of tartar

¼ cup puréed fresh or frozen raspberries

¼ cup Chambord liqueur

Confectioners' sugar for dusting

Vanilla sauce for serving (recipe follows)

MAKES 6 INDIVIDUAL SOUFFLÉS

For the soufflé base: In a medium saucepan, bring the milk to a boil over high heat, then turn off the heat. In a large bowl, combine the eggs, egg yolks, and sugar and whisk until blended. Combine the flour and cornstarch in a small bowl. Stir with a small whisk to blend. Add two-thirds of the flour mixture to the egg mixture and whisk to blend. Whisk in 1 cup of the hot milk. Add the remaining flour mixture and whisk until smooth (the mixture should be fairly liquid). Bring the remaining milk to a boil again and add it to the egg mixture all at once, whisking constantly until smooth. Immediately whisk in the butter until fully incorporated. The mixture should have the consistency of heavy cream. Let cool. Cover and refrigerate for at least 4 hours or, preferably, overnight (the base will perform better after it has rested for a day).

Preheat the oven to 375°F. Butter and sugar six 4½-ounce ramekins, tapping each to remove the excess sugar. In a large bowl, beat the egg whites until frothy. Gradually beat in the sugar and cream of tartar and continue beating until soft peaks form.

Stir the raspberry purée and liqueur into the soufflé base. Add about one-fourth of the beaten whites to the soufflé base and stir to combine. Fold in the remaining whites with a rubber spatula until just incorporated. Divide the batter among the ramekins. Place the ramekins in a baking pan, then place the baking pan in the oven and carefully pour boiling water into the pan to reach halfway up the sides of the ramekins. Bake for 20 minutes, or until puffed and golden brown.

Immediately transfer each ramekin to a serving plate, dust with confectioners' sugar, and serve with the vanilla sauce on the side. Each guest should crack open the top of his or her soufflé with a spoon, then pour about 2 tablespoons of the sauce into the soufflé.

Vanilla Sauce: In a small saucepan, combine 1 cup milk and ½ vanilla bean, split lengthwise, and cook over medium heat until bubbles form around the edges of the pan. Remove from the heat and remove the vanilla bean. Whisk 3 egg yolks and 3 tablespoons sugar together in a small bowl. Gradually whisk ¼ cup of the hot milk into the egg yolks, then whisk in the remaining milk. Return to the pan and cook over medium-low heat, stirring constantly, until the mixture coats the back of the spoon. Makes about 1 cup.

VARIATIONS

Pumpkin Soufflés: Replace the raspberry purée and the liqueur with ¼ cup pumpkin purée and ½ cup Southern Comfort.

+++++++++++

Mandarin Orange Soufflés: Replace the raspberry purée with mandarin purée (found in specialty foods stores or online) and the liqueur with ¼ cup mandarin liqueur or mandarin vodka.

+++++++++++

Chocolate Soufflés: Replace the raspberry purée with ¼ cup shaved dark chocolate and the liqueur with ¼ cup coffee liqueur.

+++++++++++

Grand Marnier Soufflés: Delete the raspberry purée and replace the liqueur with ¼ cup Grand Marnier.

+++++++++++

Pistachio Soufflés: Replace the raspberry purée with ¼ cup pistachio paste (found in specialty foods stores or online) and the liqueur with ¼ cup amaretto liqueur.

12

HIGH ROLLERS' BAR

ABSINTHE SAZERAC

BESH STEAK AT HARRAH'S NEW ORLEANS
CHEF JOHN BESH

Now that absinthe is once again legal in the United States, Besh Steak has restored the classic New Orleans Sazerac to its original recipe by using Absinthe Superior for the rinse instead of an anise-flavored liquor substitute.

Absinthe Superior, preferably Versinthe, for rinsing

Ice cubes

3 ounces rye whiskey, such as Old Overholt

Splash of Peychaud's bitters

Splash of simple syrup (recipe follows)

1 lemon twist

Rinse a rocks glass with the absinthe. In a cocktail shaker filled with ice, combine the whiskey, bitters, and simple syrup. Shake vigorously and strain into the rinsed glass. Garnish with the lemon twist.

Simple Syrup: Combine 1 cup sugar and 1 cup water in a small, heavy saucepan and bring to a boil over low heat, stirring to dissolve the sugar. Boil for 1 minute, then remove from the heat and let cool completely. Store in a tightly covered glass container in the refrigerator indefinitely. Makes about 1⅓ cups.

SERVES 1

BESH STEAK BOASTS AN ORIGINAL "BLUE DOG" PAINTING BY GEORGE RODRIGUE.

GERMAN CHOCOLATE CAKE

VIP LOUNGES & HIGH LIMIT BAR AT HARRAH'S LAKE TAHOE & HARVEYS LAKE TAHOE
BEVERAGE MANAGER CHARLOTTE ROGERS

German chocolate cake in a glass: coconut rum, crème de cacao, and hazelnut liqueur. Serve this drink in place of dessert and win the hearts of your guests.

¾ ounce Malibu coconut rum

¾ ounce white crème de cacao

¼ ounce Frangelico liqueur

Splash of half-and-half

Ice cubes

Sweetened whipped cream, unsweetened cocoa powder, and 1 maraschino cherry for garnish

In a cocktail shaker, combine the rum, crème de cacao, Frangelico, and half-and-half. Shake well and strain over ice cubes in a chilled hurricane glass. Garnish with whipped cream, dust with cocoa, and top with the cherry.

SERVES 1

HIGH ROLLERS' BAR

SEX IN THE BIGGEST LITTLE CITY

SAPPHIRE AT HARRAH'S RENO
ASSISTANT BEVERAGE MANAGER MICHAEL BAYS

The Reno ("Biggest Little City in the World") version of *Sex and the City's* Cosmo adds peach schnapps and pineapple juice to make a refreshing cocktail. It's also Sapphire's best-selling drink out of the long list on their menu.

Peach sugar for rimming glass (found at liquor stores)
Ice cubes
1 ounce Absolut vodka
1 ounce peach schnapps
1 ounce cranberry juice
1 ounce pineapple juice

Pour some peach sugar on a saucer. Wet the rim of a Cosmo glass and dip it in the sugar to coat. In a cocktail shaker filled with ice, combine the vodka, schnapps, and two juices. Shake well and strain into the prepared glass.

SERVES 1

> THE STEAKHOUSE AT HARRAH'S RESORT ATLANTIC CITY WON THE 2009 *WINE SPECTATOR* AWARD OF EXCELLENCE FOR HAVING ONE OF THE BEST WINE LISTS IN THE COUNTRY.

OASIS TROPICAL TREAT

HARRAH'S AK-CHIN
BEVERAGE SUPERVISOR JOSEPH CARUSO

You can't go wrong when pineapple juice meets refreshing melon, citrus, and coconut flavors. Ak-Chin's beverage supervisor Joseph Caruso says, "Escaping to paradise never tasted so good, or was so easy!"

Ice cubes
½ ounce Absolut Citron vodka
1 ounce Malibu rum
½ ounce melon liqueur
3 ounces pineapple juice
Splash of sweet and sour mix
Splash of Sierra Mist soft drink
1 maraschino cherry for garnish

Fill a 9-ounce cocktail glass with ice. Pour the vodka, rum, liqueur, juice, sweet and sour, and soft drink over the ice. Stir, and garnish with the cherry.

SERVES 1

MINT JULEP

Fresh mint and bourbon in a traditional silver tumbler make this cocktail a favorite all year-round. Use an ultra-premium small-batch bourbon to put this drink over the top. Chef Jon M. Kell suggests, "To begin your search for that unforgettable bourbon, check out www.smallbatch.com."

8 fresh mint leaves, plus 1 sprig

1½ tablespoons simple syrup (see page 289)

1½ ounces bourbon

¼ teaspoon Angostura bitters

Shaved ice

SERVES 1

In a blender, combine the mint leaves, simple syrup, bourbon, and bitters and blend on high speed until the mint is puréed. Strain into a silver tumbler or other decorative glass packed with shaved ice. Garnish with the mint sprig.

PARROTHEAD-CHEF MARGARITA

Chef Keith Andreasen named his version of the Margarita after himself: "I'm a huge Jimmy Buffett fan, or what is known as a 'parrothead.' Whenever there's a Buffett concert going on, you can count on me being there with several blenders of these margaritas. And if I'm having a cookout at my house, everyone looks forward to these margaritas being served."

Salt for rimming the glasses

One 6-ounce can frozen limeade, preferably Minute Maid

2 tablespoons fresh lemon juice

¼ cup sugar

6 ounces Margaritaville tequila (white or gold, depending on your preference)

2 ounces Grand Marnier liqueur

6 ounces water

¾ cup ice cubes

4 orange wedges for garnish

SERVES 4

Pour some salt into a saucer, moisten the rim of a margarita glass, and dip it in the salt to coat. In a blender, combine the limeade, lemon juice, sugar, tequila, Grand Marnier, and water, blending until smooth. Add the ice and blend. Pour into a pitcher and add more ice and water, if desired. Serve with the salt-rimmed glasses, garnished with the orange wedges.

TOP 10 TIPS
FOR PAIRING WINE AND FOOD

1   Match the weight of the dish with the body of the wine. White wine is usually best with fish and white meat while red wine works with red meat. Achieving balance is the main goal.

2   Salty and fatty foods require wines that are high in acidity, such as Chablis, Pinot Grigio, Chianti, and Sauvignon Blanc (my personal favorite is Staete Landt Sauvignon Blanc, from New Zealand.)

3   Foods served with tomato sauces require red wines that are high in acidity, such as Chianti and Barbera.

4   Duck or goose will taste less fatty with younger, tannic wines. Rare meats are also best served with younger, tannic wines.

5   Well-done meats are best served with more mature, less tannic wines.

6   Spicy foods are best served with wines that are low in acidity. For example, Gewürztraminer or sweet Riesling wines are perfect with Asian cuisine. However, if the food is very spicy, go with beer.

7   The dessert wine should always be sweeter than the dessert, otherwise it will taste tart.

8   For dinners with multiple courses, serve light wines before heavier wines, dry wines before sweet, and young wines before old.

9   Never serve white wines too cold or red wines too warm. Use the Fifteen-Minute Rule: Take whites from the fridge 15 minutes before serving. And, unless your reds are in a cellar, refrigerate them for 15 minutes before serving.

10 Champagne, the most versatile wine, can be served with every course.

Bonus tip

Regional wines match best with regional foods.

TOP 10 TIPS
FOR PAIRING BEER AND FOOD

It may seem odd for a sommelier to compile a list of beer matches, but there are times when only beer will satisfy. Every beer has its perfect moment, and that is the essence of refreshment, isn't it?

1 A savory starter: Some sharp, acidic cheeses are meant to be served with more acidic beers, such as Belgian Gueuze. These beers are elegance, complexity, and finesse in a bottle.

2 Shellfish: Since Victorian times, the English have enjoyed a Guinness with a plate of oysters. A dry porter or stout can work with a variety of shellfish, such as mussels, clams, scallops, and other crustaceans.

3 Smoked food: Not surprisingly, beers malted over an open flame pair well with the smoked foods and preserved meats found on a charcuterie platter. Try a Rauchbier, a Stone beer, or a smoked porter.

4 Fish: Serve a fine Pilsner or a clean, golden lager. Their fresh palates don't overwhelm the delicate flavor of fish.

5 White meats: Red beers are a perfect partner for lighter meats, whatever the cooking method. Some red beers have a spicy sweetness that can stand up to roasted fowl or pancetta-laced pasta.

6 Beef: Something with a bolder profile is needed in this match. As in Old World/New World wines, there are two distinct styles of pale ale. From the United Kingdom, you'll find Burton-style ales with a light maltiness and a hint of cedar. These are satisfying when accompanying steak and frites. The ales from North America are somewhat more assertive and lively, often displaying an orange-fruit edge.

7 Pizza: Go for something with a nutty, yeasty aroma. It's a symbiotic relationship if ever there was one. North American red ales and Vienna lagers come to mind.

8 Fruity desserts: Fruit beers work well with those fruit-based desserts. Think of a raspberry lambic paired with glazed raspberry flan. Heaven.

9 Chocolate and coffee: Here, pull out all the stops and look for a big, rich, not-too-dry stout. Nothing else will mirror the powerful flavors of bittersweet chocolate quite so harmoniously. Some stouts actually have chocolate and espresso added as flavorings.

10 Digestifs: Beer can work here as well. Try a double bock, Abbey-style dark ale, or barley wine. These tend to start out very dense and creamy, evolving into an almost Armagnac-like pruniness and finishing some-what dry. All have a propensity toward 8 percent and higher alcohol.

CUCUMBER-MINT SPLASH

THE STEAKHOUSE AT HARRAH'S RESORT ATLANTIC CITY
BEVERAGE OPERATIONS MANAGER JOSEPH CRILLEY

Muddled mint, minced cucumber, and vodka create a cool cocktail for warm days.

Sugar for rimming

4 fresh mint leaves

One ½-inch-thick slice peeled cucumber, finely chopped

Ice cubes

1½ ounces vodka

Club soda as needed

SERVES 1

Pour sugar into a saucer. Moisten the rim of a 12-ounce glass and dip in the sugar to coat the rim. Muddle the mint leaves in the glass. Add the cucumber. Fill the glass with ice. Add the vodka and top off the glass with club soda. Stir and serve.

THE STEAKHOUSE AT HARRAH'S RESORT
IS ALSO HOME TO THE BLUEPOINT RAW BAR,
VOTED BEST SEAFOOD BAR IN ATLANTIC CITY IN 2008
BY *CASINO PLAYER* MAGAZINE.

JEWEL OF THE DESERT

HARRAH'S AK-CHIN
BEVERAGE SUPERVISOR JOSEPH CARUSO

Enjoying this bright blue drink is like finding fresh water in the desert. It's just the cocktail to sip while relaxing by the pool.

Ice cubes

1 ounce Malibu rum

1 ounce blue curaçao

4 ounces sweet and sour mix

Splash of Sierra Mist soft drink

1 lime wedge for garnish

SERVES 1

Fill a 9-ounce cocktail glass with ice. Pour the ingredients over, stir, and garnish with the lime wedge.

HIGH ROLLERS' BAR

GOODNIGHT KISS MARTINI

TOBY KEITH'S I LOVE THIS BAR & GRILL AT HARRAH'S LAS VEGAS
TOBY KEITH & ENTERTAINMENT FLAIR BARTENDER ROB VERGARA

Finish off a great evening in style with this delectable combination of citrus vodka, vanilla vodka, and Cointreau. But be warned—this drink is so good, you may feel like having more than one Goodnight Kiss.

Sugar

Ice cubes

1 ounce citrus vodka

½ ounce vanilla vodka

1 splash Cointreau liqueur

2 ounces sweet and sour mix

Dash of sugar

Juice of ½ lemon

Lemon twist, cinnamon stick, and maraschino cherry for garnish

Pour some sugar onto a saucer. Moisten the rim of a martini glass and dip it in the sugar to coat the rim. In a cocktail shaker filled with ice, combine the vodkas, Cointreau, sweet and sour, sugar, and lemon juice. Shake well and strain into the sugar-rimmed glass. Garnish with the lemon twist and cinnamon stick.

SERVES 1

CARNAVAL COURT, AN OUTDOOR BAR AT HARRAH'S LAS VEGAS, EMPLOYS MORE CHAMPION FLAIR BARTENDERS THAN ANY PLACE ON THE LAS VEGAS STRIP, AND IT HAS NO DRESS CODE!

INVISIBLE HOMBRE

BAJA BLUE RESTAURANT & CANTINA AT HARRAH'S LAUGHLIN
BEVERAGE MANAGER DEBORAH ORAM

Take your party guests south of the border with the lemon-lime delight of this simple-to-make drink. Baja Blue's beverage manager Deborah Oram says, "The Invisible Hombre has really surprised our guests with the fresh twist it offers."

Ice cubes

1½ ounces José Cuervo white tequila

½ ounce fresh lime juice

½ ounce fresh lemon juice

Splash of tonic water

SERVES 1

Fill a cocktail shaker with ice and add the tequila and two juices. Shake well and strain into a rocks glass. Add the tonic.

GULF COAST BLOODY MARY

GRAND BILOXI CASINO, HOTEL & SPA
EXECUTIVE CHEF JASON CARLISLE

A perfect drink for the Gulf Coast: a spicy Bloody Mary garnished with an array of favorite regional foods. Chef Jason Carlisle comments, "This drink is more like a lagniappe than a beverage, but either way you take it, it is phenomenal!" The recipe makes a pitcherful for your next brunch or backyard cookout.

1½ cups tomato juice

¾ cup vodka

1½ tablespoons fresh lemon juice

1½ tablespoons fresh lime juice

1 tablespoon prepared horseradish
sauce

1½ teaspoons Worcestershire sauce

2 teaspoons hot sauce

1 teaspoon Old Bay Seasoning

½ teaspoon salt

½ teaspoon freshly ground black pepper

¼ teaspoon cayenne pepper

GARNISH

24 crawfish tails

2 to 3 shakes Tabasco sauce per drink

12 pitted green olives

6 pickled or cooked green beans

6 pickled or fresh okra pods

6 extra-large shrimp, shelled, deveined,
and steamed

12 cooked blue crab claws

SERVES 6

In a pitcher, combine all the ingredients except the garnish, stirring to combine. Refrigerate until well-chilled, about 1 hour.

For the garnish: In a small bowl, combine the crawfish tails and Tabasco. Toss to coat. Wearing rubber gloves, stuff 2 crawfish tails into each green olive. Pour the drink into rock glasses filled with ice. Divide the garnish evenly among the glasses and serve.

HARRAHCANE

MASQUERADE AT HARRAH'S NEW ORLEANS
BEVERAGE SUPERVISOR RICKIE DEANO

Southern Comfort, coconut rum, fruit juices, and grenadine join forces to create this potent drink, which can be served on the rocks or frozen. Harrahcane warning: You may want more than one.

1¼ ounces Southern Comfort whiskey

1¼ ounces Cruzan coconut rum

2 ounces orange juice

2 ounces pineapple juice

1 ounce fruit punch

Dash of grenadine

Ice cubes

SERVES 1

In a cocktail shaker, combine the whiskey, rum, juices, punch, and grenadine. Shake well and pour over ice in a Collins glass.

Frozen Harrahcane: Combine all the ingredients in a blender and blend until frozen.

CLOUD NINE

VOODOO LOUNGE AT HARRAH'S NORTH KANSAS CITY
MANAGER AARON LUND

VooDoo Lounge manager Aaron Lund comments, "Our players enjoy having a perfect meal and have been known to drink their desserts from time to time." The versatile Cloud Nine can be served either hot or cold. This version of the classic drink adds nocello, a walnut liqueur, to give flavor and depth to an already smooth libation.

½ ounce Frangelico liqueur

3 ounces Skyy vodka

½ ounce nocello liqueur

1 ounce chocolate syrup

4 cups cold brewed coffee

1 cup milk

10 ice cubes

2 tablespoons sugar

Whipped cream for garnish

In a blender, combine all the ingredients except the garnish. Blend until the ice cubes are crushed. Pour into a tall, footed coffee mug and top with a generous portion of whipped cream.

VARIATION

To serve the Cloud Nine hot, use hot coffee and steamed milk; delete the ice and the blender. Combine the hot coffee and milk in the coffee mug with all the other ingredients except the garnish; stir to blend, then top with the whipped cream.

SERVES 4

THE VOODOO LOUNGE HAS HOSTED PERFORMERS INCLUDING JAMES BROWN, THE BLACK CROWES, AND WAYNE NEWTON IN AN INTIMATE CONCERT VENUE WITH STATE-OF-THE-ART SOUND AND LIGHTING.

RASPBERRY LEMONADE

CARNAVAL COURT BAR & GRILL AT HARRAH'S LAS VEGAS
ENTERTAINMENT FLAIR BARTENDER JOSHUA A. NEMEROW

Bartender Joshua A. Nemerow explains the origin of this popular drink: "I was inspired to make this drink while I was backpacking in Canada. I was on a trail that was surrounded by fresh raspberries, which I collected in a bag to snack on later down the trail. While setting up camp, I was drinking lemonade and snacking on the raspberries, which made me think that this would be a great combination to explore with liquor when I returned to my real job as a bartender in Las Vegas. Once I returned home, I played around with the combination of flavors and ended up creating the Raspberry Lemonade. I think it is perfect for quenching your thirst on a hot summer day, while daydreaming of your next vacation."

Ice cubes
1½ ounces Bacardi Limón rum
½ ounce Chambord liqueur
3 ounces sweet and sour mix
Juice of ½ lime
Fresh raspberries for garnish
1 lime wedge for garnish

SERVES 1

Fill a cocktail shaker with ice and add all the ingredients except the raspberries and lime wedge. Shake well and strain into a Collins glass with ice cubes. Garnish with the raspberries and lime wedge.

TAHOE WABO
LAKE TAHOE'S TRADEMARK MARGARITA

SAMMY HAGAR'S THE CABO WABO CANTINA AT HARVEYS LAKE TAHOE
RESTAURANT MANAGER KEVIN MCGIRK

Harveys Lake Tahoe reimagines the classic margarita, Tahoe-style, using legendary rocker Sammy Hagar's signature Cabo Wabo blanco tequila.

Ice cubes
1½ ounces Cabo Wabo blanco tequila
½ ounce Triple Sec
Sweet and sour mix
Splash of Chambord liqueur
1 lime wedge for garnish

SERVES 1

Fill a 12- to 14-ounce margarita glass or a 12-ounce double rocks glass with ice and add the tequila and Triple Sec. Fill the remainder of the glass with the sweet and sour mix and stir to mix. Add the Chambord and garnish with the lime wedge. Serve with a straw.

TOP 10 TIPS FOR CHOOSING THE RIGHT MUSIC FOR YOUR DINING EVENT

HORSESHOE COUNCIL BLUFFS

1. Cocktail party: More than just about any other event, a cocktail party naturally lends itself to background music. For perfect cocktail-party music, try one of Michael Bublé's albums, such as *Call Me Irresponsible, Come Fly with Me*, or *It's Time.*

2. Romantic candlelight dinner: To put the finishing touch on your next romantic evening, I recommend anything by Frank Sinatra. The album *Sinatra: Nothing But the Best* is a good place to start.

3. Wine dinner: For music on the soft side, I would go with pieces by Norah Jones, such as "Come Away With Me" and "Not Too Late."

4. BBQ cookout: Enjoy Jimmy Buffett's music while hanging out at the beach, around the pool, or if you just want to chill. "Cheeseburger in Paradise," "Margaritaville," "Come Monday," and "It's Five O'Clock Somewhere" will never go out of style.

5. Italian dinner: Are you ordering pizza tonight? Why not kick it up a bit? Add a red and white checkered tablecloth, candles, a straw-wrapped bottle of Chianti, and a musical selection that includes "O Sole Mio," "That's Amore," "Volare," and "Santa Lucia." It'll make pizza or pasta night at your house something special.

6. Latin dinner: Arturo Sandoval & The Latin Train's energetic beats will get you grooving at your Latin-themed dinner with songs like "Be-Bop," "La Guarapachanga," and "The Latin Trane."

7. Louisiana Cajun dinner: Gumbo, jambalaya, dirty rice, beignets, corn bread and biscuits, and shrimp, crab, and crawfish boil all call out for The Jambalaya Trio's *Jazz Brunch at the Pizza on the Park*, with songs like "Way Down Yonder in New Orleans," "Rose Room," and "Poor Butterfly," or the Jambalaya Cajun Band's *C'est Fun*, with "C'est Fun (It's Fun)," "Jig Cadien (The Cajun Jig)," and "Oh, Ma Belle (Oh, My Belle)."

8. Fiesta dinner party: What would a fiesta be without a mariachi band? Originating in Mexico, a mariachi band is usually made up of a spirited grouping of violins, trumpets, a Spanish guitar, a vihuela (a high-pitched five-string guitar), and a guitarrón (a small-scaled acoustic bass). To add an authentic flair to your fiesta, play some selections from Plácido Domingo's *100 Years of Mariachi*. If that isn't setting the right mood, change it up with the classic sounds of Los Lobos, Ritchie Valens, or Los Lonely Boys.

9. Luau: The music you choose for your Hawaiian luau can be either traditional Hawaiian music or fun beach party music. I also suggest choosing some selections from the man who is synonymous with Hawaiian music, Don Ho. Start with Don Ho's *Hawaii's Greatest Hits, Hawaiian Favorites*, and *A Night in Hawaii with Don Ho*. For beach party music, you can never go wrong with anything by the Beach Boys, including *Sounds of Summer: The Very Best of the Beach Boys, Summer Love Songs*, and *Good Vibrations: Thirty Years of the Beach Boys* box set.

10. Chinese New Year dinner: Chinese New Year music is played on Chinese drums and other traditional instruments. Musical selections for your celebration might include pieces from Heart of the Dragon Ensemble's *Chinese New Years Music*, including "Celebration," "Lion Dance," and "New Year Is Coming."

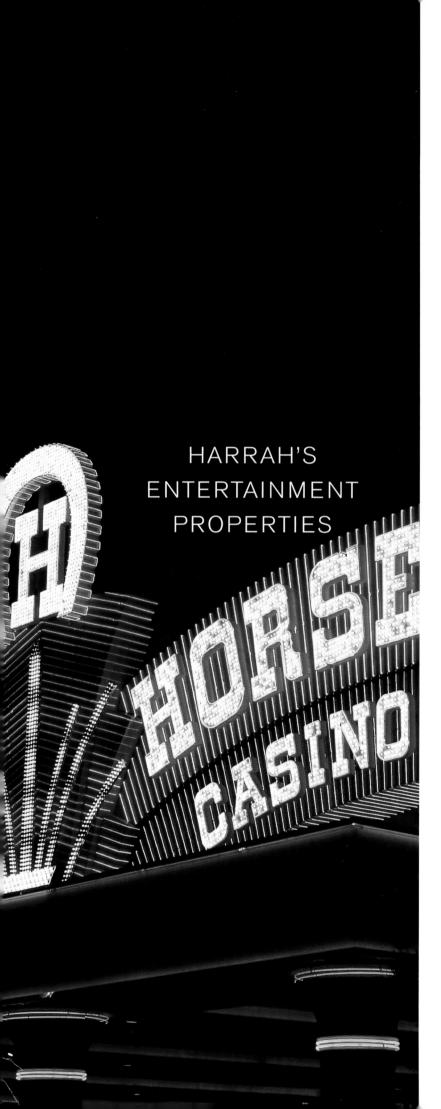

HARRAH'S
ENTERTAINMENT
PROPERTIES

Bally's Atlantic City
Park Place and the Boardwalk
Atlantic City, NJ 08401
609-340-2000
www.ballysac.com

Bally's Las Vegas
3645 Las Vegas Boulevard South
Las Vegas, NV 89109
877-603-4390
www.ballyslasvegas.com

Caesars Atlantic City
2100 Pacific Avenue
Atlantic City, NJ 08401
609-348-4411
www.caesarsac.com

Caesars Palace Las Vegas
3570 Las Vegas Boulevard South
Las Vegas, NV 89109
866-227-5938
www.caesarspalace.com

Caesars Windsor
377 Riverside Drive East
Windsor, Ontario
N9A 7H7 Canada
800-991-7777
www.caesarswindsor.com

Flamingo Las Vegas
3555 Las Vegas Boulevard South
Las Vegas, NV 89109
888-902-9929
www.flamingolasvegas.com

Grand Biloxi Casino, Hotel & Spa
280 Beach Boulevard
Biloxi, MS 39530
800-WIN-2-WIN
www.grandbiloxi.com

Harrah's Ak-Chin
15406 Maricopa Road
Maricopa, AZ 85239
480-802-5000
www.harrahsakchin.com

Harrah's Cherokee
777 Casino Drive
Cherokee, NC 28719
828-497-7777
www.harrahscherokee.com

Harrah's Chester Casino & Racetrack
777 Harrah's Boulevard
Chester, PA 19013
800-480-8020
www.harrahschester.com

Harrah's Council Bluffs
1 Harrah's Boulevard
Council Bluffs, IA 51501
712-329-6000
www.harrahscouncilbluffs.com

Harrah's Joliet
151 North Joliet Street
Joliet, IL 60432
800-HARRAHS
www.harrahsjoliet.com

Harrah's Lake Tahoe
15 Highway 50
Stateline, NV 89449
800-HARRAHS
775-588-6611
www.harrahslaketahoe.com

Harrah's Las Vegas
3475 Las Vegas Boulevard South
Las Vegas, NV 89109
800-214-9110
www.harrahslasvegas.com

Harrah's Laughlin
2900 South Casino Drive
Laughlin, NV 89029
702-298-4600
www.harrahslaughlin.com

Harrah's Louisiana Downs
8000 East Texas Street
Bossier City, LA 71111
800-HARRAHS
318-742-5555
www.harrahslouisianadowns.com

Harrah's Metropolis
100 East Front Street
Metropolis, IL 62960
800-929-5905
www.harrahsmetropolis.com

Harrah's New Orleans
8 Canal Street
New Orleans, LA 70130
800-847-5299
www.harrahsneworleans.com

Harrah's North Kansas City
One Riverboat Drive
North Kansas City, MO 64116
816-472-7777
www.harrahsnkc.com

Harrah's Reno
219 North Center Street
Reno, NV 89501
775-786-3232
www.harrahsreno.com

Harrah's Resort Atlantic City
777 Harrah's Boulevard
Atlantic City, NJ 08401
609-441-5000
www.harrahsresort.com

Harrah's Rincon Casino & Resort
777 Harrah's Rincon Way
Valley Center, CA 92082
877-777-2457
www.harrahsrincon.com

Harrah's St. Louis
777 Casino Center Drive
Maryland Heights, MO 63043
314-770-8100
www.harrahsstlouis.com

Harrah's Tunica
13615 Old Highway 61 North
Robinsonville, MS 38664
800-WIN-4WIN
www.harrahstunica.com

Harveys Lake Tahoe
18 Highway 50
Stateline, NV 89449
800-HARVEYS
www.harveys.com

Horseshoe Bossier City
711 Horseshoe Boulevard
Bossier City, LA 71111
800-895-0711
www.horseshoebossiercity.com

Horseshoe Council Bluffs
2701 23rd Avenue
Council Bluffs, IA 51501
712-323-2500
www.horseshoecouncilbluffs.com

Horseshoe Hammond
777 Casino Center Drive
Hammond, IN 46320
866-711-SHOE (7463)
www.chicagohorseshoe.com

Horseshoe Southern Indiana
11999 Casino Center Drive SE
Elizabeth, IN 47117
866-676-SHOE (7463)
www.horseshoe-indiana.com

Horseshoe Tunica
1021 Casino Center Drive
Robinsonville, MS 38664
800-303-7463
www.horseshoetunica.com

Imperial Palace Las Vegas
3535 Las Vegas Boulevard South
Las Vegas, NV 89109
800-351-7400
www.imperialpalace.com

Paris Las Vegas
3655 Las Vegas Boulevard South
Las Vegas, NV 89109
877-796-2096 (Reservations)
877-603-4386 (Hotel Main)
www.parislasvegas.com

Rio All-Suite Hotel & Casino
3700 West Flamingo Road
Las Vegas, NV 89103
866-746-7671
www.riolasvegas.com

Showboat Atlantic City
801 Boardwalk
Atlantic City, NJ 08401
800-621-0200
www.showboatac.com

Tunica Roadhouse Casino & Hotel
1107 Casino Center Drive
Tunica, MS 38676
800-391-3777
www.tunicaroadhouse.com

INDEX

A

Absinthe Sazerac, 289

Aioli Sauce, 45

Alcoholic beverages, 257
    Absinthe Sazerac, 289
    Cloud Nine, 302
    Cucumber-Mint Splash, 297
    German Chocolate Cake, 289
    Goodnight Kiss Martini, 298
    Gulf Coast Bloody Mary, 301
    Harrahcane, 302
    Invisible Hombre, 298
    Jewel of the Desert, 297
    Mint Julep, 293
    Oasis Tropical Treat, 290
    Parrothead-Chef Margarita, 293
    Raspberry Lemonade, 305
    Sex in the Biggest Little City, 290
    Tahoe Wabo, 305

Almonds
    Oreo Cookie Macaroons, 274

Antipasto, Roasted Pepper, 72

Apples
    Apple & Blood Orange Vinaigrette over Bibb Lettuce & Watercress, 60
    Coconut Crêpes with Caramelized Cinnamon Apples, Chocolate Whipped Cream & Caramel Sauce, 234

Appliances, 144

Artichoke Chicken, Mediterranean, 168

Asparagus, 108
    Lemon Sole–Wrapped Asparagus with Orange-Citrus Beurre Blanc, 205
    Pan-Roasted Dry-Aged Rib-Eye Steak with Fingerling Potatoes & Asparagus-Morel Ragout, 132
    Seared Scallops, Asparagus & Crabmeat with Hollandaise Sauce & Potato Cakes, 214

Avocados, 108
    Avocado Spring Rolls, 48

B

Bacon
    Bacon & Cream Cheese Frittata with Roasted Red Pepper Hollandaise, 230
    Poached Eggs with Bacon-Potato Hash & Hollandaise Sauce, 229

Baklava, Goat Cheese Truffled, 46

Balsamic vinegar
    Balsamic Dressing, 39
    Balsamic Reduction, 244

Beans
    Baja Blue Black Bean Dip, 36
    Crispy Fried Green Beans, 110
    Smoked Turkey & White Bean Casserole with Herbed Crumb Topping, 174

Beef, 124–25
    Beef & Onion Soup with Short Rib Croutons, 92
    The Best Steak in Kansas City, 128
    Braised Short Rib Sliders with Goat Cheese, Ricotta & Horseradish Gremolata, 141
    Cajun Skillet Filets, 143
    Grilled Citrus-Marinated Skirt Steak with Saffron–Heirloom Tomato Salad, 130
    Pan-Roasted Dry-Aged Rib-Eye Steak with Fingerling Potatoes & Asparagus-Morel Ragout, 132
    Roast Beef with Creamy Horseradish & Blue Cheese Spread, 242
    Sage Steak, 127
    Seared Beef Tenderloin & Goat Cheese Salad, 54
    Signature Lasagna, 187
    Steak & Blue Cheese Macaroni, 182
    Steak au Poivre, 134

Beer, pairing food and, 295

Bell peppers
    Cucumber–Red Pepper Salsa, 244
    Roasted Pepper Antipasto, 72
    Roasted Red Pepper Hollandaise, 230
    roasting and peeling, 196
    Smoked Red Pepper Sauce, 197

Berries, 108
    Berry Napoleon, 266
    Coconut Panna Cotta with Rum-Flamed Berries, 278
    Eiffel Tower Raspberry Soufflés, 284
    Raspberry Lemonade, 305

Biscuits
    Cornmeal–Brown Butter Biscuits, 229
    Paula Deen's Cheese Biscuits, 119

Blackening Spice, 142

Bloody Mary, Gulf Coast, 301

Bourbon
    Bourbon Sauce, 137
    Mint Julep, 293

Bread. See also Sandwiches
    Bruschetta Pomodoro, 36
    Garlic Bread Fingers, 116

Buffet tips, 237

Butter
    clarified, 43
    Compound Butter, 128

Buttermilk
    Buttermilk Dressing, 39
    Buttermilk Potatoes, 112

C

Cajun Rémoulade, 43

Cajun Seafood Pasta, 190

Cajun Skillet Filets, 143

Cakes
    Chocolate-Coconut Cake, 261
    Paula Deen's Gooey Butter Cake, 269
    Pecan Praline Cheesecake, 270
    Seven Sisters Lounge Orange Cake, 283

Caramel Sauce, 235

Cauliflower
    Cauliflower Gratin, 115
    Cauliflower Purée, 106

Caviar, Colors of, 32

Cheese
    Artisanal Cheese Platter, 241
    Bacon & Cream Cheese Frittata with Roasted Red Pepper Hollandaise, 230
    Black Forest Ham & Gruyère Cheese Feuilletées, 151
    Boursin Cheese, Lobster & Cognac Omelet, 227
    Bruschetta Pomodoro, 36
    Cheddar Béchamel Sauce, 220
    Chocolate Fun-Do, 277
    Creamy Horseradish & Blue Cheese Spread, 242
    Fiore Tomato Caprese, 74
    Garden Basket-Weave Salad with Heirloom Tomatoes & Fresh Mozzarella, 67
    Goat Cheese Truffled Baklava, 46
    Lobster Mac Casserole, 220
    Mac & Cheese, 185
    Monte Cristo Sandwich, 152
    Parmesan & Garlic Potato Chips, 109
    Parmesan Cheese Twists, 65
    Paula Deen's Cheese Biscuits, 119
    Pecan Praline Cheesecake, 270
    Ricotta Gnocchi, 189
    Ricotta Ravioli, 186
    Seared Beef Tenderloin & Goat Cheese Salad, 54
    Signature Lasagna, 187
    Steak & Blue Cheese Macaroni, 182
    Tennessee Prosciutto & Warm Goat Cheese Salad, 57
    Tiramisù, 281
    White Cheddar Cheese Sauce, 185

Chefs. See also Food and beverage personnel
    Aleman, Jose, 46
    Andreasen, Keith, 58, 96, 183, 198, 283, 293
    Annapolen, Brian, 208
    Askren, Roy, 62, 190
    Baird, Christine, 267, 272
    Bannan, Todd, 93
    Basil, Chris, 253
    Batten, Edward, 61
    Becker, William, 145
    Besh, John, 35, 289
    Bowen, Tim, 61
    Brooks, Robert, 55, 134
    Byro, Amy, 236
    Cardenas, Vernon, 47
    Carlisle, Jason, 86, 189, 259, 301
    Carlos, Olivier, 274, 277
    Carter, Raymond, 39
    Chobert, Benoit, 187
    Chung, Winston, 148
    Colello, Christopher, 112, 143, 262
    Conrad, Kevin, 205
    Coombs, James, 65
    Cortes, Armando, 93
    Craig, Jeff, 87, 128
    Daggers, Edward, 278
    Damidot, Eric, 171, 185, 241
    D'Angelo, Michael, 273
    Deen, Paula, 105, 119, 269
    Derwinski, Robert, 246
    Dimarco, Maurizio, 110
    Doumergue, Christophe, 136, 214
    Drew, Paul, 211
    Dworzan, William, 106, 128, 155, 164, 243
    Fairhurst, Brian, 207
    Feyersinger, Klaus, 82, 163, 263
    Flay, Bobby, 196
    Galate, Anthony, 270
    Galick, Jeffrey, 159
    Gillespie, J. Ryan, 88, 112, 173, 195
    Harris, Jason, 36
    Haynes, Cathy, 266
    Hencyk, Christopher J., 68, 70, 89
    Heppner, Matthew, 210
    Hughes, Jeremy, 36, 168, 194
    Jeschke, Peter, 60
    Joho, Jean, 284
    Keith, Toby, 155, 164, 298
    Kell, Jon M., 67, 108, 137, 230, 293
    Kinoshita, Sean, 162, 229, 234
    Kisner, Steven, 115
    Klinkenberg, Phil, 35

Laurenza, Mike, 116

Leadbetter, Richard, 92

Leaming, Georgeann, 186, 219

LeCompte, Scott D., 119, 124, 160, 232

Ledwon, Edward, 130

Lepore, Deron, 106

Leppala, Vesa, 74, 201, 204

Leung, Ray, 40, 223

Mai-Thanh, Thierry, 110, 254

Maltby, John, 121

Maricle, Rick, 249

McClary, Patrick, 48, 54, 84, 167

Mecinas, Honorio, 132

Mejlak, John, 72

Miragliotta, Joshua, 188, 220

Mitchell, Keith, 131, 273

Mortensen, Kurtess, 182

Nielsen, Tye, 80

Oatis, Hoyce, 90, 213, 276

Ogden, Bradley, 103

Ortiz, Steve, 166

Pairolero, Steve, 43, 139

Payard, François, 261

Pellegrino, Carla, 179

Perry, Brian, 223

Phillips, Randy, 242

Piston, Eric, 227

Priesol, Mary Therese, 281

Prudhomme, Paul, 79, 200

Reber, James, 44, 306

Reno, Hugh, 109, 128

Roxas, Jerry, 256

Savoy, Guy, 32

Scaffidi, William, 174

Schoell, Robert, 144

Secko, Matthew E., 116, 217

Shewmake, James, 42, 252

Siergey, Joshua, 109

Snuggs, James, 183

Sparks, Andy, 128

Spoor, Thomas, 71

Suscavage, David, 94

Tapia, George Alberto, 250

Tran, Trang, 50

Tucker, Stephen, 244

Ulczak, Ron, 152

Weithofer, Rolf J., 28, 98, 141, 246

Wells, Joe, 58, 127, 146, 151, 170, 180

Williams-Hansen, Tammy, 105, 119, 120, 269

Chicken

    Chanterelle & Parmesan–Crusted Chicken, 159

    Chicken & Shrimp Jambalaya, 93

    Chicken Romano, 163

    Classic Gumbo, 88

    Cream of Cilantro Chicken, 166

    Gumbo, 89

    Mediterranean Artichoke Chicken, 168

    New Orleans Gumbo, 90

Portobello Chicken Chardonnay, 160

Toby Keith's Who's Your Daddy? Chicken Wings, 164

Chili, Italian Meatball & Sausage, 98

Chocolate

    Chocolate-Coconut Cake, 261

    Chocolate Fun-Do, 277

    Chocolate Soufflés, 285

    Chocolate Whipped Cream, 234

    Cloud Nine, 302

    Friday's Peanut Butter Mousse Cups, 272

    Hot Chocolate Sauce, 277

    Oreo Cookie Macaroons, 274

    Tiramisù, 281

Chutney, Fig, 241

Citrus fruits. *See also individual fruits*

    Citrus-Basil Vinaigrette, 65

    Citrus Vinaigrette, 50

    segmenting, 50

Clam Bake for Two, Phillips, 211

Cloud Nine, 302

Coconut

    Chocolate-Coconut Cake, 261

    Coconut Crêpes with Caramelized Cinnamon Apples, Chocolate Whipped Cream & Caramel Sauce, 234

    Coconut Panna Cotta with Rum-Flamed Berries, 278

    toasting, 261

Colors of Caviar, 32

Cooking tips

    adding color, 188

    general, 183

    locally, 121

    for multicourse meals, 243

    seasonally, 120

Corn, 108

    Bradley Ogden's Blue Corn Muffins, 103

    roasted, 50

    Seared Scallops with Tempura Ramps & Roasted Corn Custard, 50

    Selu Turkey & Roasted Corn Soup, 96

    Sweet Iowa Creamed Corn, 112

Crab

    Besh Steak Oysters Casino, 35

    Cajun Seafood Pasta, 190

    Crab & Eggplant Lasagna, 219

    Crab-Stuffed Salmon Fillets, 256

    Gumbo, 89

    Jack Binion's Premium Crab Cakes, 44

    Jumbo Lump Crab Cakes, 43

    Lobster & Crab Tarts, 249

    New Orleans Gumbo, 90

    Phillips Clam Bake for Two, 211

Range Crab Cocktail, 40

Ricotta Ravioli, 186

Seared Scallops, Asparagus & Crabmeat with Hollandaise Sauce & Potato Cakes, 214

Crawfish

    Gumbo, 89

    Red Grouper with Stewed Tomatoes, Okra & Crawfish, 203

Crème brûlée

    Crème Brûlée in Tuile Cups, 259

    Passion Fruit Crème Brûlée, 273

Crème de cacao

    German Chocolate Cake, 289

Crêpes, Coconut, with Caramelized Cinnamon Apples, Chocolate Whipped Cream & Caramel Sauce, 234

Cucumbers

    Cucumber & Mint Salad, 58

    Cucumber-Mint Splash, 297

    Cucumber–Red Pepper Salsa, 244

D

Desserts

    Berry Napoleon, 266

    Chocolate-Coconut Cake, 261

    Chocolate Fun-Do, 277

    Chocolate Soufflés, 285

    Coconut Panna Cotta with Rum-Flamed Berries, 278

    Crème Brûlée in Tuile Cups, 259

    Eiffel Tower Raspberry Soufflés, 284

    Friday's Peanut Butter Mousse Cups, 272

    Grand Marnier Soufflés, 285

    Mandarin Orange Soufflés, 285

    Oreo Cookie Macaroons, 274

    Passion Fruit Crème Brûlée, 273

    Paula Deen's Gooey Butter Cake, 269

    Pecan Praline Cheesecake, 270

    Pistachio Soufflés, 285

    Prosecco Gelée, 273

    Pumpkin Soufflés, 285

    serving, 267

    Seven Sisters Lounge Orange Cake, 283

    Tiramisù, 281

Dip, Baja Blue Black Bean, 36

Duck with Porcini Mushrooms, 250

E

Eggplant

    Crab & Eggplant Lasagna, 219

    Roasted Eggplant Soup, 94

Eggs

    Bacon & Cream Cheese Frittata with Roasted Red Pepper Hollandaise, 230

    Boursin Cheese, Lobster & Cognac Omelet, 227

    Poached Eggs with Bacon-Potato Hash & Hollandaise Sauce, 229

Escargots Provençal, 246

F

Fennel, Endive & Arugula Salad, 65

Fig Chutney, 241

Filo dough

    Berry Napoleon, 266

    Goat Cheese Truffled Baklava, 46

Fish

    Blackened Mahi Mahi with Butternut Squash Polenta and Grilled Asparagus, 207

    Blue Corn–Crusted Red Snapper with Warm Tomato Relish, 196

    Bronzed Fish with Jalapeño Tartar Sauce, 200

    Chef Rolf's VIP Finger Sandwiches, 246

    choosing, 194

    Crab-Stuffed Salmon Fillets, 256

    Japanese Yellowtail Sashimi with Diced Chiles, 47

    Lemon Sole–Wrapped Asparagus with Orange-Citrus Beurre Blanc, 205

    Mahi Mahi & Grilled Shrimp, 253

    Pacific Shutome Swordfish Chops with Port Wine & Cherry Reduction, 208

    Pan-Roasted Halibut with Salsa Provençal, 204

    Parmesan-Crusted Orange Roughy, 210

    Peanut-Crusted Trout, 198

    Red Grouper with Stewed Tomatoes, Okra & Crawfish, 203

Food and beverage personnel. *See also* Chefs

    Batten, Edward, 61

    Bays, Michael, 290

    Becker, William, 145

    Bowen, Tim, 61

    Carnahan, Beverley, 294–95

    Caruso, Joseph, 290, 297

    Crilley, Joseph, 297

    Deano, Rickie, 302

    Lund, Aaron, 302

    McGirk, Kevin, 305

    Nemerow, Joshua A., 305

    Oram, Deborah, 298

    Vergara, Rob, 298

    Weithofer, Rolf J., 28, 98, 141, 246

INDEX

Frozen foods, 167

Fruits, choosing, 108. *See also individual fruits*

G

Garden Basket-Weave Salad with Heirloom Tomatoes & Fresh Mozzarella, 67

Garlic
Garlic Bread Fingers, 116
roasted, 48

Gazpacho, Grilled Shrimp, 80

Gelée, Prosecco, 273

German Chocolate Cake, 289

Gnocchi, Ricotta, 189

Goodnight Kiss Martini, 298

Grand Marnier Soufflés, 285

Gulf Coast Bloody Mary, 301

Gumbo, 89
Classic Gumbo, 88
New Orleans Gumbo, 90

H

Ham. *See also* Prosciutto
Black Forest Ham & Gruyère Cheese Feuilletées, 151
Chef Rolf's VIP Finger Sandwiches, 246
Monte Cristo Sandwich, 152
Patate Arrostite (Roasted Potatoes with Speck), 116

Harrahcane, 302

Hazelnut Pancakes, 232

Herbs, 86

Hoecakes, Paula Deen's, 105

Hollandaise Sauce, 215, 228

Honey-Walnut Truffle Dressing, 57

Host/hostess gifts, 263

I

Invisible Hombre, 298

Italian Meatball & Sausage Chili, 98

J

Jam, Onion, 69

Jambalaya, Chicken & Shrimp, 93

Japanese Yellowtail Sashimi with Diced Chiles, 47

Jewel of the Desert, 297

K

Kitchen organization, 131

Knives, 61

L

Lamb, Pistachio-Encrusted Loin of, with Mint-Infused Rice & Port Wine Reduction, 252

Lasagna
Crab & Eggplant Lasagna, 219
Signature Lasagna, 187

Leek, Sun-Dried Tomato, Shiitake Mushroom & Champagne Soup, 79

Lemons
Flavor's Buffet Lemon Squares, 236
Lemon-Basil Cream Sauce, 159

Lobster
Boursin Cheese, Lobster & Cognac Omelet, 227
Lobster & Crab Tarts, 249
Lobster Mac Casserole, 220
Phillips Clam Bake for Two, 211
Seafood Risotto, 217

M

Mac & Cheese, 185

Macaroons, Oreo Cookie, 274

Mandarin Orange Soufflés, 285

Mao Pao Tofu, 254

Margaritas
Parrothead-Chef Margarita, 293
Tahoe Wabo, 305

Marinara Sauce, 163

Martini, Goodnight Kiss, 298

Meat, choosing, 124–25. *See also individual meats*

Meatball & Sausage Chili, Italian, 98

Mediterranean Artichoke Chicken, 168

Menu planning, 28–29, 70, 71

Mint Julep, 293

Mistakes, common, 201

Monte Cristo Sandwich, 152

Mornay Sauce, 182

Muffins, Bradley Ogden's Blue Corn, 103

Mushrooms, 108
Black Pepper Fettuccine with Wild Mushrooms, 180
Chanterelle & Parmesan–Crusted

Chicken, 159
Duck with Porcini Mushrooms, 250
Fried Portobello Mushrooms, 39
Leek, Sun-Dried Tomato, Shiitake Mushroom & Champagne Soup, 79
Pan-Roasted Dry-Aged Rib-Eye Steak with Fingerling Potatoes & Asparagus-Morel Ragout, 132
Pickles' Famous Mushroom-Barley Soup, 87
Portobello Chicken Chardonnay, 160
Veal Chops Portobello, 139
Wild Mushroom Chowder, 84

Music, 306

Mussels
P.E.I. Mussels in Magners Cider, 223
Phillips Clam Bake for Two, 211

Mustard Vinaigrette, 68

N

New Orleans Gumbo, 90

Nuts, toasting, 60

O

Oasis Tropical Treat, 290

Okra
Classic Gumbo, 88
Gumbo, 89
New Orleans Gumbo, 90
Red Grouper with Stewed Tomatoes, Okra & Crawfish, 203

Onions
Beef & Onion Soup with Short Rib Croutons, 92
Five-Onion Salad, 92
Harrah's Steak House Creamy Five-Onion Soup, 82
Onion Jam, 69

Oranges
Apple & Blood Orange Vinaigrette over Bibb Lettuce & Watercress, 60
Orange-Citrus Beurre Blanc, 205
Seven Sisters Lounge Orange Cake, 283

Oreo Cookie Macaroons, 274

Oysters
Besh Steak Oysters Casino, 35
Gumbo, 89

P

Pancakes
Hazelnut Pancakes, 232
Sweet Potato & Raisin Pancakes, 119

Panna Cotta, Coconut, with Rum-Flamed Berries, 278

Parrothead-Chef Margarita, 293

Party planning tips, 276

Passion Fruit Crème Brûlée, 273

Pasta
Black Pepper Fettuccine with Wild Mushrooms, 180
Cajun Seafood Pasta, 190
Lobster Mac Casserole, 220
Mac & Cheese, 185
Pecan Herbed Orzo Salad, 62
Pennette alla Vodka, 179
Ricotta Ravioli, 186
Signature Lasagna, 187
Steak & Blue Cheese Macaroni, 182

Patate Arrostite (Roasted Potatoes with Speck), 116

Peach schnapps
Sex in the Biggest Little City, 290

Peanuts
Friday's Peanut Butter Mousse Cups, 272
Peanut-Crusted Trout, 198

Pea Soup, Seven Stars Split, 87

Pecans
Pecan Herbed Orzo Salad, 62
Pecan Praline Cheesecake, 270

Pistachios
Goat Cheese Truffled Baklava, 46
Pistachio-Encrusted Loin of Lamb with Mint-Infused Rice & Port Wine Reduction, 252
Pistachio Soufflés, 285
skinning, 252

Polenta, Butternut Squash, 207

Pork. *See also* Bacon; Ham; Prosciutto; Sausage
Applewood-Smoked Molasses & Five Peppercorn–Crusted Pork Loin, 146
Grilled Bourbon Pork Chops, 137
Ming's Glazed Chinese Pork Spareribs, 148
Signature Lasagna, 187

Potatoes
Buttermilk Potatoes, 112
Fresh Market Potato Salad, 58
Pan-Roasted Dry-Aged Rib-Eye Steak with Fingerling Potatoes & Asparagus-Morel Ragout, 132

Parmesan & Garlic Potato Chips, 109

Patate Arrostite (Roasted Potatoes with Speck), 116

Poached Eggs with Bacon-Potato Hash & Hollandaise Sauce, 229

Potatoes au Gratin, 109

Sweet Potato & Raisin Pancakes, 119

Yukon Potato Cakes, 214

Pots and pans, 145

Prosciutto
Bruschetta Pomodoro, 36
Fennel, Endive & Arugula Salad, 65
Tennessee Prosciutto & Warm Goat Cheese Salad, 57

Puff pastry
Black Forest Ham & Gruyère Cheese Feuilletées, 151
Parmesan Cheese Twists, 65

Pumpkin Soufflés, 285

R

Ragù Napolitano, 187

Raspberries
Eiffel Tower Raspberry Soufflés, 284
Raspberry Lemonade, 305

Ravioli, Ricotta, 186

Restaurants and bars
Ah Sin at Paris Las Vegas, 110, 254
Al Dente at Bally's Las Vegas, 187
Andreotti at Harrah's Reno, 36, 266
Arturo's at Bally's Atlantic City, 110
Augustus Café at Caesars Windsor, 48, 54
Baja Blue Restaurant & Cantina at Harrah's Laughlin, 36, 298
Bally's Atlantic City, 152, 246
Bally's Steakhouse at Bally's Las Vegas, 109
Banquet Kitchen at Harrah's Lake Tahoe & Harveys Lake Tahoe, 249
Besh Steak at Harrah's New Orleans, 35, 289
Boa Steakhouse at the Forum Shops at Caesars Palace Las Vegas, 46
Bobby Flay's Mesa Grill at Caesars Palace Las Vegas, 196
Bradley Ogden at Caesars Palace Las Vegas, 103
Breakaway Café at Bally's Atlantic City, 98

The Buffet at Harrah's at Harrah's New Orleans, 90

Búzios Seafood Restaurant at Rio All-Suite Hotel & Casino, 50

Caesars Atlantic City, 72, 166, 273

Caesars Windsor, 84

Carnaval Court Bar & Grill at Harrah's Las Vegas, 305

Carvings Buffet at Harrah's Reno, 163

Casa di Napoli at Showboat Atlantic City, 186, 219

Diamond Lounge at Harrah's Reno, 244

Eat Up! Buffet at Harrah's St. Louis, 223

Eiffel Tower Restaurant at Paris Las Vegas, 284

Embers at Imperial Palace, 210

Fiore at Harrah's Rincon Casino & Resort, 74, 204

Flavor's Buffet & the Range Steakhouse at Harrah's Las Vegas, 236

Forest Buffet at Harrah's Lake Tahoe, 146

French Quarter Buffet at Showboat Atlantic City, 93

Fresh Market Buffet at Harrah's North Kansas City, 87, 270

Fresh Market Square Buffet at Harrah's Cherokee, 58

Friday's Station Steak & Seafood Grill at Harrah's Lake Tahoe, 272

Grand Biloxi Casino, Hotel & Spa, 189, 259, 301

Harrah's Ak-Chin, 252, 290, 297

Harrah's Cherokee, 293

Harrah's Chester Casino & Racetrack, 229, 234

Harrah's Joliet, 119, 160, 232

Harrah's Lake Tahoe, 58, 151

Harrah's Louisiana Downs, 88, 112, 173

Harrah's Metropolis, 67

Harrah's North Kansas City, 62, 190, 256

Harrah's Steak House at Harrah's Reno, 82, 159

Harveys Lake Tahoe, 58, 151

Jack Binion's Steak House at Horseshoe Bossier City, 134

Jack Binion's Steak House at Horseshoe Council Bluffs, 44

Jack Binion's Steak House at Horseshoe Hammond, 281

Jack Binion's Steak House at Horseshoe Southern Indiana, 220

Jimmy Buffett's Margaritaville at Flamingo Las Vegas, 35

K-Paul's Louisiana Kitchen, 79, 200

Le Provençal at Paris Las Vegas, 246

Les Artistes Steakhouse at Paris Las Vegas, 182

Le Village Buffet at Paris Las Vegas, 115

Magnolia, A Delta Grille at Horseshoe Tunica, 57, 203

Magnolia Buffet at Harrah's New Orleans, 213

Masquerade at Harrah's New Orleans, 302

Ming's Table at Harrah's Las Vegas, 148

Mosaic at Harrah's Joliet, 116, 217

Murano's at Harrah's Tunica, 139

Nero's at Caesars Palace Las Vegas, 185, 241

Neros Steakhouse at Caesars Windsor, 106

Oyster Bar at Penazzi at Harrah's Las Vegas, 207

Paula Deen Buffet at Harrah's Tunica, 105, 119, 269

Payard Pâtisserie & Bistro at Caesars Palace Las Vegas, 261

Penazzi at Harrah's Las Vegas, 250

Phillips Seafood at the Pier Shops at Caesars Atlantic City, 211

Polistina's Italian Ristorante at Harrah's Resort Atlantic City, 116

The Pool at Harrah's Resort Atlantic City, 278

Preview Bar at Bally's Atlantic City, 141

The Range Steakhouse & Bar at Tunica Roadhouse Casino & Hotel, 39, 68, 89

The Range Steakhouse at Harrah's Laughlin, 168

The Range Steakhouse at Harrah's Metropolis, 137, 293

The Range Steakhouse at Harrah's North Kansas City, 106, 109, 128, 155

The Range Steakhouse at Harrah's St. Louis, 40

Rao's at Caesars Palace Las Vegas, 179

Red Pearl at Bally's Atlantic City, 273

Reflections Café at Harrah's Resort Atlantic City, 65

Reserve at Bally's Atlantic City, 208

Reserve at Harrah's Joliet, 80

Restaurant Guy Savoy at Caesars Palace Las Vegas, 32

Rib & Chophouse at Showboat Atlantic City, 130

The Rivercrest at Harrah's Metropolis, 230

Sage Room Steak House at Harveys Lake Tahoe, 127, 180

Sammy Hagar's The Cabo Wabo Cantina at Harveys Lake Tahoe, 305

Sapphire at Harrah's Reno, 290

Selu Garden Cafe at Harrah's Cherokee, 96

Seven Sisters Lounge at Harrah's Cherokee, 242, 283

The Seven Stars Club at Harrah's Resort Atlantic City, 174

Seven Stars Lounge at Horseshoe Hammond, 253

The Steakhouse at Harrah's Resort Atlantic City, 92, 297

Sterling Brunch at Bally's Steakhouse at Bally's Las Vegas, 227

Sushi Roku at the Forum Shops at Caesars Palace Las Vegas, 47

Sycamores on the Creek at Harrah's Cherokee, 198, 205

'37 at Harrah's Tunica, 43

360 Steakhouse at Harrah's Council Bluffs, 112, 143

Toby Keith's I Love This Bar & Grill at Harrah's Las Vegas, 298

Toby Keith's I Love This Bar & Grill at Harrah's North Kansas City, 155, 164

Trinity Pub & Carvery at the Pier Shops at Caesars Atlantic City, 223

VIP Lounges & High Limit Bar at Harrah's Lake Tahoe & Harveys Lake Tahoe, 289

Voga at Flamingo Las Vegas, 214, 274, 277

VooDoo Lounge at Harrah's North Kansas City, 302

VooDoo Steak & Lounge at Rio All-Suite Hotel & Casino, 132

Waterfront Buffet at Harrah's Resort Atlantic City, 94

Rice
Mint-Infused Rice, 252
Seafood Risotto, 217

Rum
Coconut Panna Cotta with Rum-Flamed Berries, 278
German Chocolate Cake, 289
Harrahcane, 302
Jewel of the Desert, 297
Oasis Tropical Treat, 290
Raspberry Lemonade, 305

S

Salad dressings
Apple & Blood Orange Vinaigrette, 60
Balsamic Dressing, 39
Buttermilk Dressing, 39
Caviar Vinaigrette, 32
Citrus-Basil Vinaigrette, 65
Citrus Vinaigrette, 50
Honey-Walnut Truffle Dressing, 57

INDEX

Mustard Vinaigrette, 68

Sherry Vinaigrette, 33

Spicy Tomato Dressing, 54

Sun-Dried Tomato Vinaigrette, 207

Salads
Apple & Blood Orange Vinaigrette over Bibb Lettuce & Watercress, 60
Cucumber & Mint Salad, 58
Fennel, Endive & Arugula Salad, 65
Fiore Tomato Caprese, 74
Five-Onion Salad, 92
Fresh Market Potato Salad, 58
Garden Basket-Weave Salad with Heirloom Tomatoes & Fresh Mozzarella, 67
Pecan Herbed Orzo Salad, 62
Roasted Pepper Antipasto, 72
Seared Beef Tenderloin & Goat Cheese Salad, 54
Tennessee Prosciutto & Warm Goat Cheese Salad, 57

Salsas. See Sauces and salsas

Sandwiches
Braised Short Rib Sliders with Goat Cheese, Ricotta & Horseradish Gremolata, 141
Chef Rolf's VIP Finger Sandwiches, 246
Monte Cristo Sandwich, 152

Sashimi, Japanese Yellowtail, with Diced Chiles, 47

Sauces and salsas
Aioli Sauce, 45
Bourbon Sauce, 137
Cajun Rémoulade, 43
Caramel Sauce, 235
Cheddar Béchamel Sauce, 220
Cucumber–Red Pepper Salsa, 244
Hollandaise Sauce, 215, 228
Hot Chocolate Sauce, 277
Jalapeño Tartar Sauce, 200
Lemon-Basil Cream Sauce, 159
Marinara Sauce, 163
Mornay Sauce, 182
Orange-Citrus Beurre Blanc, 205
Ragù Napolitano, 187
Roasted Red Pepper Hollandaise, 230
Salsa Provençal, 204
Smoked Red Pepper Sauce, 197
Vanilla Sauce, 253, 284
White Cheddar Cheese Sauce, 185
Yuzu Ponzu Sauce, 47

Sausage
Chicken & Shrimp Jambalaya, 93
Classic Gumbo, 88
Gumbo, 89
Italian Meatball & Sausage Chili, 98
New Orleans Gumbo, 90
Signature Lasagna, 187

Sazerac, Absinthe, 289

Scallops
Cajun Seafood Pasta, 190
Jumbo Lump Crab Cakes, 43
Seafood Risotto, 217
Seared Scallops, Asparagus & Crabmeat with Hollandaise Sauce & Potato Cakes, 214
Seared Scallops with Tempura Ramps & Roasted Corn Custard, 50
Smoked Scallops with Cucumber–Red Pepper Salsa, 244

Seafood. See also individual seafood
Cajun Seafood Pasta, 190
choosing, 194–95
Phillips Clam Bake for Two, 211
Seafood Risotto, 217

Serving tips, 55, 262, 267

Sex in the Biggest Little City, 290

Sherry Vinaigrette, 33

Shrimp
Barbecued Shrimp, 213
Cajun Seafood Pasta, 190
Chicken & Shrimp Jambalaya, 93
Classic Gumbo, 88
Grilled Shrimp Gazpacho, 80
Grilled Shrimp Skewers, 223
Gumbo, 89
Mahi Mahi & Grilled Shrimp, 253
New Orleans Gumbo, 90
Peel & Eat Shrimp, 35
Phillips Clam Bake for Two, 211
Ricotta Ravioli, 186
Seafood Risotto, 217
Shrimp Stock, 202

Soufflés
Chocolate Soufflés, 285
Eiffel Tower Raspberry Soufflés, 284
Grand Marnier Soufflés, 285
Mandarin Orange Soufflés, 285
Pistachio Soufflés, 285
Pumpkin Soufflés, 285

Soups
Beef & Onion Soup with Short Rib Croutons, 92
Chicken & Shrimp Jambalaya, 93
Classic Gumbo, 88

Grilled Shrimp Gazpacho, 80
Gumbo, 89
Harrah's Steak House Creamy Five-Onion Soup, 82
Leek, Sun-Dried Tomato, Shiitake Mushroom & Champagne Soup, 79
New Orleans Gumbo, 90
Pickles' Famous Mushroom-Barley Soup, 87
Roasted Eggplant Soup, 94
Selu Turkey & Roasted Corn Soup, 96
Seven Stars Split Pea Soup, 87
Wild Mushroom Chowder, 84

Spices, 136

Spring Rolls, Avocado, 48

Squash
Butternut Squash Polenta, 207
Garden Basket-Weave Salad with Heirloom Tomatoes & Fresh Mozzarella, 67

Staples, 162, 170–71

Stock, Shrimp, 202

Sweet potatoes
Mashed Sweet Potatoes, 106
Sweet Potato & Raisin Pancakes, 119

T

Table, setting the, 42

Tahoe Wabo, 305

Tartar Sauce, Jalapeño, 200

Tarts, Lobster & Crab, 249

Tennessee Prosciutto & Warm Goat Cheese Salad, 57

Tequila
Invisible Hombre, 298
Parrothead-Chef Margarita, 293
Tahoe Wabo, 305

Tiramisù, 281

Tofu, Mao Pao, 254

Tomatoes, 108
Bruschetta Pomodoro, 36
Fiore Tomato Caprese, 74
Fried Green Tomatoes, 68
Garden Basket-Weave Salad with Heirloom Tomatoes & Fresh Mozzarella, 67
Grilled Shrimp Gazpacho, 80
Gulf Coast Bloody Mary, 301
Italian Meatball & Sausage Chili, 98
Leek, Sun-Dried Tomato, Shiitake Mushroom & Champagne Soup, 79
Marinara Sauce, 163

Pennette alla Vodka, 179
Red Grouper with Stewed Tomatoes, Okra & Crawfish, 203
Salsa Provençal, 204
Signature Lasagna, 187
Spicy Tomato Dressing, 54
Sun-Dried Tomato Vinaigrette, 207
Tomato Confit Chips, 110
Warm Tomato Relish, 196

Turkey
Deep-Fried Turkey, 173
Monte Cristo Sandwich, 152
Selu Turkey & Roasted Corn Soup, 96
Smoked Turkey & White Bean Casserole with Herbed Crumb Topping, 174

U

Utensils, 61

V

Vanilla Sauce, 253, 284

Veal Chops Portobello, 139

Vegetables, choosing, 108. See also individual vegetables

Vinaigrettes. See Salad dressings

Vodka
Cloud Nine, 302
Cucumber-Mint Splash, 297
Goodnight Kiss Martini, 298
Gulf Coast Bloody Mary, 301
Oasis Tropical Treat, 290
Pennette alla Vodka, 179
Sex in the Biggest Little City, 290

W

Whiskey. See also Bourbon
Absinthe Sazerac, 289
Harrahcane, 302

Wine
pairing food and, 28, 294
Prosecco Gelée, 273

Y

Yuzu Ponzu Sauce, 47

REGISTERED TRADEMARKS

Absolut Country of Sweden vodka, Absolute Country of Sweden Pears vodka, and Absolut Country of Sweden Citron are registered trademarks of V&S Vin & Sprit Aktiebolag. Angostura Bitters is a registered trademark of Angostura Ltd. Aunt Jemima is a registered trademark of the Quaker Oats Company. Bacardi Limón rum is a registered trademark of Bacardi and Company, Ltd. Baileys Irish Cream is a registered trademark of R & A Bailey & Co., Ltd. Baileys liqueur is a registered trademark of R & A Bailey & Co. Barbecue Magic, Blackened Redfish Magic, Chef Paul Prudhomme's Magic Pepper Sauce, Chef Paul Prudhomme's Vegetable Magic, Fajita Magic, Magic Salt Free Seasoning, Magic Seasoning Salt, Pizza & Pasta Magic, Poultry Magic, Salmon Magic, Seafood Magic, and Shrimp Magic seasonings are registered trademarks of Magic Seasoning Blends, Inc. Best Foods mayonnaise is a registered trademark of Unilever Supply Chain, Inc. Boursin cheese is a registered trademark of Societe de la Fromagerie Boursin. Cabo Wabo tequila is a registered trademark of Cabo Wabo LLC. Cajun Chef is a registered trademark of Cajun Chef Products, Inc. Chambord liqueur is a registered trademark of Chatam International Inc. Cleveland tilting skillet is a registered trademark of Cleveland Range, LLC. Cointreau liqueur is a registered trademark of Cointreau Corp. Cruzan coconut rum is a registered trademark of Cruzan Viril Ltd. Cuisinart is a registered trademark of Conair Corporation. De Cecco pasta is a registered trademark of F.LLI De Cecco Filippo San Martino S.P.A. Don Julio tequila is a registered trademark of Tequila Don Julio. Durkee hot sauce is a registered trademark of ACH Food Companies, Inc. Frangelico liqueur is a registered trademark of Giorgio Barbero and Figli, S.P.A. Grand Marnier liqueur is a registered trademark of Société des Produits Marnier-Lapostolle. Guinness stout is a registered trademark of Guinness & Co. Heineken beer is a registered trademark of Heineken Brouwerijen B.V. Jack Daniel's and Old No. 7 Tennessee whiskey are registered trademarks of Jack Daniel's Properties, Inc. Jade Infrared Broiler is a registered trademark of Jade Products Company. José Cuervo tequila is a registered trademark of Tequila Cuervo la Rojena, S.A. Kahlúa is a registered trademark of the Kahlua Company. Land Shark beer is a registered trademark of Margaritaville Enterprises, LLC. Magners Irish Cider is a registered trademark of Bulmers Ltd. Margaritaville tequila is a registered trademark of Margaritaville Enterprises, LLC. Meat Magic Seasoning is a registered trademark of Tasso Travel, Inc. Minute Maid limeade is a registered trademark of The Coca-Cola Co. Muscovy Duck is a registered trademark of Epicurean Farms, LLC.

Negra Modelo beer is a registered trademark of Cervecería Modelo. Nocello liqueur is a registered trademark of Toschi Vignola S.R.L. Old Bay seasoning is a registered trademark of Old Bay Co., LLC. Old Overholt whiskey is a registered trademark of Jim Beam Brands Co. Oreo cookies is a registered trademark of Kraft Foods Global Brands, LLC. Otokoyama sake is a registered trademark of Otokoyama Co., Ltd. Parmigiano-Reggiano cheese is a registered trademark of Consorzio del Formaggio Parmigiano-Reggiano Consortium Italy. Paula Deen Collection sauces and seasonings is a registered trademark of Paula Deen Enterprises, LLC. Peychaud's bitters is a registered trademark of Sazerac Company, Inc. Phillips Seafood Restaurants is a registered trademark of S.B. Phillips, LLC. Rational Combi-Oven-Steamer is a registered trademark of Rational. Sazerac is a registered trademark of Sazerac Company, Inc. Sierra Mist soft drink is a registered trademark of Pepsico, Inc. Silpat baking mats is a registered trademark of Ets Guy DeMarle. Skyy vodka is a registered trademark of Skyy Spirits, LLC. Southern Comfort whiskey is a registered trademark of Southern Comfort Properties, Inc. Stolichnaya vodka is a registered trademark of Spirits International B.V. Tabasco sauce is a registered trademark of McIlhenny Co. Teflon is a registered trademark of E. I. du Pont de Nemours and Company. TurboChef oven is a registered trademark of TurboChef Technologies, Inc. V8 juice is a registered trademark of Campbell Soup Co. Versinthe is a registered trademark of Liquoristerie de Provence. Worcestershire sauce is a registered trademark of HP Foods Ltd. Wüsthof is a registered trademark of Ed. Wüsthof, Dreizackwerk. Zatarain's seasonings is a registered trademark of Zatarain's Partnership, L.P.

DESTINATION PHOTO INDEX

PAGE 6:   View from Eiffel Tower Restaurant, Paris Las Vegas

PAGE 14:   Paula Deen slot machine, Harrah's Tunica

PAGE 17:   Eiffel Tower, Paris Las Vegas

PAGE 18:   Eiffel Tower, Paris Las Vegas

PAGE 24:   Beijing Noodle No. 9, Caesars Palace Las Vegas

PAGE 26:   Magnolia, A Delta Grille, Horseshoe Tunica

PAGE 30:   Jubilee Showgirl, Jubilee!, Bally's Las Vegas

PAGE 52:   The Pool, Harrah's Resort Atlantic City

PAGE 70:   Jackson Square, New Orleans, LA

PAGE 76:   Pool, Flamingo Las Vegas

PAGE 78:   K Paul's Louisiana Kitchen, New Orleans, LA

PAGE 100:   Bridge, Paris Las Vegas

PAGE 122:   The Greenbacks: Winnie and Buck, Harrah's Las Vegas

PAGE 156:   Fountain, Paris Las Vegas

PAGE 222:   Trinity Pub & Carvery, The Pier Shops at Caesars Atlantic City

PAGE 224:   Theatre, Harrah's New Orleans

PAGE 238:   David, Caesars Palace Las Vegas

PAGE 264:   Jubilee Showgirls, Jubilee!, Bally's Las Vegas

PAGE 286:   Sphere Bar, Harrah's Tunica

PAGE 307:   Tahoe Star on Lake Tahoe, Harrah's/ Harveys Lake Tahoe

PAGE 308:   Las Vegas Strip at Night

PAGE 318:   Pony Express Monument, Harrah's Lake Tahoe

The exact equivalents in the following tables have been rounded for convenience.

LIQUID/DRY MEASURES

U.S.		METRIC
¼ teaspoon		1.25 milliliters
½ teaspoon		2.5 milliliters
1 teaspoon		5 milliliters
1 tablespoon	(3 teaspoons)	15 milliliters
1 fluid ounce	(2 tablespoons)	30 milliliters
¼ cup		60 milliliters
⅓ cup		80 milliliters
½ cup		120 milliliters
1 cup		240 milliliters
1 pint	(2 cups)	480 milliliters
1 quart	(4 cups, 32 ounces)	960 milliliters
1 gallon	(4 quarts)	3.84 liters
1 ounce (by weight)		28 grams
1 pound		454 grams
2.2 pounds		1 kilogram

LENGTH

U.S.	METRIC
⅛ inch	3 millimeters
¼ inch	6 millimeters
½ inch	12 millimeters
1 inch	2.5 centimeters

OVEN TEMPERATURE

FAHRENHEIT	CELSIUS	GAS
250	120	½
275	140	1
300	150	2
325	160	3
350	180	4
375	190	5
400	200	6
425	220	7
450	230	8
475	240	9
500	260	10

TABLE OF
EQUIVALENTS

ACKNOWLEDGMENTS

Countless people have lent their extraordinary talents and expertise to *The Seven Stars Cookbook*, many more than I could ever thank. This book would not have been possible without each and every one of you.

Many thanks to each of the Harrah's Entertainment executive chefs and their inspired teams of chefs and kitchen and restaurant staff, who contributed recipes, Top 10 lists, and valuable advice to this book. It is a tribute to your creativity, hard work, and amazing culinary skills.

My gratitude to David Norton, Matt Bowers, Kathy Hickman, and Mindy Rabinowitz, who were driving forces behind this project at Harrah's Entertainment. A special thanks in particular to Mindy, who spent endless hours helping to manage this project, secure recipes, fact-check, organize logistics, and make sure this book was the best it could be. I owe her a debt of gratitude that can never be repaid in this lifetime. Thanks also to the food and beverage executive teams, the property marketing teams, and the dozens of other employees at each Harrah's Entertainment property who contributed their time and talents to this project. We also appreciate Harrah's Entertainment's restaurant partners for providing recipes from their outstanding restaurants.

A big thank-you to Gary W. Loveman, CEO of Harrah's Entertainment, Inc., for his support of this project and for writing the preface. He knows well what the art of entertaining truly means and entails.

A million thanks to Paula Deen for writing such a thoughtful and entertaining foreword.

It has been a great pleasure for me and Harrah's Entertainment to work with Chronicle Books on this project. Special thanks to the amazing team they assembled to make sure this cookbook made it into your hands, including Michael Ashby, Mikayla Butchart, Ken DellaPenta, Pamela Geismar, David Hawk, Catherine Huchting, Ben Kasman, Bill LeBlond, Laurel Leigh, Carolyn Miller, Peter Perez, and Beth Weber.

I owe an enormous debt of gratitude to our photographer extraordinaire, Frankie Frankeny, and her masterful team, including her assistant, Molly Johnstone, and one of the world's most talented food stylists, Alison Richman, who all helped bring this book to life in vivid color. It was such a pleasure to work with them. And, many thanks to Public, San Francisco, for creating beautiful layouts showcasing the recipes.

Finally, thank you to literary agent Steve Troha, who understood and supported the vision for this undertaking from the very beginning.

HEALTH AND FITNESS

A Guide to a Healthy Lifestyle

Kendall Hunt

publishing company

4050 Westmark Drive • P O Box 1840 • Dubuque IA 52004-1840

LAURA BOUNDS | KIRSTIN BREKKEN SHEA | DOTTIEDEE AGNOR | GAYDEN DARNELL

Book Team
Chairman and Chief Executive Officer   Mark C. Falb
President and Chief Operating Officer   Chad M. Chandlee
Vice President, Higher Education   David L. Tart
Senior Managing Editor   Ray Wood
Assistant Editor   Lara McCombie
Vice President, Operations   Timothy J. Beitzel
Assistant Vice President, Production Services   Christine E. O'Brien
Senior Production Editor   Mary Melloy
Senior Permissions Editor   Caroline Kieler
Cover Designer   Mallory Blondin
Web Project Editor   Sarah Kress

Cover images © Shutterstock, Inc.

www.kendallhunt.com
Send all inquiries to:
4050 Westmark Drive
Dubuque, IA 52004-1840

Printed in the United States of America
10 9 8 7 6 5 4 3 2 1

Dedication

This textbook is dedicated to the memory of Dr. Emma S. Gibbons, who was a valued member of the Department of Health and Kinesiology at Texas A&M University for 25 years. She fought a 12 year battle with breast cancer and passed away on September 7, 2001.

Dr. Gibbons was known for mentoring students, faculty and staff. She had high expectations of herself and others and had the rare quality of making every individual feel appreciated. As the "glue" that held the Department together, she dedicated her life to the betterment of the department through her vision and perseverance. She lived a life of courage and faith in an attempt to give back to the world, and it is through her wisdom and inspiration that we were able to complete this textbook. Texas A&M University is a much better place because she was here.

A portion of the sales proceeds from this textbook benefit The Emma Gibbons Endowed College Scholarship Fund.

"To laugh often and much; to win the respect of
intelligent people and the affection of children;
to earn the appreciation of honest critics and
endure the betrayal of false friends;
to appreciate beauty, to find the best in others;
to leave the world a little better, whether
by a healthy child, a garden patch or a redeemed
social condition; to know even one life
has breathed easier because you have lived.
This is the meaning of success."

—Ralph Waldo Emerson

Brief Contents

CHAPTER 1
Introduction

CHAPTER 2
Stress and Psychological Health

CHAPTER 3
Personal Fitness

CHAPTER 4
Lifestyle Choices and Hypokinetic Conditions

CHAPTER 5
Nutrition

CHAPTER 6
Lifetime Weight Management

CHAPTER 7
Relationships

CHAPTER 8
Sexuality

CHAPTER 9
Drug Misuse and Abuse

CHAPTER 10
Safety Awareness

CHAPTER 11
Human Diseases

CHAPTER 12
Complementary and Alternative Medicine

Contents

Acknowledgments   xiii
About the Authors   xiv

CHAPTER 1

Introduction   1
Dimensions of Wellness   2
  Emotional   3
  Intellectual   3
  Social   3
  Spiritual   3
  Physical   3
  Occupational   3
  Environmental   4
Financial Wellness   4
  Factors That Influence Health and Wellness   4
A Wellness Profile   4
Changing Behavior and Setting Goals   5
  The Stages of Change   5
  Precontemplation   6
  Contemplation   6
  Preparation   6
  Action   6
  Maintenance   6
  Behavior Change and Goal Setting   8
Healthy People 2020: Improving the Health
  of Americans   11
Summary   13
References   14
Activities   14
  In-Class Activities   14
  Notebook Activities   14
  IN-CLASS ACTIVITY   15
  Human Bingo   15
  Journal—Goal Setting   17
NOTEBOOK ACTIVITY   19
  Dimensions of Wellness Writing
    Assignment   19
  Wellness Goal   21
  Lifestyle Assessment Inventory   23
  Behavior Change and Goal Setting   25
  If I Had It to Do Over   27

CHAPTER 2

Stress and Psychological Health   29
Wellness and Stress   30
Self-Talk Your Way to Reduced Levels of Stress
  and an Improved Life   35
  What Is Self-Talk?   35
  Negative or Positive Self-Talk   35
Stress and Its Impact on Mental Health   36
  Who Gets Mental Health Disorders?   36
  Depression and Stress   36
  Suicidal Behavior and Stress   38
  Eating Disorders and Stress   39
Body Image   40
  Anorexia Nervosa   41
  Bulimia Nervosa   42
  Binge-Eating Disorder   42
  Fear of Obesity   42
  Activity Nervosa   42
  Who Is at Risk?   43
  Causes of Eating Disorders   43
Ways to Help   46
References   46
Activities   47
  Notebook Activities   47
NOTEBOOK ACTIVITY   49
  Time Budget Sheet   49
  Stress Journal   51
  Forbidden Foods   53
  Forbidden Foods Chart   54
  Ways I Sneak   55
  What Am I Waiting For?   57
WRITING PROMPTS   58

CHAPTER 3

Personal Fitness   59
Why Is Physical Activity Important?   61
Cardiovascular Fitness   63
  How Aerobic Exercise Helps Cardiovascular
    Fitness   64
Aerobic and Anaerobic Exercise   67
Exercise Prescription, or How to Become
  FITT   68

Frequency   68
Intensity   68
Time   70
Type   70
Components of an Exercise Session   71
Warm-Up   71
Pre-Stretch   71
Activity   71
Cooldown and Stretch   72
Principles of Fitness Training—The Rules   72
Overload and Adaptation   72
Specificity   72
Individual Differences   72
Reversibility   73
Evaluating Cardiovascular Fitness   73
Muscular Fitness   75
Benefits of Muscular Fitness   76
Importance of the Core Musculature
in Functional Movement   76
What Makes Up the "Core"?   77
Effective Training   77
Training for the Best Results   77
True or False? Weight Training Myths   80
Flexibility   82
When You Should Not Exercise   84
Injuries   84
Proper Footwear   85
Environmental Conditions   87
Hyponatremia   88
Illness   89
Common Sense Concerns for Outside
Activity   89
The Biggest Risk to Exercise Is Not Starting!   90
References   91
Contacts   92
Activities   92
Notebook Activities   92
NOTEBOOK ACTIVITY   93
Safety of Exercise Participation: PAR-Q and You (A
Questionnaire for People Aged 15 to 69)   93
Calculating Your Activity Index   95
Karvonen Formula   97
Developing an Exercise Program for
Cardiorespiratory Endurance   99
Assessing Your Current Level of Muscular
Endurance   101
Check Your Physical Activity and Heart Disease
I.Q.   103
Answers to the Check Your Physical Activity and
Heart Disease I.Q. Quiz   104
Assessing Cardiovascular Fitness:
Cooper's 1.5-Mile Run   105

CHAPTER 4

Lifestyle Choices and Hypokinetic
Conditions   107
Let's Move! America's Move to Raise a Healthier
Generation of Kids   108
Types of Hypokinetic Conditions   112
Cardiovascular Disease (CVD)   112
Who Is At Risk for CVD?   114
CVD Prevention   116
Measuring Health Risk   117
Arteriosclerosis   119
Arteriosclerosis   119
Peripheral Vascular Disease   120
Hypertension   120
Heart Attack   122
Stroke   123
Risk Factors for Cardiovascular Disease   127
Controllable Risk Factors   127
Uncontrollable Risk Factors   128
Contributing Risk Factors   128
Obesity   128
Childhood Obesity   129
Causes of Obesity   132
Physiological Response to Obesity   132
Fitness or Fatness   133
Cancer   133
Who Gets Cancer?   133
Can Cancer Be Prevented?   133
Does Exercise Help?   133
Diabetes   134
Who Gets Diabetes?   134
Can Diabetes Be Prevented?   134
Does Exercise Help?   134
Metabolic Syndrome   135
Low Back Pain   135
Who Suffers from Low Back Pain?   135
Can Low Back Pain Be Prevented?   136
Does Exercise Help?   136
Osteoporosis   136
Who Gets Osteoporosis?   136
Can Osteoporosis Be Prevented?   138
Does Exercise Help?   139
Aging   139
Prevention of Hypokinetic Conditions: Planning
Your Activity Program   140
References   141
Contacts   143
Recommended Reading   143
Activities   143
Notebook Activities   143
NOTEBOOK ACTIVITY   145
Self-Assessment of Cardiovascular Fitness   145
Healthy Back Test   147
Is Your Blood in Tune?   149
Is Osteoporosis in Your Future?   151

CHAPTER 5

Nutrition   153
Dietary Guidelines for Americans   154
  Balancing Calories to Manage Weight   155
  Key Recommendations   155
  Foods and Food Components to Reduce   155
  Key Recommendations   155
  Foods and Nutrients to Increase   155
  Key Recommendations   155
  Building Healthy Eating Patterns   156
  Key Recommendations   156
Essential Nutrients   156
  Carbohydrates   157
  Fats   158
  Protein   159
  Vitamins   163
  Minerals   163
  Antioxidants   163
  Organic Foods   167
  Functional Foods   167
  Water   171
The Food Guide Pyramid   172
  Grains   172
  Vegetables   177
  Fruits   180
  Milk/Dairy   182
  Protein/Meats and Beans   184
  Oils   186
  Daily Activity   187
  What Happened to the "Fat" Group?   187
Other Issues in Nutrition   188
  Building a Healthy Plate   188
  Reading and Understanding the Nutrition Facts
    Label   191
  Vegetarianism   194
References   195
Contacts   196
Activities   196
  Notebook Activities   196
NOTEBOOK ACTIVITY   197
  Dietary Analysis Project   197
  Cholesterol Levels Measured   201
  Nutrition Assignment   203
  Super Tracker Assignment   205
WRITING PROMPTS   206

CHAPTER 6

Lifetime Weight Management   207
Causes of Obesity and Being Overweight   209
The Weight Loss 'Halo' Effect   211
What Is a Healthy Body Weight?   212
  Determining Caloric Needs   213
Obesity   213
  Obesity Prevention   214

How Does Activity Help Obesity?   214
How Do I Lose Weight?   215
Dietary Supplements   218
Energy Drinks and Nutrition Bars   219
Weight Loss Products   220
Super-Size Meals Lead to Super-Size
  Problems   222
How to Combat a Super-Sized Meal   222
Points to Ponder   222
Fad Diets   224
Healthy Habits   224
  Building a Healthy Plate   224
  Healthy Weight Gain   224
  Healthy Food Shopping   224
  Fast Foods/Eating Out   225
  Fitness or Fatness   225
References   226
Recommended Reading   227
Activities   227
  Notebook Activities   227
NOTEBOOK ACTIVITY   229
  Body Mass Index Calculator   229
  Facts about My Favorite Fast-Food Meal   231
WRITING PROMPTS   233

CHAPTER 7

Relationships   235
Healthy Relationships   236
  Positive Self-Worth   236
  Open Communication   236
  Communication Styles   237
  Differences between Males and Females   238
  Compromise   239
  Trust   239
Types of Relationships   239
  Parental Relationship Stages   239
  Before College   240
  During College   240
  After College (the Extended Visit)   241
  Peer Relationships   241
  Group Projects   242
  Roommates   243
Types of Friendships   244
Stages of Relationships   247
  Dating   247
  When and What Type of Love Is It?   247
  Rating Safe Sex Activities   250
  Date Rape   250
  Taming the Green-Eyed Monster   250
  What to Do for a Jealous Partner   250
  Rules for Arguing Fairly   251
  Ending a Relationship   251
  On the Sending End   251
  On the Receiving End   251
  I Do or I Do Not   252

Tips for a Successful Marriage   253
Ten Characteristics of a Happy Marriage   253
Unhealthy Relationships   253
Abusive Relationships   254
Additional Readings   255
References   255
Contacts   255
Activities   256
In-Class Activities   256
Notebook Activities   256
IN-CLASS ACTIVITY   257
The "Perfect" Mate   257
NOTEBOOK ACTIVITY   259
Relationship Writing Assignment   259
How Strong Is the Communication and Affection in Your Relationship?   261
Relationship Report Card   263
Relationship Report Card   265
Are You in an Abusive Relationship?   267

CHAPTER 8

Sexuality   269
Anatomy   270
Female Sexual Anatomy   270
Male Sexual Anatomy   272
Sexual Orientation   274
Readiness for Sexual Activity   275
Reproduction   277
Menstrual Cycle   277
Ovarian Cycle   278
Endometrial Cycle   278
Pregnancy   279
Sexually Transmitted Infections and Pregnancy   281
Pregnancy Prevention   282
Natural Methods   282
Abstinence from Penile/Vaginal Intercourse   282
Barrier Methods   283
Male Condom   283
Hormonal Methods   285
The Pill   285
Emergency Contraception "The Morning After Pill"   290
Unplanned Pregnancy   291
Parenthood   291
Adoption   291
Abortion   292
Sexually Transmitted Infections (STIs)   292
Levels of Risk   293
Bacterial STIs   293
Chlamydia   293
Gonorrhea   293
Pelvic Inflammatory Disease (PID)   296
Syphilis   299
Viral STIs   304

Genital Herpes   304
HIV/AIDS   305
HPV   306
HPV Vaccine   308
HPV Screening and Cancer   308
Hepatitis B   309
Parasitic STIs   314
Pubic Lice and Scabies   314
Trichomoniasis   314
STI Prevention   315
References   316
Contacts   317
Activities   318
In-Class Activities   318
Notebook Activities   318
IN-CLASS ACTIVITY   319
Can We Make Ends Meet?   319
Parents   321
Parents (2)   323
NOTEBOOK ACTIVITY   325
STI Attitudes   325
Hepatitis Risk Assessment   327

CHAPTER 9

Drug Misuse and Abuse   329
Introduction   330
Alcohol   330
What Is Alcohol?   330
Physiological Effects   331
Blood Alcohol Concentration   331
Societal Problems   333
Drinking and Driving   333
Alcohol Use in College   335
Binge Drinking   336
Alcohol Poisoning   336
Drinking Problems   337
Alcoholism   338
Chronic Effects   338
Laws Relating to Alcohol   340
Tobacco   341
Tobacco Components   341
Types of Tobacco Use   342
Environmental Tobacco Smoke   345
Smoking Cessation   345
Cannabinoids   347
Opioids   348
Heroin   348
Stimulants   348
Caffeine   348
Cocaine   350
Amphetamines   350
Methamphetamines   350
Club Drugs   351
MDMA   351

2C-B   351
Rohypnol   351
Gamma Hydroxybutyrate (GHB)   352
Dissociative Drugs   352
Ketamine Hydrochloride   352
Phencyclidine Hydrochloride   352
Hallucinogens   352
Lysergic Acid Diethylamide (LSD)   353
Other Drugs   353
Anabolic Steroids   353
Prescription Drugs   354
Opioid Pain Relievers   354
Hydrocodone   354
Morphine   354
Codeine   354
Oxycodone   355
Stimulants   355
Depressants   355
Prescription Drug Conclusion   355
References   357
Activities   358
In-Class Activities   358
Notebook Activities   358
IN-CLASS ACTIVITY   359
The Physical Effects of Smoking   359
NOTEBOOK ACTIVITY   361
Are You Addicted to Nicotine?   361
"Why Do You Smoke?" Test   363
"Do You Want to Quit?" Test   365
Addictive Behavior Questionnaire   367
Alcohol Screening Self-Assessment   369
Making Changes   371

CHAPTER 10

Safety Awareness   373
Classes of Unintentional Injuries   374
Motor Vehicle Safety   374
Distracted Driving   374
Drowsy Driving   375
Motorcycles   376
Bicycle Safety   377
Helmet Laws   377
Home Safety   378
Poisoning   378
Falls   378
Fires and Burns   378
Workplace Safety   380
Public Safety   380
Hurricanes   381
Disaster Planning   381
Personal Safety   383
Safety Tips   383

Home   383
Car   384
Campus   384
College Campuses   384
Stalking   385
Sexual Violence   386
Acquaintance Rape   387
Safety Tips   387
Steps to Take if Rape Occurs   388
Intimate/Family Violence   388
Environmental Safety   388
Reduce, Reuse, Recycle   388
References   390
Contacts   391
Activities   391
Notebook Activities   391
NOTEBOOK ACTIVITY   393
Family Emergency Plan   393
Checklist of Rape Prevention Strategies   395
A College Studen't Guide to Safety
Planning   399

CHAPTER 11

Human Diseases   403
Communicable Diseases   404
HIV/AIDS (Non-Sexual Contraction)   404
Tuberculosis   404
Mononucleosis   405
Hepatitis   406
Hepatitis A   406
Hepatitis B   408
Hepatitis C   408
Hepatitis D, E, and G   409
Meningitis   409
Common Cold   410
Influenza   410
Non-Communicable Diseases   411
Cancer   411
Skin Cancer   413
Lung Cancer   417
Breast Cancer   417
Cervical Cancer   419
Testicular Cancer   421
Colon and Rectum Cancers   422
Oral Cancers   422
Asthma   422
Diabetes   423
Anemia   425
Lupus   426
Gastrointestinal Disorders   427
References   428
Contacts   429
Activities   430
Notebook Activities   430

NOTEBOOK ACTIVITY   431
   Current Trends Writing Assignment   431
   Family Health Portrait   433
   Are You at Risk for Diabetes?   435
   At-Risk Weight Chart   436
   Family Tree Assignment   437

CHAPTER 12
Complementary and Alternative Medicine   439
Alternative Healthcare Systems   443
Manipulative and Body-Based Therapies   447
Biological-Based Therapies   449

Mind-Body Medicine   452
Energy Therapies   456
Using the Internet for Credible Medical
   Information   458
References   458
Contacts   460
Recommended Books For Further Reading   461
Appendix   463
   *College Health Risk Assessment
      Assignment   463*
Glossary   465
Index   473

Acknowledgments

The authors would like to acknowledge the following individuals for their invaluable contributions in the writing of *Health and Fitness: A Guide to a Healthy Lifestyle:*

Julie Barber, M.S.   Susan Wagner, M.S.
Roger Bounds, Ph.D.   Dianne Maddox, M.S.
William Coady, M.S.   Martha Muckleroy, M.Ed.
Tamara Franks, M.A.G.   Jeremy Nelms, M.S.
Melinda Grant, M.S.   Christine Reeves, M.S.
Janet Hardcastle, M.S.   Teresa Wenzel, M.S.
Sandra Kimbrough, Ph.D.   Brian Wigley, M.S.
Ernie Kirkham, M.S.   Nicole Wilkerson, M.S.

We also acknowledge with appreciation the continuing guidance and support from the expert review panel:

Robert Armstrong, Ph.D.   Margaret Griffith, M.S.
Danny Ballard, Ed.D   Linda Mullen, M.D.
Susan Bloomfield, Ph.D.   B.E. Pruitt, Ed.D.
Maurice Dennis, Ph.D.   Jack Wilmore, Ph.D.
Jerry Elledge, Ph.D.

Special thanks to:
Roger Bounds, Richard Darnell, Kathy Durkin, Alyssa Locklear, Beth Netherland, and Kristin Slagel for their guidance, support, and input.

Without the technical knowledge of Kristin Slagel, M.S., and Beth Netherland, M.S., the development of the Powerpoint presentation and the contribution it makes to the text would not have been possible.

Laura Bounds, M.S., MCHES, ACE

Laura Bounds is an Assistant Clinical Professor in the Health Sciences Department at Northern Arizona University (NSU). Laura currently teaches Health Principles, Human Diseases, Theories of Health Behavior, Maternal Child, and Sexual Health courses at Northern Arizona University. Prior to her time at NAU she spent fourteen years at Texas A&M University in College Station, where she earned her B.B.A. in Accounting, M.S. in Health Education, taught Health and Fitness courses, and coordinated the Health and Fitness program for five years. Outside of the classroom, Laura enjoys spending time with her children, hiking, mountain biking, scuba diving, and snow skiing.

Kirstin Brekken Shea, M.S.

Kirstin is a Senior Lecturer and Coordinator of Group Exercise Activities in the Physical Education and Activity program in the Health and Kinesiology Department at Texas A&M University. Childhood obesity, stress management through yoga/meditation, and adult fitness/nutrition are her particular areas of interest. Kirstin teaches Kinesiology majors classes as well as step aerobics, cardio-kickboxing, walking, and beginning and intermediate yoga. She especially enjoys sharing yogic principles in order to enhance her students' quality of life. Kirstin is a soccer mom of three wonderful, active kids. She loves to hang out with her family, cook, garden, and of course attend soccer practices and games.

Dottiedee Agnor, M.S.

Dottiedee has been teaching at Texas A&M University in the Health and Kinesiology Department for the past twelve years. She is coordinator for the areas of Self-Defense, Yoga, Badminton, and Basketball. She also teaches Safety Education courses as well as Alcohol Awareness programs. She received a B.S. in Physical Education and Health and an M.S. in Kinesiology at Texas A&M University. She has also been involved with the National Youth Sports program for the past thirteen years as Director and Project Administrator. Prior to returning to the college setting she was a public school teacher in the Richardson Independent School District, coaching and teaching physical education and health. Her interests are drug and alcohol prevention, personal safety awareness, and underserved youth services.

Gayden Darnell, M.S.

Gayden is currently teaching Health and Fitness and Physical Education classes at Texas A&M University. She has taught for the Physical Education Activity program at Texas A&M in College Station since 1997 and has spent several semesters coordinating racquet sports for the department during this time. Prior to teaching at TAMU, she taught and coached in the Bryan, Texas public schools. She attended Millsaps College in Jackson, Mississippi, for two years during which time she played on the varsity tennis and soccer teams. She earned both her B.S. in Kinesiology and M.S. in Health Education from Texas A&M University in College Station. Outside of the classroom, Gayden enjoys spending time with her children, coaching and attending various youth sports, training for half and full marathons, and reading.

Chapter 1
Introduction

© 2012, Shutterstock, Inc.

OBJECTIVES

Students will be able to:

- Differentiate between the definitions of health and wellness.
- Describe and discuss the seven dimensions of wellness.
- Identify the link between preventative behaviors and wellness.
- Discuss the health behaviors that increase the quality and longevity of life.
- Identify the significance of *Healthy People 2020*.
- List the five stages of change.
- Describe key elements for a successful behavior change.

> *"Take care of your body with steadfast fidelity.*
> *The soul must see through these eyes alone, and*
> *if they are dim, the whole world is clouded."*
>
> **—Johann Wolfgang Von Goethe**

Health is a universal trait. The World Health Organization defines **health** as a "state of complete physical, mental, and social well-being and not merely the absence of disease or infirmity." Webster's Dictionary offers "the condition of being sound in body, mind, or spirit; especially: freedom from physical disease or pain . . . the general condition of the body" as a definition of health. However, health also has an individual quality; it is very personal, and unique.

Early on, definitions of health revolved around issues of sanitation and personal hygiene. Today, the definition of health has evolved from a basis of physical health or absence of disease, to a term that encompasses the emotional, mental, social, spiritual, and physical dimensions of an individual. This current, positive approach to health is referred to as wellness. **Wellness** is a process of making informed choices that will lead one, over a period of time, to a healthy lifestyle that should result in a sense of well-being.

Dimensions of Wellness

Wellness emphasizes an individual's potential and responsibility for his or her own health. It is a process in which a person is constantly moving either away from or toward a most favorable level of health. Wellness results from the adoption of low-risk, health-enhancing behaviors. The adoption of a wellness lifestyle requires focusing on choices that will enhance the individual's potential to lead a productive, meaningful, and satisfying life.

It is the complex interaction of each of the seven dimensions of wellness that will lead an individual, over time, to a higher quality of life and better overall health and well-being. Constant, ongoing assessment of one's behaviors in the following dimensions is key to living a balanced life. In addition to the seven dimensions shown in Figure 1.1, there is discussion of other factors that influence wellness.

FIGURE 1.1

Seven Dimensions of Wellness

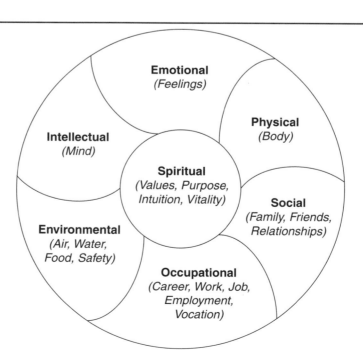

Emotional

An individual who is emotionally healthy is able to enjoy life despite unexpected challenges and problems. Effectively coping with life's difficulties and unexpected events is essential to maintaining good health. Equally important to good personal wellness is the ability to understand your feelings and express those feelings or emotions outwardly in a positive and constructive manner. "Bottled-up" negative emotions can affect the immune system and result in chronic stress, which in turn can lead to serious illnesses such as high blood pressure and can potentially lead to a premature death.

© Yuri Arcurs, 2012, Shutterstock, Inc.

The ability to relate and interact with others is important to a person's overall sense of well-being.

Intellectual

The mind can have substantial influence over the body. To be intellectually healthy, it is essential to continue to explore new avenues and interests and to regularly engage in new and ongoing learning opportunities and experiences. The more "unknowns" an individual faces or explores, the more opportunities he or she has to learn and grow intellectually.

Social

Social health is an individual's ability to relate to and interact with others. Socially healthy people are able to communicate and interact with the other people they come in contact with each day. They are respectful and caring of their family, friends, neighbors, and associates. Although reaching out and communicating with others may be difficult or uncomfortable initially, it is extremely important to a person's social health and their overall sense of well-being.

Spiritual

Spiritual health helps a person achieve a sense of inner peace, satisfaction, and confidence. It can help give the sense that all is right with the world. A person's ethics, values, beliefs, and morals can contribute to their spiritual health. Good spiritual health can help give life meaning and purpose.

Physical

Ensuring good physical health begins with devoting attention and time to attaining healthy levels of cardiovascular fitness, muscular strength and endurance, flexibility, and body composition. When coupled with good nutritional practices, good sleep habits, and the avoidance of risky social behaviors such as drinking and driving or unprotected sexual intercourse, a physically healthy body results. This is the component that is most often associated, at first glance, with a person's health.

Occupational

Attaining occupational wellness begins with determining what roles, activities, and commitments take up a majority of an individual's time. These roles, activities, or commitments could include but are not limited to being a student, parenting, volunteering in an organization, or working at a part-time job while pursuing one's degree. It is when each of these areas are integrated and balanced in a personally and professionally fulfilling way that occupational wellness occurs.

Financial wellness has an impact on an individual and society as a whole.

Environmental

An individual's health and wellness can be substantially affected by the quality of their environment. Access to clean air, nutritious food, sanitary water, and adequate clothing and shelter are essential components to being well. An individual's environment should, at the very least, be clean and safe.

Through wellness, an individual manages a wide range of lifestyle choices. How a person chooses to behave and the decisions he or she makes in each of the seven dimensions of wellness will determine their overall quality of life. Making an active effort to combining and constantly trying to balance each of the seven dimensions is key to a long and fulfilling life.

Financial Wellness

There are many different wellness models and most include multidimensional elements. One element which has typically not been included is financial wellness. Financial wellness has an impact on an individual and society as a whole. The first step to gaining financial wellness is financial responsibility. There are numerous ways to be financially responsible, some of which include:

- Have a monthly budget and do not overspend
- Wait for items to go on sale
- Use coupons
- Avoid credit card debt (pay the balance every month)
- Use credit cards only in emergency situations
- Save at least 5 percent of net income in case of an emergency
- Do not get a car loan for more than five years (three- or four-year notes are even better)
- Always pay your bills on time
- Shop and trade at resale stores
- Pay off a mortgage early
- Check out books from a library instead of purchasing them from a bookstore
- Carpool
- Ride your bike
- Eat at home
- Go for a hike instead of going to a movie

Factors That Influence Health and Wellness

In addition to the dimensions of wellness, the factors shown in Figure 1.2 also influence health and wellness, as well as physical fitness. You will see that lifestyle is only one component that works in tandem with other factors to make up good health and wellness.

A Wellness Profile

Living well requires constant evaluation and effort on an individual's part. The following list includes important behaviors and habits to include in your daily life:

- Be responsible for your own health and wellness. Take an active role in your life and well-being.
- Learn how to recognize and manage stress effectively.

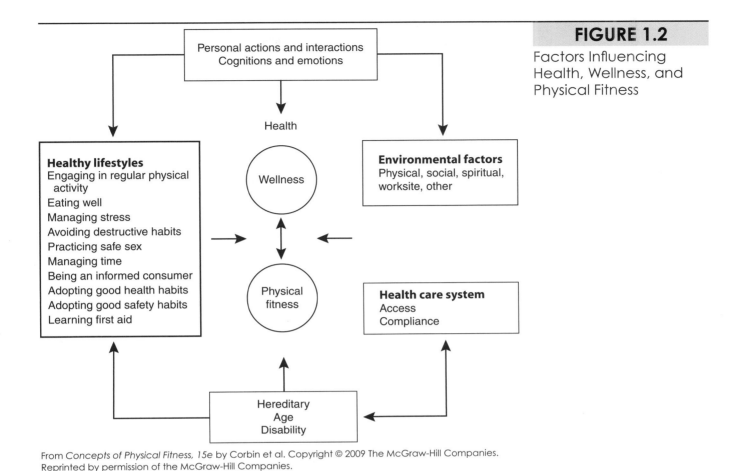

FIGURE 1.2

Factors Influencing
Health, Wellness, and
Physical Fitness

From *Concepts of Physical Fitness, 15e* by Corbin et al. Copyright © 2009 The McGraw-Hill Companies.
Reprinted by permission of the McGraw-Hill Companies.

- Eat nutritious meals, exercise regularly, and maintain a healthy weight.
- Work towards healthy relationships with friends, family, and significant others.
- Avoid tobacco and other drugs; use alcohol responsibly, if at all.
- Know the facts about cardiovascular disease, cancer, infections, sexually transmitted infections, and injuries. Utilize this knowledge to protect yourself.
- Understand how the environment affects your health and take appropriate measures to improve it.
(adapted from Insel & Roth, 2009)

Changing Behavior and Setting Goals

The Stages of Change

The Stages of Change Model (SCM) was originally developed in the late 1970s and early 1980s by James Prochaska and Carlo DiClemente when they were studying how smokers were able to quit smoking. The SCM model has been applied to many different behavior changes including weight loss, injury prevention, alcohol use, drug abuse, and others. The SCM consists of five stages of change precontemplation, contemplation, preparation, action, and maintenance. The idea behind the SCM is that behavior change does not usually happen all

© Jason Stitt, 2012, Shutterstock, Inc.

Living well requires constant
evaluation and effort.

at one time. People tend to progress through the stages until they achieve a successful behavior change or relapse. The progression through each of these stages is different depending upon the individual and the particular behavior being changed. Each person must decide when a stage is complete and when it is time to move on to the next stage.

Precontemplation

The stage at which there is no intention to change a specific behavior in the foreseeable future. Many individuals in this stage are unaware of their unhealthy behavior. They are not thinking about change and are not interested in any help. People in this stage tend to defend their current behavior and do not feel it is a problem. They may resent efforts to help them change.

Contemplation

The stage at which people are more aware of the consequences of their unhealthy behavior and have spent time thinking about the behavior but have not yet made a commitment to take action. They consider the possibility of changing, but tend to be ambivalent about change. In this stage, people straddle the fence, weighing the pros and cons of changing or modifying their behavior.

Preparation

A stage that combines intention and behavioral criteria. In this stage, people have made a commitment to make a change. This can be a research phase where people are taking small steps toward change. They gather information about what they will need to do to change their behavior. Sometimes, people skip this stage and try to move directly from contemplation to action. Many times, this can result in failure because they did not research or accept what it was going to take to make a major lifestyle change.

Action

The stage at which individuals actually modify their behavior. This stage requires a considerable commitment of time and energy. The amount of time people spend in the action stage varies. On average, it generally lasts about six months. In this stage, unhealthy people depend on their own willpower. They are making efforts to change the unhealthy behavior and are at greatest risk for relapse. During this stage, support from friends and family can be very helpful.

Along the way to a permanent behavior change, most people experience a relapse. In fact, it is much more common to have at least one setback than not. Relapse is often accompanied by feelings of discouragement. While relapse can be frustrating, the majority of people who successfully change their behavior do not follow a straight path to a lifetime free of unwanted behaviors. Rather, they cycle through the five stages several times before achieving a consistent behavior change. Therefore, the SCM considers relapse to be normal. Relapses can be important opportunities for learning and becoming stronger. This is where a behavior change journal and weekly reflections can help an individual see how much progress has been made, as well as what may trigger relapses. The main thing to remember is that the goal is getting closer. Do not get upset by life or setbacks, but keep moving forward and get closer to the end goal.

Maintenance

The stage in which people work to prevent relapse and focus on the gains attained during the action stage. Maintenance involves being able to successfully avoid temptations to return to the previous behavior. The goal of the maintenance stage is to continue the new behavior or lack there of without relapse. People are more able to successfully anticipate situations in which a relapse could occur and prepare coping or avoidance strategies in advance.

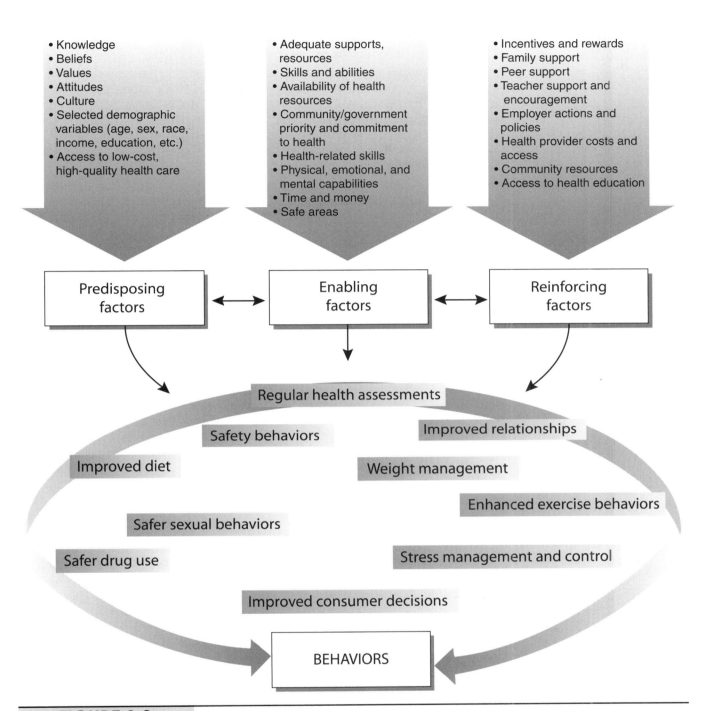

FIGURE 1.3

Factors That Influence Behavior Change Decisions

Behavior Change and Goal Setting

Listed below are some tips for successful behavior change.

Choose a behavior that an individual is really invested in. Utilize the Lifestyle Assessment Inventory at the end of this chapter to see what behavioral areas need the most attention. Ideas for behavior change include: better communication, working on a particular relationship (parent, friend, significant other), increasing exercise, quitting smoking, decreasing procrastination, decreasing or eliminating sodas, eating more fruits and/or vegetables, flossing teeth every day, stretching, and so on.

Only change one behavior at a time. After reviewing lifestyle behaviors, people tend to get excited and want to change several different behaviors. Even if the behaviors are related, it is best to choose only one to focus on at a time. After a specific behavior has become a habit (at least six months in the maintenance stage) the individual can consider working on another behavior.

The goal should be specific and measurable. The more specific the goal and the plan to achieve this goal are, the more likely the behavior change will be successful. If an individual wants to increase fitness, it would be best to be very specific about the short- and long-term goals. For example, the individual should consider their baseline (where they are right now). If someone is not exercising at all, they should not begin working out five times per week the following week. During the first week the individual may want to exercise two times for fifteen minutes each exercise session. The following week the goal could be three times at twenty minutes each exercise session. The final goal may be five days per week for thirty minutes each time. This particular goal should take at least a month or two to achieve. The Behavior Change and Goal Setting notebook activity at the end of the chapter can help outline a plan of change.

Any behavior change target should be realistic. Often, behavior change goals include weight loss. To increase the long-term success rate, the most a person should lose is two pounds per week. One pound is equal to 3,500 calories. In order to lose two pounds per week the caloric deficit would need to be 7,000 calories. This translates to a deficit of 1,000 calories per day, which is not easy to achieve. The best way to achieve this caloric deficit is to include both exercise and limit caloric consumption. For example, an individual could expend part of the needed caloric deficit with exercise (approximately 500 calories per day) as well as consume fewer (approximately 500) calories per day for a total daily caloric deficit of 1,000. Remember, this is the most an individual should lose per week.

Have a reward system. It is nice to have short- and long-term goals that have a small reward when a goal is reached. These rewards should never be counterproductive. For example, if an individual is trying to lose weight, the worst type of reward would be to have a dessert. Some constructive reward ideas could be to go to a movie, go for a specific hike, buy a new pair of shorts, purchase a book or magazine.

Keep a journal. Recording notes on a regular basis is a great way to keep a behavior change project on an individual's mind. It also creates a method to track progress and setbacks. A lot can be learned from looking at what worked and what did not in previous weeks. It is best to journal a minimum of three days per week and include a weekly reflection statement summarizing how the week progressed. This can give the individual critical insight that they may not have had without the journaling process.

Have a support group. Tell friends and family members who will be supportive about a particular behavior change. The more people who know about the behavior change, the more likely the change will be successful.

By regularly evaluating your lifestyle and making small changes, you can maintain a healthy lifestyle. There are significant benefits to choosing healthy behaviors early on. The earlier these healthy behaviors are achieved, the more graceful aging will be. In Figure 1.4 the life expectancy is differentiated between healthy life expectancy and unhealthy years. In Figure 1.5 the number one cause of death is unintentional injury until the age of 44. After age 44, the leading causes of death are cancer and heart disease. These two figures demonstrate how critical it is that healthy behavior choices are made now rather than waiting until an injury or disease has occurred.

© Brian Dixon, 2012, Shutterstock, Inc.

The best way to avoid injuries and disease is through prevention. There are three types of prevention: primary, secondary and tertiary. **Primary prevention** utilizes behaviors to avoid the development of disease. This can include getting immunizations, exercising regularly, eating healthy meals, limiting exposure to sunlight, using sunscreen, having safe drinking water, and guarding against accidents. The focus of this textbook will be primary prevention to help individuals choose behaviors that will prevent disease and premature death.

The Stages of Change Model consists of precontemplation, contemplation, preparation, action, and maintenance.

Secondary prevention is aimed at early detection of disease. This can include blood pressure screenings, mammograms, and annual pap tests to identify and detect disease in its earliest stages. This is before noticeable symptoms develop, when the disease is most likely to be treated successfully. With early detection and diagnosis, it may be possible to cure a disease, slow its progression, prevent or minimize complications, and limit disability. Another goal of secondary prevention is to prevent the spread of communicable diseases. In the community, early identification and treatment of people with communicable diseases, such as sexually transmitted infections, not only provides secondary prevention for those who are infected but also primary prevention for people who come in contact with infected individuals.

Tertiary prevention works to improve the quality of life for individuals with various diseases by limiting complications and disabilities, restoring function, and slowing or stopping the progression of a disease. Tertiary prevention plays a key role for individuals with arthritis, asthma, heart disease, and diabetes.

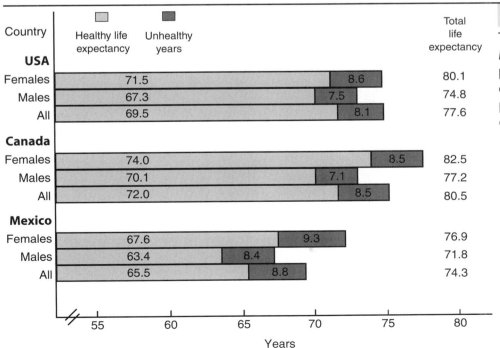

FIGURE 1.4

The Stages of Change Model consists of precontemplation, contemplation, preparation, action, and maintenance.

Country	Healthy life expectancy	Unhealthy years	Total life expectancy
USA			
Females	71.5	8.6	80.1
Males	67.3	7.5	74.8
All	69.5	8.1	77.6
Canada			
Females	74.0	8.5	82.5
Males	70.1	7.1	77.2
All	72.0	8.5	80.5
Mexico			
Females	67.6	9.3	76.9
Males	63.4	8.4	71.8
All	65.5	8.8	74.3

Years

Sources: World Health Organization and National Center for Health Statistics

FIGURE 1.5

10 Leading Causes of Death by Age Group, United States 2007

Rank	<1	1–4	5–9	10–14	15–24	25–34	35–44	45–54	55–64	65+	All Ages
1	Congenital Anomalies 5,785	Unintentional Injury 1,588	Unintentional Injury 965	Unintentional Injury 1,229	Unintentional Injury 15,897	Unintentional Injury 14,977	Unintentional Injury 16,931	Malignant Neoplasms 50,167	Malignant Neoplasms 103,171	Heart Disease 496,095	Heart Disease 616,067
2	Short Gestation 4,857	Congenital Anomalies 546	Malignant Neoplasms 480	Malignant Neoplasms 479	Homicide 5,551	Suicide 5,278	Malignant Neoplasms 13,288	Heart Disease 37,434	Heart Disease 65,527	Malignant Neoplasms 389,730	Malignant Neoplasms 562,875
3	SIDS 2,453	Homicide 398	Congenital Anomalies 196	Homicide 213	Suicide 4,140	Homicide 4,758	Heart Disease 11,839	Unintentional Injury 20,315	Chronic Low. Respiratory Disease 12,777	Cerebro-vascular 115,961	Cerebro-vascular 135,952
4	Maternal Pregnancy Comp. 1,769	Malignant Neoplasms 364	Homicide 133	Suicide 180	Malignant Neoplasms 1,653	Malignant Neoplasms 3,463	Suicide 6,722	Liver Disease 8,212	Unintentional Injury 12,193	Chronic Low. Respiratory Disease 109,562	Chronic Low. Respiratory Disease 127,924
5	Unintentional Injury 1,285	Heart Disease 173	Heart Disease 110	Congenital Anomalies 178	Heart Disease 1,084	Heart Disease 3,223	HIV 3,572	Suicide 7,778	Diabetes Mellitus 11,304	Alzheimer's Disease 73,797	Unintentional Injury 123,706
6	Placenta Cord Membranes 1,135	Influenza & Pneumonia 109	Chronic Low. Respiratory Disease 54	Heart Disease 131	Congenital Anomalies 402	HIV 1,091	Homicide 3,052	Cerebro-vascular 6,385	Cerebro-vascular 10,500	Diabetes Mellitus 51,528	Alzheimer's Disease 74,632
7	Bacterial Sepsis 820	Septicemia 78	Influenza & Pneumonia 48	Chronic Low. Respiratory Disease 64	Cerebro-vascular 195	Diabetes Mellitus 610	Liver Disease 2,570	Diabetes Mellitus 5,753	Liver Disease 8,004	Influenza & Pneumonia 45,941	Diabetes Mellitus 71,382
8	Respiratory Distress 789	Perinatal Period 70	Benign Neoplasms 41	Influenza & Pneumonia 55	Diabetes Mellitus 168	Cerebro-vascular 505	Cerebro-vascular 2,133	HIV 4,156	Suicide 5,069	Nephritis 38,484	Influenza & Pneumonia 52,717
9	Circulatory System Disease 624	Benign Neoplasms 59	Cerebro-vascular 38	Cerebro-vascular 45	Influenza & Pneumonia 163	Congenital Anomalies 417	Diabetes Mellitus 1,984	Chronic Low. Respiratory Disease 4,153	Nephritis 4,440	Unintentional Injury 38,292	Nephritis 46,448
10	Neonatal Hemorrhage 597	Chronic Low. Respiratory Disease 57	Septicemia 36	Benign Neoplasms 43	Three Tied* 160	Liver Disease 384	Septicemia 910	Viral Hepatitis 2,815	Septicemia 4,231	Septicemia 26,362	Septicemia 34,828

Age Groups

*The three causes are: Complicated Pregnacy, HIV, Septicemia

Source: National Vital Statistics System. National Center for Health Statistics, CDC. Produced by: Office of Statistics and Programming, National Center for Injury Prevention and Control, CDC.

Healthy People 2020: Improving the Health of Americans

There are twelve major public health areas, which include leading health indicators. They are:

- Access to health services
- Clinical preventive services
- Environmental quality
- Injury and violence
- Maternal, infant, and child health
- Mental health
- Nutrition, physical activity, and obesity
- Oral health
- Reproductive and sexual health
- Social determinants
- Substance abuse
- Tobacco

www.healthypeople.gov/2020/LHI.default.aspx

There are four major factors that influence personal health:

1. personal behavior
2. heredity
3. environment
4. access to professional health care personnel

The importance of prevention is made clear in *Healthy People 2020. Healthy People* was first developed in 1979 as a *Surgeon General's Report*. It has been reformulated since 1979 as *Healthy People 1990: Promoting Health/Preventing Disease, Healthy People 2000: National Health Promotion and Disease Prevention and Healthy People 2010; Objectives for Improving Health*. The original efforts of these programs were to establish national health objectives and to serve as a base of knowledge for the development of both state-level and community-level plans and programs to improve the nation's overall health. Much like the programs *Healthy People 2020* is based on, it was developed through broad consultation programs and the best and most current scientific knowledge in the public and private sectors. It is also designed in a way that will allow communities to measure the success rates, over time, of the programs they choose to implement.

Healthy People 2020 has four overarching goals. The first goal is to attain high quality, longer lives free of preventable disease, disability, injury, and premature death. The second goal is to achieve health equity, eliminate disparities, and improve the health of all groups. The third goal is to create social and physical environments that promote good health for all. One last goal is to promote quality of life, healthy development, and healthy behaviors across all life stages. In an attempt to meet these overarching goals, *Healthy People 2020* has forty-two topic areas—each with a concise goal statement that is designed to frame the overall purpose of each of the forty-two topic areas. For example:

- Topic Area Five. Cancer

Goal—Reduce the number of new cancer cases as well as the illness, disability, and death caused by cancer.

Each of the chapters in *Health & Fitness: A Guide to a Healthy Lifestyle* corresponds to one or more of the topic areas within *Healthy People 2020*. The chapters of this text and the corresponding focus areas of *Healthy People 2020* are as follows:

Chapter 1—Introduction

- Environmental Health
- Health Communication
- Health-Related Quality of Life and Well-Being
- Social Determinants of Health

Chapter 2—Stress and Psychological Health

- Mental Health and Mental Disorders
- Nutrition

Chapter 3—Personal Fitness

- Physical Activity

Chapter 4—Lifestyle Choices and Hypokinetic Conditions

- Arthritis, Osteoporosis, and Chronic Back Conditions
- Cancer
- Diabetes
- Heart Disease and Stroke
- Mental Health and Mental Disorders

Chapter 5—Nutrition

- Mental Health and Mental Disorders
- Nutrition and Weight Status

Chapter 6—Lifetime Weight Management

- Nutrition and Weight Status
- Physical Activity and Fitness

Chapter 7—Relationships

- Health Communication
- Lesbian, Gay, Bisexual, and Transgender Health

Chapter 8—Sexuality

- Family Planning
- Health Communication
- HIV
- Immunization and Infectious Disease
- Maternal, Infant, and Child Health
- Sexually Transmitted Diseases

Chapter 9—Drugs

- Chronic Kidney Disease
- Educational and Community-Based Programs
- Environmental Health
- Oral Health

Researchers at the Human Population Laboratory of the California Department of Health published the following list of health-related behaviors that have been associated with good health and a long life. These behaviors include:

1. Regular exercise
2. Adequate sleep
3. A good breakfast
4. Regular meals
5. Weight control
6. Abstinence from smoking and drugs
7. Moderate use of (or abstinence from) alcohol

It was shown that by following six of the seven listed behaviors, not only is an individual's quality of life greatly improved, but also, men could add eleven years to their lives and women could add seven years to their lives.

- Respiratory Diseases
- Substance Abuse
- Tobacco Use

Chapter 10—Safety Awareness

- Injury and Violence Prevention
- Social Determinats of Health

Chapter 11—Human Diseases

- Cancer
- Diabetes
- HIV
- Immunization and Infectious Disease

Chapter 12—Alternative and Complementary Medicine

- Health Communication

Summary

Health is "a state of complete physical, mental, and social well-being and not merely the absence of disease or infirmity" according to the World Health Organization. By definition, health is a universal trait. Due to the fact that personal behaviors are one of the four major factors that influence a person's lifespan and quality of life, health also takes on a very individual and unique quality.

The idea of wellness is an individual-based approach to health. Wellness is grounded in behavior modification strategies that result in the adoption of low-risk, health-enhancing behaviors. By balancing the seven components of wellness—emotional, intellectual, social, spiritual, physical, occupational, and environmental—a person can, to some degree, prevent disease and premature death.

Changing behaviors and setting goals to achieve healthy change are major steps to wellness. Using the SCM can be helpful in making behavior changes. The SCM consists of precontemplation, contemplation, preparation, action, and maintenance stages. These stages are very important to recognize when preparing for a behavior change project. The key elements in a successful behavior change include planning, research, and individual willpower. Healthy behaviors chosen early in life affect an individual's wellness now and in the years to come.

Prevention is a fundamental factor in promoting wellness. The three types of prevention include primary, secondary, and tertiary. Primary prevention utilizes behaviors to avoid injuries, the development of diseases, and premature death. Secondary prevention focuses on early detection of disease and tertiary prevention works to improve the quality of life for individuals with various disease processes.

Each decade, since the 1979 *Surgeon General's Report,* the nation has refined its health agenda—first through *Healthy People* 1990 through *Healthy People 2000: National Health Promotion and Disease Prevention* through *Healthy People 2010: Objectives for Improving Health,* and currently through *Healthy People 2020.* When an attempt is made to understand the four goals of *Healthy People 2020:*

- Goal 1—Attaining high-quality, longer lives free of preventable disease, disability, injury, and premature death

- Goal 2—Achieving health equity, eliminating disparities, and improving the health of all groups
- Goal 3—Creating social and physical environments that promote good health for all
- Goal 4—Promoting quality of life, healthy development, and healthy behaviors across all life stages

and connect the topic areas of this program with these goals, the overwhelming importance of prevention in promoting an individual's level of wellness is made clear.

References

Corbin, C. B., Welk, G. J., Corbin, W. R. and Welk, K. A. *Concepts of Physical Fitness* (16th ed). McBrown. 2010.

Floyd, P., Mims, S., and Yelding-Howard, C. *Personal Health: Perspectives and Lifestyles* (4th ed). Morton Publishing Co. 2007.

http://ahha.org http://wellness.ndsu.nodak.edu/education/dimensions.shtml

http://who.int/aboutwho/en/definition.html

http://www.cdc.gov/nchs/data/hp2k99.pdf

http://www.healthypeople.gov/2020/default.aspx

http://www.m-w.com/dictionary.htm

http://www.wellnesswise.com/dimensions.htm

Hyman, B., Oden, G., Bacharach, D., and Collins, R. *Fitness for Living* (3rd ed). Kendall-Hunt Publishing Co. 2006.

Insel, P. M. and Roth, W. T. *Core Concepts in Health* (12th ed). McGraw Hill Publishing. 2009.

Payne, W. A., Hahn, D. B., and Lucas, E. B. *Understanding Your Health* (10th ed). McGraw Hill Publishing. 2008.

Pruitt, B.E. and Stein, J. *Health Styles*. Allyn & Bacon. 1999.

Activities

In-Class Activities
Human Bingo
Journal—Goal Setting

Notebook Activities
Dimensions of Wellness Writing Assignment
Wellness Goal
Lifestyle Assessment Inventory
Behavior Change and Goal Setting
If I Had It to Do Over

Name _____ Section_____ Date_____

Human Bingo

After the leader says "GO!" ask individuals in the group if a statement matches a characteristic of himself or herself or if they have completed an item listed below. If someone answers "yes" to this question, have them sign their initials in that box. An individual can sign no more than two squares per piece of paper. Continue until someone completes a row, column, or diagonal line and yells "BINGO!"

can juggle	has TP'd a house	has colored his or her hair	received 4+ traffic tickets	plays tennis	sings in the shower	watched *Sesame Street*
ever slept in church	never changed a diaper	split their pants in public	has milked a cow	was born out of the country	has been to Hawaii	eats out at restaurants daily
watches reality shows	can touch tongue to nose	has driven a motorcycle	has never ridden a horse	moved twice last year	sleeps in a loft	has a hole in his or her sock
walked in the wrong restroom	loves classical music	ever skipped school	FREE	has broken an arm	has a hot tub	loves eating sushi
has two siblings	loves vegetables	has a 2-inch scar	wears P.J.'s	ever smoked a cigar	has been skinny-dipping	wears size 8 shoes
likes writing poetry	still has their tonsils	can quote a Bible verse	likes bubble gum	has a piercing	doesn't use mouth wash	often watches cartoons
doesn't like fishing	can wiggle their ears	can play the guitar	plays chess regularly	only reads the comics	can touch palms to floor	sleeps with stuffed animals

IN-CLASS ACTIVITY

Journal—Goal Setting

Locate the Stages of Change in Chapter 1 of your health textbook. Choose one health behavior in your life that you would like to change. You may choose to eliminate a behavior (ex. Smoking or eating fried food) or choose to begin a new behavior (like exercising or mediating).

Health Behavior:

What dimension of wellness encompasses this behavior?

What stage of change are you currently in?

What support, tools, or resources do you need to progress through the stages of change?

Set three specific short-term goals that will help you change this behavior

1. _____

_____

2. _____

_____

3. _____

_____

How will you measure your success?

NOTEBOOK ACTIVITY

Dimensions of Wellness Writing Assignment

Look at the website http://www.counseling.uci.edu/Students/wellness.aspx. What did you learn about the different dimensions of your wellness? Identify your strengths and areas that may need improvement.

Wellness Goal

Reflect on your own wellness. Are there any behaviors that you would like to change during the semester or in the future?

Establish one Wellness Goal to work toward this semester. Set short-term realistic goals that are easily measured to help support your long-term goal. Make sure to include behavioral goals that will help you reach your short-term goals. Be specific in how you plan to change this particular behavior.

Example 1

LT goal;
Degree from A&M

ST goal:
Earn a 3.5 this summer

Bahavior goals:

Get more sleep—I'll be in bed by 11:30 each night. I will look at my class schedules Sun. evening to determine my game plan for the week to maximize my free time.

Go to class more often—I'll attend 90% of my classes this summer.

Learn new study skills—I will schedule an appointment at SCC tomorrow afternoon and attend their study skills session on June 10th

Example 2

LT goal:
Improve body composition

ST goal:
Lose 5 pounds

Behavioral goals:

Exercise 3X a week—I'll work out every Mon, Wed, Fri after my last class of the day (4:00pm) and on Tues/Thur evening (9:30pm) before I take a shower in the evening.

3 dinners at home each week—I will make a menu and grocery list Sunday afternoon and will grocery shop Sunday evening. I will prepare those meals on Mon, Wed, & Friday.

And more veggies—At dinner 1/4 of my plate will be filled with veggies.

NOTEBOOK ACTIVITY

Lifestyle Assessment Inventory

The purpose of this lifestyle assessment inventory is to increase your awarness of areas in your life that increase your risk of disease, injury, and possibly premature death. A key point to remember is that you have control over each of the lifestyle areas discussed.

Awareness is the first step in making change. After identifying the areas that require modification, you will be able to use the behavior modification techniques presented in Chapter 1 to bring about positive lifestyle changes.

Directions

Put a check by each statement that applies to you. You may select more than one choice per category.

A. Physical Fitness

_____ I exercise for a minimum of twenty to thirty minutes at least three days per week.

_____ I play sports routinely (two to three times per week).

_____ I walk for fifteen to thirty minutes (three to seven days per week).

B. Body Fat

_____ There is no place on my body where I can pinch more than 1 inch of fat.

_____ I am satisfied with the way my body appears.

C. Stress Level

_____ I find it easy to relax.

_____ I rarely feel tense or anxious.

_____ I am able to cope with daily stresses without undue emotional stress.

D. Car Safety

_____ I have not had an auto accident in the past 4 years.

_____ I always use a seat belt when I drive.

_____ I rarely drive above the speed limit.

E. Sleep

_____ I always get seven to nine hours of sleep.

_____ I do not have trouble going to sleep.

_____ I generally do not wake up during the night.

F. Relationships

_____ I have a happy and satisfying relationship with my spouse or boy/girlfriend.

_____ I have a lot of close friends.

_____ I get a great deal of love and support from my family.

G. Diet

_____I generally eat three balanced meals per day.

_____I rarely overeat.

_____I rarely eat large quantities of fatty foods and sweets.

H. Alcohol Use

_____I consume fewer than two drinks per day.

_____I never get intoxicated.

_____I never drink and drive.

I. Tobacco Use

_____I never smoke (cigarettes, pipe, cigars, etc.).

_____I am not exposed to second-hand smoke on a regular basis.

_____I do not use smokeless tobacco.

J. Drug Use

_____I never use illicit drugs.

_____I never abuse legal drugs such as diet or sleeping pills.

K. Sexual Practices

_____ I always practice safe sex (e.g., always using condoms or being involved in a monogamous relationship).

Scoring

1. Individual areas: If there are any unchecked areas in categories A through K, you can improve those aspects of your lifestyle.

2. Overall lifestyle: Add up your total number of checks. Scoring can be interpreted as follows:

    23–29 Very healthy lifestyle

    17–22 Average healthy lifestyle

    < 16 Unhealthy lifestyle (needs improvement)

Name _____ Section _____ Date _____

Behavior Change and Goal Setting

In order to make positive changes in your life, you must identify behaviors that need to be modified, and behavior changes that would support your life change goals. This assignment has two parts: (1) Complete this page; (2) Type 1–2 pages reflecting your behavior change at the end of the semester. Besure to address the key elements that contributed to your success or lack thereof. Both parts should be submitted at the end of the semester for credit.

Setting Goals:

1. Make achievable and measurable goals.

2. Establish long-term goals, with weekly or monthly short-term goals that support the long-term goals.

3. Identify behavior changes that will directly support your short-term goals (for example: try to always carry a water bottle, don't keep soda where it is readily available).

4. Identify how you will measure your goals.

5. Set target dates and reasonable rewards for goal achievement.

Rewards:

A reward should be something that you enjoy but might not always get to do. It should be relatively inexpensive and accessible. It should not be anything that would reinforce the behavior you are trying to change. (Don't reward smoking cessation goals with a smoke!)

Goal:

My long-term goal is

_____

My short-term goal in support of my long-term goal is

_____

Specific behavior changes that will support my goals are _____,

_____, _____

I will achieve my long-term goal by _____(date). The reward I will

give myself upon completion of my long-term goal is

_____

_____

Note:

After achieving your goals, congratulate yourself and then make new goals. If you did not succeed with your goals, examine what behavior changes you were not able to do in order to support your short-term goals. Learn from your mistakes, and try again. Perhaps you made your goals too challenging.

Name _____ Section _____ Date_____

If I Had It to Do Over

A few years ago I read a piece by Nadine Stair called "If I Had It to Do Over," in which she was looking back on her life as an older woman and remarking about the things she would do differently. Some of the things she said were: "I would wear more purple; I would eat fewer beans and more ice cream; I would go barefoot earlier in spring."

And you? If you were eighty-five years old right now and you were looking back on the life you had lived, what would you want to do differently?

EXAMPLES:

1) I would want to take money less seriously.
2) I would want to tell the people I love that I love them.
3) I would want to take more vacations.

Complete the sentences:
If I had it to do over, I would:

1. _____

_____

2. _____

_____

3. _____

_____

4. _____

_____

5. _____

_____

6. _____

_____

7. _____

Of the seven items you listed, which ones can you begin doing this month?

Complete the sentence:
This month, I will:

1. _____

_____

2. _____

_____

3. _____

_____

Chapter 2
Stress and Psychological Health

© 2012, Shutterstock, Inc.

OBJECTIVES

Students will be able to:

- Define stress and describe ways in which stress can manifest itself.
- Introduce general tips to help individuals positively cope with stress.
- Describe the negative health complications that can result from unmanaged stress.
- Establish a link between preventative behaviors and stress.
- List characteristics of good stress managers.
- Establish a link between unmanaged stress and its detrimental effect on psychological health.

- Introduce the concept of self-talk and explain the effects positive and negative self-talk can have on an individual's stress level and its impact on the person's psychological health.
- Show the links between stress, depression and suicidal behaviors.
- Define eating disorders: who is at risk, what are the causes, what are the symptoms, how serious are they, and what can be done to help someone with an eating disorder.

"Take care of your body with steadfast fidelity. The soul must see through these eyes alone, and if they are dim, the whole world is clouded."

—Johann Wolfgang Von Goethe

Stress, both positive and negative forms, has always been a part of life. One cannot hope to live and thrive without facing stressful situations daily. Most Americans live a fast-paced, over-booked lifestyle each day in an attempt to make the most of their time and talents. Due to the fact that "working under the gun" has become the rule rather than the exception, stress has become one of the most common detriments to the overall health and well-being of Americans.

Wellness and Stress

Stress was defined by Hans Selye as the nonspecific response to demands placed on the body. "Nonspecific response" alludes to the production of the same physiological reaction by the body regardless of the type of stress placed on the body. Physiologically, when an individual is confronted with a stressor they will experience a surge of adrenaline that causes the discharge of cortisol and the release of endorphins. This, in turn, will increase the person's blood pressure and heart rate, preparing him or her to take immediate action.

While the physiological way in which all people react to stress is the same, the way a person physically, emotionally, or behaviorally reacts to a specific stressor can vary greatly. This is due in part to the fact that when facing the exact same event or circumstance it might be perceived as highly stressful and draining to one person but simply stimulating and exciting to someone else. The ways in which people outwardly react to stressful situations are a personal physical and emotional response to the stimuli. These responses can be either positive or negative.

Eustress is a positive stress that produces a sense of well-being. It is a healthy component of daily life. It can be harnessed to improve health and performance. Examples of activities or events that might initiate a positive stress response include competitive sports, graduation from school, dating, marriage, the birth of a baby, or a long awaited vacation. Eustress can help channel nervous energy into a top-notch performance.

Distress is negative stress. It is a physically and mentally damaging response to the demands placed upon the body. Distress is generally associated with changes that interrupt the natural flow of a person's life. Excessive schoolwork, loss of a job, breaking up with a significant other, or illness or death of a loved one are examples of activities or situations that may produce a negative stress response from an individual. When distress occurs, it is typical to see deterioration in the affected individual's health and performance.

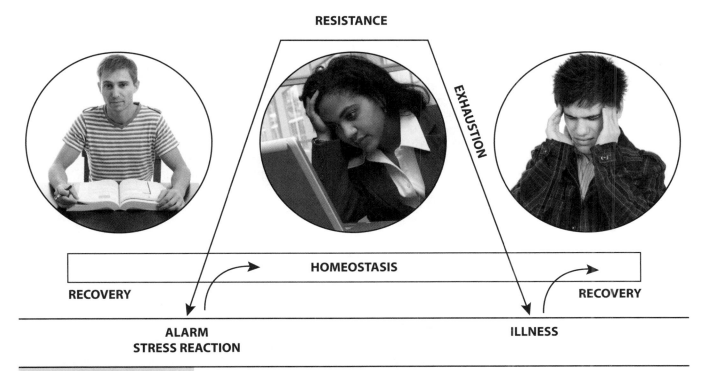

FIGURE 2.1

© Hugo Silveirinha Felix, 2009, Shutterstock, Inc.
© Rob Marmion, 2009, Shutterstock, Inc.
© Rui Vale de Sousa, 2009, Shutterstock, Inc.

The way each person chooses to manage the stressors that occur in life will, to a large degree, determine overall physical and emotional well-being. An individual's body naturally attempts to maintain a state of homeostasis, or balance, so that it can continue to function in an effective manner. When a stressful situation presents itself, an "alarm" is triggered. Then either the person deals with the situation and the body recovers and returns to a state of homeostasis, or the attempts to avoid or resist the stressor eventually result in exhaustion or illness (see Figure 2.1).

Stress is not the cause of illness, but when it goes on for long periods of time or is particularly irritating, it can become harmful by weakening an individual's immune system. This increases that person's risk of getting sick.

Uncontrolled or unmanaged stress can lead to a variety of negative health consequences such as coronary heart disease, high blood pressure, ulcers, irritable bowel syndrome, migraine headaches, and insomnia.

Certain forms of stress are not only normal but necessary in everyday life. However, the results of continual or inappropriately managed stress can cause disruptions that can be serious or severe to an individual's emotional, intellectual, social, spiritual, physical, occupational, and/or environmental health.

It is extremely important for an individual to determine how he or she handles or reacts to stressors, especially if the stress is ongoing. The way stress manifests or "shows itself" is going to vary depending on an individual's personality and past experiences.

There are typically four ways in which stress can manifest itself:

1. Emotionally
   - Do you always feel rushed, without enough time to get all that is needed done well or done at all?
   - Do you find it difficult to relax?
   - Are you irritable and moody, or easily angered?

- Do you feel helpless or hopeless?
- Do you want to cry for no apparent reason?
- Is it difficult for you to listen or pay attention to your friends without being distracted?
- Is it hard for you to fall asleep even on days when you are exhausted?
- When you do fall asleep, is it difficult to stay asleep?

2. Mentally
    - Are you indecisive in many areas of your life?
    - Is it difficult for you to concentrate?
    - Do you regularly have bad dreams or nightmares?
    - Do you have negative thoughts, including suicidal thoughts?

3. Behaviorally
    - Has your appetite changed so that you have gained or lost significant amounts of weight?
    - Are you neglecting yourself/your appearance?
    - Have you curtailed social activities?
    - Have you taken to substance abuse, such as cigarette smoking, drug use, or excessive alcohol or coffee intakes?

4. Physically
    - Do you have an increased heart rate or blood pressure?
    - Can you feel your own heart beat?
    - Do you feel out of breath or have tightness in your chest?
    - Do you suffer from frequent headaches or muscle aches due to chronic tension?
    - Is it difficult for you to digest food—leading to nausea or diarrhea?
    - Do you suffer from frequent attacks of infections such as influenza or sore throats?

Recognizing how stress affects their lives allows individuals to recognize stressful situations and to immediately deal with, or cope with, something that has the potential to compromise their overall well-being.

While uncontrolled or unmanaged stress can lead to negative health consequences, there are a number of ways to control stress. What works for one person will not necessarily be helpful to someone else. It is important to recognize the stressor (see Figure 2.2) and determine the most effective way(s) to relieve, reduce, or eliminate that particular stressor. Another key to successfully managing stressors is to use a strategy that produces positive results, rather than a strategy that creates additional stress. Also, to be successful with stress management, give a particular stressor only the amount of energy it warrants—do not give a "10 cent" stressor $10 worth of time or energy. The following are general tips that can help maintain a healthy lifestyle and can prepare an individual to cope with many of the stressors found in everyday life.

FIGURE 2.2

Stressors in the Lives of College Students

STRESSORS IN THE LIVES OF COLLEGE STUDENTS

Drug use	Military obligations
Academic competition	Social alienation, anonymity
College red tape	Love/marriage decisions
Religious conflicts	Illness and injury
Choice of major/future job	Lack of privacy
Sexual pressures	Parental conflict
Family responsibilities	Time management
Loneliness Depression Anxiety	Alcohol use
Money troubles	

Source: Adapted from W. W. K. Hoeger, L. W. Turner, and B. Q. Hafen. *Wellness Guidelines for a Healthy Lifestyle.* Wadsworth/Thomson Learning, 2007.

1. Deal with the cause:
   Finish the task, talk to the person, fix the tire, write the letter, make the call—do what needs to be done to deal with the situation. The longer a situation gets put off, the more stress it can create.
2. Put the situation into perspective: How important is it really? How important will this be tomorrow, in six months? Most situations that tax physical/mental energies will soon be inconsequential and forgotten. Determine if anything can be done about the situation, or if it is a situation that calls for acceptance.
3. Pace yourself:
   No one can be in "high gear" all the time. Too often individuals stop to "smell the roses" only after the first accident or heart attack. Set short and intermediate goals—reward yourself upon reaching these goals.
4. Laugh at life and at yourself:
   Humor is a wonderful tool. Laughing is internal jogging! She or he who laughs . . . lasts! See the humor in people and the absurdity of situations. Read the "funny pages."
5. Develop quality relationships:
   Seek social and emotional support systems—individuals who care, love, and will listen to you. Express feelings constructively. Be there for others and allow others to be there for you in the good times and in the bad times.
6. Time management needs to be life management:
   Look at goals and responsibilities from a bigger perspective; this can help with decision making. Streamline activities by breaking big, imposing jobs into small components and list each activity in a daily planner. Seek assistance when it is needed; don't try to do everything yourself—delegate! Avoid common "time killers" (see Figure 2.3).
7. Look at situations and people in a different light—try an attitude adjustment: Is your perception of the situation, event, or person correct? Is there another way to handle things, or is there another possible way to answer the problem? Go easier on yourself and on others. It is unreasonable to expect perfection from yourself or from others. Perfection is a "moving target" and causes constant stress. Take care of the things you can; don't worry about the things that are beyond your control.
8. Balance fun and responsibility:
   Family, society, and community encourage and command constant work and responsibility. It is important to contribute and to meet responsibilities, but it is also important to find enjoyment and fun in life as well. Do something you find enjoyable on a regular basis and don't feel guilty!

Reduce Stress and Improve Your Life with Positive Self-Talk
Start by following a single, simple rule: If you wouldn't say what you are thinking to someone else, don't "think it" to yourself!!

Try to take time during your day to really think about what is "running, unfiltered through your head."

If you find that you are mentally beating yourself up, stop and try to put a positive angle on your thoughts. For example, if you are thinking "I'll never get better at this," try putting a positive spin on it and change your thinking to, "It never hurts to keep trying!"

COMMON TIME KILLERS

- Watching television
- Listening to radio/music
- Sleeping
- Eating
- Daydreaming
- Shopping
- Socializing/parties
- Recreation
- Talking on the telephone
- Worrying
- Procrastinating
- Drop-in visitors
- Confusion (unclear goals)
- Indecision (what to do next)
- Interruptions
- Perfectionism (every detail must be done)

FIGURE 2.3
Behavior Modification Planning

Balance fun and responsibility. Do something you enjoy on a regular basis and don't feel guilty.

9. Exercise and eat sensibly:
Exercise is one of the best stress-busters. Schedule exercise into your life. Walk, bike, swim, stretch, and recreate. Good food in proper proportions is also essential to good health and is an excellent way to reduce the negative effects stress may have on your life.

When an individual is able to identify stress management techniques that work with her or his personality and lifestyle, it can be extremely beneficial to be proactive in recognizing potential sources of stress so that they can be dealt with before they become detrimental to the individual's overall well-being.

There are several scales or scientific instruments that have been designed in an attempt to measure an individual's level of stress. The Student Stress Scale that is shown in Figure 2.4 has been modified from the Holmes and Rahe's Life Events Scale (1967) to gauge the stress level and corresponding health consequences for collegeaged adults.

In the Student Stress Scale, each event, such as beginning or ending school, is given a score that represents the amount of readjustment a person has to make in life as a result of the change. To determine a stress score, add up the number of points corresponding to the events that have happened during the past six months or are likely to occur within the next six months.

People with scores of 300 points or higher have a high health risk. Individuals scoring between 150 and 300 points have about a fifty-fifty

FIGURE 2.4
Student Stress Scale

1.	Death of a close family member	❏	100	❏
2.	Death of a close friend	❏	73	❏
3.	Divorce between parents	❏	65	❏
4.	Jail term	❏	63	❏
5.	Major personal injury or illness	❏	63	❏
6.	Marriage	❏	58	❏
7.	Fired from job	❏	50	❏
8.	Failed important course	❏	47	❏
9.	Change in health of a family member	❏	45	❏
10.	Pregnancy	❏	45	❏
11.	Sexual problems	❏	44	❏
12.	Serious argument with close friend	❏	40	❏
13.	Change in financial status	❏	39	❏
14.	Change of major	❏	39	❏
15.	Trouble with parents	❏	39	❏
16.	New girl- or boyfriend	❏	38	❏
17.	Increased workload at school	❏	37	❏
18.	Outstanding personal achievement	❏	36	❏
19.	First quarter/semester in college	❏	35	❏
20.	Change in living conditions	❏	31	❏
21.	Serious argument with instructor	❏	30	❏
22.	Lower grades than expected	❏	29	❏
23.	Change in sleeping habits	❏	29	❏
24.	Change in social activities	❏	29	❏
25.	Change in eating habits	❏	26	❏
26.	Chronic car trouble	❏	26	❏
27.	Change in number of family get-togethers	❏	26	❏
28.	Too many missed classes	❏	25	❏
29.	Change of college	❏	24	❏
30.	Dropped more than one class	❏	23	❏
31.	Minor traffic violations	❏	20	❏

Source: Adapted from T. H. Holmes and R. H. Rahe, 1967, *Journal of Psychosomatic Research,* 11:213.

chance of developing a serious health condition within the next two years. People scoring below 150 points have a one-in-three chance of developing a serious health condition.

It is imperative that individuals recognize the potential stressors that occur in their lives. However, it is equally important that individuals also acknowledge an overall level of stress. By doing this, a proactive "deal with it" approach can be taken. This lessens the negative impact that stress can have on overall well-being and allows them to become good stress managers (see Figure 2.5).

Self-Talk Your Way to Reduced Levels of Stress and an Improved Life

What Is Self-Talk?

Self-talk is the constant interpretation of the different situations that individuals find themselves in throughout each day. It is that "inner voice" that determines one's perception of a situation. Conscious thoughts, as well as subconscious thoughts, are part of a person's inner voice. Negative or positive self-talk begins early in most individuals' lives and can determine the impact stress has on each person's life.

Negative or Positive Self-Talk

Negative self-talk such as "I am going to fail my test" or "there is no way I can run that far or fast or perform that move" is self-defeating. Negative interpretation of a situation will often make that situation more stressful than it needs to be.

Replacing negative thoughts or self-talk with positive thoughts can decrease stress levels and improve a person's productivity and overall outlook. There

---

CHARACTERISTICS OF GOOD STRESS MANAGERS

Good stress managers
- are physically active, eat a healthy diet, and get adequate rest every day.
- believe they have control over events in their life (have an internal locus of control).
- understand their own feelings and accept their limitations.
- recognize, anticipate, monitor, and regulate stressors within their capabilities.
- control emotional and physical responses when distressed.
- use appropriate stress management techniques when confronted with stressors.
- recognize warning signs and symptoms of excessive stress.
- schedule daily time to unwind, relax, and evaluate the day's activities.
- control stress when called upon to perform.
- enjoy life despite occasional disappointments and frustrations.
- look success and failure squarely in the face and keep moving along a predetermined course.
- move ahead with optimism and energy and do not spend time and talent worrying about failure.
- learn from previous mistakes and use them as building blocks to prevent similar setbacks in the future.
- give of themselves freely to others.
- have a deep meaning in life.

FIGURE 2.5

Behavior Modification Planning

is a line between thinking something and feeling it! People changing the way they think can allow them to change the way they feel.

Some tips for reducing stress and improving your quality of life through the use of positive self-talk are listed in the margin of page 33.

Thinking positively is a habit. Like any other habit, it will take time and practice to master—but health benefits such as decreased negative stress, reduced risk of coronary heart disease, and improved coping skills make it time well spent.

Stress and Its Impact on Mental Health

While stress in general, and specifically unmanaged stress, can have a negative impact on a person's physical health, the detrimental impact it can have on mental health can be equally devastating.

There are many types of mental health disorders. Schizophrenia, depression, general anxiety disorders, bipolar disorders, and panic disorders are just a few of the mental health disorders that can cause havoc in a person's life. These disorders typically include chronic or occasional dysfunctional feelings and/or a lost sense of self worth that may often limit the extent to which an individual participates in life's daily activities.

Who Gets Mental Health Disorders?

According to the 1996 Surgeon General's Report on Physical Activity and Health, one out of two Americans will suffer from some sort of mental health disorder at some point in their lifetime. The many different types of mental health disorders affect 90 million people. Mental health disorders are far-reaching. They affect not only the individual with the disorder but also the people who have intimate and social relationships with them. Mental health disorders have a far-reaching "ripple effect."

Depression and Stress

Depression is a mental health disorder that is prevalent among college populations. One of the reasons college students are particularly vulnerable to depression is that for many students, they face large amounts of unresolved stress. College is a time filled with challenging, new, different, and stressful situations (refer back to Figure 2.2).

It is important to realize that unmanaged stress and depression can quickly become a vicious cycle. The more depressed an individual is, the less day-to-day stress and the fewer activities can be coped with and the more depressed the person becomes.

While stress often plays a major roll in depression, another type of depression also has a biological basis—endogenous depression. In this instance, a person's family mental health history can help determine if a genetic predisposition toward depression exists. This knowledge allows them to take a proactive approach toward diagnosing and battling this mental health condition.

Everyone has occasional feelings of being down or sad at some point. However, when depression results in a person crying a great deal, feeling hopeless, or being unable to take pleasure in life, professional help should be sought so that a life-threatening situation does not occur.

Aside from or along with professional counseling, individual therapy or group therapy can be beneficial to an individual battling with depression. Prescription medications can be another important tool when coping with depression. They may or may not be necessary depending on each individual's situation.

Exercise has also been shown to be effective in treating mild to moderate cases of depression. Thirty-three percent of all inactive adults con-

The ability to relate and interact with others is important to a person's overall sense of well-being.

Jenny's Story

Jenny Smith was diagnosed with bipolar disorder, a condition characterized by severe mood swings from total elation to utter depression. Jenny was hospitalized off and on, and after trying all available drug therapy to no avail, Jenny was told to expect to be in and out of psychiatric hospitals for the rest of her life. Jenny decided to learn hatha yoga. Hatha yoga incorporates breathing, postures, and meditation that relax and strengthen the body. Smith noticed that her panic attacks subsided (a symptom of her bipolar disorder) with her daily yoga practice. Smith now feels better and successfully manages her disorder with the anti-depressant Paxil and daily yoga practice. She has taught her 11-year-old daughter relaxation through simple breathing techniques, and now her daughter's panic attacks have also subsided. Some mental health disorders are genetic in nature. Smith's grandmother committed suicide due to depression, and Smith is determined to spread the word that she believes yoga has literally saved her life.

(Weintraub, 2000)

sider themselves depressed. "A recent review of more than 20 years of studies found that aerobic exercise and strength training are equally effective in treating depression, can reduce anxiety in patients with panic disorders and can be an important part of treatment for people with schizophrenia" (Payne, 2000).

Recently a charity conducted a survey that found that 83 percent of those with mental health problems looked to some form of exercise to help improve their mood or reduce the amount of stress they felt they were under (news. bbc.co.uk). While exercise plays a vital role in reducing the negative impact mental health disorders have on a person's life, it should not be considered a total replacement for other treatments, and patients should always work with and under the close care of a physician.

James Blumenthal, a psychologist at Duke University Medical Center, conducted a study comparing the effects of exercise and drugs on depression. The 156 participants were broken up into three different groups:

1. exercise only,
2. antidepressants only,
3. exercise and antidepressants.

After sixteen weeks, the researchers found that all three groups showed the same amount of improvement on standard measures for depression. An interesting note concerning the participants using exercise as a method of dealing with their depression was that not only did the exercise have a positive impact on their level of depression, but it also improved their cognitive functioning ability (bbc.news.health).

It is critical to realize that for an individual dealing with any type of mental illness, therapy through counseling and/or the use of prescription medications is not a sign of weakness or personal failure. Accepting these means of help requires strength and courage to face the fact that there is a problem and to fight/prevail against a life-draining force. An individual with a mental illness receiving any type of therapy is much the same as a visually impaired person wearing glasses or contacts, or a hearing impaired individual using a hearing aid.

Suicidal Behavior and Stress

Another area in which stress can affect an individual's mental health is thoughts of or attempts at suicide. College students are particularly vulnerable to this problem. Nationwide each year, approximately one in 10,000 college students commits suicide; many more college students have suicidal thoughts.

Most people who contemplate or actually do commit suicide want something in their "world" to change. It may be one thing that will greatly impact their life if it changes or goes away, or it may be a lot of the "little things" that have added up. Often, a suicidal individual does not really want to die; it is just that the person has run out of ways or ideas on how to make that needed change occur.

Intense pressure or stress, along with feelings of depression, alcohol misuse, drug abuse, or a personal loss such as a breakup or lack of academic success, are common causative factors in suicides. Anyone expressing suicidal thoughts should be taken seriously. Friends, roommates, or whoever should seek out help for a suicidal individual immediately.

Typical signs that an individual is contemplating suicide could include:

- skipping classes,
- giving away personal possessions,
- withdrawing from friends,
- withdrawing from "normal" activities,
- engaging in risky behaviors not normal for that person.

A Simple Gesture

Everybody can be great ... because anybody can serve. You don't have to have a college degree to serve. You don't have to make your subject and verb agree to serve. You only need a heart full of grace. A soul generated by love.
Martin Luther King, Jr.

Mark was walking home from school one day when he noticed the boy ahead of him had tripped and dropped all of the books he was carrying, along with two sweaters, a baseball bat, a glove, and a small tape recorder. Mark knelt down and helped the boy pick up the scattered articles. Since they were going the same way, he helped carry part of the burden. As they walked, Mark discovered the boy's name was Bill, that he loved video games, baseball, and history, that he was having a lot of trouble with his other subjects, and that he had just broken up with his girlfriend.

They arrived at Bill's home first, and Mark was invited in for a Coke and to watch some television. The afternoon passed pleasantly with a few laughs and some shared small talk, and then Mark went home. They continued to see each other around school, had lunch together once or twice, and then both graduated from junior high school. They ended up in the same high school where they had brief contacts over the years. Finally the long awaited senior year came, and three weeks before graduation, Bill asked Mark if they could talk.

Bill reminded him of the day years ago when they had first met. "Do you ever wonder why I was carrying so many things home that day?" asked Bill. "You see, I cleaned out my locker because I didn't want to leave a mess for anyone else. I had stored away some of my mother's sleeping pills and I was going home to commit suicide. But after we spent some time together talking and laughing, I realized that if I had killed myself, I would have missed that time and so many others that might follow. So you see, Mark, when you picked up my books that day, you did a lot more. You saved my life."

John W. Schlatter

Source: From *Chicken Soup for the Soul,* © 1992 by John Schlatter. Published by Health Communication, Inc. Permission conveyed by The Permissions Company.

An effective tool for helping someone get past suicidal thoughts or desires is counseling to help change the way he or she is thinking and coping. Medications can also be very effective in the prevention of suicidal behaviors. Hospitalization may be needed as well, in order to prevent suicide. The key to helping a suicidal or potentially suicidal individual is for those around them to be aware and actively involved in seeking out help for the person who is at risk

Eating Disorders and Stress

Eating disorders are medically identifiable, potentially life-threatening mental health conditions related to obsessive eating patterns. Eating disorders are not new— descriptions of self-starvation have been found as far back as medieval times.

Even though more young men are succumbing to eating disorders each year, the mental health condition is typically thought of as a woman's disease. Unfortunately, even grade school girls can feel pressure to "fit in" or look thin. This can be very troubling and disruptive to young girls struggling to build a positive body image.

Typically, a person with an eating disorder seeks perfection and control over their life. Both anorexics and bulimics tend to suffer from low self-esteem and depression. They often have a conflict between a desire for perfection and feelings of personal inadequacy. Such persons typically have a distorted view of themselves, in that when they look into a mirror, they see themselves differently than others see them. Narcissism, or excessive vanity, can be linked to both anorexia and bulimia. (see Figure 2.6)

Eating disorders are often accompanied by other psychiatric disorders, such as depression, substance abuse, or anxiety disorders. Eating disorders are very serious and may be life-threatening due to the fact that individuals suffering from these diseases can experience serious heart conditions and/or kidney failure—both of which can result in death. Therefore, it is critically important that eating disorders are recognized as real and treatable diseases.

© Ariel Skelley/CORBIS

Anorexics and bulimics tend to suffer from low self-esteem and depression and typically have a distorted view of themselves.

FIGURE 2.6
Major Risk Factors for Eating Disorders

Biological

Dieting
Obesity/overweight/pubertal weight gain

Psychological

Body image/dissatisfaction/distortions
Low self-esteem
Obsessive-compulsive symptoms
Childhood sexual abuse

Family

Parental attitudes and behaviors
Parental comments regarding appearance
Eating-disordered mothers
Misinformation about ideal weight

Sociocultural

Peer pressure regarding weight/eating
Media: TV, magazines
Distorted images: toys
Elite athletes as at-risk groups

Source: White, Jane. "The Prevention of Eating Disorders: A Review of the Research on Risk Factors with Implications for Practice." *Journal of Child and Adolescent Psychiatric Nursing,* Vol. 13, No. 2, April 2000.

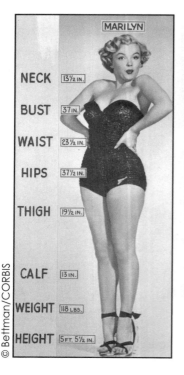

© Charles Platiau/Reuters/CORBIS

Body image is affected by a person's attitudes and beliefs, as well as outside influences such as family, social pressures, and the media.

Body Image

The media, advertising, and the fashion industry portray women, as well as men, as thin (or fit), beautiful, and youthful. This is an ideal that is difficult to attain and nearly impossible to maintain. It is important to note that glamorous magazine cover models' pictures are airbrushed with imperfections deleted, so that the final product is an almost perfect unachievable image. It wasn't too long ago that the ideal for a woman's body was "fat is where it's at" instead of the current preoccupation with "thin is in." Many of the great masters' paintings portray the female image as having desirable traits such as soft, round, and fleshy bodies. The 50's had curvy movie stars such as Marilyn Monroe. In the 60's, the Twiggy look was in. In the 70's, it was Farrah Fawcett Fit. In the 80's, it was the fit look with Cindy Crawford. In the 90's, Kate Moss exemplified the gaunt heroin look. As Americans grow in size, the current unobtainable look is very thin. The Body Mass Index of Playboy models and Miss America contestants lowered significantly from the 1970's to the 1990's. Even wealthy celebrities who can afford personal chefs, trainers, registered dieticians, and top consultants sometimes battle with their weight.

A person's body image is how a person sees him or herself in his or her mind. Body image is affected by a person's attitudes and beliefs, as well as by outside influences such as family, social pressures, and the media. It is important to have good perspective. If you are an "apple" and naturally carry excess fat in your abdominal area, when you gain weight you will become a larger "apple" or you may lose weight and become a smaller "apple." The same is true for "pear" shaped individuals who carry their excess fat in their hips and buttocks. You cannot become a different shape, nor can you diet down to a thin waif. Accept yourself for who you are; then work on behavior changes to become healthier. The fringe benefit to becoming healthier is that you will most likely fit better in your jeans. You will also feel better while you reduce your risk of heart disease and diabetes.

It's All about Balance and Portion Size!

- One small chocolate chip cookie is equivalent to walking briskly for ten minutes.
- The difference between a large gourmet chocolate chip cookie and a small chocolate chip cookie could be about forty minutes of raking leaves (200 calories).
- One hour of walking at a moderate pace (twenty min/mile) uses about the same amount of energy that is in one jelly-filled doughnut (300 calories).
- A fast-food "meal" containing a double-patty cheeseburger, extra-large fries, and a twenty-four-ounce soft drink is equal to running two and one-half hours at a ten min/mile pace (1,500 calories).

(Surgeon General, 2005)

Anorexia Nervosa

Anorexia nervosa is a state of starvation and emaciation, usually resulting from severe dieting and excessive exercise. An anorexic will literally stop eating in an effort to control body size.

Most, if not all, anorexic individuals suffer from an extremely distorted body image. People with this disease look in a mirror and see themselves as overweight or fat even when they have become dangerously thin.

Major weight loss is the most visible and the most common symptom of anorexia. Anorexic individuals often develop unusual eating habits, such as avoiding food or meals, picking out a few "acceptable" foods and eating them in small quantities, or carefully weighing and portioning foods. Other common symptoms of this disease include absent menstruation, dry skin, excessive hair on the skin, and thinning of scalp hair. Gastrointestinal problems and orthopedic problems resulting from excessive exercise are also specific to this illness.

Anorexic individuals can lose between 15 and 60 percent of their normal body weight, putting their body and their health in severe jeopardy. The medical problems associated with anorexia are numerous and serious. Starvation damages bones, organs, muscles, the immune system, the digestive system, and the nervous system.

Ways to Love Your Body

- Become aware of what your body does each day, as the instrument of your life, not just an ornament for others.
- Think of your body as a tool. Create a list of all the things you can do with this body.
- Walk with your head held high, supported by pride and confidence in yourself as a person.
- Do something that will let you enjoy your body. Stretch, dance, walk, sing, take a bubble bath, get a massage.
- Wear comfortable styles that you really like and feel good in.
- Decide what you would rather do with the hours you waste every day criticizing your body.
- Describe ten positive things about yourself without mentioning your appearance.
- Say to yourself "Life is too short to waste my time hating my body this way."
- Don't let your weight or shape keep you from doing things you enjoy.
- Create a list of people who have contributed to your life, your community, the world. Was their appearance important to their success and accomplishment? If not, why should yours be?
- If you had only one year to live, how important would your body image and appearance be?

By Margo Maine, Ph.D. and Eating Disorders' Awareness and Prevention

Between 5 and 20 percent of anorexics die due to suicide or other medical complications. Heart disease is the most common medical cause of death for people with severe anorexia.

Long-term irregular or absent menstruation can cause sterility or bone loss. Severe anorexics also suffer nerve damage and may experience seizures. Anemia and gastrointestinal problems are also common to individuals suffering from this illness.

The most severe complication and the most devastating result of anorexia is death.

Bulimia Nervosa

Bulimia nervosa is a process of bingeing and purging. This disorder is more common than anorexia nervosa. The purging is an attempt to control body weight, though bulimics seldom starve themselves as anorexics do. They have an intense fear of becoming overweight, and usually have episodes of secretive binge eating, followed by purging, frequent weight variations, and the inability to stop eating voluntarily. Bulimics often feel hunger, overeat, and then purge to rid themselves of the guilt of overeating.

Bulimic individuals are often secretive and discreet and are, therefore, often hard to identify. Typically, they have a preoccupation with food, fluctuating between fantasies of food and guilt due to overeating. Symptoms of bulimia can include cuts and calluses on the finger joints from a person sticking their fingers or hand down their throat to induce vomiting, broken blood vessels around the eyes from the strain of vomiting, and damage to tooth enamel from stomach acid.

Because purging through vomiting, the abuse of laxatives, or some other compensatory behavior typically follows a binge, bulimics usually weigh within the normal range for their weight and height. However, like individuals with anorexia, they often have a distorted body image and fear gaining weight, want to lose weight, and are intensely dissatisfied with their bodies.

While it is commonly thought that the medical problems resulting from bulimia are not as severe as those resulting from anorexia, the complications are numerous and serious. The medical problems associated with bulimia include tooth erosion, cavities, and gum problems due to the acid in vomit. Abdominal bloating is common in bulimic individuals. The purging process can leave a person dehydrated and with very low potassium levels, which can cause weakness and paralysis. Some of the more severe problems a bulimic can suffer are reproductive problems and heart damage, due to the lack of minerals in the body.

Binge-Eating Disorder

People with binge-eating disorder typically experience frequent (at least two days a week) episodes of out-of-control eating. Binge-eating episodes are associated with at least three of the following characteristics: eating much more rapidly than normal; eating until an individual is uncomfortably full; eating large quantities of food even when not hungry; eating alone to hide the quantity of food being ingested; feeling disgusted, depressed, or guilty after overeating. Not purging their bodies of the excessive calories they have consumed is the characteristic that separates individuals with binge-eating disorder from those with bulimia. Therefore, individuals suffering from this disease are typically overweight for their height and weight.

Fear of Obesity

Fear of obesity is an over-concern with thinness. It is less severe than anorexia, but can also have negative health consequences. This condition is often seen in achievement-oriented teenagers who seek to restrict their weight due to a fear of becoming obese. This condition can be a precursor to anorexia or bulimia if it is not detected and treated early.

Activity Nervosa

Activity nervosa is a condition in which the individual suffers from the ever-present compulsion to exercise, regardless of illness or injury. The desire to exercise excessively may result in poor performance in other areas of that individual's life due to the resulting fatigue, weakness, and unhealthy body weight.

Female Athlete Triad   In 1991, a team was formed by the American College of Sports Medicine to educate, initiate a change, and focus on the medical management of a triad of female disorders that included disordered eating, amenorrhea, and osteoporosis (ACSM, 1991). A triangle is used to depict these

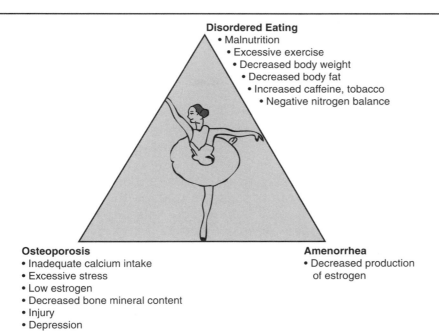

FIGURE 2.7

The Female Athlete Triad

Disordered Eating
• Malnutrition
• Excessive exercise
• Decreased body weight
• Decreased body fat
• Increased caffeine, tobacco
• Negative nitrogen balance

Osteoporosis
• Inadequate calcium intake
• Excessive stress
• Low estrogen
• Decreased bone mineral content
• Injury
• Depression

Amenorrhea
• Decreased production
  of estrogen

disorders because the three are interlinked. Disordered eating behaviors result in weight loss and subsequent loss of body fat that halts menstruation. When amenorrhea occurs, calcium is lost and a decline in bone mass occurs. This in turn causes osteoporosis and can easily result in stress fractures. Many times the inactivity necessary to allow stress fractures to heal causes depression that often leads an individual back into disordered eating behaviors, and the cycle continues (see Figure 2.7).

Who Is at Risk?

By far, more women than men succumb to eating disorders; however, the incidence of eating disorders in men is believed to be very underreported.

It is estimated that one in every hundred teenage girls is anorexic. Anorexia usually occurs in adolescent women (90 percent of all reported cases), although all age groups can be affected. It is estimated that one in every five college-bound females is bulimic.

Individuals living in economically developed nations, such as the United States, are much more likely to suffer from an eating disorder, due to the dual factors of an abundance of available food and external, societal pressure. College campuses have a higher incidence of people with eating disorders, and upper-middle-class women who are extremely self-critical are also more likely to become anorexic. Being aware of the groups at risk can be a large step toward prevention.

Activities such as dance and dance team, gymnastics, figure skating, track, and cheerleading tend to have higher instances of eating disorders. An estimate of people suffering from anorexia and bulimia within these populations is 15–60 percent. Male wrestlers and body builders are also at risk due to the unsafe practice of attempting to shed pounds quickly in an attempt to "make weight" before a competition.

Causes of Eating Disorders

The causes of anorexia and bulimia are numerous and complex. Cultural factors, family pressure, psychological factors, emotional disorders, and chemical imbalances can all contribute to eating disorders.

Forty to 80 percent of anorexics suffer from depression, as reduced levels of chemical neurotransmitters in the brain have been found in victims suffering from both eating disorders and depression. Links between hunger and

I Have Won

One Woman's Recovery from Binge-Eating Disorder

It was a constant nagging voice in my mind, whispering promises of protection, comfort and a life of numbness. I didn't realize it was my enemy, disguised as a savior. This is what my eating disorder was to me. I have been struggling with binge-eating disorder for eight years, and after a year of therapy I am learning how to tell that voice to go away and to love, trust and respect myself and my values.

I have countless memories of daytime binges when my roommates were in class, even digging through the trash to retrieve a half-eaten candy bar or piece of cake. I withdrew from my friends, missed out on beach parties, and felt lonely, scared and completely out of control every waking moment of the day. I became deeply depressed and couldn't face emotional issues that had been with me for a long time. That voice gave soothing promises of a way out, a way to forget, an excuse for any failures or disappointments, and a way to slowly. . . die.

My friends and family were aware there was a problem but I spent years denying the truth. I would tell them I just loved to eat and I just needed to start exercising more. All the while my weight kept slowly growing. I would think constantly about changing, going on a diet, but the diet day would come and I couldn't do it, so I would retreat to the voice and let it take charge. I finally accepted that I had a problem when I was in school completing a Master's Degree in Counseling. I had to constantly analyze myself and my life for projects and papers and could no longer deny the issues at hand.

I entered into therapy and honestly wasn't prepared for the difficulty that lay ahead. I had to confront my demons, that voice, examine every horrible issue that I had suppressed and once again learn how to live life. I learned that I can do other things when I find myself in front of the refrigerator and I am not physically hungry. I can take walks, call my husband, or put together a puzzle. I also had to relearn my body's signals for hunger and fullness and to trust that my body will tell me what I need and when I need it.

Although still in recovery, I can clearly see how far I've come, and I can see the light at the end of the tunnel. I now spend time speaking about eating disorders and volunteering at the Massachusetts Eating Disorder Association. I want people to know that there is hope and that recovery is possible. The voice no longer whispers to me; I now shout at it, "I don't need you anymore. I love myself. I have won!"

by Cathy King, M.S.

A special thanks to the Massachusetts Eating Disorder Association

Source: *Courtesy of the Massachusetts Eating Disorder Association*

depression have been discovered through research, which contributes to the depression a person with an eating disorder may feel.

For some bulimics, seasonality can adversely affect them, causing the disorder to worsen during the dark, winter months. Another startling statistic is that the onset of anorexia appears to peak in May, which is also the peak month for suicides.

Family factors are also critical. One study showed that 40 percent of all 9- to 10-year-old girls were trying to lose weight, many at the encouragement of their mothers. Mothers of anorexics are often overinvolved in their child's life, while mothers of bulimics are many times critical and detached.

It is clear that many people who suffer from eating disorders do not have a healthy body image. From an early age, there is enormous pressure in our culture from society, family, friends, the media, and often from one's self to

Guidelines for Helping a Friend with an Eating Disorder

DO:

- listen with understanding
- appreciate the openness and trust in sharing with you his/her distress
- share your own struggles, be open and real
- learn more about eating disorders
- give support and be available
- give hope that with help and with patience he/she can free themselves from this disorder
- give your friend a list of resources for help

DO NOT:

- tell your friend he/she is crazy
- blame him/her
- gossip about your friend
- follow him/her around to check their eating or purging behavior
- ignore your friend
- reject him/her
- tell him/her to quit this ridiculous behavior
- feel compelled to solve their problem
- make excess comments about being thin

DO heed the signs. Anorexic behavior includes extreme weight loss (often emaciation), obsessive dieting, and distorted body perception (a thin person thinks he/she is fat when they are not). Clues of bulimia are more subtle. Your friend may eat a great deal of food, then rush to the bathroom. She/ he may hide laxatives or speak outright about the "magic method" of having the cake and not gaining weight. Anorexics and bulimics tend to be preoccupied with food and many have specific rituals tied to their eating patterns.

DO approach your friend gently, but persistently. Explain that you're worried; listen sympathetically. Don't expect your friend to admit he/she has a problem right away. The first step is realizing there is a problem;

therefore, it is important to help your friend realize this.

DO focus on unhappiness as the reason your friend could benefit from help. Point out how anxious or unhappy he/she has been lately, and emphasize that it does not have to be that way.

DO be supportive, but do not try to analyze or interpret their problem. Being supportive is the most important thing you can do. Show your friend you believe in him/her—it will make a difference in recovery.

DO talk to someone about your own emotions if you feel the need. An objective outsider can emphasize the fact that you are not responsible for your friend; you can only try to help that person help him/herself.

DO be yourself. Be honest in sharing your feelings: i.e., "It's hard for me to watch you destroy yourself."

DO give non-judgmental feedback. For example, "We haven't gone to lunch together in a while, is something wrong?" instead of "You haven't gone to eat with me in a while, do you have a problem?"

DO cooperate with your friend if he/she asks you to keep certain foods out of common storage areas. This may help prevent a binge on such foods.

DON'T keep the "secret" from the family when your friend's health and thinking are impaired.

DON'T forget that denial is a form of selective "deafness."

DON'T be deceived by the excuse: "It's not really bad. I can control myself."

DON'T focus on your friend's weight or appearance. Focus on your concern about his/her health and well-being.

DON'T change your eating habits when you're around your friend. Your "normal" eating is an example to your friend of a more healthy relationship with food.

Source: *Student Health Services, Texas A&M University. Guidelines for Helping a Friend with an Eating Disorder, 2002.*

© Anita Patterson Peppers, 2012, Shutterstock, Inc.

Forty to 80 percent of anorexics suffer from depression.

achieve the unachievable and unnecessary "perfect" body. A woman's self-worth is too often associated with other people's opinions, which in many cases put unrealistic emphasis on physical attractiveness.

Ways to Help

The best course of action for a person who suspects they know someone with an eating disorder is to be patient, supportive, and not judge the individual. Learn what you can about the problem by consulting an eating disorder clinic or counseling center (common on college campuses), and offer to help the ill person seek professional help.

Often, individuals suffering from an eating disorder do not realize or will not admit that they are ill. For this reason, seeking help or continuing/completing treatment for the disorder is often difficult.

Medical treatment is often necessary for eating disorders. However, it is extremely encouraging to note that eating disorders can be treated and a healthy weight and relationship with food can be restored. Because of the complexity of eating disorders, the best and most successful treatment is usually a combination of counseling, family therapy, cognitive behavior therapy, nutritional therapy, support groups, and drug therapy. Treatment, many times, includes a hospital stay and is usually resisted by the patient. Support for the anorexic or bulimic person by friends and family and the realization of the severity of the problem is critical to successful treatment of the illness.

References

Ballard, D. "A Dozen Ways to Stress-Proof Your Life." 2002.

Corbin, C.B. and Lindsey, R. *Concepts of Physical Fitness.* McBrown. 2008.

Donatelle, R. J. *Access to Health* (9th ed). Allyn & Bacon. Boston. 2006.

Floyd, P., Mims, S., and Yelding-Howard, C. *Personal Health: Perspectives and Lifstyles.* Morton Publishing Co. 2007.

Hahn, D. B. and Payne, W. A. *Understanding Your Health.* McGraw-Hill. 2008.

Hales, D. *An Invitation to Health* (8th ed). New York: Brooks/Cole Publishing Company. 1999.

Hales, D. *An Invitation to Health* (Brief 2nd ed). Belmont, CA: Wadsworth Thomson. 2002.

Hoeger, W. and Hoeger, S. A. *Principles and Labs for Fitness and Wellness* (9th ed). Brooks/ Cole Publishing Company. 2008.

Hoeger, W. W. K. and Hoeger, S. A. *Lifetime Physical Fitness and Wellness: A Personalized Program* (8th ed). Belmont, CA: Thomson Wadsworth. 2005.

Holmes, T. H. and Rahe, R. H. Student Stress Scale. *Journal of Psychosomatic Research, 11,* 213.

http://ahha.org

http://healthed.tamu.edu/stress.htm

http://indiana.edu/~health/stress.html

http://stress.about.com/od/optimismspitituality/a/positiveselftalk.html

http://who.int/aboutwho/en/definition.html

http://www.healthdepot.com

http://www.med.nus.edu.sg/pcm/stress

http://www.m-w.com/dictionary.html

http://www.nimh.nih.gov/publicat/eatingdisorder.com

http://www.reachout.com.au/default.asp?ti=2249

http://www.selfcounseling.com/help/depression/suicide.html

http://www.acsm.org

http://www.cdc.gov/nccdphp/sgr/pdf/chap4.pdf

Hyman, B., Oden, G., Bacharach, D., and Collins, R. *Fitness for Living.* Kendall-Hunt Publishing Co. 2006.

Payne, W. A., Hahn, D. B. *Understanding Your Health* (6th ed). St. Louis, MO: Mosby. 2000.

Peterson, M. S. *Eat to Compete* (2nd ed). St. Louis, MO: Mosby. 63146

Powers, S. K., Todd, S. L., and Noland, U. J. *Total Fitness and Wellness* (2nd ed). Boston: Allyn & Bacon. 2005.

Prentice, W. E. *Fitness and Wellness for Life* (6th ed). New York: WCB McGraw-Hill. 1999.

Pruitt, B. E. and Stein, J. *Health Styles.* Boston: Allyn & Bacon. 1999.

Robbins, G., Powers, D., and Burgess, S. *A Wellness Way of Life* (4th ed). New York: WCB McGraw-Hill. 1999.

Rosato, F. *Fitness for Wellness* (3rd ed). Minneapolis: West. 1994.

Roth, G. *Why Weight? A Guide to Compulsive Eating.* New York. Penguin Group. 1989. Student Health Services, Texas A&M University. *Guidelines for Helping a Friend with an Eating Disorder,* 2002.

Webmaster@noah.cuny.edu

Weinttraub, Amy. Yoga: It's Not Just An Exercise. *Psychology Today,* Nov. 2000.

Activities

Notebook Activities

Time Budget Sheet
Stress Journal
Forbidden Foods
Ways I Sneak
What Am I Waiting For?

Name _____ Section_____ Date_____

Time Budget Sheet

Consider study, classess/labs, church, exercise, personal needs, socializing, and so on.

Time	Monday	Tuesday	Wednesday	Thursday	Friday	Saturday	Sunday
7:00 a.m.							
8:00							
8:30							
9:00							
9:30							
10:00							
10:30							
11:00							
11:30							
12:00 p.m.							
12:30							
1:00							
1:30							
2:00							
2:30							
3:00							
3:30							
4:00							
4:30							
5:00							
5:30							
6:00							
6:30							
7:00							
7:30							
8:00							
8:30							
9:00							
9:30							
10:00							
10:30							
11:00							

Name _____ Section_____ Date_____

Stress Journal

Directions: To start managing stress, you must first recognize it. Fill in the stress journal entries twice in the morning, twice in the afternoon, and twice in the evening for two weeks. When the two weeks are over, discuss your observations with your classmates. What causes YOU the most stress? (Use as many sheets as necessary to complete the task.)

Date	Time	Situation	Stress Level	Signs
5/29	9:00 a.m.	(Where? With whom? Doing what? At work . . . argued with boss.	(1–100) 85	Heart racing, headache, muscle tension

Source: From *Just for the Health of It* by Patricia Rizzo Toner, Center for Applied Research in Education.

Name _____ Section_____ Date_____

Forbidden Foods

We usually binge on the foods we won't allow ourselves to eat unless we binge. It is only when we give ourselves permission to eat them that we can choose not to eat them. If, for instance, you allow yourself to eat chocolate any time you are hungry for it, then a "chocolate charge" will not build and you won't feel the need to binge on chocolate at a later time. We forbid and forbid and forbid ourselves to have food that we like, food that brings us pleasure. It should be no surprise to us that when we feel a crack in our steely resolve to restrict ourselves—and make a decision to binge—we immediately run for those foods we have not been allowing ourselves to enjoy.

Make a list of the foods you will not allow yourself to eat freely and without guilt. Let yourself think of the food that you determined years ago to shut out of your life, perhaps as far back as childhood. Are sweets included? Bread? Take your time in making the list, remembering foods that you banished, or attempted to banish, or still berate yourself for eating whenever you "succumb."

My Forbidden Foods Are:

_____

_____

_____

_____

_____

_____

Eating My Forbidden Foods

Using the chart on the back of this page, keep a record of what you discover when you do the following:

1. Look at the list you made and decide which is the first food you would like to eat again without guilt.

2. Bring that food into your house this week. Bring more of it than you could possibly eat at one sitting—and *eat it when you are hungry and until you are satisfied*. Allow yourself the pleasure of good tastes.

3. As you eat it, notice whether you like it as much as you thought you would. Notice how it tastes, how it feels in your throat.

4. Remind yourself that you can have it again any time you are hungry.

5. Do the same next week. And the next.

6. Bring one forbidden food into your house each week, until you have no forbidden foods.

Source: From *Why Weight? A Guide to Ending Compulsive Eating* by Geneen Roth, copyright © 1989 by Geneen Roth. Used by permission of Dutton Signet, a division of Penguin Group (USA) Inc.

Forbidden Foods Chart

Week #	The food I chose from the Forbidden Foods List is	I bought plenty		I ate it when I was hungry		I stopped when I was satisfied		When I ate it, I felt:
		Yes	No	Yes	No	Yes	No	
1								
2								
3								
4								

Name _____ Section_____ Date_____

Ways I Sneak

"Eating with the intention of being in full view" means not sneaking. If you eat alone, it means not being afraid that someone will walk in the door and see what you're eating. It means telling the truth about the food you eat.

How do you sneak food?

EXAMPLES:

1. By eating modest amounts of food at a party, then coming home and eating a meal.

2. By running back and forth to the kitchen (and eating) while people are in the living room.

3. By ordering a cake at the bakery for yourself and telling the cashier that it is for your kids.

Complete the sentence: I sneak food by:

1. _____

   _____

2. _____

   _____

3. _____

   _____

4. _____

   _____

5. _____

   _____

Source: From *Why Weight? A Guide to Ending Compulsive Eating* by Geneen Roth, copyright © 1989 by Geneen Roth. Used by permission of Dutton Signet, a division of Penguin Group (USA) Inc.

NOTEBOOK ACTIVITY

What Am I Waiting For?

Most compulsive eaters are waiting until they have the "right" body to begin living the kind of life they want to live. You don't have to wait. You deserve to have what you want now. Being thin does not suddenly make you worthy of a job you like, relationships that are meaningful, clothes that you find attractive. Your decision that you are worthy is what makes you worthy.

What are you waiting to get thin to do?

Complete the following list:
I am waiting to get thin so I can:

Example:

1. go to my high school reunion and not be ashamed of myself.

2. be in a relationship.

3. make love with the lights on.

_____

_____

_____

_____

_____

_____

_____

_____

_____

Read over the list. Pick two things on it that you can begin doing this week. Make a commitment to yourself to do them on specific days. You'll find that when you begin acting as if you deserve to treat yourself and to be treated with respect and kindness you will slowly begin believing that you do.
Complete the sentence: This week I will:

1. _____

2. _____

- In general, how does stress manifest itself in you/your life? How do you deal with stress? Identify a few positive and negative stress managment techniques you use regularly.

- Do you know anyone who has been impacted by an eating disorder? Were you able to offer help? How did this illness impact your relationship?

Chapter 3
Personal Fitness

© 2012, Shutterstock, Inc.

OBJECTIVES

Students will be able to:

- Define key terms related to cardiovascular fitness, muscular fitness, and flexibility.
- Explain the benefits of regular physical activity.
- Explain the relationship between cardiovascular fitness and heart disease.
- Identify the FITT formula components.
- Identify the benefits of resistance training.
- Identify the benefits of flexibility.
- Identify the components of a workout and the importance of each component.
- Identify when the environment is not safe to exercise.

"Physical Fitness is not only one of the most important keys to a healthy body, it is the basis of dynamic and creative intellectual activity. The relationship between the soundness of the body and the activities of the mind is subtle and complex. Much is not yet understood. But we do know what the Greeks knew: That intelligence and skill can only function at the peak of their capacity when the body is healthy and strong; that hardy spirits and tough minds usually inhabit sound bodies."

—President John F. Kennedy,
"The Soft American," Sports Illustrated,
December 26, 1960

"It gives you more mental endurance and more energy to think clearly," said President Barack Obama. You might think the president was talking about the newest energy drink on the market, but he was referring to exercise. "He is quietly confident and competitive" was a description of President Barack Obama by U. S. Senator Bob Casey, D-Pa. Although it may sound like the way Mr. Obama ran his marathon election campaign, Senator Casey was actually describing Obama on the basketball court. The president commits forty-five to ninety minutes six days a week for cardio, weights, and basketball. He has good blood pressure and he eats fairly well, so President Obama told *Men's Health* magazine that "The main reason I do it is just to clear my head and relieve me of stress." The Obama children stay active with organized sports like soccer and gymnastics while wife Michelle Obama enjoys hitting the gym at least three days a week for ninety minutes doing cardio and lifting weights. The first lady calls exercise "therapeutic." The president also enjoys healthy snacks of nuts, seeds, and raisins. His vice happens to be an on-again off-again smoking habit. Perhaps the president will not only be a good example of living a fit lifestyle, but he might encourage many who may try to quit the smoking habit alongside him. The White House is, after all, a non-smoking area.

Before President George W. Bush took office for his first term, President Clinton was known for jogging through the streets of Washington. In his first term President George W. Bush jogged for fitness, but in his second term he traded in his running shoes for a mountain bike. The biking allowed him to work his heart without stressing his knees. President John F. Kennedy wrote in 1960 that hardy minds and tough spirits usually inhabit sound bodies (see quote at the beginning of this chapter). In June 2002, the Bush

President Obama commits forty-five to ninety minutes, six days a week, for cardio, weights, and basketball.

White House kicked off the ongoing "Healthier U.S. Initiative." Members of the Oval Office have a nonpartisan request, which is for Americans to increase their activity to hopefully decrease the increased prevalence of obesity and heart disease in America (see Figure 3.3 on page 64). If the president of the United States finds time to exercise, perhaps our excuse of "I don't have time" is not valid.

Why Is Physical Activity Important?

Regular physical activity decreases cardiovascular risk. Clinical, scientific, and epidemiological studies indicate that physical activity has a positive effect on the delay in development of cardiovascular disease (ACSM, 2012). In a landmark report in 1996, the Surgeon General recommended that all Americans accumulate thirty minutes of activity on most, if not all, days of the week. Recent recommendations state that thirty minutes might not be enough (see Figure 3.3 on page 64). The 2010 dietary guidelines recommend most Americans should bump activity time to sixty minutes daily and up to ninety minutes if a recent significant weight loss is to be maintained. In 2002, the Institute of Medicine issued a statement that all Americans, regardless of age, weight, size and race, should achieve a total of sixty minutes of moderately intense physical activity daily. In December 2003, the National Sports and Physical Education (NASPE) changed the previous recommendation (1998) to be increased to "at least sixty minutes, and up to several hours of physical activity per day" for children 5 to 12 years of age.

In 2007 the American College of Sports Medicine (ACSM) and the American Heart Association (AHA) together released updated physical activity guidelines that emphasize thirty minutes of moderate activity five times weekly for most Americans. An alternative would be three twenty minute vigorously intense bouts of activity. Strength training is also recommended. Both ACSM and AHA endorse recommendations by the Institute of Medicine that in order to lose weight when these guidelines are already being met, "an increase in activity is a reasonable component of a strategy to lose weight" (ACSM/AHA, 2007). *For individuals that are overweight and want to avoid becoming obese, exercise sessions of forty-five to sixty minutes may be prudent. Formerly obese individuals who are trying to avoid regaining weight should consider up to ninety minutes of aerobic activity on most days of the week.*

NASPE has released physical activity guidelines for infants and toddlers as well. Infants should interact with parents and caregivers in daily physical activities. They should not be placed in one environment for the whole day, and they should be given opportunities to encourage the development of movement skills. Toddlers should accumulate at least thirty minutes of structured activity a day, and at least sixty minutes of unstructured play. "Prevention and treatment of obesity entails changes in lifestyle that promote physical activity and minimize sedentary behavior, said Nazrat Mirza, MD, pediatrician at Children's National Medical Center in Washington, D.C. "Promoting positive behaviors early on in childhood may lead to persistence of these behaviors in to adulthood—helping alleviate the problem of obesity."

In June of 2011, the Institute of Medicine (IOM) released the Early Childhood Obesity Prevention Policies as the first document to recommend strategies to prevent obesity in children under the age of 6 years. The IOM reports that what happens to children during the first years of life is important to their current and future health and well-being. Parents and caregivers should try to keep children active throughout most of the day, feed them a diet rich in fruits, vegetables, and whole grains and one that is low in calorie-dense, nutrient poor food. Screen time should be limited and a special emphasis should be placed on adequate sleep especially for those under the age of 3 years old.

In 2008, the U.S. Department of Health and Human Services (DHHS) released new physical activity guidelines for Americans (see Figure 3.1).

FIGURE 3.1

At-A-Glance: A Fact Sheet for Professionals

U.S. Department of Health & Human Services   ▶ www.hhs.gov

Physical Activity Guidelines for Americans

These guidelines are needed because of the importance of physical activity to the health of Americans, whose current inactivity puts them at unnecessary risk. The latest information shows that inactivity among American children, adolescents, and adults remains relatively high, and little progress has been made in increasing levels of physical activity among Americans.

Adults (aged 18–64)

- Adults should do two hours and thirty minutes a week of moderate-intensity, or one hour and fifteen minutes (seventy-five minutes) a week of vigorous-intensity aerobic physical activity, or an equivalent combination of moderate- and vigorous-intensity aerobic physical activity. Aerobic activity should be performed in episodes of at least ten minutes, preferably spread throughout the week.
- Additional health benefits are provided by increasing to five hours (three hundred minutes) a week of moderate-intensity aerobic physical activity, or two hours and thirty minutes a week of vigorous-intensity physical activity, or an equivalent combination of both.
- Adults should also do muscle-strengthening activities that involve all major muscle groups performed on two or more days per week.

Source: U.S. Department of Health & Human Services

How do we define moderate or vigorous activities? Examples of each follow. **Moderate activities** (You can still speak while doing them) are activities like line dancing, biking with no hills, gardening, tennis (doubles), manual wheelchair wheeling, walking briskly, and water aerobics. **Vigorous activities** are aerobic dance or step aerobics, biking hills or going faster than ten miles per hour, dancing vigorously, hiking uphill, jumping rope, martial arts, race-walking, jogging or running, sports with continuous running such as basket-

FIGURE 3.2

Evidence abounds that everyone, all ages, can benefit from an enhanced quality of life with regular physical activity.

Health Benefits of Physical Activity—A Review of the Strength of the Scientific Evidence

Adults and Older Adults

Strong Evidence

- Lower risk of:
  - Early death
  - Heart disease
  - Stroke
  - Type 2 diabetes
  - High blood pressure
  - Adverse blood lipid profile
  - Metabolic syndrome
  - Colon and breast cancers
- Prevention of weight gain
- Weight loss when combined with diet
- Improved cardiorespiratory and muscular fitness
- Prevention of falls
- Reduced depression
- Better cognitive function (older adults)

Moderate to Strong Evidence

- Better functional health (older adults)
- Reduced abdominal obesity

Moderate Evidence

- Weight maintenance after weight loss
- Lower risk of hip fracture
- Increased bone density
- Improved sleep quality
- Lower risk of lung and endometrial cancers

Children and Adolescents

Strong Evidence

- Improved cardiorespiratory endurance and muscular fitness
- Favorable body composition
- Improved bone health
- Improved cardiovascular and metabolic health biomarkers

Moderate Evidence

- Reduced symptoms of anxiety and depression.

Source: U.S. Department of Health & Human Services.

Photo courtesy of Gayden Darnell

ball, soccer and hockey, swimming laps, and singles tennis. With vigorous activities it would be difficult to carry on a conversation due to the intensity of the exercise. Try to do all of these activities for a minimum of ten minutes at a time. It is important to recognize that moderate activity is beneficial to everyone, while vigorous activity may not be appropriate for everyone.

Regardless of recommendations, children and adults alike benefit from regular, consistent physical activity (see Figure 3.2). Choosing to seek opportunities to move such as walking, biking, swimming, gardening, and other activities can impact risk of disease as well as quality of life. In this chapter, we will discuss why you should exercise and give suggestions to help ensure your success.

Cardiovascular Fitness

Cardiovascular fitness refers to the ability of the heart, lungs, circulatory system, and energy supply system to perform at optimum levels for extended periods of time. **Cardiovascular endurance** is defined as the ability of the body to perform prolonged, large-muscle, dynamic exercise at moderate to high levels of intensity. The word **aerobic** means "in the presence of oxygen" and is used synonymously with *cardiovascular* as well as *cardiorespiratory* when describing a type of exercise.

Complete fitness is comprised of health-related fitness and skill-related fitness. **Health-related fitness** consists of cardiovascular fitness, muscular strength, muscular endurance, flexibility, and optimal body composition. The components of health-related fitness affect the body's ability to function efficiently and effectively. Optimal health-related fitness is not possible without regular physical activity. Most health clubs and fitness classes focus primarily on the health-related fitness components. **Skill-related fitness** includes agility, balance, coordination, reaction time, speed, and power. These attributes are critical for competitive athletes. Skill-related fitness is not essential in order to have cardiovascular fitness, nor will it necessarily make a person healthier. Balance is, however, important for seniors. Staying active helps seniors maintain strength and balance, which can be critical in avoiding injuries.

Cardiovascular fitness is often referred to as the most important aspect of physical fitness because of its relevance to good health and optimal performance. **Muscular fitness** is important because of its effect on efficiency of human movement and basal metabolic rate. **Flexibility** is important for everyone, athletes and non-athletes alike, especially as a person ages. Knowing how to exercise correctly for effectiveness and reduced risk of injury is also important. Physically active individuals can expect to experience a positive impact on glucose regulation, blood pressure, blood cholesterol, bone density, body weight, and their outlook on life. Small amounts of activity for sedentary individuals can have a positive impact on overall health risk. For those who are overweight or obese, a loss of 5 to 10 percent of body weight can have a significant impact on body composition and overall health risk.

How important is participation in physical activity in achieving and maintaining good health? Since 1992, the American Heart Association has considered **inactivity** as important a risk factor for heart disease as high blood

Five components of health-related fitness:

1. cardiovascular fitness,
2. muscular strength,
3. muscular endurance,
4. flexibility, and
5. body composition.

Exercising with friends can be enjoyable and help to keep you motivated and committed to your fitness program.

cholesterol, high blood pressure, and cigarette smoking. The U.S. Centers for Disease Control and Prevention (CDC) and the American College of Sports Medicine (ACSM) reported that 300,000 lives are lost each year due to inactivity (AHA, 2006). In 1996 the U.S. Surgeon General's Report made several definitive statements regarding physical activity and its impact on one's health (see Figure 3.3). Evidence is mounting that physical activity is an integral part of good health. Lack of exercise has spawned a whole new field of study termed **inactivity physiology.**

How Aerobic Exercise Helps Cardiovascular Fitness

There are many benefits associated with aerobic exercise. When one is aerobically fit, there is an overall reduction in the risk of coronary artery disease, i.e., stroke, blood vessel diseases, and heart diseases. Related to this reduction,

FIGURE 3.3

1996 U.S. Surgeon General's Report: Physical Activity and Health

1. Males and females of all ages benefit from regular physical activity.

2. Significant health benefits can be obtained by moderately increasing daily activity on most, if not all, days of the week.

3. Additional health benefits can be gained through greater amounts of physical activity.

4. Physical activity reduces the risk of premature mortality in general, and of coronary heart disease, hypertension, colon cancer, and diabetes mellitus in particular.

5. More than 60 percent of American adults are not regularly physically active.

6. Nearly half of American youth 12 to 21 years of age are not vigorously active on a regular basis.

7. *People of all ages should try to accumulate thirty minutes of activity of moderate intensity (e.g., brisk walking) on most, if not all, days of the week.*

there is a decrease in resting heart rate due to the improved efficiency of the heart. There is also an increase in **stroke volume,** which is the amount of blood pumped from the heart with each heartbeat. A decrease in **systolic blood pressure,** which is the highest arterial blood pressure attained during the heart cycle, and a decrease in **diastolic blood pressure,** or lowest arterial pressure attained during the heart cycle, also occurs. There is also an increase in collateral circulation, which refers to the number of functioning capillaries both in the heart and throughout the body. Increased capillarization is an adaptation to regular aerobic activity. Delivery of oxygen to the working muscles and removal of metabolic wastes is more efficient with increased collateral circulation. In addition to the specific physiological changes just listed, other benefits of a mental, emotional, and physical nature will increase with regular aerobic exercise. Some of the potential benefits that have been documented when aerobic fitness levels increase are:

- a decrease in percent body fat,
- an increase in strength of connective tissues,
- a reduction in mental anxiety and depression,
- improved sleep patterns,
- a decrease in the speed of the aging process,
- an improvement in stress management,
- an increase in cognitive abilities.

Heart rate becomes elevated during exercise because of the increase in demand for oxygen in the muscle tissues. Oxygen is attached to hemoglobin molecules and is transported in the blood. The heart pumps at a faster rate to meet the increased demand for oxygen. The heart is a muscle, and like other muscles, it becomes stronger due to the stress of exercise. Through regular exercise, the heart will increase slightly in size and significantly in strength, which results in an increased stroke volume. The primary difference is seen in the increased thickness and strength of the left ventricle wall. As a result

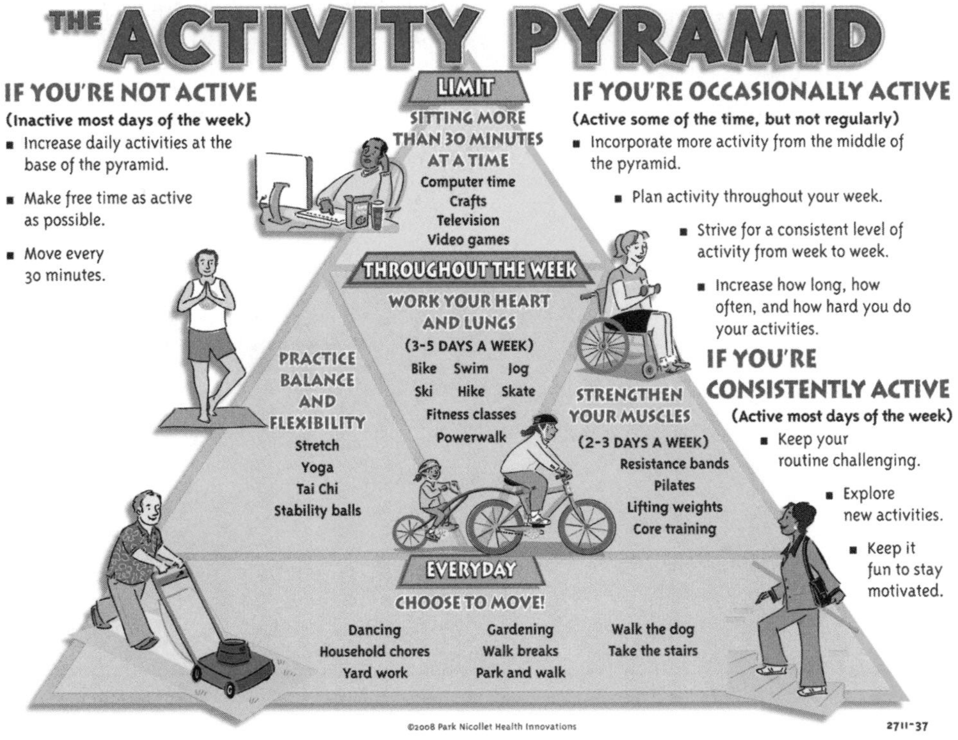

Stress and the Heart
A strong heart will be more efficient than a weak heart when demands are imposed on it through stress. Exercise makes the heart stronger. Sympathetic nerve stimulation is responsible for the *fight-or-flight* response experienced as a result of emotional or physical stress. High fitness levels decrease the impact of this stress on the heart.

THE ACTIVITY PYRAMID

IF YOU'RE NOT ACTIVE
(Inactive most days of the week)
- Increase daily activities at the base of the pyramid.
- Make free time as active as possible.
- Move every 30 minutes.

LIMIT
SITTING MORE THAN 30 MINUTES AT A TIME
Computer time
Crafts
Television
Video games

IF YOU'RE OCCASIONALLY ACTIVE
(Active some of the time, but not regularly)
- Incorporate more activity from the middle of the pyramid.
  - Plan activity throughout your week.
  - Strive for a consistent level of activity from week to week.
  - Increase how long, how often, and how hard you do your activities.

THROUGHOUT THE WEEK
WORK YOUR HEART AND LUNGS
(3-5 DAYS A WEEK)
Bike   Swim   Jog
Ski   Hike   Skate
Fitness classes
Powerwalk

PRACTICE BALANCE AND FLEXIBILITY
Stretch
Yoga
Tai Chi
Stability balls

STRENGTHEN YOUR MUSCLES
(2-3 DAYS A WEEK)
Resistance bands
Pilates
Lifting weights
Core training

IF YOU'RE CONSISTENTLY ACTIVE
(Active most days of the week)
- Keep your routine challenging.
- Explore new activities.
- Keep it fun to stay motivated.

EVERYDAY
CHOOSE TO MOVE!
Dancing
Household chores
Yard work

Gardening
Walk breaks
Park and walk

Walk the dog
Take the stairs

©2008 Park Nicollet Health Innovations   2711-37

FIGURE 3.4
Planned exercise is great, but also look for opportunities to move throughout your day. Increase lifestyle activity with simple things like taking the stairs instead of the elevator.

Source: The Activity Pyramid. Copyright © 2003 Park Nicollet *Health Innovations*, Minneapolis, U.S.A. 1-800-637-2675. Reprinted with permission.

of exercise, blood plasma volume increases, which allows stroke volume to increase. These two factors will cause resting heart rate to decrease, exercising heart rate will become more efficient, and there will be a quicker recovery to a resting heart rate after exercise ceases. Lack of exercise can contribute to many cardiovascular diseases and conditions, including **myocardial infarction,** or heart attack; **angina pectoris,** a condition caused by insufficient blood flow to the heart muscle that results in severe chest pain; and **atherosclerosis,** a build-up of fatty deposits causing blockage within the blood vessel.

Closely associated with the function and efficiency of the heart is the function and efficiency of the **circulatory system**. Blood flows from the heart to arteries and capillaries where oxygen is released and waste products are collected and removed from the tissues. The deoxygenated blood then makes the return trip to the heart through the venous system (see Figure 3.5). As a result of aerobic exercise, blood flow to the skeletal muscles improves due to an increase in stroke volume, an increase in the number of capillaries, and an increase in the function of existing capillaries. This provides more efficient circulation both during exercise and during daily activities.

Blood flow to the heart muscle is provided by two coronary arteries that branch off from the aorta and form a series of smaller vessels. With regular

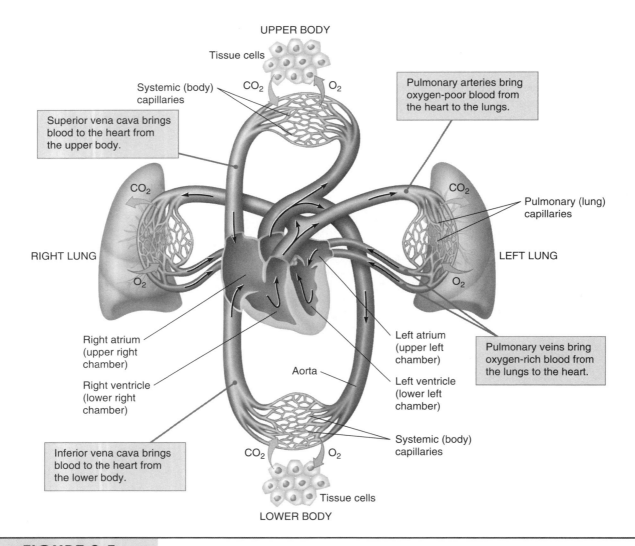

FIGURE 3.5

The Route of Blood during Gas Transport

Source: From Biology: Understanding Life by Alters and Alters, © 2006 by Alters and Alters. Reproduced with permission of John Wiley & Sons, Inc.

aerobic activity, the size of the coronary blood vessels increase and collateral circulation improves. These small blood vessels can supply oxygen to the cardiac muscle tissue when a sudden block occurs in a major vessel, such as during a heart attack. Often the degree of developed collateral circulation determines one's ability to survive a myocardial infarction, or heart attack. It appears that a regular exerciser might survive a heart attack due to collateral circulation within the heart, as the smaller collateral vessels take over when the primary artery becomes occluded, or blocked.

The lungs, air passages, and muscles involved in breathing that supply oxygen and remove carbon dioxide from the body are known as the respiratory system. During exercise, pulmonary ventilation, which is the movement of gases into and out of the lungs, increases in direct proportion to the body's metabolic needs. At lower exercise intensities, this is accomplished by increases in respiration depth. At higher intensities, the rate of respiration also increases. Although fatigue in strenuous exercise is frequently referred to as feeling "out of breath" or "winded," it appears that the normal capacity for pulmonary ventilation does not limit exercise performance (McArdle, Katch, and Katch, 1999). In a normal environment, one inhales sufficient amounts of oxygen. The breathing limitation is in the efficiency of the oxygen exchange at the cellular level. *The primary benefit of aerobic exercise to the respiratory system is an increase in strength and endurance of the respiratory muscles, not an increase in lung volume.* Maximal pulmonary ventilation volumes are dependent on body size (Wilmore and Costill, 1999). Muscles that elevate the thorax such as the diaphragm are referred to as muscles of inspiration. Muscles of expiration, including the abdominal muscles, depress the thorax. Regular aerobic training will result in an increase in both the strength and endurance of these muscles, and will also result in more efficient respiration.

Aerobic and Anaerobic Exercise

Aerobic exercise is activity that requires the body to supply oxygen to support performance over a period of time. Aerobic exercise is characterized by the use of the large muscle groups in a rhythmic mode with an increase in respiration and heart rate. *Aerobic* literally means "with oxygen." Walking, the most common form of exercise in the United States, is an aerobic activity. Other aerobic exercises include running, swimming, biking, cardiokickboxing, rowing, jump-roping, and any activity that fits the above criteria. As with most exercise, the rate of energy expenditure varies with an individual's skill level and intensity of exercise. *Aerobic activities of low intensity are ideal for the beginning or sedentary exerciser because they can be maintained for a longer period of time and have been shown to be effective in promoting weight loss and enhancing cardiovascular health.* Many activities are too intense to be maintained more than a few minutes; these activities are considered anaerobic.

Anaerobic literally means "in the absence of oxygen." **Anaerobic exercise** is exercise performed at intensity levels so great that the body's demand for oxygen exceeds its ability to supply it. Anaerobic activities are usually short in duration, high intensity, and result in the production of blood lactate. The energy for anaerobic activity is primarily from carbohydrates stored within the muscles, called **glycogen,** which is in limited supply. Fatigue rapidly sets in when glycogen stores are depleted. Examples of anaerobic activities include strength training,

© Carl Southerland, 2012, Shutterstock, Inc.

Bicycling is an aerobic exercise that uses the large muscle groups in a rhythmic mode with an increase in respiration and heart rate.

sprinting, and interval training. Sprinting requires so much energy that the intensity of the activity cannot be maintained for a long period of time. Anaerobic training can enhance the body's ability to cope with the effects of lactic acid and fatigue, thus promoting greater anaerobic fitness.

Interval training has been used for years, but now there is a new name for it–boot camp. The concept is simple: work for a shorter amount of time, but work harder. Working with a coach or personal trainer is recommended so that you also work smarter. Interval training involves high intensity cardiovascular exercise alternating between short rest or active rest periods. People who tend to get bored just running for 40 minutes often enjoy the variety and change in routine. The increased challenge of a 40-minute interval workout means increased energy expenditure. The basic variables manipulated when designing an interval training program include:

1. Duration (time/distance) of intervals
2. Duration of rest/recovery phase
3. Number of repetitions of intervals
4. Intensity (speed) of intervals
5. Frequency of interval workout sessions

Working hard with other people can be motivating due to the supportive and/or competitive nature in a class. A fringe benefit of interval training is that you will not only become more aerobically fit, but you might get stronger, faster, and more powerful. The anaerobic energy system is trained as well as the aerobic energy system in an interval type class. Due to increased caloric expenditure in a high intensity class, participants may experience weight loss success. Remember to warm up thoroughly, progress slowly, and stretch after activity.

Exercise Prescription, or How to Become FITT

To improve cardiovascular fitness, one must have a well-designed regimen of cardiovascular exercise. In order for improvement to occur, specific guidelines must be adhered to when designing a personal exercise program. As will be discussed later, the following guidelines apply not only to aerobic exercise, but to other components of physical fitness as well. The **FITT** acronym is easy to remember when identifying an appropriate cardiovascular exercise prescription: **frequency, intensity, time,** and **type.**

Frequency

Frequency refers to the number of exercise sessions per week. The American College of Sports Medicine recommends exercising three to five days per week at a moderate to vigorous level of intensity.

For individuals with a low level of aerobic fitness, beginning an exercise program by working out two times a week will result in an initial increase in aerobic fitness level. However, after some time, frequency and/or intensity will need to be increased for improvement to continue.

Intensity

Intensity refers to how hard one is working, and it can be measured by several techniques. These techniques include **measuring the heart rate** (see Figure 3.6) while exercising, **rating of perceived exertion (RPE),** and the **talk test**. To use heart rate as a measure of intensity, one's target heart rate range needs to be calculated before exercising. **Target heart rate range** is the intensity of training necessary to achieve cardiovascular improvement (see Figure 3.7). This target heart rate range indicates what an individual's heart rate should be during exercise. Calculation of target heart rate range us-

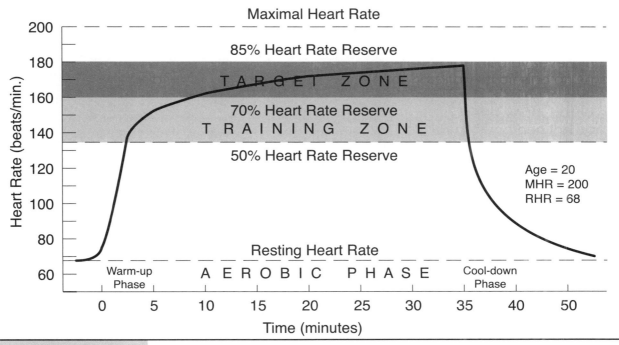

FIGURE 3.6

Cardiovascular Exercise Prescription Guidelines Tracking the Heart Rate Response Through a Typical Cardiovascular Exercise Session.

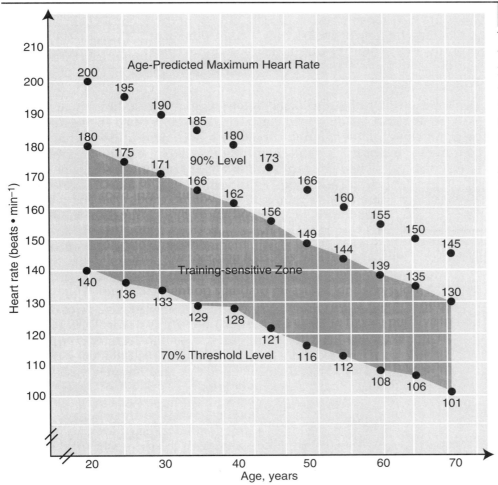

FIGURE 3.7

Target Heart Rate Zones for Individuals of Ages 20 through 70. The zones cover 70–90 percent of maximum heart rate, which is indicated above the zones for selected ages.

Source: From *Total Fitness and Wellness*, 5th Edition, by Powers and Dodd, Pearson Benjamin Cummings Publishers.

ing the Karvonen formula is done by multiplying maximum heart rate (220 minus one's age) by a designated intensity percentage. The American College of Sports Medicine guidelines for intensity recommends working between 55 and 90 percent of maximum heart rate, or between 50 and 85 percent of heart rate reserve (maximum heart rate minus resting heart rate). For individuals who are very unfit, the recommended range is 55 to 64 percent of maximum heart rate or 40 to 49 percent of heart rate reserve (Pollock, Gaesser, Butcher, Despres, Dishman, et al., 1998). Use of a heart rate monitor is also useful for specific heart rate and intensity feedback. Programs can be designed using heart rate to alleviate boredom and increase efficiency of the workout.

Another technique for measuring exercise intensity is through subjective self-evaluation of how hard one is working. Gunner Borg designed the **Rating of Perceived Exertion Scale (RPE)** (see Table 3.1) in the early 1950s. It is a numbered scale from 6 to 20, with the lowest numbers being "very, very light" exercise, the highest numbers being "maximal" exercise, and the numbers in between representing a gradual increase in exercise intensity, from low to high. Using this scale, a rating of 10 corresponds roughly to 50 percent of maximal heart rate and a rating of 16 corresponds roughly to 90 percent of maximal heart rate. A person estimates his or her exercise intensity level by taking into consideration or "perceiving" how they feel, how much sleep they have had, whether or not they have eaten, whether or not they are ill, and so on. This scale is a useful tool for estimating exercise intensity when exact measures are not needed, and it is often used in a clinical setting as well as fitness classes and health clubs. Perceived exertion is also useful when a person is taking medication that can alter the heart rate.

A third, and probably the easiest, technique to measure exercise intensity is the **talk test.** If you are exercising and must laboriously breathe rather than participate in a conversation, the exercise intensity is too high and training heart rate has probably been exceeded. Exercise at this intensity will be difficult to maintain for long periods of time. On the other hand, if you are able to sing, intensity level is probably insufficient for improvement in your fitness level.

Time

The third factor to be considered when designing a cardiovascular exercise workout is **time,** or duration. For benefits to be accrued in the cardiovascular system, exercise duration should be a minimum of twenty minutes of continuous exercise or several intermittent exercise sessions of a minimum of ten minutes each. Some beginning exercisers may not be capable of exercising continuously for twenty minutes at a prescribed intensity. While a minimum of twenty minutes is recommended, a duration of ten minutes can certainly be beneficial to people who are at a low fitness level and just beginning an exercise program. Duration and exercise intensity are interdependent, having an inverse relationship. As exercise effort increases, duration typically decreases. Distance runners exert a moderate effort for a long period of time, called long slow distance training. Sprinters exert a maximal effort for a brief period of time. Duration at a lower intensity is optimal for beginning exercisers. Exercise intensity levels should remain within recommended guidelines, while maximum duration is only limited by the participant's available fuel for energy and mental determination to keep going.

TABLE 3.1 ♦ The Borg RPE Scale	
Score	Degree of Exertion
6	No exertion at all
7	Extremely light
8	
9	Very light
10	
11	Light
12	
13	Somewhat hard
14	
15	Hard (heavy)
16	
17	Very hard
18	
19	Extremely hard
20	Maximal exertion

Source: © Gunner Borg, 1970, 1985, 1998.

Type

Another factor that should be considered in determining a cardiovascular exercise prescription is **type,** or mode, of exercise. The choice of exercise modality is up to each individual, but one must keep in mind the specific requirements of cardio-vascular exercise: use the large muscle groups via continuous and rhythmic movement, and exercise for a duration of twenty to thirty minutes or more in the target heart rate range a minimum of three to five times per week. Common types of aerobic exercise include running, walking, swimming, step aerobics, cross-country skiing, biking, or using a machine such as a rower, stairstepper, or treadmill. However, these are certainly not the only types of exercise available. Any exercise that meets the requirements of intensity and duration is acceptable. Some sports can provide aerobic exercise, depending on the nature of the sport, the position being played, and the skill level of the player. For example, an indoor soccer player could get an aerobic workout by playing a game, provided there is constant movement and training heart rate was maintained in the target heart rate range. Many sports provide an excellent way for people to expend a lot of energy and burn a significant number of calories, but the "play some and rest some" nature often prevents them from being good aerobic exercise. In order to achieve longterm cardiovascular fitness, it is good to pick a variety of activities, and to find activities that are pleasurable to the individual.

© Val Thoermer, 2012, Shutterstock, Inc.

To achieve long-term cardiovascular fitness, select a variety of activities you find pleasurable.

Components of an Exercise Session

The sequence of a cardiovascular workout should be as follows: warm-up, easy optional stretch, workout, cool down, and stretch again with more intensity for increased flexibility.

Warm-Up

A good cardiovascular workout follows a specific sequence of events. First and foremost, to prepare the body and increase the comfort level for a cardiovascular workout, a warm-up is crucial. The purpose of the warm-up is to prepare the body and especially the heart for the more vigorous work to come. The warm-up should increase body temperature, increase heart rate, increase blood flow to the muscles that will be used during the workout, and include some rhythmic movement to loosen muscles that may be cold and/or tight. A warm-up should raise the pulse from a resting level to a rate somewhere near the low end of the recommended heart rate training zone. Beginning vigorous exercise without some kind of warm-up is not only difficult physically and mentally, but it can also contribute to musculoskeletal injuries.

Pre-Stretch

It is important to warm up the muscles that will be used during the workout. Use caution when stretching prior to the workout, holding the stretches for a brief time and not stretching with much intensity. Stretching prior to the workout is optional. Many athletes choose to go through rhythmic limbering, with dynamic movements focusing on functional movement patterns that will be used in the race, sport, or fitness class rather than holding a static stretch.

Activity

When doing cardiovascular exercise, the aerobic component should be from fifteen minutes to sixty minutes, depending

© Val Thoermer, 2012, Shutterstock, Inc.

It is important to warm up muscles before stretching.

on the individual's fitness level and goals. A gradual increase in intensity and duration is recommended for beginners. It is important to pay attention to your body's signals to slow down or perhaps stop.

Cooldown and Stretch

After an aerobic exercise session, heart rate should be lowered gradually by slowly reducing the intensity of the exercise. Sudden stops are not recommended and can lead to muscle cramps, dizziness, and blood pooling in the legs. After a gradual cooldown such as walking, static stretching of the muscle groups is needed and highly recommended. *When muscle core and body core temperature are elevated, it is an optimal time to stretch for increased flexibility.* Warmer muscle core temperature increases the pliability of the muscle, allowing it to lengthen better.

Principles of Fitness Training—The Rules

There are specific principles that can be applied to any exercise program. Understanding these exercise principles will increase a person's chance of success with his/her exercise program.

Overload and Adaptation

The principle of overload and adaptation states that in order for a body system to become more efficient or stronger, it must be stressed beyond its normal working level. In other words, it must be overloaded. When this overload occurs, the system will respond by gradually adapting to this new load and increasing its work efficiency until another plateau is reached. When this occurs, additional overload must be applied for gain. The cardiovascular system can be overloaded in more than one way. For example, a person has been running for a few months and is running a distance of three miles in thirty minutes. The runner never goes farther than three miles and never runs faster than a ten-minute per mile pace. For this individual, some techniques of overloading would be: to increase distance, to run the same distance at a faster pace, or to add hills or sprint segments to the run. In terms of weight training, any time a person adds more weight to the bench press or increases the number of repetitions, that person is using the principle of overload. *In order for improvements to be realized, overload must occur.* The principle of overload and adaptation applies to muscular strength, cardiovascular and muscular endurance, and flexibility training.

Specificity

The principle of specificity refers to training specifically for an activity, or isolating a specific muscle group and/or movement pattern one would like to improve. For example, a 200-m sprinter would not train by running long, slow distances. Likewise, a racewalker would not train for competition by swimming. Workouts must be specific to one's goal with respect to the type of exercise, intensity, and duration. The warm-up should also be specific to a particular activity. Cross training, defined as using several different types of training, has recently increased in popularity. The benefits of cross training are to prevent injury from overuse and to decrease boredom. The principle of specificity does not negate participation in cross training activities; rather, it indicates that the primary training protocol should be in one's chosen activity.

Individual Differences

The principle of individual differences reminds us that individuals will respond differently to the same training protocol. Some individuals may be what is called a "low responder" to an exercise stimulus. It is not clear why

A Complete Physical Activity Program

There are three principle components to a rounded program of physical activity: aerobic exercise, strength training exercise, and flexibility training. It is not essential that all three components be performed during the same workout session. Try to create a pattern that fits into your schedule and one to which you can adhere. *Commitment to a regular physical activity program is more important than intensity of the workouts.* Therefore, choose exercises you are likely to pursue and enjoy.

ACSM/AHA recent position stand *Guideline for adults under* 65 states that **aerobic training** should be moderate intensity for thirty minutes five times per week or three times per week for twenty minutes with vigorous intensity. Remember that *if your schedule is tight, it is better to exercise for a shorter period of time than not at all.* Typical forms of aerobic exercise are walking and running (treadmills), stair climbing, bicycling (bicycle ergometers), rowing, cross-country skiing, and swimming. Many devices contain combinations of these motions.

For general purposes, **strength training** should be done two or three times per week. Strength training is performed with free weights or weight machines. For the purposes of general training, two or three upper body and lower body exercises should be done. Additionally, abdominal exercises are an important part of strength training.

Flexibility training is important and frequently neglected, resulting in increased tightness as we age and become less active. Stretching is most safely done with sustained gradual movements lasting a minimum of fifteen seconds per stretch. Strive to stretch every day.

individuals vary in response to exercise, but initial fitness level, age, gender, genetic composition, and previous history will also cause individual responses to specific activities to differ. Coaches, athletic trainers, and personal trainers should be especially aware of this principle when designing workouts in order to achieve maximum performance levels. It is also critical that individuals realize that body type is genetically determined. Body fat distribution and metabolism are individual. Lifestyle and activity can affect one's physique; however, a large-framed person will never be a small-framed person and vice versa. Focusing more on enhanced health rather than trying to change one's body type is prudent.

Reversibility

The inevitable process of losing cardiovascular benefits with cessation of aerobic activity is known as the reversibility principle. The old adage "if you don't use it you lose it" applies here. Physiological changes will occur within the first two weeks of detraining and will continue for several months. Bed rest causes this detraining process to greatly accelerate. Consider the muscle atrophy that occurs with disuse when a cast is removed from a body part that has been immobilized for several weeks. The reversibility principle is clearly the justification for off-season programs for athletes and immediate initiation of physical rehabilitation programs for individuals with limited mobility or for those individuals recovering from injury.

Evaluating Cardiovascular Fitness

There are many ways to measure a person's level of cardiovascular fitness. Over time, the body adapts to regular activity by not working as hard when given the same workload. An example would be running the mile. A person may have a goal of running the mile in eight minutes. At first an eight-minute mile may be a challenge, but with continuous practice, an eight-minute mile can be achieved, and may actually become easier. The body has adapted by allowing the pace to be maintained with less apparent effort. Working heart rate, the heart rate during activity, is lower. Oxygen delivery is increased to the working muscles. Respiration rate is less as the respiratory muscles become stronger. Muscles become stronger with use, creating ease of movement. Body composition typically becomes more favorable, which contributes to efficiency of movement. *Powers and Howley have shown that in general twelve to fifteen weeks of endurance exercise results in a 10 percent to 30 percent improvement in VO2 Max.*

VO$_2$ Max is the nomenclature for **maximum oxygen uptake,** the measure of the maximum amount of oxygen that an individual can utilize per minute of physical activity. VO$_2$ Max is expressed as mililiters of oxygen per kilogram of body weight per minute (ml/kg/min). As aerobic capacity increases, so does VO$_2$ Max. VO$_2$ Max is considered the best indicator of cardiovascular fitness. Unfortunately, measurement in a laboratory takes time, equipment, and technicians to administer the tests. Other ways to measure cardiovascular fitness include:

* 1.5-mile run (see 1.5-mile run activity (Notebook Activity on page 105)
* 1-mile walk (below)
* various submaximal tests on cycle ergometers and treadmills

The **Rockport one-mile walk test** is often used. See Table 3.2 for the Rockport Fitness test. In order to correctly evaluate cardiovascular fitness, walk the

TABLE 3.2 ♦ Rockport One-Mile Walk Test

	Age (years)			
Fitness Category	13–19	20–29	30–39	40+
Men				
Very Poor	>17:30	>18:00	>19:00	>21:30
Poor	16:01–17:30	16:31–18:00	17:31–19:00	18:31–21:30
Average	14:01–16:00	14:31–16:30	15:31–17:30	16:01–18:30
Good	12:31–14:00	13:01–14:30	13:31–15:30	14:01–16:00
Excellent	<12:30	<13:00	<13:30	<14:00
Women				
Very Poor	>18:01	>18:31	>19:31	>22:01
Poor	16:31–18:00	17:01–18:30	18:01–19:30	19:01–22:00
Average	14:31–16:30	15:01–17:00	16:01–18:00	16:31–19:00
Good	13:01–14:30	13:31–15:00	14:01–16:00	14:31–16:30
Excellent	<13:00	<13:30	<14:00	<14:30

Because the one-mile walk test is designed primarily for older or less conditioned individuals, the fitness categories listed here do not include a "superior" category.

Source: Modified from Rockport Fitness Walking Test.

distance in the shortest amount of time, find your age and corresponding time and estimated fitness level.

Recovery heart rate is taken after an exercise session is completed, typically for thirty seconds, and multiplied by two for a per minute count. The higher a person's level of cardiovascular fitness, the less time it will take after exercise for the heart rate to return to a pre-exercise level. One minute after the cessation of exercise, a conditioned male heart rate should have returned to below 90, and a female heart rate to below 100 beats per minute. Five minutes post exercise, both male and female heart rates should be below 80 beats per minute. This is an indication not only of one's fitness level, but also of the adequacy of a cooldown period.

Muscular Fitness

Muscular fitness includes two specific components: muscular strength and muscular endurance. **Muscular strength** is the force or tension a muscle or muscle group can exert against a resistance in one maximal effort. **Muscular endurance** is the ability or capacity of a muscle group to perform repeated contractions against a load, or to sustain a contraction for an extended period of time. In February 2002 ACSM released a new position stand regarding resistance training progression. The position stand reported that everyone would benefit from resistance training two to three days per week, working eight to ten muscle groups with one to two sets of eight to twelve repetitions. For more information, these statements can be found on the ACSM Web site listed at the end of this chapter.

> "Fitness isn't just for highly skilled athletes. It is for all of us. It's our natural state of being, particularly when we are young. Being out of shape is really being out of sorts with ourselves."
> —Kenneth H. Cooper, M.D.,
> The Aerobics Way

Top Ten Reasons to Work Your Muscles

1. *Gain lean body mass and lose body fat.* For each pound of muscle you gain, you'll burn 35 to 50 more calories daily.
2. *Get strong.* Extra strength makes it easier to carry suitcases and accomplish some daily activities, such as lifting children or groceries.
3. *Build denser bones.* Weight training can increase spinal bone mineral density by 13 percent in six months.
4. *Reduce risk of diabetes.* Weight training can boost glucose utilization in the body by 23 percent in four months and lower the likelihood of developing diabetes.
5. *Fight heart disease.* Strength training reduces harmful cholesterol and lowers blood pressure.
6. *Beat back pain.* In a twelve-year study, strengthening the low-back muscles had an 80 percent success rate in eliminating or alleviating low-back pain.
7. *Move easier.* Weight training can ease arthritis pain and strengthen joints, so you feel fewer aches.
8. *Improve athletic ability.* Whatever your sport, strength training may improve proficiency and decrease risk of injury.
9. *Feel younger.* Even men and women in their 80's and 90's can make significant gains in strength and mobility with weight training.
10. *Boost your spirits.* Strength training reduces symptoms of anxiety and depression and instills greater self-confidence.

Benefits of Muscular Fitness

Several **physiological adaptations** occur as a result of resistance training. *Strength gains can be seen within the first six weeks, with little or no change in muscle size, and are attributed to neural changes.* These changes include decreased activation of antagonistic muscles, learning how to perform the activity, changes in activation of the motor unit, improved recruitment patterns of muscle fibers, change in the gain of the muscle spindle and Golgi tendon organ, and reduction in the sensitivity of force-producing limiting factors.

As strength training activities continue, hypertrophy, or an increase in the size of the muscle fibers, occurs (see Figure 3.10 on page 82). Another result from training is an increase in the amount of energy available for contraction. Carbohydrates are stored in the form of **glycogen** in the muscle and can be used as the primary energy source for contraction. These muscle glycogen stores increase as a result of training. Bone and connective tissue also undergo changes with resistance training, including an increase in bone matrix, an increase in **bone mineral density,** and an increase in mass and tensile strength of ligaments and tendons. These increases help prevent injury and decrease the chance of development of osteoporosis after middle age. More muscle mass increases an individual's basal metabolic rate, which is why weight training is excellent for "dieters," or those wanting to reduce their percentage of body fat. "An increase in one pound of muscle elevates basal metabolic rate by approximately 2–3 percent" (Powers and Dodd, 2009).

Along with the physiological adaptations previously discussed come benefits that improve the quality of one's life. These benefits of muscular fitness include:

- an increase in muscular strength,
- power and endurance,
- a higher percentage of muscle mass,
- improved posture,
- increased metabolic rate,
- improved ease of movement,
- increased resistance to muscle fatigue,
- increased strength of tendons, ligaments, and bones,
- decreased risk of low back pain,
- increased energy and vitality.

Importance of the Core Musculature in Functional Movement

An important new buzzword in the group fitness and personal training field is **functional movement.** Functional movement is exercise based on real-life movement. The actions done by an athlete in his/her sport are functional. Functional movement usually involves gross motor, multi-planar, multi-joint movements which place demand on the body's core—from the hips to the sternum. The core involves the muscles of the abdomen, back, and hips (listed below). Functional exercises (medicine ball warm-up, full squat with military press, wood choppers) attempt to incorporate as many variables as possible (balance, multiple joints, multiple planes of movement). This is in contrast to weight training for a specific muscle group such as the biceps brachai when doing a biceps curl. It is important to stabilize the pelvis, train the core muscles, align the spine, and achieve muscle equity to use functional movement when exercising. *A strong core reduces the risk of injury and increases the efficiency of movement.* Training the core can lead to an increase in balance and coordination, as well as gains in strength, power, and endurance.

What Makes Up the "Core"?

- *Pelvic floor muscles*—The pelvic floor muscles run collectively from the pubic bone to the tailbone. Contraction of these muscles contributes to spinal stability, which is the foundation from which we move.
- *Abdominal wall*—The rectus abdominus, the internal and external obliques, and the transverse abdominus together are responsible for spinal flexion, extension, and rotation, as well as for assisting in stabilization.
- *Back muscles*—The erector spinae and multifidus produce spine extension, lateral flexion, and rotation. The interconnections of these muscles help contribute to stability of the lower back and pelvis.
- *Hip muscles*—The adductor and abductor muscles of the hip, when in balance, provide optimum stability and mobility to the hip and lumbopelvic area.
- *Lats and glutes*—Both of these muscle groups attach to the spine or pelvis, so each has an important role in the stability and mobility of the trunk.

These muscle groups make up the "core" and play an important role in core stabilization, muscle balance, and proper alignment, as well as strength and flexibility (see Figures 3.8a and 3.8b).

Effective Training

The following are general definitions regarding the use of weight training for developing an exercise protocol to increase muscular endurance (Cissik, 1998).

- **Frequency** refers to how often one should lift, with the recommendation being three nonconsecutive days per week.
- **Load** defines the amount of weight lifted. This will vary with each individual, with the recommended amount being a weight that will allow twelve to fifteen repetitions with good form. If form is compromised, the load should be decreased.
- **Repetition** is simply the performance of a movement from start to finish one time.
- **Set** is the specific number of repetitions performed without resting. Twelve to fifteen repetitions per set are recommended while performing two to three sets of each exercise. Each exercise session should contain eight to ten different exercises, with at least one being a full-body exercise.
- **Recovery** is the amount of time between each set. Thirty seconds is considered the optimum amount; however, taking more time is not detrimental.
- **Repetition-maximum** (also called one rep max) is the maximum amount of weight that can be lifted one time without compromising form.
- **Intensity** is the stress level of the exercise and is expressed as a percent of a one repetition-maximum. The recommended intensity level is less than 70 percent of a one repetition-maximum.

Training for the Best Results

The exercise prescription for developing muscular strength is more intense than for endurance. The number of repetitions decreases from eight to one, with the number of sets increasing from three to five. The percent of the one repetition maximum that should be lifted increases to 80 to 100 percent. Due to the increase in intensity, the rest period is extended, lasting three to five

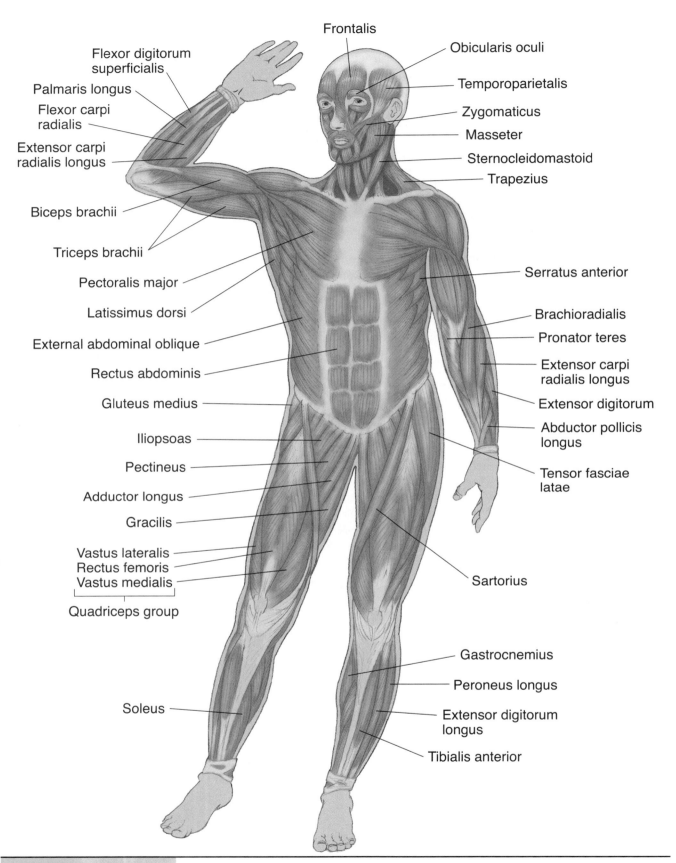

Frontalis
Flexor digitorum superficialis
Palmaris longus
Flexor carpi radialis
Extensor carpi radialis longus
Biceps brachii
Triceps brachii
Pectoralis major
Latissimus dorsi
External abdominal oblique
Rectus abdominis
Gluteus medius
Iliopsoas
Pectineus
Adductor longus
Gracilis
Vastus lateralis
Rectus femoris
Vastus medialis
Quadriceps group
Soleus
Obicularis oculi
Temporoparietalis
Zygomaticus
Masseter
Sternocleidomastoid
Trapezius
Serratus anterior
Brachioradialis
Pronator teres
Extensor carpi radialis longus
Extensor digitorum
Abductor pollicis longus
Tensor fasciae latae
Sartorius
Gastrocnemius
Peroneus longus
Extensor digitorum longus
Tibialis anterior

FIGURE 3.8a

Major Anterior Muscles in the Human Body

Source: Kendall/Hunt Publishing Company.

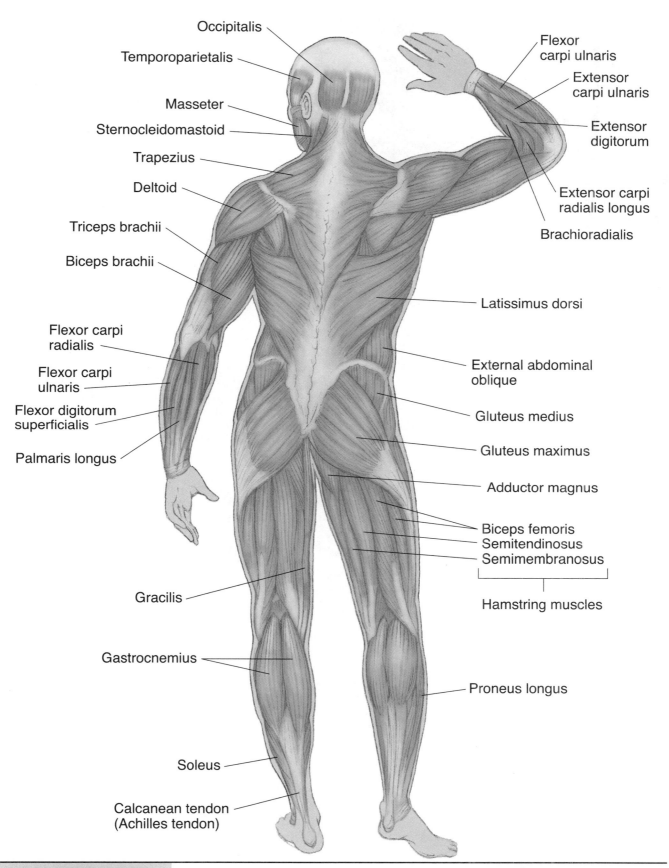

FIGURE 3.8b

Major Posterior Muscles in the Human Body

Source: Kendall/Hunt Publishing Company.

Always focus on correct form when doing resistance exercise.

minutes. Exercise prescription will vary depending on one's goals and objectives for training (see Figure 3.9 p. 81).

Muscle soreness often accompanies resistance training and will occur at various times during the training process. Muscle soreness that begins late in an exercise session and continues during the immediate recovery period is known as acute muscle soreness. This soreness will last only a brief period of time and is typically gone within twenty-four hours, while **delayed-onset muscle soreness** begins a day or two after the exercise session and can remain for several days. Eccentric contraction seems to be the primary cause of delayed-onset muscle soreness. According to Wilmore and Costill (1999), the causes of delayed-onset muscle soreness include structural damage to muscle cells and inflammatory reactions within the muscles. Muscle soreness can be prevented or minimized by: reducing the eccentric component of muscle action during early training, starting training at a low intensity and gradually increasing it, or beginning with a high-intensity, exhaustive bout, which will cause much soreness initially, but will decrease future pain. During delayed-onset muscle soreness, strength production is reduced by as much as 50 percent during the first five days and a reduction in strength can occur for as long as fourteen days. The best technique for prevention of delayed-onset muscle soreness is to maintain an appropriate training program. Diet supplements of vitamin E, an antioxidant, may also help to reduce damage to muscle fiber membranes (Evans, 2000).

As with any type of training program, watch for signs of **over-training** called burn-out. With muscular fitness training, these indicators include a decrease in physical performance, weight loss, increase in muscle soreness, increase in resting heart rate, sleeplessness, nausea after a workout, constant fatigue, and decreased interest in exercise.

True or False? Weight Training Myths

1. Myth: Weight training causes one to lose flexibility.
   Fact: Resistance training will increase muscle size, but it does not necessarily make one less flexible. In fact, proper strength training can actually increase flexibility when a full range of motion is used.

2. Myth: Resistance training or "spot reducing" is beneficial in reducing deposits of fat from specific areas on the body, such as in the hips, thighs, and waist.
   Fact: Resistance training focuses on the muscles used. Fat is not removed from one area of the body by working the muscles in that area. Creating a caloric deficit consistently, through diet, exercise, or a combination of both, loses fat. The location of fat deposits is determined genetically. The majority of women tend to be "pears" with fat deposits collecting on the hip and thigh region. The majority of men tend to be "apples" with fat deposits collecting around the torso. Abdominal fat has been shown to indicate an increased health risk.

3. Myth: Fat will be converted to muscle with resistance training.
   Fact: Fat is not converted to muscle with exercise, nor is muscle converted to fat through disuse. Muscle cells and fat cells are different entities. The size of muscle cells can be increased with resistance training. Fat cell size is increased with sedentary living combined with a poor diet.

Preparation:

- Establish goals. Why do you want to weight train? Your goals will affect the way you train.
- Don't train on an empty stomach; fuel your body and brain before working out with a healthy snack.
- Consume a balanced diet daily.
- Stay hydrated with water before, during, and after the workout.
- Dress properly in loose clothing and wear non-slip athletic shoes.
- Commit to a regularly scheduled training time weekly for best results.
- Get instruction in a safe, effective, and balanced program.
- Adjust the weight machine to your body height.

Lifting:

- Always warm up; try ten minutes of cardiovascular activity or calisthenics followed by joint-specific movements for the body parts you will target.
- Progress slowly; use common sense when overloading.
- Work all the major muscle groups; avoid focusing on just one or two areas of the body.
- Consider balance—working opposing muscle groups (biceps-triceps, hamstring-quadriceps, lower backabdominals).
- Work the larger muscle groups first, progressing to the smaller muscles.
- Complete multi-joint exercises before doing singlejoint exercises (squats before leg curls).
- Keep the weights as close to the body as required for proper form and technique.
- Use a full range of motion for each exercise.
- Make sure stretching needs are appropriate to the individual; only stretch the muscle, not the ligaments or joint capsule.
- Maintain good posture throughout each movement.
- Movement should be slow and controlled, with a smooth rhythm.
- Breathe, exhaling on the exertion phase.
- Avoid breath holding during heavy lifting.

- Expect some soreness; excessive muscle soreness may be a sign of overuse or injury.
- Allow forty-eight hours of recovery for a particular body part after heavy lifting; light activity is fine during recovery.
- Get plenty of rest, water, and good nutrition to allow for muscle repair and recovery.
- Enlist a workout buddy to help with technique, motivation, and safety.
- Use a workout log to track your progress, recording weight, sets, and repetitions.

Safety:

- Learn the rules at your facility.
- Don't overtrain; listen to your body.
- Never sacrifice form for additional repetitions or weight.
- When squatting, maintain a natural lordotic curve in your spine; descend until the thighs are parallel to the floor.
- Use collars or other locking devices to keep the plates on the bars when using free weights.
- Use experienced spotters for heavy lifting.
- Always lift free weights with a partner.
- Avoid locking out or hyperextending any joints while lifting.
- Don't lift if you are too fatigued to maintain good form.

Etiquette:

- Practice good weight room etiquette; don't drop or bang the weights.
- Always re-rack free weights.
- Use a towel to wipe equipment when you are done at an exercise station.
- Be considerate of others who are waiting to use the equipment.

(a) Standing   (b) Beginning Squat   (c) Advanced Full Squat

FIGURE 3.9

Beginning Strength Training Guidelines

4. Myth: Dietary supplements will make one bigger and stronger.
   Fact: A balanced diet and hard work in the weight room will increase muscle size and strength. Most dietary supplements will only cause the manufacturer's wallet to become bigger. Often when a person spends money on a supplement believing that supplement to work, the placebo effect might result in some apparent short-term improvement.
5. Myth: Performance-enhancing drugs such as steroids, growth hormones, diuretics, and metabolism boosters will help make one fit.
   Fact: These drugs are extremely dangerous and potentially fatal. They can contribute to aesthetic changes, but can also have a negative impact on health. Some fitness enthusiasts have lost their lives searching for a short-cut to health by using supplements.
6. Myth: Women will become masculine in appearance by participating in resistance training activities.
   Fact: Masculinity and femininity are determined through hormones, not through resistance training. Resistance training will cause an increase in muscle tone, which is perceived to increase the attractiveness of both males and females.
7. Myth: Kids should not weight train.
   Fact: Pre-adolescent children can and should use their body as resistance. Swinging on the monkey bars or climbing a tree are good examples of using one's body as resistance; push-ups, sit-ups, and tumbling activities are also great. Teaching 11- to 13-year-olds proper technique and form lifting light weight with proper supervision helps lay a strong foundation for future training. Proper training can improve flexibility, as well as strengthen muscles and the skeletal structure. Body composition and self-esteem are also usually enhanced with a training program, which can be a positive outcome with childhood obesity on the rise.

Flexibility

Can you touch your toes? Think of how much your flexibility has changed in the last ten years. How much more will it change in the next ten years? Truly, if you don't stretch or if you are not active, flexibility will be lost. Why is this a concern? Loss of flexibility with age or injury can greatly affect a person's quality of life. Simple activities such as putting on your socks, or bending to

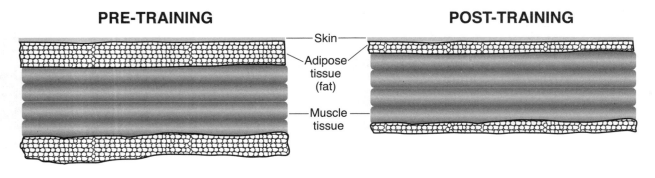

PRE-TRAINING   **POST-TRAINING**

Skin
Adipose tissue (fat)
Muscle tissue

FIGURE 3.10

Changes in Body Composition from Combined Aerobic and Strength Training Program

Yoga is gaining in popularity in the United States. Most forms of yoga encourage the buildup of heat within the body to facilitate movement and internal focus. Relaxation is a common goal of most yoga participants, yet most experience enhanced flexibility and increased strength as a fringe benefit. One style of yoga, Bikram yoga, advocates practicing yoga in rooms with temperatures as high as 105 degrees. The premise is that the heat will allow the tendons, ligaments, and muscles to loosen up more and stretch further. A common yoga truism is that even steel, when heated hot enough, will bend.

lift a toddler can be painful or worse, impossible. Individuals who are active tend to be more flexible simply because they tend to use a full range of motion in their activity. Active individuals are also more likely to engage in health-enhancing behaviors. Several factors can have an impact on the amount of flexibility a person can achieve, including gender, age, genetic composition, activity level, muscle core temperature, and previous or current injury. Old injuries often hamper flexibility for adults later in life, therefore affecting future activity.

Flexibility and balance are a concern for the aging population. Non-impact activities such as tai chi and yoga are gaining in popularity with all ages, both of which are appropriate to the aging population.

Flexibility is defined as the range of motion around a joint. Flexibility is also specific to individual joints. For instance, an individual may have complete range of motion in the wrist but be very limited or stiff in the shoulder. An individual could be very flexible on the right side of the body, and inflexible on the left side. Flexibility exercises should be included in all exercise programs regardless of the objectives. The benefits of maintaining flexibility include having the ability to perform daily activities without developing muscle strains or tears and being able to participate in sports with enhanced performance. Consider a swimmer who increases shoulder flexibility is able to reach further, pull more water, and thus swim faster.

© Alex Saberi, 2012, Shutterstock, Inc.

Strengthening and stretching the back with cobra.

The athlete, whether serious about competition or a weekend recreator, will have a greater ability to perform particular sports skills with an increased range of motion. Consider a football coach encouraging his receivers to bench press as much as possible. That receiver can be very strong in the weight room; however, if he cannot apply that strength on the football field, he will not be an effective player. Athletes should train for **functional strength.** A wide receiver should train to jump high and extend from his shoulders to catch a pass. Strength without flexibility is limiting. It is especially important to include flexibility exercises in a muscular fitness workout. Flexibility also helps to prevent injuries through a reduction in strains and muscle tears.

Stretching exercises are identified through three specific categories: **ballistic, static,** and **PNF.**

1. **Ballistic** stretching involves dynamic movements, or what is commonly referred to as "bouncing." Ballistic stretching is not recommended for the general population as a means to improve

Time, Inc reported (Aug. 5, 2002) that tai chi is the perfect exercise for seniors. **Tai chi** is an ancient martial art involving graceful movement performed slowly with great concentration and focus on breathing. The atmosphere is non-competitive, and participants are encouraged to progress at their own pace. The Oregon Research Institute reports that studies show older men and women who are inactive yet relatively healthy attain many benefits from participation in tai chi.

flexibility. An exception is athletes who have ballistic movement in their sport. This type of stretch actually stimulates receptors in the muscle that are designed to help prevent injury due to over-extending the muscle. Thus, the ballistic stretch can cause the muscle to contract rather than relax, and can contribute to muscle soreness. A more appropriate type of muscular stretching for the general population is identified as static stretching.

2. **Static** stretching involves slowly moving the joint to the point of mild discomfort in the muscle and maintaining that angle for approximately thirty seconds before allowing the muscle to relax. The entire procedure should be repeated several times for maximum benefit. As previously noted, a warmup is highly recommended prior to stretching for injury prevention and to facilitate the stretch. A warm environment and a warm muscle will greatly enhance the stretch. If the stretch hurts the muscle or the joint, then stop. Learn to distinguish between the mild tensions needed to overload from pain, indicating a potential injury.

3. A third type of stretching activity is called **proprioceptive neuromuscular facilitation** or **PNF.** This activity requires a partner to provide resistance. The basic formula for this activity is to isometrically resist against a partner using the muscle groups surrounding a particular joint, causing contraction, and then relaxing the same muscle group. For example, in stretching the hamstring, both the hamstrings and the quadriceps will be contracted and then relaxed. This contraction and relaxation process will increase the range of motion in the hamstrings. When stretching with a partner, communication is essential to avoid injury to the joint.

When You Should Not Exercise

Injuries

Although injuries do occur during exercise, the benefits of regular exercise far out-weigh the risk of injury. In most cases, proper training, clothing, and equipment will prevent injuries. Avoiding injury requires common sense and moderation. One should not attempt to self-diagnose, nor try to "train through the pain." Pain is a signal that something is wrong, and activity should be stopped until the source of the pain is identified and a trained medical professional can advise you. Some common injuries resulting from exercise include joint sprains, muscle strains, and other musculoskeletal problems. Knowing how to treat an acute, or immediate, injury is important (see Table 3.3). **RICE** most injuries, such as a twisted ankle: Rest, Ice, Compression, and Elevation.

RICE
R—Rest the injured limb, preventing further injury.
I—Ice will help reduce swelling by reducing circulation and easing pain. Apply ice in thirty-minute periods several times per day. A Styrofoam cup with frozen water can be used as an ice rub. A bag of frozen peas also works well!
C—Compression will help reduce swelling and fluid collection at the injury site. An elastic bandage works well to wrap the injured limb.
E—Elevating the injured limb will reduce swelling. Ideally, raise the injured area above the heart. Placing the injured area on pillows on a stool is helpful.

Table 3.3 ◆ Reference Guide for Exercise-Related Problems

Injury	Signs/Symptoms	Treatment*
Bruise (contusion)	Pain, swelling, discoloration	Cold application, compression, rest
Dislocations, fractures	Pain, swelling, deformity	Splinting, cold application, seek medical attention
Heat cramps	Cramps, spasms and muscle twitching in the legs, arms, and abdomen	Stop activity, get out of the heat, stretch, massage the painful area, drink plenty of fluids
Heat exhaustion	Fainting, profuse sweating, cold/clammy skin, weak/rapid pulse, weakness, headache	Stop activity, rest in a cool place, loosen clothing, rub body with cool/wet towel, drink plenty of fluids, stay out of heat for two to three days
Heat stroke	Hot/dry skin, no sweating, serious disorientation, rapid/full pulse, vomiting, diarrhea, unconsciousness, high body temperature	Seek immediate medical attention, request help and get out of the sun, bathe in cold water/spray with cold water/rub body with cold towels, drink plenty of cold fluids
Joint sprains	Pain, tenderness, swelling, loss of use, discoloration	Cold application, compression, elevation, rest, heat after thirty-six to forty-eight hours (if no further swelling)
Muscle cramps	Pain, spasms	Stretch muscle(s), use mild exercises for involved area
Muscle soreness and stiffness	Tenderness, pain	Mild stretching, low-intensity exercise, warm bath
Muscle strains	Pain, tenderness, swelling, loss of use	Cold application, compression, elevation, rest, heat after thirty-six to forty-eight hours (if no further swelling)
Shin splints	Pain, tenderness	Cold application prior to and following any physical activity, rest, heat (if no activity is carried out)
Side stitch	Pain on the side of the abdomen below the rib cage	Decrease level of physical activity or stop altogether, gradually increase level of fitness
Tendinitis	Pain, tenderness, loss of use	Rest, cold application, heat after forty-eight hours

*Cold should be applied three or four times a day for fifteen to twenty minutes. Heat should be applied three times a day for fifteen to twenty minutes.

Of course, using proper equipment, wearing proper clothing and shoes, and practicing correct technique are essential for injury prevention. Weight-bearing forms of exercise will obviously cause more stress on the joints, but also have benefits that non-weight-bearing activities do not have, such as increasing strength of the bones and other connective tissues.

Proper Footwear

It many seem trivial, but proper footwear is critical to success in weight bearing exercise. Shoe technology has come a long way in the past decade. Sport-specific shoes are highly recommended to avoid injury and to enhance performance. Unfortunately, the consumer pays for the research and technology, as well as the logo on the shoes. A good cross trainer shoe is the way to go if you like to do a variety of activities. Cross trainers are not, however, recommended for aerobic dance or running. Running shoes are also not appropriate for "studio activities" such as aerobic dance, step aerobics, BOSU activities, as well as court activities like tennis or racquetball. Running shoes have little lateral

How to Buy Athletic Shoes

For many aerobic activities, good shoes are the most important purchase you'll make. Take the time to choose well. Here are some basic guidelines:

- Shop for shoes in the late afternoon, when your feet are most likely to be somewhat swollen—just as they will be after a workout.
- For walking shoes, look for a shoe that's lightweight, flexible, and roomy enough for your toes to wiggle, with a well-cushioned, curved sole; good support at the heel; and an upper made of a material that breathes (allows air in and out).
- For running shoes (see the figure), look for good cushioning, support, and stability. You should be able to wiggle your toes easily, but the front of your foot shouldn't slide from side to side, which could cause blisters. Your toes should not touch the end of the shoes because your feet will swell with activity. Allow about half an inch from the longest toe to the tip of the shoe.
- For racquetball shoes, look for reinforcement at the toe for protection during foot drag. The sole should allow minimal slippage. There should be some heel elevation to lessen strain on the back of the leg and Achilles tendon. The shoe should have a long throat to ensure greater control by the laces.
- For tennis shoes, look for reinforcement at the toe. The sole at the ball of the foot should be well padded because that's where most pressure is exerted. The sides of the shoe should be sturdy, for stability during continuous lateral movements. The toe box should allow ample room and some cushioning at the tips. A long throat ensures greater control by the laces.

Don't wear wet shoes for training. Let wet shoes air dry, because a heater will cause them to stiffen or shrink. Use powder in your shoes to absorb moisture, lessen friction, and prevent fungal infections. Break in new shoes for several days before wearing them for a long-distance run or during competition.

Source: Canadian Podiatric Sports Medicine Academy.

What to Look for When You Buy Running Shoes

Well-molded Achilles pad prevents irritation of Achilles tendon

Well-padded tongue prevents extensor tendinitis and irritation of dorsum of foot

Laces not too long so they stay tied longer

High, rounded toe box (at least 1½" high) prevents subungual hematomas ("black toes")

Firm heel counter for hindfoot stability

Flared heel for stability and beveled or rounded heel for quick roll-off

Soft, raised heel wedge to absorb impact at heel strike

Flexible midsole helps prevent Achilles tendon problems

Studded sole absorbs shock and provides traction in mud and snow

support and the higher flared heel can actually cause a person participating in step aerobics to be more prone to twisting an ankle or knee joint. Some steps also have a rubber top which can grip the waffle sole of the running shoe and increase the risk of injury.

In any athletic shoe, fit and comfort are of the utmost importance. It is worth going to a store staffed by knowledgeable personnel. Often they can give you good insight into the type of shoe that is most appropriate for your foot and your gait.

Christopher McDougall's 2009 publication *Born to Run* started a discourse between runners regarding what is the best way to run—wearing $160.00 state-of-the-art running shoes or running barefoot? The barefoot crowd claims that a barefoot runner has a more natural gait, striking with the mid or fore-foot first. Shoes with cushioning and a high heel cause the runner to strike the ground with the heel first. Vibram's successful FiveFingers brand popularized the minimalist shoe movement in California and first-place runners in marathons have been seen wearing them. Barefoot runners using the FiveFingers shoe can "feel" the road and may run with a more natural gate and yet still have protection from irritants on the ground like small shards of glass. There are 2 categories of minimalist shoes—the FiveFingers type that fits snug on your foot, and a minimalist running shoe (a cross between a traditional running shoe and being barefoot) which has just a bit of structure and support. If you decide to try the minimalist route, progress slowly and use caution. (Ellingson, Linda, *The Basics of Barefoot/Minimalist Running,* Jan. 2012, REI expert advice online.)

Environmental Conditions

© EdBockStock, 2012, Shutterstock, Inc.

Proper footwear is critical to success in weight bearing exercise. Sport-specific shoes help prevent injury and enhance performance.

Take into consideration environmental conditions such as temperature, air pollution, wind-chill, altitude, and humidity that can affect one's health and safety. Dressing appropriately is important when exercising in extreme weather conditions.

When exercising in the cold weather, layering of clothes is advised. There are new fabrics that can wick away moisture from the body better than fabrics such as wool, polypropylene, and cotton. Avoid cotton as a base layer in cold weather because if it gets wet with perspiration it will stay wet and make you colder. The Dupont company pioneered such a fabric called ComfortMax (Powers and Dodd, 2009). This is an advantage because moisture from perspiration can be transferred away (called "wicking") from the body, allowing evaporation to occur. This type of fabric is excellent as a first layer when skiing, jogging, or hiking in cold weather. Outer layers are ideally a waterproof shell that has mesh or zippered compartments to "breathe" and can be peeled off as needed. It is advisable to limit exercise time in extremely cold weather to avoid hypothermia.

Exercising in the heat can be a challenge (see Figure 3.11). It is important to acclimate to the heat and humidity, especially when moving from an area that is cool and arid. Gradually increase duration and intensity when exercising in a new type of environment. Especially in the Southern states, heat injuries are a real concern. **Heat cramps**, **heat exhaustion**, and **heat stroke** can all occur with prolonged exposure to the heat. Heat stroke is a life-threatening condition, and necessitates hospitalization. Heat exhaustion is more common, with individuals typically suffering from dehydration. In order for the body to effectively cool, evaporation of sweat needs to occur. *In a humid environment when perspiration drips off of a person, evaporation is not occurring, and therefore cooling is not taking place.* A hot and humid environment is especially risky to the very young, the old, and those with low cardiovascular fitness levels.

Heat injuries are much less likely to occur if a person is adequately hydrated. Proper hydration is necessary for the body to function properly. Water aids in controlling body temperature, contributes to the structure and form of the body, and provides the liquid environment for cell processes. When the thirst mechanism is activated, dehydration has already begun. It is important to pre-hydrate, drink before thirst

Guidelines for Exercising in the Heat

1. Stay hydrated with cool water (cool water is absorbed best in the gut) before, during and after activity.
2. Dress appropriately in clothes that can wick moisture away from the body.
3. Limit exposure time.
4. Exercise with a buddy, or let someone know your plan and stick to it.
5. Wear lightweight sunglasses for eye protection against sun glare, dust and debris in the air. (Important if you exercise near a construction site or near traffic.)
6. Exercise in the coolest time of the day if possible.
7. Stop activity if you experience nausea, dizziness, or extreme headache.
8. Monitor your heart rate, staying within your target heart rate zone.
9. Check the heat index to make sure it is safe to exercise.

Figure 3.11

Heat and Humidity Chart

Apparent temperature (what it feels like)

Air temperature (F°)	70°	75°	80°	85°	90°	95°	100°	105°	110°	115°
0%	64°	69°	73°	78°	83°	87°	91°	95°	99°	103°
10%	65°	70°	75°	80°	85°	90°	95°	100°	105°	111°
20%	66°	72°	77°	82°	87°	93°	99°	105°	112°	120°
30%	67°	73°	78°	84°	90°	96°	104°	113°	123°	135°
40%	68°	74°	79°	86°	93°	101°	110°	123°	137°	151°
50%	69°	75°	81°	88°	96°	107°	120°	135°	150°	
60%	70°	76°	82°	90°	100°	114°	132°	149°		
70%	70°	77°	85°	93°	106°	124°	144°			
80%	71°	78°	86°	97°	113°	136°				
90%	71°	79°	88°	102°	122°					
100%	72°	80°	91°	108°						

Relative Humidity (left vertical label)

Apparent temperature:	Heat stress risk with exertion:
90°–105°	Heat cramps and heat exhaustion possible.
105°–130°	Heat cramps or heat exhaustion likely; heat stroke possible.
130° and above	Heat stroke highly likely with continued exposure.

To determine the risk of exercising in the heat, locate the outside air temperature on the top horizontal scale and the relative humidity on the left vertical scale. Where these two values intersect is the apparent temperature. For example, on a 90°F day with 70 percent humidity, the apparent temperature is 106°F. Heat cramps or heat exhaustion are likely to occur, and heat stroke is possible during exercise under these conditions.

Source: Adapted from U.S. Department of Commerce, National Oceanic and Atmospheric Administration, Heat index chart, in *Heat wave: A major summer killer.* Washington, D.C.: Government Printing Office, 1992.

occurs, and especially drink before exercising. The standard recommendation is to drink at least eight eight-ounce glasses of water a day. Exercise increases the body's demand for water due to an increase in metabolic rate and body temperature. Therefore, this amount should be increased. Drinking water every waking hour is a good habit for individuals who exercise on a regular basis. Hydration is very critical in a humid environment. Before, during, and after aerobic exercise, increase the amount of water consumed. *Water is necessary for the efficient functioning of the body; thus, the importance of hydration cannot be overstated.* Electrolyte levels, especially calcium, sodium, and potassium, are critically important in muscle contraction and should also be carefully maintained. This may be accomplished through re-hydrating with sports drinks. Sports drinks are useful for glycogen replacement when the duration of an activity is sixty to ninety minutes or longer or if the athlete is in a tournament with multiple events.

Hyponatremia

Avoiding dehydration is critical when exercising, especially in the heat and high humidity. There is, however, a possibility of over-hydration, which can be just as critical. Due to the popularity of marathon and triathlon training programs, more people are participating in longer road races. There are more marathon walkers than ever before. A walker can be on the course for a much longer time than a runner—perhaps six or seven hours. If the walker is hydrating the entire time, it is possible to over-hydrate. This over-hydration can lead to a condition called hyponatremia, also called **water intoxication**. Hyponatremia is characterized by a low sodium concentration in the blood. Hyponatremia is seen in some medical conditions such as certain forms of lung cancer. Exercise-associated hyponatremia involves excess ADH (antidiuretic hormone) being secreted from the pituitary gland. The longer a person sweats, the higher the risk of hyponatremia due to lost electrolytes. Hyponatremia can be life-threatening, and unfortunately the hyponatremia symp-

Adverse Effects of Dehydration

Exercise in the heat can be extremely dangerous, depending on exercise intensity, ambient temperature, relative humidity, clothing, and state of hydration (water content of the body). Although some forms of heat injury can occur prior to significant weight loss due to sweating, the table in this box shows how weight loss during exercise can be a predictor of some of the dangers associated with exercise in the heat. The loss of body weight during exercise in the heat is simply due to water loss through sweating. Thus, prolonged, profuse sweating is the first warning signal of impending dehydration.

% Body Weight Loss	Symptoms	% Body Weight Loss	Symptoms
0.5	Thirst	6.0	Impaired temperature regulation, increased heart rate
2.0	Stronger thirst, vague discomfort, loss of appetite	8.0	Dizziness, labored breathing during exercise, confusion
3.0	Concentrated blood, dry mouth, reduced urine output	10.0	Spastic muscles, loss of balance, delirium
4.0	Increased effort required during exercise, flushed skin, apathy	11.0	Circulatory insufficiency, decreased blood volume, kidney failure
5.0	Difficulty in concentrating		

Source: From Total Fitness and Wellness, 5th Edition, by Powers and Dodd, Benjamin Cummings Publishers.

toms mimic the symptoms of heat illness (fatigue, light headedness, nausea, cramping, headache, dizziness). If you treat a hyponatremia victim the same way you would a heat illness victim, you could accelerate their decline. The best way to avoid hyponatremia, or dehydration for that matter, is to be aware of fluid loss and fluid intake. After approximately sixty minutes of activity, it is best to rehydrate in part with sports drinks that contain electrolytes such as sodium and chloride. It is also prudent to eat a normal diet including salt-containing foods unless you are restricted by your physician from sodium in your diet. When competing in races, avoid ingesting aspirin, ibuprofen, or acetaminophen, which can interfere with kidney functioning. As with other things in life, balance is the key.

Illness

Use common sense when ill. If you have cold symptoms with no fever, then possibly a light workout might make you feel better. If fever is present, you have a headache, extreme fatigue, muscle aches, swollen lymph glands, or if you have flu-like symptoms, then bed rest is recommended. Marathon efforts of high intensity and long duration have been shown to temporarily suppress the immune system. Mild to moderate exercise has been shown to enhance the immune system and to reduce risk of respiratory infections (ACSM, 1989).

Common Sense Concerns for Outside Activity

- **Lightning**—DO NOT exercise if there is lightning in the area. Stay indoors.
- **Air pollution**—When the air quality is poor, exercise early in the morning, later in the evening, or preferably indoors, especially for those with lung or heart disease. Pay attention to air pollution alerts. Avoid high traffic areas.

- *Allergens*—Check weather reports for pollen counts, and avoid outdoor vigorous exercise when the pollen count is high.
- *Night exercise*—It is common for some to walk, jog, or bike on the shoulder of roads. Drivers need to use caution; sometimes the glare from oncoming traffic can obscure visibility. However, night exercisers must be responsible and make themselves more visible at night:

1. Use a flashlight.
2. Dress in *white* clothing—there is an amazing difference in visibility between gray and white shirts at night.
3. Wear a reflective vest or reflective arm bands.
4. Walk in a well-lit, safe area if possible.
5. Be safe, be aware of your surroundings, and use common sense.
6. Don't go alone; go with friends or borrow a dog if you don't have your own.
7. Carry ID with you.
8. Do NOT let headphones distract you from traffic or safety concerns.
9. Use flashing lights that can be attached to a belt or arm band.
10. Remember when walking to face the oncoming traffic if possible.
11. Let someone know your route and expected time back.
12. Be aware that drivers may have difficulty seeing you at twilight.

Use common sense when environmental conditions are significant!

The Biggest Risk to Exercise Is Not Starting!

If you're interested in training for a 5K or 10K fun run, visit Smart Coach at runnersworld.com. You will find a beginning runner's training guide that includes free advice according to your personal fitness and training level.

The internal conditions of the body before and during exercise are even more crucial than exercising with the proper external conditions. Eating a regular meal immediately before exercising will usually result in poor performance, stomach cramps, and sometimes even vomiting. The days of a steak and potato pre-game meal are gone. It is important to fuel your body with high quality protein, low fat, and high complex carbohydrate foods prior to competition; however, even more important is fueling your body on a daily basis. *Everyday good nutrition will cause an athlete to perform better in practice, thereby optimizing training that may result in a better performance in competition.* This is also sound advice for non-athletes trying to stay active. The recommendations for individuals involved in a regular exercise program are: 55 to 60 percent of total calories consumed should be from carbohydrates, 25 to 30 percent from fat, and 12 to 15 percent from protein. Individuals who are involved in a high-intensity muscular training program should consume a higher amount of protein and less fat for muscle growth and maintenance. Adequate hydration is also critical and can make a difference in the quality of exercise and performance.

Staying active has clearly been shown to enhance a person's quality of life. **Exercise is for everyone; it is never too early or too late to start.** Most people know that they would benefit from participating in an exercise program, but for many it is difficult to get started. Find an activity you enjoy. Make a plan. Write it down. Get a workout buddy. Start slowly, and listen to your body. Pain is usually a signal that something is wrong. The old adage 'no pain, no gain' can cause beginners to become frustrated. Balance activity, leisure time, and rest each week. With consistency, activity can have a positive impact on reducing risk for many conditions associated with too little activity, called hypokinetic conditions. And most importantly, you should experience increased stamina, enthusiasm, and enhanced mental well-being in your daily life.

References

American College of Sports Medicine (ACSM). *Exercise and the Common Cold.* 1989.

ACSM/AHA Joint Position Stand "Exercise and Acute Cardiovascular Events: Placing Risks into Perspective." *Medicine and Science in Sports and Exercise.* 2007.

American Heart Association. *Heart and Stroke Statistical Update.* Dallas: American Heart Association. 2012.

Bishop, J. G. and Aldana, S. G. *Step Up to Wellness.* Needham Heights, MA: Allyn & Bacon. 1999.

Cissik, J. M. *The Basics of Strength Training.* New York: McGraw-Hill Companies, Inc. 1998.

Corbin, C. B. and Lindsey, R. *Concepts of Fitness and Wellness: Active Lifestyles for Wellness* (15th ed). McGraw Hill. 2009.

Corbin, C. et al. Physical Activity for Children: A Statement of Guidelines for Children Age 5–12, NASPE. Dec. 2003.

Ellingsen, Jan, The Basics of Barefoot/Minimalist Running Jan. 2012, REI expert advice online. www.physicalactivityplan.org

Evans, W. J. Vitamin E, Vitamin C, and Exercise. *American Journal of Clinical Nutrition,* Vol. 72, 647s-652s. August 2000.

Fox, E., Bowers, R., and Merle, F. *The Physiological Basis for Exercise and Sport* (5th ed). Madison, WI: WCB Brown & Benchmark Publishers. 1989.

Haskell, W. L. et al. Physical Activity and Public Health: Updated Recommendations for Adults from the American College of Sports Medicine. *Medicine and Science in Sports and Exercise* 39 (8):1424–1434 Belmont, CA: Wadsworth/Thompson Learning. 2007.

Healthier U.S. Initiative; www.whitehouse.gov

Journal of Obesity Vol 2012, Article ID 480467. doi:10.1155/2012/480467

McArdle, W. D., Katch, F. I., and Katch, V. L. *Exercise Physiology: Energy, Nutrition, and Human Performance.* Baltimore: Williams and Wilkins. 1999.

Pate, R., Pratt, M., Blair, S., Haskell, W., Macera, C., et al. Physical Activity and Public Health: A Recommendation from the Centers for Disease Control and Prevention and the American College of Sports Medicine. *Journal of the American Medical Association,* 273: 402–407. 1995.

Payne, W. A. and Hahn, D. B. *Understanding Your Health* (6th ed). St. Louis, MO: Mosby. 2000.

Physical Activity and Health: A Report of the Surgeon General. Atlanta: U.S. Department of Health and Human Services, Centers for Disease Control and Prevention, National Center for Chronic Disease Prevention and Health Promotion. 1996.

Pollock, M. L., Gaesser, G. A., Butcher, J. D., Despres, J-P., Dishman, R. K., et al. ACSM Position Stand on the Recommended Quantity and Quality of Exercise for Developing and Maintaining Cardiorespiratory and Muscular Fitness, and Flexibility in Adults. *Medicine & Science in Sports & Exercise, 30:* 975–991. 1998.

Powers, S. K., and Dodd, S. L. *Total Fitness and Wellness* (5th ed). San Francisco: Pearson Benjamin Cummings. 2009.

Powers, S. K., and Howley, E. T. *Exercise Physiology: Theory and Application to Fitness and Performance* (6th ed). New York: McGraw-Hill Companies, Inc. 2006.

Rosato, F. *Fitness to Wellness: The Physical Connection* (3rd ed.) Minneapolis: West. 1994.

Sabo, E. *Good Exercises for Bad Knees.* www.healthology.com; Retrieved June 14, 2005.

Sharkey, B. J. *Fitness and Health*. Champaign, IL: Human Kinetics Publishing. 1997.

Sieg, K. W., and Adams, S. P. *Illustrated Essentials of Musculoskeletal Anatomy.* Gainesville, FL: Megabooks Inc. 1985.

2005 Dietary Guidelines, www.health.gov.

Why We Are Losing the War on Obesity; Health Annual Editions 05/06, 26th edition, McGraw-Hill/Dushkin.

Wilmore, J. H. and Costill, D. L. *Physiology of Sport and Exercise.* Champaign, IL: Human Kinetics Publishing Company. 1999.

Contacts

American College of Sports Medicine (ACSM)
http://www.acsm.org/index.asp

American Council of Exercise

Cardiovascular Fitness Facts
www.acefitness.org/fitfacts/fitfacts_list.cfm#1

American Running Association
http://www.americanrunning.org

American Heart Association
www.americanheart.org/statistics/

American Heart Association Web site for tips, health facts, a personal trainer, and more
www.justmove.org/fitnessnews

American Medical Association
http://www.ama-assn.org

Centers for Disease Control and Prevention
http://www.cdc.gov/nccdphp/sgr/mm.thm

National Institute of Arthritis and Musculoskeletal and Skin Diseases
http://www.healthfinder.gov/

National Institute for Health Web site for lowering blood pressure.
http://www.nhlbi.nih.gov/hbp/

President's Council on Physical Fitness and Sports

Fitness Fundamentals
http://www.hoptechno.com/book11.htm

President's Council on Physical Fitness and Sports
The Link Between Physical Activity and Morbidity and Mortality
http://www.cdc.gov/nccdphp/sgr/mm.htm

Tucker Center—Women in Sport
http://www.kls.coled.umn.edu/crgws/

Results from the President's Council on Physical Fitness
http://www.girsite.org/Html/nike2.htm

Shape Up America!
http://www.shapeup.org

Excellent current information regarding osteoporosis treatment and prevention.
www.osteo.org/osteo.html
www.nhlbi.nih.gov
www.healthfinder.gov
www.medlineplus.gov
www.nutrition.gov
www.fitness.gov

UCBerkelyWellnessLetter.com

Women's Health womenshealth.gov
exercisemedicine.com

Activities

Notebook Activities

Safety of Exercise Participation: PAR-Q and YOU
Calculating Your Activity Index
Karvonen Formula
Developing an Exercise Program for Cardiorespiratory Endurance
Assessing Your Current Level of Muscular Endurance
Check Your Physical Activity and Heart Disease I.Q.
Assessing Cardiovascular Fitness: Cooper's 1.5-Mile Run

Name _____ Section_____ Date_____

Safety of Exercise Participation: PAR-Q and You
(A Questionnaire for People Aged 15 to 69)

Regular physical activity is fun and healthy, and increasingly more people are starting to become more active every day. Being more active is very safe for most people. However, some people should check with their doctor before they start becoming much more physically active.

If you are planning to become much more physically active than you are now, start by answering the seven questions in the box below. If you are between the ages of 15 and 69, the PAR-Q will tell you if you should check with your doctor before you start. If you are over 69 years of age, and you are not used to being very active, check with your doctor.

Common sense is your best guide when you answer these questions. Please read the questions carefully and answer each one honestly: Check YES or NO.

YES	NO	
❏	❏	1. Has your doctor ever said that you have a heart condition and that you should only do physical activity recommended by a doctor?
❏	❏	2. Do you feel pain in your chest when you do physical activity?
❏	❏	3. In the past month, have you had chest pain when you were not doing physical activity?
❏	❏	4. Do you lose your balance because of dizziness, or do you ever lose consciousness?
❏	❏	5. Do you have a bone or joint problem that could be made worse by a change in your physical activity?
❏	❏	6. Is your doctor currently prescribing drugs (for example, water pills) for your blood pressure or heart condition?
❏	❏	7. Do you know of any other reason why you should not do physical activity?

If

you

answered

YES to one or more questions

Talk with your doctor by phone or in person BEFORE you start becoming much more physically active or BEFORE you have a fitness appraisal. Tell your doctor about the PAR-Q and which questions you answered YES.
- You may be able to do any activity you want—as long as you start slowly and build up gradually. Or, you may need to restrict your activities to those that are safe for you. Talk with your doctor about the kinds of activities you wish to participate in and follow his/her advice.
- Find out which community programs are safe and helpful for you.

NO to all questions

If you answered NO honestly to all PAR-Q questions, you can be reasonably sure that you can:
- start becoming much more physically active—begin slowly and build up gradually. This is the safest and easiest way to go.
- take part in a fitness appraisal—this is an excellent way to determine your basic fitness so that you can plan the best way for you to live actively.

DELAY BECOMING MUCH MORE ACTIVE:
- if you are not feeling well because of a temporary illness such as a cold or a fever—wait until you feel better, or
- if you are or may be pregnant—talk to your doctor before you start becoming more active.

Please note: If your health changes so that you then answer YES to any of the above questions, tell your fitness or health professional. Ask whether you should change your physical activity plan.

Informed Use of the PAR-Q: The Canadian Society for Exercise Physiology, Health Canada, and their agents assume no liability for persons who undertake physical activity, and if in doubt after completing this questionnaire, consult your doctor prior to physical activity.

You are encouraged to copy the PAR-Q but only if you use the entire form.

Note: If the PAR-Q is being given to a person before he or she participates in a physical activity program or a fitness appraisal, this section may be used for legal or administrative purposes.

I have read, understood and completed this questionnaire. Any questions I had were answered to my full satisfaction.

Name _____

Signature _____ Date _____

Signature of parent _____ Witness _____
or Guardian (for participants under the age of majority)

© *Canadian Society for Exercise Physiology*   *Supported by:*   Health   Santé
Société canadienne de physiologie de l'exercice   Canada   Canada

Source: Physical Activity Readiness Questionnaire (PAR-Q). © 2002. Used with permission from the Canadian Society for Exercise Physiology. www.csep.ca.

Name _____ Section_____ Date_____

Calculating Your Activity Index

Frequency: How often do you exercise?

If you exercise:	Your frequency score is:
Less than 1 time a week	0
1 time a week	1
2 times a week	2
3 times a week	3
4 times a week	4
5 or more times a week	5

Duration: How long do you exercise?

If your total duration of exercise is:	Your duration score is:
Less than 5 minutes	0
5–14 minutes	1
15–29 minutes	2
30–44 minutes	3
45–59 minutes	4
60 minutes or more	5

Intensity: How hard do you exercise?

If exercise results in:	Your intensity score is:
No change in pulse from resting level	0
Slight increase in pulse from resting level	1
Slight increase in pulse and breathing	2
Moderate increase in pulse and breathing	3
Intermittent heavy breathing and sweating	4
Sustained heavy breathing and sweating	5

Multiply your three scores:

Frequency _____ × Duration _____ × Intensity _____ = Activity index _____

To determine your activity index, refer to the following table:

If your activity index is:	Your estimated level of activity is:
Less than 15	Sedentary
15–24	Low active
25–40	Moderate active
41–60	Active
Over 60	High active

NOTEBOOK ACTIVITY

Karvonen Formula

Determining Target Heart Rate Zone (THRZ)

Take your resting heart rate early in the morning before you rise, counting for sixty seconds. Use your index and middle finger to palpate either your carotid (neck) or radial (wrist) artery. It is best to do this three different times and then average the three resting heart rates.

Finding your target heart rate zone is beneficial so that you can determine at any given time during a workout how hard your heart is working. This gives you feedback that helps you construct a proper workout that matches your goals. Working out with intensity high enough to bring the heart rate above the minimum threshold is important to attain cardiovascular benefits of exercise.

EXAMPLE:

AGE: 20 yr. old RESTING HEART RATE: 68 bpm

Formula for calculating Maximum Heart Rate (Max HR)
220 – age (in years) = Maximum Heart Rate

Example
220 – 20 = 200 beats per minute (bpm)

Formula for calculating Heart Rate Reserve
Max HR – Resting HR = Heart Rate Reserve

Example
200 – 68 = 132 beats per minute

Formula for calculating Threshold of Training HR
HR Reserve × 60%
Plus Resting HR = Threshold of Training HR

Example
132 × .60 = 80 bpm
80 + 68 = 148 bpm

Formula for calculating the Upper Limit of the THRZ
HR Reserve × 85%
Plus Resting HR = Upper Limit for the THRZ

Example
132 × .85 = 112
112 + 68 = 180 bpm

The target zone for this 20-year-old with a resting HR of 68 bpm is 148 – 180 bpm.

Divide these numbers to get a 10-second working heart rate 24–30 bpm/10 sec

Your age: _____ Your Resting HR _____ bpm

Max HR = 220 – _____ = _____

Max HR – RHR = HR Reserve _____ – _____ = _____

HR Reserve × 60% + RHR = Minimum Threshold
_____ × .60 = _____ + _____ = _____

HR Reserve × 85% + RHR = Upper Limit
_____ × .85 = _____ + _____ = _____

Your target heart rate zone is _____ bpm (60%) to _____ bpm (85%)

Now, divide these numbers by 6 to determine your working heart rate for 10 seconds _____ bpm/10 sec to _____ bpm/10 sec

Name _____ Section_____ Date_____

Developing an Exercise Program for Cardiorespiratory Endurance

Goals: Identify three goals you want to accomplish as a result of this program. Goals should be accomplished by the end of the semester.

1. _____

    _____

2. _____

    _____

3. _____

    _____

Activities: Identify three different activities you will perform.

1. _____

2. _____

3. _____

Duration: Fill in an amount of time for each exercise session and activity.
Activity   Duration

1. _____

2. _____

3. _____

NOTEBOOK ACTIVITY

Assessing Your Current Level of Muscular Endurance

Push-up Test:

Men should use the standard push-up position with hands shoulder-width apart and feet on the floor. Women may modify the standard push-up position by putting their knees on the floor. Complete as many push-ups as possible without stopping, and evaluate your performance according to the following.

MEN					WOMEN				
Age	20s	30s	40s	50s	Age	20s	30s	40s	50s
Good	40	36	30	27	Good	38	33	27	22
Fair	35	30	25	22	Fair	32	27	22	18
Poor	30	25	21	18	Poor	27	22	18	15

Curl-up Test:

Begin by lying on your back, arms by your sides with palms down and on the floor and fingers straight. Your knees should be bent at about ninety degrees, with your feet twelve inches away from your buttocks. To perform a curl up, curl your head and upper back upward, keeping your arms straight. Slide your fingers forward along the floor until you touch the back of your heels. Then curl back down until your back and head reach the floor. Palms, feet, and buttocks remain on the floor the entire time. Perform as many curlups as you can in one minute without stopping to rest, and evaluate your performance according to the following.

MEN					WOMEN				
Age	20s	30s	40s	50s	Age	20s	30s	40s	50s
Good	25	25	25	25	Good	25	25	25	25
Fair	22	22	21	19	Fair	22	21	20	15
Poor	13	13	11	09	Poor	13	11	06	04

Name _____ Section_____ Date_____

Check Your Physical Activity and Heart Disease I.Q.

Test how much you know about how physical activity affects your heart. Mark each statement true or false. See how you did by checking the answers on the back of this sheet.

1. Regular physical activity can reduce your chances of getting heart disease.   T   F

2. Most people get enough physical activity from their normal daily routine.   T   F

3. You don't have to train like a marathon runner to become more physically fit.   T   F

4. Exercise programs do not require a lot of time to be very effective.   T   F

5. People who need to lose some weight are the only ones who will benefit from regular physical activity.   T   F

6. All exercises give you the same benefits.   T   F

7. The older you are, the less active you need to be.   T   F

8. It doesn't take a lot of money or expensive equipment to become physically fit.   T   F

9. There are many risks and injuries that can occur with exercise.   T   F

10. You should consult a doctor before starting a physical activity program.   T   F

11. People who have had a heart attack should not start any physical activity program.   T   F

12. To help stay physically active, include a variety of activities.   T   F

Source: Department of Health and Human Services, National Institutes of Health.

Answers to the Check Your Physical Activity and Heart Disease I.Q. Quiz

1. **True.** Heart disease is almost twice as likely to develop in inactive people. Being physically inactive is a risk factor for heart disease along with cigarette smoking, high blood pressure, high blood cholesterol, and being overweight. The more risk factors you have, the greater your chance for heart disease. Regular physical activity (even mild to moderate exercise) can reduce this risk.

2. **False.** Most Americans are very busy but not very active. Every American adult should make a habit of getting thirty minutes of low to moderate levels of physical activity daily. This includes walking, gardening, and walking up stairs. If you are inactive now, begin by doing a few minutes of activity each day. If you only do some activity every once in a while, try to work something into your routine everyday.

3. **True.** Low- to moderate-intensity activities, such as pleasure walking, stair climbing, yardwork, housework, dancing, and home exercises can have both short- and long-term benefits. If you are inactive, the key is to get started. One great way is to take a walk for ten to fifteen minutes during your lunch break, or take your dog for a walk every day. At least thirty minutes of physical activity everyday can help improve your heart health.

4. **True.** It takes only a few minutes a day to become more physically active. If you don't have thirty minutes in your schedule for an exercise break, try to find two fifteen-minute periods or even three ten-minute periods. These exercise breaks will soon become a habit you can't live without.

5. **False.** People who are physically active experience many positive benefits. Regular physical activity gives you more energy, reduces stress, and helps you to sleep better. It helps to lower high blood pressure and improves blood cholesterol levels. Physical activity helps to tone your muscles, burns off calories to help you lose extra pounds or stay at your desirable weight, and helps control your appetite. It can also increase muscle strength, help your heart and lungs work more efficiently, and let you enjoy your life more fully.

6. **False.** Low-intensity activities—if performed daily—can have some long-term health benefits and can lower your risk of heart disease. Regular, brisk, and sustained exercise for at least thirty minutes, three or four times a week, such as brisk walking, jogging, or swimming, is necessary to improve the efficiency of your heart and lungs and burn off extra calories. These activities are called aerobic—meaning the body uses oxygen to produce the energy needed for the activity. Other activities, depending on the type, may give you other benefits such as increased flexibility or muscle strength.

7. **False.** Although we tend to become less active with age, physical activity is still important. In fact, regular physical activity in older persons increases their capacity to do everyday activities. In general, middle-aged and older people benefit from regular physical activity just as young people do. What is important, at any age, is tailoring the activity program to your own fitness level.

8. **True.** Many activities require little or no equipment. For example, brisk walking only requires a comfortable pair of walking shoes. Many communities offer free or inexpensive recreation facilities and physical activity classes. Check your shopping malls, as many of them are open early and late for people who do not wish to walk alone, in the dark, or in bad weather.

9. **False.** The most common risk in exercising is injury to the muscles and joints. Such injuries are usually caused by exercising too hard for too long, particularly if a person has been inactive. To avoid injuries, try to build up your level of activity gradually, listen to your body for warning pains, be aware of possible signs of heart problems (such as pain or pressure in the left or mid-chest area, left neck, shoulder, or arm during or just after exercising, or sudden light-headedness, cold sweat, pallor, or fainting), and be prepared for special weather conditions.

10. **True.** You should ask your doctor before you start (or greatly increase) your physical activity if you have a medical condition such as high blood pressure, have pains or pressure in the chest and shoulder, feel dizzy or faint, get breathless after mild exertion, are middle-aged or older and have not been physically active, or plan a vigorous activity program. If none of these apply, start slow and get moving.

11. **False.** Regular physical activity can help reduce your risk of having another heart attack. People who include regular physical activity in their lives after a heart attack improve their chances of survival and can improve how they feel and look. If you have had a heart attack, consult your doctor to be sure you are following a safe and effective exercise program that will help prevent heart pain and further damage from overexertion.

12. **True.** Pick several different activities that you like doing. You will be more likely to stay with it. Plan short-term and long-term goals. Keep a record of your progress, and check it regularly to see the progress you have made. Get your family and friends to join in. They can help keep you going.

NOTEBOOK ACTIVITY

Assessing Cardiovascular Fitness: Cooper's 1.5-Mile Run

(Please note: If you are not comfortable with the run, use the Rockport Fitness test found in Table 3.2 on page 74.)

This test is optimally done on a track for six laps.

Prior to testing, get a good night's rest, drink water, and try to choose a time of day when the weather is agreeable. If you cannot run the entire test, you may walk-run as best you can. It may be advisable to practice running a 1.5-mile distance prior to testing to determine a reasonable pace for you. Use a stopwatch for accuracy in timing. The objective of this test is to complete the six laps as quickly as possible.

Warm up first.

Run; note time.

Recover, stretch, drink water.

Fitness Categories for Cooper's 1.5-Mile Run Test to Determine Cardiorespiratory Fitness

Fitness Category	Age (years)					
	13–19	20–29	30–39	40–49	50–59	60+
Men						
Very poor	>15:30	>16:00	>16:30	>17:30	>19:00	>20:00
Poor	12:11–15:30	14:01–16:00	14:46–16:30	15:36–17:30	17:01–19:00	19:01–20:00
Average	10:49–12:10	12:01–14:00	12:31–14:45	13:01–15:35	14:31–17:00	16:16–19:00
Good	9:41–10:48	10:46–12:00	11:01–12:30	11:31–13:00	12:31–14:30	14:00–16:15
Excellent	8:37–9:40	9:45–10:45	10:00–11:00	10:30–11:30	11:00–12:30	11:15–13:59
Superior	<8:37	<9:45	<10:00	<10:30	<11:00	<11:15
Women						
Very poor	>18:30	>19:00	>19:30	>20:00	>20:30	>21:00
Poor	16:55–18:30	18:31–19:00	19:01–19:30	19:31–20:00	20:01–20:30	20:31–21:31
Average	14:31–16:54	15:55–18:30	16:31–19:00	17:31–19:30	19:01–20:00	19:31–20:30
Good	12:30–14:30	13:31–1554	14:31–16:30	15:56–17:30	16:31–19:00	17:31–19:30
Excellent	11:50–12:29	12:30–13:30	13:00–14:30	13:45–15:55	14:30–16:30	16:30–18:00
Superior	<11:50	<12:30	<13:00	<13:45	<14:30	<16:30

Times are given in minutes and seconds. (> = greater than; < = less than)

From Cooper, K. *The aerobics program for total well-being.* Bantam Books, New York, 1982.

Date _____ Temperature _____ Relative Humidity _____

Location of test _____

Finish time _____

Fitness category _____

Chapter 4
Lifestyle Choices and Hypokinetic Conditions

© 2012, Shutterstock, Inc.

OBJECTIVES

Students will be able to:

◆ Discuss the major hypokinetic diseases afflicting Americans.
◆ List the six major cardiac risk factors and the three unalterable cardiac risk factors.
◆ Know the warning signs for a heart attack.
◆ Discuss three ways to combat obesity.
◆ Discuss ways to prevent osteoporosis and achieve a high peak bone mass.
◆ Explain three ways to prevent low back pain.
◆ List and discuss four lifestyle choices that prevent hypokinetic conditions.

"When health is absent wisdom cannot reveal itself, art cannot become manifest, strength cannot be exerted, wealth is useless and reason is powerless"

—Herophilies, 300 B.C.

Let's Move! America's Move to Raise a Healthier Generation of Kids

The health of American children should be a bipartisan initiative in every administration

Today's kids live differently than kids raised a generation ago. Most children, 30 years ago, walked to and from school, had homemade meals at home, and maybe one snack a day (3–6 snacks are common today). Fast food meals were a rarity. Kids played at recess and had gym class. Today, budget cuts require gym class, librarians, and after-school activities to be cut. Sweetened drinks are the norm for many kids and can be a source of extra calories. Parents are busy and the average American child spends 7.5 hours with electronic devices for entertainment. Less than 1/3 of high school students get the recommended amount of daily physical activity. In the last 30 years, our society has changed dramatically.

With the Let's Move! Campaign, the goal is to end the epidemic of childhood obesity in one generation. Mrs. Obama hopes kids can put "play" back into their lives by having the children experience "that exercise and eating good stuff" can be fun. The first lady quoted a young 7-year-old Penacook, New Hampshire resident, Caitlyn Habel, remarking that, "I like being able to play games before school because it's really fun and it helps me wake up my heart." 3/9/12 (whitehouse.gov/the press-office)

It has taken 3 decades to create an environment where childhood obesity rates have tripled. Programs such as Let's Move! strive to work with schools, families, communities, and the corporate sector to change the circumstances for this generation and also for generations to come. So choose to get involved in your community. Ask a kid to help you plant a community garden!

"The physical and emotional health of an entire generation and the economic health and security of our nation is at stake."
—First Lady Michelle Obama at the Let's Move! Launch on February 9, 2010.

© Jim Cole/AP/Corbis

The life expectancy for someone born at the beginning of the twenty-first century is almost double the life expectancy of those born at the beginning of the twentieth century. Modern medicine has, for the most part, wiped out the threat from infectious diseases. Modern technology has made life easy. Life is so automated that we move less, and therefore we conserve lots of energy. The more sedentary people become, the higher the health risk. It is no longer polio, smallpox, or tuberculosis that are a large-scale threat to survival (see Figure 4.1), it is our own poor lifestyle choices. The Centers for Disease Control and Prevention (CDC) has determined that *lifestyle is the single largest factor affecting longevity of life*. "If exercise could be packed into a pill, it would be the single most widely prescribed, and most beneficial, medicine in the nation" (National Institute on Aging). More than half of the population will die from coronary heart disease—a disease that for many can be prevented with simple healthy lifestyle choices. The choices we make daily determine not only the longevity of our lives but also the quality of our lives—now and in the future.

The life expectancy of this baby is almost double that of a baby born one hundred years ago.

Results of the Surgeon General's Report on Physical Activity and Health:

- More than 60 percent of U.S. adults do not engage in the recommended amount of activity.
- Approximately 25 percent of U.S. adults are not active at all.
- Physical inactivity is more common among:
  —Woman than men
  —African American and Hispanic adults than whites
  —Older than younger adults
  —Less affluent than more affluent people
- Social support from family and friends has been consistently and positively related to regular physical activity.

FIGURE 4.1

Adults and Physical Activity

Regular Vigorous*

Both Regular Vigorous* and Regular Sustained†

Regular Sustained†

Inactive

Not Regularly Active

*Regular Vigorous–20 minutes 3 roles per week of vigorous intensity

†Regular Sustained–30 minutes 5 times per week of any intensity

Source: Behavioral Risk Factor Survey, 1992, CDC.

© Supri Suharjoto, 2012, Shutterstock, Inc.

Daily, we determine whether or not we will eat breakfast, use tobacco, abuse drugs, hold a grudge, or make time for exercise. As Westerners living in an industrialized nation, we are fortunate to have choices. We have the privilege to choose from at least eighteen brands of toothpaste. Toothpaste brands may not have a significant impact on the quality of our life, but other daily decisions do. How we handle ourselves when stressed is a significant factor in whether or not we become ill. Nutrition choices at dinnertime and in between meals . . . Cheetos, Cheerios, or cheese? Choosing to be more active daily, such as gardening, taking the stairs instead of the elevator, walking rather than riding, can make a surprising dent in our energy reserves. The 1996 Surgeon General's Report (Satcher, 1996) encouraged all individuals to try and expend 150 calories extra each day, above and beyond a normal routine. **Lifestyle activity** is searching for opportunities to expend some extra energy, rather than searching for opportunities to conserve energy with convenient devices such as cell phones and electric pencil sharpeners. Students who walk across big campuses between classes rather than take a bus expend more energy. One day might not have a significant impact; however, at the end of the semester the cumulative effects of walking can add up to enhanced health.

Planned exercise is important for fitness benefits. It is important to find an activity that is enjoyable because that will ensure a more sincere commitment—one that may become permanent over a lifetime. Plan it! Don't leave your exercise to chance, because chances are, you won't have time. If you hate to run, don't train for a marathon. Set realistic goals. Research has shown that specific goal setting greatly enhances the chances of achieving said goals. Use the goal activity at the end of Chapter 1. Be reasonable and look for behaviors to change in support of your goals. Enlist the help and support of friends and family. Walking is the most popular activity in the United States, most likely because it is easy and requires no special training or equipment except a good pair of shoes. Choose an activity you enjoy and as the shoe company says, "Just do it!"

Lifestyle activity, planned exercise, stress management, and good nutrition choices can make a difference in whether or not an individual suffers from a hypokinetic condition. **Hypokinetic** literally means too little activity. Kraus and Rabb first coined the term hypokinetic in 1961. Hypokinetic diseases include the leading causes of death, such as coronary heart disease and cancer, as well as debilitating conditions such as low back pain, osteoporosis, obesity, diabetes, and mental health disorders. Simply changing an individual's lifestyle to one that includes more physical activity can reduce the incidence of many hypokinetic conditions. *Regular consistent activity can decrease the potential of contracting a hypokinetic disease.*

For example, expending an extra 500–1,000 calories per week can decrease health risk (see Figure 4.2). Expending an extra 1,000–2,000 calories per week can decrease overall health risk more and also moderately increase cardiovascular fitness. An expenditure of 2,000–3,500 calories per week can decrease overall health risk, as well as significantly increase cardiovascular fitness over time. Typically expending beyond 3,500 calories can increase risk of musculoskeletal injuries and burnout.

Caloric expenditure from both lifestyle activity and planned exercise has a significant impact on health. Participating in a little extra activity helps by decreasing overall health risk and by enhancing self-confidence. Expending more extra energy does the same as expending a little extra activity with further decreased risk, added fitness benefits, and potential weight loss, particularly if exercise is within the target heart rate zone (see Figure 4.3). However, doing too much activity can cause burnout, injury, or possibly an obsession with exercise. As in all areas of life, balance and common sense are important.

It has been previously noted that the CDC reported that life-style is the single greatest factor affecting longevity of life. This is especially critical to note

Examples of Lifestyle Activity: Looking for Opportunities to Expend More Calories

- Taking the stairs instead of the elevator.
- Parking farther from your destination to increase walking distance.
- Walking rather than riding.
- Vacuuming with vigor, taking big lunging steps.
- Doing sit-ups during the commercials of your favorite program.
- Playing Frisbee or planting a garden instead of watching TV.

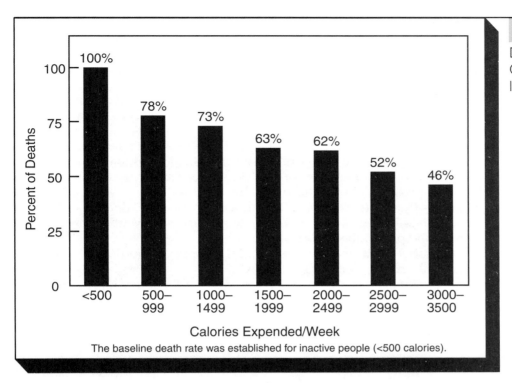

FIGURE 4.2

Deaths Decrease as Caloric Expenditure Increases

Source: Data from C. Bouchard et al. *Exercise Fitness and Health*. Champaign, IL: Human Kinetics Publishers, 1990.

for future generations as America's children are more sedentary and at higher risk for developing hypokinetic diseases than their parents or grandparents. Childhood obesity is a national epidemic; this is partially due to technology (think energy-saving remote controls and cell phones) and the ease with which tasks are performed. To combat this trend, parents can help plan activities to ensure their children accumulate at least sixty minutes of activity a day. The best way to accomplish this is for parents to be good role models and to lead active lifestyles. Parents can plan active family outings and participate with children, as well as limit sedentary activities.

Documentation from many organizations and research facilities support the benefits of a healthy lifestyle. The following are just a few of the significant groups that have contributed to our current knowledge of lifestyle choices related to health. The "Rules" or Guidelines have changed over the years, but the documentation from all of the following organizations reveals that physical activity is a major key to a healthy lifestyle:

- 1961—*Hypokinetic*—term coined by Krause and Rabb relating to "too little activity."
- 1979—*World Health Organization* (WHO) classified obesity as a disease.
- 2010—*Healthy People 2010* (National Health Promotion and disease Prevention Objectives) developed statements by expert groups representing over 300 national organizations that include realistic health goals to be achieved by the year 2010, and now for the year 2020.
- 1992—*The American Heart Association* (AHA) identified inactivity as a major cardiac risk factor.

Students who walk to class rather than ride are increasing their lifestyle activity as well as their metabolic rate.

© Michael Jung, 2012, Shutterstock, Inc.

- 1995—*American College of Sports Medicine* (ACSM) established physical activity guidelines, updated periodically. Promotes and integrates scientific research, education, and practical applications of sports medicine and exercise science to maintain and enhance physical performance, fitness, health, and quality of life.
- 1996—*Surgeon General's Report*—landmark report that, after a thorough review of literature, traced the link between physical activity and good health.
- Ongoing—*Centers for Disease Control* (CDC) provides scientific and technical leadership and assistance to help states, national organizations, and professional groups reduce major risk factors associated with chronic diseases in the U.S.
- 2007—*Exercise Is Medicine* (EIM) launched by medical doctors in conjunction with ACSM, to integrate exercise as preventive medicine as a regular part of medical treatment.
- 2008—*U.S. Department of Health and Human Services* (HHS) released the current physical activity guidelines.
- 2011—*2011 Dietary Guidelines for Americans* (USDA Center for Nutrition Policy and Promotion) long-awaited, evidence-based guidelines encouraging Americans to reduce calorie consumption and increase physical activity.
- 2011—*Million Hearts Initiative* launched with HHS and public and private partners, a commitment to prevent 1 million cardiovascular events (including stroke) in 5 years.
- 2011—*2020 Health Impact Goal*—AHA/ASA (American Stroke Association) launched to improve health of all American by 20% while reducing deaths due to cardiovascular disease and stroke by 20%.
- 2012—*American Cancer Society Guidelines on Nutrition and Physical Activity for Cancer Prevention*—updated every 5 years; most cancer risk is due to factors that are not inherited, but lifestyle-related. Focuses on environment and community for support in choosing healthy behaviors.
- 2012—Heart Disease and Stroke Statistics Update (AH)—updated yearly; comprehensive analysis of health data.
- 2012—*Inactivity Physiology* is added to the medical lexicon.

The fact that Americans need these guidelines at all is evidence that we are not following them. The health of most Americans in the past 30 years has declined as we have eaten more, as we have become more sedentary, and as we have had an explosion in technology. Regardless of what a government agency deems or what research says, the bottom line is that we all have to make the choice, daily, to move more. Our life depends on it.

Types of Hypokinetic Conditions

Cardiovascular Disease (CVD)

The cardiovascular system is responsible for delivering oxygen and other nutrients to the body. The major components of the cardiovascular system are the heart, blood, and the vessels that carry the blood. Cardiovascular disease (CVD) is a catch-all term that includes several disease processes including various diseases of the heart, stroke, high blood pressure, congestive heart failure, and atherosclerosis. The heart muscle may become damaged or lose its ability to contract effectively. The vessels that supply the heart with oxygen may become blocked or damaged and subsequently compromise the heart muscle. Finally, the peripheral vascular system (all of the vessels outside the heart) may become damaged and decrease the ability to provide oxygen to other parts of the body.

The great news is that between 1998–2008, deaths due to cardiovascular disease declined 30.6% (AHA, 2012). Americans are also on the whole, living

The "ABCS" of heart disease and stroke prevention

Aspirin therapy
Blood pressure control
Cholesterol control
Smoking cessation

CVD and stroke are largely preventable for a significant part of the lifespan. High blood pressure, high cholesterol, and smoking continue to put people at risk of heart attack and stroke. To address these risk factors, the Centers for Disease Control and Prevention is focusing many of its efforts on the "ABCS" of heart disease and stroke prevention: **appropriate Aspirin therapy, Blood pressure control, Cholesterol control, and support for Smoking cessation** for those trying to quit and, even more generally, comprehensive tobacco prevention and control efforts. (CDC, 2012)

The American Heart Association projects that by 2030, 40.5% of the U.S. population will have some form of CVD, costing the healthcare system an estimated $1 trillion every year. (AHA, 2012)

Benefits of Exercise

Consistent physical activity affects cardiovascular disease by one or more of the following mechanisms:

- Improved cardiovascular fitness and health
- Greater lean (fat-free) body mass
- Improved strength and muscular endurance
- Stronger heart muscle
- Lower heart rate
- Increased oxygen to the brain
- Reduced blood fat including low-density-lipoprotein cholesterol (LDL-C)
- Increased protective high-density-lipoprotein cholesterol (HDL-C)
- Delayed development of atherosclerosis
- Increased work capacity
- Improved peripheral circulation
- Improved coronary circulation
- Reduced risk of heart attack
- Reduced risk of stroke
- Reduced risk of hypertension
- Greater chance of surviving a heart attack
- Greater oxygen carrying capacity of the blood

Exercise improves your body and mind more than you might expect.

longer, as life expectancy increases. The bad news is that many of the risk factors for CVD are lifestyle-related and therefore preventable, and Americans, including women, are much more likely to die from CVD than anything else. The cost of CVD is very high, both in dollars and in productivity lost. Health Impact Goals 2020 and the Million Hearts Initiative are efforts to coordinate public, private, and governmental resources to focus on the positives, on prevention. As part of Health Impact Goals 2020, the AHA developed **7 Metrics of Cardiovascular Health** (see Figure 4.3). The good news is that you have choices daily that can help in CVD prevention. MyLifeCheck.org is a part of a campaign to increase awareness of positive attributes of health. Check it out.

Who Is At Risk for CVD?

The Surgeon General's Report (Satcher, 1996) placed **physical inactivity** as a significant risk factor for cardiovascular diseases and other health disorders. Most sedentary Americans are at risk as stated previously. There are an estimated 82,600,000 Americans that have some form of CVD. Many factors can predispose a person to be at risk for CVD. Sedentary living, habitual stress, smoking, poor diet, high blood pressure, diabetes, obesity, high cholesterol, and family history can all increase risk. Advancing age increases risk. Males

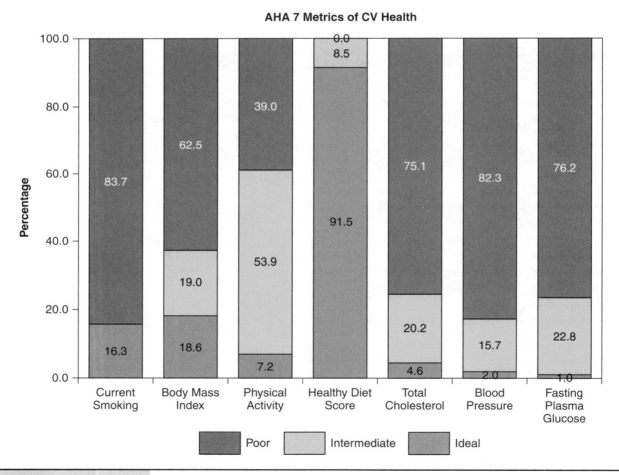

FIGURE 4.3

Prevalence (unadjusted) estimates for poor, intermediate, and ideal cardiovascular health for each of the 7 metrics of cardiovascular health in the American Heart Association 2020 goals, US children aged 12 to 19 years, National Health and Nutrition Examination Survey (NHANES) 2007–2008 (available data as of June 1, 2011).

Claudette's Story

"I consider myself to be relatively healthy and I exercise for about ninety minutes every morning. I started having pain in my chest and face during my exercising, and finally went to the cardiologist. I never thought that the pain in my face could be related to my heart, so I was shocked when the tests showed that I had had a heart attack. I thought I was too young, but my father died of a heart attack when he was only 38, so I had family history as a risk factor. After my second heart attack, I knew that I needed to help get the message out. Women need to know that heart disease is their biggest health threat."

Source: National Heart, Lung and Blood Institute, National Health Institute.

typically have a higher risk than women until women are post-menopausal, then risk evens out. Misconceptions still exist that CVD is not a real problem for women. Because more women have heart attacks when they are older, the initial heart attack is more likely to be fatal. It is important for women to realize that CVD is an equal opportunity killer. Just like men, more women die from heart disease than anything else.

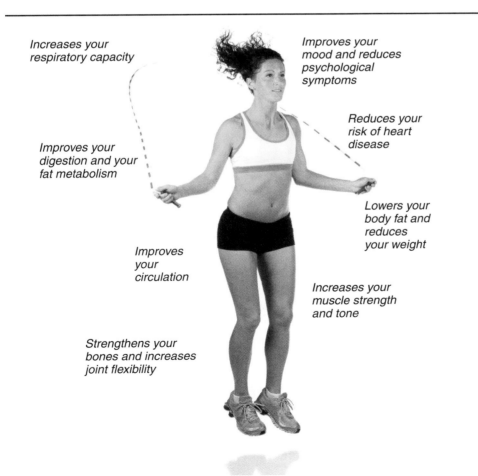

Increases your respiratory capacity

Improves your mood and reduces psychological symptoms

Reduces your risk of heart disease

Improves your digestion and your fat metabolism

Improves your circulation

Lowers your body fat and reduces your weight

Increases your muscle strength and tone

Strengthens your bones and increases joint flexibility

FIGURE 4.4

The Benefits of Exercise
© ATurner, 2012, Shutterstock, Inc.

Increasing lifestyle activity by spending less time on the couch and doing something active daily will have a positive impact on your health.

© Ieva Geneviciene, 2012, Shutterstock, Inc.

Certain populations have an inherently higher health risk such as African Americans and Hispanics. Genetic predisposition is a strong factor; familial tendencies toward elevated triglycerides, fat distribution (abdominal fat accumulation denotes a higher health risk than hip/thigh accumulation of fat), and high **low-density lipoprotein cholesterol (LDL-C)** levels increase risk. LDL-C is a blood lipid that indicates a higher cardiac risk. Saturated fat intake tends to increase LDL cholesterol. Dr. William Franklin of Georgetown University Medical School in Washington claims that anyone who has a close relative who has had a heart attack should begin monitoring his heart with regular stress tests when he is 45. If your father died in his 40's of a heart attack, then you should be concerned a decade earlier in your 30's. Variables such as age, gender, race, and genetic makeup may place you at a higher or lower risk but cannot be changed. These can be termed unalterable risk factors.

CVD Prevention

Since you cannot change your age, your sex, and who your parents are, focus on what you *can* change. These risk factors include but are not limited to: diet, drug use, smoking history, cholesterol levels, obesity, high blood pressure, and last but definitely not least, physical inactivity (see pages 16 and 19). This is a critical point, since activity level is a risk factor that can be easily modified and is often overlooked. Increasing an individual's activity level can prevent many of the diseases discussed in this chapter. Cardiovascular disease is the leading cause of death in the United States. "About every 25 seconds an American will experience a coronary event, and about every minute someone will die from one" (AHA, 2012) (see Figure 4.5). With this being the case, consider your own risk. How can you adjust your current lifestyle habits to decrease your risk? Read the Benefits of Exercise (on page 113) and Figure 4.4 to determine how exercise helps CVD.

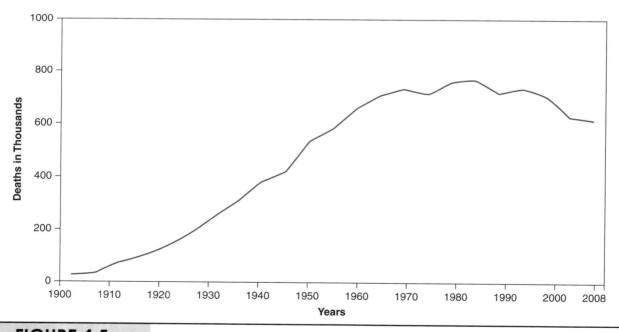

FIGURE 4.5

Deaths attributable to diseases of the heart (United States: 1990–2008)

Source: National Center for Health Statistics

FIGURE 4.6

Determining Your Waist to Hip Ratio

Equipment
1. Tape measure
2. Partner to take measurements

Preparation
Wear clothes that will not add significantly to your measurements.

Instructions
Stand with your feet together and your arms at your sides. Raise your arms only high enough to allow for taking the measurements. Your partner should make sure that the tape is horizontal around the entire circumference and pulled snugly against your skin. The tape shouldn't be pulled so tight that it causes indentations in your skin. Record measurements to the nearest millimeter or one-sixteenth of an inch.

Waist. Measure at the smallest waist circumference. If you don't have a natural waist, measure at the level of your navel.
Hip. Measure at the largest hip circumference.

Calculating Your Ratio
You can use any unit of measurement (for example, inches or centimeters), as long as you're consistent. Waist-to-hip ratio equals waist measurement divided by hip measurement.

Determine Your Relative Risk
Find the risk category that corresponds to your ratio and age group on the appropriate figure below.

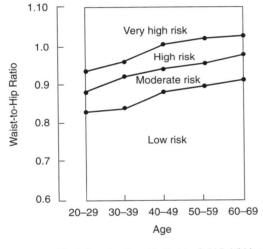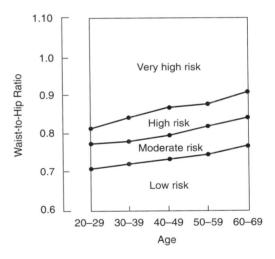

Source: from *Fit & Well* by Fahey, Insel and Roth, Mayfield Publishing.

Measuring Health Risk

There are two simple measures of overall health risk: **Waist-to-Hip Ratio** and **Body Mass Index (BMI).** See Figure 4.6 to determine your Waist-To-Hip ratio, and see the activity Body Mass Index Calculator in Chapter 6 to determine your BMI. Increasing lifestyle activity by spending less time on the couch and doing something daily will have a positive impact on your health. It is true that overweight and obesity are associated with complications and high risk factors such as hypertension, high blood cholesterol, and diabetes. *A growing body of evidence, however, indicates physical inactivity is more critical than excess weight in determining health risk.* Longitudinal studies such as the ongoing research by epidemiologist Steven Blair, previously of the Cooper Institute in Dallas, Texas, and information from the ongoing Harvard alumni study indicate that lifestyle is more significant than weight. **Fitter people have lower**

Waist-to-Hip Ratio

Recent evidence from a study done at the University of Manchester in the United Kingdom indicates that abdominal obesity is a strong independent risk factor for heart disease. "A large waist with large hips is much less worrisome than a large waist with small hips." The conclusion of the study determined that the simple waist-to-hip ratio is a strong predictor of heart disease (AHA, 2007).

death rates regardless of weight (see Figure 4.7). Indeed, the mortality rate for low fit males is more than 20% higher than for those that are high fit. While this effect is smaller for women, the decrease in mortality rate for high fit females is more than 6% compared to those who are low fit. Previously sedentary Harvard alumni (Sesso and Paffenbarger, 1956) who became active reduced their all-cause mortality rate by 23 percent. The alumni who lost weight (but were not active) did not improve their mortality rate. Improvements in metabolic fitness (glucose tolerance, blood pressure, and cholesterol) are often seen with just moderate amounts of physical activity. The good news is that

FIGURE 4.7

Relationship between Different Levels of Fitness and Death Due to Cardiovascular Disease among Men and Women

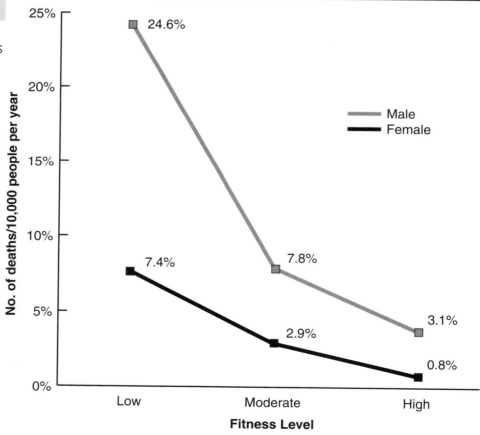

Source: Blair et al., Physical fitness and all-cause mortality: A prospective study of healthy men and women. *Journal of the American Medical Association* 262(17): 2395–2401, 1989. (Adapted from S. N. Blair, H. W. Kohl, III, R. S. Paffenbarger, Jr., D. G. Clark, K. H. Cooper, and L. W. Gibbons. Physical fitness and all-cause mortality: A prospective study of healthy men and women.)

overweight Americans don't need to go on a crash diet, buy a gym member-ship, or totally give up Twinkies. Increasing lifestyle activity and walking regu-larly, spending less time on the couch, and doing something active daily can have a positive impact on health.

Arteriosclerosis

Arteriosclerosis

Arteriosclerosis is a term used to describe the thickening and hardening of the arteries. Healthy arteries are elastic and will dilate and constrict with changes in blood flow, which allows proper maintenance of blood pressure. Hardened, non-elastic arteries do not expand with blood flow and can in-crease intrarterial pressure causing high blood pressure. Both high blood pres-sure and arteriosclerosis increase the risk of an **aneurysm**. With an aneu-rysm, the artery loses its integrity and balloons out under the pressure created by the pumping heart, in much the same way as an old garden hose might if placed under pressure. If an aneurysm occurs in the vessels of the brain, a stroke might occur. Aneurysms in the large vessels can place a person at risk of sudden death. Maintaining normal elasticity of the arteries is very impor-tant for good health. Exercise helps to manage symptoms and the factors that contribute to cardiac risk.

Atherosclerosis   Atherosclerosis is a type of arteriosclerosis. Atherosclerosis is the long-term buildup of fatty deposits and other substances such as cho-lesterol, cellular waste products, calcium, and fibrin (clotting material in the blood) on the interior walls of arteries (see Figure 4.8). The leading theory states that plaque develops when the endothelium (a thin layer of cells that line the interior vessel wall) is damaged due to major fluctuations in blood pressure, increased levels of blood triglycerides, cholesterol, and cigarette smoking. Conditions such as these accelerate the development of atheroscle-rosis. Due to this plaque development, the flow of blood within the artery decreases because the diameter of the vessel is decreased. This may create a partial or total blockage (called an occlusion) that may cause high blood pres-sure, a heart attack, or stroke. This process can occur in any vessel of the body. If it occurs outside of the brain or heart, it is termed peripheral vascular dis-

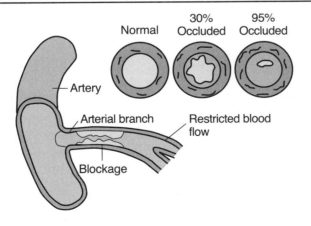

FIGURE 4.8

Atherosclerosis

Atherosclerosis occurs in stages. Plaque deposits in a normal "clean" artery can partially block the flow of blood. As the size of the blockage increases, blood supply decreases until tissues downstream from the block fail to receive adequate blood and are damaged.

ease. Within the heart the gradual narrowing of the coronary arteries to the myocardium, or heart muscle, is called coronary artery disease. Atherosclerosis is a disease that can start early in childhood. The rate of progression of the disease depends on family history and lifestyle choices. Exercise helps manage symptoms as well as increase coronary collateral circulation. Collateral arteries are the vessels that form preceding the blockage as an artery slowly becomes occluded. Collateral vessels such as these can help lessen the severity of a heart attack when the artery becomes totally blocked. High cholesterol levels can increase risk of atherosclerosis, and low-density lipoprotein cholesterol is thought to contribute to the arterial occlusion. Triglycerides are another type of blood fat which at high levels is associated with high risk (see Figure 4.9). Regular physical activity has been shown to lower risk by lowering blood lipid (fat) levels.

Peripheral Vascular Disease

Peripheral vascular disease is simply a term attributed to disease of the peripheral vessels. The lack of proper circulation may cause fluids to pool in the extremities. Associated leg pain, cramping, numbness, tingling, coldness, and loss of hair to affected limbs are common signs. The restrictions in blood flow are typically caused by years of arteriosclerosis and atherosclerosis in the vessels of the extremities. The risk factors are the same as those for cardiovascular disease. One difference is that the disease process may progress extensively before the affected person begins to notice any problems. The heart and brain are much more sensitive to compromised blood flow than are the extremities.

Hypertension

Hypertension, or high blood pressure, is often called the "silent killer" because typically there are no symptoms. Because hypertension is asymptomatic, it is important to get your blood pressure checked on a regular basis. In 2009, the estimated prevalence of hypertension (a blood pressure reading of 140/90 mm or higher) was one in 3 adults. High blood pressure is associated with a shortened life span. Interestingly, under the age of 45 more males typically have a higher blood pressure, while after age 55, more females tend to have a higher blood pressure (AHA, 2008). High blood pressure causes the heart to work harder. Chronic, untreated hypertension can lead to aneurysms in blood vessels, heart failure from an enlarged heart, kidney failure, atherosclerosis, and blindness.

Teens, Sleep, and Blood Pressure In the News

A new study finds that teens who get too little sleep or erratic sleep may elevate their blood pressure. "Our study underscores the high rate of poor quality and inadequate sleep in adolescence coupled with the risk of developing high blood pressure and other health problems which may lead to cardiovascular disease," says Susan Redline, M.D., professor of medicine and pediatrics and director of University Hospital's Sleep Center at Case Western Reserve University in Cleveland, Ohio. Researchers say technology in bedrooms (phone, games, computers, music) may be part of the problem (AHA, 2008).

Total Cholesterol Level	Category
Less than 200 mg/dL	Desirable level that puts you at lower risk for heart disease.
	A cholesterol level of 200 mg/dL or higher raises your risk.
200–239 mg/dL	Borderline high
240 mg/dL and above	High blood cholesterol. A person with this level has more than twice the risk of heart disease as someone whose cholesterol is below 200 mg/dL.

Cholesterol levels are measured in milligrams (mg) of cholesterol per deciliter (dL) of blood.

LDL Cholesterol Level	Category
Less than 100 mg/dL	Optimal
100–129 mg/dL	Near or above optimal
130–159 mg/dL	Borderline high
160–189 mg/dL	High
190 mg/dL and above	Very High

mg/dL = milligrams per deciliter of blood

HDL Cholesterol Level	Category
Less than 40 mg/dL	A major risk factor for heart disease.
40–59 mg/dL	The higher your HDL level, the better.
60 mg/dL and above	An HDL of 60 mg/dL and above is considered protective against heart disease.

mg/dL = milligrams per deciliter of blood

Triglyceride Level	Category
Less than 150 mg/dL	Normal
150–199 mg/dL	Borderline high
200–499 mg/dL	High
500 mg/dL and above	Very high

mg/dL = milligrams per deciliter of blood

FIGURE 4.9

Cholesterol and Triglyceride Levels and Risk of Heart Disease

If you don't smoke, don't start. **If you do smoke, get help to quit now!** Many effective programs, nicotine patches, and other medications are available to help you quit. As soon as you stop smoking, your risk of heart disease starts to drop. In time your risk will be about the same as if you'd never smoked.

The top number is the **systolic** reading, which represents the arterial pressure when the heart is contracting and forcing the blood through the arteries. The bottom number is the **diastolic** reading, which represents the force of the blood on the arteries while the heart is relaxing between beats. In 2003 new blood pressure guidelines were issued, with a new "prehypertensive" category identified (see Figure 4.11). A blood pressure reading of 115/75 is the new threshold above which cardiovascular complication can occur. The prehypertensive category includes a systolic pressure from 120–139 and a diastolic pressure from 80–89 as a warning zone. If your are considered prehypertensive, it is time to take action by modifying your lifestyle. Any reading consistently over 139/89 mm Hg is high blood pressure and indicates a high risk. With persons over 50 years old, a systolic reading of 140 or above is a more important CVD risk factor than the diastolic reading (JNC VII, 2003).

$\frac{117}{76}$ **mm Hg**

Read as "117 over 76 millimeters of mercury"

Systolic

The top number, which is also the higher of the two numbers, measures the pressure in the arteries when the heart beats (when the heart muscle contracts).

Diastolic

The bottom number, which is also the lower of the two numbers, measures the pressure in the arteries between heartbeats (when the heart muscle is resting between beats and refilling with blood).

Source: American Heart Association

FIGURE 4.10

Blood Pressure is known as the 'silent killer' because many people do not realize that they have high BP. Do you know your BP?

Blood Pressure Category	Systolic mm Hg (upper #)		Diastolic mm Hg (lower #)
Normal	less than **120**	and	less than **80**
Prehypertension	120–139	or	80–89
High Blood Pressue (Hypertension) **Stage 1**	140–159	or	90–99
High Blood Pressue (Hypertension) **Stage 2**	**160** or higher	or	**100** or higher
Hypertensive Crisis (Emergency care needed)	Higher than **180**	or	Higher than **110**

* Your doctor should evaluate unusually low blood pressure readings.

FIGURE 4.11

This chart reflects blood pressure categories defined by the American Heart Association.
Source: American Heart Association

Hypertension cannot be cured, but it can be successfully treated and controlled. Most people with hypertension have additional risk factors for cardiovascular disease. Some of the risk factors for high blood pressure include Hispanic or African American heritage, older age, family history, a diet high in fat and sodium, alcoholism, stress, obesity, and inactivity. Exercise has been shown to help symptoms of high blood pressure in mild to moderate hypertension.

Heart Attack

A heart attack or **myocardial infarction** occurs when an artery that provides the heart muscle with oxygen becomes blocked or flow is decreased (see Figure 4.12). The area of the heart muscle served by that artery does not receive adequate oxygen and becomes injured and may eventually die. The heart attack may be so small as to be imperceptible by the victim, or so massive that the victim will die. It is often reported that heart attack victims delay seeking medical help with the onset of symptoms. Every minute counts! In one study, men waited an average of three hours before seeking help. Women waited four hours. It is important to seek medical help at the first sign of a heart attack.

Women who smoke and take oral contraceptives are ten times more likely to have a heart attack (Payne and Hahn, 2000). "Smoking and oral contraceptives (OC) appear to act synergistically in increasing the risk of arterial thrombotic disease, particularly in heavy smokers and with old OC formulations," Ojvind Lidegaard reported in 1998. In addition to the classic symptoms of heart attack listed in the box on page 124, women were more likely than men to report throat discomfort, pressing on the chest, and vomiting.

Exercise is the cornerstone therapy for the primary prevention, treatment, and control of hypertension, according to the Position Stand *Exercise and Hypertension* released from the American College of Sports Medicine (ACSM). Adults with hypertension should seek to gain at least thirty minutes of moderate-intensity physical activity on most, if not all, days of the week, but they should be evaluated, treated, and monitored closely.

FIGURE 4.12

Narrowed or Blocked
Arteries in the Heart
Result in a Heart Attack

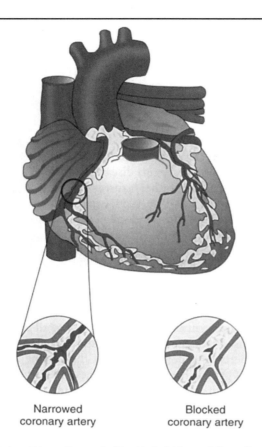

Narrowed
coronary artery

Blocked
coronary artery

Source: Bishop, Jan Galen; Aldana, Steven G., *Step Up To Wellness: A Stage-Based Approach,* 1st Edition, © 1999. Printed and electronically reproduced by permission of Pearson Education, Inc., Upper Saddle River, New Jersey.

Each person may experience heart disease in a different way and unfortunately, a fatal sudden cardiac arrest may be the only symptom. Heart attack symptoms for women may be different than the classic symptoms that are commonly known such as chest, jaw, or left arm pain with shortness of breath and weakness. Women may experience more subtle symptoms such as fatigue, depression, back pain, or pain throughout the chest. Don't wait to get help, as time is critical when experiencing a heart attack.

Some findings suggest that coronary collateral circulation is increased with regular physical activity (Corbin and Welk, 2009). This increased vascularization may decrease the risk of having a heart attack, as well as increase the chances of survival if a heart attack does occur. This happens because the new vessels, which form as a result of exercise, can take over if a major coronary artery is blocked. Since 1951, the death rate from heart attacks has declined by 51 percent, yet more Americans die from coronary artery disease than from any other disease. Both treatment and prevention for heart attacks has increased due to revolutionary new surgical treatments, new drugs, and new information about the etiology of heart disease (see Figure 4.13). Many of the drugs reserved for treating cardiac patients in the past are now used as aggressive prevention in high-risk patients. The AHA has developed Heart Attack Symptoms and Warning Signs (see box on next page).

Stroke

Do you know the warning signs of a stroke? There is a public awareness campaign to increase knowledge of stroke warning signs and symptoms (see box on page 124). Stroke, or more recently called "**brain attack**," is the third leading cause of death affecting 795,000 Americans per year (AHA, 2012). This

Heart Attack Symptoms and Warning Signs

If you think you're having a heart attack, call 9-1-1 or your emergency medical system immediately.

Some heart attacks are sudden and intense—the "movie heart attack," where no one doubts what's happening—but most heart attacks start slowly, with mild pain or discomfort. Often people affected aren't sure what's wrong and wait too long before getting help. Here are signs that can mean a heart attack is happening:

© imageegami, 2012, Shutterstock, Inc.

- **Chest discomfort.** Most heart attacks involve discomfort in the center of the chest that lasts more than a few minutes, or that goes away and comes back. It can feel like uncomfortable pressure, squeezing, fullness, or pain.
- **Discomfort in other areas of the upper body.** Symptoms can include pain or discomfort in one or both arms, the back, neck, jaw, or stomach.
- **Shortness of breath.** This feeling often comes along with chest discomfort. But it can occur before the chest discomfort.
- **Other signs:** These may include breaking out in a cold sweat, nausea, or lightheadedness.

If you or someone you're with has chest discomfort, especially with one or more of the other signs, don't wait longer than a few minutes (no more than five) before calling for help. Call 9-1-1... Get to a hospital right away.

Calling 9-1-1 is almost always the fastest way to get lifesaving treatment.

Source: Reprinted with permission, www.heart.org
© 2010, American Heart Association, Inc.

Famed television host David Letterman was not overweight when he had quintuple bypass surgery at age 52 in 2000. Although Mr. Letterman didn't look like the typical person who has a heart attack, he had several risk factors going against him. He had a family history—his father, Harry, died of a heart attack in his 50's. Mr. Letterman had high cholesterol. Most likely his job would be considered high stress. David Letterman credits Dr. Wayne Isom, who operated on his heart, with saving his life. In an interview with another talk show host, Larry King (who coincidentally also was operated on by Dr. Isom for quadruple bypass surgery) asked Dr. Isom what was important in avoiding heart disease. Besides exercise, controlling stress, managing weight, and eating well, Dr. Isom said that attitude is very, very important. Post-heart surgery, the patient must decide for himself that he is going to get well. An important part of cardiac rehabilitation is a **positive attitude**.

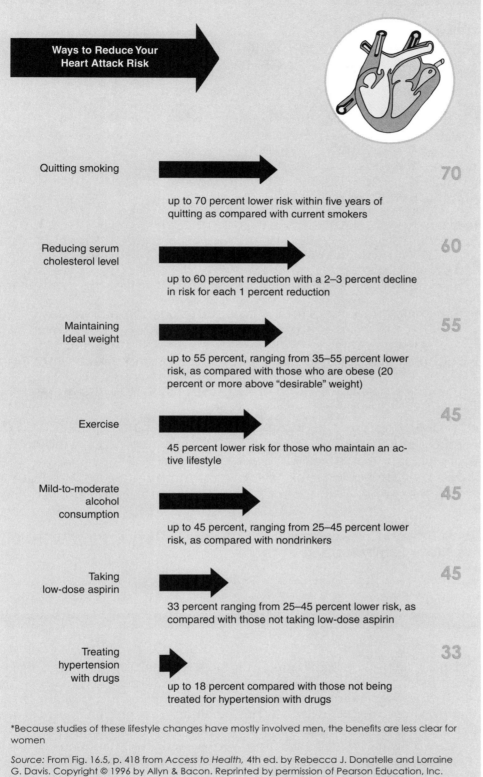

FIGURE 4.13

Estimated Average Reduction in Risk for Heart Attack*

*Estimated risk reductions refer to the independent contribution of each risk factor to heart attack and do not address the wide range of known or hypothesized reactions among them.

Ways to Reduce Your Heart Attack Risk

Quitting smoking — 70
up to 70 percent lower risk within five years of quitting as compared with current smokers

Reducing serum cholesterol level — 60
up to 60 percent reduction with a 2–3 percent decline in risk for each 1 percent reduction

Maintaining Ideal weight — 55
up to 55 percent, ranging from 35–55 percent lower risk, as compared with those who are obese (20 percent or more above "desirable" weight)

Exercise — 45
45 percent lower risk for those who maintain an active lifestyle

Mild-to-moderate alcohol consumption — 45
up to 45 percent, ranging from 25–45 percent lower risk, as compared with nondrinkers

Taking low-dose aspirin — 45
33 percent ranging from 25–45 percent lower risk, as compared with those not taking low-dose aspirin

Treating hypertension with drugs — 33
up to 18 percent compared with those not being treated for hypertension with drugs

*Because studies of these lifestyle changes have mostly involved men, the benefits are less clear for women

Source: From Fig. 16.5, p. 418 from *Access to Health,* 4th ed. by Rebecca J. Donatelle and Lorraine G. Davis. Copyright © 1996 by Allyn & Bacon. Reprinted by permission of Pearson Education, Inc.

Stroke Symptoms / Warning Signs

IF YOU NOTICE ONE OR MORE OF THESE SIGNS, DON'T WAIT. STROKE IS A MEDICAL EMERGENCY. CALL 9-1-1 OR YOUR EMERGENCY MEDICAL SERVICES. GET TO A HOSPITAL RIGHT AWAY!

The American Stroke Association wants you to learn the warning signs of stroke:

- Sudden numbness or weakness of the face, arm, or leg, especially on one side of the body
- Sudden confusion, trouble speaking or understanding
- Sudden trouble seeing in one or both eyes
- Sudden trouble walking, dizziness, loss of balance or coordination
- Sudden, severe headache with no known cause

Be prepared for an emergency.

- Keep a list of emergency rescue service numbers next to the telephone and in your pocket, wallet, or purse.
- Find out which area hospitals are primary stroke centers that have twenty-four-hour emergency stroke care.
- Know (in advance) which hospital or medical facility is nearest your home or office.

Take action in an emergency.

- Not all the warning signs occur in every stroke. Don't ignore signs of stroke, even if they go away!
- Check the time. When did the first warning sign or symptom start? you'll be asked this important question later.
- If you have one or more stroke symptoms that last more than a few minutes, don't delay! Immediately call 9-1-1 or the emergency medical service (EMS) number so an ambulance (ideally with advanced life support) can quickly be sent for you.
- If you're with someone who may be having stroke symptoms, immediately call 9-1-1 or the EMS. Expect the person to protest—denial is common. Don't take "no" for an answer. Insist on taking prompt action.

For stroke information, call the American Stroke Association at 1-888-4-STROKE. For information on life after stroke, ask for the Stroke Family Support Network.

Source: Reprinted with permission, www.heart.org © 2010, American Heart Association, Inc.

occurs when the vessels that supply the brain with nutrients become damaged or occluded and the brain tissue dies because of insufficient oxygen (see Figure 4.14). The cerebral artery, the main supply of nutrients to the brain, can be narrowed due to atherosclerosis. The conditions that precipitate stroke may take years to develop. Stroke has the same risk factors as heart disease. Hypertension is the most notable risk factor. Like heart disease, conditions favorable to stroke also respond favorably to exercise. Ischemic (thrombosis and embolism) strokes are the most common form of stroke (87 percent) and occur as a result of a blockage to the cerebral artery (AHA, 2009). The process is similar to that which occurs in a heart attack. Intracerebral hemorrhage, or aneurysm, in which the vessel may rupture and cause bleeding inside the head and result in pressure on the brain, are 10 percent of strokes. Three percent of strokes are caused by hemorrhage. The least common form of stroke results from compression that can occur as a result of a hemorrhage or brain tumor. African Americans have the highest risk at 44% (AHA, 2012). African Americans also

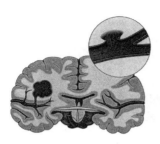

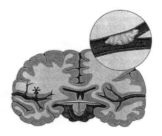

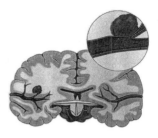

Cerebral Hemorrhage as the Cause of Stroke:

A blood vessel in the brain ruptures.

Cerebral Embolism as the Cause of Stroke: A clot or foreign body forms in some other part of the body and travels to the brain.

Cerebral Thrombosis as the Cause of Stroke: There is a blood clot in the brain.

Compression as the Cause of Stroke

FIGURE 4.14

Causes of Stroke

Source: Hafen, Brent Q.; Karren, Keith J.; Frandsen, Kathryn J., *First Aid for Colleges and Universities*, 7th Edition, © 1999. Printed and electronically reproduced by permission of Pearson Education, Inc., Upper Saddle River, New Jersey.

have a high incidence of stroke risk factors such as high blood pressure. On the average, someone in the United States has a stroke every forty seconds, and every three to four minutes someone dies of a stroke (AHA, 2012). One-third of all stroke victims die, one-third of stroke victims suffer permanent disability, and one-third of stroke victims gradually return to their normal daily routines (Bishop and Aldana, 1999). Stroke is also a leading cause of serious disability. Various studies have shown significant trends toward lower stroke risk with moderate and high levels of leisure time physical activity.

Risk Factors for Cardiovascular Disease

Controllable Risk Factors

- *Cigarette Smoking*—Smokers have two to four times the risk of developing cardiovascular disease than do nonsmokers (AHA, 2009). Cigarette smoking is the most "potent" of the preventable risk factors. Former U.S. Surgeon General C. Everett Koop claims that cigarette smoking is the number one preventable cause of death and disease in the United States and the most important health issue of our time. Smoking accounts for 50 percent of the female deaths due to heart attack before the age of 55 (Rosato, 1994).
- *Hypertension*—The AHA (2012) reports that approximately 76.4 million American adults and children have high blood pressure. Reports from the Harvard Alumni Study (1986) show that subjects who did not engage in vigorous sports or activity were 35 percent more likely to develop hypertension than those who were regularly active. Hypertension is the most important modifiable risk factor for stroke.
- *Cholesterol*—Dietary cholesterol contributes to blood serum cholesterol (cholesterol circulating in the blood), which can contribute to heart disease. Every 1 percent reduction in serum cholesterol can result in a 2–3 percent reduction in the risk of heart disease (AHA, 2009). To lower cholesterol, reduce intake of dietary saturated fat, increase consumption of soluble fiber, maintain a healthy weight, do not smoke, and exercise regularly.

- *Inactivity*—Physical inactivity can be very debilitating to the human body. The changes brought about by the aging process can be simulated in a few weeks of bed rest for a young person. Aerobic exercise on a regular basis can favorably influence the other modifiable risk factors for heart disease. Consistent, moderate amounts of physical activity can promote health and longevity. The Surgeon General's report (Satcher, 1996) states that as few as 150 extra calories expended daily exercising can dramatically decrease CVD risk.
- *Obesity*—Highly correlated to heart disease, mild to moderate obesity is associated with an increase in risk of CVD. Fat distribution can also predict higher risk. A waist-to-hip ratio that is greater than 1.0 for men and greater than 0.8 for women constitutes a higher risk because abdominal fat is more easily mobilized and dispersed into the bloodstream, thereby elevating serum cholesterol levels. A BMI over 30 is considered obese.
- *Diabetes*—At least 65 percent of diabetics die of some form of CVD (CDC, 1999). Exercise is critical to help increase the sensitivity of the body's cells to insulin. 18.3 million Americans have diabetes (AHA, 2012.)

The Surgeon General Encourages Americans to Know Health History—In the fall of 2008 the acting Surgeon General encouraged all Americans to take advantage of family gatherings to speak with family members to discuss, identify, and make a record of health problems that seem to run in the family. Doing this can offer insight into your health risk. Check out the Web-based tool "My Family Health Portrait" at www.hhs.gov/familyhistory/

Uncontrollable Risk Factors

- *Age*—Risk of CVD rises as a person ages.
- *Gender*—Men have a higher risk than women until women reach postmenopausal age. Remember that CVD is an equal opportunity killer!
- *Heredity*—A family history of heart disease will increase risk.

Contributing Risk Factors

- *Stress*—Although difficult to measure in concrete form, stress is considered a factor in the development and acceleration of CVD. Without stress-management techniques, constant stress can manifest itself in a physical nature in the human body. Stress contributes to many of today's illnesses.
- *Triglycerides*—Most of the fat in the human body is stored in the form of triglycerides. Elevated triglyceride levels are thought to increase CVD risk by being involved in the plaque formation of atherosclerosis.

Obesity

Since 1979 the World Heath Organization (WHO) has classified obesity as a disease. "Obesity is a complex condition, one with serious social and psychological dimensions, that affects virtually all age and socioeconomic groups and threatens to overwhelm both developed and developing countries. As of 2000, the number

---

Health Risks of Obesity
Each of the diseases listed below is followed by the percentage of cases that are caused by obesity.

Colon cancer	10%
Breast cancer	11%
Hypertension	33%
Heart disease	70%
Diabetes	90%
(Type II, non-insulin-dependent)	

As these statistics show, being obese greatly increases the risk of many serious and even life-threatening diseases.

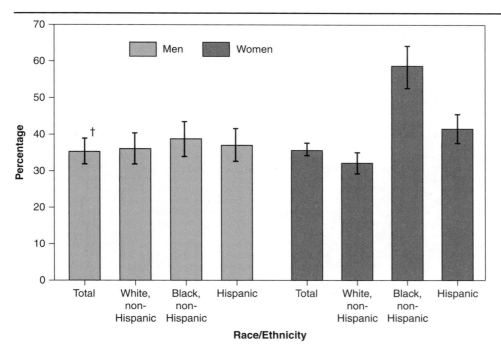

FIGURE 4.15

Prevalence of Obesity Among Adults Aged ≥20 Years, by Race/Ethnicity and Sex—National Health and Nutrition Examination Survey, United States, 2009–2010

Source: National Health and Nutrition Examination Survey, 2009–2010.

of obese adults has increased to over 300 million" (WHO, 2008). "Globesity" may be the new term coined for the world's heavy populations. While malnutrition still contributes to an estimated 60 percent of deaths in children ages 5 and under globally, in the United States the excess body weight and physical inactivity that leads to obesity cause more than 112,000 deaths each year, making it the second leading cause of death in our county.

The figure above shows the prevalence of obesity among adults aged ≥20 years, by race/ethnicity and sex in the United States during 2009–2010, according to the National Health and Nutrition Examination Survey. Among adults aged ≥20 years in 2009–2010, 35.5% of men and 35.8% of women were obese. Among men, 38.8% of non-Hispanic blacks, 37.0% of Hispanics, and 36.2% of non-Hispanic whites were obese. Among women, 58.5% of non-Hispanic blacks, 41.4% of Hispanics, and 32.3% of non-Hispanic whites were obese.

Obesity causes, contributes to, and complicates many of the diseases that afflict Americans. Obesity is associated with a shortened life, serious organ impairment, poor self-concept, and a higher risk of cardiovascular disease and diabetes, as well as colon and breast cancer.

Fat distribution is related to health risk (Canoy, 2007). "Apples" describe male-fat patterned distribution with fat accumulating mostly around the torso. "Pears" describe female-fat patterned distribution with fat accumulating mostly on the hips and upper thighs (see Figure 4.16). Apples have a higher health risk especially if they have visceral fat located around internal organs.

Childhood Obesity

We are a society of excesses. Unfortunately, everyone seems to be getting bigger—all ages, sexes, races independent of socioeconomic status, gender, or locale. The increase in overweight children causes the most concern. For some parents, childhood obesity has become a bigger concern than smoking or drug abuse. In the last 30 years, school age children (ages 6–11) have increased obesity rates from 4% to 20%.

The causes of **childhood obesity** are complex. As with adult obesity, the bottom line is that if there is a caloric intake surplus, weight will be gained.

Childhood Obesity: How bad is it? About one in three children and teens in the U.S. is overweight or obese. Overweight kids have a 70–80 percent chance of staying overweight their entire lives. Obese and overweight adults now outnumber those at a healthy weight; nearly seven in 10 U.S. adults are overweight or obese. Reprinted with permission, www. heart.org, © 2010, American Heart Association, Inc.

FIGURE 4.16

Body Shape and
Associated Health Risk

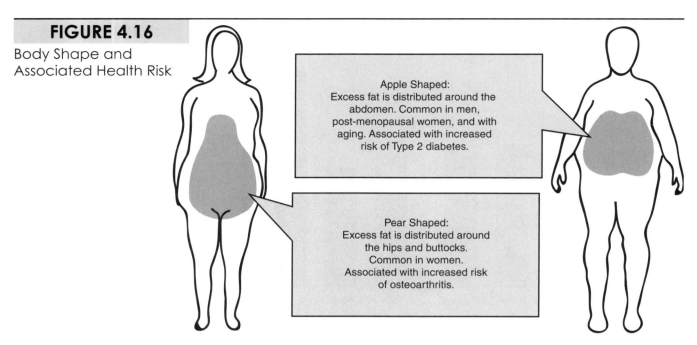

Apple Shaped:
Excess fat is distributed around the
abdomen. Common in men,
post-menopausal women, and with
aging. Associated with increased
risk of Type 2 diabetes.

Pear Shaped:
Excess fat is distributed around
the hips and buttocks.
Common in women.
Associated with increased risk
of osteoarthritis.

Source: From National Institute of Diabetes and Kidney Disease.

Infants can be overfed, toddlers can be pacified with candy, and teenagers love soft drinks and junk food. Overweight parents are more likely to have overweight children because the children learn eating and activity patterns from parents. To try to combat childhood obesity, adults should look at their own lifestyle habits: 44 oz sodas several times a day, fast food throughout each week, and lots of time spent playing video games or watching TV will increase the risk of obesity for children and adults alike. These behaviors are not the way to encourage kids to become healthy. Simple things such as eating balanced meals together at home, recreating as a family, and not having junk food always accessible at home are good places to start. Childhood obesity can have a negative impact on overall health risk including psychosocial

Excess weight at young ages has been linked to higher and earlier death rates in adulthood. Perhaps one of the most sobering statements regarding the severity of the childhood obesity epidemic came from former Surgeon General Richard Carmona, who characterized the threat as follows:

"Because of the increasing rates of obesity, unhealthy eating habits, and physical inactivity, we may see the first generation that will be less healthy and have a shorter life expectancy than their parents."

Obesity has also risen dramatically in adults. Today over 144 million Americans, or 66 percent of adults age 20 and older, are overweight or obese (BMI at or above 25). That is nearly seven out of every 10 adults. Additionally, 33 percent (over 71 million) of adults are classified as obese (BMI at or above 30). Obese Americans now outnumber overweight Americans, which means that individuals who are above a healthy weight are significantly, not slightly, above a healthy weight. Some experts project that by 2015, 75 percent of adults will be overweight, with 41 percent obese.

Source: Reprinted with permission, www.heart.org, © 2010, American Heart Association, Inc.

Stand2Learn

One simple thing can help a child build and maintain healthy bones and muscles, reduce risk of developing obesity and chronic diseases, reduce feelings of depression and anxiety, and promote feelings of well-being. That same thing can help improve academic achievement, and also improve academic behavior such as time on task, concentration, and attentiveness in the classroom. What is that one thing? Exercise. Savvy school districts should make sure kids are active every day at school! Perhaps those school districts should speak with some researchers at the Texas A&M Health Science Center involved in Stand2Learn.

In College Station, TX, a pilot study was conducted by researchers at College Hills Elementary School. Mark Benden, Ph.D., CPE, assistant professor at the TAMHSC-School of Rural Public Health, examined the effect giving students in several first grade classrooms the option to stand at a tall desk rather than sit during the day while in class.

"Students in classrooms with the standing-height desks are choosing to stand more than two-thirds of the time and are burning an average of 17 percent more calories overall than their classmates in traditional seated classrooms," Dr. Benden said. "More importantly, overweight and obese students are burning 32 percent more calories while working at standing desks than their peers who work in traditional seated classrooms." Besides expending more calories the students are also experiencing some fringe benefits which the teachers must like. "In addition to increasing physical activity, teachers in these classrooms note that standing desks seem to increase alertness and attentiveness of students while decreasing disruptive behavior."

Perhaps in the not too distant future classrooms will be full of stand up desks and the rest of us will all be working at treadmill desks.

Source: Courtesy of Stand2Learn

consequences. Perhaps as individuals, families, schools, communities, and as a nation we should emphasize being more active. Overweight by some arbitrary standard may or may not mean cardiovascular or diabetic risk. Sedentary living, however, almost always predicates poor health in the future, if not sooner. "School aged youth should participate daily in 60 minutes or more of moderate to vigorous physical activity that is developmentally appropriate, enjoyable, and involves a variety of activities" (*Journal of Pediatrics*, 2005). How ironic that we should have to tell our kids to go out and play! Adults would do well to follow this same advice.

Causes of Obesity

Is it your genes or your fast-food lunches every day? Most likely it is both. Since you cannot change who your parents are, change your lifestyle habits. *Physical inactivity is certainly a major, if not the primary, cause of obesity in the United States today* (Wilmore, 1994). Most often caloric intake exceeds caloric expenditure. Glandular disorders affect 2 percent of the obese population. Genetically we are predisposed to a certain somatotype, fat distribution, size, and weight.

In every person, body weight is the result of many factors; genetic, metabolic, behavioral, environmental, cultural as well as socioeconomic influences (Surgeon General, 2005). An individual's lifestyle choices can help to modify these tendencies. Nineteen out of twenty overweight teenagers will be overweight adults (Texas A&M University Human Nutrition Conference, 1998).

Physiological Response to Obesity

For an obese person, more blood vessels are needed to circulate blood. The heart has to pump harder, therefore increasing blood pressure. Extra weight can be tough on the musculoskeletal joints, causing problems with arthritis, gout, bone and joint diseases, varicose veins, gallbladder disease, as well as complications during pregnancy. Obese individuals often are heat intolerant and experience shortness of breath during heavy exercise. Obesity increases most cancer risks (Bishop and Aldana, 1999).

Can You Make a Difference?

Get involved in your local school district as an activist for good health. When school budgets are tight, P.E. teachers are often the first to be let go. Often we think one person can't make a difference. Molly Barker didn't let that stop her from forming a grassroots organization that targets the emotional and the mental fitness as well as developing the physical fitness of young girls. The program, called *Girls on the Run*, is a twelve-week program that culminates in the participants running or walking a 5-km road race. The road race is secondary to what the girls experience in the twelve weeks leading up to the race. Positive preteen emotional development is the focus. The girls might warm up by running/walking around a track, and then have focused girl talk. They discuss positive people in their lives. Issues such as pressures to look a certain way, anorexia, bullying, nutrition, the role of women in society, and what makes each girl special are contemplated as a group. *Girls on the Run* is now in over one-hundred cities across Canada and the United States. One person can make a difference. Be a good role model for your kids, your siblings, your relatives, for any children that you come in contact with. Like Molly Barker, choose to be involved not only with your own health, but also with the health of your community.

Fitness or Fatness

Dr. Steven Blair is convinced we are too focused on obesity and overweight. Physical activity is much more crucial than a high BMI. People who are active, yet have a high BMI, have lower death rates than those who have a normal BMI but are sedentary. It is clear that if a sedentary person begins an exercise program, blood glucose and cholesterol could improve, yet that person might not loose any weight. *"Fitness is a more important indicator of health outcomes than fatness"* says Steven Ball, University of Missouri exercise physiologist.

Cancer

Cancer is characterized by the uncontrollable growth and spread of abnormal cells. Cancer cells do not follow the normal code of DNA that is encrypted in noncancerous cells.

Who Gets Cancer?

Possibly in the future people will be able to go to the doctor for a simple blood test to determine whether they will have cancer or not. Unfortunately there seems to be no rhyme or reason for some cancer cases. Lifestyle choices, as well as heredity and also luck, play a big role in a person's risk of developing cancer. Even personality can influence if a person is prone to cancer. With health promotion and prevention, fewer people may develop cancer, and more cancer patients may survive.

Can Cancer Be Prevented?

It is theorized that 80 percent of cancers can be prevented with positive life-style choices. Avoiding tobacco and over-exposure to sunlight are two major examples. Eating a varied diet, consuming antioxidants, having a positive attitude, and participating in regular physical activity are simple choices that can have a large impact on cancer prevention. Thirty-five percent of the total cancer death toll is associated with diet (Rosato, 1994), and fit individuals may have a decreased risk of reproductive organ cancers (Bishop and Aldana, 1999). Cancer is the second leading cause of death in the United States, accounting for about 23 percent of all deaths yearly (Hoeger et al., 2009).

Does Exercise Help?

Recognition of the potential of exercise to prevent cancer came in 1985 when the American Cancer Society began recommending exercise to protect against cancer. Regular activity has been shown to reduce risk of colon cancer (see Table 4.1). Active people have lower death rates from cancer than inactive people—50 to 250 percent lower. Colon, breast, rectal, and prostate cancers each have an established link with inactivity.

Exercising early in life also seems to have an impact in reducing risk of breast cancer in post-menopausal women. A study at the USC Norris Cancer Center reported that one to three hours of exercise a week over a woman's reproductive lifetime (between the teens and age 40) may result in a 20 to 30 percent risk reduction for breast cancer. Exercise that averaged four or more hours per week resulted in a 60 percent reduction! A woman starting to exercise in her 20's or 30's can also experience reduced risk. Active females, such as a dancer or track athlete, may put off the age of onset of menstruation, and if they continue to be active, they may experience earlier menopause than their inactive counterparts. This results in a lower lifetime exposure to estrogen, which also reduces cancer risk. Ironically lower estrogen levels may contribute to osteoporosis.

It is also thought that exercise can boost immunity that can help kill abnormal cancer cells (Bishop and Aldana, 1999). Dr. Steven Blair at the Institute for Aerobics Research in Dallas, Texas, has done long-term epidemiological studies

"Exercise is a known remedy for the weakness and low spirits that cancer patients experience during their recovery. It boosts energy and endurance, and also builds confidence and optimism. But, within the past five years, several medical investigations have revealed a surprising new fact: Exercise may also help prevent cancer" (Rosato, 1994).

TABLE 4.1 ♦ Physical Activity and Cancer

Cancer Type	Effect of Physical Activity
Colon	Exercise speeds movement of food and cancer-causing substances through the digestive system, and reduces prostaglandins (substances linked to cancer in the colon).
Breast	Exercise decreases the amount of exposure of breast tissue to circulating estrogen. Lower body fat is also associated with lower estrogen levels. Early life activity is deemed important for both reasons. Fatigue from therapy is reduced by exercise.
Rectal	Similar to colon cancer, exercise leads to more regular bowel movements and reduces "transit time."
Prostate	Fatigue from therapy is reduced by exercise.

that show rate of death due to cancer is significantly lower in patients with elevated levels of fitness. It must also be noted that people who are active tend to also participate in other healthy behaviors, such as eating a varied diet low in fat and high in fiber. These other behaviors may also influence cancer risk and help those with cancer lead more fulfilling and productive lives. The American Cancer Society reports that people with healthy lifestyles (non-smokers, regular physical activity, and sufficient sleep) have the lowest cancer mortality rates.

Diabetes

Diabetes is a disorder that involves high blood sugar levels and inadequate insulin production by the pancreas or inadequate utilization of insulin by the cells (Wilmore, 1994). Type II diabetes will be discussed in this chapter.

Who Gets Diabetes?

Eighty percent of the adults who develop Type II diabetes are obese (Surgeon General, 2005). The mortality rate is greater in diabetics with CVD—68% of people with diabetes die from some form of CVD. Each year, 1.6 million new cases of diabetes are diagnosed (AHA, 2012). Diabetes is the seventh leading cause of death in people over 40 (Corbin and Welk, 2009). Due to the surge in childhood obesity in the decade of the 90's, children are more at risk for diabetes. Diabetes is one of the most important risk factors for stroke in women.

Can Diabetes Be Prevented?

Research shows that changing lifestyle habits to decrease risk for heart disease also decreases risk for diabetes. "According to research, a seven percent loss of body weight and 150 minutes of moderate-intensity physical activity a week can reduce the chance of developing diabetes by 58 percent in those who are at high risk. These lifestyle changes cut the risk of developing type II diabetes regardless of age, ethnicity, gender, or weight." Type II diabetes may account for 90–95 percent of all diagnosed cases of diabetes (AHA, 2012).

Does Exercise Help?

Exercise plays an important role in managing this disease, as exercise helps control body fat and improves insulin sensitivity and glucose tolerance. Exercise does not prevent Type II diabetes; however, exercise does help manage the disorder.

Diabetic Walkers Gain Fitness

Diabetics who **walked moderately for thirty-eight minutes** (4,400 steps or 2.2 miles) did not lose weight; however, they showed significant effects: risk of heart disease decreased; cholesterol improved; triglycerides improved; and they saved $288.00 in health costs per year.

© Tyler Olson, 2012, Shutterstock, Inc.

Diabetics who **walked ninety minutes** (10,000 steps or 5 miles) saw bigger benefits: the number of walkers needing insulin therapy decreased by 25 percent; those receiving insulin therapy reduced the dosage by an average of eleven units per day; cholesterol, triglycerides, blood pressure, and heart disease risk decreased; and they saved over $1,200.00 per year.

Diabetics in the control group that **walked 0 minutes** saw health care costs rise $500.00; insulin use, cholesterol, blood pressure, triglycerides, and heart disease risk all increased. This study was conducted for two years. (Sullivan et al., 2009)

Metabolic Syndrome

Moderate and vigorous activity is associated with a lower risk of developing **metabolic syndrome**. Metabolic syndrome is a "cluster" of cardiovascular risk factors including overweight or obesity (waist circumference above 102 cm for men or above 88 cm for women), high blood pressure (above 130/85 mm Hg or current drug treatment for hypertension), elevated triglycerides (150 mg/dL or higher), low levels of high-density lipoprotein (below 40 mg/dL in men and below 50 mg/dL in women), and high fasting glucose levels (100 mg/dL or higher) (AHA, 2009). Having three or more of these risk factors puts you at higher risk of developing CVD or diabetes. In studies done at the Cooper Institute in Dallas, the risk of metabolic syndrome for men with moderate fitness was 26 percent lower, and for men with high fitness the risk was 53 percent lower compared to their lower fitness counterparts. For women the risk was 20 percent and 63 percent lower, respectively. It is clear that to prevent metabolic syndrome, improving cardiovascular fitness through regular physical activity is critical.

Low Back Pain

Low back pain is characterized by chronic discomfort in the lumbar region of the back. Chronic back pain may be the result of an injury; however, back pain is most often due to a lack of fitness. The National Safety Council data indicates that the back is the most frequently injured of all the body parts, with the injury rate double that of other body parts. Intervertebral disks can suffer degeneration from overuse, which is more common in men than in women. Backache is the second leading medical complaint when visiting a physician (Corbin and Welk, 2009).

Who Suffers from Low Back Pain?

More than eight out of ten Americans will suffer some back-related pain at some point in their lifetime (Corbin and Welk, 2009). Low back pain is epidemic throughout the world and is the major cause of disability in people aged 20 through 45 in the United States. Ninety percent of back injuries occur in the lumbar region (Donatelle and Davis, 2007). Thirty to 70 percent of all Americans have recurring back problems; two million Americans cannot hold a job as a result. Back pain is the most frequent cause of inactivity in individuals under the age of 45 (Corbin and Welk, 2009). Improper lifting, faulty work habits, heredity, diseases such as scoliosis, and excess weight are other causes of low back pain. Undue psychological stress can cause back pain via tight muscles and constricted blood vessels (Hoeger et al., 2009).

Can Low Back Pain Be Prevented?

Lack of activity is the most common reason for low back pain, so movement is critical to good back health. Staying active, using common sense regarding lifting heavy objects, and managing weight all are important in low back pain prevention. Decrease occupational risks. Use caution, as it is often employees new to a job who injure their back. Another factor in low back pain is poor posture while sitting, standing, or walking.

Does Exercise Help?

How much calcium does a college student need? **1,300 mg daily**

- Good sources of calcium: low-fat dairy products, dark green leafy vegetables, tofu, sardines, and salmon.
- Calcium-fortified foods: cereals, breads, orange juice, and some antacids.

Exercise helps with enhancing posture, balance, strength, and flexibility. Strengthening abdominal muscles, which are the complimentary muscle group to the lower back, helps support the spine. Stretching the hip flexors and the hamstrings are important to help tilt the anterior portion of the pelvis back. Low back pain and tight hamstrings are highly correlated. Excess weight around the torso and abdominal region pulls the pelvis forward, causing potential strain in the lumbar region. In general, strengthening the "core" (all the muscles from the shoulders and the hips) helps prevent back pain. A regular exercise and flexibility program can help to manage weight over a lifetime.

Osteoporosis

Osteoporosis is a disease characterized by low bone density and structural deterioration of bone tissue, which can lead to increased bone fragility and increased risk of fractures to the skeletal structure. Osteoporosis is sometimes called the "silent disease" because there are often no symptoms as bone density decreases. The *Dallas Morning News* (August 26, 2001) describes osteoporosis as an "epidemic of young women with old bones." Many young women delay the onset of menstruation due to high activity levels, which in turn lowers body fat and estrogen levels. Your physician may recommend a bone mineral density test. The test is noninvasive, painless, and safe (Otis and Goldingay, 2000).

Bone is living, growing tissue. With adequate nutrition and activity, bone formation continues to occur throughout a lifetime. Old bone is removed through **resorption**, and new bone is formed through a process called **formation**. Bones need to be fed and cared for just as the rest of our body. Childhood and teenage years are when new bone is developed more quickly than the old bone is resorbed. Bones become stronger and denser until peak bone mass is attained at approximately age 30. Thereafter, bone loss exceeds bone formation. *Adequate calcium intake, minimal exposure to sunlight for vitamin D, and regular physical activity are critical for young adults because the higher peak bone mass is at age 30, the less likely it is that osteoporosis will develop in later years.*

Who Gets Osteoporosis?

For 34 million Americans, osteoporosis is a major public health threat (Surgeon General, 2004). Considered to afflict mostly women, this disease can affect males as well. Of the women with osteoporosis, 80 percent are post-

Bone Loss during Spaceflight

In the 1980's, NASA scientists observed a dramatic spike in calcium excreted by astronauts after the first seven days of spaceflight. Researchers have since confirmed that humans lose bone mineral density during spaceflight at a rate ten-fold faster than does a post-menopausal woman; the lack of gravitational forces, even with daily exercise during space missions, has a very dramatic effect on bone mass. There are also changes in the cross-sectional geometry of long bones, for instance, the femoral neck near the hip joint, that further reduce bone strength and increase risk of a hip fracture should that astronaut fall soon after returning to earth. Some of this bone loss may be due to reduced blood flow to bone with the shifts in body fluids while in microgravity, according to a study by Dr. Michael Delp at Texas A&M University. This reduced blood flow in turn may affect in various ways the activity of bone cells responsible for bone formation and bone resorption, altering the balance in favor of resorption (Colleran et al., 2000). Related studies conducted by Dr. Susan Bloomfield at Texas A&M University demonstrated that this bone loss is not uniform across the skeleton but focused in trabecular ("spongy") bone sites (for instance, in the ends of the long bones) (Bloomfield et al., 2002). This is the same type of bone that is lost first with the development of osteoporosis here on earth. Another potential contributor to bone loss in astronauts might be reduced caloric intake, quite common during busy missions. Restricting caloric intake by 40 percent causes reductions in trabecular bone formation rate similar in magnitude to that observed with the unloading of microgravity (Baek et al., 2008). This finding has important implications for the many Americans who attempt long-term restriction of caloric intake to achieve weight loss.

Colleran, P.N., M.K. Wilkerson, S.A. Bloomfield, L.J. Suva, R.T. Turner, and M.D. Delp. Alterations in skeletal perfusion with simulated microgravity: a possible mechanism for bone remodeling. *J. Appl. Physiol.* 89: 1046–1054, 2000.

Bloomfield, S.A., M.R. Allen, H.A. Hogan, and M.D. Delp. Site-and compartment-specific changes in bone with hindlimb unloading in mature adult rats. *Bone* 31: 149–157, 2002.

Baek, K., A.A. Barlow, M.R. Allen, and S.A. Bloomfield. Food restriction and simulated microgravity: effects on bone and serum leptin. *J. Appl. Physiol.* 104: 1086–1093. 2008.

menopausal. One out of two women and one out of eight men over 50 will get osteoporosis in their lifetime.

Risk increases with age. Have you observed older women who seem to slump? Many women with low bone density have kyphosis (also called dowager's hump), or a rounding of the upper back. The head tilts forward because often the cervical vertebrae in the upper spine actually suffer compression fractures. This keeps older women from being able to stand up straight or to get a full breath. Small, thin-boned women are at higher risk, and there may also be a genetic factor. If there are people in a family with weak, thin bones then relatives with the same body type may have an inherently higher risk. Post-menopausal Caucasian and Asian women are at the highest risk. It is unknown why these particular groups are more susceptible to osteoporosis. African Americans have bone that is 10 percent more dense than Caucasians (Greenberg et al., 1998). Others at risk include those with poor diets, especially if calcium and vitamin D are low over a long period of time. It is estimated that 75 percent of adults do not consume enough calcium on a daily basis (Bishop and Aldana, 1999). An inactive lifestyle contributes greatly. A history of excessive use of alcohol or cigarette smoking can also increase risk.

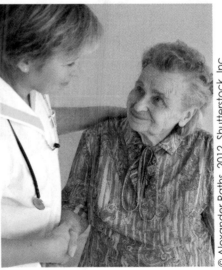

© Alexander Raths, 2012, Shutterstock, Inc.

An estimated 10 million Americans—8 million women and 2 million men have osteoporosis.

Another growing group of high-risk individuals is the eating disordered. Many active young women suffer stress fractures, which can be a sign of osteoporosis. If a person is extremely active with a low percentage of body fat, then hormone levels may be askew. Prolonged **amenorrhea** (absence of menstruation) can signal low body fat or an eating disorder. Low estrogen levels characterize fracture, it is not typical to administer a bone density test. If other symptoms such as amenorrhea, disordered eating, or abuse of exercise are suspected, then it would be prudent for the physician to order or for the athlete to consider asking for a bone density test.

Can Osteoporosis Be Prevented?

The good news is that osteoporosis can be both prevented and treated. Regular physical activity reduces the risk of developing osteoporosis. A lifetime of low calcium intake is associated with low bone mass (www.osteo.org). Adequate calcium intake is critical for optimal bone mass. Growing children, adolescents, and pregnant and breast-feeding women need more calcium. It is estimated by the National Institutes of Health that less than 10 percent of girls age 10–17 years are getting the calcium they need each day. A varied diet with green leafy vegetables and plenty of dairy will help ensure good calcium intake. Many calcium-fortified foods are now available. A varied diet will also ensure adequate intake of vitamin D, which aids in prevention. It is also advisable to limit caffeine and phosphate-containing soda, which may interfere with calcium absorption. Prolonged high-protein diets may also contribute to calcium loss in bone. A high-sodium diet is thought to increase calcium excretion through the kidneys. For post-menopausal women, some physicians consider hormone replacement therapy to help strengthen bones. Weightbearing exercise such as walking, running, tennis, and basketball is an excellent way to strengthen bones to help prevent osteoporosis.

Current Recommendations to Decrease Osteoporosis Risk
- Engage in daily weight-bearing aerobic activity
- Weight training (the ACSM recommends ten–twelve reps, two sets two times weekly)
- Vitamin D (wellbalanced diet and adequate exposure to sunlight)
- Estrogen replacement therapy (for some women, especially post-menopausal women)

Shape Up America!

Try using digital technology—there are numerous free apps and some pricey high tech options for tracking your fitness progress. If you like gimmicks and gadgets, the cheapest option is probably a pedometer. A pedometer is a small device that clips on your belt and counts your steps. The average American walks approximately 900–3,000 steps per day in daily normal activities. The former U.S. Surgeon General, C. Everett Koop, developed Shape Up America! in 1994 to highlight health risks of obesity. The extra 150 calories or thirty minutes per day recommended by the Surgeon General's 1996 Report may not be enough for you to reach your fitness or weight loss goals. Studies indicate that a sufficient goal would be to walk 10,000 steps per day. Shape Up America! challenges you to walk 10,000 steps. Without a conscious effort, 10,000 steps would be a difficult task. Be sure and log your steps each day to work up to 10,000. Give it a try; if you like the latest thing, a pedometer is much cheaper than an ab roller or a treadmill!

It's Never Too Late

He was a world champion. Jesse Coon of College Station, Texas, passed away on July 30, 2005, after a long, full, and active life. He was 94. Coon started swimming competitively at the ripe old age of 64, and he started breaking world records in his early 80's.

The former physics professor at Texas A&M University broke five world records at his last major swim meet in Munich, Germany, in the 90 through 94 age group. His stroke? The butterfly. When competing, Coon worked out in the pool ninety minutes five times per week. Jesse Coon was an active sailor and he mowed his own lawn.

Not all mature Americans need to be world record holders to benefit from a more active lifestyle. Recent studies indicate that regular exercise and physical activity can reduce or slow down the biological process of aging. Older adults can experience increased life satisfaction, happiness, and self-esteem, along with reduced stress with a regular activity. A friend noted that it never occurred to Jesse that he was old. He celebrated life and always had a positive attitude. Coon himself said "the older you get, the more important it is to exercise." Coon is an example not only to others of the gray-haired set, but to all of us of all ages.

Does Exercise Help?

The stress caused by working against gravity during activity strengthens and causes bones to be more dense, just as any other living tissue. Weight-training is highly recommended to keep the bones strong and to build bone mass. Consider the muscle atrophy experienced when a person is confined to bed rest, or a limb that is in a cast for a period of time. Bones deteriorate just as muscles deteriorate without the stimulation of movement. An interesting current topic of study is the effect of zero gravity in space on bone mass. It appears that even a short duration in space can impact bone density (see Bone Loss during Spaceflight, on page 137).

Physical activity is presented as the only known intervention that can potentially increase bone mass and strength in the early years of life and reduce the risk of falling in older populations according to a new Position Stand from the American College of Sports Medicine (ACSM). The official ACSM position stand encourages the adoption of specific exercise prescriptions designed for various ages to best capitalize on the chances to accrue and preserve bone throughout the various stages of life (Surgeon General, 2004).

Aging

Although aging is a completely natural and inevitable process, some people age more gracefully than others. As the typical American's lifespan expands, quality of life for many is compromised due to habits and lifestyle choices made earlier in life. Ensure your independence as you age by choosing how you live your life now. Balancing work, family commitments, and leisure time can be stressful. Stress takes a toll on our bodies, our minds, and our relationships.

Everyone experiences age-related decline in biological functions of the body. Chronological age is our true age in years. Biological age can be different depending on our lifestyle choices. **Biological age** can be younger than chronological age with good nutrition, adequate rest on a regular basis, stress-management techniques, and consistent exercise (see Table 4.2). Biological age can be older than chronological age when unhealthy habits are the norm: poor diet, inadequate sleep, excessive alcohol use, smoking, and obesity. You are in charge of your biological age. What will your biological age be in ten, twenty, and thirty years from now? How about fifty years from now? It is interesting to note that physiological changes with aging are similar to those changes seen with inactivity or prolonged weightlessness, such as experienced by the astronauts (Bloomfield et al., 2002). An integrative biology professor at Berkeley, 78-year-old Marian Diamond, lists five **essentials for staying mentally vigorous:**

1. **diet,**
2. **exercise,**
3. **challenge,**
4. **novelty,**
5. **love.**

These five essentials seem to be critical to maintain quality of life at retirement age, but perhaps they are essentials for us all, at any age (Springen and Seibert, 2005).

Prevention of Hypokinetic Conditions: Planning Your Activity Program

Most adults know that they should be active, and they may be aware that a more active life would make them feel better. The truth is that sometimes it is very difficult to know how to get started and how to incorporate activity into busy lives. *The most important thing is to get started.* Remember that lifestyle activity is easier to incorporate into a hectic schedule; walk during a coffee break, grab ten minutes to move around while on break, or jump rope for a study break. Planned exercise can be more of a challenge. The following are a few suggestions to help jump-start the new you.

1. Establish why you want to exercise.
2. Write down reasonable long-term goals.
3. Write down short-term goals that support the long-term goals.
4. Record the behaviors that need to change in order to support the goals. (A person wanting to quit smoking may want to quit working at a bar and work in a nonsmoking environment.)
5. Write in a log: feelings, food, activity and goal progress are all appropriate.
6. Develop a weekly plan for the activity that supports your goals.

TABLE 4.2 ♦ Effects of Physical Activity and Inactivity on Older Men

	Exercisers	Non-Exercisers
Age (yrs)	68.0	69.8
Weight (lbs)	160.3	186.3
Resting heart rate (bpm)	55.8	66.0
Maximal heart rate (bpm)	157.0	146.0
Heart rate reserve* (bpm)	101.2	80.0
Blood pressure (mm Hg)	120/78	150/90
Maximal oxygen uptake (ml/kg/min)	38.6	20.3

*Heart rate reserve = maximal heart rate – resting heart rate.

Source: From *Principles and Labs for Fitness & Wellness*, 6th edition, Wadsworth Publishing.

Creativity and Aging

Typically mental processes being to slow down with age; however, some characteristics such as creativity can flourish with age. There are many examples of great creative accomplishments by elderly artists. Michaelangelo completed his final frescoes for the vatican's Pauline Chapel at 75. Georgia O'Keeffe painted into her 90's despite failing eyesight. Benjamin Franklin invented bifocal glasses at 78 to correct his poor vision. Folks that have lived longer and have had more experience tend to be more comfortable in their own skin. Because mature adults seldom experience the adolescent need to "fit in," they are more likely to have the freedom to express themselves. This may enhance creative endeavors. So look forward to good health and artful aging in your golden years.

"Real Age"
Dr. Michael Roizen has developed a "real" age test. Log on to www.realage.com to take the free test. According to Roizen, exercising regularly can make your "real" age as much as nine years younger.

7. Tell your friends and family about your goals and ask for their support; or ask them to join you.
8. Reward yourself when any goals are met (rewards should be non-food items, and should not be a day "off" from behaviors that promote your goals).
9. When goals are not met, check your log. What can you change to more effectively support your goals?
10. Periodically re-evaluate goals.

It has been firmly established that physical activity should be a part of our daily lives. Exercise enhances weight management and overall wellness by burning calories, speeding up metabolism, building muscle tissue, and balancing appetite with energy expenditure. More importantly, an active life decreases health risk and typically makes you feel good, and feel good about yourself. Look for opportunities to be active and have fun at the same time.

References

Alters, S. and Schiff, W. *Essential Concepts for Healthy Living* (5th ed). Sudbury, MA., Jones and Bartlett. 2009.

American College of Sports Medicine (ACSM). *Exercise and Hypertension.*

American Heart Association (AHA). *Poor Teen Sleep Habits May Raise Blood Pressure, Lead to CVD.* News release December 10, 2008.

American Heart Association (AHA). *Heart Disease and Stroke Statistics—2012 Update.* 2012. www.aha.com

Canoy, M. P. et al. Abdominal Fat Distribution Predicts Heart Disease, *Circulation*, 2007. Castelli, W. P., Chair, Women, smoking and oral contraceptives; Highlights of a consensus conference, Montreal, November 1997.

Center for Health and Health Care in Schools, School of Public Health and Health Services, George Washington University Medical Center. *Childhood Overweight: What the Research Tells Us.* September 2007 Update. *www.healthinschools.org*

Corbin, C. and Welk G. *Concepts of Physical Fitness* (15th ed). New york: McGraw-Hill. 2009.

Donatelle, R. J. and Davis, L. G. *Access to Health* (10th ed). Boston: Benjamin Cummings. 2007.

Flegal, K. M., Carrol, M. D., Kuczmarski, R. J., and Johnson, C. L. Overweight and Obesity in the United States: Prevalence and Trends, 1960–1994. *International Journal of Obesity and Related Metabolic Disorders,* 22: 39–47. 1998.

Frye, D. W. Contracting Officer. NHANES Iv, Central Lipid Laboratory for National Health and Nutrition Survey. October 1999.

Gaesser, G. Obesity, Health, and Metabolic Fitness, *www.thinkmuscle.com/ articles* Gibbs, W. W. Obesity: An Overblown Epidemic? *Scientific American,* May 23, 2005. Greenberg, J. et al. *Physical Fitness and Wellness* (2nd ed). Boston: Allyn and Bacon. 1998.

Hafen, B. Q., Karren, K. J., and Frandsen, K. J. *First Aid for Colleges and Universities* (7th ed). Boston: Allyn and Bacon. 1999.

The Heart Truth for Women: Women and Heart Disease, *www.hearttruth.gov*

Hoeger, W. W. K., Turner, L. W., and Hafen, B. Q. *Wellness Guidelines for a Healthy Lifestyle* (4th ed). Belmont, CA: Thomson Wadsworth. 2009.

Koop, C. E. Shape Up America! http://www.shapeupamericastore.org, 1994.

National Center for Health Statistics, U.S. Department of Health and Human Services, Centers for Disease Control and Prevention. Hyattsville, MD.

National Institutes on Aging, NIH, www.nia.nih.gov 2008.

National Institutes of Health, http://www.nhlbi.nih.gov/actintime/rhar/md.htm

National Institutes of Health. *Sixth Report on the Joint National Committee on Prevention, Detection, Evaluation and Treatment of High Blood Pressure.* 1997.

National Institutes of Health. Osteoporosis and Related Bone Disease, http://www.osteo.org

Ochoa, L. W., editor. Women's Health and Wellness, an Illustrated Guide (26th ed).

Skokie, IL: Lippincott Williams & Wilkins. 2002.

Otis, C. L. and Goldingay, R. *The Athletic Woman's Survival Guide.* Champaign, IL: Human Kinetics Publishers. 2000.

Paffenbarger, R. et al. Physical Activity and Physical Fitness as Determinants of Health and Longevity. In C. Bouchard et al. *Exercise Fitness and Health.* Champaign, IL: Human Kinetics Publishers. 1990.

Payne, W. A. and Hahn, D. B. *Understanding Your Health* (6th ed). St. Louis, MO: Mosby. 2000.

Powers, S. K. and Dodd, S. L. *Total Fitness and Wellness.* San Francisco: Pearson Benjamin

Cummings. 2009.

Rosato, F. *Fitness to Wellness: The Physical Connection* (3rd ed). Minneapolis: West. 1994. Satcher, D. *Surgeon General's Report on Physical Activity and Health.* Atlanta, GA: CDC. 1996.

Sesso, H. D. and Paffenbarger, R. S. The Harvard Alumni Health Study, Harvard School of Public Health. Boston: 1956.

Seventh Report of the Joint National Committee on Prevention, Detection, Evaluation, and Treatment of High Blood Pressure (JNC vII). *Hypertension,* December 2003.

Springen, K. and Seibert, S. Artful Aging, *Newsweek,* January 17, p. 57. 2005.

Sullivan, P. W. et. al. Obesity, Inactivity, and the Prevalence of Diabetes and Diabetes-related Cardiovascular Comorbidities in the U.S., 2000–2002, *Diabetes Care,* 28: 1599–1603, 2009.

Surgeon General's Call to Action to Prevent and Decrease Overweight and Obesity, www.surgeongeneral.gov

Surgeon General's Report on Bone Health and Osteoporosis: What It Means to You. Washington, DC: U.S. DHHS. October, 2004.

Texas A&M University Human Nutrition Conference. College Station, TX. 1998. Weinttraub, A. yoga: It's Not Just An Exercise. *Psychology Today.* November, 2000. Wilmore, J. H. Exercise, Obesity, and Weight Control, *Physical Activity and Research*

Digest. Washington D.C.: President's Council on Physical Fitness & Sports. 1994.

World Health Organization (WHO). *Controlling the Obesity Epidemic.* Geneva: Author December 2008.

www.exerciseismedicine.com

www.osteo.org

Contacts

American College of Sports Medicine (ACSM)
http://www.acsm.org

American Heart Association
http://www.americanheart.org

American Medical Association
http://www.ama-assn.org

Franklin Institute of Science: interactive multimedia tour of the heart
http://www.fi.edu/biosci/heart.html

Dr. Koop's Community: health improvement info
http://www.drkoop.com

Stayhealthy.com: comprehensive Internet resources continuously updated
http://www.stayhealthy.com/

Go Ask Alice: sponsored by Columbia University Health Service; question & answer format
http://www.alice.columbia.edu/index. html

Centers for Disease Control and Prevention: Information and national health statistics plus more
http://www.cdc/gov

National Health Information Center: 100 organizations listed here to provide answers to health-related questions
http://nhic-nt.health.org/

Weight-control Information Network
www.win.niddk.nih.gov

1 WIN Way
Bethesda, MD 20892-3665
(toll-free number) 877-946-4627

Recommended Reading

Working Out, Working Within by Jerry Lynch (Archer/Putnam, 1998)
The Athletic Woman's Survival Guide by Carol Otis & Roger Goldingay (Human Kinetics Publishers, 2000)
Strong Women Stay Young by Miriam E. Nelson (Bantam, 1997)
Habits Not Diets by James M. Ferguson (Bell, 1988)

Activities

Notebook Activities

Self-Assessment of Cardiovascular Fitness
Healthy Back Test
Is Your Blood in Tune?
Is Osteoporosis in Your Future?

NOTEBOOK ACTIVITY

Self-Assessment of Cardiovascular Fitness

Once you've been exercising regularly for several weeks, you might want to assess your cardiovascular fitness level. Find a local track, typically one-quarter mile per lap, to perform your test. You may either run/walk for one and a half miles and measure how long it takes to reach that distance, or run/walk for twelve minutes and determine the distance you covered in that time. Use the chart below to estimate your cardiovascular fitness level based upon your age and gender. Note that females have lower standards for each fitness category because of their higher levels of essential fat.

	1.5-Mile Run (min:sec)		12-Minute Run (miles)	
Age*	Female (min:sec)	Male (min:sec)	Female (miles)	Male (miles)
Good				
15–30	<12:00	<10:00	>1.5	>1.7
31–50	<13:30	<11:30	>1.4	>1.5
51–70	<16:00	<14:00	>1.2	>1.3
Adequate for most activities				
15–30	<13:30	<11:50	>1.4	>1.5
31–50	<15:00	<13:00	>1.3	>1.4
51–70	<17:30	<15:30	>1.1	>1.3
Borderline				
15–30	<15:00	<13:00	>1.3	>1.4
31–50	<16:30	<14:30	>1.2	>1.3
51–70	<19:00	<17:00	>1.0	>1.2
Need extra work on cardiovascular fitness				
15–30	>17:00	>15:00	<1.2	<1.3
31–50	>18:30	>16:30	<1.1	<1.2
51–70	>21:00	>19:00	<0.9	<1.0

Please list the date, location, and amount of time it took you to complete 1.5 miles. _____

_____

or

Please list the date, location, and distance you traveled in twelve minutes. _____

_____

*Cardiovascular fitness declines with age.

If you are now at the Good level, your emphasis should be on maintaining this level for the rest of your life. If you are now at lower levels, you should set realistic goals for improvement.

Source: From *Health/Fitness Instructor's Handbook* by Edward Howley and B. Don Franks. Copyright © 1986. Reprinted by permission of Human Kinestics, Inc.

NOTEBOOK ACTIVITY

Healthy Back Test

These tests are among the ones used by physicians and therapists to make differential diagnoses of back problems. You and your partner can use them to determine if you have muscle tightness that may make you "at risk" for back problems. Discontinue any of these tests if they produce pain or numbness, or tingling sensations in the back, hips, or legs. Experiencing any of these sensations may be an indication that you have a low back problem that requires diagnosis by your physician. Partners should use great caution in applying force. Be gentle and listen to your partner's feedback.

Test 1—Back to Wall

Stand with your back against a wall, with head, heels, shoulders, and calves of legs touching the wall as shown in the diagram. Try to flatten your neck and the hollow of your back by pressing your buttocks down against the wall. Your partner should just be able to place a hand in the space between the wall and the small of your back.

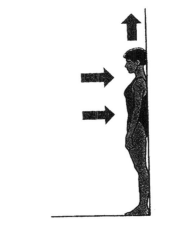

- If this space is greater than the thickness of his/her hand, you probably have lordosis with shortened lumbar and hip flexor muscles.

     ❑ **Pass**   ❑ **Fail**

Test 2—Straight Leg Lift

Lie on your back with hands behind your neck. The partner on your left should stabilize your right leg by placing his/her right hand on the knee. With the left hand, your partner should grasp the left ankle and raise your left leg as near to a right angle as possible. In this position (as shown in the diagram), your lower back should be in contact with the floor. Your right leg should remain straight and on the floor throughout the test.

- If your left leg bends at the knee, short hamstring muscles are indicated. If your back arches and/or your right leg does not remain flat on the floor, short lumbar muscles or hip flexor muscles (or both) are indicated. Repeat the test on the opposite side. (Both sides must pass in order to pass the test.)

     ❑ **Pass**   ❑ **Fail**

Test 3—Thomas Test

Lie on your back on a table or bench with your right leg extended beyond the edge of the table (approximately one-third of the thigh off the table). Bring your left knee to your chest and pull the thigh down tightly with your hands. Your lower back should remain flat against the table as shown in the diagram. Your right thigh should remain on the table.

- If your right thigh lifts off the table while the left knee is hugged to the chest, a tight hip flexor (iliopsoas) on that side is indicated. Repeat on the opposite side. (Both sides must pass in order to pass the test.)

     ❑ **Pass**   ❑ **Fail**

Test 4—Ely's Test

Lie prone; flex right knee. Partner gently pushes right heel toward the buttocks. Stop when resistance is felt or when partner expresses discomfort.

- If pelvis leaves the floor or hip flexes or knee fails to bend freely (135 degrees) or heel fails to touch buttocks, there is tightness in the quadriceps muscles. Repeat with left leg. (Both sides must pass to pass the test.)

     ❑ **Pass**   ❑ **Fail**

Test 5—Ober's Test

Lie on left side with left leg flexed ninety degrees at the hip and ninety degrees at the knee. Partner places right hip in neutral position (no flexion) and right knee in ninety-degree flexion; partner then allows the weight of the leg to lower it toward the floor.

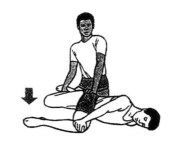

- ■ If there is no tightness in the iliotibial band (fascia and muscles on lateral side of leg), the knee touches the floor without pain and the test is passed. Repeat on the other side. (Both sides must pass in order to pass the test.)

  ❏ **Pass** ❏ **Fail**

Test 6—Press-Up (Straight Arm)

Perform the press-up.

- ■ If you can press to a straight-arm position, keeping your pubis in contact with the floor, and if your partner determines that the arch in your back is a continuous curve (not just a sharp angle at the lumbosacral joint), then there is adequate flexibility in spinal extension.

  ❏ **Pass** ❏ **Fail**

Test 7—Knee Roll

Lie supine with both knees and hips flexed ninety degrees, arms extended to the sides at shoulder level. Keep the knees and hips in that position and lower them to the floor on the right and then on the left.

- ■ If you can accomplish this and still keep your shoulders in contact with the floor, then you have adequate rotation in the spine, especially at the lumbar and thoracic junction. (You must pass both sides in order to pass the test.)

  ❏ **Pass** ❏ **Fail**

Healthy Back Ratings

Classification	Number of Tests Passed
Excellent	7
Very good	6
Good	5
Fair	4
Poor	1–3

NOTEBOOK ACTIVITY

Is Your Blood in Tune?

Instructions: The composition of your blood is very important when it comes to preventing CHD. You can easily have your physician check your blood-fat levels. Sometimes, this is done with a simple finger prick, but to be as accurate as possible, it should be done by having blood drawn from a vein after you have fasted for about twelve hours. Record the results of that assessment below by checking the appropriate rating.

_____ Total cholesterol is below 200: No further evaluation necessary, recheck in five years.

Total cholesterol is 200–239 (borderline high cholesterol): Evaluate risk factors to see what lifestyle changes you can make (diet, exercise, and so forth). If your physician says you are not in high-risk
_____ category for CHD, active treatment is not necessary, but recheck in one to eight weeks.

Total cholesterol is above 240 (high cholesterol): Analyze and measure HDL, LDL, and
_____ triglycerides.

Once the above is completed, answer the following questions:

Yes   No

_____   _____   1. Is your total cholesterol no more than $4.5 \times$ HDL cholesterol?

_____   _____   2. Is your cholesterol-to-HDL ratio at least five to one?

_____   _____   3. Is your HDL reading above 35?

_____   _____   4. Is your LDL cholesterol less than 160?

If the answers to these questions are yes, your lipid profile is good. Regardless of how your lipid profile turned out, list the important changes you can make to lower your total cholesterol and increase your HDL cholesterol over the next twelve months.

1. _____

2. _____

3. _____

4. _____

5. _____

Source: From *Physical Fitness & Wellness, 2nd Edition,* by Greenberg, Dintiman & Oakes, Allyn and Bacon Publishers.

Name _____ Section_____ Date_____

NOTEBOOK ACTIVITY

Is Osteoporosis in Your Future?
Risk Factors You CANNOT Control:
1. Are you female?
2. Do you have a family history of osteoporosis?
3. Are your ancestors from the British Isles, northern Europe, China, or Japan?
4. Are you very fair-skinned?
5. Are you small-boned?
6. Are you over age 35?
7. Have you had your ovaries removed, or did you have an early menopause?
8. Are you allergic to milk and milk products?
9. Have you never been pregnant?
10. Do you have cancer or kidney disease?
11. Do you have to take chemotherapy, steroids, anticonvulsants, or anticoagulants?

Risk Factors You CAN Control:
12. Do you smoke?
13. Do you drink alcohol?
14. Do you avoid milk and cheese in your diet?
15. Do you get very little exercise?
16. Do you drink a lot of soft drinks?
17. Is your diet high in protein?
18. Do you consume a lot of caffeine (five or more cups of coffee per day or equivalent)?
19. Are you amenorrheic (without a monthly period)?
20. Do you get less than 1,000 mg of calcium a day?
21. Is your body weight very low?
22. Do you go on extreme or crash diets?
23. Do you have a high sodium (salt) intake?

If you answered "yes" to three (3) of the above questions, you are at risk for osteoporosis and may want to ask your doctor to give you a bone density screening test. The more questions you answered "yes" to, the higher your risk of developing osteoporosis in the future.

Many clinical studies suggest that osteoporosis is a preventable disease. As you can see from the quiz, you can do several things right now to help prevent osteoporosis in your future.

Source: Adapted from Marion Laboratories, Inc.

Chapter 5
Nutrition

© 2012, Shutterstock, Inc.

OBJECTIVES

Students will be able to:

- Define the essential nutrients (carbohydrates, fats, proteins, vitamins, and minerals) and describe their roles in daily nutrition.
- Introduce and explain the USDA Food Guide Pyramid.
- Introduce guidelines for food labeling and explain how food labels describe the nutritional values of food.
- Define the four styles of vegetarianism.
- Discuss the roles of organic and functional foods.

"A man's health can be judged by which he takes two at a time—pills or stairs."

—Joan Welsh

Good, sound nutritional choices are necessary for maintaining a healthy lifestyle. Making the effort to obtain the essential nutrients through daily dietary intake is not something in which most Americans are proficient. In general, Americans eat too much salt, sugar, and fat and do not consume the recommended daily allowance (RDA) of vitamins and minerals.

Poor dietary habits, along with being physically inactive, are major factors that result in Americans becoming increasingly overweight and obese. As noted in Chapter 4, being overweight or obese is a major risk factor for chronic health problems such as hypertension, cardiovascular disease, diabetes, and certain types of cancers. With this in mind, the importance of building a knowledge base that will allow an individual to develop sound, life-long nutritional habits and practices becomes clear.

Once an individual has made the effort to gather information that will allow him or her to make good nutritional choices, he or she must then make a concentrated effort to obtain the essential macronutrients and micronutrients through their daily food selections. **Macronutrients** provide energy in the form of calories. Carbohydrates, fats, and proteins make up the sources of macronutrients. **Micronutrients**, which include vitamins and minerals, regulate bodily functions such as metabolism, growth, and cellular development. Together, macronutrients and micronutrients are responsible for the following three tasks that are necessary for the continuance of life:

1. growth, repair, and maintenance of all tissues,
2. regulation of body processes, and
3. providing energy.

Because nutrition information is often filled with scientific terminology and unfamiliar jargon, it is many times misleading or appears to be overly complicated. Several government agencies, such as the U.S. Department of Agriculture (USDA) and the U.S. Department of Health and Human Services (DHHS), have teamed up in an effort to simplify and streamline nutritional information widely available to the general public in an effort to decrease the amount of misinformation on nutrition and increase the prevalence of practical, easy-to-apply, user-friendly information.

Dietary Guidelines for Americans

In 1980 the *Dietary Guidelines for Americans* was first published as a scientifically-based health promotion that attempted to reduce an individual's risk for chronic diseases through diet and increased levels of physical activity. The USDA and the DHHS have updated and republished these *Dietary Guidelines* every five years since their inception in 1980.

The most current version of the *Dietary Guidelines* was published in early 2005 (www.health.gov/dietaryguidelines/dga2005/html/executivesummary.htm). Despite the 2005 report containing more scientific and technical information than it has in the past, it continues to be an excellent source to aid in the building of a nutritious and healthy diet for the general population.

The recommendations stated by the *Dietary Guidelines* are interrelated and depend on each other. Therefore, it is the intent of the *Guidelines* to be used together in planning a healthy diet. However, it is still possible to achieve health benefits if just some of the recommendations are followed.

Dietary Guidelines for Americans (pp. 120–124) from www.health.gov

The following is a list of the key recommendations of the *Dietary Guidelines*.

Balancing Calories to Manage Weight

Key Recommendations

- Prevent and/or reduce overweight and obesity through improved eating and physical activity behaviors.
- Control total calorie intake to manage body weight. For people who are overweight or obese, this will mean consuming fewer calories from foods and beverages.
- Increase physical activity and reduce time spent in sedentary behaviors.
- Maintain appropriate calorie balance during each stage of life—childhood, adolescence, adulthood, pregnancy and breastfeeding, and older age.

Foods and Food Components to Reduce

Key Recommendations

- Reduce daily sodium intake to less than 2,300 milligrams (mg) and further reduce intake to 1,500 mg among persons who are 51 and older and those of any age who are African American or have hypertension, diabetes, or chronic kidney disease. The 1,500 mg recommendation applies to about half of the U.S. population, including children, and the majority of adults.
- Consume less than 10 percent of calories from saturated fatty acids by replacing them with monosaturated and polysaturated fatty acids.
- Consume less than 300 mg per day of dietary cholesterol.
- Keep trans fatty acid consumption as low as possible by limiting foods that contain synthetic sources of trans fats, such as partially hydrogenated oils, and by limiting other solid fats.
- Reduce the intake of calories from solid fats and added sugars.
- Limit the consumption of foods that contain refined grains, especially refined grain foods that contain solid fats, added sugars, and sodium.
- If alcohol is consumed, it should be consumed in moderation—up to one drink per day for women and two drinks per day for men—and only by adults of legal drinking age.[1]

Foods and Nutrients to Increase

Key Recommendations

Individuals should meet the following recommendations as part of a healthy eating pattern while staying within their calorie needs.

- Increase vegetable and fruit intake.
- Eat a variety of vegetables, especially dark green and red and orange vegetables and beans and peas.
- Consume at least half of all grains as whole grains. Increase whole-grain intake by replacing refined grains with whole grains.
- Increase intake of fat-free or low-fat milk and milk products, such as milk, yogurt, cheese, or fortified soy beverages.[2]

[1]See Chapter 3, Foods and Food Components to rEduce, for additional recommendations on alcohol consumption and specific population groups. There are many circumstances when people should not drink alcohol.

[2]Fortified soy beverages have been marketed as "soymilk," a product name consumers could see in supermarkets and consumer materials. However, FDA's regulations do not contain provisions for the use of the term soymilk. Therefore, in this document, the term "fortified soy beverage" includes products that may be marketed as soymilk.

- Choose a variety of protein foods, which include seafood, lean meat and poultry, eggs, beans and peas, soy products, and unsalted nuts and seeds.
- Increase the amount and variety of seafood consumed by choosing seafood in place of some meat and poultry.
- Replace protein foods that are higher in solid fats with choices that are lower in solid fats and calories and/or are sources of oils.
- Use oils to replace solid fats where possible.
- Choose foods that provide more potassium, dietary fiber, calcium, and vitamin D, which are nutrients of concern in American diets. These foods include vegetables, fruits, whole grains, and milk and milk products.

Recommendations for specific population groups

Women capable of becoming pregnant[7]

- Choose foods that supply heme iron, which is more readily absorbed by the body, additional iron sources, and enhancers of iron absorption such as vitamin C-rich foods.
- Consume 400 micrograms (mcg) per day of synthetic folic acid (from fortified foods and/or supplements) in addition to food forms of folate from a varied diet.[8]

Women who are pregnant or breastfeeding[7]

- Consume 8 to 12 ounces of seafood per week from a variety of seafood types.
- Due to their high methyl mercury content, limit white (albacore) tuna to 6 ounces per week and do not eat the following four types of fish: tilefish, shark, swordfish, and king mackerel.
- * If pregnant, take an iron supplement, as recommended by obstetrician or other health care provider.

Individuals ages 50 years and older

- Consume foods fortified with vitamin B_{12}, such as fortified cereals, or dietary supplements.

Building Healthy Eating Patterns
Key Recommendations

- Select an eating pattern that meets nutrient needs over time at an appropriate calorie level.
- Account for all foods and beverages consumed and assess how they fit within a total healthy eating pattern.
- Follow food safety recommendations when preparing and eating foods to reduce the risk of food borne illnesses.

Essential Nutrients

It is necessary for an individual to ingest more than forty different nutrients in order to maintain good health. Because no single food source contains all of these nutrients, variety in one's diet is essential. Eating a wide variety of foods will help ensure adequate intake of carbohydrates, fats, proteins, vitamins, and minerals.

---

[7]Incudes adolescent girls.

[8]"Folic acid" is the synthetic form of the nutrient; whereas, "folate" is the form found naturally in foods.

Carbohydrates

Carbohydrates should be the body's main source of fuel. Between 55 and 60 percent of an individual's diet should be composed of carbohydrates. Of this 55 to 60 percent, 45 to 50 percent of total daily caloric intake should be from complex carbohydrates, leaving simple carbohydrates to account for less than 10 percent of the daily carbohydrate intake.

Complex carbohydrates are relatively low in calories (4 calories per gram), nutritionally dense, and are a rich source of vitamins, minerals, and water. Complex carbohydrates provide the body with a steady source of energy for hours. The best sources of complex carbohydrates are breads, cereals, pastas, and grains.

Dietary fiber, also known as roughage or bulk, is a type of complex carbohydrate that is present mainly in leaves, roots, skins, and seeds and is the part of a plant that is not digested in the small intestine. Dietary fiber helps decrease the risk of cardiovascular disease and cancer, and may lower an individual's risk of coronary heart disease. Table 5.1 lists good sources of dietary fiber.

Dietary fiber is either soluble or insoluble. **Soluble fiber** dissolves in water. It helps the body excrete fats and has been shown to reduce levels of blood cholesterol and blood sugar, as well as helping to control diabetes. Water-soluble fiber travels through the digestive tract in gel-like form, pacing the absorption of cholesterol, which helps prevent dramatic shifts in blood sugar levels. Soluble fiber is found primarily in oats, fruits, barley, and legumes.

TABLE 5.1 ◆ Good Sources of Dietary Fiber

Fruits	Grams	Grains	Grams
1 medium apple	4–5	1 bagel	1
1 banana	3	1 whole-grain slice of bread	1–3
1 cup blueberries	5	4 graham crackers	3
10 dates	7	1 bran muffin	2
1 orange	3	hot dog/hamburger bun	1
1 pear	5	1 cup cooked oatmeal	7–9
1 cup strawberries	3	1/2 cup Grape Nuts cereal	3.5
1 watermelon slice	2–3	1 cup Nature Valley granola	7.5
Vegetables	**Grams**	3/4 cup Shredded Wheat cereal	4
		1 cup cooked macaroni	1
1 artichoke	4	1 cup cooked rice	2.5–4
1 raw carrot	2	1 cup cooked spaghetti	1–2
1/2 cup cream style corn	6	**Other**	**Grams**
1 cup chopped lettuce	1		
1/2 cup green peas	6	1 cup almonds	15
1 cup cooked spinach	6	1 cup cashews	8
1 cup cooked squash	5–6	1 cup shredded coconut	11
1 tomato	2	1 tbsp peanut butter	1
Legumes	**Grams**		
1 cup cooked black beans	15		
1 cup cooked green beans	3		
1 cup pork and beans	18		
1 cup cooked blackeyed peas	11		
1 cup kidney beans	20		
1 cup cooked navy beans	16		
1 cup cooked pinto beans	19		

Insoluble fiber does not dissolve easily in water; therefore, it cannot be digested by the body. Insoluble fiber causes softer, bulkier stool that increases peristalsis. This, in turn, reduces the risk of colon cancer by allowing food residues to pass through the intestinal tract more quickly, limiting the exposure and absorption time of toxic substances within the waste materials. Primary sources of insoluble fiber include wheat, cereals, vegetables, and the skins of fruits.

The recommended daily intake of fiber is 25–30 g per day. Health disorders associated with low fiber intake include constipation, diverticulitis, hemorrhoids, gall bladder disease, and obesity. Problems associated with ingesting too much fiber include losses of calcium, phosphorous, iron, and disturbances of the gastrointestinal system.

Simple carbohydrates are sugars that have little nutritive value beyond their energy content. Sugars that are found naturally in milk, fruit, honey, and some vegetables are examples of simple carbohydrates. Foods high in simple sugars are sometimes dismissed as "empty calories." Examples of these foods include candy, cakes, jellies, and sodas.

Fats

Fats are the body's primary source of energy, and supply the body with 9 calories of energy per gram ingested. While many Americans consume too many of their daily calories from fats (37 to 40 percent), dietary fat is not necessarily a "bad" component of an individual's diet at moderate levels of consumption. At moderate amounts, between 25 and 30 percent of daily calories, fat is crucial to good nutrition.

Fat has many essential functions: providing the body with stored energy, insulating the body to preserve body heat, contributing to cellular structure, and protecting vital organs by absorbing shock. Fat not only adds flavor and texture to foods and helps satisfy an individual's appetite because it is digested more slowly, it also supplies the body with essential fatty acids and transports fat-soluble vitamins A, E, D, and K. Fat is also necessary for normal growth and healthy skin, and is essential in the synthesis of certain hormones.

There are different types of dietary fat. **Saturated fats** are found primarily in animal products such as meats, lard, cream, butter, cheese, and whole milk. However, coconut and palm oils are two plant sources of saturated fat. A defining characteristic of saturated fats is that they typically do not melt at room temperature (an exception being the above mentioned oils that are "almost solid" at room temperature). Saturated fats increase low-density lipoproteins (LDL) or "bad cholesterol" levels and in turn increase an individuals risk for heart disease and colorectal cancer.

Trans fat is different from other types of fat in that it typically does not occur naturally in plant or animal products. While a small amount of trans fat is found naturally, the majority of trans fat is formed when liquid oils are made into solid fats (i.e., shortening and some margarines). Trans fat is made during hydrogenation—when hydrogen is added to vegetable oil. This process is used to increase the shelf life of foods and to help foods maintain their original flavor. Many fried foods and "store bought" sweets and treats have high amounts of this type of fat. While most individuals consume four to five times more saturated fat than trans fat, it is important to be aware of the amount of trans fat in one's diet because it raises LDL, "bad," cholesterol and increases the risk of coronary heart disease. Starting January 1, 2006, the Food and Drug Administration (FDA) requires all foods to list the amount of trans fat contained in the product on the Nutrition Facts panel. The exception to this new requirement is that if the total fat in a food is less than 0.5 g per serving and no claims are made about fat, fatty acid, or cholesterol content, trans fat does not have to be listed.

Unsaturated fats are derived primarily from plant products such as vegetable oils, avocados, and most nuts, and do not raise the body's blood cho-

TABLE 5.2 ◆ What Is Your Upper Limit on Fat for the Calories You Consume?

Total Calories per Day	Saturated Fat in Grams	Total Fat in Grams
1,600	18 or less	53
2,000*	20 or less	65
2,200	24 or less	73
2,500*	25 or less	80
2,800	31 or less	93

*Percent Daily Values on Nutrition Facts Labels are based on a 2,000 calorie diet. Values for 2,000 and 2,500 calories are rounded to the nearest 5 grams to be consistent with the Nutrition Facts Label.

lesterol. Unsaturated fats include both monounsaturated and polyunsaturated fats. **Monounsaturated fats** are found in foods such as olives, peanuts, canola oil, peanut oil, and olive oil. **Polyunsaturated fats** are found in margarine, pecans, corn oil, cottonseed oil, sunflower oil, and soybean oil (see Table 5.3).

Fats become counterproductive to good health when they are consumed in excess. Too much fat in many Americans' diets is the reason Americans lead the world in heart disease. Excess fat intake elevates blood cholesterol levels and leads to atherosclerosis. Diets with excess fat have attributed to 30 to 40 percent of all cancers in men and 60 percent of all cancers in women, and have also been linked to cancer of the breast, colon, and prostate more frequently than any other dietary factor.

By following the guidelines listed in Table 5.2 of this chapter, the level of saturated fat and trans fat consumed each day can be limited to 10 percent of that day's total calories.

Protein

Even though **proteins** should make up only 12–15 percent of total calories ingested, they are the essential "building blocks" of the body. Proteins are needed for the growth, maintenance, and repair of all body tissues, that is, muscles, blood, bones, internal organs, skin, hair, and nails. Proteins also help maintain the normal balance of body fluids and are needed to make enzymes, hormones, and antibodies that fight infection.

Proteins are made up of approximately twenty amino acids. An individual's body uses all twenty of these amino acids in the formation of different proteins. Eleven of the twenty are **non-essential amino acids**—they are manufactured in the body if food proteins in a person's diet provide enough nitrogen. Nine of the twenty are **essential amino acids**—the body cannot

TABLE 5.3 ◆ Composition of Oils (%)

Type	Sat	Poly	Mono
safflower	9	75	16
sunflower	10	66	24
corn	13	59	28
soybean	14	58	28
sesame	14	42	44
peanut	17	32	51
palm	49	9	42
olive	14	8	78
canola	7	35	58

TABLE 5.4 ◆ Percentage of Fat Calories in Foods

Type of Food	Less than 15% of Calories from Fat	15%–30% of Calories from Fat	30%–50% of Calories from Fat	More than 50% of Calories from Fat
Fruits and Vegetables	Fruits, plain vegetables, juices, pickles, sauerkraut		French fries, hash browns	Avocados, coconuts, olives
Bread and Cereals	Grains and flours, most breads, most cereals, corn tortillas, pitas, matzoh, bagels, noodles, and pasta	Corn bread, flour tortillas, oatmeal, soft rolls and buns, wheat germ	Breakfast bars, biscuits and muffins, granola, pancakes and waffles, donuts, taco shells, pastries, croissants	
Dairy Products	Nonfat milk, dry curd cottage cheese, nonfat cottage cheese, nonfat yogurt	Buttermilk, low-fat yogurt, 1% milk, low-fat cottage cheese	Whole milk, 2% milk, creamed cottage cheese	Butter, cream, sour cream, half & half, most cheese, (including part-skim and lite cheeses)
Meats		Beef round; veal loin, round, and shoulder; pork tenderloin	Beef and veal, lamb, fresh and picnic hams	All ground beef, spareribs, cold cuts, beef, hot dogs, pastrami
Poultry	Egg whites	Chicken and turkey (light meat without skin)	Chicken and turkey (light meat with skin, dark meat without skin), duck and goose (without skin)	Chicken/turkey (dark meat with skin), chicken/turkey bologna and hot dogs, egg yolks, whole eggs
Seafood	Clams, cod, crab, crawfish, flounder, haddock, lobster, perch, sole, scallops, shrimp, tuna (in water)	Bass and sea bass, halibut, mussels, oyster, tuna (fresh)	Anchovies, catfish, salmon, sturgeon, trout, tuna (in oil, drained)	Herring, mackerel, sardines
Beans and Nuts	Dried beans and peas, chestnuts, water chestnuts		Soybeans	Tofu, most nuts and seeds, peanut butter
Fats and Oils	Oil-free and some lite salad dressings			Butter, margarine, all mayonnaise (including reduced-calorie), most salad dressings, all oils
Soups	Bouillons, broths, consomme	Most soups	Cream soups, bean soups, "just add water" noodle soups	Cheddar cheese soups, New England clam chowder
Desserts	Angel food cake, gelatin, some new fat-free cakes	Pudding, tapioca	Most cakes, most pies	
Frozen Desserts	Sherbert, low-fat frozen yogurt, sorbet, fruit ices	Ice milk	Frozen yogurt	All ice cream
Snack foods	Popcorn (air popped), pretzels, rye crackers, rice cakes, fig bars, raisin biscuit cookies, marshmallows, most hard candy, fruit rolls	Lite microwave popcorn, Scandinavian "crisps," plain crackers, caramels, fudge, gingersnaps, graham crackers	Snack crackers, popcorn (popped in oil), cookies, candy bars, granola bars	Most microwave popcorn, corn and potato chips, chocolate, buttery crackers

Source: American Heart Association/USDA.

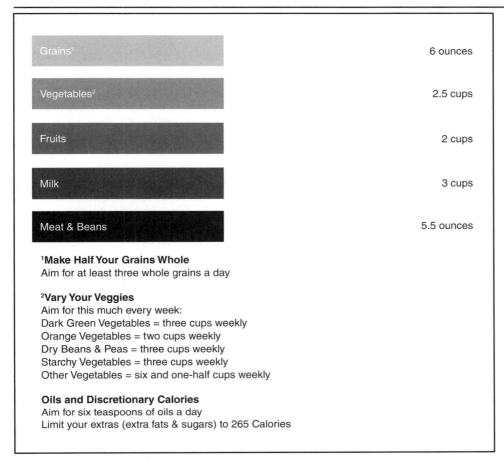

Grains[1]	6 ounces
Vegetables[2]	2.5 cups
Fruits	2 cups
Milk	3 cups
Meat & Beans	5.5 ounces

FIGURE 5.1

Daily Diet Recommendations based on a 2,000-calorie pattern of a 19-Year-Old Female Who Does Less Than Thirty Minutes of Physical Activity a Day.

Go to MyPyramid. gov to get your personalized diet recommendation.

[1]**Make Half Your Grains Whole**
Aim for at least three whole grains a day

[2]**Vary Your Veggies**
Aim for this much every week:
Dark Green Vegetables = three cups weekly
Orange Vegetables = two cups weekly
Dry Beans & Peas = three cups weekly
Starchy Vegetables = three cups weekly
Other Vegetables = six and one-half cups weekly

Oils and Discretionary Calories
Aim for six teaspoons of oils a day
Limit your extras (extra fats & sugars) to 265 Calories

Source: From www.mypyramid.gov

produce these, and thus must be supplied through an individual's diet. All amino acids must be present at the same time for particular protein synthesis to occur.

The suggested RDA of protein for adults is 45 through 65 g per day (intake should not exceed 1.6 g/kg of body weight (1kg. = 2.2 lbs). A few exceptions to this rule should be noted: Overweight individuals need slightly less than the calculated "norm," and women who are pregnant or lactating need slightly more protein per pound of body weight than the calculation indicates.

It is inadvisable to consume more protein than the daily recommended dosage (45–65 g/day), particularly in the form of protein supplements. Excessive protein supplementation can damage the kidneys, increase calcium excretion, negatively affect bone health, inhibit muscle growth, and can be detrimental to endurance performance.

Individuals who are trying to maximize muscular strength, endurance, and growth should take in the recommended 1.5 g of protein per kilogram of body weight, as well as an additional 500 calories of complex carbohydrates. The recommended protein and additional complex carbohydrates will work together to provide the extra nutrients and glucose needed for the increased muscular work load.

Fat-soluble vitamins, such as A, E, D and K, are stored in the body for relatively long periods of time.

Choose Sensibly for Good Health

- Choose a diet that is low in saturated fat and cholesterol and moderate in total fat.
- Choose beverages and foods to moderate your intake of sugars.
- Choose and prepare foods with less salt.
- If you drink alcoholic beverages, do so in moderation.

Fats and Oils

- Choose vegetable oils rather than solid fats (meat and dairy fats, shortening).
- If you need fewer calories, decrease the amount of fat you use in cooking and at the table.

Meat, Poultry, Fish, Shellfish, Eggs, Beans, and Nuts

- Choose two to three servings of fish, shellfish, lean poultry, other lean meats, beans, or nuts daily. Trim fat from meat and take skin off poultry. Choose dry beans, peas, or lentils often.
- Limit your intake of high-fat processed meats such as bacon, sausages, salami, bologna, and other cold cuts. Try the lower fat varieties (check the Nutrition Facts Label).
- Limit your intake of liver and other organ meats. Use egg yolks and whole eggs in moderation. Use egg whites and egg substitutes freely when cooking since they contain no cholesterol and little or no fat.

Dairy Products

- Choose fat-free or low-fat milk, fat-free or low-fat yogurt, and low-fat cheese most often. Try switching from whole to fat-free or low-fat milk. This decreases the saturated fat and calories but keeps all other nutrients the same.

Prepared Foods

- Check the Nutrition Facts Label to see how much saturated fat and cholesterol are in a serving of prepared food. Choose foods lower in saturated fat and cholesterol.

Foods at Restaurants or Other Eating Establishments

- Choose fish or lean meats as suggested. Limit ground meat and fatty processed meats, marbled steaks, and cheese.
- Limit your intake of foods with creamy sauces, and add little or no butter to your food.
- Choose fruits as desserts most often.

Following the tips here will help you keep your intake of saturated fat at less than 10 percent of calories. They will also help you keep your cholesterol intake less than the Daily Value of 300 mg/day listed on the Nutrition Facts Label.

Vitamins

Vitamins are necessary for normal body metabolism, growth, and development. They do not provide the body with energy, but they do allow the energy from consumed carbohydrates, fats, and proteins to be released. Although vitamins are vital to life, they are required in minute amounts. Due primarily to adequate food supply, vitamin deficiencies in Americans are rare. However, there are some situations that may alter an individual's requirements, including pregnancy and smoking. Non-smokers need to consume 60 mg of vitamin C each day; a smoker must ingest 100 mg of vitamin C each day in order to gain the same nutritional benefits. A man or a non-pregnant woman should consume 180–200 mcg of folic acid, while a pregnant woman should consume approximately 400 mcg of folic acid per day.

Vitamins are grouped as either fat soluble or water soluble. **Fat-soluble vitamins** are transported by the body's fat cells and by the liver. They include vitamins A, E, D, and K. Fat-soluble vitamins are not excreted in urine; therefore, they are stored in the body for relatively long periods of time (many months), and can build up to potentially toxic levels if excessive doses are consumed over time.

Water-soluble vitamins include the B vitamins and vitamin C. These vitamins are not stored in the body for a significant amount of time, and the amounts that are consumed and not used relatively quickly by the body are excreted through urine and sweat. For this reason, water-soluble vitamins must be replaced daily. Table 5.5 summarizes the functions of vitamins, lists the best sources for each vitamin, and outlines associated deficiency symptoms.

Minerals

Minerals are inorganic substances that are critical to many enzyme functions in the body. Approximately twenty-five minerals have important roles in bodily functions. Minerals are contained in all cells and are concentrated in hard parts of the body—nails, teeth, and bones—and are crucial to maintaining water balance and the acid-base balance. Minerals are essential components of respiratory pigments, enzymes, and enzyme systems, while also regulating muscular and nervous tissue excitability, blood clotting, and normal heart rhythm. Table 5.6 outlines the major sources and functions of specific minerals, as well as lists deficiency symptoms for those minerals.

Two groups of minerals are necessary in an individual's diet: macrominerals and microminerals. **Macrominerals** are the seven minerals the body needs in relatively large quantities (100 mg or more each day). These seven minerals are: calcium, chloride, magnesium, phosphorus, potassium, sodium, and sulfur. In most cases, these minerals can be acquired by eating a variety of foods each day.

While **microminerals** are essential to healthy living, they are needed in smaller quantities (less than 100 mg per day) than macrominerals. Examples of these minerals include chromium, cobalt, copper, fluoride, iodine, iron, manganese, molybdenum, selenium, and zinc.

Antioxidants

Antioxidants are compounds that aid each cell in the body facing an ongoing barrage of damage resulting from daily oxygen exposure, environmental pollution, chemicals and pesticides, additives in processed foods, stress hormones, and sun radiation. Studies continue to show the ability of antioxidants to suppress cell deterioration and to "slow" the aging process. Realizing the potential power of these substances should encourage Americans to take action by eating at least five servings of a wide variety of fruits and vegetables each day (see Table 5.7 on page 166).

There are many proven health benefits of antioxidants. Vitamin C speeds the healing process, helps prevent infection, and prevents scurvy. Vitamin E helps prevent heart disease by stopping the oxidation of low-density lipoprotein (the harmful form of cholesterol); strengthens the immune system; and

TABLE 5.5 ◆ Facts about Vitamins

Vitamin	Functions	Deficiency Problems
Fat Soluble		
Vitamin A	Allows normal vision in the dark; promotes health and growth of cells and tissues; protects health of skin and tissues in the mouth, stomach, intestines, and respiratory and urogenital tract	Night blindness and other eye problems; dry, scaly skin; reproduction problems; poor growth
Vitamin D	Promotes absorption of calcium and phos phorus to develop and maintain bones and teeth	Osteoporosis and softening of the bones, rickets, defective bone growth
Vitamin E	Antioxidant and may protect against heart disease and some types of cancer	Nervous system problems
Vitamin K	Helps blood clotting	Thin blood that does not clot
Water Soluble		
Vitamin C	Helps produce collagen; maintenance and repair of red blood cells, bones, and other tissues; promotes healing; keeps immune system healthy	Scurvy, excessive bleeding, swollen gums, improper wound healing
Thiamin	Conversion of carbohydrates into energy	Fatigue, weak muscles, and nerve damage
Riboflavin	Energy metabolism, changes tryptophan into niacin	Eye disorders, dry and flaky skin, red tongue
Niacin	Helps the body use sugars and fatty acids, produce energy, enzyme function	Diarrhea, mental disorientation, skin problems
Vitamin B6	Converts tryptophan into niacin and serotonin, helps produce other body chemicals such as insulin, hemoglobin, and antibodies	Depression, nausea, mental convulsions in infants; greasy, flaky skin
Folate	Produces DNA and RNA to make new body cells, works with vitamin B12 to form hemoglobin in red blood cells	Impaired cell division and growth, anemia
Vitamin B12	Works with folate to make red blood cells, vital part of body chemicals	Anemia, fatigue, nerve damage, smooth tongue, very sensitive skin
Biotin	Metabolize fats, protein, and carbohydrates	Heart abnor malities, appetite loss, fatigue, depressions, and dry skin
Pantothenic Acid	Metabolize protein, fat, and carbohydrates	Rare

Effect of Excess Amounts	Dietary Sources
Birth defects, headaches; vomiting, double vision; hair loss; bone abnormalities; liver damage	Liver; fish oil; eggs; milk fortified with vitamin A; red, yellow, and orange fruits and vegetables; many dark green leafy vegetables
Kidney stones or damage, weak muscles and bones, exces sive bleeding	Sunlight on the skin, cheese, eggs, some fish, fortified milk, breakfast cereals, and margarine
May interfere with vitamin K action and en hance the effect of some anticoagulant drugs	Vegetable oils and margarine, salad dressing and other foods made from vegetable oils, nuts, seeds, wheat germ, leafy green vegetables
None observed	Green leafy vegeta bles, smaller amounts widespread in other foods
Diarrhea, gastrointestinal discomfort	Citrus fruits, berries, melons, peppers, dark leafy green vegetables, tomatoes, potatoes
None reported	Whole-grain, enriched grain products, pork, liver, and other organ meats
None reported	Milk and other dairy products; enriched bread, cereal, and other grain products; eggs; meat; green leafy vegetables; nuts; liver; kidney; and heart
Flushed skin, liver damage, stomach ulcers and high blood sugar	Poultry, fish, beef, peanut butter, and legumes
Nerve damage	Chicken, fish, pork, liver, kidney, whole grains, nuts, and legumes
Medication in terference, masking of vitamin B12 deficiencies	Leafy vegetables, orange juice and some fruits, legumes, liver, yeast breads, wheat germ, and some fortified cereals
None reported	Animal products and some fortified foods
None reported	Eggs, liver, yeast breads, and cereal
Diarrhea and water retention	Meat, poultry, fish, whole-grain cereals, and legumes; smaller amounts in milk, vegetables, and fruits

TABLE 5.6 ♦ Facts about Selected Minerals

Mineral	Functions	Deficiency Problems
Calcium	Helps build strong bones and teeth, control of muscle contractions and nerve function, supports blood clotting	Stunted growth in children, bone mineral loss in adults
Fluoride	Formation and maintenance of bones and teeth	Higher occurrence of tooth decay
Iron	Helps carry oxygen to body tissues	Anemia, weakness impaired immune function, cold hands and feet, gastrointestinal distress
Iodine	Component of thyroid hormones that help regulate growth, development, and metabolic rate	Enlarged thyroid, birth defect
Magnesium	Facilitates many cell processes	Neurological disorders, impaired immune function, kidney disorders nausea, weight loss
Phosphorus	Works with calcium to build and maintain bones and teeth, helps convert food to energy	Bone loss, kidney disorders
Potassium	Vital for muscle contractions and nerve transmission, important for heart and kidney function, helps regulate fluid balance and blood pressure	Muscular weakness, nausea, drowsiness, paralysis, confusion, disruption of cardiac rhythm
Sodium	Maintains fluid and electrolyte balance, supports muscle contraction and nerve impulse transmissions	Muscle weakness, loss of appetite, nausea, vomiting
Zinc	Involved in production of genetic material and proteins, ability to taste, wound healing, sperm production, normal fetus development	Night blindness, loss of appetite, skin rash, impaired immune function, impaired taste, poor wound healing

TABLE 5.7 ♦ Antioxidants and Their Primary Food Sources

Vitamin A	Fortified milk; egg yolk; cheese; liver; butter; fish oil; dark green, yellow, and orange vegetables and fruits
Vitamin C	Papaya, cantaloupe, melons, citrus fruits, grapefruit, strawberries, raspberries, kiwi, cauliflower, tomatoes, dark green vegetables, green and red peppers, asparagus, broccoli, cabbage, collard greens, orange juice, and tomato juice
Vitamin E	Vegetable oils, nuts and seeds, dried beans, egg yolk, green leafy vegetables, sweet potatoes, wheat germ, 100 percent whole wheat bread, 100 percent whole grain cereal, oatmeal, mayonnaise
Carotenoids	Sweet potatoes, carrots, squash, tomatoes, asparagus, broccoli, spinach, romaine lettuce, mango, cantaloupe, pumpkin, apricots, peaches, papaya
Flavenoids	Purple grapes, wine, apples, berries, peas, beets, onions, garlic, green tea
Selenium	Lean meat, seafood, kidney, liver, dairy products, 100 percent whole grain cereal, 100 percent whole wheat bread

Effect of Excess Amounts	Dietary Sources
Muscle and abdominal pain, calcium kidney stones	Milk and milk products, tofu, green leafy vegetables, fortified orange juice, and bread
Increased bone density, mottling of teeth, impaired kidney function	Fluoridated drinking water, tea, seafood
Liver disease, arrhythmias, joint pain	Red meat, seafood, dried fruit, legumes, fortified cereals, green vegetables
Depression of thyroid activity, sometimes hyperthyroidism	Salt, seafood, bread, milk, cheese
Nausea, vomiting, nervous system depression, coma, death in people with impaired kidney function	Widespread in foods
Lowers blood calcium	Dairy products, egg yolks, meat, poultry, fish, legumes, soft drinks
Slower heart beat, kidney failure	Milk and yogurt, many fruits and vegetables (especially oranges, bananas, and potatoes)
Edema, hypertension	Salt, soy sauce, bread, milk, meats
Nausea and vomiting, abdominal pain	Seafood, meats, eggs, whole grains

may play a role in the prevention of Alzheimer's disease, cataracts, and some forms of cancer, providing further proof of the benefits of antioxidants.

Adequate amounts of vitamins, minerals, and antioxidants are crucial to good overall health.

Organic Foods

Organic foods are foods that are grown without the use of pesticides. These chemical-free foods are much more difficult to grow because they are more vulnerable to disease and pests. Thus, they are not "high yield" crops. Due to the fact that they are less common, and harder to grow successfully, they are more expensive. Whether the expense is justified by the improved nutritional quality and overall health benefits is yet to be determined.

Functional Foods

Functional foods are foods that have benefits that go above and beyond basic nutrition. A person's overall health can be greatly affected by the food choices they make. Functional benefits of foods that have been consumed for decades are being discovered and new foods are being developed for their helpful dietary components. Table 5.8 lists examples of functional food components, their sources, and their potential benefits.

The ability to relate and interact with others is important to a person's overall sense of well-being.

TABLE 5.8 ◆ Examples of Functional Components*

Class/Components	Source*	Potential Benefit
Carotenoids		
Beta-carotene	Carrots, pumpkin, sweet potato, cantaloupe	Neutralizes free radicals, which may damage cells; bolsters cellular antioxidant defenses; can be made into vitamin A in the body
Lutein, zeaxanthin	Kale, collards, spinach, corn, eggs, citrus	May contribute to maintenance of healthy vision
Lycopene	Tomatoes and processed tomato products, watermelon, red/pink grapefruit	May contribute to maintenance of prostate health
Dietary (functional and total) Fiber		
Insoluble fiber	Wheat bran, corn bran, fruit skins	May contribute to maintenance of a healthy digestive tract; may reduce the risk of some types of cancer
Beta glucan**	Oat bran, oatmeal, oat flour, barley, rye	May reduce risk of coronary heart disease (CHD)
Soluble fiber**	Psyllium seed husk, peas, beans, apples, citrus frui	May reduce risk of CHD and some types of cance
Whole grains**	Cereal grains, whole wheat bread, oatmeal, brown rice	May reduce risk of CHD and some types of cancer; may contribute to maintenance of healthy blood glucose levels
Fatty Acids		
Monounsaturated fatty acids (MUFAs)**	Tree nuts, olive oil, canola oil	May reduce risk of CHD
Polyunsaturated fatty acids (PUFAs)—omega-3 fatty acids—ALA	Walnuts, flax	May contribute to maintenance of heart health; may contribute to maintenance of mental and visual function
PUFAs—omega-3 fatty acids—DHA/EPA**	Salmon, tuna, marine, and other fish oils	May reduce risk of CHD; may contribute to maintenance of mental and visual function
Conjugated linoleic acid (CLA)	Beef and lamb; some cheese	May contribute to maintenance of desirable body composition and healthy immune function
Flavonoids		
Anthocyanins—cyanidin, delphinidin, malvidin	Berries, cherries, red grapes	Bolsters, cellular antioxidant defenses; may contribute to maintenance of brain function
Flavanols—catechins, epicatechins, epigallocatechin, procyanidins	Tea, cocoa, chocolate, apples, grapes	May contribute to maintenance of heart health
Flavanones—hesperetin, naringenin	Citrus foods	Neutralize free radicals, which may damage cells; bolster cellular antioxidant defenses

TABLE 5.8 ♦ Examples of Functional Components*

Class/Components	Source*	Potential Benefit
Flavonols—quercetin, kaempferol, isorhamnetin, myricetin	Onions, apples, tea, broccoli	Neutralize free radicals, which may damage cells; bolster cellular antioxidant defenses
Proanthocyanidins	Cranberries, cocoa, apples, strawberries, grapes, wine, peanuts, cinnamon	May contribute to maintenance of urinary tract health and heart health
Isothiocyanates		
Sulforaphane	Cauliflower, broccoli, broccoli sprouts, cabbage, kale, horseradish	May enhance detoxification of undesirable compounds; bolsters cellular antioxidant defenses
Minerals		
Calcium**	Sardines, spinach, yogurt, low-fat dairy products, fortified foods and beverages	May reduce the risk of osteoporosis
Magnesium	Spinach, pumpkin seeds, whole-grain breads and cereals, halibut, brazil nuts	May contribute to maintenance of normal muscle and nerve function, healthy immune function, and bone health
Potassium**	Potatoes, low-fat dairy products, whole-grain breads and cereals, citrus juices, beans, bananas	May reduce the risk of high blood pressure and stroke, in combination with a low-sodium diet
Selenium	Fish, red meat, grains, garlic, liver, eggs	Neutralizes free radicals, which may damage cells; may contribute to healthy immune function
Phenolic Acids		
Caffeic acid, ferulic acid	Apples, pears, citrus fruits, some vegetables, coffee	May bolster cellular antioxidant defenses; may contribute to maintenance of healthy vision and heart health
Plant Stanols/Sterols		
Free stanols/sterols**	Corn, soy, wheat, wood oils, fortified foods and beverages	May reduce risk of CHD
Stanol/sterol esters**	Fortified table spreads, stanol ester dietary supplements	May reduce risk of CHD
Polyols		
Sugar alcohols**—xylitol, sorbitol, mannitol, lactitol	Some chewing gums and other food	Applications may reduce risk of dental caries
Prebiotics		
Inulin, fructo-oligosaccharides (FOS), polydextrose	Whole grains, onions, some fruits, garlic, honey, leeks, fortified foods and beverages	May improve gastrointestinal health; may improve calcium absorption
Probiotics		
Yeast, *Lactobacilli*, *Bifidobacteria*, and other specific strains of beneficial bacteria	Certain yogurts and other cultured dairy and non-dairy applications	May improve gastrointestinal health and systemic immunity; benefits are strain-specific

(continued)

TABLE 5.8 ◆ Examples of Functional Components*

Class/Components	Source*	Potential Benefit
Phytoestrogens		
Isoflavones—daidzein, genistein	Soybeans and soy-based foods	May contribute to maintenance of bone health, healthy brain and immune function; for women, may contribute to maintenance of menopausal health
Lignans	Flax, rye, some vegetables	May contribute to maintenance of heart health and healthy immune function
Soy Protein		
Soy protein**	Soybeans and soy-based foods	May reduce risk of CHD
Sulfides/Thiols		
Diallyl sulfide, allyl methyl trisulfide	Garlic, onions, leeks, scallions	May enhance detoxification of undesirable compounds; may contribute to maintenance of heart health and healthy immune function
Dithiolthiones	Cruciferous vegetables	May enhance detoxification of undesirable compounds; may contribute to maintenance of healthy immune function
Vitamins		
A***	Organ meats, milk, eggs, carrots, sweet potato, spinach	May contribute to maintenance of healthy vision, immune function, and bone health; may contribute to cell integrity
B1 (Thiamin)	Lentils, peas, long-grain brown rice, brazil nuts	May contribute to maintenance of mental function; helps regulate metabolism
B2 (Riboflavin)	Lean meats, eggs, green leafy vegetables	Helps support cell growth; helps regulate metabolism
B3 (Niacin)	Dairy products, poultry, fish, nuts, eggs	Helps support cell growth; helps regulate metabolism
B5 (Pantothenic acid)	Organ meats, lobster, soybeans, lentils Helps regulate metabolism and hormone synthesis	Helps regulate metabolism and hormone synthesis
B6 (Pyridoxine)	Beans, nuts, legumes, fish, meat, whole grains	May contribute to maintenance of healthy immune function; helps regulate metabolism
B9 (Folate)**	Beans, legumes, citrus foods, green leafy vegetables, fortified breads and cereals	May reduce a woman's risk of having a child with a brain or spinal cord defect
B12 (Cobalamin)	Eggs, meat, poultry, milk	May contribute to maintenance of mental function; helps regulate metabolism and supports blood cell formation
Biotin	Liver, salmon, dairy, eggs, oysters	Helps regulate metabolism and hormone synthesis

TABLE 5.8 ♦ Examples of Functional Components*

Class/Components	Source*	Potential Benefit
C	Guava, sweet red/green pepper, kiwi, citrus fruit, strawberries	Neutralizes free radicals, which may damage cells; may contribute to maintenance of bone health and immune function
D	Sunlight, fish, fortified milk and cereals	Helps regulate calcium and phosphorus; helps contribute to bone health; may contribute to healthy immune function; helps support cell growth
E	Sunflower seeds, almonds, hazelnuts, turnip greens	Neutralizes free radicals, which may damage cells; may contribute to healthy immune function and maintenance of heart health

*Examples are not an all-inclusive list.

**FDA approved health claim established for component.

***Preformed vitamin A is found in foods that come from animals. Provitamin A carotenoids are found in many darkly colored fruits and vegetables and are a major source of vitamin A for vegetarians.

Source: Reprinted from International Food Information Council Foundation, 2007–2009. Originally printed in the 2007–2009 Foundation Media Guide on Food Safety and Nutrition.

Water

In many cases, **water** is the "forgotten nutrient." Although water does not provide energy to the body in the form of calories, it is a substance that is essential to life. Among other things, water lubricates joints, absorbs shock, regulates body temperature, maintains blood volume, and transports fluids throughout the body, while comprising 60 percent of an individual's body.

While it is clear that adequate hydration is crucial to proper physiological functioning, many people are in a semi-hydrated state most of the time. Whether exercising or not, hydration should be a continuous process. Prolonged periods of dehydration can result in as much as a 10 percent loss of intracellular water concentration and can result in death. Individuals more susceptible to dehydration include: persons who are overweight; deconditioned or unacclimatized to heat; very old and very young; and individuals who do not eat breakfast or drink water.

To ensure proper water balance and prevent dehydration, approximately six to eight eight-ounce glasses of water should be consumed each day an individual is not exercising. When working out, current recommendations for water intake are two to three eight-ounce cups of water before exercising, four to six ounces of cool water every fifteen minutes during the workout, and rehydrating thoroughly after the activity.

© Andrei Mihalcea, 2009, Shutterstock, Inc.

Water lubricates joints, absorbs shock, regulates body temperature, maintains blood volume, transports fluids throughout the body, and comprises 60 percent of your body.

Progressive Effects of Dehydration

Percent loss of body water	Some progressive effects of dehydration
0–1 percent	Thirst
2–5 percent	Dry mouth, flushed skin, fatigue, headache, impaired physical performance
6 percent	Increased body temperature, breathing rate, and pulse rate; dizziness, increased weakness
8 percent	Dizziness, increased weakness, labored breathing with exercise
10 percent	Muscle spasms, swollen tongue, delirium
11 percent	Poor blood circulation, failing kidney function

Source: Adapted from "The American Dietetic Association's Complete Food and utrition Guide" (Minneapolis: Chronimed Publishing, 1996), p. 168.

Visual Cues for 1 Serving of Grains

1 large egg = muffin

© Petr Malyshev, 2012, Shutterstock, Inc.

Handful of rubber bands = ½ cup pasta

© Brent Hofacker, 2012, Shutterstock, Inc.

CD = 1 slice bread, waffle, or pancake

© Novitech, 2012, Shutterstock, Inc.

6 in. plate = 1 tortilla

© Artur Synenko, 2012, Shutterstock, Inc.

The Food Guide Pyramid

The Food Guide Pyramid was originally created in 1992 by the federal government in an attempt to arm more Americans with the knowledge that would allow them to create a healthy, balanced, and tasty diet. Twelve years later, in 2004, the U.S. Department of Agriculture produced an expanded and updated version of that original Food Guide Pyramid (see Figure 5.2). Key to the new pyramid is the acknowledged necessity of balancing what an individual eats with the amount of physical activity in which he or she engages.

To make the pyramid portray the changes deemed necessary by the USDA, to promote optimal health, the pyramid was "flipped" onto its side so that all the food group bands run from the top of the pyramid to its base. The different size of each of the bands indicates how much food should be consumed from each food group. The bands are all wider at the base of the pyramid. This symbolizes the importance of eating, when possible, foods without solid fats and added sugar in each of the six bands or groups within the pyramid.

Grains

The color orange represents grains within the pyramid. When examining options of food choices within this group it is important to not only choose a majority on one's daily calories from grains, but also to remember that it is nutritionally prudent to make half of the grains chosen whole grains. Whole grains are defined by the American Association of Cereal Chemists as "food made from the entire grain seed, usually called the kernel, which consists of the bran, germ, and endosperm (AACC International Board of Directors, 1999) (see Figure 5.3 on page 176). If the kernel has been cracked, crushed, or flaked, it must retain nearly the same relative proportions of bran, germ, and endosperm as the original grain." Examples of easy-to-find whole grains include brown rice, bulgur (cracked wheat), popcorn, whole rye, wild rice, whole oats/oatmeal, whole-grain barley, and whole wheat. Selections of whole-grain products from this group will help an individual maximize their intake of dietary fiber as well as other nutrients. One serving from the grain group equals one slice of bread, half a bagel or one sixteen-inch tortilla.

MyPyramid
STEPS TO A HEALTHIER YOU
MyPyramid.gov

| GRAINS | VEGETABLES | FRUITS | MILK | MEAT & BEANS |

GRAINS	VEGETABLES	FRUITS	MILK	MEAT & BEANS
Make half your grains whole	Vary your veggies	Focus on fruits	Get your calcium-rich foods	Go lean with protein
Eat at least 3 oz. of whole-grain cereals, breads, crackers, rice, or pasta every day 1 oz. is about 1 slice of bread, about 1 cup of breakfast cereal, or ½ cup of cooked rice, cereal, or pasta	Eat more dark-green veggies like broccoli, spinach, and other dark leafy greens Eat more orange vegetables like carrots and sweetpotatoes Eat more dry beans and peas like pinto beans, kidney beans, and lentils	Eat a variety of fruit Choose fresh, frozen, canned, or dried fruit Go easy on fruit juices	Go low-fat or fat-free when you choose milk, yogurt, and other milk products If you don't or can't consume milk, choose lactose-free products or other calcium sources such as fortified foods and beverages	Choose low-fat or lean meats and poultry Bake it, broil it, or grill it Vary your protein routine — choose more fish, beans, peas, nuts, and seeds

For a 2,000-calorie diet, you need the amounts below from each food group. To find the amounts that are right for you, go to MyPyramid.gov.

| Eat 6 oz. every day | Eat 2½ cups every day | Eat 2 cups every day | Get 3 cups every day; for kids aged 2 to 8, it's 2 | Eat 5½ oz. every day |

Find your balance between food and physical activity
- Be sure to stay within your daily calorie needs.
- Be physically active for at least 30 minutes most days of the week.
- About 60 minutes a day of physical activity may be needed to prevent weight gain.
- For sustaining weight loss, at least 60 to 90 minutes a day of physical activity may be required.
- Children and teenagers should be physically active for 60 minutes every day, or most days.

Know the limits on fats, sugars, and salt (sodium)
- Make most of your fat sources from fish, nuts, and vegetable oils.
- Limit solid fats like butter, stick margarine, shortening, and lard, as well as foods that contain these.
- Check the Nutrition Facts label to keep saturated fats, *trans* fats, and sodium low.
- Choose food and beverages low in added sugars. Added sugars contribute calories with few, if any, nutrients.

MyPyramid.gov
STEPS TO A HEALTHIER YOU

U.S. Department of Agriculture
Center for Nutrition Policy and Promotion
April 2005
CNPP-15

USDA

FIGURE 5.2
Source: From www.mypyramid.gov.

How many grain foods are needed daily?

The amount of grains you need to eat depends on your age, sex, and level of physical activity. Recommended daily amounts are listed in the chart. Most Americans consume enough grains, but few are whole grains. At least half of all the grains eaten should be whole grains.

		Daily recommendation*	Daily minimum amount of whole grains
Children	2–3 years old	3 ounce equivalents**	1½ ounce equivalents**
	4–8 years old	5 ounce equivalents**	2½ ounce equivalents**
Girls	9–13 years old	5 ounce equivalents**	3 ounce equivalents**
	14–18 years old	6 ounce equivalents**	3 ounce equivalents**
Boys	9–13 years old	6 ounce equivalents**	3 ounce equivalents**
	14–18 years old	8 ounce equivalents**	4 ounce equivalents**
Women	19–30 years old	6 ounce equivalents**	3 ounce equivalents**
	31–50 years old	6 ounce equivalents**	3 ounce equivalents**
	51+ years old	5 ounce equivalents**	3 ounce equivalents**
Men	19–30 years old	8 ounce equivalents**	4 ounce equivalents**
	31–50 years old	7 ounce equivalents**	3½ ounce equivalents**
	51+ years old	6 ounce equivalents**	3 ounce equivalents**

*These amounts are appropriate for individuals who get less than 30 minutes per day of moderate physical activity, beyond normal daily activities. Those who are more physically active may be able to consume more while staying within calorie needs.

What counts as an ounce equivalent of grains?

In general, 1 slice of bread, 1 cup of ready-to-eat cereal, or ½ cup of cooked rice, cooked pasta, or cooked cereal can be considered as 1 ounce equivalent from the Grains Group.

The chart lists specific amounts that count as 1 ounce equivalent of grains towards your daily recommended intake. In some cases the number of ounce-equivalents for common portions are also shown.

		Amount that counts as 1 ounce equivalent of grains	Common portions and ounce equivalents
Bagels	WG*: whole wheat RG*: plain, egg	1 "mini" bagel	1 large bagel = 4 ounce equivalents
Biscuits	(baking powder/ buttermilk—RG*)	1 small (2" diameter)	1 large (3" diameter) = 2 ounce equivalents
Breads	WG*: 100% Whole wheat RG*: white, wheat, French, sourdough	1 regular slice 1 small slice French 4 snack-size slices rye bread	2 regular slices = 2 ounce equivalents

		Amount that counts as 1 ounce equivalent of grains	Common portions and ounce equivalents
Bulgur	cracked wheat (WG*)	½ cup cooked	
Cornbread	(RG*)	1 small piece (2½" x 1¼" x 1¼")	1 medium piece (2½" x 2½" x 1¼") = 2 ounce equivalents
Crackers	WG*: 100% whole wheat, rye RG*: saltines, snack crackers	5 whole wheat crackers 2 rye crispbreads 7 square or round crackers	
English muffins	WG*: whole wheat RG*: plain, raisin	½ muffin	1 muffin = 2 ounce equivalents
Muffins	WG*: whole wheat RG*: bran, corn, plain	1 small (2½" diameter)	1 large (3½" diameter) = 3 ounce equivalents
Oatmeal	(WG)	½ cup cooked 1 packet instant 1 ounce (1/3 cup) dry (regular or quick)	
Pancakes	WG*: Whole wheat, buckwheat RG*: buttermilk, plain	1 pancake (4½" diameter) 2 small pancakes (3" diameter)	3 pancakes (4½" diameter) = 3 ounce equivalents
Popcorn	(WG*)	3 cups, popped	1 mini microwave bag or 100-calorie bag, popped = 2 ounce equivalents
Ready-to-eat breakfast cereal	WG*: toasted oat, whole wheat flakes RG*: corn flakes, puffed rice	1 cup flakes or rounds 1¼ cup puffed	
Rice	WG*: brown, wild RG*: enriched, white, polished	½ cup cooked 1 ounce dry	1 cup cooked = 2 ounce equivalents
Pasta—spaghetti, macaroni, noodles	WG*: whole wheat RG*: enriched, durum	½ cup cooked 1 ounce dry	1 cup cooked = 2 ounce equivalents
Tortillas	WG*: whole wheat, whole grain corn RG*: Flour, corn	1 small flour tortilla (6" diameter) 1 corn tortilla (6" diameter)	1 large tortilla (12" diameter) = 4 ounce equivalents

*WG = whole grains, RG = refined grains. This is shown when products are available both in whole grain and refined grain forms.

FIGURE 5.3

A Grain of Wheat

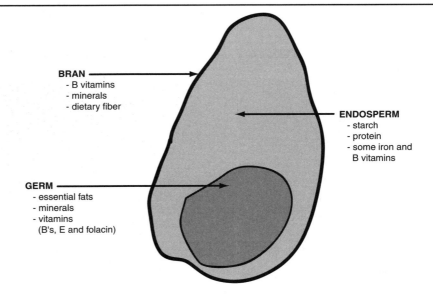

BRAN
- B vitamins
- minerals
- dietary fiber

ENDOSPERM
- starch
- protein
- some iron and
  B vitamins

GERM
- essential fats
- minerals
- vitamins
  (B's, E and folacin)

What Counts as a Whole Grain Serving

- Cheerios – 2/3 cup
- Wheat Chex – 2/3 cup
- Oatmeal (hot, cooked) – 1/2 cup
- Quaker Oatmeal Squares or Toasted Oatmeal Cereal – 1/2 cup
- Grape Nuts – 1/5 cup
- Frosted Mini-Wheats (bite-sized) – 9 biscuits
- 100% whole-grain bread – 1 slice
- 100% whole-grain English muffin – 1 half
- Popcorn (popped) – 2 cups
- Sun Chips or baked tortilla chips – 1 oz. (about 15 chips)
- 100% whole-grain crackers (like Triscuits) – 4 crackers
- Whole-wheat pasta – 1/3 cup cooked
- Brown rice, bulgur, sorghum, or barley – 1/3 cup cooked

Vegetables

Green is the color within the pyramid that stands for vegetables. Vegetables are an excellent source of natural fiber, they are low in fat, and provide the body with vitamins, especially vitamins A and C. While all vegetables are good nutritional choices, to maximize the benefits of eating vegetables, one should vary the type of vegetables eaten. It is also important when choosing vegetables to ingest not only a variety of the brightly colored vegetables such as corn, squash, and peas, but also the green and orange vegetables such as carrots, yams, and broccoli. One serving from the vegetable group equals one cup of raw, lefty greens; half cup of other chopped vegetables; or three-quarter cup of vegetable juice.

tennis ball = 1 serving of vegetable

© Ljupco Smokovski, 2012. Shutterstock, Inc

How many vegetables are needed daily or weekly?

The amount of vegetables you need to eat depends on your age, sex, and level of physical activity. Recommended total daily amounts are shown in the first chart.

Daily recommendation*

Children	2–3 years old	1 cup**
	4–8 years old	1½ cups**
Girls	9–13 years old	2 cups**
	14–18 years old	2½ cups**
Boys	9–13 years old	2½ cups**
	14–18 years old	3 cups**
Women	19–30 years old	2½ cups**
	31–50 years old	2½ cups**
	51+ years old	2 cups**
Men	19–30 years old	3 cups**
	31–50 years old	3 cups**
	51+ years old	2½ cups**

*These amounts are appropriate for individuals who get less than 30 minutes per day of moderate physical activity, beyond normal daily activities. Those who are more physically active may be able to consume more while staying within calorie needs.

What counts as a cup of vegetables?

In general, 1 cup of raw or cooked vegetables or vegetable juice, or 2 cups of raw leafy greens can be considered as 1 cup from the Vegetable Group. The chart lists specific amounts that count as 1 cup of vegetables (in some cases equivalents for ½ cup are also shown) towards your recommended intake:

	Amount that counts as 1 cup of vegetables	Amount that counts as ½ cup of vegetables
Dark Green Vegetables		
Broccoli	1 cup chopped or florets	
	3 spears 5" long raw or cooked	
Greens (collards, mustard greens, turnip greens, kale)	1 cup cooked	
Spinach	1 cup, cooked	
	2 cups raw is equivalent to 1 cup of vegetables	1 cup raw is equivalent to ½ cup of vegetables
Raw leafy greens: Spinach, romaine, watercress, dark green leafy lettuce, endive, escarole	2 cups raw is equivalent to 1 cup of vegetables	1 cup raw is equivalent to ½ cup of vegetables
Red and Orange Vegetables		
Carrots	1 cup, strips, slices, or chopped, raw or cooked	
	2 medium	1 medium carrot
	1 cup baby carrots (about 12)	About 6 baby carrots
Pumpkin	1 cup mashed, cooked	
Red peppers	1 cup chopped, raw, or cooked	1 small pepper
	1 large pepper (3" diameter, 3¾" long)	
Tomatoes	1 large raw whole (3") 1 cup chopped or sliced, raw, canned, or cooked	1 small raw whole (2¼" diameter) 1 medium canned
Tomato juice	1 cup	½ cup
Sweet potato	1 large baked (2¼" or more diameter)	
	1 cup sliced or mashed, cooked	
Winter squash (acorn, butternut, hubbard)	1 cup cubed, cooked	½ acorn squash, baked = ¾ cup

	Amount that counts as 1 cup of vegetables	Amount that counts as ½ cup of vegetables
Beans and Peas		
Dry beans and peas (such as black, garbanzo, kidney, pinto, or soy beans, or black eyed peas or split peas)	1 cup whole or mashed, cooked	
Starchy Vegetables		
Corn, yellow or white	1 cup	
	1 large ear (8" to 9" long)	1 small ear (about 6" long)
Green peas	1 cup	
White potatoes	1 cup diced, mashed 1 medium boiled or baked potato (2½" to 3" diameter)	
	French fried: 20 medium to long strips (2½" to 4" long) (Contains added calories from solid fats.)	
Other Vegetables		
Bean sprouts	1 cup cooked	
Cabbage, green	1 cup, chopped or shredded raw or cooked	
Cauliflower	1 cup pieces or florets raw or cooked	
Celery	1 cup, diced or sliced, raw or cooked	
	2 large stalks (11" to 12" long)	1 large stalk (11" to 12" long)
Cucumbers	1 cup raw, sliced or chopped	
Green or wax beans	1 cup cooked	
Green peppers	1 cup chopped, raw or cooked	
	1 large pepper (3" diameter, 3¾" long)	1 small pepper
Lettuce, iceberg or head	2 cups raw, shredded or chopped = equivalent to 1 cup of vegetables	1 cup raw, shredded or chopped = equivalent to ½ cup of vegetables
Mushrooms	1 cup raw or cooked	
Onions	1 cup chopped, raw or cooked	
Summer squash or zucchini	1 cup cooked, sliced or diced	

Baseball = 1 serving of fruit

© Alex Staroseltsev, 2012, Shutterstock, Inc.

Fruits

Fruits are represented in the pyramid by the color red. Fresh, canned, frozen, or dried fruits are all excellent sources of vitamins and minerals, most notably vitamin C. It is, however, important to watch for heavy, sugary syrups when selecting canned fruits. Fruits canned in lite syrups or the fruit's own natural juice allow an individual to take in the same amount of vitamins and minerals as their heavily syruped counterparts without adding unnecessary and/or unwanted sugar, fat, and calories to their diet. Fruit juices are another important part of many people's diet that should be monitored for "hidden" sugars and calories. When possible, freshly squeezed juices are an ideal alternative. Serving equivalents for the fruit group are: one serving equals one medium apple, banana, or orange; one melon wedge; half cup of chopped berries, or three-quarter cup of fruit juice.

How much fruit is needed daily?

The amount of fruit you need to eat depends on age, sex, and level of physical activity. Recommended daily amounts are shown in the chart.

Recommended amounts are shown in the table below.

		Daily recommendation*
Children	2–3 years old	1 cup**
	4–8 years old	1 to 1½ cups**
Girls	9–13 years old	1½ cups**
	14–18 years old	1½ cups**
Boys	9–13 years old	1½ cups**
	14—18 years old	2 cups**
Women	19–30 years old	2 cups**
	31–50 years old	1½ cups**
	51+ years old	1½ cups**
Men	19–30 years old	2 cups**
	31–50 years old	2 cups**
	51+ years old	2 cups**

*These amounts are appropriate for individuals who get less than 30 minutes per day of moderate physical activity, beyond normal daily activities. Those who are more physically active may be able to consume more while staying within calorie needs.

What counts as a cup of fruit?

In general, 1 cup of fruit or 100% fruit juice, or ½ cup of dried fruit can be considered as 1 cup from the Fruit Group. The following specific amounts count as 1 cup of fruit (in some cases equivalents for ½ cup are also shown) towards your daily recommended intake:

	Amount that counts as 1 cup of fruit	**Amount that counts as ½ cup of fruit**
Apple	½ large (3.25" diameter)	
	1 small (2.5" diameter)	
	1 cup sliced or chopped, raw or cooked	½ cup sliced or chopped, raw or cooked
Applesauce	1 cup	1 snack container (4 oz)
Banana	1 cup sliced	1 small (less than 6" long)
	1 large (8" to 9" long)	
Cantaloupe	1 cup diced or melon balls	1 medium wedge (1/8 of a med. melon)
Grapes	1 cup whole or cut-up	
	32 seedless grapes	16 seedless grapes
Grapefruit	1 medium (4" diameter)	½ medium (4" diameter)
	1 cup sections	
Mixed fruit (fruit cocktail)	1 cup diced or sliced, raw or canned, drained	1 snack container (4 oz) drained = 3/8 cup
Orange	1 large (3-1/16" diameter)	1 small (2-3/8" diameter)
	1 cup sections	
Orange, mandarin	1 cup canned, drained	
Peach	1 large (2 ¾" diameter)	1 small (2" diameter)
	1 cup sliced or diced, raw, cooked, or canned, drained	1 snack container (4 oz) drained = 3/8 cup
	2 halves, canned	
Pear	1 medium pear (2.5 per lb)	1 snack container (4 oz) drained = 3/8 cup
	1 cup sliced or diced, raw, cooked, or canned, drained	
Pineapple	1 cup chunks, sliced or crushed, raw, cooked or canned, drained	1 snack container (4 oz) drained = 3/8 cup
Plum	1 cup sliced raw or cooked	
	3 medium or 2 large plums	1 large plum
Strawberries	About 8 large berries	
	1 cup whole, halved, or sliced, fresh or frozen	½ cup whole, halved, or sliced
Watermelon	1 small wedge (1" thick)	6 melon balls
	1 cup diced or balls	

	Amount that counts as 1 cup of fruit	Amount that counts as ½ cup of fruit
Dried fruit (raisins, prunes, apricots, etc.)	½ cup dried fruit is equivalent to 1 cup fruit: ½ cup raisins ½ cup prunes ½ cup dried apricots	¼ cup dried fruit is equivalent to ½ cup fruit 1 small box raisins (1.5 oz)
100% fruit juice (orange, apple, grape, grapefruit, etc.)	1 cup	½ cup

Milk/Dairy

6 dice = 1½ oz. cheese
= 1 serving of dairy

© Dmitrydesign, 2012. Shutterstock, Inc

Milk and other calcium-rich foods such as yogurt and cheese now make up the blue portion of the Food Guide Pyramid. Milk products are not only the body's best source of calcium, they are also an excellent source of protein and vitamin B12. To maximize the benefits of calcium-rich foods and minimize the calories, cholesterol, fat, and saturated fat per selection, low-fat and skim alternatives should be chosen. One serving from the milk group equals one cup of milk or yogurt, or one and a half ounces of cheese.

How Much Food from the Dairy Group Is Needed Daily?

The amount of food from the Dairy Group you need to eat depends on age. Recommended daily amounts are shown in the chart below. See what counts as a cup in the Dairy Group.

	Daily recommendation	
Children	2–3 years old	2 cups
	4–8 years old	2½ cups
Girls	9–13 years old	3 cups
	14–18 years old	3 cups
Boys	9–13 years old	3 cups
	14–18 years old	3 cups
Women	19–30 years old	3 cups
	31–50 years old	3 cups
	51+ years old	3 cups
Men	19–30 years old	3 cups
	31–50 years old	3 cups
	51+ years old	3 cups

What counts as a cup in the Dairy Group?

In general, 1 cup of milk or yogurt, 1 ½ ounces of natural cheese, or 2 ounces of processed cheese can be considered as 1 cup from the Dairy Group. Additionally, 1 cup of soymilk counts as 1 cup in the Dairy Group.

The chart below lists specific amounts that count as 1 cup in the Dairy Group towards your daily recommended intake.

	Amount that counts as 1 cup in the Dairy Group	Common portions and cup equivalents
Milk *[choose fat-free or low-fat milk]*	1 cup milk or calcium-fortified soymilk (soy beverage) 1 half-pint container milk or soymilk ½ cup evaporated milk	
Yogurt *[choose fat-free or low-fat yogurt]*	1 regular container (8 fluid ounces) 1 cup yogurt	1 small container (6 ounces) = ¾ cup 1 snack size container (4 ounces) = ½ cup
Cheese *[choose reduced-fat or low-fat yogurt]*	1½ ounces hard cheese (cheddar, mozzarella, Swiss, Parmesan) 1/3 cup shredded cheese 2 ounces processed cheese (American) ½ cup ricotta cheese 2 cups cottage cheese	1 slice of hard cheese is equivalent to ½ cup milk 1 slice of processed cheese is equivalent to 1/3 cup milk ½ cup cottage cheese is equivalent to ¼ cup milk
Milk-based desserts *[choose fat-free or low-fat types]*	1 cup pudding made with milk 1 cup frozen yogurt 1½ cups ice cream	1 scoop ice cream is equivalent to 1/3 cup milk
Soymilk	1 cup calcium-fortified soymilk	

Visual Cues for 1 Serving of Protein

Deck of cards = 3 oz. meat

Golf ball = 2 Tb. peanut butter

Checkbook = 3 oz. thin fish

Protein/Meats and Beans

Purple is the designated color for meats and beans within the pyramid. Meats and beans are excellent sources of protein, iron, zinc, and B vitamins. It is important to be aware of the fact that many food selections within this food group can be relatively high in fat content, especially saturated fats. Lower fat alternatives within this group that remain a rich source of vitamins and minerals include beans, fish, poultry, and lean cuts of beef. Serving equivalents for the meat and beans group are as follows: one serving equals two to three ounces of cooked lean beef, poultry, or fish; one egg; half cup of cooked beans; or two tablespoons of seeds or nuts.

How much food from the Protein Foods Group is needed daily?

The amount of food from the Protein Foods Group you need to eat depends on age, sex, and level of physical activity. Most Americans eat enough food from this group, but need to make leaner and more varied selections of these foods. Recommended daily amounts are shown in the chart.

		Daily recommendation*
Children	2–3 years old	2 ounce equivalents**
	4–8 years old	4 ounce equivalents**
Girls	9–13 years old	5 ounce equivalents**
	14–18 years old	5 ounce equivalents**
Boys	9–13 years old	5 ounce equivalents**
	14–18 years old	6 ½ ounce equivalents**
Women	19–30 years old	5 ½ ounce equivalents**
	31–50 years old	5 ounce equivalents**
	51+ years old	5 ounce equivalents**
Men	19–30 years old	6½ ounce equivalents**
	31–50 years old	6 ounce equivalents**
	51+ years old	5½ ounce equivalents**

*These amounts are appropriate for individuals who get less than 30 minutes per day of moderate physical activity, beyond normal daily activities. Those who are more physically active may be able to consume more while staying within calorie needs.

What counts as an ounce equivalent in the Protein Foods Group?

In general, 1 ounce of meat, poultry or fish, ¼ cup cooked beans, 1 egg, 1 tablespoon of peanut butter, or ½ ounce of nuts or seeds can be considered as 1 ounce equivalent from the Protein Foods Group.

The chart lists specific amounts that count as 1 ounce equivalent in the Protein Foods Group towards your daily recommended intake:

	Amount that counts as 1 ounce equivalent in the Protein Foods Group	Common portions and ounce equivalents
Meats	1 ounce cooked lean beef	1 small steak (eye of round, filet) = 3½ to 4 ounce equivalents
	1 ounce cooked lean pork or ham	1 small lean hamburger = 2 to 3 ounce equivalents
Poultry	1 ounce cooked chicken or turkey, without skin	1 small chicken breast half = 3 ounce equivalents
	1 sandwich slice of turkey (4½ x 2½ x 1/8")	½ Cornish game hen = 4 ounce equivalents
Seafood	1 ounce cooked fish or shell fish	1 can of tuna, drained = 3 to 4 ounce equivalents
		1 salmon steak = 4 to 6 ounce equivalents
		1 small trout = 3 ounce equivalents
Eggs	1 egg	3 egg whites = 2 ounce equivalents 3 egg yolks = 1 ounce equivalent
Nuts and seeds	½ ounce of nuts (12 almonds, 24 pistachios, 7 walnut halves)	1 ounce of nuts or seeds = 2 ounce equivalents
	½ ounce of seeds (pumpkin, sunflower or squash seeds, hulled, roasted)	
	1 Tablespoon of peanut butter or almond butter	
Beans and peas	¼ cup of cooked beans (such as black, kidney, pinto, or white beans) ¼ cup of cooked peas (such as chickpeas, cowpeas, lentils, or split peas) ¼ cup of baked beans, refried beans	1 cup split pea soup = 2 ounce equivalents 1 cup lentil soup = 2 ounce equivalents 1 cup bean soup = 2 ounce equivalents
	¼ cup (about 2 ounces) of tofu 1 oz. tempeh, cooked ¼ cup roasted soybeans 1 falafel patty (2¼", 4 oz) 2 Tablespoons hummus	1 soy or bean burger patty = 2 ounce equivalents

1/2 business card =
1 brownie = 1 serving

© Petr Vaclavek, 2012, Shutterstock, Inc.

Oils

Oils are depicted by the yellow band within the Food Guide Pyramid. As in all other areas of the pyramid, it is important to choose your source(s) of oils carefully. As a general rule, oils such as olive oil, peanut oil, and canola oil contain unsaturated fats. These oils do not raise an individual's blood cholesterol and are therefore a healthier option.

How much is my allowance for oils?

Some Americans consume enough oil in the foods they eat, such as:

- nuts
- fish
- cooking oil
- salad dressings

Others could easily consume the recommended allowance by substituting oils for some solid fats they eat. A person's allowance for oils depends on age, sex, and level of physical activity. Daily allowances are shown in the chart.

		Daily allowance*
Children	2–3 years old	3 teaspoons
	4–8 years old	4 teaspoons
Girls	9–13 years old	5 teaspoons
	14–18 years old	5 teaspoons
Boys	9–13 years old	5 teaspoons
	14–18 years old	6 teaspoons
Women	19–30 years old	6 teaspoons
	31–50 years old	5 teaspoons
	51+ years old	5 teaspoons
Men	19–30 years old	7 teaspoons
	31–50 years old	6 teaspoons
	51+ years old	6 teaspoons

*These amounts are appropriate for individuals who get less than 30 minutes per day of moderate physical activity, beyond normal daily activities. Those who are more physically active may be able to consume more while staying within calorie needs.

How do I count the oils I eat?

The chart gives a quick guide to the amount of oils in some common foods:

	Amount of food	Amount of oil	Calories from oil	Total calories
		Teaspoons/ grams	Approximate calories	Approximate calories
Oils:				
Vegetable oils (such as canola, corn, cottonseed, olive, peanut, safflower, soybean, and sunflower)	1 Tbsp	3 tsp/14 g	120	120
Foods ric in oils:				
Margarine, soft (trans fat free)	1 Tbsp	2½ tsp/11 g	100	100
Mayonnaise	1 Tbsp	2½ tsp/11 g	100	100
Mayonnaise-type salad dressing	1 Tbsp	1 tsp/5 g	45	55
Italian dressing	2 Tbsp	2 tsp/8 g	75	85
Thousand Island dressing	2 Tbsp	2½ tsp/11 g	100	120
Olives*, ripe, canned	4 large	½ tsp/ 2 g	15	20
Avocado*	½ med	3 tsp/15 g	130	160
Peanut butter*	2 T	4 tsp/ 16 g	140	190
Peanuts, dry roasted*	1 oz	3 tsp/14 g	120	165
Mixed nuts, dry roasted*	1 oz	3 tsp/15 g	130	170
Cashews, dry roasted*	1 oz	3 tsp/13 g	115	165
Almonds, dry roasted*	1 oz	3 tsp/15 g	130	170
Hazelnuts*	1 oz	4 tsp/18 g	160	185
Sunflower seeds*	1 oz	3 tsp/14 g	120	165

*Avocados and olives are part of the Vegetable Group; nuts and seeds are part of the Protein Foods Group. These foods are also high in oils. Soft margarine, mayonnaise, and salad dressings are mainly oil and are not considered to be part of any food group.

Daily Activity

The steps along the side of the pyramid symbolize the importance of including exercise into each and every day of a person's life. When daily exercise does not occur, the benefits of even the wisest food or nutrition choices are minimized.

What Happened to the "Fat" Group?

When looking at the new Food Guide Pyramid, it appears that foods like cookies, candies, and sodas found in the former pyramid's "Fat Group" no longer are a part of the pyramid. These foods are typically high in fat, sugars, and "empty" calories, and though they are not mentioned or specifically depicted in the new pyramid, they should only be enjoyed sparingly or in moderation. These foods often taste great but, in general, they provide the body with very little nutritionally.

Due to the fact that one pyramid could not possibly match or meet the needs of all Americans, twelve different pyramids have been created. To determine which Food Guide Pyramid is the best match, you can go to the USDA's Web site at MyPyramid.gov and enter your age, gender, and activity level. This process takes only a few seconds and can personalize the amounts and types of grains, vegetables, fruits, milk products, meats, and beans you should consume each day to maximize your health benefits.

Because an individual's nutritional requirements vary based on their life circumstances, there is a range in the number of servings within each food group. Examples of factors that might influence the number of servings viewed as healthy for an individual could be age, activity level, gender—if the person is a woman, is she pregnant or lactating?

Determining the appropriate number of servings from each of the food groups is extremely important when planning a healthy diet. However, this information is of little practical value unless a person also knows what constitutes an accurate serving size.

Other Issues in Nutrition

Building a Healthy Plate

MyPlate is an idea based on the 2010 Dietary Guidelines for Americans. The idea behind MyPlate is to simplify the concept of making better/healthier food choices.

MyPlate uses the familiar place setting, using a plate 9 inches in diameter, shown in Figure 5.4 to illustrate the five food groups and the relative proportions in which they should be consumed. When used in conjunction with the ChooseMyPlate.gov website, consumers have access to practical, easy to understand information that will enable them to easily build a healthier diet.

Some select messages ChooseMyPlate uses to help consumers focus in on key behaviors include:

choosemyplate.gov

- Balancing Calories
  Eat the right amount of calories for you Everyone has a personal calorie limit. Staying within yours can help you get to or maintain a healthy weight. People who are successful at managing their weight have found ways to keep track of how much they eat in a day, even if they don't count every calorie.

  Enjoy your food, but eat less.
  - Get your personal daily calorie limit at www.ChooseMyPlate.gov and keep that number in mind when deciding what to eat.
  - Think before you eat . . . is it worth the calories?
  - Avoid oversized portions.
  - Use a smaller plate, bowl, and glass.
  - Stop eating when you are satisfied, not full.

  Cook more often at home, where you are in control of what's in your food. When eating out, choose lower calorie menu options.
  - Check posted calorie amounts.
  - Choose dishes that include vegetables, fruits, and/or whole grains.
  - Order a smaller portion or share when eating out.

© Kurhan, 2012, Shutterstock, Inc.

Choose MyPlate: 10 Tips to a Great Plate
Making food choices for a healthy lifestyle can be as simple as using these 10 Tips. Use the ideas in this list to *balance your calories,* to choose foods to eat more often, and to cut back on foods to *eat less often.*

1. balance calories
   Find out how many calories YOU need for a day as a first step in managing your weight. Go to www.ChooseMyPlate.gov to find your calorie level. Being physically active also helps you balance calories.
2. enjoy your food, but eat less
   Take the time to fully enjoy your food as you eat it. Eating too fast or when your attention is elsewhere may lead to eating too many calories. Pay attention to hunger and fullness cues before, during, and after meals. Use them to recognize when to eat and when you've had enough.
3. avoid oversized portions
   Use a smaller plate, bowl, and glass. Portion out foods before you eat. When eating out, choose a smaller size option, share a dish, or take home part of your meal.
4. foods to eat more often
   Eat more vegetables, fruits, whole grains, and fat-free or 1% milk and dairy products. These foods have the nutrients you need for health—including potassium, calcium, vitamin D, and fiber. Make them the basis for meals and snacks.
5. make half your plate fruits and vegetables
   Choose red, orange, and dark-green vegetables like tomatoes, sweet potatoes, and broccoli, along with other vegetables for your meals. Add fruit to meals as part of main or side dishes or as dessert.
6. switch to fat-free or low-fat (1%) milk
   They have the same amount of calcium and other essential nutrients as whole milk, but fewer calories and less saturated fat.
7. make half your grains whole grains
   To eat more whole grains, substitute a whole-grain product for a refined product—such as eating whole wheat bread instead of white bread or brown rice instead of white rice.
8. foods to eat less often
   Cut back on foods high in solid fats, added sugars, and salt. They include cakes, cookies, ice cream, candies, sweetened drinks, pizza, and fatty meats like ribs, sausages, bacon, and hot dogs. Use these foods as occasional treats, not everyday foods.
9. compare sodium in foods
   Use the Nutrition Facts label to choose lower sodium versions of foods like soup, bread, and frozen meals. Select canned foods labeled "low sodium," "reduced sodium," or "no salt added."
10. drink water instead of sugary drinks
    Cut calories by drinking water or unsweetened beverages. Soda, energy drinks, and sports drinks are a major source of added sugar, and calories, in American diets.

Write down what you eat to keep track of how much you eat. If you drink alcoholic beverages, do so sensibly—limit to 1 drink a day for women or to 2 drinks a day for men.

© Elena Larina, 2012. Shutterstock, Inc.

- Foods to Increase

Build a healthy plate Before you eat, think about what goes on your plate or in your cup or bowl. Foods like vegetables, fruits, whole grains, low-fat dairy products, and lean protein foods contain the nutrients you need without too many calories. Try some of these options.

Make half your plate fruits and vegetables.

- Eat red, orange, and dark-green vegetables, such as tomatoes, sweet potatoes, and broccoli, in main and side dishes.
- Eat fruit, vegetables, or unsalted nuts as snacks—they are nature's original fast foods.

© Eduardo Alexandre Piccoli, 2012. Shutterstock, Inc.

Switch to skim or 1% milk.

- They have the same amount of calcium and other essential nutrients as whole milk, but less fat and calories.
- Try calcium-fortified soy products as an alternative to dairy foods.

Make at least half your grains whole.

- Choose 100% whole-grain cereals, breads, crackers, rice, and pasta.
- Check the ingredients list on food packages to find whole-grain foods.

Vary your protein food choices.

- Twice a week, make seafood the protein on your plate.
- Eat beans, which are a natural source of fiber and protein.
- Keep meat and poultry portions small and lean.

Keep your food safe to eat—learn more at www.FoodSafety.gov.

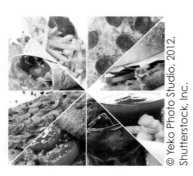

© Yeko Photo Studio, 2012. Shutterstock, Inc.

- Foods to Reduce

Cut back on foods high in solid fats, added sugars, and salt Many people eat foods with too much solid fats, added sugars, and salt (sodium). Added sugars and fats load foods with extra calories you don't need. Too much sodium may increase your blood pressure.

Choose foods and drinks with little or no added sugars.

- Drink water instead of sugary drinks. There are about 10 packets of sugar in a 12-ounce can of soda.
- Select fruit for dessert. Eat sugary desserts less often.
- Choose 100% fruit juice instead of fruit-flavored drinks.

Look out for salt (sodium) in foods you buy—it all adds up.

- Compare sodium in foods like soup, bread, and frozen meals—and choose the foods with lower numbers.
- Add spices or herbs to season food without adding salt.

Eat fewer foods that are high in solid fats.

- Make major sources of saturated fats—such as cakes, cookies, ice cream, pizza, cheese, sausages, and hot dogs—occasional choices, and not every day foods.
- Select lean cuts of meats or poultry and fat-free or low-fat milk, yogurt, and cheese.
- Switch from solid fats to oils when preparing food.*

*Examples of solid fats and oils	
Solid Fats	**Oils**
Beef, pork, and chicken fat Butter, cream, and milk fat Coconut, palm, and palm kernel oils Hydrogenated oil Partially hydrogenated oil Shortening Stick margarine	Canola oil Corn oil Cottonseed oil Olive oil Peanut oil Safflower oil Sunflower oil Tub (soft) margarine Vegetable oil

- Physical Activity

© Monkey Business images, 2012, Shutterstock, Inc.

Be physically active your way Pick activities that you like and start by doing what you can, at least 10 minutes at a time. Every bit adds up, and the health benefits increase as you spend more time being active.

Note to parents
What you eat and drink and your level of physical activity are important for your own health, and also for your children's health.

You are your children's most important role model. Your children pay attention to what you **do** more than what you **say.**

You can do a lot to help your children develop healthy habits for life by providing and eating healthy meals and snacks. For example, don't just **tell** your children to eat their vegetables—**show** them that you eat and enjoy vegetables every day.

Reading and Understanding the Nutrition Facts Label

Beginning in May 1993, the federal government has required food manufacturers to provide accurate nutritional information about their products on their product labels. Because food labels are standardized, relatively straightforward, and easy to read, much of the guesswork has been taken out of good nutrition.

Ingredients are listed on food labels by percentage of total weight, in order from heaviest or highest to lowest. By reading the listing of ingredients, an individual can determine whether a food is relatively high in fat, sugar, salt, and so on.

Food labels are legally required to include the number of servings per container, serving size, and the number of calories per serving. They must also list the percentage of the daily value of total fat, saturated fat, and, beginning in January 2006, trans fat. Nutrition Facts Labels must also list the percentage of the daily value of cholesterol, sodium, total carbohydrates (including dietary fiber and sugars), proteins, vitamins, and minerals. Figure 5.5 on page 194 provides an example of the required nutrition information found on packaged foods.

The bottom part of Nutrition Facts Labels on larger packages (typically any item that is not packaged for individual sale) contains a footnote with Daily Values (DVs) for 2,000- and 2,500-calorie-a-day diets. Because this information is not about a specific food product, it does not change from product to product. It shows recommended advice for all Americans. In the footnote section of the Nutrition Facts Label, the nutrients that have an upper limit or a set amount one wants to stay below are listed first. These nutrients include total fat, saturated fat, trans fat, sodium, and cholesterol. The amount of dietary fiber listed in this section is a minimum amount that should be con-

Why Is There No Percentage of Daily Value for Trans Fats?

There have been scientific findings and reports that confirm a link between trans fats and an increased risk of coronary heart disease. However, none of the reports have recommended an amount of trans fat that the Food and Drug Administration could use to establish a daily value, and without a daily value, a percentage of that daily value cannot be calculated.

sumed each day. The daily value for carbohydrates listed is a recommendation based on a 2,000-calorie-a-day diet, but it can vary slightly depending on the amount of fat and protein consumed.

When an individual takes the time to use the main body of the Nutrition Facts Label in conjunction with the footnote section of the label, he or she can get a very accurate picture of not only what source (carbohydrate, fat, or protein) their calories are coming from, but also how close they are coming to meeting the daily requirements necessary to maintain a high level of health.

Although product labels do have accuracy requirements, mistakes can be made and sometimes do occur. For this reason, it is wise to check the accuracy of food labels. One quick and easy way to do this is to divide the number of servings within the container—does it equal the serving size? For example, you have a product that the Nutrition Facts Label shows having a serving size of one-half cup and the number of servings per container is four. If you open the product and check it, does it contain two cups of that food? If so, the label is correct. Another way to check the accuracy of a nutrition label is to calculate the calories (grams of fat times nine, grams of protein and carbohydrates times four). Does the number calculated match the reported calories within 10 to 20 calories? If the numbers are way "off" one should be aware that the label is incorrect. See Figure 5.5 (Nutrition Facts Label) for an example of how to check for label accuracy based on reported calories.

Reported Total Calories per Serving = 250
Reported Calories from Fat = 110

Reading labels while grocery shopping is important in preparing healthy meals.

The product contains a total of 12 g of fat. Fat contains 9 calories per gram of fat, so to check for accuracy of reported fat calories, multiply 12 × 9. This equals 108.

To check for accuracy of total number of calories, multiply the total grams of carbohydrates . . . 31 in this product, by 4 (the amount of calories per gram of carbohydrate). This equals 124 calories.

The total grams of protein . . . 5 in this product, by 4 (the amount of calories per gram of protein). This equals 20 calories.

To check for accuracy of the total number of calories per serving, add calories from fat, protein, and carbohydrates. If they are close to the number of calories per serving listed on the Nutrition Fact Label, the label is accurate.

108 + 124 + 20 = 252 actual vs. 250 reported

FIGURE 5.5   Food Label: Nutrition Facts

Serving Size
Is your serving the same size as the one on the label? If you eat double the serving size listed, you need to double the nutrient and calorie values. If you eat one-half the serving size shown here, cut the nutrient and calorie values in half.

Calories
Are you overweight? Cut back a little on calories! Look here to see how a serving of the food adds to your daily total. A 5'4", 138-lb. active woman needs about 2,200 calories each day. A 5'10", 174-lb. active man needs about 2,900. How about you?

Total Carbohydrate
When you cut down on fat, you can eat more carbohydrates. Carbohydrates are in foods like bread, potatoes, fruits, and vegetables. Choose these often! They give you more nutrients than sugars like soda pop and candy.

Dietary Fiber
Grandmother called it "roughage," but her advice to eat more is still up-to-date! That goes for both soluble and insoluble kinds of dietary fiber. Fruits, vegetables, whole-grain foods, beans, and peas are all good sources and can help reduce the risk of heart disease and cancer.

Protein
Most Americans get more protein than they need. Where there is animal protein, there is also fat and cholesterol. Eat small servings of lean meat, fish, and poultry. Use skim or low-fat milk, yogurt, and cheese. Try vegetable proteins like beans, grains, and cereals.

Vitamins and Minerals
Your goal here is 100 percent of each for the day. Don't count on one food to do it all. Let a combination of foods add up to a winning score.

Nutrition Facts

Serving Size 1 cup (228g)
Servings Per Container 2

Amount Per Serving

Calories 250	Calories from Fat 110

	% Daily Value*
Total Fat 12g	**18%**
Saturated Fat 3g	**15%**
Trans Fat 3g	
Cholesterol 30mg	**10%**
Sodium 470mg	**20%**
Total Carbohydrate 31g	**10%**
Dietary Fiber 0g	**0%**
Sugars 5g	
Protein 5g	

Vitamin A	4%
Vitamin C	2%
Calcium	20%
Iron	4%

*Percent Daily Values are based on a 2,000 calorie diet. Your Daily Values may be higher or lower depending on your calorie needs:

	Calories	2,000	2,500
Total Fat	Less than	65g	80g
Sat Fat	Less than	20g	25g
Cholesterol	Less than	300mg	300mg
Sodium	Less than	2,400mg	2,400mg
Total Carbohydrate		300g	375g
Fiber		25g	30g

Calories per gram:
Fat 9 • Carbohydrates 4 • Protein 4

More nutrients may be listed on some labels.

Total Fat
Aim low. Most people need to cut back on fat! Too much fat may contribute to heart disease and cancer. Try to limit your calories from fat. For a healthy heart, choose foods with a big difference between the total number of calories and the number of calories from fat.

Saturated Fat
A new kind of fat? No—saturated fat is part of the total fat in food. It is listed separately because it's the key player in raising blood cholesterol and your risk of heart disease. Eat less!

Cholesterol
Too much cholesterol—a second cousin to fat—can lead to heart disease. Challenge yourself to eat less than 300 mg each day.

Sodium
You call it "salt," the label calls it "sodium." Either way, it may add up to high blood pressure in some people. So, keep your sodium intake low—2,400 to 3,000 mg or less each day.*

*The AHA recommends no more than 3,000 mg sodium per day for healthy adults.

Daily Value
Feel like you're drowning in numbers? Let the Daily Value be your guide. Daily Values are listed for people who eat 2,000 or 2,500 calories each day. If you eat more, your personal daily value may be higher than what's listed on the label. If you eat less, your personal daily value may be lower.

For fat, saturated fat, cholesterol, and sodium, choose foods with a low percent Daily Value. For total carbohydrate, dietary fiber, vitamins, and minerals, your daily value goal is to reach 100 percent of each.
g = grams (About 28 g = 1 ounce)
mg = milligrams (1,000 mg = 1 g)

You Can Rely on the New Label

Rest assured, when you see key words and health claims on product labels, they mean what they say as defined by the government. For example:

Key Words	What They Mean
Fat Free	Less than 0.5 g of fat per serving
Low Fat	3 g of fat (or less) per serving
Lean	Less than 10 g of fat, 4 g of saturated fat, and 95 mg of cholesterol per serving
Light (Lite)	one-third less calories or no more than one-half the fat of the higher-calorie, higher-fat version; or no more than one-half the sodium of the higher-sodium version
Cholesterol Free	Less than 2 mg of cholesterol and 2 g (or less) of saturated fat per serving

To Make Health Claims About...	The Food Must Be . . .
Heart Disease and Fats	Low in fat, saturated fat, and cholesterol
Blood Pressure and Sodium	Low in sodium
Heart Disease and Fruits, Vegetables, and Grain Products	A fruit, vegetable, or grain product low in fat, saturated fat, and cholesterol, that contains at least 0.6 g soluble fiber, without fortification, per serving

Other claims may appear on some labels.

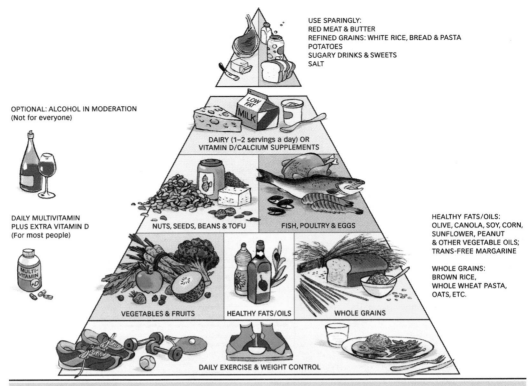

USE SPARINGLY:
RED MEAT & BUTTER
REFINED GRAINS: WHITE RICE, BREAD & PASTA
POTATOES
SUGARY DRINKS & SWEETS
SALT

OPTIONAL: ALCOHOL IN MODERATION
(Not for everyone)

LOW FAT MILK

DAIRY (1–2 servings a day) OR
VITAMIN D/CALCIUM SUPPLEMENTS

DAILY MULTIVITAMIN
PLUS EXTRA VITAMIN D
(For most people)

MULTI-VITAMIN +D

NUTS, SEEDS, BEANS & TOFU   FISH, POULTRY & EGGS

HEALTHY FATS/OILS:
OLIVE, CANOLA, SOY, CORN,
SUNFLOWER, PEANUT
& OTHER VEGETABLE OILS;
TRANS-FREE MARGARINE

WHOLE GRAINS:
BROWN RICE,
WHOLE WHEAT PASTA,
OATS, ETC.

VEGETABLES & FRUITS   HEALTHY FATS/OILS   WHOLE GRAINS

DAILY EXERCISE & WEIGHT CONTROL

FIGURE 5.4

The Healthy Eating Pyramid

Source: Copyright © 2008 Harvard University. For more information about The Healthy Eating Pyramid, please see The Nutrition Source, Department of Nutrition, Harvard School of Public Health, http://www. thenutritionsource.org, and Eat, Drink, and Be Healthy, by Walter C. Willett, M. D. and Patrick J. Skerrett (2005), Free Press/Simon & Schuster Inc.

Both the total calories and fat calories listed on the Nutrition Facts Label were slightly low. Knowing this, an individual can more accurately determine when he or she has reached their nutritional limit.

Vegetarianism

There have always been people who, for one reason or another (religious, ethical, or philosophical), have chosen to follow a vegetarian diet. However, in recent years, a vegetarian diet has become increasingly popular.

Salmon is a good source of Omega-3 fatty acids.

There are four different types of vegetarian diets. **Vegans** are considered true vegetarians. Their diets are completely void of meat, chicken, fish, eggs, or milk products. A vegan's primary sources of protein are vegetables, fruits, and grains. Because vitamin B12 is normally found only in meat products, many vegans choose to supplement their diet with this vitamin.

Lactovegetarians eat dairy products, fruits, and vegetables but do not consume any other animal products (meat, poultry, fish, or eggs).

Ovolactovegetarians are another type of vegetarians. They eat eggs as well as dairy products, fruits, and vegetables, but still do not consume meat, poultry, or fish.

A person who eats fruits, vegetables, dairy products, eggs, and a small selection of poultry, fish, and other seafood is a partial or **semivegetarian.** These individuals do not consume any beef or pork.

Vegetarians of all four types can meet all their daily dietary needs through the food selections available to them. However, because certain foods or groups of foods that are high in specific nutrients are forbidden, it is critical that a vegetarian is diligent in selecting his or her food combinations so that the nutritional benefits of the foods allowed are maximized. If food combinations from a wide variety of sources are not selected, nutritional deficiencies of proteins, vitamins, and minerals can rapidly occur and proper growth, development, and function may not occur. While a vegetarian diet can certainly be a healthy, low-fat alternative to the typical American diet, without diligent monitoring, it is not a guarantee of good health.

For many individuals who choose a vegetarian diet, it is more than simply omitting certain foods or groups of food, it is a way of living that they have embraced.

References

Donatelle, R. J. & Davis, L. G. *Access* to *Health* (9th ed). Boston: Allyn & Bacon. 2006. Floyd, P. A., Mimms, S. E., and Yelding-Howard, C. *Personal Health: Perspectives & Life-*

styles., Englewood, CO: Morton Publishing Company. 2007.

Hales, D. *An Invitation to Health* (8th ed). New York: Brooks/Cole Publishing Company. 1999.

Hoeger, W. and Hoeger, S. A. *Principles and Labs for Fitness and Wellness* (9th ed). Belmont, CA: Thomson Wadsworth. 2008.

Hoeger, W. W. K. and Hoeger, S. A. *Lifetime Physical Fitness and Wellness: A Personalized Program* (8th ed). Belmont, CA: Thomson Wadsworth. 2005.

Hyman, B., Oden, G., Bacharach, D., and Collins, R. *Fitness for Living.* Dubuque, Iowa: Kendall/Hunt. 2006.

http://www.ific.org/nutrition/functional/index.cfm?rederforprint = 1

Powers, S. K., Todd, S. L. and Noland, J. J. *Total Fitness and Wellness* (2nd ed). Boston: Allyn & Bacon. 2005.

Prentice, W. E. *Fitness and Wellness for Life* (6th ed). New York: WCB McGraw-Hill. 1999.

Pruitt, B. E. & Stein, J. *HealthStyles* (2nd ed). Boston: Allyn & Bacon. 1999.

Robbins, G., Powers, D., and Burgess, S. *A Wellness Way of Life (*4th ed). New York: WCB McGraw-Hill. 1999.

Rosato, F. *Fitness for Wellness* (3rd ed). Minneapolis: West. 1994.

Webmaster@noah.cuny.edu

http://www.cfsan.fda.gov/~dms/transfat.html

http://www.ganesa.com/food/foodpyramid.gif

http://www.healthdepot.com

http://www.health.gov/dietaryguidelines/dga2010.htm

http://www.health.gov/dietaryguidelines/dga2010/document/aim.htm

http://www.health.gov/dietaryguidelines/dga2010/document/choose.htm

http://www.capp.usda.gov/Publications/DietaryGuidelines/2010/PolicyDoc/ExecSumm.pdf

http://www.health.gov/dietaryguidelines/dga2005/document/html/chapter1.htm

http://vm.cfsan.fda.gov/~dms/foodlab.html

http://www.ers.usda.gov/AmberWaves/June05/Features?Will2005WholeGrain.htm

http://www.aaccnet.org/definitions/wholegrain.asp

http://www.capp.usda.gov/Pubications/MyPlate/GettingStartedWithMyPlate.pdf

http://www.choosemyplate.gov/foodgroups/downloads/MyPlate/DG2010Brochure.pdf

Contacts

American Dietetic Association Get Nutrition Fact Sheets at American Dietetic Association Consumer Education Team
216 West Jackson Boulevard
Chicago, IL 60606
(send a self-addressed, stamped envelope), call 800–877–1600, ext. 5000 for other publications or 800–366–1655 for recorded food/nutrition messages

American Obesity Association
1250 24th Street, NW, Suite 300
Washington, DC 20037
800–98–OBESE

Department of Nutrition Sciences University of Alabama at Birmingham Birmingham, AL 35294
Calorieking.com Fitday.com http://www.caloriesperhour.com/index_food.html

Activities

Notebook Activities

Dietary Analysis Project
Cholesterol Levels Measured
Nutrition Assignment
Super Tracker Assignment

Name _____ Section _____ Date_____

Dietary Analysis Project

I. Carbohydrates

1. Look at your analysis sheet and list below each day's intake, then find the average calories that you consumed for the time period you entered.

   Day 1 ___, 2 ____3, _____(ex. credit 4, __5, _____6, _____7, _____)

   Total calories divided by 3(7) days = _____Average intake

2. Look at your analysis sheet and list below each day's carbohydrate intake, then find the average grams of carbs that you consumed for the time period you entered

   Day 1 ___, 2 ____3, _____(ex. credit 4, _____5, _____6, _____7, _____g)

   Total carbs divided by 3(7) days = _____Average intake

3. Now calculate the percentage of energy in your diet from carbohydrate. Use the formula below and use your **average** carb grams and your average calorie intake.

   Average grams of CHO (   ) × 4   × 100 = _____% of energy from carbohydrates average calories consumed (_____)

4. Did your carb intake meet the RDA's recommendations that 55–65 percent of your total calories come from carbohydrate? _____yes ___no

5. If not, what carbohydrate-rich foods do you need to eat more or less of to meet these requirements?

   _____

   _____

6. List below each day's fiber intake and then determine the average grams of fiber you consumed

   Day 1 ___, Day 2 , Day 3 , Day 4 , Day 5 , Day 6 , Day 7

   Total grams of fiber/days (i.e., 30 g/3 days = 10 grams per day average intake)

   ___/_____= _____g fiber

7. Did this amount meet the recommendations to consume 20–35 g of fiber a day? _____ If not, what foods do you need to eat more of to increase your fiber intake?

   _____

   _____

II. Fats

8. Look at your analysis and list your daily intakes of the following types of fat, and then determine the average intakes for the period recorded.

	Total Fat	Saturated Fat	Cholesterol	MUS	PUS
Day 1	_____	_____	_____	____	____
Day 2	_____	_____	_____	____	____
Day 3	_____	_____	_____	____	____
Day 4	_____	_____	_____	____	____
Day 5	_____	_____	_____	____	____
Day 6	_____	_____	_____	____	____
Day 7	_____	_____	_____	____	____
Average	_____	_____	_____	____	____

9. Now calculate the percentage of energy in your diet from fat. Use the formula below and use your **average** total fat grams (as listed in #7 and your average calorie intake).

$$\frac{\text{Average of fat (\_\_\_\_)} \times 9}{\text{Average calories consumed (\_\_\_\_)}} \times 100 = \text{_____\% of energy from fat}$$

10. Did your fat intake meet the RDA's recommendations that 20–30 percent of your total calories come from fat? ____yes ____no

11. If not, what foods do you need to eat less of to meet these requirements?

_____

_____

12. What was your average intake of cholesterol? _____ Does your cholesterol intake fall within the recommendations of consuming no more than 300 mg of cholesterol each day? ____yes ____no

13. If your intake was above 300 mg per day, what foods do you need to eat less of to reduce your cholesterol intake?

_____

_____

Name _____ Section_____ Date_____

III. Protein

14. List each day's protein intake below.

    Day 1 _____, Day 2 _____, Day 3 _____, Day 4 _____, Day 5 _____, Day 6 _____, Day 7 _____

    According to your Dietary Analysis, how many grams of protein did you consume per day (average) during this time? _____ (i.e., total protein intake = 300 g/3 days = 100 g per day average)

15. Now calculate the percentage of energy in you diet from protein. Use the formula below and use your **average** protein grams (as listed in #1 and your average calorie intake).

    $$\frac{\text{Average g of protein (\_\_\_\_\_)}}{\text{Average calories consumed (\_\_\_\_\_)}} \times 4 \quad \times 100 = \text{_____} \% \text{ of energy from protein}$$

    Does this amount follow the dietary recommendations for protein intake (12–15 percent of your total calorie intake)? _____

16. The minimum recommendations for protein intake are as follows:

    .8 g – .9 g of protein per kg of body weight

    Determine your protein needs according to these recommendations (kg = #/2.2)

    Body weight in #/2.2 = _____ × .8 or .9) = _____ g needed minimum

    My minimum protein needs are _____. I consumed _____ g of protein for a difference of +, – _____ g.

17. What foods do you need to consume more/less of to meet your protein requirements?

    _____

    _____

18. Did your protein come more from animal or plant sources? _____

19. If you would exercise regularly (3 × week for 30 minutes), you would need about 1.2–1.4 g of protein/kg of body weight. Calculate your protein requirements.

    Body weight (kg) × 1.2–1.4 g protein = _____ g needed.

20. Look at your food printout and calculate your average servings of fruits and veggies according to the food guide pyramid's serving sizes suggestions. Then compare your averages to the USDA's analysis of your fruits and veggies intake. Remember French fries and chips are not veggies. One-half cup cooked red, yellow, or green veggies or one cup leafy is a serving of veggies and one medium fruit or one-half or three-quarter cup juice is a serving of fruit.

    Average fruit intake _____USDA intake _____

    Average veggie intake _____USDA intake _____

21. Based on the total analysis of your diet, what health problems might you experience if you continue to eat in this manner?

_____

_____

22. What is the most important thing you learned about your diet after doing this analysis?

_____

_____

_____

_____

_____

_____

_____

_____

_____

_____

_____

_____

_____

_____

_____

_____

_____

_____

_____

_____

NOTEBOOK ACTIVITY

Cholesterol Levels Measured

Have a cholesterol test performed by a licensed individual, and turn in the actual results from the test.

Name _____ Section_____ Date_____

Nutrition Assignment (____ points)

Go to *choosemyplate.gov*

On the top of the page in the green box, click on "SuperTracker & other Tools"; *Click on "Daily Food Plans"; click on the blue highlighted "Daily Food Plans";* enter your age, sex, weight, height, and physical activity level, and click "submit."

On the right hand side where it says, "view, print, and learn more," click on "print PDF version of your results." Print this page out.

Go back to previous page and print out "PDF meal tracking worksheet" (print out 3 copies of this).

Pick two weekdays and one weekend day and record what you eat on those days as accurately as possible. Try to eat as you normally do and see how close (or far) you are from what is recommended for you.

This assignment should help some of you ensure you are within the guidelines. For others, **hopefully** help you re-evaluate how you are currently eating and hopefully get you on the right track of healthy eating!!

Good Luck!!

NOTE: This assignment is graded on completion, so be sure you do that, if you want credit. Don't forget to add comments on the bottom of each printout.

NOTEBOOK ACTIVITY

Super Tracker Assignment (____ points)

Write down everything you eat and drink for 3 days. You must include at least one weekend day (Saturday or Sunday) in your list. Be sure to include as much detail as possible about the type of food and serving size.

Go to https://www.choosemyplate.gov/SuperTracker/default.aspx

Create your profile.

Click on Food Tracker. When the tracking page opens, make sure the date on the left hand corner matches the date of the foods you are entering in. Enter in all of your foods from that day, being as accurate as possible.

Click on Physical Activity Tracker. Include your exercises from that day.

Repeat these steps for the 3 days of food tracking.

Click on My Reports. Open the **Food Groups and Calories** report. Enter the date range. Click Create Report. After the report opens, click on Export as PDF. Save this file to your computer.

Go back to My Reports. Open the **Nutrients Report.** Enter the date range. Click Create Report. After the report opens, click on Export as PDF. Save this file to your computer.

You should have 2 documents saves—one Food Groups and Calories Report and one Nutrients Report. Upload both documents to eLearning.

NOTE: Make sure to specify the date for the foods that you are entering in. You may enter more than one day at a time, but be sure to finish one day and then move onto the next and change the date on the screen.

In the eLearning textbox, write a 3-5 sentence reflection of your results. Indicate if you plan to make any dietary changes based on the reports, and if you were surprised by any of the results.

If you have problems accessing the website, be sure to let me know BEFORE your assignment is due. Do not wait until the last minute to do this!

- Is it possible to eat healthy on a budget? Why or why not?

- What are proactive ways you could ensure good nutrition throughout the day on a busy day and/or evening when you don't have time to go home and prepare meals?

Chapter 6
Lifetime Weight Management

© 2012, Shutterstock, Inc.

OBJECTIVES

Students will be able to:

- Identify problems associated with fast food dining.
- Discuss diet supplements.
- Present guidelines for a successful weight-loss program.
- Identify a healthy Body Mass Index.
- Identify causes of obesity and complications associated with obesity.
- Discuss the importance of activity for weight management.
- Recognize the pitfalls of Fad Dieting.

> *"Thou shouldst eat to live;*
> *not live to eat."*
>
> —*Socrates, 469 bc–399 bc*

Why have Americans gained so much weight over the last fifty years? Approximately two-thirds of adult Americans are overweight, and typically so are their children. The causes of obesity are numerous and complex. The bottom line is nutritional balance (see Figure 6.2): calories eaten versus calories expended. However, even if some folks exercise and attempt to eat healthy, it is more complicated than that. Because our society has become increasingly automated, Americans are saving lots of energy in the form of stored fat. "Easier," "automated," "instant," and "remote control" are all terms which describe using less energy. Saving energy relates to moving less, which means saving calories. A person who moves less typically stores more energy in the form of fat. Chapter 3 discusses lifestyle activity, which means looking for opportunities to expend more energy—like taking the stairs instead of the elevator. Every time you drive through for fast food, think of all of the energy you are saving. Another culprit in contributing to larger Americans is the Internet, games, texting, and so on. Balancing sedentary activities with playing baseball, tag, and climbing trees is important.

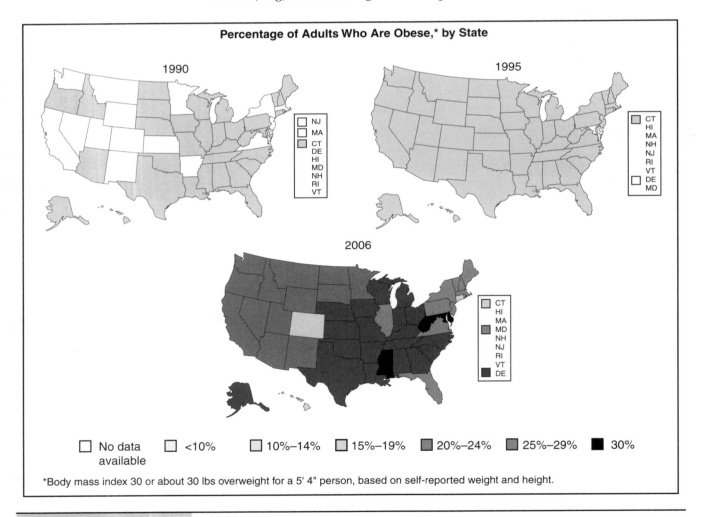

*Body mass index 30 or about 30 lbs overweight for a 5' 4" person, based on self-reported weight and height.

FIGURE 6.1

Percentage of Adults Who Are Obese,* by State from 1990 to 2006.

Source: Behavioral Risk Factors Surveillance System, CDC.

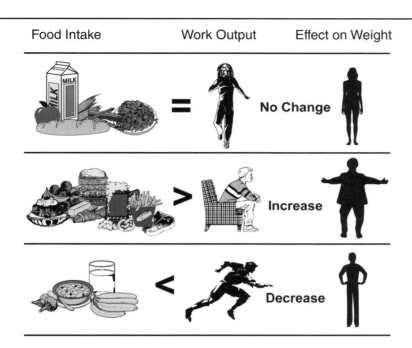

Food Intake	Work Output	Effect on Weight

= No Change

> Increase

< Decrease

FIGURE 6.2
Caloric Balance: Caloric intake should equal caloric expenditure in order to maintain weight.

Causes of Obesity and Being Overweight

Patrick O'Neil, director of the Weight Management Center at the Medical University of South Carolina in Charleston, determined that 40 percent of people's weight problems are due to whom they choose for their parents. Gene pool plays a big role in body size. Through evolution we are programmed to hunt and gather, then eat plenty as the food is available to store energy. Dr. O'Neil quotes the old adage, "Genes load the gun, but environment pulls the trigger." We typically learn eating patterns and develop a familiarity with certain types of foods that we eat when we are younger. Starting with what we eat as infants through adulthood, we learn particular eating styles.

Foods have changed. Fifty years ago foods were less processed. There was less convenience food. Foods were eaten more in their wholesome state. Portion sizes were smaller than they are today. Today's small McDonald's Happy Meal French fries were the "regular" size when McDonald's opened. A McDonald's Super Size serving of French fries contains 540 calories with 230 calories coming from fat. It is only in the last 25 years that convenience stores and fast-food eateries have offered the 42-ounce size of sweetened soft drinks. A 42-ounce Dr. Pepper has 525 calories. Many in the health industry think that the increase in corn syrup sweetened soft drink consumption has contributed to America's obesity problem, especially childhood obesity. Portion control is a critical component in weight management. Check product labels to determine how much food is considered a serving, as well as how many calories, grams of fat, and so on, are in a serving. Many prepackaged foods contain two or more servings—always read the label! See What Counts as a Serving on page 175. Trans-fatty acids have entered the diet via hydrogenation, a process by which liquid oils (which are unsaturated and healthy) are reconstituted to a solid convenient form. As you recall from the nutrition chapter, the problem with ingesting trans-fatty acid is that it raises LDL (the bad cholesterol) and lowers HDL (the good cholesterol). Results from Nurses' Health Study determined that a diet high in trans-fatty acids is highly associated with an increase in cardiovascular risk. A diet high in trans fats also may be linked to an increased abdominal fat measurement, as well as to an increase in the risk of Type 2 diabetes (IUFOST, 2006). What you eat, when

Calories Count
Between 1971 and 2004, the average American woman increased her caloric consumption by 22%. Between 1971 and 2004, the average American man increased his caloric consumption by 10%. *Men, women, and children are eating more carbohydrates in the form of starches, more refined grains and sugars, larger portion sizes, more fast food, and more sugar sweetened beverages (AHA, 2012).* To combat this, consider eating more foods the way nature made them. Try adding more raw foods to your diet and minimizing processed foods. Limit high sugar drinks, including juices, and drink more water.

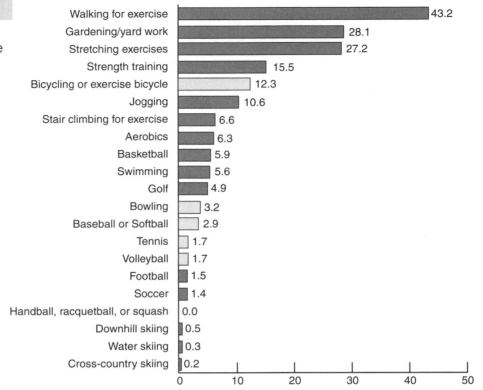

FIGURE 6.3

Most Popular Adult Physical Activities in the United States

Note: Data are weighted to the U.S. population and age-adjusted to the year 2000 population standard. "Participation" in activity reported as being done at least once during the past two weeks.

Source: Centers for Disease Control and Prevention, National Health Interview Survey (NHIS), 1998, Atlanta.

you eat, and how much you eat make a difference. How you choose to eat makes a difference as well. Do you sit down and enjoy your food, or do you eat on the run?

Although the causes of overweight and obesity are complex and numerous, the risks of being overweight or obese are very real and tangible. An individual who is overweight is at increased risk for conditions such as high blood pressure, high cholesterol, stroke, heart disease, diabetes, and certain types of cancers. For most Americans, food is plentiful. Americans are typically not malnourished due to a lack of food, but the World Health Organization (WHO) predicts that there will soon be a world epidemic of overweight and malnourished people resulting from the unhealthy types of foods that are being eaten. A person living on only fast food that is high in sodium, fat, and cholesterol and low in vitamins and fiber can experience a lack of some essential nutrients. *Eating a variety of foods such as vegetables, fruits, whole grains, low-fat dairy, fish, lean cuts of meat (or other quality protein), and beans are the building blocks of a solid nutritional practice.*

Chapters 3 and 4 emphasized the importance of regular activity for overall health. Exercise can help you get fit and stay fit and is a critical aid in efforts to lose weight. The three largest contributors to overweight are lack of exercise, eating choices and behaviors, and genetics. Exercise may be the most significant. Sobering studies show that most people who successfully lose weight will have gained it back within two years time. The 5 percent that successfully maintain weight loss have exercise in their life—it is part of their lifestyle (see Figure 6.3). It isn't important to take up running or any activity you are uncomfortable doing. The important thing is to just move!

The Weight Loss 'Halo' Effect

Bariatrics is the field of medicine that specializes in treating morbid obesity. A surgeon may perform bariatric surgery to assist in weight loss only after lifestyle changes and other conventional methods are unsuccessful. There is associated short term and long term risks with this type of surgery and this option must be considered carefully. Patti Neighmond reported for NPR on a study directed by Dr. John Morton, Stanford Bariatric Surgery Director. Dr. Morton considers obesity a "family disease." We typically sit around the table together, sharing and learning eating patterns. He noticed that after his patients' surgeries, family members seemed to mimic the patient's new weight loss habits such as eating smaller portions and being more physically active. Dr. Morton calls this a 'halo' effect; where good habits rub off on family members so much so that in a study of 35 of his bariatric patients one year post-surgery, family members had lost an average of 5% of their body weight. Five percent is enough to significantly enhance health and reduce risk of heart disease and diabetes. Being supportive is positive for the weight loss patient, but due to the 'halo' effect supportive family members often benefit as well (NPR, 2012).

Being supportive is positive for the weight loss patient, but due to the 'halo' effect supportive family members often benefit as well.

What Is a Healthy Body Weight?

There is no single ideal body weight; rather there is a range of healthy body weights that are acceptable for a certain height. Activity level, age, eating patterns, body composition, pregnancy or lactation, and gender, as well as genetic predisposition, can determine weight. You may find that your body seems to change, but it hovers around the same weight. The **set-point theory** postulates that the body regulates metabolism in order to maintain a certain weight, much the same as a thermostat regulates temperature. If fat stores fall below the "set" point, then the body responds by increasing appetite. If we overeat, then appetite may be reduced or all of the calories available may not be stored. Set-point gradually creeps up with poor health habits. Lowering your set-point takes patience and regular physical activity.

Body Mass Index or **BMI** is a simple way of using a ratio between height and weight to determine if your body weight falls within a healthy range. BMI is not meant to be used alone as a sole parameter of healthy body weight. Used with other measures like percentage of body fat, diet history, and exercise patterns, BMI is an easy, economical, and reproducible value to measure health risk. BMI does not take into account body type, age, sex, gender, bone density, or muscle mass. For that reason, BMI results are not good indicators for athletes, children, pregnant or lactating women, or the elderly. Fat distribution is not considered with a BMI measure. A person with abdominal obesity (an

TABLE 6.1

Body Mass Index Table

To use the table, find the appropriate height in the left-hand column labeled Height. Move across to a given weight (in pounds). The number at the top of the column is the BMI at that height and weight. Pounds have been rounded off.

BMI	19	20	21	22	23	24	25	26	27	28	29	30	31	32	33	34	35
Height (inches)							Body Weight (pounds)										
58	91	96	100	105	110	115	119	124	129	134	138	143	148	153	158	162	167
59	94	99	104	109	114	119	124	128	133	138	143	148	153	158	163	168	173
60	97	102	107	112	118	123	128	133	138	143	148	153	158	163	168	174	179
61	100	106	111	116	122	127	132	137	143	148	153	158	164	169	174	180	185
62	104	109	115	120	126	131	136	142	147	153	158	164	169	175	180	186	191
63	107	113	118	124	130	135	141	146	152	158	163	169	175	180	186	191	197
64	110	116	122	128	134	140	145	151	157	163	169	174	180	186	192	197	204
65	114	120	126	132	138	144	150	156	162	168	174	180	186	192	198	204	210
66	118	124	130	136	142	148	155	161	167	173	179	186	192	198	204	210	216
67	121	127	134	140	146	153	159	166	172	178	185	191	198	204	211	217	223
68	125	131	138	144	151	158	164	171	177	184	190	197	203	210	216	223	230
69	128	135	142	149	155	162	169	176	182	189	196	203	209	216	223	230	236
70	132	139	146	153	160	167	174	181	188	195	202	209	216	222	229	236	243
71	136	143	150	157	165	172	179	186	193	200	208	215	222	229	236	243	250
72	140	147	154	162	169	177	184	191	199	206	213	221	228	235	242	250	258
73	144	151	159	166	174	182	189	197	204	212	219	227	235	242	250	257	265
74	148	155	163	171	179	186	194	202	210	218	225	233	241	249	256	264	272
75	152	160	168	176	184	192	200	208	216	224	232	240	248	256	264	272	279
76	156	164	172	180	189	197	205	213	221	230	238	246	254	263	271	279	287

Source: www.nhlbi.gov

apple-shaped person) has a higher health risk than a person with fat accumulation around the hips and thighs (pear shape). Two people with different shapes could have the same BMI but not the same health risk. This is why an athlete with lean muscle and very little fat could have a high or "unhealthy" BMI. Even so, BMI is considered superior to traditional height-weight charts. See Table 6.1 to determine your BMI.

A BMI over 25 is considered overweight and a BMI over 30 is considered obese. A higher BMI may indicate you are at an elevated risk for heart disease, Type 2 diabetes, and most of the conditions related to obesity. Underweight is a BMI of 18.5 or below. It is interesting to note that on the catwalks of New York and Paris, models now have to weigh in and are unable to participate if they are below a BMI of 18. It is encouraging that the fashion world is participating in increasing awareness regarding the dangers of being too thin.

> 1 kg = 2.2 lbs
> 1 meter = 39.37 inches

$$BMI = \frac{\text{weight in kilograms}}{\text{height in meters squared}}$$

Body composition is one of the five health-related fitness components discussed in Chapter 3. A person's body composition is a measure of health, estimating the amount of fat mass relative to the lean body mass. Lean body mass is comprised of muscle, bone, and internal organs. Body composition is a more accurate indicator of overall fitness than using a person's body weight.

The ideal range for college-aged females is 18–23 percent body fat and 12–18 percent body fat for college-aged men. Essential fat is that fat which is necessary for normal physiological functioning. If a female gets below 11–13 percent of essential body fat, she typically experiences hormonal disturbances and may have menstruation cessation. Essential fat for men is around 3 percent body fat.

There are numerous different methods to determine an estimate of percent body fat. Skinfold calipers are commonly used in schools. At health fairs, bioelectrical impedence is a simple and inexpensive test to administer. The accuracy of this method is highly questionable due to variations in hydration levels in people throughout the day. The air displacement method uses pressure sensors inside an airtight chamber to measure the amount of air displaced by the person inside the chamber. This is a bulky and expensive container. Hydrostatic weighing is popular with laboratories and athletic centers. The clinicians determine how much a person weighs under water. Dual energy X-ray absorptiometry (DEXA) is the preferred method in research facilities. Each method has pros and cons. If measuring a percentage of body fat in a pre- and post-comparison, it is important to replicate the same environment and to use the same technique in the post-test that was used for the pre-test.

© Gerald Bernard, 2012. Shutterstock, Inc.

Body composition is a more accurate indicator of overall fitness than is a person's body weight.

Determining Caloric Needs

Caloric needs are different for every individual. To a large degree, each person's need is determined by their current body weight and by the level of physical activity they choose to engage in. See Table 6.2 to determine your own daily caloric needs. Notice the different caloric requirements for active individuals compared to sedentary individuals.

Obesity

Overweight is defined as an excess of body weight to some height standard, or a BMI between 25 and 30. **Obesity** is a term that refers to excess fat with an accompanying loss of function and an increase in health problems (see

> Some health profesionals think **waist measurement alone** is a valuable indicator of future health risk. High risk for women is a waist measurement over 35", and over 40" for men (National Institute for Health).

TABLE 6.2

Estimated Calorie Requirements (in Kilocalories) for Each Gender and Age Group at Three Levels of Physical Activity[a]

Estimated amounts of calories needed to maintain energy balance for various gender and age groups at three different levels of physical activity. The estimates are rounded up to the nearest 200 calories and were determined using the Institute of Medicine equation.

Gender	Age (years)	Sedentary[b]	Moderately Active[c]	Active[d]
Child	2–3	1,000	1,000–1,400e	1,000–1,400e
Female	4–8	1,200	1,400–1,600	1,400–1,800
	9–13	1,600	1,600–2,000	1,800–2,200
	14–18	1,800	2,000	2,400
	19–30	2,000	2,000–2,200	2,400
	31–50	1,800	2,000	2,200
	51+	1,600	1,800	2,000–2,200
Male	4–8	1,400	1,400–1,600	1,600–2,000
	9–13	1,800	1,800–2,200	2,000–2,600
	14–18	2,200	2,400–2,800	2,800–3,200
	19–30	2,400	2,600–2,800	3,000
	31–50	2,200	2,400–2,600	2,800–3,000
	51+	2,000	2,200–2,400	2,400–2,800

[a]These levels are based on Estimated Energy Requirements (EER) from the Institute of Medicine Dietary References Intakes macro- nutrients report, 2002, calculated by gender, age, and activity level for reference-sized individuals. "Reference-size," as determined by IOM, is based on median height and weight for ages up to age 18 years of age and median height and weight for that height to give a BMI of 21.5 for adult females and 22.5 for adult males.

[b]Sedentary means a lifestyle that includes only the light physical activity associated with typical day-to-day life.

[c]Moderately active means a lifestyle that includes physical activity equivalent to walking about 1.5 to 3 miles per day at 3 to 4 miles per hour, in addition to the light physical activity associated with typical day-to-day life.

[d]Active means a lifestyle that includes physical activity equivalent to walking more than 3 miles per day at 3 to 4 miles per hour, in addition to the light physical activity associated with typical day-to-day life.

[e]The calorie ranges shown are to accommodate needs of different ages within the group. For children and adolescents, more calories are needed at older ages. For adults, fewer calories are needed at older ages.

Source: USDA.

Figure 6.4), or a BMI of 30 or more. **Creeping obesity** is a gradual increase of percent body fat as activity decreases with age. This typically results in a one-half to one pound fat gain per year, with an approximate simultaneous loss of one-half pound of fat-free mass or muscle. Consider that if you overeat just 100 calories per day, you will gain one pound in a month. An extra ten pounds can sneak up on you in one year.

Obesity Prevention

Activity is the optimal way to manage current weight or successfully lose weight. The key is to exercise, maintain a healthy diet throughout your life, and avoid gaining excess weight. Participate in planned exercise as well as increased lifestyle activity. Establish support systems to help you with exercise adherence and healthy lifestyle habits.

How Does Activity Help Obesity?

There is only a 2 to 3 percent success rate for people who lose weight to actually maintain weight loss (Texas A&M University Human Nutrition Conference, 1998). Those who are successful are usually committed to a regular

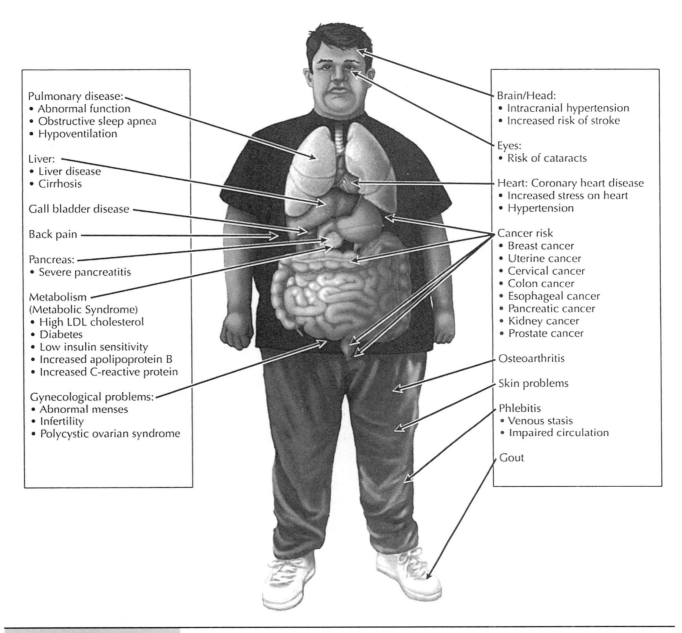

FIGURE 6.4

Medical Cost Associated with Obesity $100 Billion

Source: From *Concepts of Physical Fitness* 15th edition, by Charles Corbin et al. Copyright © 2009 by McGraw-Hill Companies. Reprinted by permission of The McGraw-Hill Companies, Inc.

exercise routine. Exercise greatly increases the likelihood of success with a maintenance program after weight loss. Weight gain occurs with inactivity; activity is the best way to reduce the size of fat stores. Even a small weight loss, 10 percent of your weight, helps boost the basal metabolic rate, which is often suppressed when a person diets without exercise. Activity, specifically weight training, has been shown to increase a person's confidence and self-esteem, regardless of actual weight loss.

How Do I Lose Weight?

The bottom line is that in order to lose weight, the calories you take in must be less than the calories that you expend. Once you have determined what your daily caloric needs are, then estimate how many calories you are actually

The bottom line is that in order to lose weight, the calories you take in must be less than the calories you expend.

© Saniphoto, 2012, Shutterstock, Inc.

eating on a regular basis. The recommended weight loss is one-half to one pound per week. Losing weight faster often signifies a short-term fix, indicating that the weight loss will be difficult to maintain. Fast weight loss is often followed by fast weight gain. This is called **yo-yo dieting,** and often the weight gain is a bit more than what was initially lost. Repeated bouts of weight loss/gain like this can gradually add unwanted excess weight. Studies have shown that yo-yo dieting through the years can make it more difficult to lose weight in the future. This also adds stress to your cardiovascular system because the workload on your heart constantly fluctuates.

In order to change your lifestyle habits to lose weight, you must change your behaviors. Determine what behaviors and everyday patterns seem to sabotage your efforts. Is it the donut cart mid-morning at the office? Is it going through the drivethrough at 2 a.m. after going out with friends? Anticipate these challenges and plan ahead. Use the behavior change activity at the end of Chapter 1 in order to focus on your goal. Most likely your goal will include examining your current diet. Use your results from the diet analysis activity at the end of Chapter 5 (Nutrition).

In order to lose a pound, there needs to be an approximate 3,500 caloric deficit. Eating 500 calories less per day over the week may cause that to occur, or expending an extra 500 calories per day may cause that to occur. The best option is to include both. Exercise is the key to losing weight, and is also the key to maintaining weight loss. The importance of movement illustrates how critical it is to find an activity that you enjoy so that you can embrace it for the rest of your life. Walking is the most popular activity in the United States (refer back to Figure 6.3). See Table 6.3 to determine a reasonable schedule for you to lose weight with a walking and caloric restriction program.

If you eat less food than you regularly eat as you might on a calorie restricted diet, the body's natural tendency is to slow the basal metabolic rate up to 30 percent. Exercise does the opposite—it will increase your metabolism. Staying active when trying to lose weight is critical because it burns calories, increases metabolism, and preserves muscle (see Table 6.4). Fad diets accompanied by no exercise often result in weight lost with an actual increase in percent body fat due to the loss of lean body mass. See the example below of Sally and the school dance to see the effects of fad diets versus a change in lifestyle.

Sally was invited to the annual spring dance with her sweetheart. She wanted desperately to lose the "freshman 15"—the extra pounds she had put on in the previous year in order to fit into her favorite little black dress.

TABLE 6.3 ♦ Countdown to Weight Loss

The combination of walking and cutting calories results in greater weight loss than either alone.

If you walk (minutes)	&	If you cut daily calories by	Days to Lose Weight				
			5 lb.	10 lb.	15 lb.	20 lb.	25 lb.
30		400	27	54	81	108	135
30		800	16	32	48	64	80
45		400	23	46	69	92	115
45		800	14	28	42	56	70
60		400	21	42	63	84	105
60		800	13	26	39	54	65

Source: cdc.gov

TABLE 6.4 ◆ How Much Physical Activity Do I Need?	
It really depends on what your health goals are. Here are some guidelines to follow:	
Goal	**Physical Activity Level for Adults**
Reduce the risk of chronic disease Manage body weight and prevent gradual unhealthy body weight gain	At least 30 minutes of a moderate intensity physical activity, above usual activity, most days of the week. Approximately 60 minutes of moderate intensity physical activity most days of the week while not exceeding calorie needs.
Maintain weight loss	At least 60 to 90 minutes of moderate intensity physical activity most days of the week while not exceeding calorie needs. Some people may need to talk to their healthcare provider before participating in this level of physical activity.

Source: cdc.gov

Option 1: Sally has two weeks before the event. She decides to crash diet. Sally drinks water and two ounces of fruit juice a day. She succeeds in losing thirteen pounds of water, fat, and muscle weight. Along the way, Sally is hungry, which leads to headaches and severe moodiness. She has little energy and sleeps through class. At the dance, Sally fits into her dress, but she is extremely fatigued. Because severe dieting can also cause an individual's blood pressure to plummet, resulting in dizziness, light-headedness, and fatigue, Sally has no energy. After the dance, Sally engages in some binge-eating behaviors. In several days' time, she gains back all the weight she lost. Unfortunately she does not gain back the muscle she lost, so her body fat increases.

Option 2: Sally can think now of next year's dance. She begins a program of walkjogging for thirty minutes five days a week. With each workout, she burns approximately 150–200 calories. Those 150 calories burned five days a week equals 750 calories each week. It will take Sally about a month to lose one pound if she does not limit her eating. If she sticks to this rather conservative program, Sally will have lost about twelve pounds in a year's time. Not only will Sally fit into her dress, but she will have established a habit and she has positively changed her lifestyle, her attitude, her body composition, her measurements, her lean body mass, and she has:

- increased her energy
- increased her muscular endurance
- increased her cardiovascular endurance
- reduced her risk of mental anxiety and depression
- improved her sleep patterns
- dealt with her stress in a positive manner
- increased her cognitive abilities
- reduced her risk of dying prematurely
- reduced her risk of heart disease, diabetes, high blood pressure
- reduced the risk of some cancers
- helped reduce risk of osteoporosis
- most likely decreased her mile time

Dieting or cutting back on calories is considered "severe" when an individual ingests fewer than 800 calories in a day. It is impossible to get all the nutrients you need with less than 1,000–1,200 calories daily. Physiological and psychological problems can result from chronic caloric restriction. Much of the weight lost with severe caloric restriction is in the form of muscle. Cardiac

Top Ten Reasons to Give Up Dieting

10. DIETS DON'T WORK. Even if you lose weight, you will probably gain it all back, and you might gain back more than you lost.
 9. DIETS ARE EXPENSIVE. If you didn't buy special diet products, you could save enough to get new clothes, which would improve your outlook right now.
 8. DIETS ARE BORING. People on diets talk and think about food and practically nothing else. There's a lot more to life.
 7. DIETS DON'T NECESSARILY IMPROVE YOUR HEALTH. Like the weight loss, health improvement is temporary. Dieting can actually cause health problems.
 6. DIETS DON'T MAKE YOU BEAUTIFUL. Very few people will ever look like models. Glamour is a look, not a size. You don't have to be thin to be attractive.
 5. DIETS ARE NOT SEXY. If you want to be more attractive, take care of your body and your appearance. Feeling healthy makes you look your best.
 4. DIETS CAN TURN INTO EATING DISORDERS. The obsession to be thin can lead to anorexia, bulimia, bingeing, and compulsive exercising.
 3. DIETS CAN MAKE YOU AFRAID OF FOOD. Food nourishes and comforts us, and gives us pleasure. Dieting can make food seem like your enemy, and can deprive you of all the positive things about food.
 2. DIETS CAN ROB YOU OF ENERGY. If you want to lead a full and active life, you need good nutrition, and enough food to meet your body's needs. And the number one reason to give up dieting:
 1. LEARNING TO LOVE AND ACCEPT YOURSELF JUST AS YOU ARE will give you self-confidence, better health, and a sense of well-being that will last a lifetime.

Source: From Council on Size & Weight Discrimination with permission. www.cswd.org

muscle can be weakened to the point that it is no longer able to pump blood through the body—resulting in death. See complications of eating disorders in Chapter 2.

Australian researchers have published a study that indicates our hormones can work against us to make us hungrier after weight loss, making it all the harder to maintain the new weight. The hormone **leptin** is in charge of letting the brain know how much body fat is present. With weight loss, leptin levels decrease which causes the appetite to increase and the metabolism to decrease. Even a year after the weight loss, the leptin levels were still lower. The study, although small, may shed some light on why it is so hard to lose weight. (*New York Times*, 2011)

Dietary Supplements

Eating a healthy diet with fruits, vegetables, whole grains, quality proteins, and unsaturated fats, as well as restricting refined white flour and sugar, is the best method for obtaining an adequate supply of nutrients in your diet. Dietary supplements are popular and provide a means for delivering these nutrients in a more convenient, but often less effective, form. It is a good idea to check with a health professional before beginning supplemention. Taken in concentrations higher than the recommended daily allowance, some nutrients have undesirable side effects, and some are even toxic.

Guidelines for a Successful Weight Loss Program

The American College of Sports Medicine has put together the following eleven guidelines in an effort to help individuals recognize potentially successful weight loss programs and avoid unsound or dangerous weight loss programs.

1. Prolonged fasting and diet programs that severely restrict caloric intake are scientifically unsound and can be medically dangerous.

2. Fasting and diet programs that severely restrict caloric intake result in the loss of large amounts of water, electrolytes, minerals, glycogen stores, and other fat-free tissues, but with minimal amounts of fat loss.

3. Mild caloric restriction (500–1,000 calories less than usual per day) results in smaller loss of water, electrolytes, minerals, and other fat-free tissues and is less likely to result in malnutrition.

4. Dynamic exercise of large muscle groups helps to maintain fat-free tissue, including lean muscle mass and bone density, and can result in a loss of body weight (primarily body fat).

5. A nutritionally sound diet resulting in mild caloric intake restrictions, coupled with an endurance exercise program, along with behavior modification of existing eating habits, is recommended for weight reduction. The rate of weight loss should never exceed two pounds per week.

6. To maintain proper weight control and optimal body fat levels, a lifetime commitment to proper eating habits and regular physical activity is required.

7. A successful weight loss plan can be followed anywhere—at home, work, restaurants, parties, and so on.

8. For a plan to be successful, the emphasis must be on portion size.

9. Successful weight loss plans incorporate a wide variety of nutritious foods that are easily accessible in the supermarket.

10. A weight loss plan must not be too costly if it is to be successful.

11. The most essential aspect of a weight loss program is that it can be followed for the rest of an individual's life.

Unfortunately some individuals think that if one pill is good, two or more must be better. In most cases this is simply not true. Sometimes, an excess of nutrients can be detrimental as is the case with fat-soluble vitamins A, D, E and K. Megadoses of many vitamins, minerals, and other supplements can cause kidney and liver damage and interact adversely with other supplements, herbs, and drugs. It is possible to interfere with absorption of other nutrients when ingesting megadoses of some supplements. In general, consuming more than the RDA of vitamins and minerals is discouraged. A registered dietician or physician may prescribe supplements for some populations or certain medical conditions (for instance, people who are pregnant, have anemia, are elderly, or are certain types of vegetarians).

Energy Drinks and Nutrition Bars

Energy drinks and nutrition bars have gained popularity with the public and college students in particular over the past several years. It is easy to see why—they are relatively inexpensive, easy and convenient to obtain and consume, and are reported to increase energy and alertness, boost academic and athletic performance, and offer extra nutrition (supplementation).

The fast-paced lifestyle of many college students makes the convenience of energy-on-the-go by way of drinks and bars especially appealing.

© Andresr, 2012, Shutterstock, Inc.

The most essential aspect of a weight loss program is that it can be followed for the rest of an individual's life.

While consuming an occasional energy drink is okay for most individuals and eating a protein/nutrition bar for breakfast is a better option than skipping breakfast, drinking 2 or 3 energy drinks daily and/or consuming a substantial amount of daily calories from bars is poor nutritional planning and will take its toll on your long-term health.

Many of the nutrition bars and caffeine drinks contain excessive amounts of caffeine, sugar, and calories. Excessive sugar and calories will result in unwanted weight gain and poor dental health and large amounts of caffeine can cause an individual to be "jittery," have headaches, an upset stomach, high blood pressure, or even irregular heartbeats.

Nutrition bars and energy drinks, in general, do not make good meal replacements. They lack the variety of nutrients that are needed for brain development and function and good physical performance.

Weight Loss Products

Appetite suppressants claim to help diminish a person's appetite, cut cravings, and increase overall energy and possibly increase metabolism. Over time this may result in weight loss, but consider the negative side effects. Appetite suppressants often contain high levels of caffeine, guarana, or Ma Huang (an herbal form of ephedra) that can cause hypertension, cardiac arrhythmia, myocardial infarction, and/or stroke that can and has led to premature death of the person consuming this type of dietary supplement. Examples of commonly used supplements include Hydroxycut, Xenadrine-EFX, and Trim Spa.

In 1997, fenfluramine and dexfenfluramine (fen/phen) were withdrawn from the market due to a link to the development of a heart valve problem. Serious illness and, in some cases, death occurred. Even FDA-approved drugs need to be used cautiously. In the 1960's and the 1970's amphetamines were often prescribed for weight loss, and in the 1920's weight loss pills were found to contain tapeworm eggs (Hales, 2007). Diet aids and supplements that have gone through rigorous testing and been approved by the FDA still need to be approached with common sense and caution.

Metabolism boosters are various supplements that speed up or boost an individual's basal metabolism. Most of these types of products claim to act in a way that increases the building of lean muscle mass. Examples of such supplements are creatine phosphate, chromium picolinate, and HMB. Megathin, Microlean, and Metabolife (now banned by the FDA) have appetite suppressants as well as metabolism boosters. Long-term effectiveness and safety of these types of supplements are unknown.

There are two types of weight loss programs, clinical and nonclinical. A clinical program is typically offered in a healthcare facility with a team of licensed health professionals. The following are examples of nonclinical programs: Jenny Craig, Nutrasystem, Weight Watchers, and Slimfast. Jenny Craig and Nutrasystem sell prepackaged foods which are convenient, but typically are higher in cost. Weight Watchers teaches participants the value of foods on a point system. The positive aspect of Weight Watchers is that participants are taught how to choose, shop, and prepare foods. Group support is essential and highly recommended after the goal weight is attained. Weight loss maintenance is one of the most difficult aspects of dieting, so support from others is often a significant help. Two other programs that offer group support are TOPS (Take Off Pounds Sensibly) and Overeaters Anonymous (OA). Programs such as Slimfast replace one or two meals with shakes or bars. Unless a person learns to make wise choices on their own, it is doubtful that weight loss will be maintained.

Low-carbohydrate high-protein diets are popular. The Zone, Atkins, Sugar-Busters, Protein Power, and the South Beach Diet are all examples of this type of diet. Although there are some variation in the diets, all advocate severely limiting carbohydrate foods such as pasta, potatoes, bread, cereals, juices,

Tips to Weight Loss Success

Be a SMART Planner!

SMART means being **S**pecific, **M**easured, **A**ppropriate, **R**ealistic, and **T**ime-bound about what you plan to achieve. For example, if your goal is to increase your physical activity, then write down the type of activity you plan to do, how many times you can realistically do it each week, and for how long each time. Start with small, short, and easier goals, and work your way up.

Make Yourself an Offer You Can't Refuse

Before starting to reach your next goal, offer yourself a promise like this, "If I reach my goal this (day, week, month), I will treat myself to a well-deserved (fill in a reward here, but not a food reward)." Think of something you want, such as an afternoon off, a massage, a movie, or even a deposit toward a larger reward. Be creative, set up rewards for yourself frequently, and make sure you give them to yourself when you reach your goal.

Balance Your (Food) Checkbook

Keep a diary of what you eat and how much physical activity you get each day. Then, at the end of each week, record your weight in the same diary. You and your healthcare provider can use this information to adjust your eating and physical activity plan to find the best way to reach your goal.

Keep an Eye on the Size!

Did you know that we eat most of what is on our plate, no matter what the size of the plate? When at home, try using smaller plates; they will help you take smaller portions. When eating out, share an entrée! Studies show that portions today are often super-sized—enough for two or more people to share.

How Much Is Enough Activity?

You need to get at least 30 minutes of moderate physical activity per day, most days of the week to help burn up extra calories. But give yourself credit for the activities that you're already doing. Common activities such as climbing stairs, pushing a stroller, gardening, and walking all count as physical activity. Just make sure you do enough of them.

Am I Full Yet?

The question may take longer to answer than you think. It takes 15 minutes or more for the message that we're full to get from our stomachs to our brains. So take a few minutes before digging in for that next helping. Having trouble feeling full? Eight glasses (8 ounces each) or more of water or other non-caloric beverages daily fills you up and keeps you refreshed. Also, vegetables and fruits can help you feel fuller, especially when eaten raw.

Source: www.nhlbi.nih.gov/health/public/heart/obesity/lose_wt/index.htm.

sweets, and even fruits and vegetables. Protein-rich foods are plentiful. Steak, ham, bacon, eggs, fish, chicken, and cheese are allowed to be eaten in unlimited quantities for some diets.

The basis for the low-carbohydrate diet is that during digestion, carbohydrates are converted into glucose, which serves as fuel for every cell in a person's body. When blood glucose levels begin to rise, insulin, the hormone that allows the entry of glucose into the cells, is released. This process lowers the level of glucose in the bloodstream. If the available glucose is not rapidly used for normal cellular functions or physical activity, the glucose is converted to and stored as body fat. Individuals who support this type of diet believe that if a person eats fewer carbohydrates and more protein, they will produce less insulin, and as insulin levels drop, the body will look to its own fat stores to meet energy needs.

While research has shown that people participating in low-carbohydrate high-protein diets do initially lose weight more rapidly than an individual who maintains a more nutritionally balanced diet but decreases calorie intake and increases physical activity, these same studies show that at the one-year mark weight loss for many of the dieters in both groups was not significantly different. Low carbohydrate diets also have the potential to result in the loss of B vitamins, calcium, and potassium. This can lead to osteoporosis, constipation, bad breath, and fatigue. Before starting on this type of diet, consider that because the diet is high in protein, and therefore high in fat, it may carry an increased risk for heart disease.

Super-Size Meals Lead to Super-Size Problems

Most days, you're mindful of what you eat. Some days, though, if you're out of your routine, you may be tempted to go overboard on high-calorie, fatty foods. Can one big meal at your favorite restaurant be so bad? Research shows that it may.

Just one bad meal choice can have immediate effects that are most dangerous for people who are at risk for or already have heart disease. After just one large fatty meal, you may have:

- **Stiffer arteries, reduced blood flow.** Blood vessel dilation and expansion is hampered by a big high-fat meal. Large meal digestion forces your heart to work harder, increasing the heart rate, to meet the needs of the digestive tract. Sometimes people who have cardiovascular disease and eat a large meal before exercising will suffer angina or possibly a heart attack.
- **Higher blood pressure.** Norepinephrine is a stress hormone that can be released by a big meal. This hormone raises blood pressure and heart rate.
- **High triglycerides.** Triglycerides are fats in the blood, and any meal elevates levels. A super-size meal loaded with fat or refined carbohydrates boosts levels most and keeps them elevated for up to twelve hours.
- **Blood sugar effects.** A diabetic's ability to process glucose can be impaired by a large meal.
- **Heartburn.** The bigger the meal, the more you'll suffer from gastric reflux if you are susceptible to heartburn.

How to Combat a Super-Sized Meal

There have been some studies that indicate taking high doses of vitamin C and E before eating a fatty meal help maintain arterial blood flow. However, it is not conclusive that these vitamins—or any others—can protect your heart in either the short- or long-run. Another study determined that young, healthy people who ate a super-size meal (1,000 calories' worth) and then walked quickly for 45 minutes had the benefit of having their arteries' ability to dilate restored. That being said, exercise is not going to wipe out all the bad effects of overeating. It's also worth noting that exercising after eating a big meal may cause more problems for those of us who are older or have less than perfect health.

Points to Ponder

Overdoing it at the buffet table on occasion shouldn't be a problem if you're healthy. For those who have conditions such as diabetes, high cholesterol or blood pressure, heart disease, or if you smoke and/or are very overweight, ordering your meals super-sized is never a good idea. Plan before you go to a

Fad diets

Fad diets are risky because they...

- tend to be very low in calories
- are limited to a few foods, limiting key nutrients and minerals
- produce only short-term, rapid weight loss—not long-term weight management
- ignore the importance of physical activity in healthy weight loss
- increase risks for certain diseases or health complications
- take the pleasure and fun out of eating
- alter metabolism, making it easier to regain the weight after the diet has ceased

Diets That Don't Work

1. **"Magical"/Same Foods Diets** (i.e., grapefruit, cabbage soup, Subway diet)
   - *Pros*—usually the single food is a nutritious food
   - *Cons*—too few calories, risk of overeating, lacking of specific nutrients, lack variety, do not teach healthy eating habits, do not encourage exercise
2. **High-Protein Diets** (i.e., Atkins)
   - *Pros*—weight loss does occur
   - *Cons*—high in saturated fat and cholesterol increasing risk for heart disease; high protein puts strain on liver and kidneys; lacks vitamins, minerals, complex carbohydrates, and fiber; weight loss is water weight, not fat; lack of carbs causes a condition called ketosis with symptoms of nausea, weakness, and dehydration
3. **Liquid Diets** (i.e., Slimfast)
   - *Pros*—drinks have vitamins, minerals, and high-quality protein
   - *Cons*—do not teach new ways of eating, no long-term weight loss, very low in calories
4. **Gimmicks, Gadgets, and Other "Miracles"**
   - *Pros*—none
   - *Cons*—may be harmful, expensive, do not teach healthy eating, do not encourage exercise

Effective Weight Loss Questionnaire

1. ***Could you follow the diet for the rest of your life?*** Good health and permanent weight loss require a lifestyle change, not just a temporary modification.
2. ***Does the diet promise quick results?*** If so, you're probably losing water and lean muscle tissue. Weight loss of one-half to two pounds a week is safe and will more likely be kept off.
3. ***Does the diet accommodate your lifestyle?*** Any diet that does not allow much freedom or flexibility is less likely to be followed permanently.
4. ***Is the diet very low in calories?*** Any diet that is below 1,200 calories per day could be dangerous. You may not be getting enough energy and nutrients. You may feel deprived and frustrated, both physically and mentally. In the long run, metabolism slows in order to conserve energy with very low calorie diets.
5. ***Does the diet eliminate or restrict certain food groups?*** Many diets leave out one or more food groups. Restricting a type of food may result in elimination of essential nutrients in the diet causing health risks. A balanced diet modeled after the Food Guide Pyramid and including a variety of foods should be followed.
6. ***Does the diet call for unusual items or require you to go to a specialty store?*** Unusual foods or supplements may be very costly and hard to obtain. They may also contain dangerous ingredients that are not regulated by the Food and Drug Administration.
7. ***Will someone make money on the diet?*** If yes, BEWARE! The diet could be a quick way for someone to make a lot of money.
8. ***Is the author or supplier reputable?*** To check for validity and credibility of a book, diet, or supplement, view the list of references provided and check the credentials of the author.

party or out to that favorite restaurant so you're not starving when you get there. Fill your plate with foods high in water content that will serve to fill you up—stick with mainly fruits and vegetables. Take your time eating and enjoy the food so you notice when your body tells your brain that you're full. Once you're finished, take a nice walk.

Fad Diets

Each year billions of dollars are spent in the weight loss industry. Unfortunately, many of these dollars are spent on diet plans that are unhealthy, cannot be maintained long term, or simply do not work. The lure of a quick and easy way to "melt away" the pounds is too tempting for many individuals, and although the diets are more times than not ineffective in the long term, weight loss hopefuls are willing to give almost anything a chance. To avoid the pitfalls of an unsuccessful, unreliable, or even dangerous weight loss plan, one should always take the time to check out as much factual information as possible from a variety of sources. The boxed information on page 223 contains a list of some fad diets that are currently popular and the theories and possible shortcomings within these diets.

Healthy Habits

Building a Healthy Plate

The concept of building a healthy plate was introduced on page 188 in Chapter 5. This practice is a key healthy habit to form early on and stick with throughout one's lifetime. A "healthy plate" is typically smaller in size, about 9" in diameter, than a typical dinner plate found in most homes and is certainly smaller than the average size plate served in restaurants. Filling half of the plate with fruits and vegetables and making half of the grains consumed whole grains are essential components to building a healthy plate. Eating a variety of small, lean, natural sources of protein and switching to skim or fat free dairy products are also important when building a healthy plate.

Healthy Weight Gain

Although they are in the minority, many people struggle to gain weight. It is important for individuals who feel that they are "too thin" to recognize that there are healthy and unhealthy ways of accomplishing their goal of weight gain. Overeating all types of foods will simply result in an increase in body fat.

Adding lean body mass through strength training and a slight caloric increase is a much healthier alternative. Chapter 3 outlines the benefits of muscular fitness, as well as presents helpful guidelines for beginning a strength training regimen. Nutrition information on page 194 of Chapter 5 identifies ways to add calories in an appropriate portion and manner to maximize their benefits.

Healthy Food Shopping

The National Heart, Lung, and Blood Institute Obesity Guidelines (www. nhlbi.nih. gov/health/public/heart/obesity/lose_wt/shop.htm) list the following suggestions to help individuals prepare healthier home cooked meals in shorter periods of time. They recommend reading labels while shopping—paying particular attention to serving sizes and the number of servings in the container. Comparing the total number of calories in similar products and choosing the product containing the lower number of total calories will result in a healthier meal. Finally, make cooking at home easier and healthier by shopping for quick, low-fat food items and filling kitchen cabinets with a supply of lower calorie staples such as:

- fat-free or low-fat milk, yogurt, cheese, and cottage cheese
- light or diet margarine
- sandwich breads, bagels, pita bread, English muffins, low-fat tortillas
- plain cereal, dry or cooked
- rice and pastas, dry beans, and peas
- fresh, frozen, canned fruits in light syrup or juice
- fresh, frozen, or no-salt-added canned vegetables
- low-fat or no-fat salad dressings and sandwich spreads
- mustard and ketchup
- jam, jelly, or honey
- salsa, herbs, and spices

Fast Foods/Eating Out

People eat more meals outside the home than ever before. Due to their quick service and relatively low food prices, fast-food chains are the most frequent source for meals eaten away from home. Each day 50 million people line up inside or drive through outside service lanes of one of the over 160,000 fast-food establishments in this country.

When meals are prepared with speed and convenience as the primary focus, good nutrition will, in most cases, suffer. A great majority of fast foods are high in fat, calories, and salt, and low in many of the essential nutrients and dietary fiber.

However, fast food does not have to mean "junk food." While it may take a little more thought and discretion, quick and healthy alternatives do exist. Depending on what ingredients are used and how the food is prepared, fast foods served in restaurants can be healthy. Most restaurants have nutritional information about the foods they serve posted in the dining area or on their menus. By taking a couple of extra minutes to think about their best and most nutritious options, an individual can make dining out more nutritious, filling, and healthy.

Another pitfall of eating meals prepared away from home is the quality of food an individual is served. In an effort to be competitive, many restaurants serve well beyond an adequate portion size. To control portion sizes when eating out, order from the senior citizens or kids menus, share the entrée with a friend, or take part of the food home for a later meal.

Another way to eat healthy when dining out is to select foods that are steamed, broiled, baked, roasted, or poached rather than foods that are fried or grilled. Asking if the restaurant will trim visible fat off the meat or serve butter, sauces, or dressings "on the side" is another way to ensure a healthy and tasty meal.

Fitness or Fatness

Our food choices and habits, our exercise habits, and our genetic make-up all play a role in our ability to maintain a healthy weight. Managing weight is brought about most successfully by a lifestyle choice, not a short-term diet. Even if both of your parents are overweight and you didn't have good nutrition emphasized when you were young, you can make wise choices for yourself today.

Make small positive changes to encourage healthful behaviors. If you are over-weight or obese, even a small 5 percent to 10 percent weight loss can have a favorable effect on your overall health risk.

© Jason Stitt, 2012. Shutterstock, Inc.

Everyday choices make a difference!

Tips for Healthy Dining at Home and Away

When restaurant eating, ask for a to-go box right away and put half of your order in it as soon as it comes.

Order a dinner salad, but share the entree with a friend when eating out.

Order water with your meal rather than a soda—save money and calories.

Opt for your traditional foods made in a "light" version. Use a smaller plate to encourage smaller portions. Drink a glass of water before your meal.

Eat your salad first.

Eat slowly. Put your eating utensil down and enjoy your meal or converse between bites.

Eat breakfast regularly.

Always have healthy snacks in your backpack or briefcase or car.

Try eating fruits for dessert.

Trim visible fat off meat and take skin off poultry before cooking.

Try to use less refined sugar and processed flour in food preparation. Try whole wheat flour or unbleached white flour.

Wean yourself off sodas—or try to cut way down on your intake.

Read labels: minimize corn syrup, trans fat, coconut oil, palm kernel oil, and cocoa butter.

Use added fats like salad dressings minimally—try dipping your fork into the dressing before skewering the lettuce.

Avoid supersizing your meal.

References

American Heart Association. Heart Disease and Stroke Statistics. 2012 Update.

Bishop, A. *Step Up to Wellness: A Stage Based Approach* (1st ed). Needham Heights, MA: Allyn & Bacon. 1999.

The Center for Health and Healthcare in Schools, School of Public Health and Health Services, George Washington University Medical Center. *Childhood Overweight: What the Research Tells Us*. March 2005 Update. www.healthinschools.org

Corbin, C. and Welk, G. *Concepts of Physical Fitness* (15th ed). Dubuque, IA: McGraw-Hill. 2009.

Donatelle, R. J. *Access to Health* (9th ed). Boston: Allyn & Bacon. 2006.

Flegal, K. M., Carrol, M. D., Kuczmarski, R. J., and Johnson, C. L. Overweight and Obesity in the United States: Prevalence and Trends, 1960–1994. *International Journal of Obesity and Related Metabolic Disorders* 22:39–47. 1998.

Floyd, P., Mims, S., and Yelding-Howard, C. *Personal Health: Perspectives and Lifstyles*. Morton Publishing Co. 2007.

Gibbs, W. W. Obesity: An Overblown Epidemic? *Scientific American*, May 23, 2005.

Hahn, D. B. and Payne, W. A. *Understanding Your Health*. McGraw-Hill. 2008.

Hales, D. *An Invitation to Wellness* (Instructor Ed.). Thomson-Wadsworth, 2007.

Hoeger, W. W. K. and Hoeger, S. A. *Lifetime Physical Fitness and Wellness: A Personalized Program* (10th ed). Belmont, CA: Wadsworth. 2009.

http://ahha.org

http://www.cdc.gov/nccdphp/dnpa/healthyweight/physical_activity/index.htm

http://www.nhlbi.nih.gov/health/public/heart/obesity/lose_wt/shop.htm

http://kidshealth.org/pagemanager.jsp?dn-kidsHealthbSlic

http://www.foodinsight.org/Resources

http://www.reachout.com.au/default.asp?ti=2249

http://www.cfsan.fda.gov/~dms/foodlab.html

http://www.win.niddk.nih.gov/publications/tools.htm

http://www.womhealth.org.au/studentfactsheets/bodyimage.htm

Hyman, B., Oden, G., Bacharach, D., and Collins, R. *Fitness for Living*. Dubuque, IA: Kendall-Hunt Publishing Co. 2006.

IUFOST, International Union of Food Science and Technology Bulletin. Trans-fatty Acids, May 2006.

Neighmond, *Patti, Gain together, Lose Together: The Weight-Loss 'Halo' Effect,* Health Blog: NPR http://www.npr.org/blogs/health/2012/03/12, retrieved 3/17/12.

Nordestgaard, B. G., Benn, M., Schnohr, P., Tybjærg-Hansen, A. Nonfasting triglycerides and risk of myocardial infarction, ischemic heart disease, and death in men and women. *JAMA*. 2007; 298(3):299–308, PubMed.

O'Neil, Patrick. Weight Management Center, Medical University of South Carolina. 2009. www.muschealth.com

Powers, S. K., Todd, S. L., and Noland, U. J. *Total Fitness and Wellness* (2nd ed). Boston: Allyn & Bacon. 2005.

Prentice, W. E. *Fitness and Wellness for Life* (6th ed). New York: WCB McGraw-Hill. 1999.

Pruitt, B. E. and Stein, J. *Health Styles*. Boston: Allyn & Bacon. 1999.

Rosato, F. *Fitness for Wellness* (3rd ed). Minneapolis: West. 1994.

Satcher, D. Surgeon General's Report on Physical Activity and Health. Atlanta: U.S. Department of Health and Human Services, CDC. 1996.

Texas A&M University, Student Health Services. Fad Diets: Promise or Profit, 77, 2002.

Texas A&M University Human Nutrition Conference. College Station, TX. 1998.

Wilmore, J. H. Exercise, Obesity, and Weight Control, *Physical Activity and Research Digest*. Washington, DC: President's Council on Physical Fitness and Sports. 1994.

World Health Organization (WHO). Management of Severe Malnutrition: A Manual for Physicians and other Senior Health Workers. Geneva: Author. 1999.

World Health Organization (WHO). Obesity: Preventing and Managing the Global Epidemic — Report of WHO Consultation on Obesity. Geneva, June 1997.

Surgeon General's Call to Action to Prevent and Decrease Overweight and Obesity. 2005. www.surgeongeneral.gov

Diet Books: What the Experts Say, *Consumer Reports*, June 2007, 14–15.

Diet Plans: What the Studies Say, *Consumer Reports*, June 2007, 16–17.

Recommended Reading

Eat, Drink and Be Healthy: The Harvard Medical School Guide to Healthy Eating by Walter C. Willett, M.D. Simon and Schuster Source, 2001.

The Spectrum: A Scientifically Proven Program to Feel Better, Live Longer, Lose Weight, and Gain Health. Ballantine Books, 2007.

Activities

Notebook Activities

Body Mass Index Calculator

Facts about My Favorite Fast-Food Meal

Name _____ Section _____ Date _____

Body Mass Index Calculator

In order to complete this Body Mass Index assignment, go to http://www.cdc.gov/nccdphp/dnpa/bmi/calc-bmi.htm

Body Mass Index is a mathematical formula that correlates highly with body fat. This weight calculation helps determine whether you are at a healthy weight or have too much fat.

The formula for BMI =

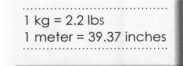

1 kg = 2.2 lbs
1 meter = 39.37 inches

$$\frac{\text{Weight (kg)}}{\text{Height (m)}^2}$$

Note:

If you are under the age of 20 years, you have the option of using the BMI-by-age calculator.

1. Enter your weight and height using English or metric measurements. What is your BMI? _____

2. What is your weight status according to your BMI calculation? _____

3. Click on "What does this all mean?"
   How can two individuals, one fit and one unfit, who weigh the same and are the same height have the same BMI?

4. What does your BMI tell you about your health risk?

<18	Underweight
19–26	Healthy Weight (low risk)
27–29	Overweight (medium risk)
30–40	Obese (high risk)
>40	Morbidly obese (very high risk)

A BMI of 25 or higher is associated with an increased health risk of conditions that include coronary heart disease, certain forms of cancer, stroke, high blood pressure, and non insulin-dependent diabetes.

NOTEBOOK ACTIVITY

Facts about My Favorite Fast-Food Meal

1. List your favorite fast-food meal in the space provided below—be specific and detailed. Include anything you consume with the meal and the quantity (i.e., large beverage, four ketchup or salsa packets, etc.).

2. Go to the restaurant and obtain a nutritional analysis of their foods. This information is generally available as a pamphlet. You might also be able to obtain this information from the restaurant's Web site.

3. Determine and list the following for your meal:

   A. total number of calories

   B. grams of total fat

   C. grams of saturated fat

   D. grams of trans fat

4. Use Table 6.2 on page 214 to determine your daily calorie allowance based on your age, gender, and activity level. List that information in the space provided below.

   Age:

   Gender:

   Activity Level:

   Estimated Daily Caloric Allowance:

5. Using Table 5.2 on page 159 of Chapter 5 (What Is Your Upper Limit on Fat for the Calories You Consume) and your estimated daily caloric allowance, judge how "healthy" your food choice was in relation to the total number of calories it contains and the number of grams of total fat, saturated fat, and trans fat it contains. When you are looking at these numbers, remember that the calorie allowance and the limit on fat is for all food consumed within a twenty-four-hour period, and the meal listed is probably only about one-third of the calories and fat you will consume during this time period. In the space below, use the numbers you compared and briefly describe how "healthy" your choice was.

6. Other than never eating this meal, what modifications could reasonably be made to keep this meal in your diet but make it a more nutritionally sound choice?

WRITING PROMPTS

- What is your favorite restaurant? What do you typically order? List at least 3 ways, other than not eating the meal, you could realistically improve the nutritional quality of this meal.

- Why are fad diets ineffective for long-term weight loss? Identify successful weight loss programs in your community.

Chapter 7
Relationships

© 2012, Shutterstock, Inc.

OBJECTIVES

Students will be able to:

♦ List and describe the three elements of a healthy relationship.

♦ List five ways to reduce the risk of date rape.

♦ Identify the differences between males and females and how these differences relate to communication.

♦ List warning signs of an unhealthy relationship.

♦ Identify types of abuse and describe the cycle of abuse and why it's difficult for the victim to end the relationship.

"It's not about getting what you want, it's about wanting what you've got."

—Sheryl Crow

Healthy Relationships

There are numerous types of relationships that exist. They range from casual acquaintances to life-long partners. It is important to realize the different types and stages that relationships grow into, as well as what represents a healthy relationship.

Positive Self-Worth

The first step to having a healthy relationship is developing a positive self-worth. This self-worth comes from many different sources. These may include family members, close friends, co-workers, occupation, achievements, and so on. A couple of questions to answer might include: (1) Whom do you see in the mirror? (2) Would you want a relationship with you? A positive self-worth is represented in confidence, a healthy body, and a positive attitude about yourself and others. This is not to say that one has to be completely healthy in order to have a healthy relationship, but the closer to this goal the better relationships typically will be.

Healthy relationships include open communication, compromise, trust, respect, caring, selflessness, as well as many other attributes. Researchers have found that 70 to 93 percent of messages sent come from nonverbal communication. Non-verbal communication includes unwritten and unspoken information; these can be both intentional and unintentional. Some examples include smiling, eye contact, nodding, leaning closer, crossed arms, looking off in another direction, and even rolling eyes. Mismatch of verbal and non-verbal communication can cause confusion. When this happens, people tend to believe the nonverbal communication more readily, which comes from the old saying, "Actions speak louder than words." With this in mind, pay attention to the messages you are sending nonverbally. As mentioned earlier, some individuals will lean closer to let a person know they are interested in them or in what is being said. There are different spatial zones that exist. There is an acceptable amount of space or a "zone" that individuals claim as their personal space. Depending upon the circumstance, geographic location (such as a crowded city), or culture one grew up in, this zone changes. For example, this zone is larger when an individual is in a public or social environment, but typically becomes smaller when they are in a more personal or intimate setting. If your personal zone becomes too small for your comfort level, take two steps backward to increase the size of the space.

Open Communication

Open communication involves actively listening, talking effectively, and body language. Minimize or alleviate other distractions in order to maximize open communication with your partner or friend. This may include turning off the radio, the television, or maybe getting away from other friends and/or roommates. During a discussion truly listen to the other person. Do not interrupt or simply wait until they are finished speaking to interject your thought or advice. So much of the time people only hear the first part of a sentence or a concept because they are busy forming their thoughts and ideas of how they are going to reply. Periodically confirm the main points that you are hearing. Do this before proceeding with the conversation. Do this several times during the discussion, as well as at the end, to make certain that you agree on the conclusion and the important points discussed. Be open to questions. Do not continuously lead the conversation. Let the other person talk and listen to what they have to say.

Communication Styles

There are numerous ways to communicate with one another. Each individual has their own style of communication. Four basic communication styles include: assertive, aggressive, passive, and passive-aggressive. The type of communication an individual chooses to use at any given time is dependent upon the current situation, how important the concept or information is to them, and their personality. Communication styles are learned throughout one's life from parents, siblings, peers, and co-workers and are blended into a style that is preferred and compatible with one's personality.

Communication styles tend to differ between genders. Males tend to be more assertive while females tend to use more passive communication styles.

Spelling a Healthy Relationship

(adapted from Kuriansky, 2002)

Honesty—always tell the truth even if it will initially hurt.
Harmony—enrich one another's differences.
Heart—give your whole heart.
Honor—hold others in high regard.
Happy—be happy with each other.

Empathy—be able to understand what each other feel.
Equality—treat the other as your equal.
Energetic—be spontaneous, relationships take energy.
Enthusiasm—be excited about being together.
Empowerment—support each other.

Acceptance—know that you approve of each other just the way they are.
Accommodation—make adjustments for each other's needs.
Appreciation—be grateful for each other.
Adaptability—be able to make changes when necessary.
Agreements—make an agreement and hold to it.

Love—should be unconditional.
Loyalty—be devoted, never betray each other.
Listening—actively listen, it makes the other person feel important.
Laughter—have fun together.
Lust—sparks the union.

Trust—being able to relax around the other person.
Talking—communication is the key.
Time—spend time together. Nothing is more important than time.
Tenderness—treat each other with kindness.
Thoughtfulness—show consideration in thoughts and actions.

Home—create a safe haven.
Healing—work together to heal new and old wounds.
Humility—admit when you are wrong.
Hope—for a better tomorrow when things are not at their best.
Homework—relationships are not easy, they do require constant work.

YES! Say yes as often as you can.

These generalizations do not always hold true. There are always exceptions to these ideas. It is helpful to recognize and understand communication styles and differences early in relationships regardless if they are personal or professional to help strengthen communication and minimize miscommunication.

Left-brain vs. Right-brain.   Men typically are associated with left-brained dominance (see Table 7.1), with their cognitive style being more logical (focusing more on problems and solutions). Whereas, women typically are associated with rightbrained dominance, with emphasis on communication and emotions (Kuriansky, 2003).

So, what does this mean? Men and women approach simple as well as complex relationships very differently. The first step to a healthy relationship is to realize these differences exist. Secondly, respect these differences. Then you can begin to understand the differences, where they come from, and make your relationship a healthier one. Always work toward compromise and find the best solution to fulfill your relationship. As stated earlier, the above characteristics are simply generalizations, not the rule. In the recent past there have been trends to meet more in the middle with some of these characteristics. Inevitably when you have two different sets of ideas and philosophies arguments will occur. Realize that long-term stress can have a detrimental effect on your relationship. Try to engage in stress-relieving techniques discussed in Chapter 2. A typical response to increased stress is arguing. Always try to argue fairly, which sometimes is hard to do when individuals are tired and stressed.

Differences between Males and Females

(Adapted from Godek, 1997)
The following are generalizations, trends, and some personal observations.

- **Men** hear "sex" when you say "romance."
- **Women** hear "love" when you say "romance."

- **Men** can easily separate their sexuality from their feelings.
- **Women** connect many emotional issues with their sexuality.

- **Men** communicate to gather information.
- **Women** communicate to create relationships.

- **Men** view relationships in a hierarchical manner.
- **Women** view relationships as a vast interlocking network.

- **Men** are aroused visually and quickly.
- **Women** are aroused through sensation and slowly.

- **Men** have been taught to hide their tender feelings.
- **Women** have been taught to hide their angry feelings.

- **Men** have been taught to suppress their gentle side.
- **Women** have been taught to suppress their aggressive side.

TABLE 7.1 ◆ How Differences in Brain Dominance Affect Behavior

Left Brain (Male)	Right Brain (Female)
Values power or being in control	Values love and communication
Needs approval and acceptance	Needs appreciation and attention
Fulfilled by achieving goals	Fulfilled by expression and relating
More interested in news and sports	More interested in romance novels and self-help
Comfortable with gadgets and hi-tech	Comfortable with gab groups

Source: Adapted from Kuriansky, 2003.

As for talking effectively, be straightforward and say what you mean. Do not beat around the bush and hope that your friend or partner can read your mind. If you say you do not care about a certain situation, then mean that you do not care. If you have an opinion, let your friend or partner know what it is. Friends and partners will not always agree on every decision; therefore, compromise is important in a healthy relationship.

Compromise

In order to come to an appropriate compromise, discuss the pros and cons about a certain situation and then come to a mutual agreement. An individual will not always get what they want, but sometimes an idea synthesizes from the two and is much better. Sometimes it is important to concede and let the other individual get what they desire, and other times this gesture must be returned. Problems typically occur when one person is always conceding.

Trust

Trust is an integral element in a healthy relationship. From friendship to life-long partner, individuals must be able to trust the people they spend time with. Trust takes time to develop. Be cautious and do not expose deep feelings and internal ideas too early, but at the same time give others a chance to build trust little by little. In a relationship built upon trust one can discuss issues with confidence and know that these ideas will be kept private if necessary. Another element associated with trust is that in this person's absence one can trust the friend's ideas and actions. A relationship built upon trust can have incredible rewards. With this added element each person is comfortable being himself or herself and the relationship can develop to a completely different level. When complete trust exists many problems such as jealousy are non-existent in the relationship.

Healthy relationships include open communication, compromise, trust, respect, and caring.

Types of Relationships

There are many types of relationships, which fulfill many different needs. We begin with our family relationships, parents, siblings, aunts, uncles, and so on. This is the core of our foundation. In today's society we have many different structures that represent "family." Some individuals are raised by both of their biological parents, or maybe just one parent, others by grandparents, and others are adopted, to name a few. These initial relationships have a huge impact upon how we relate with others. What type of relationship do you have with your parents? Is it close? What changes would you make in your relationships with family members if you had the chance? Who has impacted you the most in your family? Was this a positive or negative impact? When there is a good foundation of healthy relationships with family members this typically carries over to friendships and intimate relationships.

Parental Relationship Stages

Similar to most relationships, the parental and child relationship has many stages in which it progresses through in an individual's life. These different stages can have easy, routine, or difficult transitions. As with most situations, open, honest, and respectful communication is one of the key elements to a successful relationship. It is helpful when both parties recognize the ever-changing dynamics of this very unique relationship. Problems can arise when one party is ready or needs to transition to the next stage, but the other half of the relationship is not ready or does not recognize the need for a change. It only takes one side of the equation to be unaware of the change in the relationship for communication problems to develop. This section will try to bring awareness to the transitions in hopes of facilitating the normal developmental cycle.

Before College

Since this is a textbook targeting a college population, the transitions before college are already in the past. Take a moment to think back on how you communicate with your parents now compared to just 10 years ago. Obvious, a lot has changed. This will likely continue.

The initial stage of the parent-child relationship is that of complete dependency during infancy and early childhood. As the child grows older and develops more independence, it is necessary for the relationship to change. During the elementary years, it is critical for the parent to teach and guide a child. This is the foundational time for the rest of an individual's life.

As the child transitions to middle school (ear4ly transition of independence) there is a tendency to move back and forth toward independence. A middle-school-aged individual still needs a large amount of guidance (possibly more than in the early years), but they are also trying to become more independent. This is the stage that peer influence becomes much stronger. This change in influence can compliment or undermine the lessons parents have taught for many years. Parental involvement and guidance is still import, but at a distance.

As an individual matures into high school (intermediate transition of independence) years, the amount of influence a parent has is quickly diminishing. The teenager traditionally lives at home, but is likely to have a part-time job, attend school, and is becoming more independent. The peer influence is almost at the peak of an individual's life and parental influence, and sometimes even parental guidance, is minimal to none. During this stage, communication and respect are critical from both parties. Parents need to respectfully communicate their expectations and rules and teenagers need to respectfully communicate their needs to their parents.

During College

One the young adult has moved to college (late or almost complete transition to independence), it can be more difficult to decipher boundaries and expectations. This is especially true if the parents are still paying for living and college expenses. The young adult is experiencing complete independence for the first time in their life. No one is there to tell them when to be home, what and when to eat, who to hang out with, etc. This is refreshing and exhilarating to most students, but it can also be a significant unrecognized stressor. It is not uncommon for the new college student to feel anxiety from the new situation, but not immediately recognize its source. Many college freshmen report an internal struggle between their need for complete independence and the relative comfort of the past parent-child bond. This unfamiliar situation can result in a new form of tension when the college student returns home for winter and summer break.

It is important to remember that both the college student and the parents have gone through significant transitions in their lives. Confusion and conflict can come from two different realities. Some parents assume the past relationships will be unchanged when the student returns home and hold onto the former expectations. It is still the parent's house and their child is coming back. Many parents believe that if they are under their roof, then the parent's rules apply. The college student, however, has become accustomed to complete freedom and typically does not life the increased control in their life. On the other hand, some parents have moved on to the next stage of their lives. They become accustomed to an empty house with fewer obligations to a dependent child in the home. In this case, tension may arise when the student comes home with the expectation, or even the need, for everything to be as it was when they left. Anxiety can be inadvertently increased when the student realizes that their safety net is no longer the same place they remember. It is likely still there, it just feels or looks different.

One way to bridge this gap of expectations is to recognize that different perspectives exist and have open dialogue with one another about each other's needs and wants prior to visiting or shortly after arriving. Try to keep emotions calm and allow everyone ample time to speak. It may be helpful for everyone involved to write down and prioritize their expectations and needs before having a discussion. By doing this, it can help identify the areas that are less important and thus can be compromised upon and the areas that cannot be compromised. If at all possible, it is best to try and meet in the middle on the majority of the differing expectations. Recognizing that everyone is in a different stage of life than they were just a year or two before can help ease this transition.

After College (the Extended Visit)

A new consequence of the current economic situation is that many college graduates do not immediately find work after college. In 2011, 14.2 percent of young adults, aged 25 and younger were living with their parents, up from 11.8 percent in 2007.

Living at home after college graduation can create many more challenges than shorter visits. Many times, there is an expectation by both parties that financial independence will be achieved upon successful graduation from college. When this doesn't happen, there is disappointment on both sides of the parental and the former student (now college graduate) relationship. Unfortunately, because of higher unemployment rates, this living situation is becoming more common than in the past. Fortunately, the unemployment rate of 4.3 percent in August 2011 (bureau of Labor Statistics) for bachelor degree recipients, is still high when compared to the unemployment rates in 2007 of just 2 percent and the unemployment rates in the 19902 (the years of the Internet/tech boom) between 1.5 and 3 percent. The news for graduates is still good. The unemployment rates college graduates are substantially lower than the 9.6 percent rate for high school graduates and 14.6 percent for high school dropouts.

In order to help minimize the challenges that may arise when moving back home, it is important to set aside some time to visit about each person's expectations of the new living arrangement. Since a college graduate is more capable and would typically have more time available to help than they did in high school, it is beneficial to do more around the house to help one's parents and show gratitude for the place to live. When a child moves back home and does not have a part-time job and does not help the parents around the house, it makes the parents feel taken for granted and can create long-term relationship problems. It is very important to show that one is a responsible adult and that they are trying to reach their independence potential by working part-time and applying for full-time job opportunities.

Peer Relationships

As you already know, there are many different relationships that must be navigated while in college. Some of these are similar to, but slightly different from those experienced earlier in life. Other relationships are entirely new to the college student. Navigating these relationships can be just as important to college success as navigating the classroom or academic environment.

Group Projects

The dreaded group project is a common experience in college. Class require-ments and even student organizations generate demands where students are asked to work together in collaborative groups. When taken seriously, the skills learned in these situations can be critical to lifelong abilities and strengths. In most cases, this is the point of the activity. Many students, however, re-port negative experience with such projects and often do not come away with any new cooperative group work skills. A potential barrier to successful group work is the failure to recognize various work styles and differing expectations. When not acknowledged and dealt with in a proactive way, the group process fails, the products of the group are less than optimal, and the experience fails in its ability to help the student later in life.

One of the best ways to avoid conflict is to have an organized approach to group work and make sure all group members are in agreement with the ap-proach.

Steps to help organize group projects:

1. Clarify the project and goals to be completed by the group. Are all of the group members expecting and shooting for the same grade?
2. Work together to break the project up into separate or slightly overlapping tasks. Do all group members feel they have been assigned a fair share?
3. Assign people and due dates for each part of the project. Be sure to give ample time for unanticipated delays based on technology, illnesses, and school and work schedules. Does everyone in the group understand what they need to do and by when?
4. Consider using technology to support the group process; e.g., Google docs, wikis, etc. There are various ways that a group can work together and not be in the same place. Most of this technology allows for multiple versions of a document or product and saves all drafts. This is a very good option for larger groups. It also provides an option to track individual group member contributions.
5. Decide who will compile the information into one document prior to the due date. Dividing tasks may be good initially, but the project must be compiled at the end and organized and written in a consistent manner. Many student projects lose points due to lack of a cohesive approach. Assign at least one or two members to the task of reading and polishing everything before submission.
6. Have predetermined ways of keeping in touch (texting, email, phone, etc.). See number 4 above.
7. Meet weekly or bi-weekly to make sure the project is moving in the right direction. This can be very helpful especially if one or more of the members are headed in the wrong direction, have questions, or are not meeting the set deadlines. If you wait until the night before a group project is due to finalize everything, it may be too late to complete the project.

If problems arise during group work:

1. Listen to everyone's perspective. Be sure that everyone can attend the meeting.
2. Try to see the situation from the other person's point of view. They may have things going on in their life that you are not aware of.
3. Avoid blaming other people for the problem. This puts the other person on the defensive and undermines forward progress.
4. Discuss each other's perceptions to make sure you understand. This is where you check in and let the other person know what you have heard from the conversation.
5. Review the tasks to be completed by each individual and see if any tasks need to be changed. A task that earlier seemed very small or simple may have turned out to be very time consuming.

6. A person may need help with time management in order to get their portion of the project done. Try to help each other out; time management can be a tricky skill to learn and practice.
7. Look for creative solutions to the problem. Consider changing tasks or timelines. This may be more difficult to do if many of the tasks have already been completed by other group members. Celebrate! Go out for ice cream or pizza once you have met the half-way point or finished the project.
8. Negotiate a solution that works for everyone. Be sure that everyone has time to express their concerns and ideas, even if you have a quiet person in the group.

Roommates

Another important relationship that is typically new to a college student is that of a roommate. Many people think that if they were best friends in high school, they will make perfect college roommates. There are more complicated dynamics that exist with roommates far beyond that of a traditional friendship. Making this assumption can set one up for possible roommate struggles. In some cases, the prior friendship creates barriers to living together harmoniously. Various hygiene habits, different sleep patterns, and different expectations for dorm or apartment cleanliness can make the best of friends experience difficulty. In addition to adjusting to a new living arrangement, one must also learn to balance new-found freedom, and the responsibilities that go along with college education al demands. With the list of suggestions below, you will see several things that might seem minor (i.e., trash or dish responsibility). All of the little things can add up over time and create conflict if not dealt with constructively. All of these things can be very challenging in the first year of college. It is helpful to recognize these adjustments and work toward a smooth transition. Any of these changes can cause stress and friction between roommates which can interrupt sleep, study time, and crate uncomfortable living arrangements. Interpersonal skills and open communication (talking versus social networking, e.g., texting, Facebook messages, etc.) are critical for conflict resolution. Some of the key elements for successful roommates are setting boundaries and expectations early in the relationship.

Within the first month of living together, develop a roommate agreement. At a minimum, address the following questions:

1. Who will take out the trash and how often?
2. Who will unload the dishwasher and how often?
3. What are the expectations of the shared space (e.g., living room)? How late can the TV be on? Is there designated "study or quiet" time" Does this space need to remain clean or is it okay to leave personal items (clothes, textbooks, dishes) in the shared space?
4. Are overnight guests (same or opposite gender) allowed?
5. Are pets allowed? If so, what type?
6. If you share a bathroom, who will clean it and how often?
7. Are you going to purchase your own food or buy together and share?
8. Are you allowed to borrow each other's clothes? What if something gets stained, torn, or ruined? Are there certain items that are off limits?
9. Other items?

Have each roommate sign the agreement and keep a copy for future reference. At a minimum, review and update the agreement once a year.

If conflict arises, address your concerns early and in a respectful and calm manner. If the concern is relatively minor, don't make too big of a deal out of it, but be sure to address it if it will bother you if the behavior continues. Remember, your roommate cannot read your mind. A simple reminder (verbal or writ-

There are many types of relationships, which fulfill many needs.

ten) may be all that is needed. If the problem persists or is more serious in nature, decide which method of communication is best based upon the personalities involved. Usually open, face-to-face communication is preferred so that everyone has time to contribute to the conversation. Find a time that everyone has at least 30 minutes to an hour to try and fully discuss and resolve the concerns. If a face-to-face meeting is not possible, then email or text may be another option. Since 70 percent of communication is non-verbal, it is important to clearly explain your concerns and some options for resolving your concerns in a diplomatic manner. It is important to discuss each roommate's opinion openly and work toward a compromise. Typically, class and work schedules will change from semester to semester and roommate agreements will likely need to be updated or revisited. These revisions and compromises need to benefit all parties. One person should not feel like they are always giving in to the other roommate's requests.

When discussions and compromise do not resolve more serious problems, then it is time to consider consulting a third party or a new living arrangement. Most dorms have a resident assistant (RA) to help with these types of situations. Be sure that the RA is able to hear all sides of the situation so that they have a good understanding of what is actually happening. Remember, there are always two sides (or more) to every story. If you do not believe that this type of conflict resolution will be helpful to the problem, then it is probably time to consider moving to a different room or find a new roommate (adapted from http://bailey-shoemaker-richards.suite101.com/dorm-life-conflict-resolution-strategies-a275040).

Types of Friendships

There are different levels of friendship: casual, close, and intimate. Each of these friendships can be very beneficial. The key ingredients to a successful friendship include steadfastness, honesty, reliability, and trust. Casual friendships are good for camaraderie, someone to see a movie with, or eat lunch. In

The Ten Commandments of a Healthy Relationship
(Kuriansky, 2002)
1. I will do my best to be the happiest person I can be.
2. I will be honest in my dealings with my partner.
3. I will keep my agreements.
4. I will have integrity about my actions.
5. I will honor all others I am in a relationship with.
6. I will practice forgiveness for others and myself.
7. I will nurture my spiritual soul and that of others.
8. I will accept others for who they are without judging them or insisting they change to suit me.
9. I will be open to suggestions and change when it's in the best interest for both of us.
10. I will trust in the powers that be what happens is for the best.

close friendships, there is typically a greater investment of time and emotional energy. Benefits typically seen with close friendships are those that can stand the test of time. There is a connection beyond the surface and a history with this person. Typically close friends know more about you than a casual acquaintance and can be called upon more easily in a time of need.

This chapter would not be complete without the mention of Internet relationships. More often people are meeting others and developing relationships over the Internet. This can be very beneficial in that you can express your opinions and thoughts anonymously and receive feedback. It can also help fill a void on a lonely Friday night. Use this method of meeting people with extreme caution and never give your full name, address, or other personal information for the entire world to see. As detailed in this chapter, a student was murdered by an individual he had met over the Internet. Remember, you never know exactly to whom you are talking through the Internet. Be cautious when using Facebook, MySpace, or posting personal information on the Internet. It is relatively easy for criminals to piece together random information and figure out where you live or what your usual routine is.

Don't Be Fooled! There Are Risks!

The following are things to be aware of:

DON'T disclose:
- phone number
- address
- actual email address (use Hotmail or other free email service)

Also, watch out that your personal signature lines on those services do not include the personal information you are trying to guard.

How Do I Know They're Legit?
- Use on-line services to do background checks.
- Ask the person if they'd be willing for you to contact some personal references.
- Make sure that you have numerous contacts with the individual prior to agreeing to meet in person. This should include several contacts of different sorts, including phone or snail mail.

The Big Meeting

So, you think you've met your match. You've checked him out and allowed him to check you out. You have sent pictures and email and talked on the phone.

Just as with a blind date, let someone know where you are and whom you are with. Better yet, bring them along and have them be in the same restaurant to keep their eyes peeled.

Meet in a public place.

Carry your cell or pager and have someone page you at a certain time. Tell your friend if you don't answer, they should worry.

Take your own car or cab.

If things get uncomfortable, leave (even if it's through the back door).

Meet on your home turf if you can. This, of course, follows the above guidelines of a public place and such.

If you meet them at their place away from your city, don't stay with them. Get a hotel and arrange your own transportation. The expense of that is worth the safety. Don't tell them where you are staying.

Source: www.selfcounseling.com with permission.

True-Life Stories

Man Indicted in Death of A&M Student

31-year-old could get life in Internet-luring incident.

A San Antonio man accused of posing as a woman on the Internet and luring a Texas A&M University junior to an out-of-town rendezvous was indicted Wednesday on charges of murdering the student.

A San Marcos grand jury handed up the first-degree felony indictment, saying there was enough evidence for Kenny Wayne Lockwood, 31, to be charged with the early-April shooting death of Kerry Jason Kujawa, 20, of Richmond, Texas.

If convicted, Lockwood faces five to 99 years or life in prison for the crime.

Hays County Sheriff's Department authorities said evidence shows Lockwood probably shot and killed Kujawa between April 7 and 9 in San Antonio, put the body in the trunk of a car and then dumped it west of Dripping Springs.

Kujawa's body was recovered April 19, almost two weeks after he left College Station for San Antonio.

Concerns about Kujawa's disappearance were not reported to police for almost two weeks, a delay perpetuated by Lockwood, according to police who said friends and family received e-mail messages from a person they presumed to be Kujawa.

Authorities said Lockwood was logging on to the computer as Kujawa.

A&M police and the Texas Rangers knew Kujawa had excitedly told friends and family that he was meeting face-to-face for the first time with a female friend he met in January over the Internet.

That person was Kelley Lynn McCauley, a 21-year-old female pre-law student at A&M who had several online suitors during the past year, but existed only in Lockwood's mind, according to the investigation. Lockwood pretended to be "Kelley."

The inquiry led to Lockwood's doorstep in San Antonio where he lived with his parents. Computer records showed Lockwood would regularly log on the Internet as Kelley, often spending hours in chat rooms talking to strangers.

The break in the case came when A&M students came forward with a telephone number and details of the Kelley they thought Kujawa met while online.

Lockwood's carefully crafted online identity was flirtatious and imaginative. Authorities said Lockwood continued to lie after killing Kujawa, telling others online that "she" and Kujawa were engaged and "she" would soon meet his parents.

Authorities said Lockwood confessed to the crime a week after Kujawa's body was discovered. Texas Ranger Frank Malinak, who is based in Bryan and assisted in the case, said it's unfortunate it took Kujawa's death for people to learn about the dangers of meeting others over the Internet.

"I just hope people are more wary of these chat rooms, because you never know who you are communicating with," Malinak said. "You may be talking to a truthful and forthright individual or you may be talking to murder.com."

Lockwood has been in the Hays County Jail on $500,000 bail since April 27, when he was arrested for Kujawa's murder.

Source: From Bryan-College Station Eagle, July 6, 2000 by Kelly Brown. Copyright © 2000 by Bryan-College Station Eagle. Reprinted by permission.

Stages of Relationships

These are some of the most common stages of a relationship. Not all relationships will have all of these stages, nor will they all proceed in this exact order.

- The first look
- Getting to know one another
- Finding out you like this person
- Establishing boundaries—who needs more or less space?
- Sexual attraction
- Falling in love
- Looking beyond the surface
- Commitment
- Playing house
- Living together
- Valleys and mountains—the ups and downs of a long-term relationship

Dating

Dating is the process of getting to know other people as well as yourself while growing with and from each relationship. Typically a date is stimulated by physical attraction, which can lead to emotional and physical intimacy. One of the outcomes of this process can be finding someone with whom we can happily spend the rest of our life. This process can be incredibly exciting and frustrating all at the same time. There are so many people with whom to meet and enjoy their company. Each new relationship exposes one to new and exciting experiences. While dating, your abilities, strengths, and interests can be maximized. As you are learning who you are and what you like, you should prioritize which characteristics are important and which are not. There is so much to be learned during the dating process. How do you relate to your partner in an intimate setting? What expectations do you have for the person with whom you want to live the rest of your life? As mentioned earlier, after the initial physical attraction, individuals may choose to become emotionally and/ or physically intimate. There are many responsibilities that follow when taking this next step. There is more at risk—mentally, physically, and financially. A scenario to contemplate is: How long does it take the average person to decide to buy a car? Or maybe a house? How long will these items be an influence on an individual's life? How long does the average person contemplate sexual intercourse? What are some of the repercussions associated with intercourse and how long will this affect an individual's life? It is best to fully consider the consequences before proceeding. Make sure that you and your partner are ready to deal with the consequences. For more information on protection against sexually transmitted infections and pregnancy, see Chapter 8.

Some of the best places to meet people: doing something you enjoy—for example, music store, coffee shop, workout facility, sporting events, bookstore, museum, lake, church, club, concert, class, or convention.

When and What Type of Love Is It?

There are probably as many different definitions of love as there are people in this world. For this reason, it makes answering "When is it love?" very difficult. One definition of love is a strong affection or liking for someone or something. Some signs it might be love include: verbally expressing affection, such as saying "I love you"; feeling happier or more secure when this person is present; putting the other person's interests before yours (in a healthy give-and-take relationship); respecting the other person for who they are; and not minding the other person's idiosyncrasies (adapted from Yarber et al., 2009).

Historically, there are several different models of love. Two common ones are described below. The first is Sternberg's (1988) love triangle which includes three

---

Rules about Sexual Health

Smart sex requires that you:

- Protect yourself (through abstinence or condoms).
- Never make a mistake or allow an exception to safe sex practices.
- Ease up on using protection only if both partners were virgins when they met, or if both have tested negative for AIDS and other STIs, and then had sex with each other exclusively.
- Talk about your sexual history. Say something like, "Before we have sex, we need to talk about diseases, safe sex, and our sexual pasts."
- Discuss what method you are going to use for safe sex.
- Find ways to enjoy intimacy other than through sex.

An Easy Recipe for Day-to-Day Relationship Success: 11 Tips

"The Pleasure of Your Company"

1. Pay attention to your partner.
2. Do a daily check-in and share your day.
3. Enjoy the simple pleasure of each other's company and do things the easy way.
4. Discuss the inevitable problems and concerns of your relationship.
5. Make plans for activities and fit within the context of your relationship.
6. Plan for daily skin time and eye contact.
7. Eat together.
8. Be in each other's presence for a reasonable amount of time each day.
9. Share a task together.
10. Understand the power of sacrifice and devotion.
11. Expect and find the magic and miracle in your relationship.

Source: www.selfcounseling.com with permission.

© Stephen Coburn, 2012, Shutterstock, Inc.

Levels of passion, intimacy, and commitment change over time as a relationship matures.

components: passion, intimacy, and commitment. Passion tends to occur at the beginning of relationships, peaks relatively quickly, and then reduces to a stable level. Passion generates romance, physical attraction, and sometimes intercourse. Intimacy is the feeling of closeness that exists between two people. Intimacy tends to peak slower than passion and then gradually reduces to a lower level. This level typically changes throughout a relationship. Commitment is the decision to further a loving relationship with another individual. The level of commitment typically rises slowly in the beginning, speeds up, and then gradually levels off. Sternberg describes the various types of love as a composition of different combinations of these three components. These various kinds of love change over time as the relationship matures.

John Lee (1973) describes six styles of loving:

EROS – passionate love
> Becomes sexually involved quickly
> Intense focus on partner and shares all of him/herself
> Quick to develop, quick to end

LUDUS – game-playing love
> Love and sex are seen only as fun, an activity, a diversion
> Move from partner to partner and often have several at a time
> Passion for the game, not the partner

STORGE – friendship love
> Long-term commitment
> Strong and secure, places less emphasis on passion

MANIA – obsessive love
> Turbulent and ambivalent
> Intense mental preoccupation, but little satisfaction
> Likely to be possessive and jealous

PRAGMA – realistic love
> Rational and practical
> Often for evolutionary and economic purposes
> Intense feelings may develop once a partner is chosen

AGAPE – altruistic love
> Generous, unselfish giving of oneself
> Less emphasis on passion and sexuality

Some Things to Do on a Date

1. Sit outside and visit.
2. Feed the ducks at the park.
3. Make a meal together.
4. Go for a bike ride.
5. Go to a baseball game.
6. Draw a picture together.
7. Enjoy a romantic moonlit picnic.
8. Play a game of pool.
9. Sightsee in a nearby town.
10. Grill some steaks outside for dinner together.
11. Go see a comedian.
12. Make s'mores (over a campfire or stove).
13. Have dinner at a very quaint restaurant.
14. Go to the zoo.
15. Go to an amusement park.
16. Take a recreational class together.
17. Go hiking.
18. Stop and read all of the historic landmarks.
19. Lie in a hammock.
20. Tie-dye two T-shirts.
21. Play I Spy.
22. Go to the ballet.
23. Play chess.
24. Host a dinner buffet for your closest friends.
25. Make a cake together.
26. Go white-water rafting.
27. Play games at the local arcade.
28. Share a five-course meal.
29. Wait in line all night together for tickets.
30. Rent a jeep and go to the lake.
31. Discuss the three most memorable events in your life.
32. Finger-paint a picture.
33. Go to a yoga class.
34. Gather food for a good cause.
35. Dress up for Halloween and hand out candy.
36. Read a book together.
37. Teach a Sunday school class together.
38. Go scuba diving.
39. Have your cholesterol levels checked.
40. Volunteer for a fund-raiser.
41. Go roller blading.
42. Rent his and her movies and watch them together.
43. Play a board game.
44. Go ice-skating.
45. Play tennis.
46. Go canoeing.
47. Spend an evening counting your blessings.
48. Visit your state capitol.
49. Run a 5K.
50. Go to the circus.
51. Visit a national park.
52. Study religious texts together.
53. Donate blood.
54. Go to a water park.
55. Take a class in self-defense.
56. Pick fruit from an orchard.
57. Adopt your own clean-up spot.
58. Baby-sit together.
59. Go to a county fair.
60. Spend an evening massaging each other.
61. Play hide-and-seek.
62. Make homemade ice cream.
63. Go to church/temple/mosque together.
64. Ride a tandem bike.
65. Dress up as clowns and visit the children's ward at a hospital.
66. Go Hawaiian by hosting a luau.
67. Play Frisbee.
68. Go to a basketball game.
69. See a talent show.
70. Go fishing.
71. Take a hot-air balloon ride.
72. Visit a haunted house.
73. Go play in the rain (and get drenched)!
74. Dress up for a special night out on the town.
75. Write a poem.
76. Go on a hayride.
77. Pick out and cut a Christmas tree.
78. Do laundry together.
79. Go for a walk on campus on a foggy night.
80. Go for a moonlight swim.
81. Lend support during a tough time.
82. Go to a bed and breakfast.
83. Share what you wish to have accomplished by the time you are 30, 40, and so on.
84. Pray together.

Rating Safe Sex Activities

Safer sex activities include:
- Dry kissing
- Hugging
- Frottage (rubbing against each other)
- Massage
- Telephone sex
- Tantric sex (extended love-making techniques from the Orient that don't involve penetration)

Riskier activities include:
- Open mouth or deep tongue kissing
- Oral sex (with condoms or dental dams)
- Vaginal intercourse with a condom

Unsafe sex activities include:
- Vaginal intercourse without a condom (even if pulling out before ejaculation)
- Oral sex without a condom (even if pulling out before ejaculation)
- Oral sex or vaginal penetration without a condom during a woman's period
- Anal sex without a condom

Date Rape

How to decrease the odds for date rape (Floyd et al., 2007):
- Develop clear lines of communication with the person you are dating.
- Communicate and clearly understand what each of you want and expect from the date.
- Do not use psychoactive substances, including alcohol, in dating situations.
- Do not give clues or display body language that is flirtatious or indicates you are interested in having sex when you are not. For example, allowing a date to visit your bedroom may send a message that you are interested in becoming intimate.
- Do not be coerced into unwanted sexual activities.

If you are the victim of date rape, remember it is not your fault. Seek medical treatment and counseling immediately. There are hotlines and other contact information listed at the end of this chapter.

Taming the Green-Eyed Monster

Jealousy typically comes from a lack of self-esteem and/or lack of confidence. Jealousy will undermine an otherwise healthy relationship and drive potential partners away. Realizing you are the jealous type is the first step in solving the problem. Then you can begin work on your self-confidence. Realize what your strong points are and focus on them. Exercise on a regular basis. Studies show that individuals who exercise on a regular basis feel better about themselves. Walk with confidence and feel good about who you are. Look in your past, is there anything that has happened to make you insecure? Evaluate what happened and what could be different in the future so those past "ghosts" do not haunt you.

What to Do for a Jealous Partner

Reassure their importance to you on a regular basis and let them know there is no need for their jealous tendencies. Let your partner know in a constructive manner that you do not care for their jealous tendencies. Take your partner to meet your friends and co-workers and include them in social gatherings.

Rules for Arguing Fairly

(Adapted from Godek, 1997)

1. Stay with the initial issue, do not bring up everything that is bothering you.
2. Stay in the present, do not bring up past problems and issues.
3. Say what you feel.
4. Do not generalize. ("You always…" "You are just like your mother…")
5. Do not threaten (verbally or physically).
6. Absolutely, no violence. (Men: Not even the slightest touch.
   Women: This includes slapping his face.)
7. State your needs as specific requests for different behavior.
8. Work toward a solution. Do not add fuel to the fire.

Always try to be fair when arguing.

The most common topics couples argue about include:

- When to see each other
- How often to see each other
- Flirting with other people
- Being late
- Forgetting important dates (birthdays and anniversaries)
- Being faithful
- Who spends how much money and on what
- How you spend time (watching too much TV and going out with friends)
- The amount or type of sex you have
- Family (when and whom to visit) (Kuriansky, 2003)

Disagreements happen in every relationship.

Ending a Relationship

In most cases the first individual you date will not be the person you marry. There are many reasons that exist to end a relationship. Some of these include initial misperceptions, changes in life routes, surfacing unattractive behaviors, infidelity, or even boredom. Typically only one individual sees a need for the change in the relationship, which makes ending a relationship a difficult situation.

On the Sending End

Always try to be as tactful as possible. Remember that at one point you were interested enough in this person to pursue a relationship. Be open and honest about the reason(s) you wish to end the relationship. The worst way to end a relationship is to ignore the other person. This leads your partner on and fosters confusion.

On the Receiving End

Listen carefully to what the person is saying and do not respond desperately or defensively. If your partner has brought up some characteristics that *you* would like to change, slowly work toward this change for yourself. If this truly is the end of this relationship, realize and accept that there will be a better match for you at some point in the future.

One definition of **love** is a passionate affection of one person for another. Another definition is "The emotion evoked when two souls resonate or 'fit together' naturally. It is close, but still not perfect" (Godek, 1997). There is no one exact definition that sums up all of the meanings of the word *love*. It is very different and personal to each individual.

Different types of love exist with regard to partners, parents, children, and friends. Within a loving relationship there are five important elements:

1. honesty,
2. loyalty,
3. thoughtfulness,
4. sharing,
5. sacrifice.

Honesty is the foundation that relationships are formed upon. Without this one cannot deepen or enrich a relationship further. Loyalty is also incredibly important. Your partner must always realize where your loyalty lies regardless if they are present. This loyalty also builds the foundation to further enhance your relationship. Thoughtfulness is an expression of how you feel about the other person. These actions should indicate to your partner how important they are to you. Another fulfilling element of a loving relationship includes sharing. This includes sharing possessions as well as experiences. Most experiences are enhanced if accompanied by someone you love. This could include a trip, dinner, sporting activity, and the menial tasks that go along with life. Finally sacrifice, loving someone enough to do without so they may have what they desire. This is sacrificing without being a martyr, because it is freely given without strings attached.

I Do or I Do Not

In today's society, it is unfortunate that many individuals treat marriage as a dating game. If the relationship gets too rough, they will just get a divorce. This casual attitude toward marriage diminishes the meaning of the vows that are taken when a couple marries.

There are many things to consider when contemplating marriage. Is this the person with whom you truly want to spend the rest of your life? Are we compatible? Do we have similar values? These are just a few of the questions that should be asked.

The question of compatibility is one that takes time to answer. Some characteristics that comprise compatibility include similar interests, ways of doing things, as well as the ability to compromise when you do not see "eye to eye." Do you both like to participate in outdoor or indoor activities? Are your activity levels similar? Do you need structure to your life or is spontaneity more your style? Are you both outgoing or do you complement each other with some differences? What are your long-term goals and are they similar to your partner's? Do you have similar views on finances? Are you thrifty or extravagant? Do both of you want children? This is not to say that you and your ideal partner have to be identical. In fact, it is helpful to have some differences (within reason) to help complement the other's weaknesses. For example, if one of you is somewhat overreactive and the other one is more grounded, then you will probably balance one another out. Problems arise when there are so many differences that you cannot relate or the differences simply irritate one another. With this said, it is very helpful to have similar interests and ways of doing things that can carry past the initial infatuation stage.

Values are defined as beliefs or standards. Are your values similar? For example, how you treat other people, volunteer work, religion, and child rearing. What do you hold very dear to your heart? Are there any specific lines that you would never cross and expect the same out of a life-long partner? Some examples include drug use, infidelity, or lying. What are your views of marriage? What does this word mean to you, and is it similar to the meaning your partner places on it?

Tips for a Successful Marriage

- Always respect your spouse.
- Not only love your spouse, but like him or her too.
- Remember that a relationship is not 50/50, it is 100/100 (Godek, 1997). If you only try to give 50 percent (or your fair share) you will definitely fall short of the combined 100 percent that is needed.
- Don't expect perfection from yourself or your partner.

Ten Characteristics of a Happy Marriage

(Floyd et al., 2007)

People in successful marriages are willing to grow, change, and work hard at their marriages. A good relationship requires flexibility and effort to keep it alive.

1. They are giving people, meeting their emotional needs by doing for others—and they do not keep score.
2. They have a strong sense of commitment, do not take their happiness for granted, and are determined to make their marriages work.
3. They do not lose themselves in the relationship. They value their independence—the right to form their own opinions, make their own decisions, pursue their own goals—marital harmony is a top priority.
4. They have vigorous sexual drives. Sex plays a central and profoundly important role in the marriage.
5. They like to talk, sharing their thoughts about all sorts of subjects. They are open and direct, not manipulative.
6. They have a positive outlook on life.
7. They express appreciation and are generous with praise.
8. They have strong spiritual or religious convictions and commit themselves to a spiritual lifestyle, though they may not be affiliated with an organized church.
9. They recognize the needs of others, respect their differences, consider their feelings, and put themselves in the other person's shoes.
10. They are willing to grow, change, and work hard at their marriages. They know that a good relationship requires flexibility and effort to keep it alive.

Unhealthy Relationships

As discussed earlier it takes a lot to have a healthy relationship. Many times there is a process of growing through unhealthy relationships in order to achieve your final goal. Some signs of an unhealthy relationship include (Kuriansky, 2002):

- You feel insecure and weak around each other.
- You suffer from low self-esteem as a result of what happens between you.
- You are dishonest with each other.
- You spend more time feeling hurt than feeling good about how you treat each other.
- You find yourself complaining to others about your relationship.
- You are unable to talk about your feelings or problems with your partner, much less solve them.
- You are unable to resolve your differences together.
- You become unenthusiastic about life because of what goes on between you.

- Your trust is irrevocably broken.
- Seemingly small things erode your relationship, like trickling water that wears away at a rock over time.
- Priorities other than each other constantly present themselves.
- What goes on between you interferes with other aspects of your life.

Abusive Relationships

Sometimes unhealthy relationships progress further into abusive relationships (see Table 7.2). This can be physical, emotional, or both in nature and typically cycles through repetitive phases. These phases include:

- **The honeymoon phase** may consist of flowers, apologies, and acting in a manner that originally attracted the abused to the abuser. This phase may last a day, a week, or sometimes longer.
- **The tension phase** typically builds slowly over time. This phase may consist of small insults that build into public humiliation and belittling.
- **The explosion phase** typically happens in the privacy of a home or away from witnesses. Behaviors during this phase can include but are not limited to hitting, throwing down stairs, rape, and in some cases death. This is a dangerous cycle with high stakes.

As mentioned earlier, this cycle typically continues to repeat itself many times with each cycle increasing in intensity.

When this happens, it is definitely time to get out of the relationship. Sometimes this is incredibly hard for the abused partner because their self-esteem is so low. They honestly feel the only person that would "put up" with them is their partner, so they feel very trapped. The abusing partner typically isolates their partner from friends and family over an extended period of time. This evolves into a very controlling and abusive relationship. Many times the abuser will threaten their partner's life if they try to leave. If this is the case, do not let your partner know you are thinking about leaving. Wait until you know your partner will be gone for an extended period of time and call someone whom your partner does not know for help. There are numerous help lines listed at the end of this chapter.

In some instances restraining orders are necessary to keep an individual from stalking or harassing. Be very careful in these situations because they can and have become life threatening. Remember that if you are in an abusive relationship more likely than not this individual will continue to abuse you until the relationship is over. Also, the abuse will typically escalate over time. The incidence of physical violence in college dating relationships is reported as 20 percent to 50 percent, varying from slapping and hitting to more life-threatening violence (Floyd et al., 2007).

TABLE 7.2 ♦ Warning: This Relationship May Be Dangerous to Your Health

What you see:	What your partner says:
Blaming	"I love you, but you make me hit you."
Hypermasculine behavior	"I make all the decisions in this family."
Emotional abuse	"You are so stupid. I don't know why I married you."
Isolation	"I don't like your friend Linda, and I don't want you going to the store with her."
Intimidation	"Just like I kicked that dog, I can kick you."
Coercion and threats	"If you don't do what I say, I'll leave you. You can't make it without me."
Economic abuse	"You don't need to make any more money. I can give you what you need when you ask me for it."

Source: Floyd et al., 2007.

Additional Readings

Carter, S. *Getting to Commitment.* New York: M. Evans and Co. 2000.

Hammond, M. and Brooks, J. *What Women Don't Know (And Men Don't Tell You): The Unspoken Rules of Finding Lasting Love,* Colorado Springs, CO. 2007.

Gray, J. *Men Are from Mars, Women Are from Venus.* New York: HarperCollins. 2004.

Tannen, D. *You Just Don't Understand: Women and Men in Conversation.* New York: William Morrow. 2001.

References

Floyd, P. et al. *Personal Health: Perspectives & Lifestyles* (4th ed). Englewood, CO: Morton Publishing Co. 2007.

Godek, G. *Love: The Course They Forgot to Teach You in School.* Naperville, IL: Casablanca Press. 1997.

Kuriansky, J. *The Complete Idiot's Guide to a Healthy Relationship* (2nd ed). New York: Alpha Books. 2002.

Kuriansky, J. *The Complete Idiot's Guide to Dating* (3rd ed). New York: Alpha Books. 2003.

Lee, J. A. *Colours of love: an exploration of the ways of loving.* New York: New Press. 1973.

Sternberg, R. J. *The Triangle of Love: Intimacy, Passion, Commitment.* New York: Basic Books. 1988.

Yarber, W., Sayad, B., and Strong, B. *Human Sexuality: Diversity in Contemporary America* (7th ed). McGraw-Hill. 2009.

http://bailey-shoemaker-richards.suite101.com/dorm-life-conflict-resolution-strategies-a275040)

http://www.nytimes.com/2011/ 11/17/business/economy/as-graduates-move-backhome-economy-feels-the-pain.html.

http://www.ibtimes.com/articles/214426/20110915/unemployment-jobs-economy-college-graduate.htm.

www.scribd.com/doc/26177419/Group-Projects-a-Conflict-Resolution-Guide-For

http://bailey-shoemaker-richards.suite101.com/dorm-life—conflict-resolutlon-strategles-a275040.

Contacts

American Association for Marriage and Family Therapy
www.aamft.org

American Social Health Association
800-227-8922
www.ashastd.org

Christian Singles International
www.christiansinglesinternational.com

Family Violence Prevention Information
800-777-1960

Gay and Lesbian Medical Association
459 Fulton Street, Suite 107
San Francisco, CA 94102
415-255-4547
www.glma.org

National Domestic Violence Hotline
800-799-SAFE (7233)

National Victim Center
800-FYI-CALL

Parents, Families, and Friends of Lesbians and Gays (PFLAG)
202-638-4200
www.pflag.org

TAMU Student Life Gender Issues Education Services (GIES)
979-845-1107
www.glbtpn.tamu.edu/resources.html

ACTIVITIES

In-Class Activities

Discussion questions:

What do you value most in a friendship?

What is the most mysterious thing about the opposite sex?

What is the one thing that the opposite gender simply doesn't "get" about your gender?

Describe your idea of a perfect date.

Have you ever been infatuated? Describe the feeling. Describe the relationship. Have you ever been in love? Describe the feeling. Describe the relationship.

The "Perfect" Mate

Notebook Activities

Relationship Writing Assignment

How Strong Is the Communication and Affection in Your Relationship?

Relationship Report Card

Are You in an Abusive Relationship?

IN-CLASS ACTIVITY

The "Perfect" Mate

Directions: In the space below, write down all the qualities of a "perfect" mate for you. Then go back over the list and write the codes that apply in the blank to the left.

Qualities of my "Perfect" Mate:

_____ 1.

_____ 2.

_____ 3.

_____ 4.

_____ 5.

_____ 6.

_____ 7.

_____ 8.

_____ 9.

_____ 10.

_____ 11.

_____ 12.

_____ 13.

_____ 14.

_____ 15.

_____ 16.

_____ 17.

_____ 18.

_____ 19.

_____ 20.

Codes:
D   Your dad has this quality.
M   Your mom has this quality.
+   You have this quality.
–   You wish you had this quality.
B   You think both partners need this quality to be happy.
*   These are the three most important qualities.

NOTEBOOK ACTIVITY

Relationship Writing Assignment

Look at the website http://www.revolutionhealth.com/conditions/mental-behavior-health/college-health/students/relationships. Which relationship information did you find most helpful? How do you plan to use this information?

Name _____ Section_____ Date_____

How Strong Is the Communication and Affection in Your Relationship?

Effective, caring communication and loving affection markedly enhance a couple's relationship. The following self-test may help you to assess the degree of good communication, love, and respect in your intimate relationship. If you agree or mostly agree with a statement, answer yes. If you disagree or mostly disagree, answer no. You may wish to have your partner respond to this assessment as well. If so, mark your answers on a separate sheet.

1.	My partner seeks out my opinion.	Yes	No
2.	My partner cares about my feelings.	Yes	No
3.	I don't feel ignored very often.	Yes	No
4.	We touch each other a lot.	Yes	No
5.	We listen to each other.	Yes	No
6.	We respect each other's ideas.	Yes	No
7.	We are affectionate toward one another.	Yes	No
8.	I feel my partner takes good care of me.	Yes	No
9.	What I say counts.	Yes	No
10.	I am important in our decisions.	Yes	No
11.	There's lots of love in our relationship.	Yes	No
12.	We are genuinely interested in one another.	Yes	No
13.	I love spending time with my partner.	Yes	No
14.	We are very good friends.	Yes	No
15.	Even during rough times, we can be empathetic.	Yes	No
16.	My partner is considerate of my viewpoint.	Yes	No
17.	My partner finds me physically attractive.	Yes	No
18.	My partner expresses warmth toward me.	Yes	No
19.	I feel included in my partner's life.	Yes	No
20.	My partner admires me.	Yes	No

Scoring

A preponderance of yes answers indicates that you enjoy a strong relationship characterized by good communication and loving affection. If you answered yes to fewer than seven items, it is likely that you are not feeling loved and respected and that the communication in your relationship is decidedly lacking.

Source: Gottman, John. *Why Marriages Succeed or Fail.* New York: Simon & Schuster, 1994. See Hyde and DeLameter, 1997, 6th ed., p. 272.

Getting Your Signals Straight

- *Tune into your body talk.* Notice details about the way you speak, gesture, and move. If possible, watch yourself on videotape. Analyze the emotions you're feeling at the time and think of how they may be influencing your body language.

- *Learn to establish good eye contact, but don't glare or stare.* If you sense that someone feels uncomfortable with an intense eye grip, shift your focus so that your gaze hits somewhere between the eyes and the chin, rather than pupil-to-pupil.

- *Avoid putting up barriers.* If you fold your arms across your chest, you'll look defensive or uninterested in contact. Crossing your legs or ankles also can seem like a way of keeping your distance.

- *Identify the little things you characteristically do when you're tense.* Some people pat their hair or pick at their ears; others rub their necks, twist a ring or watch, twirl a lock of hair, or play with a pen. Train yourself to become aware of what you're doing (have a friend give you a signal, if necessary) and to control your mannerisms.

NOTEBOOK ACTIVITY

Relationship Report Card

Grade yourself and your partner in twenty-five key relationship skills.

A = Passionate, exciting, fulfilling; not perfect—but clearly excellent

B = Very good, solid, better-than-most, consistent, improving

C = Average, adequate, acceptable, okay, ho-hum, static

D = Below average, dismal, unhappy, bad—but not hopeless

F = Hopeless, dangerous; tried everything, didn't work

Description

The Relationship Report Card allows you to grade yourself and your partner on *a number of very specific skills* that contribute to successful relationships. It measures *actions,* not *emotions.* It is an exercise that will give you a realistic picture of how you act in your relationship. And by *comparing* how both you and your partner act in your relationship, it will give you insights into the dynamics of yourselves as a unique couple.

The Relationship Report Card measures *behavior,* not *character.* It is a technique for allowing you to focus on specific aspects of behavior, one-at-a-time. It does *not* judge *personality!* You're not a *bad person* if you have a C+ sense of humor; and you're not a *superior person* if you have A+ communication skills.

The goals of this exercise are: 1) to raise your awareness by giving you an objective look at how the two of you act as a couple, 2) to identify strengths and help you appreciate them, 3) to identify areas that need improvement, 4) to help your partner see you as you perceive yourself, 5) to help your partner see himself or herself as you see him or her, 6) to help you see your partner as he or she perceives himself or herself, and 7) to help you see yourself through your partner's eyes.

Instructions

- Each of you grades yourself and your partner.

- While grading, ask yourself, "How well do I (or my partner) exemplify/act on this particular skill?"

- Regarding choosing grades: Your first inclination is probably the right one. Rely more on your intuitive side—your gut reaction—than on your analytical side.

- Use "pluses" and "minuses" to fine-tune your grading. (A "B" is clearly a "B"—but a "B+" is nearly an "A"!)

- During the grading process, don't talk about the grades you're giving. You may talk about the process, but don't share your grades until later.

- Customize the Relationship Report Card. There are blanks at the bottom of the form where you can add topics and skills that you consider to be important.

- Most people take six to ten minutes to complete the grading process. (Although some folks fly through it in sixty seconds, and others ponder it for half an hour!)

- Note: The goal is not to get "straight A's." We all have a wide variety of characteristics, strengths, and weaknesses. The goal is to improve, not to be perfect!

- When you have both completed the grading process, compare your grades. Start at the top of the list, and share the grades you gave yourself and your partner.

- For each skill, discuss the discrepancies between how you graded yourself compared to how your partner graded you.

- Some questions to consider: What was your reasoning behind various grades? Are you satisfied, dissatisfied, happy, embarrassed, or proud of your grades? What might you do to get a better grade? What kind of help can you offer your partner?

NOTEBOOK ACTIVITY

Relationship Report Card

Grade yourself—and your partner—using the school-type evaluation of A+ through F.

Relationship skill	Grade yourself	Grade your partner
❏ Affection	_____	_____
❏ Arguing skills	_____	_____
❏ Attitude	_____	_____
❏ Commitment	_____	_____
❏ Communication	_____	_____
❏ Considerateness	_____	_____
❏ Couple thinking	_____	_____
❏ Creativity	_____	_____
❏ Financial responsibility	_____	_____
❏ Flexibility	_____	_____
❏ Generosity	_____	_____
❏ Gift-giving	_____	_____
❏ Honesty	_____	_____
❏ Household management	_____	_____
❏ Listening skills	_____	_____
❏ Lovemaking	_____	_____
❏ Patience	_____	_____
❏ Playfulness	_____	_____
❏ Romance	_____	_____
❏ Self-awareness	_____	_____
❏ Self-esteem	_____	_____
❏ Sense of humor	_____	_____
❏ Sensitivity	_____	_____
❏ Spontaneity	_____	_____
❏ _____		
❏ _____		
❏ _____		
❏ _____		
❏ _____		

Name _____ Section_____ Date_____

Are You in an Abusive Relationship?

Check any of the questions below to which you can truthfully answer "yes."

_____Are you afraid of your partner?

_____Does your partner monitor your comings and goings?

_____Does your partner control who you can and cannot talk to?

_____Are you forced to have sex against your will?

_____Are you told what you can and cannot wear?

_____Are you verbally or physically abused for looking at another man (woman)?

_____Has your partner threatened to harm your children?

A "yes" response to any of these questions signals trouble and the need to get help.

Source: Dr. Carolyn Ramsey, in an article by Laura B. Randolph, "Battered Women: How to Get and Give Help," *Ebony,* September, 1994.

Chapter 8
Sexuality

© Supri Suharjoto, 2012. Shutterstock, Inc.

OBJECTIVES

Students will be able to:

- Identify structures of the female and male sexual anatomy.
- Describe the stages of the menstrual cycle and pregnancy.
- Explain the benefits and drawbacks of each barrier method and hormonal method of pregnancy prevention.
- Identify the options in the case of an unplanned pregnancy.
- Identify and discuss the following issues concerning sexually transmitted infections: transmission, prevention, type, vaccines, asymptomatic infections, treatment, and consequences if left untreated.
- Discuss the influence the media have on attitudes and beliefs about relationships and sexuality.

"A healthy attitude is contagious but don't wait to catch it from others. Be a carrier."

—Source Unknown

The purpose of this chapter is to familiarize students with the female and male anatomy and gender-specific cycles. Information will be presented on parenthood and the options that exist when pregnancy prevention is not effective. Additional material will be presented detailing various sexually transmitted infections (STIs), the health risks associated with contraction of STIs, and various preventative measures and techniques in sexually transmitted infections and pregnancy.

Anatomy

Female Sexual Anatomy

The female anatomy consists of multiple integral parts both externally and internally (see Figure 8.1). The **vulva** includes visible external genitalia. The **mons pubis** is the soft fatty tissue covering the pubic symphysis (joint of the pubic bones). This area is covered with pubic hair that begins growing during puberty. The **labia majora** include two longitudinal folds of skin that extend on both sides of the vulva and serve as protection for the inner parts of the vulva. The **labia minora** are the delicate inner folds of skin that enclose the urethral opening and the vagina. These skin flaps, which contain sweat and oil glands, extensive blood vessels, and nerve endings, are hairless and sensitive to touch. When sexually stimulated, the labia minora swell and darken. The **clitoris** is usually the most sensitive part of the female genitalia. The clitoris consists of erectile tissue, which becomes engorged with blood, resulting in swelling during sexual arousal that enables it to double in size. The **clitoral hood** consists of inner lips, which join to form a soft fold of skin, or hood, covering and connecting to the clitoris. The **urethra** is approximately

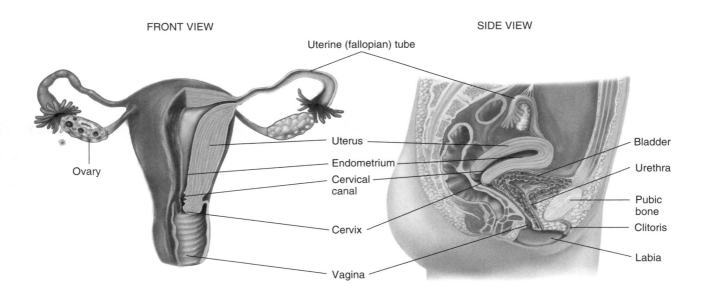

FRONT VIEW   SIDE VIEW

Uterine (fallopian) tube

Ovary

Uterus

Endometrium

Cervical canal

Cervix

Vagina

Bladder

Urethra

Pubic bone

Clitoris

Labia

FIGURE 8.1

The Human Female Reproductive System

Source: From *Biology: Understanding Life* by Alters and Alters, © 2006 by Alters and Alters. Reproduced with permission of John Wiley & Sons, Inc.

2.5 cm below the clitoris and functions as the opening for urine to be excreted from the bladder. Because the urethra is located close to the vaginal opening, some irritation may result from vigorous or prolonged sexual activity. The most common problem associated with this is the development of urinary tract infections. The **vagina** is located between the urethral opening and the anus. The **hymen** is the small membrane around the vaginal opening that is believed to tear during initial intercourse, with tampon use, while riding a horse, or other various types of athletic activities. The only function of the hymen is to protect the vaginal tissues early in life. The **perineum** is the smooth skin located between the labia minora and the anus. During childbirth this area may tear or be cut (episiotomy) as the newborn passes out of the vagina. The **anal canal** is located just behind the perineum and allows for elimination of solid waste. The anal canal is approximately an inch long with two sphincter muscles, which open and close like valves.

Internally, just past the vagina, is the cervix, which connects the vagina and the uterus. The uterus is the hollow, pear-shaped muscular organ about the size of a fist when a female is not pregnant. This is the organ in which the fetus develops during pregnancy. The upper expanded portion is referred to as the fundus (see Figure 8.2), and the lower constricted part is the cervix. On each side of the uterus there is a **fallopian tube,** which is quite narrow and approximately four inches in length. Because of the narrow passageway within these tubes, infection and scarring may cause fertility problems. Most women have a right and a left fallopian tube. These tubes extend from the ovaries to the uterus and transport mature ovum. Fertilization usually takes place within the fallopian tubes. The opening between the fallopian tube and

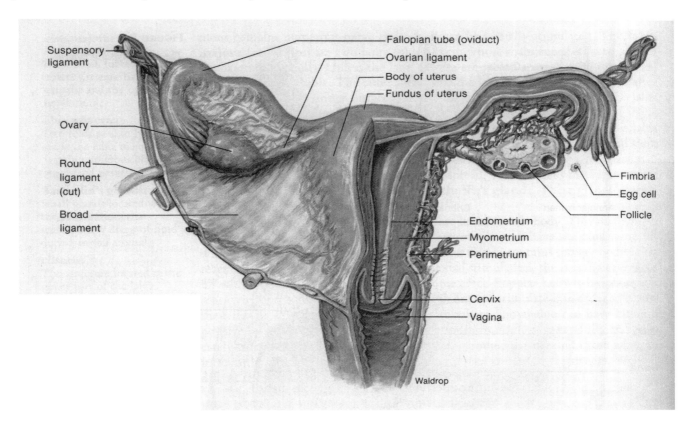

FIGURE 8.2

An Anterior View of the Female Reproductive Organs Showing the Relationship of the Ovaries, Uterine Tubes, Uterus, Cervix, and Vagina

Fig 1.3, p. 18 from Access to Health, 6th edition by Rebecca J. Donatelle and *Source: From Sexuality: Insights and Issues,* third edition. Copyright © 1993 by Jerrold Greenberg, Clint Buess, and Kathleen D. Mullen. Reprinted by permission of the authors.

the uterus is only about as wide as a needle. On each end of the fallopian tubes are the **ovaries,** where eggs are produced and released usually once a month. Each ovary is about the size of a large olive. At birth, a female's ovaries contain 40,000 to 400,000 immature ova, of which approximately 450 will mature and be released during the reproductive years. The ovaries also produce the hormones estrogen and progesterone, both of which help regulate the menstrual cycle (Crooks and Baur, 2009).

The female *sexual response* consists of four phases:

1. **Excitement:**
   Vaginal lubrication begins and the vagina, clitoris, labia majora and minora all fill with blood. The nipples swell, and there is increased tension in many voluntary muscles.

2. **Plateau:**
   The vaginal opening usually decreases in diameter due to swelling, the uterus usually increases in size, and the labia majora and minora become more swollen and engorged.

3. **Orgasm:** and
   The muscles of the vaginal wall undergo rhythmic contractions. The number of contractions may range from three to as many as twelve. Involuntary contraction of other muscles may take place as well.

4. **Resolution:**
   Blood rapidly returns to the rest of the body from the vagina, clitoris, labia majora, and minora, resulting in reduced swelling. At this time the breasts also return to their original size.

Male Sexual Anatomy

The external male sexual structures include the penis and scrotum. The **penis** is an organ through which semen and urine pass, and is structured into three main sections: the root, the shaft, and the glans penis (see Figure 8.3). The root attaches the penis within the pelvic cavity at the base, while the shaft, or the tube-shaped body of the penis, hangs freely. The **glans penis** is covered by a loose portion of tissue called the **foreskin,** which may be removed during a surgery known as circumcision. A penis without foreskin is circumcised, while one with the foreskin intact is uncircumcised. Uncircumcised men should gently pull the foreskin back when they bathe to wash the foreskin and tip of the penis. At the base of the glans is a rim known as the corona. On the underside is a triangular area of highly sensitive skin called the frenulum, which attaches the glans to the foreskin. The glans penis is the soft, fleshy, enlarged tissue at the end of the shaft, with the urethral opening at the tip. The **scrotum** is the pouch of skin, which hangs from the root of the penis and holds the two testicles. Covered sparsely with hair, the scrotum is divided in the middle by a ridge of skin, showing the separation of the testes. The surface changes of the scrotum help maintain a moderately constant temperature within the testes (~93 degrees F), which is important for maintaining good sperm production (Crooks and Baur, 2009).

The male internal sexual structures include the testes, epididymus, vas deferens, seminal vesicles, and prostate and Cowper's glands. The **testes** are the reproductive ball-shaped glands inside the scrotum, which are also referred to as testicles. Sperm and hormone production are the two main functions of the testes (Crooks and Baur, 2007). Sperm are formed constantly, beginning during puberty, inside the highly coiled thin tubes called seminiferous tubules within each testis. Between the seminiferous tubules are cells that produce sex hormones. One such important sex hormone is testosterone, which stimulates the production of sperm. On top of each testis is another tightly coiled tube, the **epididymis,** where nearly mature sperm complete the maturation process (Crooks and Baur, 2009). Mature sperm are stored in the epididymis until

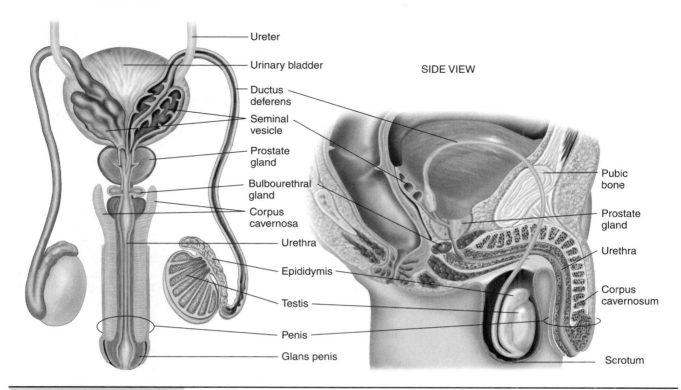

FRONT VIEW

- Ureter
- Urinary bladder
- Ductus deferens
- Seminal vesicle
- Prostate gland
- Bulbourethral gland
- Corpus cavernosa
- Urethra
- Epididymis
- Testis
- Penis
- Glans penis

SIDE VIEW

- Pubic bone
- Prostate gland
- Urethra
- Corpus cavernosum
- Scrotum

FIGURE 8.3

The Human Male Reproductive System

Source: From *Biology: Understanding Life by Alters and Alters,* © 2006 by Alters and Alters. Reproduced with permission of John Wiley & Sons, Inc.

they are released during ejaculation. The **vas deferens** is a long tube through which sperm travel during ejaculation. The epididymis is connected to the **seminal vesicle** via the vas deferens, which is responsible for contracting and pushing the sperm to the seminal vesicle. Located beneath the bladder are the two small seminal vesicles, which secrete a fluid that provides nourishment as well as an environment conducive to sperm mobility. After the sperm have combined with the seminal fluid, they reach the prostate where another substance is added. A thin, milky fluid is produced by the prostate and secreted into the urethra during the time of emission of semen, which enhances the swimming environment for the sperm (Crooks and Baur, 2009). Below the prostate and attached to the urethra are the two pea-sized **Cowper's glands,** responsible for depositing a lubricating fluid for sperm and a coating for the urethra. If there are sperm in the urethra from a previous ejaculation, they will mix with the Cowper's fluid and become a pre-ejaculate lubricant fluid. Ejaculation occurs at peak sexual excitement when the prostate muscle opens and sends the seminal fluid to the urethra where it is then forced out through the urethral opening, forming semen.

Sperm facts:

- Sperm are produced at an average rate of 1,500 per second per testicle.
- It takes about one hundred days for sperm to mature.
- The average ejaculation contains about a teaspoon of semen and 200–500 million sperm.
- At least thirty-two different chemicals have been found in semen. They include more than twenty amino acids, glucose, citric acid, fructose, vitamin C, vitamin B12, zinc, potassium, calcium, and copper.
- The average time a sperm survives in the female reproductive tract is three to five days.
- Sperm can live in the man's body up to six weeks.

- Sperm that are not ejaculated get broken down and reabsorbed or are washed away in urine. (ETR Associates, 2007a)

The shaft of the penis can change dramatically during *sexual arousal.* During sexual excitement, tiny muscles inside the shaft tissue called corpus spongiosum and corpus cavernosa relax and open, allowing inflow of blood. As these tissues fill with blood, the penis becomes longer, thicker, and less flexible, resulting in an erection. Although sexual sensitivity is unique among individuals, the glans penis is particularly important in sexual arousal due to its high concentration of nerve endings. When a man is either sexually aroused or cold, the testes are pulled close to the body (Crooks and Baur, 2009).

Sexual Orientation

The components of sexuality are gender identity (biological gender, as determined by chromosomes and sexual organs), social sex role (adherence to cultural norms for feminine and masculine behavior), and sexual orientation. Sexual orientation is distinguished by emotional, romantic, sexual, or affectionate attraction to individuals of a particular gender. Sexual orientation often becomes apparent during puberty, when hormonal changes are taking place in the body. Three sexual orientations are commonly recognized:

1. "heterosexual," attraction to individuals of the opposite gender;
2. "homosexual," attraction to individuals of the same gender;
3. "bisexual," attraction to members of both genders.

Persons with a homosexual orientation are sometimes referred to as "gay" (both men and women) or "lesbian" (women only). Sexual orientation is different from sexual behavior because it refers to feelings and self-concept. Persons may or may not express their sexual orientation in their behaviors. Homosexual orientation is not limited to a particular type of person. Gay men and lesbians are of all ages, cultural backgrounds, races, religions, and nationalities.

Alfred Kinsey, a sex researcher in the mid-1900s, developed a 7-point continuum representing sexual orientation (see Figure 8.4). He used this scale to study the sexual behaviors and preferences of the American population. The scale ranges from 0 to 6, with 0 representing exclusive heterosexual behavior, 3 representing bisexual behavior, and 6 representing exclusive homosexual behavior. This scale recognizes that many individuals do not fit solely into one of the three previously described sexual orientations.

A term often witnessed in association with homosexuality is homophobia. In general, *phobia* means an irrational, excessive, or persistent fear of something or a particular situation. *Homophobia* is defined as irrational fear of homosexuals or homosexuality. An additional component of this definition, however, is hatred since many homophobic individuals express their emotions of fear in physically aggressive ways. Homophobic behaviors range from avoiding hugging same-gender friends to name-calling, as well as physical attacks. Homophobia can also be explained as a continuum, which at one end is described as feeling uncomfortable around a homosexual individual, the middle representing fear, and finally the other end of the continuum representing hatred. Homophobia has led to many discriminatory practices toward homosexuals in employment, housing, and insurance coverage, as well as in many other facets of life.

© Anton Gvozhikov, 2012. Shutterstock, Inc.

People may or may not express their sexual orientation in their behaviors.

0	1	2	3	4	5	6
Exclusive heterosexual experience	Heterosexual with incidental homosexual experience	Heterosexual with substantial homosexual experience	Equal heterosexual and homosexual experience	Homosexual with incidental heterosexual experience	Homosexual with substantial heterosexual experience	Exclusively homosexual experience

FIGURE 8.4

Kinsey Scale of Sexual Behavior Kinsey believed that some people did not fit into strict same-gender oropposite-gender sexual behavior. His scale of sexual behavior reflects this belief.

Readiness for Sexual Activity

Deciding whether you are ready for sexual activity is a very important and personal decision. It is a decision that has numerous physical, spiritual, and emotional implications and should not be taken lightly. Typically individuals have very different timelines at which they feel comfortable participating in different types of sexual activity. Different sexual activities include: vaginal/penal, anal/penal, oral/ vaginal, or oral/penal intercourse. Some individuals consider themselves "virgins" if they have not had vaginal/penal intercourse, but have participated in other sexual activities. It is important to realize there are very real risks associated with all forms of sexual activity, which include and are not limited to sexually transmitted infections (STIs). It is also important that you decide what you would like out of a relationship and when you feel comfortable with beginning a specific sexual activity. Some individuals view sexual activity as a very casual event and others wait until they are married to participate in any sexual activity.

When making this decision it is important that the individual has considered most if not all of the implications of their actions. Examples of these implications will be provided throughout this chapter.

One of the most important tools to use with your partner is communication. An individual must be able to talk openly and honestly to their prospective sexual partner about their wishes and beliefs on this subject. Talking can bring you closer because it develops a sense of trust. It can also help you learn more about your partner and remind both of you about the risks of sexual activity. The benefits of waiting include: more time to get to know your partner without the pressures sex can add to a relationship, freedom from worries about unplanned pregnancy and STIs, as well as building a stronger relationship based on friendship and trust, without the confusion sex can add (ETR Associates, 2007b). According to the 2007 Youth Risk Behavior Survey conducted by the CDC, the percentage of high school students who had ever had sexual intercourse decreased from 57.4 percent for males and 50.8 percent for females in 1991 49.8 percent and 45.9 percent, respectively, in 2007. This decline has also decreased the number of teenage pregnancies, as well as the spread of STIs in this age group.

If you decide the time is right to become sexually active, you should stay informed about and decide which contraception method and STI protection makes sense for you and your partner. Think about how an unplanned pregnancy, STI, or a break-up would affect you and your long-term plans. Purchase some condoms. Learn the difference between "YES" and "NO". If you hear "no", "maybe", or if you hear nothing, STOP and talk to your partner. Always respect and adhere to

© iofoto, 2012, Shutterstock, Inc.

It is important to decide what you would like out of a relationship and if/when you feel comfortable beginning a specific sexual activity.

what a person is saying. Make sure any "yes" is absolute and certain. Do not use mindaltering substances such as drugs and alcohol (including beer). These substances decrease your decision-making ability. This is problematic for using a condom consistently and correctly and for listening for the "yes" answer described above (ETR Associates, 2008).

Sex, Lies, and Condom Use

In a series of focus groups with 92 sexually active, young, ethnically and racially diverse individuals, aged 15 to 20, in five American cities, researchers focused on their views and motivations for sex and for condom use. Most found it difficult to believe that people their age used condoms every single time they had sex. Although they acknowledged that everyone is at risk for sexually transmitted diseases, the young people saw their own risk as minimal.

The genders had very different motives both for engaging in sex and for using condoms. In the interviews, young women said they engaged in sexual relations because of a desire for physical intimacy and a committed relationship. They generally reported having sex only with men they cared for and deeply trusted and expected that these men would be honest and forthright about their sexual history. This trust played a significant role in their decision whether to insist on condom use. In contrast, few of the young men said "relationships" were an important dimension of their sexual involvements. Their primary motivation was a desire for physical and sexual satisfaction. Most said they were not interested in commitment and viewed emotional expectations as a complication of becoming sexually involved with a woman. The young men also admitted to making judgments about "types" of girls. To them, young women they didn't care about were "sluts" with whom they used a condom for their own protection.

Which partner determined whether a couple would use a condom? In these interviews, the answer was the women—if they chose to do so. Regardless of race or ethnicity, many of the young women were adamant in demanding that their partners use condoms–and many young men said they would not challenge such a demand out of fear of losing the opportunity for sex. Men often expected potential partners to want to use condoms and described themselves as "suspicious" of women who did not.

Both sexes named two primary reasons for using condoms: preventing pregnancy and protecting against sexually transmitted diseases. Young women saw an unwanted pregnancy as an occurrence that would be disruptive, expensive, and could "ruin" their lives and their parents' lives. Young men saw condom use as a way of protecting themselves against emotional entanglements and paternity issues.

The young people were most strongly motivated to use condoms when they did not know a potential sexual partner well or were at the earliest states of sexual involvement with others. Nearly all said they solicited information about a potential partner's sexual history from this person or from friends. Rather than directly asking about the number of past partners, they more often relied on feelings and visual observations. Some admitted to lying when asked about their own sexual experience in order to avoid being seen as promiscuous. Once a couple had sex without a condom, both partners—but especially women—found it awkward to resume condom use because doing so would imply a lack of trust.

Source: "In the Heat of the Moment: A Qualitative Study on Motivating Condom Use Among Sexually Active Young People," (#3126) The Henry J. Kaiser Family Foundation, June 2001. This information was reprinted with permission from the Henry J. Kaiser Family Foundation. The Kaiser Family Foundation is a non-profit private operating foundation, based in Menlo Park, CA, dedicated to producing and communicating the best possible information, research, and analysis on health issues.

Reproduction

Menstrual Cycle

The menstrual cycle typically lasts twenty-eight days, with a range of twenty-five to forty days. Day one of the cycle is the first day of menstruation. The cycle ends with the next menstruation (see Figure 8.5). The follicular phase begins with menstruation and terminates when ovulation occurs. The follicular phase can be very unpredictable (typically fourteen days, but can be as little as ten or as long as twenty-five). Stress, illness, and many other factors can change when a female ovulates. This can cause problems when individuals are trying to control whether they become pregnant or not. The length of

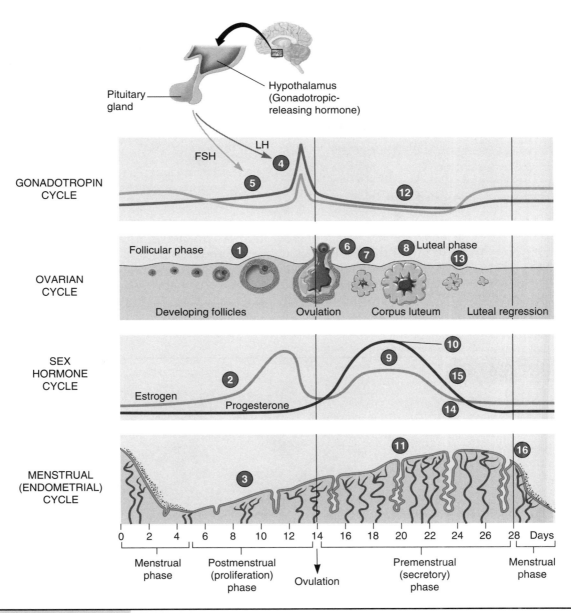

FIGURE 8.5

The Human Menstrual (Reproductive) Cycle

Source: From *Biology: Understanding Life by Alters and Alters,* © 2006 by Alters and Alters. Reproduced with permission of John Wiley & Sons, Inc.

the luteal phase is much more predictable (typically thirteen to fifteen days), beginning with ovulation and ending when the next menstrual cycle begins.

Premenstrual syndrome (PMS) can occur from one to ten days before a woman's period. This syndrome can consist of feeling bloated, diarrhea, nausea, backache, and/or cramping. Behaviors that can help ease PMS symptoms include:

- decrease salt and sugar intake,
- do not consume caffeine, and
- exercise regularly.

Ovarian Cycle

During the ovarian cycle immature eggs (follicles) are maturing and moving toward the surface of the ovary. The follicle and the ovarian surface open and allow the egg to float out. At the time of ovulation some women may feel a twinge or pain in the lower abdomen or back. After ovulation, the egg is swept into a fallopian tube (where fertilization typically occurs; see Figure 8.6) by fimbrae and the cilia (tiny hairs) and travels to the uterus. If the egg is not fertilized, it simply disintegrates or flows out with vaginal secretions, usually before menstruation. If the egg is fertilized, it will attach itself to the endometrium (internal lining of the uterus) in order to develop (see Figure 8.7).

Endometrial Cycle

The endometrial cycle consists of three phases:

1. the menstrual,
2. proliferative, and
3. progestational (secretory).

The menstrual phase lasts approximately four to seven days, when the lining of the uterus is sloughed off and flows out of the uterus through the vagina, along with blood and other vaginal secretions. The proliferative phase lasts from the completion of the menstrual phase until a day or two after ovulation. During this time the endometrium is regenerating the layer that was

---

FIGURE 8.6

The Egg

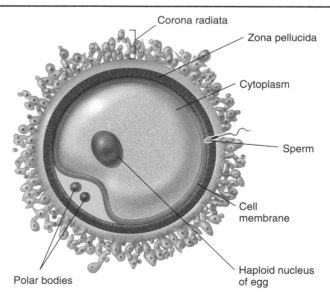

Corona radiata
Zona pellucida
Cytoplasm
Sperm
Cell membrane
Haploid nucleus of egg
Polar bodies

Source: Alters, Sandra, *Biology: Understanding Life,* 1999: Jones & Bartlett Learning, Burlington, MA. www.jblearning.com. Reprinted with permission.

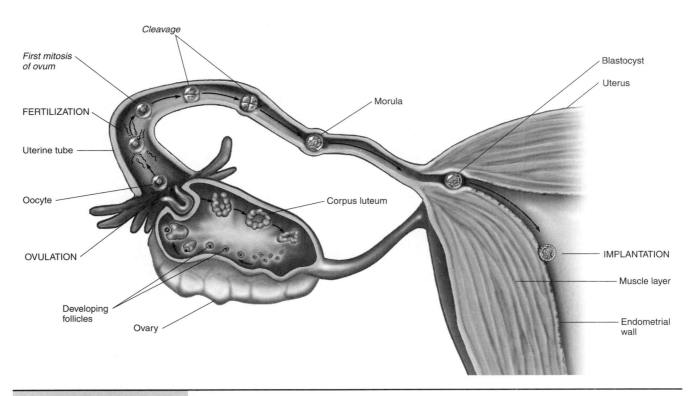

Cleavage

First mitosis
of ovum

FERTILIZATION

Uterine tube

Oocyte

OVULATION

Developing
follicles

Ovary

Morula

Corpus luteum

Blastocyst

Uterus

IMPLANTATION

Muscle layer

Endometrial
wall

FIGURE 8.7

From Fertilization to Implantation

Source: From Biology: Understanding Life by Alters and Alters, © 2006 by Alters and Alters. Reproduced with permission of John Wiley & Sons, Inc.

sloughed off with new epithelial cells. During the progestational phase the endometrium becomes twice as thick as it did during the proliferative phase. It develops a cushion-like surface, thereby possessing the ability to nourish an implanted fertilized ovum. During the end of the progestational phase, if fertilization has not occurred, the endometrium begins to deteriorate. These phases repeat throughout the reproductive years until fertilization or menopause occurs.

Pregnancy

Pregnancy is usually divided into three trimesters, each of which last approximately three months or thirteen weeks (see Figure 8.8). Typically fertilization occurs twelve to eighteen days after the beginning of the menstrual cycle. There are many variables that can impact the timing of fertilization, including irregular periods, extreme exercise, illness, stress, a missed contraceptive pill, as well as many other factors. As soon as fertilization occurs the cells begin to divide and multiply. The fertilized egg implants in the uterus after approximately one week after fertilization. For most women the first sign(s) of pregnancy include a missed period, nausea, or excessive fatigue. Home pregnancy kits are 97–99 percent accurate if used correctly. These tests can detect human chorionic gonadotropin (HCG) within two to three weeks of fertilization. HCG is the hormone secreted by the placenta to help sustain the pregnancy for the first trimester. During the second and third trimesters the HCG levels decrease and the levels of estrogen and progesterone are sufficient to sustain the pregnancy to term. This is believed to be the reason morning sickness ends for most women after the first trimester. The embryo develops very rapidly during the first trimester. During these three months, all of the major organs are formed. Therefore, it is imperative to see a physician as soon as an

FIGURE 8.8

Prenatal Development
of Fetus

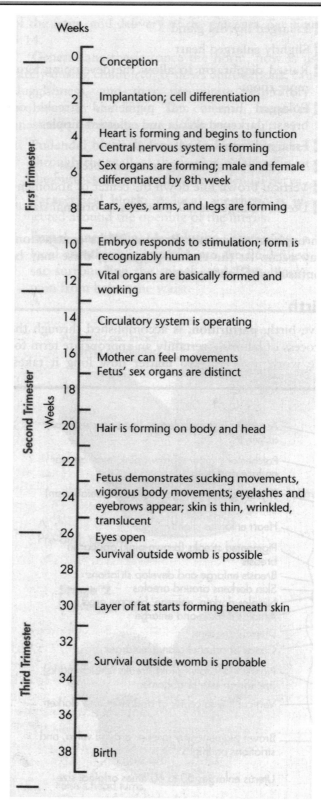

Weeks

First Trimester

0 — Conception

2 — Implantation; cell differentiation

4 — Heart is forming and begins to function
Central nervous system is forming

6 — Sex organs are forming; male and female differentiated by 8th week

8 — Ears, eyes, arms, and legs are forming

10 — Embryo responds to stimulation; form is recognizably human

12 — Vital organs are basically formed and working

Second Trimester

Weeks

14 — Circulatory system is operating

16 — Mother can feel movements
Fetus' sex organs are distinct

18

20 — Hair is forming on body and head

22

24 — Fetus demonstrates sucking movements, vigorous body movements; eyelashes and eyebrows appear; skin is thin, wrinkled, translucent

26 — Eyes open
Survival outside womb is possible

28

Third Trimester

30 — Layer of fat starts forming beneath skin

32

34 — Survival outside womb is probable

36

38 — Birth

Source: From Personal Health: Perspectives and Lifestyles by Floyd et al. (2007).

individual thinks she may be pregnant to begin taking prenatal vitamins and change any habits that could be harmful to the developing embryo. The pregnancy is dated utilizing the first day of the last menstrual period (LMP). The heartbeat can be seen during a sonogram as early as the sixth or seventh week when the embryo is approximately 5 mm long. During the second and third trimesters the fetus is growing larger and stronger in preparation for delivery. Typically the mother will begin to feel the movements of the fetus between the sixteenth and twentieth weeks. This is referred to as "quickening." After an additional month or so, these movements can be felt externally by friends or family members. Thirty-six weeks is considered a full-term pregnancy, but typically delivery does not occur until around the fortieth week.

Sexually Transmitted Infections and Pregnancy

Sexually transmitted infections (STIs) can be passed from a pregnant woman to the baby before, during, or after the baby's birth. Syphilis can cross the placenta and infect the baby while it is in the uterus. Chlamydia, gonorrhea, genital herpes, and hepatitis B can be transmitted from the mother to the baby during delivery as the baby passes through the birth canal. HIV can cross the placenta during pregnancy, during the delivery, and can infect the baby through breast milk. If an STI is transmitted, it can result in stillbirth, low birth weight (less than five pounds), conjunctivitis, pneumonia, infection of the baby's blood stream, neurological damage, blindness, deafness, acute hepatitis, meningitis, chronic liver disease, and cirrhosis. Most of these can be prevented if the mother receives routine prenatal care, including screening tests for STIs. The CDC *Guidelines for Treatment of Sexually Transmitted Infections* (2006a) recommend that pregnant women be screened on their first prenatal visit for STIs, which may include: chlamydia, gonorrhea, syphilis, hepatitis B and C, and HIV. Chlamydia, gonorrhea, and syphilis can be treated and cured with antibiotics during pregnancy. There is no cure for most viral STIs, such as genital herpes and HIV. Below is a list of annual occurrences of specific STIs and the estimated number of pregnant women who are infected in the United States:

STIs	Estimated Number of Pregnant Women
Herpes	880,000
Chlamydia	100,000
Gonorrhea	13,200
Hepatitis B	16,000
HIV	6,400
Syphilis	<1,000

Source: (CDC, 2008)

Pregnancy Prevention

Natural Methods*

Abstinence from Penile/Vaginal Intercourse

Effectiveness:
- in preventing pregnancy: 100 percent
- in preventing STIs—100 percent

Advantages:
- No worries
- No medical or hormonal side effects
- Protects against unwanted pregnancy

Disadvantages:
- Very few people choose lifetime celibacy or abstinence from sexual intercourse.
- People often forget to protect themselves against pregnancy or STIs when they stop abstaining.

Withdrawal Method

The man will pull his penis out of the vagina before he ejaculates to keep sperm from joining an egg.

Effectiveness:
- in preventing pregnancy: 73–96 percent
- in preventing STIs—NONE

Advantage:
- Can be used when no other method is available

Disadvantages:
- Requires great self-control, experience, and trust
- Not for men who ejaculate prematurely
- Not for men who do not know when to pull out
- Not recommended for teenagers

Fertility Awareness-based Methods (FAMs)

- A woman must chart her menstrual cycle and must be able to detect certain physical signs in order to predict "unsafe" days.
- She must abstain from intercourse or use barrier contraceptives during nine or more "unsafe" days each menstrual cycle.
- Check temperature daily. Before ovulation waking temperatures remain low, after ovulation temperatures rise until the next menstrual cycle begins.
- Check cervical mucus daily. Before ovulation the mucus is wet and similar to a raw egg white, after ovulation the cervical fluid dries up quickly.
- Record menstrual cycles on calendar to determine if she has regular or irregular cycles. This method is more effective for those with regular menstrual cycles.
- Remember that the sperm can live up to 120 hours after ejaculation. If a female ovulates within 120 hours after unprotected sexual intercourse the possibility of pregnancy exists.

Effectiveness:
- in preventing pregnancy: 75–99 percent
- in preventing STIs—NONE

Advantages:
- No medical or hormonal side effects
- Calendars, thermometers, and charts are easy to obtain

*More specific information can be found at www.birth-control-comparison. info/fam.htm

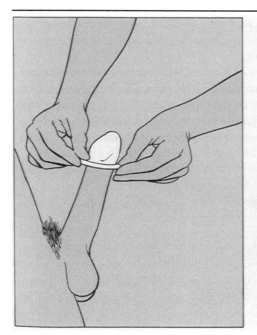

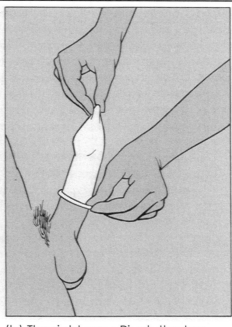

FIGURE 8.9
Using a Condom
Source: From Sexuality: Insights and Issues, third edition. Copyright © 1993 by Jerrold Greenberg, Clint Buess, and Kathleen D. Mullen. Reprinted by permission of the authors.

(a) The wrong way

(b) The right way: Pinch the top of the condom, leaving 1/2 inch at the top to catch the semen; hold the tip of the condom and unroll the condom until it reaches the pubic hair.

Disadvantages:
- Requires expert training before effective use
- Taking risks during "unsafe" days
- Poor record keeping
- Illness and lack of sleep affect body temperatures
- Vaginal infections and douches change mucus
- Cannot use with irregular periods or temperature patterns

Barrier Methods

Male Condom

The male condom is a latex sheath, placed over the penis prior to intercourse (see Figure 8.9).

Effectiveness:
- in preventing pregnancy: 83–98 percent
- in preventing STIs—85–98 percent

To increase pregnancy prevention effectiveness also use spermicide or have female utilize another form of contraception.

Do not use oil-based lubricants such as Vaseline or lotion, which will cause the condom to break. Use only water-based lubricants such as KY jelly once the condom is on the penis.

Advantages:
- Most effective way to prevent STIs besides abstinence
- Easy to buy (inexpensive)
- Easy to carry
- Only way for male to protect himself from unplanned pregnancy
- Can help relieve premature ejaculation

© ZTS, 2012, Shutterstock, Inc.

Other than abstinence, use of a condom is the most effective way to prevent STIs.

Problems:
- Possible allergies to latex
- Less sensation
- Condom breakage
- Sometimes interrupts "the mood"
- Human error: withdrawal without holding the condom in place; using after the expiration date; opening the package with teeth, fingernails, or sharp objects can damage the condom; storage of condoms in a warm place such as a wallet in a back pocket can decrease effectiveness.

Diaphragm and Femcap

Latex cup (diaphragm) or silicone cup (Femcap) requires fitting by a clinician. The diaphragm or cap is coated with spermicide before placement in the vagina. The diaphragm or cervical cap combined with spermicide act by destroying the sperm and preventing the sperm from reaching the egg. After intercourse, the Femcap should be left in place for eight hours.

Effectiveness:
in preventing pregnancy:
- Diaphragm with spermicide—86–94 percent
- Femcap with spermicide—84–91 percent for women who have never given birth; 68–74 percent for women who have given birth
- in preventing STIs—NONE

Advantages:
- Femcap can be inserted many hours before sexual intercourse
- Diaphragm can be inserted two hours before sexual intercourse
- Does not alter the menstrual cycle; easy to carry with you, comfortable
- No major health concerns
- Can last several years

Disadvantages:
- Can be messy
- Possibility of allergies to latex, silicone, or spermicide
- Cannot use with vaginal bleeding or an infection
- Diaphragm—can only be left in place for up to twenty-four hours
- Diaphragm—increased risk of bladder infection
- Femcap—difficult for some women to use
- Femcap—can only be left in place for up to forty-eight hours

Over-the-Counter Contraceptives for Women
- Female condom—insert vaginal pouch deep into vagina prior to intercourse
- Spermicide, foam, jelly, or cream—insert deep into vagina prior to intercourse

Effectiveness:
in preventing pregnancy:
- Female condom—79–95 percent
- Spermicide, foam, jelly, or cream—71–82 percent in preventing STIs:
- Female condom—similar to the male condom, but not quite as effective, due to possible folding
- Spermicides, foam, jelly, and cream in preventing STIs—NONE

Advantages:
- Easy to purchase in drugstores, supermarkets, etc.
- Increased sensation compared to the male condom
- Erection not necessary to keep female condom in place

Disadvantages:
- Outer ring of female condom may slip into vagina during intercourse
- Possible difficulty inserting the pouch
- More difficult preparation
- Possible allergies to spermicide

Hormonal Methods

The Pill

The pill (oral contraceptive pills) is a prescription medication containing the hormones estrogen and/or progesterone, which usually prevent the release of the egg, thickens the cervical mucus, and reduces the buildup of the endometrial lining within the uterus. The sperm is thus unable to penetrate the egg, and/or the fertilized egg is prevented from implanting in the uterus.

Effectiveness:
- in preventing pregnancy: 92–99.7 percent
- in preventing STIs—NONE

Advantages:
- Nothing to put into place before intercourse
- Regular and shorter periods
- Decreases chances of developing ovarian and endometrial cancers, non-cancerous breast tumors, ovarian cysts, pelvic inflammatory disease, and osteoporosis
- Decreased incidence of tubal pregnancies
- Ability to become pregnant returns quickly when use is stopped

Disadvantages:
- Less effective when taken with some drugs
- Must be taken daily (within the same two hour period)
- Rare but serious health risks, including: blood clots, heart attack, and stroke, which are more common for women over 35 and/or who smoke cigarettes (ARHP, 2008). This increased risk is found in most of the hormonal contraceptive methods. This is due to an increased correlation of cardiovascular disease most likely from the formation of atherosclerosis in women who smoke and use hormonal contraceptive methods. This risk also increases as women age, smoke, and use hormonal contraceptive methods.
- Side effects can include temporary irregular bleeding, weight gain, breast tenderness, and nausea.

Women who experience any of the following symptoms while taking the pill should call their physician immediately:
- Abdominal pains (severe)
- Chest pain or shortness of breath
- Headaches (severe)
- Eye problems, such as blurred vision
- Severe leg or arm pain or numbness (http://www.fwhc.org/birth-control/thepill.htm)

Mini-pills

Mini-pills (oral contraceptive pills) are a prescription medication containing progesterone only, which usually prevents the release of the egg, thickens the cervical mucus, and reduces the buildup of the endometrial lining within the uterus. The sperm is thus unable to penetrate the egg, and/or the fertilized egg is prevented from implanting in the uterus.

Effectiveness:
- in preventing pregnancy: 87–99.7 percent (slightly less than regular birth control pills)
- in preventing STIs—NONE

Advantages:
- Nothing to put into place before intercourse
- Avoids typical side effects of regular birth control pills
- Has no estrogen
- Ability to become pregnant returns quickly when use is stopped

Disadvantages:
- Less effective when taken with some drugs
- MUST be taken at the same time every day
- Increased risk of ectopic pregnancy
- Increased risk of functional ovarian cysts

Vaginal Ring
The female will insert a small, flexible ring deep into the vagina for three weeks and take it out for the fourth week. It releases combined hormones that protect against pregnancy for one month. The ring uses hormones similar to the estrogen and progesterone made by a woman's ovaries to prevent the ovaries from releasing an egg, thickens the cervical mucus, and reduces the buildup of the endometrial lining within the uterus. The sperm is thus unable to penetrate the egg, and/or the fertilized egg is prevented from implanting in the uterus.

Effectiveness:
- in preventing pregnancy: 92–99.7 percent
- in preventing STIs—NONE

Advantages:
- Protects against pregnancy for one month
- No pill to take daily
- Does not require a "fitting" by a clinician
- Does not require the use of spermicide
- Ability to become pregnant returns quickly when use is stopped
- Nothing to put into place before intercourse
- More regular and shorter periods
- Reduces the risk of ovarian and endometrial cancers, pelvic inflammatory disease, non-cancerous growths of the breasts, ovarian cysts, and osteoporosis
- Fewer occurrences of ectopic pregnancy

Disadvantages:
- Increased vaginal discharge
- Vaginal irritation or infection
- Cannot use a diaphragm or cap for a backup method of birth control
- Rare but serious health risks, including blood clots, heart attack, and stroke— women who are 35 and older and/or smoke are at a greater risk. This increased risk is found in most of the hormonal contraceptive methods. This is due to an increased correlation of cardiovascular disease most likely from the formation of atherosclerosis in women who smoke and use hormonal contraceptive methods. This risk also increases as women age, smoke, and use hormonal contraceptive methods.
- Temporary irregular bleeding, weight gain, breast tenderness, and nausea

Women who experience any of the following symptoms while using the ring should call their physician immediately:
- Abdominal pains (severe)
- Chest pain or shortness of breath
- Headaches (severe)
- Eye problems, such as blurred vision
- Severe leg or arm pain or numbness
  (http://www.fwhc.org/birth-control/vaginal-ring.htm)

Contraceptive Patch
The female will place a thin plastic patch on the skin of the buttocks, stomach, upper outer arm, or upper torso once a week for three weeks in a row. Use a new patch each week. Do not use a patch for the fourth week. The patch releases combined hormones that protect against pregnancy for one month. The patch uses hormones similar to the estrogen and progesterone made by a woman's ovaries to prevent the ovaries from releasing an egg, thickens the cervical mucus, and re-

duces the buildup of the endometrial lining within the uterus. The sperm is thus unable to penetrate the egg, and/or the fertilized egg is prevented from implanting in the uterus.

Effectiveness:
- in preventing pregnancy: 99 percent (for women who weigh 197 pounds or less) 92 percent (for women who weigh 198 pounds or more)
- in preventing STIs—NONE

Advantages:
- Protects against pregnancy for one month
- No pill to take daily
- Nothing to put into place before intercourse
- Ability to become pregnant returns quickly when use is stopped
- More regular and shorter periods
- Reduce the risk of ovarian and endometrial cancers, pelvic inflammatory disease, non-cancerous growths of the breasts, ovarian cysts, and osteoporosis
- Fewer occurrences of ectopic pregnancy

Disadvantages:
- Skin reaction at the site of application
- Menstrual cramps
- May not be effective for women who weigh more than 198 pounds
- Rare but serious health risks, including blood clots, heart attack, and stroke— women who are 35 and older and/or smoke are at a greater risk. This increased risk is found in most of the hormonal contraceptive methods. This is due to an increased correlation of cardiovascular disease most likely from the formation of atherosclerosis in women who smoke and use hormonal contraceptive methods. This risk also increases as women age, smoke, and use hormonal contraceptive methods.
- Temporary irregular bleeding, weight gain, breast tenderness, and nausea

Some women may not be able to use contraceptive patches because of the risk of serious health problems. Women over 35 who smoke or have any of the following conditions should not use the patch:

- History of heart attack or stroke
- Chest pain
- Blood clots
- Unexplained vaginal bleeding
- Severe high blood pressure
- Diabetes with kidney, eye, nerve, or blood vessel complications
- Known or suspected cancer
- Known or suspected pregnancy
- Liver tumors or liver disease
- Headaches with neurological symptoms
- Hepatitis or jaundice
- Disease of the heart valves with complications
- Require long bed rest following surgery
- Allergic reaction to the patch

Women who have a family history of breast cancer, diabetes, high blood pressure, high cholesterol, headaches or epilepsy, depression, gallbladder disease, kidney disease, heart disease, irregular periods, or are breast-feeding may not be able to use the patch.

Women who experience any of the following symptoms while using the contraceptive patch should call their physician immediately:

- Abdominal pains (severe)
- Chest pain or shortness of breath
- Headaches (severe)

- Eye problems, such as blurred vision
- Severe leg or arm pain or numbness
  (http://www.fwhc.org/birth-control/patch.htm)

Depo-Provera

Depo-Provera is a hormone shot injected into the arm or buttocks every twelve weeks, which will prevent the release of the egg, less often thickens the cervical mucus and reduces the build up of the endometrial lining within the uterus thereby preventing conception, and/or the fertilized egg from implanting in the uterus.

Effectiveness:
- in preventing pregnancy: 97–99.7 percent
- in preventing STIs—NONE

Advantages:
- Protects against pregnancy for twelve weeks
- No daily pill
- Nothing to put into place before intercourse
- Can be used by some women who cannot take the pill (oral contraceptive)
- Decreases incidence of endometrial and ovarian cancer, as well as iron deficiency anemia (ARHP, 2008)
- Can be used while breast-feeding

Disadvantages:
- Studies released in 2004 show that Depo-Provera is associated with a loss of bone density resulting in an increased risk of osteoporosis. The bone loss appears not to be reversed when the woman stops the Depo-Provera injections (U.S. Department of Health and Human Services).
- Side effects include irregular bleeding, headaches, depression, nausea, loss of monthly period, weight gain, nervousness, and dizziness
- Side effects cannot be reversed until medication wears off (up to twelve weeks)
- May cause delay in getting pregnant after shots are stopped (up to twelve to eighteen months)
- Should not be used continuously for more than two years

IUD

The intrauterine device (IUD) requires a health care professional to insert a small plastic device through the cervix and into the uterus. The IUD contains copper or hormones that impede conception or rarely prevent implantation of a fertilized egg. IUDs can last one to ten years.

Effectiveness:
- in preventing pregnancy: 99.2–99.9 percent
- in preventing STIs—NONE

Advantages:
- Nothing to put into place before intercourse
- Para Gard (copper IUD) may be left in place for up to ten years; Mirena (hormone IUD) may be left in place for up to five years
- No daily pills
- Ability to become pregnant returns quickly when use is stopped

Disadvantages:
- May cause cramping (copper IUD)
- Spotting between periods
- Heavier and longer periods
- Increased risk of tubal infection, which may lead to infertility if inserted when a women has an STI
- Rarely, the wall of the uterus is punctured

Contraceptive Implant

Contraceptive implants are soft capsules, about 1.5 inch long, placed under the skin in a woman's upper inner arm. The capsules release progestin, which usually prevents the release of the egg, thickens the cervical mucus, and reduces the buildup of the endometrial lining within the uterus. The sperm is thus unable to penetrate the egg, and/or the fertilized egg is prevented from implanting in the uterus. Implanon is currently being used in the United States and is a single rod that releases a hormone called etonogestrel which lasts three years. Contraceptive implants can be removed at any time.

Effectiveness:
- in preventing pregnancy: 99 percent
- in preventing STIs—NONE

Advantages:
- Can be worn for three years
- Affects fertility one month at a time
- Has no estrogen

Disadvantages:
- Increased risk of heart attack
- Increased risk of stroke

TABLE 8.1 ♦ Prevention of Sexually Transmitted Infections (STIs) and Pregnancy

Birth Control Method	Effectiveness in Preventing Pregnancy (Perfect Use)	Effectiveness in Preventing Pregnancy (Typical Use)	Effectiveness in Preventing Sexually Transmitted Infections (Typical Use)	
Abstinence from Penile/ Vaginal Intercourse		100%	100%	
Withdrawal Method	99%	75%	0%	Natural Methods
Fertility-based Methods (FAMs)	99%	75%	0%	
Male Condom	98%	85%	less than 100%	
Diaphragm w/ Spermicide	94%	84%	0%	
Femcap w/ Spermicide	91%	68%	0%	
Intrauterine Device		99%	0%	Barrier Methods
Female Condom	95%	79%	less than 100%	
Spermicides used alone	82%	71%	0%	
Contraceptive Implant		99%	0%	
Sterilization		over 99%	0%	
Oral Contraceptive Pill	99%	92–99%	0%	
Mini-Pill		87–89%	0%	
Vaginal Ring		92–99%	0%	Hormonal Methods
Contraceptive Patch		99%	0%	
Depo-Provera Injection		97–99%	0%	

Source: (Planned Parenthood, 2005) (www.youngwomanshealth.org/sexuality_menu.html, 2003).

Sterilization

Sterilization is an operation performed on the female (tubal ligation) or male (vasectomy). The tubal ligation is intended to permanently block a woman's fallopian tubes, where sperm typically unite with the eggs.

A vasectomy is performed to permanently block a man's vas deferens tubes, which transport sperm.

Effectiveness:
- in preventing pregnancy: 99.5–99.9 percent
- in preventing STIs—NONE

Advantages:
- Permanent protection against pregnancy
- No lasting side effects
- No effects on sexual pleasure
- Protects woman whose health would be seriously threatened by a pregnancy

Disadvantages:
- Mild bleeding or infection after the surgery
- Some people eventually regret being unable to have children later in life
- Reaction to anesthetic
- Not usually reversible if you change your mind
- Rarely, tubes reopen, allowing pregnancy to occur
- Rare complications with tubal ligation include bleeding and injury to the bowel
- Vasectomy—infection or blood clot can occur in or near the testicles; often there is temporary bruising, swelling, or tenderness of the scrotum

Go to www.arhp.org/Method Match and use this interactive program to help you choose the birth control method that is right for you.

Emergency Contraception "The Morning After Pill"

There is considerable public confusion about the difference between emergency contraception (EC) pills and medication abortion (RU-486). Pregnancy begins when a pre-embryo completes implantation into the lining of the uterus (ACOG, 1998). EC helps prevent pregnancy, whereas medication abortion terminates pregnancy. Hormonal methods of contraception, including EC, prevent pregnancy by inhibiting ovulation and fertilization (ACOG, 2011). More specifically, EC works by delaying or inhibiting ovulation, and/or altering tubal transport of sperm and/ or ova (thereby inhibiting fertilization), and/or altering the endometrium (thereby inhibiting implantation) (Trussell and Jordan, 2006).

After unprotected intercourse, emergency contraception may be utilized. This treatment has been in place for several years in other countries, but only recently became available in the United States. The medication should be taken within 120 hours of unprotected sexual intercourse. The sooner the medication is begun, the higher the effectiveness for pregnancy prevention. There are two types of ECs. The first one contains both estrogen and progestin. When taken within seventy-two hours of unprotected intercourse, ECs that contain both estrogen and progestin reduce the risk of pregnancy by 75 percent. The combination pills are taken in two doses, twelve hours apart.

The other type of ECs only contains progestin. When taken within twenty-four hours of unprotected intercourse, progestin-only ECs were found to reduce the risk of pregnancy by 95 percent (Ellertson et al., 2003). The progestin-only ECs are taken in two doses, twelve hours apart or at the same time.

The emergency contraceptive method is typically used in cases of unanticipated sexual intercourse, contraceptive failure, or sexual assault.

Some common side effects include substantial nausea and vomiting. These side effects generally subside within forty-eight hours. This is not to be used as a regular method of birth control. As with many of the other pregnancy prevention methods, this one offers no protection against the contraction of STIs.

Unplanned Pregnancy

This can be a very exciting and/or frightening time in an individual's life. The thought of pregnancy conjures up many emotions, such as the realization of life changes, increased responsibility, happiness, and worry all at the same time. Pregnancy and the responsibilities of parenthood are tremendous. It is important to realize these potential consequences of unprotected intercourse or failed pregnancy prevention. It is a good idea to discuss how you might handle this situation with your potential sexual partner. In the event of an unplanned pregnancy, there are several options, none of which are easy and all can be life altering. These will be discussed in the following sections.

Parenthood

Parenthood has been described in many words. Many agree it is one of the best things that can happen, while for others parenthood is quite difficult and challenging. For most, this phase of life (given its rewards and demands) is a blend of these two perspectives. These differences of opinion are often influenced by the stage of life during which the individual becomes a parent, combined with factors such as other life circumstances (whether the parent will be a single parent or not), as well as the personality and financial situation of the new parent. Parenthood usually will dramatically alter the lifestyle to which an individual has become accustomed. Initially, it is an end to restful nights, spur-of-the-moment trips, and many social activities. New parents now have an individual who is solely dependent upon them twenty-four hours a day for attention, love, food, clothing, safety, and shelter.

Parenthood can be both overwhelming and a time of tremendous joy.

This can be overwhelming physically, mentally, and financially even for the most prepared parents. It is also a time of tremendous joy, as well as many special moments, such as your baby's first smile, giggle, word, or step. As the child grows they are less dependent upon you for the basic necessities, but those needs change into dance lessons, soccer practice, and slumber parties, to name a few. The commitment to becoming a parent is large and one that never ends and can be very difficult to face alone.

Adoption

For many, present life circumstances do not permit them to remain the caregiver in the best interest of their child. Many factors, such as the age of the parent and economic circumstance, come to bear upon this complex and often difficult decision. For the vast majority this is indeed a most difficult decision to reach. The bond that ties the newborn child and parent(s) is enormous. Usually this course is taken in an attempt to be unselfish and provide the child with improved opportunities in life which might otherwise be unavailable to them. Many adoption agencies exist to help make this option as painless as possible. There are many different types of adoptions. Some allow the biological parents to remain a part of the child's life; others do not, but provide a mechanism whereby the child can eventually obtain information regarding the biological parents. Often this information can be made available only after the adopted child enters adolescence or adulthood.

Abortion

Some individuals cannot (due to medical reasons) or do not want to carry the embryo to term, and therefore choose abortion. This decision is reached for various reasons. Sometimes this is felt to be the best decision because of the circumstances of conception (such as a rape resulting in pregnancy). Some believe they cannot disclose a pregnancy to their parents or partner and see no other alternative. Others are not ready to become parents and do not want to complete the pregnancy.

Abortion was made legal throughout the United States in 1973. Since that time, abortion has become the most often performed outpatient surgery. Today, abortion is about ten times safer than giving birth. The cost of an abortion depends upon the stage of the pregnancy and which clinic is providing the service. During the first trimester (up to twelve weeks) the cost is usually between $450 and $1,275. During the second trimester (thirteen to twenty-four weeks) the cost increases to $600 to $6,000. Some insurance plans will cover abortion costs. There are some potential complications associated with abortion. The complications can include an incomplete abortion, which means the procedure would need to be repeated; an infection, which can usually be treated with antibiotics; or perforation of the uterine wall.

There are several types of abortion procedures available, depending on the stage of the pregnancy. Medical abortion (Mifepristone, RU-486, or nonsurgical abortion) is an option up to eight weeks since the last menstrual period (LMP). Surgical vacuum aspiration abortion is the procedure used to empty the uterus and can be performed between six and twelve weeks since the LMP. Last, the dilation and evacuation procedure can be performed between thirteen and twenty-four weeks since the LMP. After and during an abortion there is typically mild to very strong cramping for one to three hours, as well as bleeding and/or spotting for three to six weeks. A normal menstrual period should begin within four to eight weeks. Usually clinics will offer counseling before and after an abortion. Due to the emotional nature of any decision associated with pregnancy, counseling is highly recommended.

As mentioned earlier, pregnancy is accompanied by many emotions and lasting effects for both partners. There is no easy route once pregnancy has occurred. It is a good idea to discuss your values and ideas of what you would do in the event of an unplanned pregnancy with your prospective sexual partner. It is best to fully consider all of the options before making a decision.

Sexually Transmitted Infections (STIs)

There are more than thirty infections that are primarily spread through sexual activity (see Table 8.8 on pages 310–313, near the end of this chapter, for a partial listing). In the United States, there are more than 65 million people currently living with an incurable STI. An additional 19 million people become infected with one or more STIs each year (see Figure 8.17, on page 301), of which approximately half are not curable (SIECUS, 2008) or www.siecus.org. STIs are transmitted during vaginal, oral, anal sexual activity, or in some cases by simply touching an infected area. STIs can be transferred not only to the genitalia area, but also to the mouth, eyes, nose, and other orifices of the body. You can become infected if someone's blood, semen, vaginal secretions, or precum goes into your body during vaginal, anal, or oral sex. Many individuals who become infected with STIs are asymptomatic (without symptoms) and thus become silent carriers. This is one of the reasons STIs have reached epidemic proportions. There are many health problems that can result if an asymptomatic STI carrier is not treated. Some of these health problems include infertility, ectopic pregnancies, and genital cancers, particularly cervical cancer in women. Therefore, it is very important to know your sexual history and be tested for STIs regularly.

Levels of Risk

Sexual behaviors have different levels of risk for different STIs (Figure 8.12 on page 296). Using condoms lowers the risk of transmitting STIs in association with anal, oral, or vaginal intercourse. The following list depicts risk, assuming no protection is used for the following behaviors.

High Risk
- Anal intercourse
- Vaginal intercourse
- Oral sex on a man with ejaculation
- Oral sex on a man without ejaculation
- Oral sex on a woman
- Oral-anal contact

Low Risk
- Intimate kissing
- Casual kissing
- Touching, massage

No Risk
- Masturbation
- Talking, fantasy (ACHA, 2004)

Bacterial STIs

Chlamydia

Chlamydia is caused by a bacteria-like intracellular parasite called *Chlamydia trachomati*. Chlamydia is typically spread during vaginal, oral, or anal sex and can infect other body parts such as the eyes, nose, or throat where chlamydia can also be contracted. Symptoms in males include a thin, clear-whitish urethral discharge, itching or burning during urination, pain, or swelling in the testes and a low-grade fever. In females, symptoms include moderate vaginal discharge, itching or burning during urination, abdominal pain, bleeding between periods, nausea, headaches, and a low-grade fever. If symptoms occur, they will typically begin one to three weeks after infection. Seventy-five percent of infected females and 51 percent of infected males are asymptomatic (without symptoms). The long-term effects of untreated chlamydia can include infertility in both males and females from scarring in the testicles and fallopian tubes. Chlamydia infections are the leading cause of preventable infertility and ectopic pregnancies. In up to 40 percent of women with untreated chlamydia, infection can spread into the uterus and fallopian tubes, causing pelvic inflammatory disease (PID). Most infections respond to tetracycline, doxycycline, or erythromycin, but not penicillin. It is very important that all partners be treated to decrease the spread of infection, as well as prevent reinfection. Chlamydia is estimated to be the most common bacterial STI in the United States (Figure 8.10), with approximately three million new cases occurring each year (ASHA, 2009). Adolescents and young adults have the highest infection rates (Figure 8.11). College students account for over 10 percent of the infected cases which are on the rise (Donatelle, 2010).

Gonorrhea

Gonorrhea is caused by the bacterium called *Neisseria gonorrhea*. Infection is found primarily in the linings of the urethra, vagina, mouth, and rectum (Crowley, 2009). Symptoms in males include a foul-smelling thick, creamy white, yellow, or yellow-green discharge from the penis, painful urination, blood or pus in

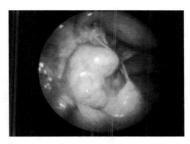

Hydrosalpinx—resulting from Chlamydia—closed, swollen and water-filled left fallopian tube in a young woman.

Excerpted from *The Secret Epidemic; STIs on Campus* © American College Health Association, PO Box 28927, Baltimore, MD 21240.

TABLE 8.2 ♦ Chlamydia—Reported Cases and Rates by State, Ranked by Rates, United States, 2009

Rank*	State	Cases	Rate per 100,000 Population
1	Mississippi	23,589	802.7
2	Alaska	5,166	752.7
3	Louisiana	27,628	626.4
4	South Carolina	26,654	595.0
5	Alabama	25,929	556.2
6	Delaware	4,718	540.4
7	Arkansas	14,354	502.7
8	New Mexico	9,493	478.4
9	Tennessee	29,711	478.1
10	New York	92,069	472.4
11	Illinois	60,542	469.3
12	Hawaii	6,026	467.8
13	Michigan	45,714	457.0
14	North Carolina	41,045	445.1
15	Missouri	25,868	437.6
16	Texas	105,910	435.4
17	Maryland	23,747	421.5
18	Ohio	48,239	420.0
19	Oklahoma	15,023	412.5
20	Georgia	39,828	411.2
	U.S. TOTAL†	**1,244,180**	**409.2**
21	Colorado	19,998	404.9
22	Arizona	26,002	400.0
23	California	146,796	399.4
24	Florida	72,931	397.9
25	Virginia	30,903	397.8
26	Nevada	10,045	386.3
27	Kansas	10,510	375.1
28	South Dakota	3,015	374.9
29	Wisconsin	20,906	371.5
30	Wyoming	1,963	368.5
31	Connecticut	12,127	346.4
32	Pennsylvania	43,068	346.0
33	Rhode Island	3,615	344.0
34	Indiana	21,732	340.8
35	Washington	21,387	326.6
36	Iowa	9,406	313.3
37	Kentucky	13,293	311.4
38	Montana	2,988	308.9
39	Nebraska	5,443	305.2
40	North Dakota	1,957	305.1
41	Oregon	11,497	303.3
42	Massachusetts	19,315	297.2
43	New Jersey	23,974	276.1
44	Minnesota	14,197	272.0
45	Idaho	3,842	252.1
46	Utah	6,145	224.6
47	West Virginia	3,604	198.6
48	Vermont	1,186	190.9
49	Maine	2,431	184.7
50	New Hampshire	2,102	159.7

Source: www.CDC.gov

*States were ranked in descending order by rate, number of cases, and alphabetically.
†Total includes cases reported by the District of Columbia with 6,549 cases and a rate of 1,106.6, but excludes outlying areas (Guam with 620 cases and rate of 352.3, Puerto Rico with 7,302 cases and rate of 184.7, and Virgin Islands with 488 cases and rate of 444.3).

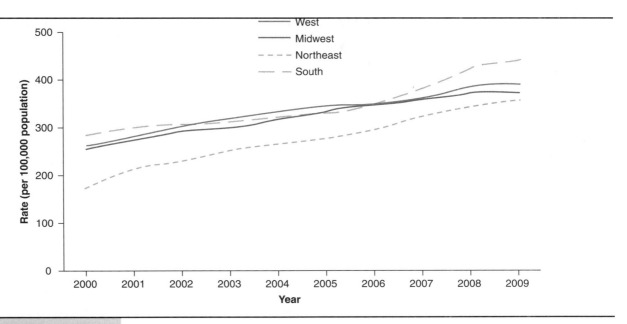

FIGURE 8.10

Chlamydia—Rates by Region, United States, 2000–2009

Source: www.CDC.gov

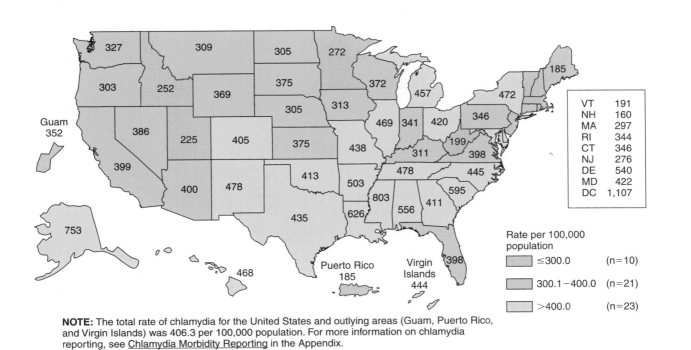

NOTE: The total rate of chlamydia for the United States and outlying areas (Guam, Puerto Rico, and Virgin Islands) was 406.3 per 100,000 population. For more information on chlamydia reporting, see Chlamydia Morbidity Reporting in the Appendix.

FIGURE 8.11

Chlamydia—Rates by State, United States and Outlying Areas, 2009

Source: www.CDC.gov

the urine, and enlarged lymph nodes in the groin area. In females, the symptoms include similar discharge from the vagina, pain during urination, pelvic pain, or irregular and painful menstruation. If symptoms are present, they usually appear about one week after exposure. Many individuals are asymptomatic *(5 to 20 percent of infected males and 60 to 80 percent of females)*. The long-term effects of untreated gonorrhea can cause infertility in both males and females, as a result of infection and scarring in both testicles and in the fallopian tubes. Gonorrhea remains one of the major causes of PID (Figure 8.13 and 8.15). Most infections respond to penicillin, tetracycline, spectinomycin, cefixime, or ceftriaxone. It is very important that all partners be treated to decrease the spread of the infection, as well as to prevent reinfection.

Pelvic Inflammatory Disease (PID)

PID is a general term that refers to an infection of the uterus, fallopian tubes, or other reproductive organ. Chlamydia and gonorrhea are the most common STIs (if left untreated) that lead to PID. Damage to the fallopian tubes and tissues in and near the uterus and ovaries can result from PID. This damage occurs from the inflammation and results in scarring of these tissues. This scarring can lead to serious consequences including infertility, ectopic pregnancy, abscess formation, and chronic pelvic pain. Each year, it is estimated that more than 1 million women will experience an episode of PID.

More than 100,000 women become infertile each year as a result of PID (CDC, 2011 or www.cdc.gov/std/PID/STDFact-PID.htm). Annually more than 150 women die from PID or complications associated with this infection.

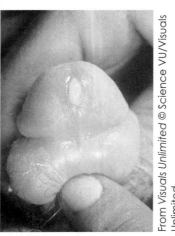

From *Visuals Unlimited* © Science VU/Visuals Unlimited.

Gonorrheal discharge from the penis.

FIGURE 8.12

STI Risk Sheet

Unprotected vaginal or anal intercourse:
Bacterial Vaginosis
Chlamydia
Cytomegalovirus (CMV)
Gonorrhea
Hepatitis B
Herpes Simplex
Human Immunodeficiency Virus (HIV)
Human Papilloma Virus (HPV, Warts)
Pelvic Inflammatory Disease (PID)
Pubic Lice
Scabies
Syphilis
Trichomoniasis
*Safer Sex Tip: Always use condoms.

Unprotected oral sex:
("blow job," "giving head," "going down," "rimming")
Cytomegalovirus (CMV)
Gonorrhea
Hepatitis B
Herpes (including cold sores)
Human Immunodeficiency Virus (HIV)
Human Papilloma Virus (HPV, Warts)
Syphilis
*Safer Sex Tip: Use dental dams, non-lubricated or flavored condom, or female condoms.

Unprotected manual sex:
("hand job" or "fingering")
Bacterial Vaginosis
Cytomegalovirus (CMV)
Herpes Simplex
Human Papilloma Virus (HPV, Warts)
Pubic Lice
Scabies
*Safer Sex Tip: Use gloves or condoms.
Source: Adapted from www.scarleteen.com.

TABLE 8.3 ♦ Gonorrhea—Reported Cases and Rates by State, Ranked by Rates, United States, 2009

Rank*	State	Cases	Rate per 100,000 Population
1	Mississippi	7,241	246.4
2	Louisiana	8,996	204.0
3	South Carolina	8,318	185.7
4	Alabama	7,498	160.8
5	Arkansas	4,460	156.2
6	Illinois	19,962	154.7
7	North Carolina	13,870	150.4
8	Michigan	14,704	147.0
9	Alaska	990	144.3
10	Georgia	13,687	141.3
11	Ohio	15,988	139.2
12	Oklahoma	4,673	128.3
13	Tennessee	7,926	127.5
14	Texas	29,295	120.4
15	Florida	20,878	113.9
16	Maryland	6,395	113.5
17	Delaware	971	111.2
18	Missouri	6,488	109.8
19	Indiana	6,835	107.2
20	Virginia	7,789	100.3
	U.S. TOTAL†	**301,174**	**99.1**
21	Wisconsin	5,201	92.4
22	Kentucky	3,827	89.6
23	Kansas	2,505	89.4
24	New York	17,004	87.2
25	Pennsylvania	10,138	81.4
26	Nebraska	1,376	77.2
27	Connecticut	2,558	73.1
28	Nevada	1,726	66.4
29	California	23,228	63.2
30	Colorado	2,823	57.2
31	Iowa	1,658	55.2
32	New Jersey	4,762	54.8
33	New Mexico	1,082	54.5
34	Arizona	3,250	50.0
35	Hawaii	631	49.0
36	Minnesota	2,303	44.1
37	South Dakota	344	42.8
38	Washington	2,285	34.9
39	Rhode Island	322	30.6
40	Massachusetts	1,976	30.4
41	Oregon	1,113	29.4
42	West Virginia	475	26.2
43	North Dakota	151	23.5
	YEAR 2010 TARGET		**19.0**
44	Wyoming	74	13.9
45	Utah	341	12.5
46	Maine	143	10.9
47	New Hampshire	113	8.6
48	Montana	80	8.3
49	Vermont	50	8.0
50	Idaho	110	7.2

*States were ranked in descending order by rate, number of cases, and alphabetically.

Source: www.CDC.gov

†Total includes cases reported by the District of Columbia with 2,561 cases and a rate of 432.7, but excludes outlying areas (Guam with 59 cases and rate of 33.5, Puerto Rico with 230 cases and rate of 5.8, and Virgin Islands with 115 cases and rate of 104.7).

FIGURE 8.13

Gonorrhea—Rates by Sex, United States, 1990–2009

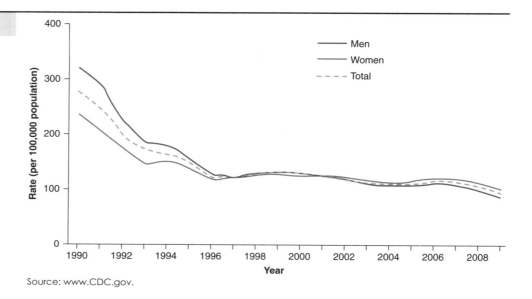

Source: www.CDC.gov.

FIGURE 8.14

Gonorrhea—Rates by Region, United States, 2000–2009

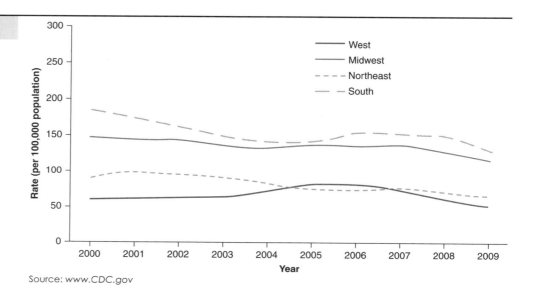

Source: www.CDC.gov

FIGURE 8.15

Gonorrhea—Rates by Age Among Women Aged 15–44 Years, United States, 2000–2009

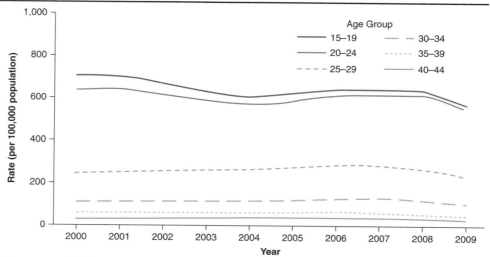

Source: www.CDC.gov.

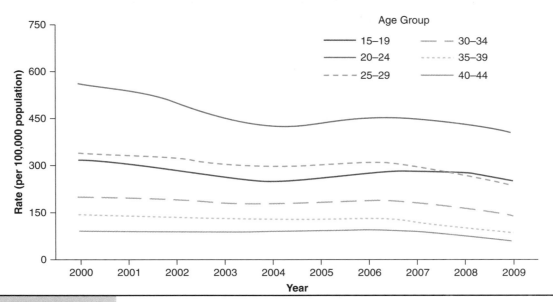

Gonorrhea—Rates by Age Among Men Aged 15–44 Years, United States, 2000–2009

Note: The *Healthy People 2010* target for P&S syphilis is 0.2 cases per 100,000 population.
Source: www.CDC.gov.

The more sexual partners a woman has had, the higher her risk of developing PID. This is because of the potential for more exposure to STIs. Most of the time there are no symptoms associated with PID. Meanwhile, the infection is causing serious long-term damage to the woman's reproductive organs. If symptoms exist, they can include lower abdominal pain, fever, unusual vaginal discharge, painful intercourse or urination, irregular menstrual bleeding, or pain in the right upper abdomen. PID can be cured with Ofloxacin, Levofloxacin, or Metronidazole. Antibiotic treatment does not reverse any damage that has already occurred to the reproductive organs.

It is critical for any woman who has symptoms of PID to be evaluated by a physician immediately. The longer treatment is delayed for PID the more likely she is to become infertile due to the damage to the reproductive organs.

Syphilis

Syphilis is a serious bacterial infection caused by the spirochete *Treponema pallidum*. Syphilis can be contracted and spread through vaginal, oral, or anal sex, as well as through blood and blood products. This disease can be debilitating and even fatal if left untreated. A person may be unknowingly infected with syphilis and transmit it to others. In the United States, over 36,000 cases of syphilis were reported in 2006 (CDC, 2008) or www.cdc.gov/std/syphilis/STDFact-syphilis.htm. The actual incidence of syphilis is much higher than reported (see Figures 8.19 and 8.20). It is estimated that for every case of syphilis that is reported, three are not (Crooks and Baur, 2009).

This disease has three stages.

1. During the first stage, a painless sore (chancre) about the size of a dime may appear at the point where the bacteria first entered the body, usually three weeks after contact. This sore may appear around or in the vagina, on the penis, or inside the mouth or anus. Sores inside the vagina or anus are often unnoticed and may disappear on their own if not treated; however, the bacterial infection remains.

2. The second stage occurs two to eight weeks after the exposure and includes flu-like symptoms and possible hair loss, a rash on the palms of hands and soles of feet, as well as over the entire body.

TABLE 8.4 ◆ Primary and Secondary Syphilis—Reported Cases and Rates by State, Ranked by Rates, United States, 2009

Rank*	State	Cases	Rate per 100,000 Population
1	Louisiana	741	16.8
2	Georgia	953	9.8
3	Arkansas	275	9.6
4	Alabama	417	8.9
5	Mississippi	237	8.1
6	Texas	1,644	6.8
7	Tennessee	403	6.5
8	North Carolina	579	6.3
9	New York	1,182	6.1
10	Illinois	750	5.8
11	Florida	1,041	5.7
12	Maryland	314	5.6
13	California	1,900	5.2
	U.S. TOTAL†	**13,997**	**4.6**
14	Virginia	299	3.8
15	Massachusetts	238	3.7
16	Arizona	231	3.6
17	Nevada	91	3.5
18	Ohio	360	3.1
19	Delaware	27	3.1
20	New Mexico	61	3.1
21	Missouri	173	2.9
22	South Carolina	123	2.7
23	Pennsylvania	341	2.7
24	Oklahoma	97	2.7
25	Hawaii	33	2.6
26	Indiana	158	2.5
27	New Jersey	212	2.4
28	Michigan	230	2.3
29	Kentucky	92	2.2
30	Colorado	105	2.1
31	Washington	139	2.1
32	Rhode Island	20	1.9
33	Connecticut	65	1.9
34	Oregon	57	1.5
35	Minnesota	71	1.4
36	Kansas	32	1.1
37	Utah	31	1.1
38	New Hampshire	14	1.1
39	Wisconsin	44	0.8
40	Iowa	23	0.8
41	North Dakota	4	0.6
42	Wyoming	3	0.6
43	West Virginia	8	0.4
44	Montana	4	0.4
45	Maine	4	0.3
46	Nebraska	5	0.3
	YEAR 2010 TARGET		**0.2**
47	Idaho	3	0.2
	Alaska	0	0.0
	South Dakota	0	0.0
	Vermont	0	0.0

Source: www.CDC.gov
*States were ranked in descending order by rate, number of cases, and alphabetically.
†Total includes cases reported by the District of Columbia with 163 cases and a rate of 27.5, but excludes outlying areas (Guam with 2 cases and rate of 1.1, Puerto Rico with 227 cases and rate of 5.7, and Virgin Islands with 0 cases and rate of 0.0).

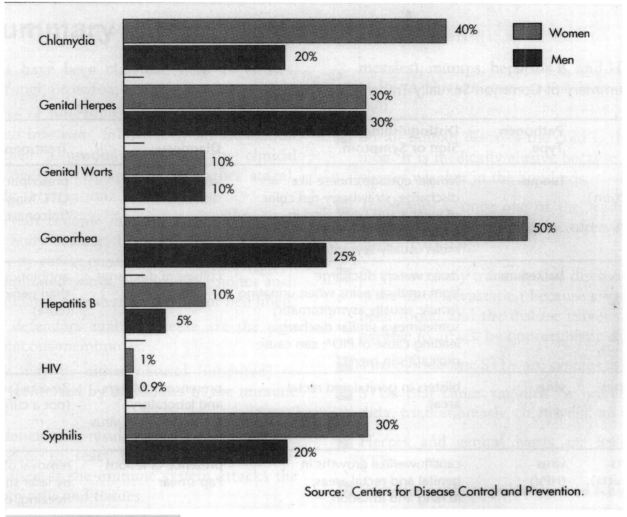

FIGURE 8.17

Rates for Contracting Various STIs after One Heterosexual Unprotected Intercourse with an Infected Partner

Source: Centers for Disease Control and Prevention.

3. The tertiary (third stage) syphilis can appear five to twenty-five years after the initial exposure. Symptoms of this stage may include skin lesions, mental deterioration, loss of balance and vision, loss of sensation, shooting pains in the legs, and heart disease (Crooks and Baur, 2009).

See a physician immediately if there is any chance you have been exposed to syphilis. A simple blood test can usually determine whether or not you have the disease. However, if you become infected two to three weeks prior to testing, the blood test may not be sensitive enough to detect the antibodies. Syphilis can be treated with the proper antibiotics, most commonly penicillin injections.

There have been several resistant strains that have developed when individuals did not take the full prescription dose. Always take all of the antibiotics that are prescribed to you; don't save them for later or stop them just because you feel better and NEVER take someone else's medication.

Go to www.thebody.com/surveys/sexsurvey.html to take this absolutely anonymous test and discover your risk for HIV or other STIs.

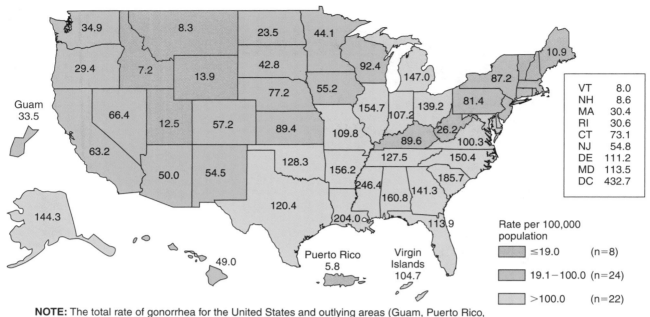

NOTE: The total rate of gonorrhea for the United States and outlying areas (Guam, Puerto Rico, and Virgin Islands) was 97.8 per 100,000 population.

FIGURE 8.18

Gonorrhea—Rates by State: United States and Outlying Areas, 2004

Source: www.CDC.gov.

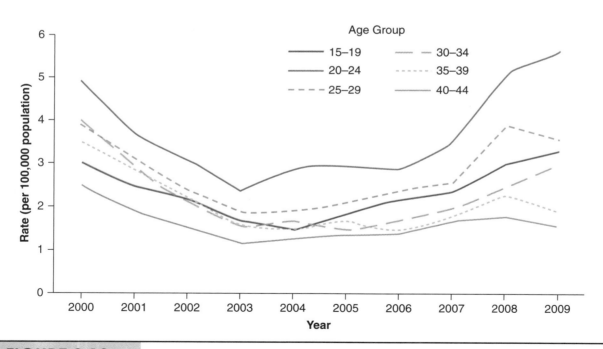

FIGURE 8.19

Primary and Secondary Syphilis—Rates by Age Among Women Aged 15–44 Years, United States, 2000–2009

Source: www.CDC.gov

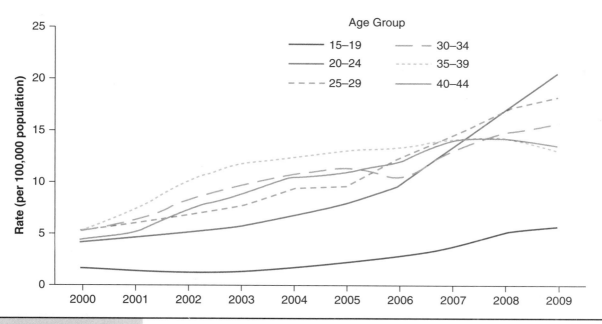

FIGURE 8.20

Primary and Secondary Syphilis—Rates by Age Among Men Aged 15–44 Years, United States, 2000–2009

Source: www.CDC.gov

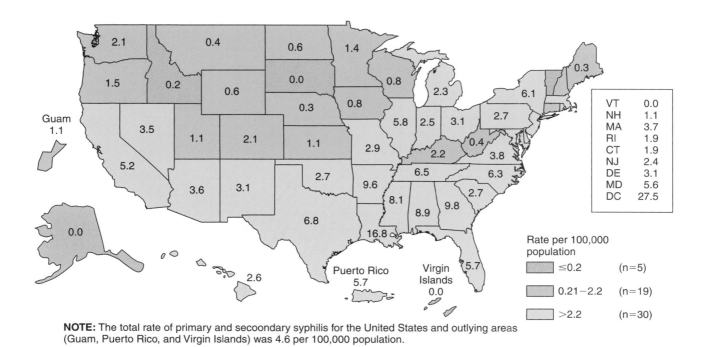

NOTE: The total rate of primary and secoondary syphilis for the United States and outlying areas (Guam, Puerto Rico, and Virgin Islands) was 4.6 per 100,000 population.

FIGURE 8.21

Primary and Secondary Syphilis—Rates by State, United States and Outlying Areas, 2009

Source: www.CDC.gov

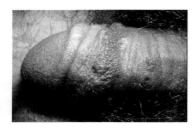

Genital herpes infection characterized by recurring cycles of painful blisters on the genitalia.

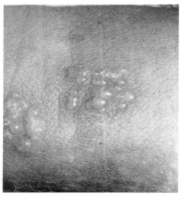

Penis with vesicles (blisters) from genital herpes.

Viral STIs
Genital Herpes

Genital herpes is a chronic, life-long infection caused by the herpes simplex virus (HSV). There are two types of HSV (Type 1 and Type 2), both of which can infect any area of the body, producing lesions (sores) in and around the vaginal area, on the penis, around the anal opening, on the buttocks or thighs, in or around the mouth, and in the eyes possibly causing blindness (Donatelle, 2010). Herpes can be contracted and spread through vaginal, oral, or anal sex, as well as skin-to-skin contact.

A newborn may be infected with genital herpes while passing through the birth canal (Crooks and Baur, 2009). Infection in the newborn can cause mental retardation, blindness, or even death (Crooks and Baur, 2009). Therefore, it is important that an infected pregnant female inform her physician of the infection so that the physician can watch for an outbreak and perform a cesarean section (C-section) if necessary. Current estimates indicate that 45 million people (approximately one in six Americans) have genital herpes (CDC, 2010) or www.cdc.gov/std/herpes/STDFact-herpes.htm. Each year there are approximately one million new cases of genital herpes (ASHA, 2004). There are many more individuals who have genital herpes and are asymptomatic. The symptoms vary, and many people have no noticeable symptoms. Symptoms will most commonly occur within two to twenty days after infection. Early symptoms may include a tingling or burning sensation in the genitals, lower back pain, pain when urinating, and flu-like symptoms. A few days later, small red bump(s) may appear in the genital area. Later, these bumps can develop into painful blisters, which then crust over, form a scab, and heal. Sometimes the diagnosis can be made by physical examination alone. For testing, the physician collects a small amount of fluid from the sores to see if the herpes virus is present. It may take up to two weeks to receive the results. If no sores are present, testing may be difficult. However, a blood test does exist to determine if an individual does have the herpes virus. It is expensive and does not indicate the location of the infection. Although herpes is a chronic, life-

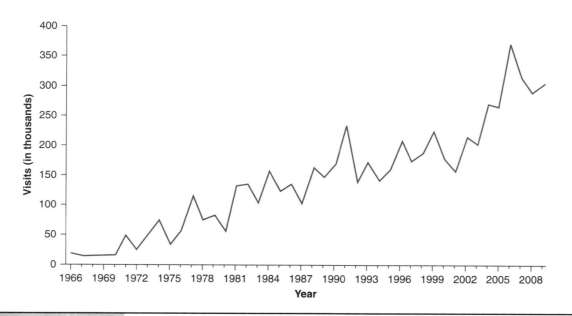

FIGURE 8.22

Genial Herpes—Initial Visits to Physicians' Offices, United States, 1966–2009

Source: www.CDC.gov

long viral infection, the symptoms can be treated. Treatment of genital herpes outbreaks, especially when begun early, shortens the duration of the outbreak and reduces the symptoms (Marr, 2007). Medications used include acyclovir, famcyclovir, and valacyclovir. Individuals with more than six outbreaks per year may be treated with preventative (prophylactic) suppressive therapy.

HIV/AIDS

Human Immunodeficiency Virus (HIV)/Acquired Immune Deficiency Syndrome (AIDS) was first identified in the United States in June 1981 by the Centers for Disease Control and Prevention (CDC). HIV is the virus that causes AIDS and is transmitted in one of four ways:

1. vaginal, oral, or anal sex;
2. sharing a needle for piercing, tattoos, or drugs including steroids;
3. blood products infected with HIV;
4. from mother to child during pregnancy, delivery or breast milk.

The highest concentrations of HIV are found in bodily fluids such as blood, semen, vaginal secretions, and breast milk (Floyd et al., 2007). Infection can occur when any of these fluids from an infected person comes into direct contact with the bloodstream or mucous membranes of another person (see Table 8.5). Trace amounts are found in tears, saliva, and other body fluids but have not been found to transmit infection. HIV is *not* spread by casual contact. It is not known if all individuals infected with this virus will develop AIDS. Women are more likely to become infected with HIV during heterosexual sex than males, because the concentration of virus is higher in semen than it is in vaginal secretions (Floyd et al., 2007).

An individual may be asymptomatic or may have some of the symptoms, which include:

- fatigue,
- dry cough,
- fever,
- night sweats,
- diarrhea,
- skin rashes,
- swollen lymph nodes,
- recurrent vaginal yeast infections,
- unexplained weight loss.

Typically six weeks to six months is required after the initial infection to detect the HIV antibodies in a blood test (Floyd et al., 2007). The average time from infection until AIDS diagnosis is about ten years. There is no known cure at the present for HIV or AIDS. There are numerous drugs/cocktails (mixture of different types of drugs) that exist to boost the immune system and interfere with the replication of the virus, therefore delaying the onset of AIDS.

The best way to avoid contracting HIV is to abstain from vaginal, oral, or anal sex or have a mutually monogamous relationship with an uninfected partner. Other ways to protect yourself include HIV testing before becoming sexually active, consistent and correct use of latex condoms with all sexual acts (vaginal, oral, and anal), avoid sharing needles for anything, and do not have sex with anyone known or suspected of using injectable drugs including steroids.

More than 45 percent of those diagnosed with AIDS were infected with HIV in their teens and twenties (Floyd et al., 2007). (See Tables 8.6 and 8.7.) About 56,000 people became infected with HIV in the past year (CDC, 2008) or www.cdc.gov/nchhstp/newsroom/WADPressrelease-112408.htm.

TABLE 8.5 ◆ AIDS Cases by Transmission Category

Six common transmission categories are male-to-male sexual contact, injection drug use, male-to-male sexual contact and injection drug use, high-risk heterosexual (male-female) contact, mother-to-child (perinatal) transmission, and other (includes blood transfusions and unknown cause).

Following is the distribution of the estimated number of cases of AIDS among adults and adolescents by transmission category in the fifty states and the District of Columbia. A breakdown by sex is provided where appropriate.

Transmission Category	Estimated # of AIDS Cases, in 2006		
	Adult and Adolescent Male	Adult and Adolescent Female	**Total**
Male-to-male sexual contact	16,001	-	16,001
Injection drug use	4,410	2,385	6,795
Male-to-male sexual contact and injection drug use	1,803	-	1,803
High-risk heterosexual contact*	4,558	7,196	11,754
Other**	217	220	437

*Heterosexual contact with a person known to have, or to be at high risk for, HIV infection.
**Includes hemophilia, blood transfusion, perinatal exposure, and risk not reported or not identified.

Transmission Category	Estimated # of AIDS Cases, through 2006*		
	Adult and Adolescent Male	Adult and Adolescent Female	Total
Male-to-male sexual contact	465,965	-	465,965
Injection drug use	170,171	74,718	244,889
Male-to-male sexual contact and injection drug use	68,516	-	68,516
High-risk heterosexual contact**	65,241	108,252	173,493
Other***	13,893	6,596	20,489

*Includes persons with a diagnosis of AIDS from the beginning of the epidemic through 2006.
**Heterosexual contact with a person known to have, or to be at high risk for, HIV infection.
***Includes hemophilia, blood transfusion, perinatal exposure, and risk not reported or not identified.

Source: From the CDC *HIV/AIDS Surveillance Report: Cases of HIV Infection and AIDS in the United States and Dependent Areas.* 2006b.

HPV

Papillary (HPV) genital warts of female.

Excerpted from *The Secret Epidemic; STIs on Campus* © American College Health Association, PO Box 28927, Baltimore, MD 21240

The Human Papilloma Viruses (HPV) are the most common sexually transmitted infections (CDC, 2011). There are more than one hundred types of HPV, about half of which can cause genital infections (Crooks and Baur, 2009). These viruses can be transmitted by vaginal, oral, or anal sex, as well as skin-to-skin contact. Genital warts or condyloma may appear three weeks to eight months after infection, with an average of three months (Crooks and Baur, 2009). As with many of the other STIs, an individual may be infected and never show signs or symptoms of the virus. Genital warts may be brown, pink, red, yellow, or grayish in color. The warts are typically found on the vaginal opening, cervix, perineum, labia, inner walls of the vagina, or anal area in females and on the foreskin or shaft of the penis, anal area, or urethra in males. Genital warts can cause bleeding and obstruction in the urinary and/or anal openings. There is a strong association between HPV infection and cancers of the cervix, vagina, vulva, penis, and anus (Crooks and Baur, 2009).

TABLE 8.6 ◆ AIDS Cases by Age

Of the **estimated number** of AIDS cases in the fifty states and the District of Columbia persons' ages at time of diagnosis were distributed as follows.

Age (Years)	Estimated # of AIDS Cases in 2006	Cumulative Estimated # of AIDS Cases, through 2006*
Under 13	38	9,156
Ages 13–14	73	1,078
Ages 15–19	401	5,626
Ages 20–24	1,669	36,225
Ages 25–29	3,423	117,099
Ages 30–34	4,349	197,530
Ages 35–39	6,402	213,573
Ages 40–44	7,298	170,531
Ages 45–49	5,628	107,207
Ages 50–54	3,687	59,907
Ages 55–59	2,071	32,190
Ages 60–64	955	17,303
Ages 65 or older	835	15,074

*Includes persons with a diagnosis of AIDS from the beginning of the epidemic through 2006.

Source: From the CDC HIV/AIDS Surveillance Report: Cases of HIV Infection and AIDS in the United States and Dependent Areas. 2006b.

TABLE 8.7 ◆ AIDS Cases by Top Ten States/Dependent Areas

The ten states or dependent areas **reporting** the highest number of AIDS cases were:

State/Dependent Area	# of AIDS Cases in 2006
New York	5,495
Florida	4,932
California	3,960
Texas	2,998
Pennsylvania	1,893
Maryland	1,626
Georgia	1,605
Illinois	1,382
North Carolina	1,229
New Jersey	1,065

State/Dependent Area	# of Cumulative AIDS Cases through 2006*		
	Adults or Adolescents	Children (<13)	Total
New York	174,908	2,354	177,262
California	142,254	664	142,918
Florida	104,084	1,530	105,614
Texas	69,735	392	70,127
New Jersey	48,750	778	49,528
Illinois	33,620	282	33,902
Pennsylvania	33,417	365	33,782
Georgia	31,734	231	31,965
Maryland	30,252	319	30,571
Puerto Rico	29,511	400	29,911

*Includes persons with a diagnosis of AIDS from the beginning of the epidemic through 2006.

Source: From the CDC HIV/AIDS Surveillance Report: Cases of HIV Infection and AIDS in the United States and Dependent Areas. 2006b.

Genital warts on the penis.
From Visuals Unlimited © Science VU/
Visuals Unlimited

HPV Vaccine

In 2006, the FDA approved Gardasil, the first vaccine developed to prevent certain types (16 and 18) of HPV, which cause 70 percent of cervical cancers and against types 6 and 11, which cause approximately 90 percent of genital warts. Gardasil has also been shown to protect against anal, vaginal, and vulvar cancers (CDC, 2011). The vaccine is designed for females and males age 9–26. Ideally, the vaccine would be given before an individual becomes sexually active and is exposed to the viruses. In order for the vaccine to be effective, it must be given in three different doses over a six month period.

HPV Screening and Cancer

In 2009, the FDA approved Cervarix, a second vaccine to prevent cervical cancer and pre-cancers caused by HPV types 16 and 18. This vaccine is designed for only females age 9–25. As with Gardasil, Cervarix must be given in three different does over a six-month period. Both vaccines are most effective when given at 11 or 12 years of age. As of 2011, the retail price of the vaccine is about $130 per does ($390 for the full series). Most health insurance plans cover the cost of vaccines. It is imperative that all sexually active females receive an annual Pap test with the first test occurring three years after the onset of sexual activity. Numerous studies show there are many false positive results from Pap tests detecting precancerous cells on the cervix if performed too close to the first vaginal intercourse experience. Ninety percent of HPV infections appear to be temporary and are most likely eradicated by the body's immune system (CDC, 2011). It is important to continue getting screened for cervical cancer with regular Pap tests since 30% of HPV types that cause cervical cancer are not prevented by the HPV vaccine. During this exam HPV is typically the only STI that can be detected visually, with the exception of genital herpes, if the female is having an outbreak. It is typically necessary to receive a blood or

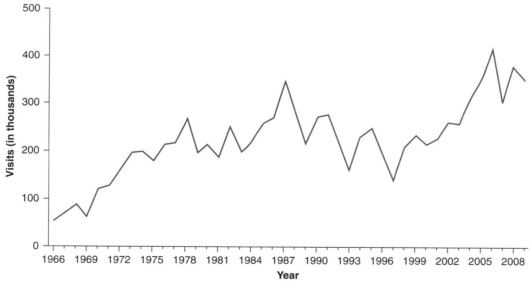

NOTE: The relative standard errors for genital warts estimates of more than 100,000 range from 18% to 30%. See Other Surveillance Data Sources in the Appendix and Table 43.

Source: IMS Health, Integrated Promotional Services™. IMS Health Report, 1966–2009.

FIGURE 8.23

Genital Warts—Initial Visits to Physicians' Offices, United States, 1966–2009
Source: www.CDC.gov

urine test to detect other types of STIs. It is not known if HPV directly causes cancer or if it combines with other cofactors such as infections or smoking to increase the risk of developing cancer. A few HPV types have been found to be at least partly responsible for more than 90 percent of cancers of the cervix. These HPV types seem to be the same ones found in oral cancers. The types of HPV found in cervical cancer are found in about 20 percent to 30 percent of oral cancers. The current view is that HPV may be a factor that contributes to the development of oral cavity and oropharyngeal cancers in around 20 percent of people (American Cancer Society, 2005). No cure exists at present for genital warts; however, there are treatments that decrease the size and the risk of spreading. Some of these include topical applications of Aldara TM cream, trichloracetic/bichloracetic acid (TCA/BCA), cryotheraphy (freezing with a probe or liquid nitrogen), and podophyllin. Other less common treatments include laser surgery and interferon (ACHA, 2005). Genital and anal HPV are an extremely common viral STI in the United States (Crooks and Baur, 2009). Approximately 20 million people in the United States are infected with HPV and each year 6.2 million more are infected (CDC, 2011) or www.cdc.gov/STD/HPV/STDFact-HPV.htm.

Hepatitis B

Hepatitis B is a potentially serious and, at times, fatal illness. Fortunately, this is one of the few viruses that can be eradicated. Ninety percent of people infected with hepatitis B eliminate the virus. This is done by developing antibodies, called immunoglobulins, which the body produces in response to the presence of the virus. These immunoglobulins (IgG and IgM) can be measured in the bloodstream and can detect whether someone has had a hepatitis B infection. However, the remaining 10 percent of individuals infected with hepatitis B become chronic carriers. There were approximately 43,000 new cases in 2007, down from 260,000 new cases in the 1980s due to the increased use of vaccinations (CDC, 2009). One out of one hundred U.S. residents is an infectious asymptomatic chronic carrier of hepatitis B (Crowley, 2009).

The illness is transmitted through exposure to infected blood or secretions. The disease is primarily spread through sexual contact, followed by injecting drug use (IDU). The following summarizes the routes of transmission in the United States:

Heterosexual contact	41%
Homosexual contact	14%
IDU (Injecting drug use)	12%
Household contacts	4%
Health care workers	2%
Unknown	25%

The concentration of hepatitis B is high in blood and serum, and lower in semen, vaginal secretions, and saliva. It can be transmitted through bites, but transmission through kissing is unlikely. Exposure to blood from cuts, nosebleeds, menstrual bleeding, and blood present on IV needles or personal items such as toothbrushes, razors, and manicuring instruments may result in infection. Pregnant women pass the virus to their babies in 20 to 90 percent of pregnancies, dependent upon the presence or absence of certain viral components. Ninety percent of these infants become chronic carriers, and 15 to 25 percent die of liver failure (CDC, 2009). Other means of spreading hepatitis B include tattooing, body piercing, sharing straws for inhaling cocaine, and hemodialysis machines.

Hepatitis B is diagnosed by elevated liver enzymes (caused when liver cells are damaged and release their enzymes into the bloodstream), and the presence of hepatitis B surface antigen (pieces of the protein coat of the virus),

TABLE 8.8 ♦ What Are the Common Sexually Transmitted Infections (STIs)?

STI	Transmission (Body Fluids and/or Direct Contact)	Symptoms
Chlamydia	**Fluids**—contact of mucous membranes (cervix, urethra) with infected person's fluids (semen and mucus). Most common with exposure through vaginal or anal sex. Casual contact considered to be safe.	Most patients have no symptoms. If present, they may be: *Women*—pain or dull aching in lower abdomen, heavy feeling in pelvic area, pain with urination or intercourse, heavier menstrual flow, breakthrough bleeding, heavy cervical discharge. *Men*—urethral discharge, pain with urination, pain in scrotum (epididymitis).
Human Papillomavirus (HPV)/Genital Warts/Precancerous Tissue Change (Intraepithelial Neoplasia)	**Contact**—touching (hands/genital, genital/genital, or ano-genital) an infected person's lesions can transmit cells containing the virus. Can be transmitted through non-penetrative sexual contact.	Usually no symptoms, but external lesions may itch. Lesions on the skin can be either raised or flat. Most lesions on the cervix can be seen only with the use of acetic acid and magnification.
Herpes Simplex (HSV) both types I and II	**Contact**—touching (hand/genital, genital/genital, oral/genital, or ano-genital) an infected person's lesions. Can be transmitted through non-penetrative sexual contact. Transmission commonly occurs in the absence of lesions.	Single or multiple fluid-filled blisters appear typically in the ano-genital area and mouth. They rupture, sometimes leaving extremely painful shallow ulcers, which heal in about twelve days.
Pelvic Inflammatory Disease (PID)	**Fluids**—contact of mucous membranes with infected person's body fluids (mucus, semen). Transmission most common with exposure through anal and vaginal sex, or rarely, oral sex. Casual contact considered to be safe.	There may be no symptoms, but PID is usually characterized by moderate to severe lower abdominal pain, fever, chills, and possibly bowel symptoms. May mimic appendicitis, ureteral stones, twisted or ruptured ovarian cyst, and other acute lower abdominal conditions.

Source: From *Sexually Transmitted Infections: What Everyone Should Know* by American College Health Association. Copyright © 2011 by American College Health Association. Reprinted by permission.

Potential Complications/ Course of Infection	Treatment	Prevention—For all STIs, abstinence is the best protection
In women, serious complications can occur if spread to fallopian tubes. May result in tubal scarring, infertility, and risk of tubal pregnancy.	A number of commonly used antibiotics are effective. Partners **must** be treated at the same time.	Condoms (latex or polyurethane) reduce but do not eliminate risk.
Cervix—Most cervical infections are invisible to the naked eye. Occasionally, visible cervical warts may be present. Cervical cancer can be prevented by detection and treatment of pre-cancerous changes. *External skin and anus of men and women, and the vagina*—warty lesions, flat or raised. Some may be pre-cancers, but natural history of lesions is not to become cancers until advanced age. Long-term complications are not yet known.	Many treatments are available. The most expensive does not necessarily mean the best. *Cervix*—cryo (freezing), laser, and LEEP. *External*—Aldara, cryo, laser, liquid N, TCA/BCA, podophyllin, and interferon. In some individuals, the virus is cleared from the body. In others, viral particles remain latent after treatment. Lesions can be eliminated. It is unlikely that the presence of latent viral particles without lesions can result in transmission.	Barrier methods reduce but do not eliminate risk. With condoms, for example, lesions may be present in uncovered areas. Only total absence of any touching of infected tissue will avoid transmission. When both partners are infected, they probably do not continue to transmit to each other.
Recurrent painful attacks. Infants infected at or before delivery may sustain severe neurological damage or death.	Antiviral drugs are effective if taken early in the infection or continuously in a preventive regimen. Topical anesthetics may be helpful in reducing discomfort.	Barrier methods reduce but do not eliminate risk. With condoms, for example, lesions may be present in uncovered areas.
May progress to abscesses and injury resulting in infertility, ectopic pregnancy, chronic pain, and even death.	Therapy with one or more antibiotics with broad coverage. Individuals must always be treated for chlamydia and gonorrhea; management sometimes requires hospitalization. Partners **must** be treated at the same time.	Condoms (latex or polyurethane) reduce but do not eliminate risk.

(continued)

TABLE 8.8 ♦ What Are the Common Sexually Transmitted Infections (STIs)? *(continued)*

STI	Transmission (Body Fluids and/or Direct Contact)	Symptoms
Human Immunodeficiency Virus (HIV)/AIDS	**Fluids**—contact of open skin or mucous membranes with infected person's body fluids (blood, mucus, semen). Most common with exposure through anal or vaginal sex, and, though uncommon, oral sex. Casual contact considered to be safe. Health care workers at risk through scalpel cuts and needle sticks.	Divided into four stages: *Infection and Seroconversion*—flu-like illness for approximately two weeks. *Symptom-Free*—few months to many years. *Early Symptoms*—fevers, shingles, yeast infections—few months to several years. *AIDS*—opportunistic infections, neoplasia (Kaposi's sarcoma, lymphoma, cervical cancer), dementia, and other neurological symptoms—few months to several years.
Gonorrhea	**Fluids**—contact of mucous membranes (cervix, urethra) with infected person's fluids (semen, mucus). Most common with exposure through vaginal or anal sex. Casual contact considered to be safe.	Very similar to chlamydia for both women and men.
Hepatitis B (HBV)	**Fluids**—contact with mucous membranes (cervix, urethra, anal area) with infected person's fluids (semen, saliva, blood, mucus). Most common with exposure through vaginal or anal sex. Casual contact considered to be safe. Health care workers at risk through scalpel cuts and needle sticks.	At first, usually no symptoms. If disease progresses, symptoms may occur—fatigue, nausea, and jaundice (yellowing of the skin and eyes) with dark urine.
Syphilis	**Fluids** and **Contact**—Also, 50% risk of transmission from mother to infant in utero.	Occurs in three stages: *Primary*—painless ulcer. *Secondary*—rash, condylomata lata, lymph node enlargement, spotty baldness. *Late/Latent*—vascular and neurological damage may be occurring.

which is the most common test for detecting an acute infection or carrier status. Hepatitis B surface antigen can be detected as early as one to two weeks and as late as eleven to twelve weeks after exposure. If this test is positive, the person is infectious.

Once infected, the incubation period is 6 weeks to 6 months, with an average of approximately 120 days. Thirty percent of adults infected are asymptomatic (CDC, 2010). For those who are symptomatic, some or all of the following symptoms may be present. Initially (approximately two weeks after exposure) there may be diminished appetite with an approximately five to ten pound weight loss, fatigue, headache, nausea, vomiting, muscle aches, cough, low grade fever and right-sided upper abdominal pain. This is known as the 'prodrome' phase. Following the prodrome is the icteric

Potential Complications/ Course of Infection	Treatment	Prevention—For all STIs, abstinence is the best protection
Signs and symptoms of AIDS, death (current medications lengthening survival). Treatment of pregnant women with HIV greatly reduces the risk of maternal-fetal transmission.	Antivirals and specific medications for complications.	Condoms (latex or polyurethane) reduce but do not eliminate risk. Avoid contact with needles, particularly IV drug use.
In women, serious complications can occur if spread to fallopian tubes. May result in tubal scarring, infertility, and risk of tubal pregnancy.	A number of commonly used antibiotics are very effective. Partners **must** be treated at the same time.	Condoms (latex or polyurethane) reduce but do not eliminate risk.
Cirrhosis, liver cancer, liver failure, death.	Antiviral medications are indicated in certain circumstances.	Vaccination of infants and non-immunized adolescents and adults is highly recommended. Avoid contact with blood, needles, etc.
Late complications include: severe neurologic dysfunction, aortic aneurysm.	Penicillin or doxycycline—based on darkfield or blood test. Very important that pregnant women with positive blood tests be treated to prevent congenital syphilis. **Must** treat all contacts.	Condoms, spermicides.

phase, approximately one to two weeks later, which lasts two to six weeks. The urine darkens and the stools become a clay color. The liver becomes enlarged and tender. Itching is common. There may be a yellow cast to the skin or eyes. The recovery phase then follows about six to eight weeks after exposure, at which time the individual usually recovers, but may develop chronic disease.

If a person develops a chronic disease (infection longer than six months), treatment may be necessary to diminish the risk of permanent liver damage. Interferon, which is given in these cases, is made by the body to boost immunity. The interferon, which is used for treatment, is manufactured and given by injection for sixteen weeks to stimulate the immune system to attack the infected liver cells. The virus is completely eradicated in approximately 58 percent of these cases. However, even if there is not total elimination of the virus, the health of the liver is often improved by this treatment. New agents being currently studied are the antivirals ganciclovir and famciclovir, which appear to be promising treatments.

It is imperative that someone with chronic hepatitis B receive the vaccine for hepatitis A to reduce the risk of a very serious complication called acute fulminant hepatitis, in which the liver is rapidly destroyed. The death rate is 63 to 93 percent with this condition. Liver transplantation is rarely an option due to the high rate of reinfection and rapid progression of the disease after transplantation.

The CDC recommends vaccination against hepatitis B for newborns, infants, and non-immunized adolescents and adults.

To prevent risk of exposure, one should practice 'safer sex' as detailed in the STI prevention section, avoid IV drug usage, as well as sharing of toothbrushes, eating utensils, razors, nail files, and clippers. If there is exposure to hepatitis B, an immunoglobulin with a high concentration of antibody against hepatitis B should be given within two weeks of exposure.

Parasitic STIs

Pubic Lice and Scabies

Pubic lice (often called "crabs") and scabies (itch mites) are parasitic insects that live on the skin. They are sometimes spread sexually, but are also transmitted by contact with infected bed linens, clothes, or towels. Pubic lice infect hairy parts of the body, especially around the groin area and can be transmitted by fingers to the armpits or scalp (Crooks and Baur, 2009). With scabies, an itchy rash is the result of a female mite burrowing into a person's skin to lay her eggs. The eggs can be seen on the hair close to the skin, where they hatch in five to ten days. Some individuals infected with pubic lice have no symptoms, while others may experience considerable itching in the area infected. Yellowish-gray insects the size of a pinhead moving on the skin or oval eggs attached to body hair may be visible. The primary symptom of scabies is itching, especially at night. A rash may appear in the folds of skin between the fingers or on the wrists, elbows, abdomen, or genitals. If you think you may have pubic lice or scabies, see your physician. They can determine whether treatment is necessary or not. The most effective treatments include shampoos and creams that contain lindane or a related compound. Pubic lice can be treated at home with special creams, lotions, and shampoos that are available in drugstores without a prescription. Be certain to follow the instructions carefully and do not exceed the recommended applications. The infestation may be stubborn, requiring an additional treatment. Avoid close contact with others if you have pubic lice or scabies until it is treated. Wash clothes, bed linens, and any other materials that may have been infected in hot water and dry on the hottest setting. If you have pubic lice or scabies be sure to tell your sexual partner(s) or anyone with whom you have had close contact or who has shared your bed linens, clothes, or towels. These individuals should be seen by a physician even if they do not have an itch or rash. The best way to protect yourself is to know your partner's sexual history, don't share towels, swimsuits, or underwear and thoroughly wash any materials that you think may carry pubic lice or scabies in hot water.

Trichomoniasis

Trichomoniasis is caused by a protozoan parasite, *Trichomonas vaginalis*. The most common sites of infection are the vagina (in women) and the urethra (in men). The parasite is sexually transmitted through the penis to the vagina during intercourse or vulva to vulva contact with an infected partner. Most men infected with trichomoniasis are asymptomatic, but have the parasites and can infect their sexual partners. Some women will have signs or symptoms from the infection which include a yellowish-green vaginal discharge, a slight burning after urination, or itching in the genital area. These signs or symptoms typically appear five to twenty-eight days after exposure.

A health care provider must perform a physical exam and laboratory tests to diagnose trichomoniasis. The treatment for trichomoniasis is a prescription drug (either Metronidazole or Tinidazole) taken by mouth in a single dose. It is important for both partners to be treated at the same time to eliminate the parasite.

The best way to avoid contracting trichomoniasis is to abstain from vaginal, oral, or anal intercourse or have a mutually monogamous relationship with an uninfected partner. Utilizing male condoms consistently and correctly can reduce the risk of transmission of trichomoniasis.

© The best way to prevent STIs is to practice sexual abstinence, or have a mutually monogamous relationship with an uninfected person.

STI Prevention

Preventing the spread of STIs requires responsibility in sexual relationships. The best way to prevent contraction of an STI is to practice sexual abstinence or have a mutually monogamous relationship with an uninfected person and do not share needles for any reason. If an individual chooses to be sexually active, limit the number of sexual partners and use condoms consistently and correctly (see Figure 8.9 on page 283). If you think you are infected, avoid any sexual contact until you visit your physician, a local STI clinic, or hospital for testing. Remember that many STIs are spread by those with no noticeable symptoms. It only takes one infected partner to contract a sexually transmitted infection.

A major problem for health care providers is persuading sexually active people to seek testing for STIs early after exposure. While some STIs such as genital herpes, HIV/AIDS, and genital warts are chronic with no cure, early diagnosis can help to prevent further transmission of the infections, and in the case of herpes, early treatment of the lesions can lessen the symptoms. Symptoms of STIs can be slow to develop or may not manifest themselves at all. Thus, an individual can be infected with a number of STIs with only minor or no symptoms. For these reasons, regular and accurate evaluations are necessary to prevent the spread of STIs. Methods of testing for STIs vary with the type of infection suspected. These tests fall loosely into three categories: visual inspection, blood or urine testing, and/or examination of the fluids within the sores themselves or smears of fluids from the vagina or urethra of the male. Symptomatic genital warts, herpes, and pubic lice can usually be identified during an examination by a health care provider. A blood test is used to test for hepatitis B, HIV, and syphilis. If the testing is done less than six months after contracting HIV and less than three weeks after contracting syphilis, there is a possibility the blood test will not be sufficiently sensitive to detect the presence of the infection. A urine test for chlamydia and gonorrhea are available at many health clinics. Often, chlamydia, gonorrhea, and herpes require fluid collection from the infected site for a conclusive diagnosis (Marr, 2007). The importance of testing cannot be overemphasized. As discussed earlier, many of these infections have dangerous complications and are easily cured. To decrease your risk of infection with an STI, you and your sexual partner(s) should know and communicate your sexual history. The only way to have adequate knowledge of your history is to be tested if there is a chance of a previous exposure regardless of the presence or absence of signs or symptoms.

There is no single test that can be administered for all sexually transmitted infections. Listed below are the different STIs and the type of test that is required to determine if an individual is infected.

STI	Type of Test
Chlamydia	Urine test and/or culture
Genital Herpes	Visual inspection, culture and/or blood test
Gonorrhea	Urine test and/or culture
Hepatitis B	Blood test
HIV	Blood test
HPV	Visual inspection
Pubic Lice/Scabies	Visual inspection
Syphilis	Blood test

Most individuals at some point in their lives will strongly desire to have children. An STI can affect the ability to conceive and have children. Chlamydia and gonorrhea can cause both males and females to become sterile. Further complications can arise for pregnant women who are infected with STIs. Herpes and hepatitis B, for example, in rare instances can be fatal to the fetus. There is a very real risk of passing HIV to a newborn. Early treatment of STIs can reduce the risk of infertility, but fertility cannot be guaranteed.

References

American Cancer Society. 2005.

American College Health Association (ACHA). *Sexually Transmitted Infections: What Everyone Should Know.* 2005.

American College Health Association (ACHA). 2004.

American College of Obstetricians and Gynecology (ACOG). 2011.

American Social Health Association (ASHA). 2009.

Association of Reproductive Health Pofessionals (ARHP). 2008. www.arhp.org

Centers for Disease Control and Prevention (CDC). 2008. www.cdc.gov/std/syphilis/STDFact-syphilis.htm www.cdc.gov/std/herpes/STDFact-herpes.htm www.cdc.gov/std/PID/STDFact-PID.htm

Centers for Disease Control and Prevention (CDC). *Youth Risk Behavior Survey.* 2007. www.cdc.gov/nchhstp/Newsroom/WADPressrelease-112408.htm

Centers for Disease Control and Prevention (CDC). *Guidelines for Treatment of Sexually Transmitted Infections.* 2006a.

Centers for Disease Control and Prevention (CDC). *HIV/AIDS Surveillance Report: Cases of HIV Infection and AIDS in the United States and Dependent Areas.* 2006b.

Crooks, R. and Baur, K. *Our Sexuality* (11th ed). Pacific Grove, CA: Brooks/Cole. 2009.

Crowley, L. *An Introduction to Human Disease: Pathology and Pathophysiology Correlations* (8th ed). Boston: Jones and Bartlett Publishers, Inc. 2009.

Donatelle, R. *Access to Health* (12th ed). San Francisco: Benjamin Cummings. 2010.

Ellertson, C. et al. Extending the Fine Limit for Starting the Yuzpe Regimen of Emergency Contraception to 120 Hours. *Obstetrics and Gynecology, 101,* 1168-1171. 2003.

ETR Associates. "Men's Health, What's Normal, What's Not." 2007a.

ETR Associates. "Not Ready for Sex, Talking with Your Partner." 2007b.

ETR Associates. "Women's Health, What's Normal, What's Not." 2007c.

ETR Associates. "Nine Sexually Responsible Behaviors." 2008.

Floyd, P. et al. *Personal Health: Perspectives & Lifestyles* (4th ed). Englewood, CO: Morton Publishing Co. 2007.

Herek, G. et al. Psychological Sequelae of Hate-Crime Victimization among Lesbian, Gay, and Bisexual Adults. *Journal of Consulting and Clinical Psychology, 67*, 6. 1999.

Marr, L. Sexually *Transmitted Diseases: A Physician Tells You What You Need to Know.* (2nd ed). Baltimore: Johns Hopkins University Press. 2007.

Sexuality Information and Education Council of the United States (SIECUS). 2008. www. siecus.org/index.cfm?fuseaction=Page.viewPage+pageId=598+ParentID=477

Trussell, J. and Jordan, B. Mechanism of Action of Emergency Contraceptive Pills. *Contraception, 74*, 87-89. 2006.

U.S. Department of Health and Human Services. "Bone Health and Osteoporosis: A Report of the Surgeon General." 2004.

www.cdc.gov/STD/HPV/STDFact-HPV.htm

www.cdc.gov/vaccines/recs/acip/downloads/mtg-slides-feb08/15-4-hpv.pdf

www.cdc.gov/vaccines/ed/ciinc/specialtopics/downloads/Feb_06_HepB_JC.ppt#262,6 Modes of HBV Transmission in Early Childhood

www.fwhc.org/birth-control

Contacts

AIDS Treatment Information Service
800-HIV-0440
http://www.aidsinfo.nih.gov

American Social Health Association and CDC National Hotline
800-227-8922
http://www.ashastd.org

Brazos County Health Department
201 North Texas Avenue
Bryan, TX 77803
979-361-4440

CDC National AIDS Hotline
800-342-AIDS (2437)
http://www.ashastd.org

Centers for Disease Control and Prevention
http://www.cdc.gov

Emergency Contraception Hotline
800-584-9911

Gay and Lesbian Medical Association
459 Fulton Street, Ste 107
San Francisco, CA 94102
415-255-4547
www.glma.org

Gladney Center for Adoption
817-922-6000

Good Samaritan Gabriel Project Life Center
1314 E 29th St.
Bryan, TX 77802
979-822-9340

Healthfinder
http://www.healthfinder.gov

National Herpes Resource Center
800-227-8922

Hope Pregnancy Centers of Brazos County
205 Brentwood Drive
College Station, TX 77840
979-695-9193

International Childbirth Education Association
800-624-4934
http://www.ICEA.org

National Abortion Federation
800-772-9100

National Council For Adoption
703-299-6633
www.adoptioncouncil.org

National Directory of LGBT Community Centers
www.lgbtcenters.org

North American Council on Adoptable Children (NACAC)
651-644-3036

Parents, Families and Friends of Lesbians and Gays (PFLAG)
1726 M Street, NW, Suite 400
Washington, DC 20036
202-467-8180
979-694-2617 (College Station, TX)

Planned Parenthood
4112 East 29th
Bryan, TX 77802
979-846-1744
http://www.plannedparenthood.org

Shanti Project
(Counseling and assistance for persons with AIDS)
415-674-4700
http://www.shanti.org

Texas A&M University Student Health
  Services
979-458-8250
http://shs.tamu.edu/

TAMU A.P. Beutel Health Center Health
  Education Division
979-847-8910
http://healthed.tamu.edu/

TAMU Student Life Gender Issues
Education Services (GIES)
979-845-1107

Activities

In-Class Activities

Apply percent incidence of STIs, HIV, unplanned pregnancy, adoption, and
  abortion to class size.
Can We Make Ends Meet?
Parents

Notebook Activities

STI Attitudes
Hepatitis Risk Assessment

Can We Make Ends Meet?

Concept/
Description: Being a parent can drastically change a person's life socially, emotionally, physically, and financially.

Objective: To explore the financial strain that being a parent would cause the typical college student.

Materials: Classified section of the newspaper
Parents sheet
Parents (2) sheet
Pens or pencils

Directions:
1. Divide the class into groups of four and give each group the Parents sheets.
2. Ask each group to choose a job from the classified section for which they would be qualified. Assuming that they got the job, they estimate how much money they would make in a year. (Call the company, if possible.)
3. Give students a few days to research the information on the sheets by asking people, calling various companies to get rates, and so on.
4. Have students fill in the sheets and figure out if "income" could cover "expenses."
5. Ask students to list the many difficulties parents face, besides financial strain.
6. Discuss.

IN-CLASS ACTIVITY

Parents

Directions: Being a parent can drastically change your life. Figure out the financial aspect of being a parent by filling in the information below:

H
O
U
S
I
N
G

1.	Rent		$ _____ per month
2.	Utilities		
		Gas	$ _____ per month
		Electricity	$ _____ per month
		Garbage	$ _____ per month
		Water	$ _____ per month
		Sewer	$ _____ per month
3.	Approximate phone bill		$ _____ per month
4.	Cable television		$ _____ per month
		TOTAL	$ _____ per month

A
U
T
O

1.	Car payment		$ _____ per month
2.	Gasoline		
3.	Car repairs		$ _____ per month
4.	License and insurance		$ _____ per month
		TOTAL	$ _____ per month

B
A
B
Y

1.	Day care		$ _____ per month
2.	Diapers		
3.	Baby clothing		$ _____ per month
		TOTAL	$ _____ per month

IN-CLASS ACTIVITY

Parents (2)

G
E
N
E
R
A
L

1.	Food bill	$ _____ per month
2.	Health care	$ _____ per month
3.	Entertainment	$ _____ per month
4.	Savings	$ _____ per month
5.	Miscellaneous (gifts, toys, etc.)	$ _____ per month
	TOTAL	$ _____ per month

TOTALS:

Housing	$ _____
Auto	$ _____
Baby	$ _____
General	$ _____
TOTAL MONTHLY COSTS	$ _____

Do you think that a typical college student could make ends meet? Why or why not?

Name _____ Section_____ Date_____

STI Attitudes

Directions: Please read each statement carefully. STI means sexually transmissible infection. Record your reaction by circling the number.

Use This Key: 1 = Strongly Agree 2 = Agree 3 = Undecided 4 = Disagree 5 = Strongly Disagree

1 2 3 4 5   1.   How one uses one's sexuality has nothing to do with getting an STI.

1 2 3 4 5   2.   It is easy to use the prevention methods that reduce one's chances of getting an STI.

1 2 3 4 5   3.   Responsible sex is one of the best ways of reducing the risk of STIs.

1 2 3 4 5   4.   Getting early medical care is the main key to preventing harmful effects of STIs.

1 2 3 4 5   5.   Choosing the right sex partner is important in reducing the risk of getting an STI.

1 2 3 4 5   6.   A high rate of STI should be a concern for all people.

1 2 3 4 5   7.   People with an STI have a duty to get their sex partners to medical care.

1 2 3 4 5   8.   The best way to get a sex partner to STI treatment is to take him/her to the doctor with you.

1 2 3 4 5   9.   Changing one's sex habits is necessary once the presence of an STI is known.

1 2 3 4 5   10. I would dislike having to follow the medical steps for treating an STI.

1 2 3 4 5   11. If I were sexually active, I would feel uneasy doing things before and after sex to prevent getting an STI.

1 2 3 4 5   12. If I were sexually active, it would be insulting if a sex partner suggested we use a condom to avoid STI.

1 2 3 4 5   13. I dislike talking about STIs with my peers.

1 2 3 4 5   14. I would be uncertain about going to the doctor unless I was sure I really had an STI.

1 2 3 4 5   15. I would feel that I should take my sex partner with me to a clinic if I thought I had an STI.

1 2 3 4 5   16. It would be embarrassing to discuss STIs with one's partner if one were sexually active.

1 2 3 4 5   17. If I were to have sex, the chance of getting an STI makes me uneasy about having sex with more than one person.

1 2 3 4 5   18. I like the idea of sexual abstinence (not having sex) as the best way of avoiding STIs.

1 2 3 4 5   19. If I had an STI, I would cooperate with public health people to find the source of STIs.

1 2 3 4 5   20. If I had an STI, I would avoid exposing others while I was being treated.

1 2 3 4 5   21. I would have regular STI checkups if I were having sex with more than one partner.

1 2 3 4 5   22. I intend to look for STI signs before deciding to have sex with anyone.

1 2 3 4 5   23. I will limit my sex activity to just one partner because of the chances I might get an STI.

1 2 3 4 5   24. I will avoid sexual contact anytime I think there is even a slight chance of getting an STI.

1 2 3 4 5   25. The chance of getting an STI would not stop me from having sex.

1 2 3 4 5   26. If I had a chance, I would support community efforts toward controlling STIs.

1 2 3 4 5   27. I would be willing to work with others to make people aware of STI problems in my town.

Calculate your total points using the following point values. For items 1, 10–14, 16, and 25: reverse the scoring of your circled response (1 becomes 5, 2 becomes 4, and so on). For Items 2–9, 15, 17–24, 26, and 27: add the points as you have them circled. The higher your score, the stronger your predisposition to engage in high-risk STI behaviors. The lower your score, the stronger your predisposition to practice low-risk STI behaviors. The range for the score is 27–135.

Name _____ Section _____ Date _____

Hepatitis Risk Assessment

Check your Risk of Hepatitis A	Yes	No
1. Do you believe you have been exposed to hepatitis A in the past 2 weeks?		
2. Do you live with someone currently ill with hepatitis A?		
3. Have you had sex with someone currently ill with hepatitis A?		
4. Do you currently live in a region of the United States where hepatitis A rates are very high?		
5. Do you travel or work in an area outside of the United States where hepatitis A is a problem? (This includes everywhere EXCEPT Australia, New Zealand, Western Europe, Japan, and Canada)		
6. If you are a man, do you have sex with other men?		
7. Are you an injecting or a non-injecting (snort cocaine) drug user?		

If you check yes to any of the questions, you are at risk and should see your doctor.

Check your Risk of Hepatitis B	Yes	No
1. Is someone in your household infected with hepatitis B?		
2. Have you ever been diagnosed with a sexually transmitted infection?		
3. Have you had sex with more than one partner in a 6-month period?		
4. If you are a man, do you have sex with other men?		
5. Have you or any of your sex partner(s) ever injected illegal drugs?		
6. Have you ever shared equipment (needles, syringes, cotton, water, etc.) when injecting drugs with someone else?		
7. Have you ever received hemodialysis?		
8. Did your mother have hepatitis B when you were born?		
9. Have you worked in a health care job or other occupation where you had a needlestick injury or other sharps exposures on the job?		
10. Have you shared a toothbrush, razor, or any other item that might have blood on it (visible or not) with a person who has hepatitis B?		

If you check yes to any of the questions, you are at risk and should see your doctor.

Check your Risk for Hepatitis C	Yes	No
1. Did you receive a blood transfusion or solid organ transplant (heart, lung, liver, pancreas, kidney) before July 1992?		
2. Did you receive clotting factor concentrates produced before 1987?		
3. Have you ever received hemodialysis?		
4. Have you had blood tests that showed a liver problem?		
5. Have you had a needlestick injury working in a health care setting?		
6. Did your mother have hepatitis C when you were born?		
7. Have you shared a toothbrush, razor, or any other item that might have blood on it (visible or not) with a person who has hepatitis C?		
8. Have you or any of your sex partner(s) injected illegal drugs, even if it was only one time many years ago?		

If you check yes to any of the questions, you are at risk and should see your doctor.

Chapter 9
Drug Misuse and Abuse

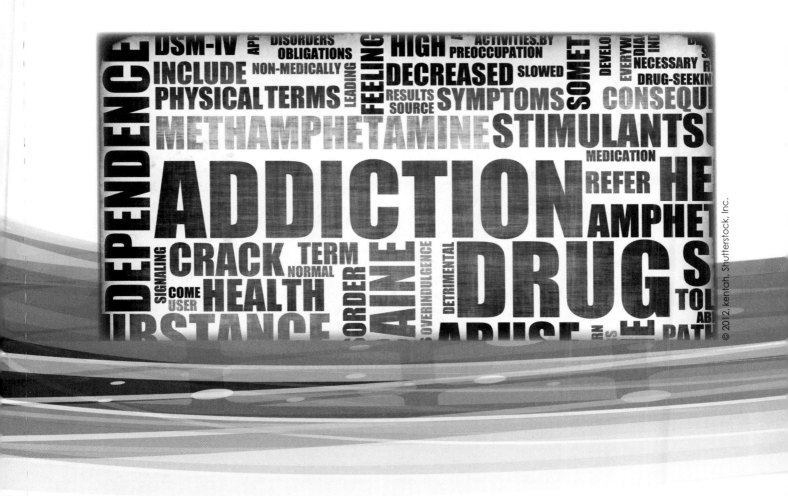

© 2012, kentah, Shutterstock, Inc.

OBJECTIVES

Students will be able to:
- Identify types of alcoholic beverages and the alcohol content for each.
- Identify the physiological and societal effects of alcohol.
- Identify risks of drinking and driving.
- Identify factors relating to binge drinking and alcohol poisoning.
- Identify alcohol-related offenses.
- Identify the adverse effects of tobacco use.
- Identify types of tobacco use.
- Identify the effects of environmental tobacco smoke.

 ◆ Identify types of drugs and their physiological effects.
 ◆ Identify the adverse effects of club drugs
 ◆ Identify common sources of caffeine.
 ◆ Identify commonly abused prescription drugs.

"First we form habits, then they form us. Conquer your bad habits, or they'll eventually conquer you."

—Dr. Rob Gilbert

Introduction

America has always had some opposition to the non-medicinal use of drugs. Alcohol and tobacco created outcries throughout the Country during colonial times and through the Civil War, which provoked prohibition legislation. Warnings of alcohol and tobacco use did not seem to deter the prevalence in American society.

Early prohibitionists were the precursors to the twentieth century "war on drugs" but it was hard to categorize the variety of substances until Congress passed The Controlled Substance Act in 1970.

Richard Evans, a Professor from the University of Houston, created a model that included teaching students to resist social influences and peer pressure. The slogan "Just Say No" was adopted and The National Institutes of Health supported this model. This program that emerged from the substance abuse model created by Evans, became a campaign throughout college campuses. First Lady, Nancy Reagan, became involved in the program in 1980 during her husband's presidency.

This campaign had a positive outcome with a significant decline in drug use during the late 70's and 80's. However, illicit drug use continues to rise in our country.

The World Health Organization's survey of legal and illegal drug use in 17 countries, including the Netherlands and other countries with less stringent drug laws, shows Americans report the highest level of cocaine and marijuana use.

Despite tough anti-drug laws, this survey shows the U.S. has the highest level of illegal drug use in the world.

> "Understanding what drugs can do to your children, understanding peer pressure and understanding why they turn to drugs is ... the first step in solving the problem." Nancy Reagan

Alcohol

What Is Alcohol?

Approximately 51.8% of Americans 12 and over, 131.3 million people, reported being current drinkers in the 2010 National Survey on Drug Use and Health (SAMHSA, 2010).

Ethyl alcohol, or ethanol, has been prevalent in our society for centuries. Except for the Prohibition Era in the United States from 1917 to 1932 when alcohol was considered an illegal substance, it has become the legal and accepted drug of choice. There are three major types of alcoholic beverages:

1. beer,
2. distilled spirits or hard liquor,
3. wine or wine coolers.

Distilled spirits include scotch, gin, rum, vodka, tequila, and whiskey. The alcohol content varies according to the proof of the beverage, which is twice the percent of alcohol. For example, if whiskey is 80 proof, then that particular beverage is 40 percent alcohol by volume. The average mixed drink contains a one-ounce shot of hard liquor.

Wine usually averages 12 percent alcohol by volume, and wine coolers average approximately 5 percent alcohol by volume. The average glass of wine is four ounces, and wine coolers are usually served in twelve-ounce bottles

Beer is usually served in twelve-ounce cans or bottles. The average alcohol content of beer is 4.5 percent by volume. To be considered a beer, the alcohol content must not exceed 5 percent by weight by volume. If the amount of alcohol is greater, it is considered an ale.

Physiological Effects

Alcohol is a drug that has two major effects on the body. Being a depressant, it slows down the nervous system (respiratory and cardiovascular systems). Alcohol and its by-products also **irritate** the nerve endings and eventually **sedate** or deaden them. **Vision** is another sense that alcohol affects quickly. This is an important ability for driving because 90 percent of the information we receive is obtained through vision. Alcohol has a direct effect on our vision by causing the loss of fine muscle control in the eyes accounting for eye focus, visual acuity, peripheral vision, color distinction, night vision, distance judgment, and double vision (Dennis and the Texas Commission on Alcohol and Drug Abuse, 2005). Other physiological effects are impaired mental and physical reflexes, increased risk of diseases such as cancer of the brain, tongue, mouth, esophagus, larynx, liver, and the bladder. Heart and blood pressure problems are also associated with alcohol consumption.

Blood Alcohol Concentration

(BAC) is a measure of the concentration of alcohol in blood, expressed in grams per 100 ml. An example would be 100 mg of alcohol in 10 ml of blood would be reported as .10 percent. The higher the alcohol content of the drink, the higher BAC it will produce.

© Roman Sigaev, 2012, Shutterstock, Inc.

12 oz. Beer	12 oz. Wine cooler
×.045	× .05
.54 oz. Alcohol	.60 oz. Alcohol

1 oz. Whiskey	4 oz. Wine
× .40	× .12
.40 oz. Alcohol	.48 oz. Alcohol

The alcoholic content of some other typical drinks:

one ounce shot 86 proof liquor	.43 oz.
Light beer 12 oz.	.46 oz.
Champagne 4 oz.	.58 oz.
Malt liquor 12 oz.	.75 oz.
Margarita	.75 oz.

Alcoholic content varies according to the type of drink and the proof of the beverage.

Factors influencing a person's BAC are body weight, alcohol content of the drink, size of the drink, time spent drinking, and food (see chart below). Gender is also a factor in determining one's BAC. Women do not process alcohol as well as men because of the enzyme alcohol dehydrogenase, which breaks down alcohol. Men produce more alcohol dehydrogenase than women; therefore, men can eliminate alcohol at a slightly faster rate (Dennis and the Texas Commission on Alcohol and Drug Abuse, 2005). Women also have less water content, so a woman at the same weight as a man will have a higher BAC. The higher alcohol content of a drink, the higher BAC it will produce. For example, a one-ounce shot of a 100 proof beverage has more alcohol than a one-ounce shot of an 80 proof beverage. The larger an alcoholic drink, the more alcohol it will contain and produce a higher BAC. For example, a twenty-four ounce beer will have twice the amount of alcohol of a twelve-ounce beer. The liver begins to process alcohol shortly after it is absorbed into the bloodstream. The longer time factor will result in a lower BAC. For example, if a person drinks a six-pack in three hours, they will have a lower BAC than if they had consumed a six-pack in one hour. Having food in the stomach may coat the lining of the stomach, therefore slowing down the absorption of alcohol. Food will not absorb or soak up the alcohol, so the alcohol will eventually reach the bloodstream.

There are three ways that alcohol is removed or eliminated from the body. Ninety percent of alcohol is eliminated through the oxidation process of the liver at .015 percent per hour. The alcohol dehydrogenase then converts alco-

How to Calculate Your Estimated Blood Alcohol Content/BAC

Showing estimated percent of alcohol in the blood by number of drinks in relation to body weight. This percent can be estimated by:
1. Count your drinks (1 drink *equals* 1 ounce of 100-proof liguor, one five ounce glass of table wine or one 12-ounce bottle of regular beer).
2. Use the chart below and under number of "drinks" and opposite "body weight" find the percent of blood alcohol listed.
3. Subtract from this number the percent of alcohol "burned up" during the time elapsed since your first drink. This figure is .015% per hour. (Example: 180 lb. man—8 drinks in 4 hours / .167% minus (.015 × 4) = .107%

Drinks

Body weight	1	2	3	4	5	6	7	8	9	10	11	12
100 lb.	.038	.075	.113	.150	.188	.225	.263	.300	.338	.375	.413	.450
110 lb.	.034	.066	.103	.137	.172	.207	.241	.275	.309	.344	.379	.412
120 lb.	.031	.063	.094	.125	.156	.188	.219	.250	.281	.313	.344	.375
130 lb.	.029	.058	.087	.116	.145	.174	.203	.232	.261	.290	.320	.348
140 lb.	.027	.054	.080	.107	.134	.161	.188	.214	.241	.268	.295	.321
150 lb.	.025	.050	.075	.100	.125	.151	.176	.201	.226	.251	.276	.301
160 lb.	.023	.047	.070	.094	.117	.141	.164	.188	.211	.234	.258	.281
170 lb.	.022	.045	.066	.088	.110	.132	.155	.178	.200	.221	.244	.265
180 lb.	.021	.042	.063	.083	.104	.125	.146	.167	.188	.208	.229	.250
190 lb.	.020	.040	.059	.079	.099	.119	.138	.158	.179	.198	.217	.237
200 lb.	.019	.038	.056	.075	.094	.113	.131	.150	.169	.188	.206	.225
210 lb.	.018	.036	.053	.071	.090	.107	.125	.143	.161	.179	.197	.215
220 lb.	.017	.034	.051	.068	.085	.102	.119	.136	.153	.170	.188	.205
230 lb.	.016	.032	.049	.065	.081	.098	.115	.130	.147	.163	.180	.196
240 lb.	.016	.031	.047	.063	.078	.094	.109	.125	.141	.156	.172	.188

Source: National Highway Traffic Safety Administration.

hol to acetaldehyde. Alcohol is then metabolized at approximately .25 to .30 ounces per hour, regardless of the blood alcohol concentration. The rate of metabolism is based on the activity of alcohol dehydrogenase, working at its own pace (Ray and Kisr, 1999). Eight percent of alcohol is eliminated through breath, which is why a breath test is used to determine BAC. A small amount of alcohol, approximately 2 percent, is eliminated through sweat. For the average individual, elimination will reduce a given blood alcohol concentration by .015 per hour. Contrary to popular belief, cold showers, black coffee, aspirin, or exercise will not speed up this elimination process (see Figure 9.1).

Tolerance is when an individual adapts to the amount consumed so that larger quantities are needed to achieve the same effect. This basically means that a person needs to drink more alcohol to achieve the same effect. This can take place over several months or years of consuming alcohol, depending on the amount consumed and at what age the individual begins to drink. At some point, after a person's tolerance has increased over a period of time, it begins to drop, allowing the effects of alcohol to be felt after only a few drinks. This reverse tolerance is caused by the natural aging process or liver disease after years of abusive drinking (Dennis and the Texas Commission Alcohol and Drug Abuse, 2005).

Intoxication is defined as a transient state of physical and mental disruption due to the presence of a toxic substance, such as alcohol (Maisto, 2005). As BAC increases, the central nervous system alters behavior and physical function. Change can occur as low as .02 BAC in some people, while everyone is impaired to some degree at .05 BAC.

© Monika Olszewska, 2012, Shutterstock, Inc.

Alcohol slows down the nervous system, impairs vision, and increases the risk of certain cancers, heart, and blood pressure problems.

Societal Problems

The dangers of alcohol consumption are a major problem in our society. Drinking too much alcohol can cause a range of very serious problems, in addition to the obvious health issues. Alcohol is a contributing factor in motor vehicle accidents, violence, and school/work problems, as well as family problems.

Drinking and Driving

Driving under the influence of alcohol is the most frequently committed and deadliest crime in America. In the Federal Bureau of Investigation's (FBI) Uniform Crime Report, more than 1.4 million people were arrested in 2009 for alcohol-impaired driving. The National Highway Traffic Safety Administration (NHTSA) reported in 2009 that 10,839 people were killed in alcohol impaired

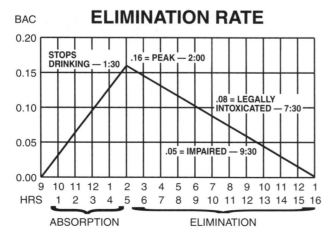

ELIMINATION RATE

Source: Texas Commission on Alcohol and Drug Abuse

FIGURE 9.1
Alcohol Absorption and Elimination

A Snapshot of Annual High-Risk College Drinking Consequences (NIAAA, 2010)

Academic Problems: About 25 percent of college students report academic consequences of their drinking including missing classes, falling behind, doing poorly on exams or papers, and receiving lower grades overall.

Police Involvement: About 5 percent of 4-year college students are involved with the police or campus security as a result of their drinking, and 110,000 students between the ages of 18 and 24 are arrested for an alcohol-related violation such as public drunkenness or driving under the influence.

Alcohol Abuse and Dependence: 31 percent of college students met criteria for a diagnosis of alcohol abuse and 6 percent for a diagnosis of alcohol dependence in the past 12 months, according to questionnaire-based self-reports about their drinking.

driving crashes. This is 32 percent of the nation's total traffic fatalities for the year. The 10,839 deaths in 2009 represent an average of one alcohol-related fatality every 22 minutes (NHTSA, 2011). Even small amounts of alcohol impair driving (see Table 9.1)

Drunk driving is no accident; it is a crime. The greatest tragedy is that these crashes are preventable, predictable, and 100 percent avoidable.

Although most drivers involved in fatal crashes have no prior convictions for DUI, about one-third of all drivers arrested for DUI are repeat offenders, which greatly increases their risk of causing a drunk driving accident. As a nation, we have seen a downward trend in alcohol-related fatalities. Today, all states have lowered their legal level of intoxication to .08 BAC. All states have some form of the zero tolerance law, as well as an open container law. These laws, in addition to stricter enforcement of existing laws, have helped in changing behavior. High school and university education programs, such as non-alcoholic activities for prom nights and designated driver organizations, have also contributed in raising awareness to combat such a serious problem.

The NHTSA and the Advertising Council's Innocent Victims public service campaign stresses the need to get the keys from someone who is about to drive. Here are some tips:

- If it is a close friend, try to use a soft, calm approach. Suggest to them that they have had too much to drink and it would be better if someone else drove, or call a cab.
- Be calm. Joke about it. Make light of it.

TABLE 9.1 ♦ Some Likely Effects on Driving

Blood Alcohol Concentration (BAC) Levels		Effect
.15%	About 7 beers	Serious difficulty controlling the car and focusing on driving
.10%	About 5 beers	Marked slowed reaction time Difficulty staying in lane and braking when needed
.08%	About 4 beers	Trouble controlling speed Difficulty processing information and reasoning.
.05%	About 3 beers	Reduced coordination and ability to track moving objects Difficulty steering
.02%	About 2 beers	Loss of judgment Trouble doing two tasks at the same time

Source: Adapted from The ABCs of BAC, National Highway Traffic Safety Administration, 2005, and How to Control Your Drinking, WR Miller and RF Munoz, University of New Mexico, 1982.

- Try to make it sound like you are doing them a favor.
- If it is somebody you do not know well, speak to their friends; usually they will listen.
- If it is a good friend, tell them if they insist on driving, you are not going with them.
- Locate their keys while they are preoccupied and take them away. Mostly they will think they lost them and will be forced to find another mode of transportation.
- Avoid embarrassing the person or being confrontational.

Alcohol Use in College

The legal drinking age in all states is 21 years old, but that does not mean individuals under 21 do not consume alcohol. Studies suggest that substance use, including alcohol, tobacco, and other drug use, is common among college-aged youth. Students who use any of these substances are at significantly greater risk than non-substance using peers to: drive after drinking and with a driver who has been drinking, and are less likely to use a seatbelt. These consistently poor and risky choices increase their risk of being in a motor vehicle crash and having crash-related injuries (Everett, 1999). College students and administrators struggle with the problems associated with alcohol abuse, binge drinking, and drunk driving (see Figure 9.2). These actions put students at risk for many serious problems, such as date rape violence and possibly death.

The National Institute on Alcohol Abuse and Alcoholism (NIAAA) reports that 1,825 college students die annually from alcohol-related unintentional injuries, including motor vehicle crashes, with 3.36 million students driving under the influence of alcohol. Another 599,000 between the ages of 18 and 24 are injured, and approximately 696,000 students per year are assaulted by a drinking student. Also, approximately 400,000 students between 18 and 24 years old reported having unprotected sex as a result of drinking. More than 97,000 students are victims of alcohol-related sexual assault or date rape.

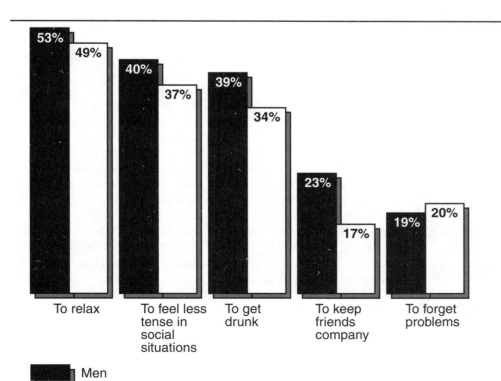

FIGURE 9.2

Why College Freshmen Drink

Source: Adapted from Weschler and McFadden for AAA Foundation for Traffic Safety. Survey of 1,669 college freshmen at 14 Massachusetts institutions.

More than 150,000 college students develop an alcohol-related health problem, with 1.5 percent attempting suicide because of alcohol (NIAAA, 2010).

Binge Drinking

College presidents agree that **binge drinking** is the most serious problem on campus. The National Institute on Alcohol Abuse and Alcoholism defines **binge drinking** as a pattern of drinking that brings a person's blood alcohol concentration to .08 or above. This typically happens when men consume five or more drinks and women consume four or more drinks in about two hours (NIAAA, 2010). Binge drinkers usually experience more alcohol-related problems than their non-drinking counterparts. These problems affect their health, education, safety, and interpersonal relationships. According to the Harvard School of Public Health College Alcohol Study, these problems include driving after drinking, damaging property, getting injured, missing classes, and getting behind in school work. According to the same Harvard study, one in five students surveyed experienced five or more different alcohol-related problems and more than one-third of the students reported driving after drinking.

The study also found that the vast majority of non-binge drinking students are negatively affected by the behavior of binge drinkers. It was reported that four out of five students who were non-binge drinkers and who lived on campus experienced secondary effects of binge drinking such as being the victim of a sexual assault or an unwanted sexual advance, having property vandalized, and having sleep or study interrupted.

Alcohol Poisoning

For more information on 911 Lifeline Legislation visit awareawakealive.org

The most serious consequence of binge drinking is **alcohol poisoning.** This results when an overdose of alcohol is consumed. When excessive amounts of alcohol are consumed, the brain is deprived of oxygen, which causes it to shut down the breathing and heart rate functions. Many think that the only deadly mix is alcohol and driving, but an alcohol overdose can be lethal. It can happen to anyone.

Some symptoms of alcohol poisoning are:

- Person does not respond to talking, shouting, or being shaken.
- Person cannot stand up.
- Person has slow, labored, or abnormal breathing—less than eight breaths/minute or ten or more seconds between each breath.
- Person's skin feels clammy.
- Person has a rapid pulse rate and irregular heart rhythm.
- Person has lowered blood pressure.
- Vomiting.

The most serious consequence of binge drinking is alcohol poisoning. Alcohol overdose can be lethal.

If you think a friend is experiencing alcohol poisoning, seek medical attention immediately. Stay with the person until help arrives. Turn the victim onto one side in case of vomiting. Choking to death on one's own vomit after an alcohol overdose is quite common. Death by asphyxiation occurs when alcohol depresses and inhibits the gag reflex to the point that the person cannot vomit properly. **Do not leave the victim alone.** Be honest in telling medical staff exactly how much alcohol the victim consumed. This is an extreme medical emergency and one that is a matter of life and death. Some states have passed legislation providing limited immunity for a minor who calls 911 for someone who is a possible victim of alcohol poisoning.

Colleges are attempting to make progress in preventing some of these problems. Many sororities and fraternities as well as other student organizations have taken action by banning alcohol at many functions. By implementing alcohol awareness programs, stronger hazing policies, and tougher enforcements on drinking violations and alcohol restrictions on campus and with the student body, some of these tragedies may be prevented.

Drinking Problems

Nearly 14 million Americans, one in every thirteen adults, abuse alcohol or are alcoholics. Rates of alcohol problems are highest among young adults ages 18 to 29 and lowest in adults ages 65 and older (NIAAA, 2006).

The National Institute on Alcohol Abuse and Alcoholism (NIAAA) found that the earlier young people begin to drink alcohol, the more likely they are to become an alcohol abuser or alcoholic. According to the report:

- Young people who start drinking before age 15 are four times more likely to become an alcoholic than if they start after age 21.
- Forty percent who drink before age 15 become alcohol dependent; 10 percent if they wait until 21.
- Fourteen percent decreased risk of alcoholism for each year drinking is delayed until age 21.

How can you tell if someone has a drinking problem? An individual does not have to be an alcoholic to have problems with alcohol. Problems linked to abuse are neglecting work, school, or family responsibilities. Legal issues such as alcohol violations and drinking-and-driving-related problems can also be a result of alcohol abuse. There are many "red flags" that can point to a problem with alcohol. One way is to answer these questions developed by Dr. John Ewing:

- Have you ever felt you should CUT down on your drinking?
- Have people ANNOYED you by criticizing your drinking?
- Have you ever felt bad or GUILTY about your drinking?
- Have you ever had a drink first thing in the morning to steady your nerves or to get rid of the hangover ("EYE OPENER")?

Michael Wagener Story

On August 3, 1999, Michael Wagener, a student at Texas A&M University celebrating his 21st birthday, died as a result of alcohol poisoning. He was an intelligent and insightful young man with many friends and his whole life ahead of him. He was not an alcoholic, nor did he abuse alcohol. Michael was typically a responsible drinker.

On August 2nd, the eve of his 21st birthday, friends joined Michael at a local establishment. While having a few beers, some friends bought him a couple of shots for his birthday. His friends had bought him eight or nine (four-ounce) shots in a matter of thirty to forty-five minutes. Michael had many friends who wanted to share in his celebration; no one wanted him to die.

By the time he was taken home, Michael's body had begun to shut down. He could no longer move and had to be carried into the house. His friends thought they had taken all the precautions: designated driver, turn him on his side in case he vomits. They even stayed the night to ensure his safety.

At 7:00 a.m. his mother called to wish Michael a happy birthday. The call stirred his friends. At 7:10 a.m. the call was made to 911—Michael never woke up. One fun-filled night of celebration turned deadly.

This can happen to anyone. Consuming excessive amounts of alcohol, even one night, can kill you. We often think the only way alcohol can kill is if someone drinks and drives or abuses alcohol for many years. Educating yourself about alcohol will help you make informed decisions and hopefully prevent this tragedy from occurring again.

To help remember these questions, notice that the first letter of each key word spells CAGE. One "yes" answer suggests a possible alcohol problem. More than one "yes" means it is highly likely that a problem exists (Ewing, 1995).

Other signs and symptoms also could indicate that a person could be misusing or abusing alcohol or other drugs. One or two of them does not necessarily point to a problem, but several, combined with the right circumstances, need to be addressed. Some of these signs may include a grade decline or a sudden drop in grades, frequently missing class because of hangovers, binge drinking, legal problems associated with alcohol, or a significant increase in tolerance to alcohol. Other major signs of a drinking problem could be frequently drinking alone, drinking to forget about personal problems, or avoiding activities where alcohol is not available. Another more serious physical sign of alcohol abuse is a **blackout**. This occurs when an individual has amnesia about events after drinking, even though there was no loss of consciousness.

Alcoholism

Alcoholism, also known as alcohol dependence, is a chronic, progressive disease with symptoms that include a strong need to drink and continued drinking despite repeated negative alcohol-related consequences. There are four symptoms generally associated with alcoholism:

1. a craving or a strong need to drink,
2. impaired control or the inability to limit one's drinking,
3. a physical dependence accompanied by withdrawal symptoms such as nausea, sweating, shakiness, and anxiety when alcohol use is stopped, and
4. an increased tolerance.

Can alcoholism be hereditary? Alcoholism has a biological base. The tendency to become an alcoholic is inherited. Men and women are four times more likely to become alcoholics if their parents were (NIAAA, 2008). Currently, researchers are finding the genes that influence vulnerability to alcohol. A person's environment may also play a role in drinking and the development of alcoholism. This is not destiny. A child of an alcoholic parent will not automatically develop alcoholism, and a person with no family history of alcohol can become alcohol dependent.

There are ways to avoid becoming alcohol dependent. It is important to know your limit and stick to it. If choosing to drink, drink slowly and alternate an alcoholic beverage with a non-alcoholic beverage, eat while drinking, and most importantly find more effective ways of dealing with problems instead of turning to alcohol.

If you feel this is a problem, the sooner you stop the better the chances of avoiding serious psychological effects.

- Admit to your drinking—first step in avoiding serious problems.
- Change your lifestyle—try to stay out of situations where alcohol is prominent until you can control your drinking.
- Get involved in self-help groups.

Chronic Effects

Drinking too much alcohol can cause a wide range of chronic health problems including liver disease, cancer, heart disease, nervous system problems, as well as alcoholism (see Figure 9.3).

Although moderate amounts of alcohol may not be harmful, there are some major health issues associated with chronic alcohol use and abuse.

- ***Liver disease*** is commonly associated with alcohol abuse. The liver has many vital functions in the body. It is a common mistake for

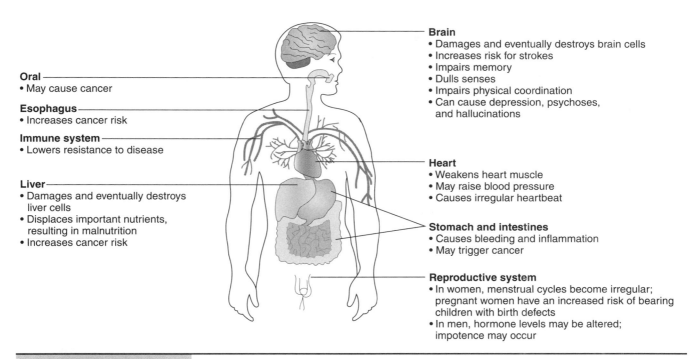

Brain
- Damages and eventually destroys brain cells
- Increases risk for strokes
- Impairs memory
- Dulls senses
- Impairs physical coordination
- Can cause depression, psychoses, and hallucinations

Oral
- May cause cancer

Esophagus
- Increases cancer risk

Immune system
- Lowers resistance to disease

Liver
- Damages and eventually destroys liver cells
- Displaces important nutrients, resulting in malnutrition
- Increases cancer risk

Heart
- Weakens heart muscle
- May raise blood pressure
- Causes irregular heartbeat

Stomach and intestines
- Causes bleeding and inflammation
- May trigger cancer

Reproductive system
- In women, menstrual cycles become irregular; pregnant women have an increased risk of bearing children with birth defects
- In men, hormone levels may be altered; impotence may occur

FIGURE 9.3

Long-term Risks Associated with Alcohol Abuse

Source: Adapted from "Long-Term Risk Associated with Alcohol Abuse" *Lifetime Physical Fitness & Wellness* by Hoeger and Hoeger, Wadsworth Publishers.

people to think that only those individuals who abuse alcohol can harm the liver. Individuals who are heavy social drinkers may run the risk of liver damage as well.

- *Hepatotoxic trauma* or "fatty liver" is the most common alcohol-related disorder causing enlargement of the liver. Some damage can be reversed if alcohol is completely avoided.

- *Alcoholic hepatitis* is an enlarged and tender liver with an elevation of white blood cells. Symptoms can include nausea, vomiting, abdominal pain, fever, and jaundice. If alcohol use continues, this could progress to cirrhosis.

- *Alcohol cirrhosis* results from continued alcohol use and may cause permanent scar tissue to form when the liver cells are damaged. This problem usually occurs in 10 to 15 percent of people who consume large quantities and can develop in as little as five years of heavy drinking.

- *Alcohol pellagra* is a deficiency of protein and niacin. Symptoms may include skin inflammation, gastrointestinal disorders, diarrhea, and mental and nervous disorders.

- *Malnutrition* occurs from a lack of needed nutrients through prolonged alcohol consumption, by depressing the appetite and attacking the lining of the stomach. Heavy drinkers do not get the calories they need, which triggers increased mineral loss and increases fatty acids because of the interference of the transfer of glucose into energy.

- *Polyneuritis* is a condition caused by thiamin deficiency, which causes inflammation of several nerves and causes the drinker to become weak and have a tingling sensation.

- *Cancers*—It is established that 2 to 4 percent of all cancer cases could be caused by alcohol use. Cancer of the upper digestive tract such as mouth, esophageal, pharynx, and larynx can be attributed to alcohol use. Liver cancer as well as breast cancer may be caused by excessive alcohol consumption. Studies indicated that a woman's risk of developing breast cancer increases with age and alcohol consumption (JAMA, 1995).

- ***Fetal alcohol syndrome.*** The alcohol crosses the placenta but experts don't know exactly how drinking causes problems for the fetus. It may directly affect the fetus or it may be acetaldehyde, the metabolic by-product of alcohol that is harmful to the fetus. Some researchers believe that alcohol effects on the placenta cause blood flow and nutrient deficiencies. Whatever the reason, drinking during pregnancy clearly puts infants at risk for birth defects (Herman, 2003).

Neurological disorders associated with alcohol use are:

- ***Wernickes disease*** is caused by a thiamine deficiency. Some symptoms include decreased mental functions, double vision, and involuntary oscillation of the eyeballs.
- ***Korsakoff's syndrome*** is caused by a B complex vitamin deficiency. Symptoms are amnesia, personality alterations, and a loss of reality. This person may become apathetic and have difficulty walking.

Organizations For information regarding alcohol use and abuse contact:

- National Institute on Alcohol Abuse and Alcoholism (NIAAA) www. niaaa.org
- *Alcoholics Anonymous (AA)* is an organization designed to support and help individuals become sober and stay sober. AA has over 19,000 affiliated groups and more than 350,000 members across the United States AA (212) 870-3400 www.alcoholic-anonymous.org
- *Al-Anon* and *Alateen* are organizations designed to help family members of alcoholics to cope with problems. 800-344-2666 www.al-anon-alateen.org

Laws Relating to Alcohol

In every state in the United States, it is illegal for a person under the age of 21 to attempt to purchase, possess, or consume alcohol. In Texas, this violation is a **minor in possession** (MIP). This offense is punishable by fines, community service, loss of driver's license, alcohol awareness class, and possibly jail.

The **Zero Tolerance Law** prohibits the use of alcohol by a minor operating a motor vehicle. In Texas, it is illegal for a minor to operate a motor vehicle in a public place with *any* **detectable** amount of alcohol. This violation is referred to as **driving under the influence** (DUI). This may be determined by a blood/breath test or simply smelling alcohol on the minor's breath. The penalties are very similar to MIP with fine, loss of license, education courses, and community service.

By operating a motor vehicle in a public place, the driver has given consent to take a breath/blood test to determine alcohol in his/her system. Refusing or failing the test is considered a violation, and penalties will result in loss of license, regardless of the outcome of the violation.

In many states, the legal definition of **driving while intoxicated (DWI)** is not having normal use of your mental or physical faculties because of alcohol or other drugs; or a blood alcohol concentration of .08 or more. It is, however, illegal in all states to drink and drive. In addition, in most states, it is also illegal for anyone in the vehicle to possess an **open container** of alcohol regardless of age.

When someone is injured in an alcohol-related motor vehicle accident, the intoxicated driver can be charged with **intoxication assault.** If there were a fatality in a drinking-and-driving accident, the offense would be elevated to **intoxication manslaughter**. Each state may have different terminology, but the offense is the same throughout the country. In Texas, both offenses are considered felonies.

Tobacco

The U.S. Surgeon General reported in 1970 that cigarette smoking is dangerous to your health. Over the years we have come to realize just how dangerous. Cigarette smoking is the leading preventable cause of death in the United States, responsible for one in five deaths annually. Through study after study, reports have proven that tobacco use is one of the biggest public health issues that faces the world today (CDC, 2006) (see Figure 9.4). Tobacco is a risk factor for six of the eight leading causes of death, with smokers dying thirteen to fourteen years earlier than non-smokers. Worldwide, there are 5.4 million deaths annually because of tobacco use with current trends estimating an increase to 8 million deaths by 2030 (CDC, 2006). In the U.S. there are 443,000 deaths annually due to smoking (CDC, 2012).

Tobacco Components

The toxic components of tobacco include tar, nicotine, and carbon monoxide. **Tar** is a by-product of burning tobacco. Its composition is a dark, sticky substance that can be condensed from cigarette smoke. Tar contains many potent carcinogens and chemicals that irritate tissue in the lungs and promote chronic bronchitis and emphysema. These substances paralyze and destroy the cilia that line the bronchi, causing "smoker's cough." Long-term exposure of extremely toxic tar to lung tissue can lead to the development of cancer.

Nicotine is a colorless, oily compound that is extremely poisonous in concentrated amounts. This highly addictive drug is a major contributor to heart and respiratory diseases causing short-term increases in blood pressure, heart rate, and blood flow from the heart, resulting in narrowing of the arteries. A strong dependence on nicotine can occur after as little as three packs of cigarettes, and it is more addictive than cocaine or heroin. Because of its addictive effects, the Food and Drug Administration (FDA) has determined nicotine should be regulated.

At first, nicotine acts as a stimulant and then it tends to tranquilize the nervous system. The effects depend largely on how one chooses to smoke. Shallow puffs seem to increase alertness because low doses of nicotine facilitate the release of acetylcholine, which creates feelings of alertness. Long, deep drags tend to relax the smoker because high doses of nicotine block the flow of acetylcholine. Ninety percent of the nicotine inhaled while smoking is absorbed into the body, while 20 to 30 percent of nicotine is absorbed if the smoke is drawn only into the mouth, not the lungs.

Other side effects include inhibiting formation of urine, discoloration of the fingers, dulling the taste buds, and irritating the membranes in the mouth and throat. Because nicotine constricts blood vessels, it causes the skin to be clammy and have a pallid appearance, as well as reducing body temperature. The highly addictive nature of nicotine can cause withdrawal symptoms to occur quite suddenly. These symptoms include irritability, anxiousness, hostility, food cravings, headaches, and the inability to concentrate.

Carbon monoxide is an odorless, tasteless gas that is highly toxic. It reduces the amount of oxygen the blood can carry, causing shortness of breath. Carbon monoxide ultimately damages the inner walls of the arteries, thus encouraging a buildup of fat on the walls of the arteries; this is called atherosclerosis. Over time, this causes the arteries to narrow and harden, which may lead to a heart attack.

Approximately 1 percent of cigarette smoke and 6 percent of cigar smoke is carbon monoxide. It impairs normal function of the nervous system and is

partially responsible for the increased risk of heart attacks and strokes in smokers.

Types of Tobacco Use

Smokeless tobacco comes in two forms: snuff and chewing tobacco. Snuff is a fine grain of tobacco, and chewing tobacco is shredded or bricked; either choice is placed in the mouth and the user sucks on the tobacco juices, spitting out the saliva. The sucking allows the nicotine to be absorbed in the bloodstream. It can be equally as dangerous and harmful as smoking. Smokeless tobacco is addictive. According to the Centers for Disease Control and Prevention (CDC) estimates, 6.1 percent of high school students are current smokeless tobacco users. Nationally, an estimated 3.5 percent of adults are current smokeless tobacco users. (CDC, 2009).

The National Cancer Institute reports there are three thousand chemical compounds in smokeless tobacco. Nicotine is the addictive drug in all forms of tobacco. Holding one pinch of smokeless tobacco in your mouth for thirty minutes delivers as much nicotine as three to four cigarettes (National Cancer Institute, 2011). There have been at least twenty-eight cancer-causing agents found in smokeless tobacco:

- Nitrosamines—20 to 43,000 more nitrosamines are found in smokeless tobacco. Other consumer products like beer or bacon only contain five parts per billion
- Polonium 210—radioactive particles that turn into radon
- Formaldehyde—embalming fluid
- Cadmium—metallic element; its salts are poisonous
- Arsenic—poisonous element

Immediate effects from chewing tobacco are bad breath and stains on your teeth. Mouth sores also accompany smokeless tobacco users. The complications of long-term use can be very serious. These complications include increased gum and teeth problems, increased heart rate, irregular heartbeat, heart attacks, and cancer. Oral cancer can occur in the mouth, lips, tongue, cheeks, or gums. Other cancer possibilities resulting from smokeless tobacco can be stomach cancer, bladder cancer, and cancer of the esophagus.

Another major problem caused by smokeless tobacco is **leukoplakia**, a precancerous condition that produces thick, rough, white patches on the gums, tongue, and inner cheeks. A variety of cancers such as lip, pharynx, larynx, esophagus, and tongue can be attributed to smokeless tobacco. Dental and gum problems are major side effects as well. Smokeless tobacco used during pregnancy increases the risk for preeclampsia, a condition that includes high blood pressure, fluid retention, and swelling. It also puts the mother and newborn at higher risk for premature birth and low birth weight. In men, smokeless tobacco reduces sperm count and increases the liklihood of abnormal sperm cell. (CDC, 2010).

Cigarette smoking greatly impairs the respiratory system and is a major cause of chronic obstructive pulmonary diseases (COPD), including emphysema and chronic bronchitis.

Problems associated with cigarette smoking (see Figure 9.2) include mouth, throat, and other types of cancer, cirrhosis of the liver, stomach, and duodenal ulcers, gum and dental disease, decreased HDL cholesterol and decreased platelet survival and clotting time, as well as increased blood thickness.

Cigarette smoking increases problems such as heart disease, atherosclerosis, and blood clots. It increases the amount of fatty acids, glucose, and various hormones in the blood, cardiac arrhythmia, allergies, diabetes, hypertension, peptic ulcers, and sexual impotence. Smoking doubles the risk of heart disease,

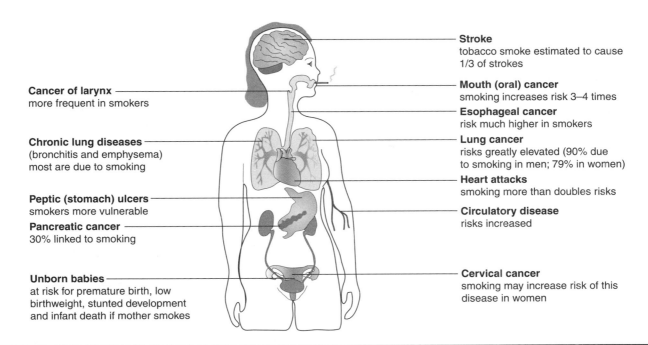

Cancer of larynx
more frequent in smokers

Chronic lung diseases
(bronchitis and emphysema)
most are due to smoking

Peptic (stomach) ulcers
smokers more vulnerable

Pancreatic cancer
30% linked to smoking

Unborn babies
at risk for premature birth, low
birthweight, stunted development
and infant death if mother smokes

Stroke
tobacco smoke estimated to cause
1/3 of strokes

Mouth (oral) cancer
smoking increases risk 3–4 times

Esophageal cancer
risk much higher in smokers

Lung cancer
risks greatly elevated (90% due
to smoking in men; 79% in women)

Heart attacks
smoking more than doubles risks

Circulatory disease
risks increased

Cervical cancer
smoking may increase risk of this
disease in women

FIGURE 9.4

The Health Effects of Smoking

Source: Adapted from "The Health Effects of Smoking" Lifetime Physical Fitness & Wellness by Hoeger and Hoeger, Wadsworth Publishing.

and those who smoke have only a 50 percent chance of recovery. Smokers also have a 70 percent higher death rate from heart disease than non-smokers (CDC, 2006). Smoking also causes cardiomyopathy, a condition that weakens the heart's ability to pump blood.

Life expectancy of smokers parallels smoking habits in that the younger one starts smoking and the longer one smokes, the higher the mortality rate. Also, the deeper smoke is inhaled and the higher the tar and nicotine content, the higher the mortality rate. On average, smokers die 13–14 years earlier than non-smokers (CDC, 2012).

The risk and mortality rates for lip, mouth, and larynx cancers for **pipe and cigar smoking** are higher than for cigarette smoking. Pipe smoke, which is 2 percent carbon monoxide, is more irritating to the respiratory system than cigarette smoking, but for those who do not inhale, the risk for developing cancer is just as likely.

Cigars have recently gained popularity in the United States among younger men and women with approximately 4.5 billion cigars consumed yearly.

Clove cigarettes are erroneously believed to be safer because they do not contain as much tobacco. In actuality, clove cigarettes are most harmful because they contain **eugenol**, which is an active ingredient of clove. Eugenol deadens sensations in the throat, which allows smokers to inhale more deeply and hold smoke in the lungs longer. Clove cigarettes also contain twice as much tar, nicotine, and carbon monoxide as most moderate brands of American cigarettes.

Once thought of as a less harmful way to smoke tobacco, **water pipes** have regained popularity in

© Wallenrock, 2012, Shutterstock, Inc.

The younger someone is when they start smoking, and the longer they continue to smoke, the greater their chance of dying from a smoking-related illness.

Smokeless Tobacco Users

Check Monthly for Early Signs of Disease

The early signs of cancer in the mouth and tongue may be detected by self-examination. Dr. Elbert Glover, director of the Tobacco Research Center at West Virginia University, and the American Cancer Society recommend that the following self-check procedures be conducted every month.

- Check your face and neck for lumps on either side. Both sides of your face and neck should be the same shape.
- Look at your lips, cheeks, and gums. Look for sores, white or red patches, or changes in your gums by pulling down your lower lip. Check your inner cheeks, especially where you hold your tobacco. Gently squeeze your lip and cheeks to check for lumps or soreness.
- Put the tip of your tongue on the roof of your mouth. Place one finger on the floor of your mouth and press up under your chin with a finger from your other hand. Feel for bumps, soreness, or swelling. Check around the inside of your teeth from one side of your jaw to the other.
- Tilt your head back and open your mouth wide. Check for color changes or bumps or sores in the roof of your mouth.
- Stick out your tongue and look at the top. Gently grasp your tongue with a piece of cloth and pull it to each side. Look for color changes. Feel both sides of your tongue with your finger for bumps.

If you use smokeless tobacco and find anything that looks or feels unusual, see your dentist or physician as soon as possible.

From Decisions for Healthy Living by Pruitt, Stein and Pruitt, Addison Wesley Longman Educational Publishers, Inc.

many cities across the United States. In 2005 the World Health Organization (WHO) published its findings emphasizing the harmful effects of waterpipe smoking, also known around the world as narghile, shisha, goza, and hookah. For centuries, smokers have been lead to believe that water pipe smoking is a safer alternative to cigarette smoking, but research shows that this method exposes the smoker to high rates of lung cancer and heart disease, as well as other tobacco-related diseases. There is also a high risk of communicable diseases like tuberculosis and hepatitis because of shared mouthpieces (WHO, 2005).

When smoking tobacco through a water pipe, some nicotine is absorbed as it passes through a water bowl. Because most smokers stop when their nicotine craving has been satisfied, this may actually lead to longer smoking sessions, exposing the user to more smoke over a longer period of time (see Figure 9.5).

Some water pipe products and accessories are marketed and sold with claims of reducing the harmful effects of hookah, but according to the WHO, none have been shown to reduce the smoker's risk of exposure to toxins.

FIGURE 9.5 Comparison of Cigarette Smoking Session and Water Pipe Smoking Session	**Cigarette Smoking Session**	**Water Pipe Smoking Session**
	8–12 puffs	50–100 puffs
	5–7 minutes	20–80 minutes
	0.5–0.6 liter of smoke inhaled	.015–1.0 liter of smoke inhaled

Note: Upon analysis, it is possible for a water pipe session to expose the smoker to the equivalent of up to one hundred cigarettes in a single session.

Environmental Tobacco Smoke

Environmental tobacco smoke (ETS), or secondhand smoke, contains more than 7,000 chemicals, including hundreds that are toxic and 70 carcinogens. Secondhand smoke exposure to non-smoking adults can cause heart disease, a 20–30 percent increased risk of lung cancer, and a 25–30 percent increased risk of heart attacks. Approximately 126 million non-smokers are exposed to secondhand smoke in homes, workplaces, and public places, resulting in an estimated 38,000 deaths and healthcare costs exceeding $10 billion annually. To those individuals with existing health issues, second-hand smoke exposure is an extremely high risk. There is no "risk-free" exposure to secondhand smoke; even brief exposure can be dangerous (CDC, 2006).

© Jonathan Brizendine, 2012, Shutter-stock, Inc.

There is no "risk-free" exposure to secondhand smoke.

Secondhand smoke is especially dangerous to infants and children. In the United States, almost 22 million children are exposed to secondhand smoke. Globally almost half of the world's children breathe air polluted by tobacco smoke. This exposure can cause sudden infant death syndrome, acute respiratory infections, ear problems, slow lung growth, and severe asthma attacks. Each year in the United States, secondhand smoke is responsible for an estimated 150,000–300,000 new cases of bronchitis and pneumonia in children less than 18 months, resulting in nearly 15,000 hospitalizations annually (CDC, 2012).

Smoking Cessation

Each year an estimated 1.3 million smokers quit successfully. More than four out of five smokers say they want to quit (AHA, 2006). Although there are various pharmacological agents used to aid smokers in quitting, nicotine replacement therapy has been shown to be the most effective. The transdermal nicotine patch is safe, as well as nicotine gum, although the patch appears to be preferred by most. In addition to the patch and gum, a nicotine nasal spray and nicotine inhalers are also available.

Of the 46 million Americans who currently smoke cigarettes, most are either actively trying to quit or want to quit (CDC, 2012). Quitting can bring a major reduction in the occurrence of coronary heart disease and other forms of cardio-vascular diseases. Quitting reduces the risk for repeat heart attacks and death from heart disease by 50 percent or more (CDC. 2012). Quitting can also aid in the management of contributors to heart attacks such as atherosclerosis, thrombosis, and cardiac arrhythmia.

By choosing to quit smoking, the American Heart Association (AHA) reports that after one year off cigarettes, risk for heart attacks is reduced by 50 percent (see Figure 9.6). After fifteen years of abstinence from smoking, your risks are similar to that of a person who never smoked. In five to fifteen years of being smoke-free, the risk of stroke is the same as for non-smokers.

The National Center for Chronic Disease Prevention and Control (part of the CDC) has shown that these five steps will help you quit and quit for good. You have the best chance if you use these together:

1. Get ready—set a quit date, get rid of all your cigarettes, do not let people smoke in your home; once you quit, do not smoke!
2. Get support and encouragement—tell family, friends, and co-workers. Ask them not to smoke around you.
3. Learn new skills and behaviors—change your routine, get busy with new tasks, reduce stress.

FIGURE 9.6

When Smokers Quit

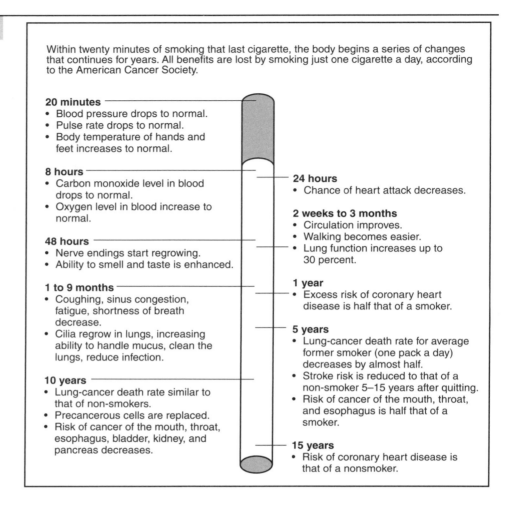

Within twenty minutes of smoking that last cigarette, the body begins a series of changes that continues for years. All benefits are lost by smoking just one cigarette a day, according to the American Cancer Society.

20 minutes
- Blood pressure drops to normal.
- Pulse rate drops to normal.
- Body temperature of hands and feet increases to normal.

8 hours
- Carbon monoxide level in blood drops to normal.
- Oxygen level in blood increase to normal.

48 hours
- Nerve endings start regrowing.
- Ability to smell and taste is enhanced.

1 to 9 months
- Coughing, sinus congestion, fatigue, shortness of breath decrease.
- Cilia regrow in lungs, increasing ability to handle mucus, clean the lungs, reduce infection.

10 years
- Lung-cancer death rate similar to that of non-smokers.
- Precancerous cells are replaced.
- Risk of cancer of the mouth, throat, esophagus, bladder, kidney, and pancreas decreases.

24 hours
- Chance of heart attack decreases.

2 weeks to 3 months
- Circulation improves.
- Walking becomes easier.
- Lung function increases up to 30 percent.

1 year
- Excess risk of coronary heart disease is half that of a smoker.

5 years
- Lung-cancer death rate for average former smoker (one pack a day) decreases by almost half.
- Stroke risk is reduced to that of a non-smoker 5–15 years after quitting.
- Risk of cancer of the mouth, throat, and esophagus is half that of a smoker.

15 years
- Risk of coronary heart disease is that of a nonsmoker.

4. Get medication and use it correctly—ask your healthcare provider for advice; FDA approved medications:
   - Bupropion SR—prescription only
   - Nicotine gum—over the counter
   - Nicotine inhaler—prescription
   - Nicotine nasal spray—prescription
   - Nicotine patch—prescription and over the counter
5. Be prepared for relapse or difficult situations—most relapses occur within the first three months after quitting. Don't be discouraged, most people try several times before they finally quit. Keep trying!

For more information visit smokefree.gov.

There is some irreversible damage to virtually every organ system in the body. There are dangers from smoking that remain even after quitting. Although it is never too late to quit smoking, the damage that has been done may never entirely disappear. It is best to choose to never light up!

For more information on smoking and the health problems associated with tobacco products, contact these agencies:

- American Heart Association (AHA)
  www.aha.org
  National Center
  7272 Greenville Avenue
  Dallas, TX 75231
  1-800-AHA-USA1
- American Lung Association (ALA)
  www.lungusa.org/
  1740 Broadway
  New York, NY 10019-4274
  (212) 315-8700
  1-800-LUNG-USA
- American Medical Association (AMA)
  www.ama-assn.org/
  515 North State Street
  Chicago, IL 60610
  (312) 464-5000

- Centers for Disease Control and Prevention
  www.cdc.gov/tobacco
- American Cancer Society (ACS)
  http://www.cancer.org
  1599 Clifton Road, N.E.
  Atlanta, GA 30329
  1-800-ACS-2345
- Cancer Research Foundation of America (CRFA)
  www.preventcancer.org
  1600 Duke Street
  Alexandria, VA 22314
  (703) 836-4412
- Doctors Ought to Care (DOC)
  www.bcm.tmc.edu/doc/
  5615 Kirby Drive
  Suite 440
  Houston, TX 77005
  (713) 528-1487

Cannabinoids

Marijuana is a naturally occurring plant called *Cannabis sativa*, whose leaves and stems can be dried, crushed, and the mixture rolled in cigarettes (joints) and smoked. The fibers of this plant are also used to manufacture hemp rope and paper. The resins scraped from the flowering tops of the plant yield **hashish**, a form of marijuana that can be smoked in a pipe. The amount of the active ingredient, tetrahydrocannabinol (THC), determines the potency of the hallucinogenic effect. Because THC is a fat-soluble substance, it is absorbed and retained in the fat tissues of the body for up to a month. Drug tests can detect trace amounts of THC for up to three weeks after consumption. Medicinal uses include relief of the nausea caused by chemotherapy, improvement of appetite in AIDS patients, and the relief of pressure in the eyes of glaucoma patients. The effects of marijuana use vary from user to user, but usually result in some similar experiences. Acute effects include euphoria, relaxation, slowed reaction time, distorted sensory perception, impaired balance and coordination, increased heart rate and appetite impaired learning and memory, anxiety, panic attacks and psychosis (NIDA, 2011).

The long-term effects are still being studied; however, chronic abuse may lead to a motivational syndrome in some. Marijuana smoke is irritating to the lung tissues and may be more damaging than cigarette smoke. There are four hundred chemicals in marijuana linked to lung cancer development. In

© Kuzma, 2012, Shutterstock, Inc.

The behavioral effects on marijuana users include an impairment of shortterm memory, an overestimation of the passage of time, and loss of the ability to focus on a task.

addition, the immune system and reproductive systems are damaged. There is an increase in birth defects among children whose mothers smoke marijuana during pregnancy. The biggest concern related to marijuana use is the perception that there is no risk or harm associated with occasional use. Other health risks include possible mental health decline and addiction.

Opioids

Derived from poppy seeds, **opium** is the base compound used for all narcotics. Opiates, which are narcotics, include opium and other drugs derived from opium, such as morphine, codeine, and heroin. Methadone is a synthetic chemical that has a morphine-like action, and also falls into this category of drugs.

Heroin

Heroin is considered a semi-synthetic narcotic because it is derived from a naturally occurring substance in the Oriental poppy plant called opium. It is a highly effective, fast-acting analgesic (painkiller) if injected when used medicinally; however, its benefits are outweighed by its risk of toxicity and high dependence rate. Heroin can be injected, snorted, or smoked. When heroin enters the brain it produces a dream-like euphoria (NIDA, 2010). Abuse is common because this drug creates a strong physical and psychological dependence and tolerance. Recently heroin has become more popular among young people. The risks of heroin use are increased due to the use of needles for injection. There is an increased likelihood of transmission of communicable diseases like HIV and hepatitis due to the practice of sharing needles. Although abrupt withdrawal from heroin is rarely fatal, the discomfort associated with going "cold turkey" is extremely intense.

Heroin users are at high risk for addiction. It is estimated that approximately 23% of heroin users become dependent. Anyone can become dependent, and life expectancy of the heroin addict who injects the drug intravenously is significantly lower than that of one who does not. Overdosing on heroin can result in death within minutes.

Stimulants

Caffeine

Caffeine is a stimulant as well as a psychotropic (mind affecting) drug. Caffeine is generally associated with coffee, tea, and cola, but can also be found in chocolate, cocoa, and other carbonated beverages (see Table 9.2), as well as some medications, both prescription and non-prescription, i.e., Excedrin®. Approximately 65–180 mg of caffeine are found in one cup of coffee, compared to tea, which contains 40–100 mg per cup, and cola, which contains 30–60 mg per twelve ounce serving. Caffeine is readily absorbed into the body and causes stimulation of the cerebral cortex and medullary centers in the brain, resulting in mental alertness.

Moderation is the key when using caffeine. Researchers agree that 300 mg of caffeine is considered moderate intake, which is equivalent to approximately three cups of coffee. Some individuals are more sensitive to caffeine than others and may feel the effects at smaller doses. According to research, caffeine in beverage form is not dehydrating, but if ingesting caffeine from food or tablets, be sure to rehydrate from the drug's diuretic action.

Excessive consumption of caffeine increases plasma levels of epinephrine, norepinephrine, and renin. It also can cause serious side effects, such as tremors, nervousness, irritability, headaches, hyperactivity, ar-

Moderation is the key when using caffeine.

TABLE 9.2 ♦ Caffeine Content of Selected Beverages

Drink	Ounces	Caffeine (mg)	mg/oz
5 Hour Energy	2	138	69.0
Amp	8.4	75	8.9
AriZona Green Tea Energy	16	200	12.5
Coca-Cola Classic	12	35	2.9
Coffee (Drip)	8	145	18.1
Coffee (Espresso)	1.5	77	51.3
Diet Coke	12	45	3.8
Diet Mountain Dew	12	55	4.6
Dr. Pepper	12	41	3.4
Full Throttle	16	144	9.0
Lipton Iced Teas	20	50	2.5
Mountain Dew	12	55	4.6
NOS	16	260	16.2
Red Bull	8.46	80	9.5
Rockstar	16	160	10.0
SoBe No Fear	16	174	10.9
Starbucks Double Shot	6.5	130	20.0
Starbucks Grande Coffee	16	330	20.6
Tea (Brewed)	8	47	5.9
VitaminWater Energy Citrus	20	42	2.1

Modified from Caffeine In Energy Drinks—How Much Caffeine Is In Your Energy Drink? www.ShapeFit.com

rhythmia, dizziness, and insomnia. It can elevate the blood pressure and body temperature, increase the breathing rate, irritate the stomach and bowels, and dehydrate the body.

A study by researchers at Duke University Medical Center shows that caffeine taken in the morning has effects on the body that persist until bedtime and amplifies stress throughout the day. In addition to the body's physiological response in blood pressure elevations and stress hormone levels, it also magnifies a person's perception of stress. According to this study, caffeine enhances the effects of stress and can make stress even more unhealthy (Lane, Pieper, Phillips-Butte, Bryant, and Kuhn, 2002).

Excessive amounts of caffeine may increase the incidence of premenstrual syndrome (PMS) in some women and may increase fibrocystic breast disease (noncancerous breast lumps) as well. The U.S. Surgeon General recommends that women avoid or restrict caffeine intake during pregnancy. Withdrawal symptoms from caffeine may include headaches, depression, drowsiness, nervousness, and a feeling of lethargy.

In 2006, more than five hundred new energy drinks were released on the market worldwide. College students have been known to use caffeinated products like these for extra energy when studying, driving long distances, or needing more energy in general. A common practice of mixing energy drinks and alcohol is of special concern. Drinking large amounts of caffeine (a stimulant) combined with large amounts of alcohol (a depressant) can cause people to misjudge their level of intoxication. The combination of drugs may mask symptoms such as headache, weakness, and muscle coordination, but in reality visual reaction time and motor coordination are still negatively affected by alcohol. Driving or making any other important decisions under these circumstances can be extremely dangerous.

How can I reduce my caffeine consumption?

- Keep a log of how much caffeine you consume daily
- Limit your consumption to 200–300 mg/daily
- Substitute herbal tea or decaf coffee
- Stop smoking— caffeine and smoking often go together
- Remember coffee does not help sober up after drinking (McKinley, 2005)

Cocaine

It is a naturally occurring psychoactive substance contained in the leaves of the South American coca plant. Crack cocaine, a rock-like crystalline form of cocaine made by combining cocaine hydrochloride with common baking soda, can be heated in the bowl of a pipe, enabling the vapors to be inhaled into the lungs. Cocaine is used occasionally as a topical anesthetic medicinally; however, more commonly it is inhaled (snorted), injected, or smoked illegally. The effects of cocaine use are rapid and short lived (from five to thirty minutes). Snorting enables only about 60 percent of the drug to be absorbed because the nasal vessels constrict immediately. Cocaine use causes dopamine and norepinephrine to be released into the brain, causing a feeling of euphoria and confidence; however, at the same time electrical impulses to the heart that regulate its rhythm are impaired. There is evidence that both psychological and physical dependence on cocaine occurs rapidly.

Today, the smoking of crack cocaine is more prevalent than inhalation. When smoked, the drug reaches the central nervous system immediately, affecting several neurotransmitters in the brain. The effects are short lived (usually around five to ten minutes), leaving the user with feelings of depression. Abuse of this drug can result in convulsions, seizures, respiratory distress, and sudden cardiac failure.

The relatively short-lived "high" from cocaine requires frequent use to maintain feelings of euphoria and is therefore quite costly for the addict. A single dose of crack sells for $30 or more, so to maintain a habit would cost hundreds of dollars a day. To pay for their habit, addicts will often turn to criminal activities such as dealing drugs, stealing, or prostitution. Crack houses are known for promoting the spread of HIV infection, and thousands of babies are born to crack-addicted mothers. These babies have severe physical and neurological problems, requiring significant medical attention. The cost of this drug is high, not just for the user, but for society as well.

Amphetamines

Amphetamines are drugs that speed up the nervous system. They do not occur naturally and must be manufactured in a laboratory. When used in moderation, amphetamines stimulate receptor sites for two naturally occurring neurotransmitters, having the effect of elevated mood, increased alertness, and feelings of well-being. In addition, the activity of the stomach and intestines may be slowed and appetite suppressed. When amphetamines are eliminated from the body, the user becomes fatigued. With abuse, the user will experience rapid tolerance and a strong psychological dependence, along with the possibility of impotence and episodes of psychosis. When use stops, the abuser may experience periods of depression.

Methamphetamines

An extremely addictive and powerful drug that stimulates the central nervous system is commonly known as "meth." In its smoked form, it is called "crystal," "crank," or "ice." It is chemically similar to amphetamines but much stronger. The effects from methamphetamine can last up to eight hours or in some cases even longer. It comes in many forms and can be injected, inhaled, orally ingested, or snorted.

Methamphetamine is considered to be the fastest growing drug in the United States. According to the director of the Substance Abuse and Mental Health Services Administration (SAMHSA), the growth and popularity of this drug is because of its wide availability, easy production, low cost, and highly addictive nature.

Methamphetamine is a psychostimulant but different than others like cocaine or amphetamine. Methamphetamine, like cocaine, results in an accumulation of dopamine. Dopamine is a neurotransmitter in regions of the brain that deal with emotion, movement, motivation, and pleasure. The large release of dopamine is presumed to help the drug's toxic effects on the brain. However, unlike cocaine, which is removed and metabolized quickly from the body, methamphetamine has a longer duration of action, which stays in the body and brain longer, leading to prolonged stimulant effects. Chronic methamphetamine abuse significantly changes the way the brain functions (NIDA, 2010).

Methamphetamine abusers may display symptoms that include violent behavior, confusion, hallucinations, and possible paranoid or delusional feelings, also causing severe personality shifts. These feelings of paranoia can lead to homicidal or suicidal thoughts or tendencies.

Methamphetamines are highly addictive and can be fatal with a single use. Deadly ingredients include antifreeze, drain cleaner, fertilizer, battery acid, or lantern fuel. The results when overused can cause heart failure and death. Long-term physical effects can lead to strokes, liver, kidney, and lung damage. Abuse can also lead to permanent and severe brain and psychological damage.

Club Drugs

MDMA

MDMA, also known as **ecstasy**, has a chemical structure similar to methamphetamines and mescaline, causing hallucinogenic effects. As a result, it can produce both stimulant and psychedelic effects. In addition to its euphoric effects, MDMA can lead to disruptions in body temperature and cardiovascular regulation causing panic, anxiety, and rapid heart rate. It also damages nerves in the brain's serotonin system and possibly produces long-term damage to brain areas that are critical for thought and memory (NIDA, 2010). Physical effects can include muscle tension, teeth clenching, nausea, blurred vision, and faintness. The psychological effects can include confusion, depression, sleep disorders, anxiety, and paranoia that can last long after taking the drug. It is most often available in tablet form and usually taken orally. Occasionally it is found in powder form and can be snorted or smoked, but it is rarely injected. An overdose can be lethal, especially when taken with alcohol or other drugs, for instance heroin ("H-bomb").

2C-B

This is a psychedelic drug synthesized by a chemist in 1974 and is considered both a psychedelic and a drug similar to MDMA. 2C-B is a white powder found in tablets or gel caps and is taken orally. The visual effects can be more intense than those created by LSD and can cause nausea, trembling, chills, and nervousness.

Rohypnol

Flunitrazepam is an illegal drug in the United States, but an approved medicine in other parts of the world where it is generally prescribed for sleep disorders. A 2-mg tablet is equal to the potency of a six-pack of beer. Rohypnol is a tranquilizer, similar to Valium, but ten times more potent, producing sedative effects including muscle relaxation, dizziness, memory loss, and blackouts. The effects occur twenty to thirty minutes after use and lasts for up to eight hours.

Rohypnol, more commonly known as "roofies," is a small, white, tasteless, pill that dissolves in food or drinks. It is most commonly used with other drugs, such as alcohol, ecstasy, heroin, and marijuana to enhance the feeling of the other drug. Although Rohypnol alone can be very dangerous, as well as physically addicting, when mixed with other drugs it can be fatal. It is also referred to as the "date rape" drug because there have been many reported cases of individuals giving Rohypnol to someone without their knowledge. The effects incapacitate the victim, and therefore they are unable to resist a sexual assault. It produces an "anterograde amnesia," meaning they may not remember events experienced while under effects of the drug (NIDA, 2010).

Gamma Hydroxybutyrate (GHB)

GHB is a fast-acting, powerful drug that depresses the nervous system. It occurs naturally in the body in small amounts.

Commonly taken with alcohol, it depresses the central nervous system and induces an intoxicated state. GHB is commonly consumed orally, usually as a clear liquid or a white powder. It is odorless, colorless, and slightly salty to taste. Effects from GHB can occur within fifteen to thirty minutes. Small doses (less than 1 g) of GHB act as a relaxant with larger doses causing strong feelings of relaxation, slowing heart rate, and respiration. There is a very fine line to cross to find a lethal dose, which can lead to seizures, respiratory distress, low blood pressure, and coma.

According to the Drug Abuse Warning Network, The Drug Induced Rape Prevention and Punishment Act of 1996 was enacted into federal law in response to the abuse of Rohypnol. This law makes it a crime to give someone a controlled substance without his/her knowledge and with the intent to commit a crime. The law also stiffens the penalties for possession and distribution of Rohypnol and GHB. Used in Europe as a general anesthetic and treatment for insomnia, GHB is growing in popularity and is widely available underground. Manufactured by non-professional "kitchen" chemists, concerns about quality and purity should be considered.

Dissociative Drugs

Ketamine Hydrochloride

"Special K" or "K" was originally created for use in a medical setting on humans and animals. Ninety percent is legally sold for veterinary use. Ketamine usually comes in liquid form and is cooked into a white powder for snorting. Higher doses produce a hallucinogenic effect and may cause the user to feel far away from their body. This is called a "K-hole" and has been compared to near-death experiences. Low doses can increase heart rate and numbness in the extremities with higher doses depressing consciousness and breathing. This makes it extremely dangerous if combined with other depressants such as alcohol or GHB.

Phencyclidine Hydrochloride

Also known as PCP or angel dust, phencyclidine hydrochloride is sometimes considered a hallucinogen, although it does not easily fit into any category. First synthesized in 1959, it is used intravenously and as an anesthetic that blocks pain without producing numbness. Taken in small doses, it causes feelings of euphoria. The harmful side effects include depression, anxiety, confusion, and delirium. High doses of PCP cause mental confusion, hallucinations, and can cause serious mental illness and extreme aggressive and violent behavior, including murder.

Hallucinogens

Hallucinogens, also called psychedelics, are drugs that affect perception, sensation, awareness, and emotion. Changes in time and space and hallucinations may be mild or extreme depending on the dose, and may vary on every occasion. There are many synthetic as well as natural hallucinogens in use.

Synthetic groups include LSD, which is the most potent; mescaline, which is derived from the peyote cactus, and psilocybin, derived from mushrooms, have similar effects.

Lysergic Acid Diethylamide (LSD)

LSD is a colorless, odorless, and tasteless liquid that is made from lysergic acid, which comes from the ergot fungus. It was first converted to lysergic acid diethylamide (LSD) in 1938. In 1943, its psychoactive properties accidentally became known (NIDA, 2009).

Hallucinations and illusions often occur, and effects vary according to the dosage, personality of the user, and conditions under which the drug is used. A flashback is a recurrence of some hallucinations from a previous LSD experience days or months after the dose. Flashbacks can occur without reason, occurring to heavy users more frequently. After taking LSD, a person loses control over normal thought process. Street LSD is often mixed with other substances and its effects are quite uncertain (NIDA, 2009).

Other Drugs

Inhalants are poisonous chemical gases, fumes, or vapors that produce psychoactive effects when sniffed. When inhaled, the fumes take away the body's ability to absorb oxygen. Inhalants are considered delerients, which can cause permanent damage to the heart, brain, lungs, and liver. Common inhalants include model glue, acetone, gasoline, kerosene, nail polish, aerosol sprays, Pam™ cooking spray, Scotchgard™ fabric protectant, lighter fluids, butane, and cleaning fluids, as well as nitrous oxide (laughing gas). These products were not created to be inhaled or ingested. They were designed to dissolve things or break things down, which is exactly what they do to the body.

Inhalants reach the lungs, bloodstream, and other parts of the body very quickly. Intoxication can occur in as little as five minutes and can last as long as nine hours. Inhaled lighter fluid/butane displaces the oxygen in the lungs, causing suffocation. Even a single episode can cause asphyxiation or cardiac arrhythmia and possibly lead to death.

The initial effects of inhalants are similar to those of alcohol, but they are very unpredictable. Some effects include dizziness and blurred vision, involuntary eye movement, poor coordination, involuntary extremity movement, slurred speech, euphoric feeling, nosebleeds, and possible coma.

Health risks involved with the use of inhalants may include hepatitis, liver and/or kidney failure, as well as the destruction of bone marrow and skeletal muscles. Respiratory impairment and blood abnormalities, along with irregular heartbeat and/or heart failure, are also serious side effects of inhalants. Regular use can lead to tolerance, the need for more powerful drugs, and addiction (NIDA, 2011).

Anabolic Steroids

Anabolic androgenic steroids are man-made and very similar to male sex hormones. The word *anabolic* means "muscle building," and *androgenic* refers to masculine. Legally, steroids are prescribed to individuals to treat problems occurring when the body produces abnormally low amounts of testosterone and problems associated with delayed puberty or impotence. Other cases for prescribed steroids use would involve individuals with whom a disease has resulted in a loss of muscle mass (NIDA, 2005).

Although steroids are a banned substance in all professional and collegiate sports, most people who use steroids do so to enhance physical performance in sports or other activities. Some choose to use steroids to improve physical appearance or to increase muscle size and to reduce body fat. Some steroids can be taken orally or injected into the muscle. There are also some forms of steroid creams and gels that are to be rubbed into the skin. Most doses taken by abusers are ten to one hundred times the potency of normal doses used for medicinal purposes.

Consequences from steroid abuse can cause some serious health issues. There can be some problems with the normal hormone production in the individual, which can be very severe and irreversible. Major side effects of steroid abuse can lead to cardiovascular disease, high blood pressure, and stroke because it increases the LDL cholesterol levels while decreasing the HDL levels. There can also be liver damage, muscular and ligament damage, as well as stunted bone growth. In addition to these problems, the side effects for males can be shrinkage of the testes and a reduction in sperm count. For females, steroid use can cause facial hair growth and the cessation of the menstrual cycle.

Research also suggests some psychological and behavioral changes. Steroid abusers can become very aggressive and violent and have severe mood swings. Users are reported to have paranoid and jealous tendencies along with irritability and impaired judgment. Depression has also been linked to steroid use once the individual stops taking the drug, therefore leading to continued use. This depressed state can lead to serious consequences, and in some cases it has been reported to lead to suicidal thoughts (NIDA, 2005).

Some of the most commonly abused prescription drugs are pain killers such as morphine, codeine, Oxycodone, Vicodin, and Demerol.

Prescription Drugs

According to the National Institute on Drug Abuse (NIDA), approximately 16 million Americans misuse and abuse prescription drugs for non-medicinal purposes. To add to the severity of the problem, many of those who abuse prescription drugs abuse alcohol and other drugs as well (NIDA, 2009).

It is not that these drugs should not be used for the purpose intended, as "they have an important place in the treatment of debilitating conditions," says Richard Brown, M.D., associate professor at the University of Wisconsin (FDA, 2005). It is generally uncommon for addiction to occur to patients using the drug as prescribed. It is the individuals abusing and misusing these drugs that can lead to problems. Some of these problems occur because prescription drugs are received through false prescriptions, over-prescribing, and pharmacy theft. Sometimes problems arise because there is a lack of communication or information provided to the patient (FDA, 2005).

Opioid Pain Relievers

Hydrocodone

Hydrocodone is a narcotic used to relieve pain and suppress cough. This drug, which can lead to both physiological and psychological dependence, saw a dramatic increase in legal sales between 1991 and 2010 with prescriptions topping 100 million (NIDA, 2011).

Morphine

This is the main alkaloid found in opium. It is ten times stronger than opium and brings quick relief from pain. It is most effectively used as an anesthetic during heart surgery, to relieve pain in post-operative patients, and sometimes used to relieve pain for cancer patients.

Codeine

A natural derivative of opium. Codeine is medically used as a mild painkiller or a cough suppressant. Although widely used, there is potential for physical dependence.

Oxycodone

Oxycodone, a drug used for moderate to severe pain relief, has a high potential for abuse. Tablets should be take orally, but when crushed and injected intravenously or snorted, a potentially lethal dose is released (FDA, 2004).

Stimulants

According to recent reports from the FDA, a highly abused stimulant among middle and high school students is methylphenidate, commonly known as **Ritalin.** This drug is more powerful than caffeine but not as potent as amphetamines and is prescribed for individuals with attention-deficit/hyperactivity disorders, ADHD, and sometimes to treat narcolepsy. Researchers speculate that Ritalin increases the slow and steady release of dopamine, therefore improving attention and focus for those in need of the increase. "Individuals abuse Ritalin to lose weight, increase alertness and experience the euphoric feelings resulting from high doses" (U.S. Dept. of Justice, 2006). When abused, the tablets are either taken orally or crushed and snorted; some even dissolve the tablets in water and inject the mixture. Addiction occurs when it induces large and fast increases of dopamine in the brain (DOJ, 2006).

Adderall is another stimulant used to treat ADHD as well as narcolepsy. Physical and psychological dependence may occur with this drug. Symptoms of Adderall overdose include dizziness, blurred vision, restlessness, rapid breathing, confusion, hallucinations, nausea, vomiting, irregular heartbeat, and seizures.

Depressants

Depressants are sedatives or anxiolytic (anti-anxiety) drugs that depress the central nervous system. Benzodiazepines such as Valium and Xanax and barbituates like Nembutal, Secobarbital, and Phenobarbibtal can be prescribed to relieve tension, induce relaxation and sleep, or treat panic attacks. All of these differ in action, absorption, and metabolism, but all produce similar intoxication and withdrawal symptoms.

Depressants can produce both a physical and psychological dependence within two to four weeks. Those with a prior history of abuse are at greater risk of abusing sedatives, even if prescribed by a physician. If there is no previous substance abuse history, one rarely develops problems if prescribed and monitored by a physician. Depressants can be very dangerous, if not lethal, if used in combination with alcohol, leading to respiratory depression, respiratory arrest, and death.

Some of the physiological effects of depressants include drowsiness, impaired judgment, poor coordination, slowed breathing, confusion, weak and rapid heartbeat, relaxed muscles, and pain relief.

A major health risk associated with the use of depressants is the development of a dependence to the drug, leading to serious side effects, such as stupors, coma, and death.

Prescription Drug Conclusion

The danger from prescription and over-the-counter drugs is often underestimated by students. Many assume that if the drug is legal and prescribed by a physician, even if for someone else, it must be safe. However, what they fail to realize is that medications and dosages are tailored to each patient and may not be appropriate in the manner they intend to use them.

For more information:

National Institutes of Health
www.nih.gov

Web of Addictions
www.well.com/user/woa.

Substance Abuse and Mental Health
Services Administration
www.samhsa.gov

National Institute on Drug Abuse
www.nida.gov

Ethical Considerations of Illicit Prescription Use

Gabriel Neal, MD

The rise in the diagnosis of cognitive deficits such as Attention Deficit and Hyperactivity Disorder over the past two decades has resulted in more students being treated with prescription nootropics (medications that improve cognitive function). Although safely treating deficient cognitive function does not raise ethical concern, the use of the same medications to improve normal cognitive function does, and the rise in use of prescription nootropics is getting the attention of high school and college administrators and faculty. Recent surveys suggest that 6–16% of college students are using prescription nootropics illicitly at some point during their studies.[i, ii] These studies demonstrated that while Ritalin and Adderall were the prescription drugs of choice, they were also used both for studying and partying. Students who used prescription medications illicitly were more likely to engage in illegal drugs such as marijuana and cocaine as well.

The illicit use of nootropic medications raises ethical concern in the areas of authenticity (the degree to which a student may take credit for work done) and fairness in the classroom. The argument for lesser authenticity is the claim that the more one is enhanced, the less credit one can receive. Could one use a calculator and still take credit for work? What if only a pencil and paper were used? The line between significant and insignificant enhancement is not perfectly clear. A response to the challenge of authenticity is that even with the use of nootropics, some level of study and hard work is still required, which could authenticate the achievement.

A student who uses Adderall to enhance her studying may be able to argue that her ideas are still authentically hers, but it remains to be answered whether it is fair that she use Adderall while other students are denied access to it. The magnitude of the enhancement becomes important. In competitive arenas such as the classroom, rules are created to keep out advantages that are of improper magnitude. Consider the use of caffeine. Although caffeine can heighten alertness, no one complains to the professor if they see someone drinking some coffee before an exam. The reason for this is that caffeine does not confer cognitive benefit of such magnitude that anyone thinks it is unfair to use it in class, and caffeine is accessible to any student. But as better, more potent enhancers such as Adderall emerge, the rules to ensure fairness may need to be updated. Some have suggested that those using prescription enhancers disclose it when submitting academic work.[iii] How professors would grade work differently remains to be seen.

While no one wishes to keep students with legitimate cognitive deficits from receiving proper treatment, students should be concerned about the unfair advantage that illicit use of prescription nootropics offers their classmates; and for those students engaged in illicit use of prescription nootropics, they would do well to consider whether they are cheating themselves out of authentic work and others out of a proper grade.

[i] McCabe, S.E."Non-Medical Use of Prescription Stimulants among US College Students: Prevalence and Correlates from a National Survey." *Addiction* 100, January (2005): 96–106.

[ii] Prudhomme White, B., Becker-Blease, K., Grace-Bishop, K. "Stimulant Medication Use, Misuse, and Abuse in an Undergraduate and Graduate Student Sample." *Journal of American College Health* 54, no. 5 (2006): 261–268.

[iii] Farah, M.J., Illes, J., Cook-Deegan, R., Gardner, H., Kandel, E., King P. et al. "Neurocognitive Enhancement: what can we do and what should we do about it?" *Nature Reviews: Neuroscience* 5, May (2004): 421–425.

Source: *Gabriel A. Neal, M.D., Family Medical Practice: Obstestrics, St. Joseph Regional Health Center, Bryan, TX*

FDA Guidelines on How to Use Prescription Drugs Safely:
- Always follow medication directions
- Do not increase or decrease doses without consulting your physician
- Do not stop taking medication on your own
- Do not crush or break pills
- Be clear about the drug's effect on driving and other tasks
- Know the drug's potential interactions with alcohol and other drugs
- Inform your doctor if you have had past problems with substance abuse
- Do not use others' prescription medications, and do not share yours.

References

American Heart Association (AHA). *Annual Report*. 2006.

Center on Addiction and Substance Abuse at Columbia University. Commission on Substances Abuse at Colleges and Universities.

Centers for Disease Control and Prevention. *Behavioral Risk Factor Surveillance System*, 2010.

Centers for Disease Control and Prevention. *National Health Interview Survey*, 2010.

Centers for Disease Control and Prevention. *Smokeless Tobacco*, 2009 and 2010.

Centers for Disease Control and Prevention. *Second Hand Smoke*, 2012.

Department of Justice. National Drug Intelligence Center. Ritalin Fast Facts, 2006.

Everett, S. A., Lowry, R., Cohen, L. R., Dellinger, A. M. Unsafe motor vehicle practices among substance-using college students. *Accident Analysis,* 1999.

Ewing, J. Detecting Alcoholism: the CAGE Questionnaire. *Journal of the American Medical Association,* 1984.

Dennis, M. E. and the Texas Commission on Alcohol and Drug Abuse. *Instructor Manual, Alcohol Education Program for Minors*. Austin: TCADA. 2005.

Herman, A., et al. In an ongoing search to understand the mechanisms of fetal alcohol syndrome. National Institute on Alcohol Abuse and Alcoholism, 2003.

Hoeger, W. and Hoeger, S. *Principles and Labs for Fitness and Wellness* (5th ed). Englewood, CO: Morton Publishing Company. 1999.

Journal of the American Medical Association. Moderate alcohol intake and lower risk of coronary heart disease, 1994.

Journal of the American Medical Association. Lifetime alcohol consumption and breast cancer risk among postmenopausal women in Los Angeles, 1995.

Lane, J., Pieper, C., Phillips-Butte, B, Bryant, J., and Kuhn, C. Caffeine's Effects Are Long-Lasting and Compound Stress. *Psychosomatic Medicine*. National Institutes of Health, July /August, 2002.

McCusker, R., Goldberger, B., and Cone, E. The Content of Energy Drinks, Carbonated Sodas, and Other Beverages. *Journal of Analytical Toxicology*, Vol. 30, March 2006.

McKinley Health Center. University of Illinois at Urbana-Champaign, 2005.

Miller, W., Tonigan, J., Longabaugh, R. Drinking Inventory of Consequences. An instrument for assessing adverse consequences of alcohol abuse. Test manual. Rockville, MD: National Institute on Alcohol Abuse and Alcoholism, 1995.

Miller, E. K., Erickson, C. A., & Desimone, R. Neural mechanisms of visual working memory in prefrontal cortex of the macaque. *Journal of Neuroscience,* 1996.

National Cancer Institute, U.S National Institutes of Health, 2008.

National Highway Traffic and Safety Administration (NHTSA). *Annual Report.* 2010.

National Institute on Alcohol Abuse and Alcoholism. National Institutes of Health. Statistic Snapshot of College Drinking, 2010.

National Institute on Alcohol Abuse and Alcoholism (NIAAA). College Drinking— Changing the Culture. "A Snapshot of Annual High-Risk College Drinking Consequences." 2010.

National Institute on Alcohol Abuse and Alcoholism. National Institutes of Health. Integrative Genetic Analysis Of Alcohol Dependence Using the Genenetwork Web Resources, 2008.

National Institute of Drug Abuse (NIDA). U.S. Dept. of Health and Human Services, 2008.

National Institute on Drug Abuse. The Science of Drug Abuse & Addiction. NIDA Info Facts: Hallucinogens, 2010.

National Institute on Drug Abuse. The Science of Drug Abuse & Addiction. NIDA Info Facts: Anabolic Steroids, 2010.

National Institute of Drug Abuse (NIDA). Update on Ecstacy. *NIDA Notes,* Volume 16, Number 5, Dec. 2001.

National Traffic Safety Administration. Traffic Safety Facts. Annual Assessment of Alcohol Related Fatalities, 2012.

Ray, O. and Ksir, C. *Drugs, Society, and Human Behavior* (8th ed). New York: WCB McGraw-Hill. 1999.

SAMHSA, National Clearinghouse for Alcohol and Drug Abuse; www.health.org

Centers for Disease Control and Prevention (CDC). Smoking and Tobacco Use. Fast Facts. Atlanta: Author. 2006.

U.S. Food and Drug Administration. Prescription Drug Use and Abuse: Complexities of Addiction, 2005.

U.S. Food and Drug Administration. Oxycodone. FDA Statement. Statement on Generic Oxycodone Hydrochloride Extended Release Tablets, 2004.

U.S. Food and Drug Administration, Department of Health and Human Services. FDA Issues Regulation Prohibiting Sale of Dietary Supplements Containing Ephedrine Alkaloids and Reiterates Its Advice That Consumers Stop Using These Products, 2005.

World Health Organization (WHO). *Waterpipe Tobacco Smoking: Health Effects, Research Needs and Recommended Actions by Regulators.* Geneva: Author. 2005.

Activities

In-Class Activities
The Physical Effects of Smoking

Notebook Activities
Are You Addicted to Nicotine?
"Why Do You Smoke?" Test
"Do You Want to Quit?" Test
Addictive Behavior Questionnaire
Alcohol Screening Self-Assessment
Making Changes

Name _____ Section_____ Date_____

The Physical Effects of Smoking

This test consists of twenty statements about the effects of smoking. Put a check to show whether you think each statement is true or false. If you don't know whether a statement is true or false, put a check under "Don't know."

	True	False	Don't Know
1. Smoking low-tar and low-nicotine cigarettes reduces the risk of all smoking-related diseases.	_____	_____	_____
2. Carbon monoxide is inhaled when a person smokes.	_____	_____	_____
3. How deeply a smoker inhales is not related to his or her chance of developing lung cancer.	_____	_____	_____
4. Most experts agree that the harmful effects of smoking on health are not as great for women as for men.	_____	_____	_____
5. Cigarette smoking increases the risk of developing breathing problems.	_____	_____	_____
6. Cigarette smoke can increase air pollution in homes and offices.	_____	_____	_____
7. Cigarette smoking increases the health dangers associated with taking birth control pills.	_____	_____	_____
8. Frequent pipe and cigar smokers are more likely than nonsmokers to develop lung cancer.	_____	_____	_____
9. The average life expectancy of a smoker is the same as that of a non-smoker.	_____	_____	_____
10. People who smoke filter cigarettes inhale less carbon monoxide than do people who smoke nonfilter cigarettes.	_____	_____	_____
11. Most people gain weight when they quit smoking.	_____	_____	_____
12. Smokers have an increased risk of developing a lung infection after an operation.	_____	_____	_____
13. Smoking during pregnancy does not increase a baby's risk of death.	_____	_____	_____
14. Pipe smokers have a greater risk of developing cancer of the mouth than do cigarette smokers.	_____	_____	_____
15. Smoking causes the heart to beat more slowly.	_____	_____	_____
16. The health risks due to smoking do not change even after a person stops smoking.	_____	_____	_____
17. The more a person smokes, the greater the chance of developing heart disease.	_____	_____	_____
18. Cigarette smoke in the air can cause eye soreness in nonsmokers.	_____	_____	_____
19. On average, babies born to mothers who smoke during pregnancy are smaller than babies born to nonsmokers.	_____	_____	_____
20. Nicotine does not cause dependence similar to other addictive drugs.	_____	_____	_____

Source: U.S. Department of Health and Human Services.

Answers
1 F; 2 T; 3 F; 4 F; S T; 6 T; 7 T; 8 T; 9 F; 10 F; 11 T; 12 T; 13 F; 14 T; 15 F; 16 F; 17 T; 18 T; 19 T; 20 F

Name _____ Section_____ Date_____

Are You Addicted to Nicotine?

Answer the following questions as honestly as you can by placing a checkmark in the appropriate column:

	Yes	No
1. Do you smoke every day?		
2. Do you smoke because of shyness and to build self-confidence?		
3. Do you smoke to escape from boredom and worries or while under pressure?		
4. Have you ever burned a hole in your clothes, carpet, furniture, or car with a cigarette?		
5. Have you ever had to go to the store late at night or at another inconvenient time because you were out of cigarettes?		
6. Do you feel defensive or angry when people tell you that your smoke is bothering them?		
7. Has a doctor or dentist ever suggested that you stop smoking?		
8. Have you ever promised someone that you would stop smoking, then broken your promise?		
9. Have you ever felt physical or emotional discomfort when trying to quit?		
10. Have you ever successfully stopped smoking for a period of time, only to start again?		
11. Do you buy extra supplies of tobacco to make sure you won't run out?		
12. Do you find it difficult to imagine life without smoking?		
13. Do you choose only those activities and entertainments during which you can smoke?		
14. Do you prefer, seek out, or feel more comfortable in the company of smokers?		
15. Do you inwardly despise or feel ashamed of yourself because of your smoking?		
16. Do you ever find yourself lighting up without having consciously decided to?		
17. Has your smoking ever caused trouble at home or in a relationship?		
18. Do you ever tell yourself that you can stop smoking whenever you want to?		
19. Have you ever felt that your life would be better if you didn't smoke?		
20. Do you continue to smoke even though you are aware of the health hazards posed by smoking?		

If you answered Yes to one or two of these questions, there's a chance that you are addicted or are becoming addicted to nicotine. If you answered Yes to three or more of these questions, you are probably already addicted to nicotine.

Source: Reprinted by permission of Nicotine Anonymous World Service. www.nicotine-anonymous.org. P.O. Box 126338, Harrisburg, PA 17112-6338. 415-750-0328.

NOTEBOOK ACTIVITY

"Why Do You Smoke?" Test

		Always	Frequently	Occasionally	Seldom	Never
A.	I smoke cigarettes to keep myself from slowing down.	5	4	3	2	1
B.	Handling a cigarette is part of the enjoyment of smoking it.	5	4	3	2	1
C.	Smoking cigarettes is pleasant and relaxing.	5	4	3	2	1
D.	I light up a cigarette when I feel angry about something.	5	4	3	2	1
E.	When I have run out of cigarettes, I find it almost unbearable until I can get them.	5	4	3	2	1
F.	I smoke cigarettes automatically without even being aware of it.	5	4	3	2	1
G.	I smoke cigarettes for the stimulation, to perk myself up.	5	4	3	2	1
H.	Part of the enjoyment of smoking a cigarette comes from the steps I take to light up.	5	4	3	2	1
I.	I find cigarettes pleasurable.	5	4	3	2	1
J.	When I feel uncomfortable or upset about something, I light up a cigarette.	5	4	3	2	1
K.	I am very much aware of the fact when I am not smoking a cigarette.	5	4	3	2	1
L.	I light up a cigarette without realizing I still have one burning in the ashtray.	5	4	3	2	1
M.	I smoke cigarettes to give me a "lift."	5	4	3	2	1
N.	When I smoke a cigarette, part of the enjoyment is watching the smoke as I exhale it.	5	4	3	2	1
O.	I want a cigarette most when I am comfortable and relaxed.	5	4	3	2	1
P.	When I feel "blue" or want to take my mind off cares and worries, I smoke cigarettes.	5	4	3	2	1
Q.	I get a real gnawing hunger for a cigarette when I haven't smoked for a while.	5	4	3	2	1
R.	I've found a cigarette in my mouth and didn't remember putting it there.	5	4	3	2	1

Source: U.S. Department of Health and Human Services.

Scoring Your Test

Enter the numbers you have circled on the test questions in the spaces provided below, putting the number you circled for question A on line A, for question B on line B, etc. Add the three scores on each line to get a total for each factor. For example, the sum of your scores for lines A, G, and M gives you your score on "Stimulation," lines B, H, and N give the score on "Handling," etc. Scores can vary from 3 to 15. Any score 11 and above is high; any score 7 and below is low.

A _____ + G _____ + M _____ = _____ Stimulation

B _____ + H _____ + N _____ = _____ Handling

C _____ + I _____ + O _____ = _____ Pleasure/Relaxation

D _____ + J _____ + P _____ = _____ Crutch: Tension Reduction

E _____ + K _____ + Q _____ = _____ Craving: Psychological Addiction

F _____ + L _____ + R _____ = _____ Habit

"Do You Want to Quit?" Test

		Strongly Agree	Mildly Agree	Mildly Disagree	Strongly Disagree
A.	Cigarette smoking might give me a serious illness.				
B.	My cigarette smoking sets a bad example for others.				
C.	I find cigarette smoking to be a messy kind of habit.				
D.	Controlling my cigarette smoking is a challenge to me.				
E.	Smoking causes shortness of breath.				
F.	If I quit smoking cigarettes, it might influence others to stop.				
G.	Cigarettes damage clothing and other personal property.				
H.	Quitting smoking would show that I have willpower.				
I.	My cigarette smoking will have a harmful effect on my health.				
J.	My cigarette smoking influences others close to me to take up or continue smoking.				
K.	If I quit smoking, my sense of taste or smell would improve.				
L.	I do not like the idea of feeling dependent on smoking.				

Scoring Your Test

Write the number you have circled after each statement on the test in the corresponding space to the right. Add the scores on each line to get your totals. For example, the sum of your scores A, E, I gives you your score for the Health factor. Scores can vary from 3 to 12. Any score of 9 or over is high, and a score of 6 or under is low.

A _____ + E _____ + I _____ = _____ Health

B _____ + F _____ + J _____ = _____ Example

C _____ + G _____ + K _____ = _____ Aesthetics

D _____ + H _____ + L _____ = _____ Mastery

Source: U.S. Department of Health and Human Services.

NOTEBOOK ACTIVITY

Addictive Behavior Questionnaire

Could You Be an Addict?

I. Recognizing Addictive Behavior*

Instructions. The following test, designed by Dr. Lawrence J. Hatterer, is not a way to diagnose whether you are in the early, middle, or chronic stages of addictive disease. It is meant merely to help you understand addictive behavior better so you can recognize it in yourself or perhaps in people you know.

1. I am a person of excesses. I can't regulate what I do for pleasure and often use a substance or indulge in an activity heavily to get high.
2. I am an extremely self-involved person. People tell me I am into myself too much.
3. I am compulsive. I must have what I want when I want it, regardless of the consequences.
4. I am excessively dependent on or independent of others.
5. I am preoccupied. I spend a lot of time thinking or fantasizing about a particular activity or substance. Also, I will work my day around doing it or go to pains to make sure it's available.
6. I deny that I do this and lie about it to others who ask me.
7. I have been involved in this behavior for a least a year.
8. I've told myself I could easily stop, even though I've shown no signs of slowing down.
9. Once I start indulging in this behavior or substance, I find I have trouble stopping.
10. One or more members of my family are also involved in some kind of excessive behavior or substance abuse.
11. I find I gravitate mostly toward people who have the same behavior or take the same substance as I do.
12. I seem to be developing a tolerance of the behavior or substance. I have had a need to steadily increase the amounts I take or the time I spend doing it.
13. I have found that my excessive use of highs has, in fact, only made my problems worse.
14. If someone tries to keep me from obtaining the substance or practicing the activity, I get angry and reject or abuse that person.
15. I experience withdrawal symptoms if I cannot indulge in the substance or activity.
16. This has gotten in the way of my functioning. I have missed something important—days at work or time with my friends, family, children—because of it.
17. The substance/activity is destroying my home life. I know I am hurting those closest to me.
18. I have failed in many goals in life, lost money, given up many social and occupational contracts, all because of my excessive behavior.
19. I have tried to stop or cut down on my excesses but have been unsuccessful.
20. I have physically endangered myself or others in accidents that were a direct result of my excessive behavior.

Evaluation: If you answer "yes" to half or more of the questions, you may have a problem with addictive disease and should seek immediate professional help. For a referral, contact your local mental health clinic (look in the Yellow Pages) or speak to your doctor.

Source: From *McCall's* magazine, 1986.

II. Stage of Change for Addictive Behavior

If chemical dependency is a problem in your life, use Figure 2.4 (page 41) and Table 2.3 (page 41) to identify your current stage of change for participation in a treatment program for addictive behavior.

III. Changing Addictive Behavior

On a separate sheet of paper indicate the steps that you are going to take to correct addictive behavior(s) and identify people or organizations that you will contact to help you get started.

NOTEBOOK ACTIVITY

Alcohol Screening Self-Assessment

This self-assessment tool is designed to assist you in understanding your use of alcohol.

The following ten questions pertain to your use of alcoholic beverages during the past year. Check your answers and record the score (the number next to each choice) for each question. In the questions, a "drink" is equal to 10 oz. of beer, 4 oz. of wine, or 1.25 oz. of 80 proof liquor.

1. How often do you have a drink containing alcohol?

    _____ Never (0)

    _____ Monthly or less (1)

    _____ 2 to 4 times a month (2)

    _____ 2 to 3 times a week (3)

    _____ 4 or more times a week (4)

2. How many drinks containing alcohol do you have on a typical day when you are drinking?

    _____ Never (0)

    _____ 1 or 2 (1)

    _____ 3 or 4 (2)

    _____ 5 or 6 (3)

    _____ 7 to 9 (4)

    _____ 10 or more (5)

3. How often do you have six or more drinks on one occasion?

    _____ Never (0)

    _____ Less than monthly (1)

    _____ Monthly (2)

    _____ Weekly (3)

    _____ Daily or almost daily (4)

4. How often during the last year have you found that you were unable to stop drinking once you had started?

    _____ Never (0)

    _____ Less than monthly (1)

    _____ Monthly (2)

    _____ Weekly (3)

    _____ Daily or almost daily (4)

5. How often during the last year have you failed to do what was normally expected from you because of drinking?

    _____ Never (0)

    _____ Less than monthly (1)

    _____ Monthly (2)

    _____ Weekly (3)

    _____ Daily or almost daily (4)

Source: Courtesy of the World Health Organization.

6. How often during the last year have you needed a drink first thing in the morning to get yourself going after a heavy drinking session?

_____ Never (0)

_____ Less than monthly (1)

_____ Monthly (2)

_____ Weekly (3)

_____ Daily or almost daily (4)

7. How often during the last year have you had a feeling of guilt or remorse after drinking?

_____ Never (0)

_____ Less than monthly (1)

_____ Monthly (2)

_____ Weekly (3)

_____ Daily or almost daily (4)

8. How often during the last year have you been unable to remember what happened the night before because you had been drinking?

_____ Never (0)

_____ Less than monthly (1)

_____ Monthly (2)

_____ Weekly (3)

_____ Daily or almost daily (4)

9. Have you or someone else been injured as the result of your drinking?

_____ Never (0)

_____ Less than monthly (1)

_____ Monthly (2)

_____ Weekly (3)

_____ Daily or almost daily (4)

10. Has a relative, friend, or a doctor or other health worker been concerned about your drinking or suggested you cut down?

_____ Never (0)

_____ Less than monthly (1)

_____ Monthly (2)

_____ Weekly (3)

_____ Daily or almost daily (4)

Scoring and Interpretation

Determine your total score by adding up the scores for all ten questions. A score of eight or more indicates that a harmful level of alcohol consumption is likely and that you should seek help.

About This Instrument

This self-assessment tool is the Alcohol Use Disorders Identification Test (AUDIT) developed by the World Health Organization and tested in a world-wide trial.

NOTEBOOK ACTIVITY

Making Changes

Breaking the Habit

Here's a six-point program to help you or someone you love quit smoking. (Caution: Don't undertake the quit-smoking program until you have a two- to four-week period of relatively unstressful work and study schedules or social commitments.)

1. *Identify your smoking habits.* Keep a daily diary (a piece of paper wrapped around your cigarette pack with a rubber band will do) and record the time you smoke, the activity associated with smoking (after breakfast, in the car), and your urge for a cigarette (desperate, pleasant, or automatic). For the first week or two, don't bother trying to cut down; just use the diary to learn the conditions under which you smoke.

2. *Get support.* It can be tough to go it alone. Phone your local chapter of the American Cancer Society, or otherwise get the names of some ex-smokers who can give you support.

3. *Begin by tapering off.* For a period of one to four weeks, aim at cutting down to, say, twelve or fifteen cigarettes a day; or change to a lower-nicotine brand, and concentrate on not increasing the number of cigarettes you smoke. As indicated by your diary, begin by cutting out those cigarettes you smoke automatically. In addition, restrict the times you allow yourself to smoke. Throughout this period, stay in touch, once a day or every few days, with your ex-smoker friend(s) to discuss your problems.

4. *Set a quit date.* At some point during the tapering-off period, announce to everyone—friends, family, and ex-smokers—when you're going to quit. Do it with flair. Announce it to coincide with a significant date, such as your birthday or anniversary.

5. *Stop.* A week before Q-day, smoke only five cigarettes a day. Begin late in the day, say after 4:00 p.m. Smoke the first two cigarettes in close succession. Then, in the evening, smoke the last three, also in close succession, about fifteen minutes apart. Focus on the negative aspects of cigarettes, such as the rawness in your throat and lungs. After seven days, quit and give yourself a big reward on that day, such as a movie or a fantastic meal or new clothes.

6. *Follow-up.* Stay in touch with your ex-smoker friend(s) during the following two weeks, particularly if anything stressful or tense occurs that might trigger a return to smoking. Think of the person you're becoming—the very person cigarette ads would have you believe smoking makes you. Now that you're quitting smoking, you're becoming healthier, sexier, more sophisticated, more mature, and better looking—and you've earned it!

Sources: American Cancer Society; National Cancer Institute.

Chapter 10
Safety Awareness

© Andresr, 2012. Shutterstock, Inc.

OBJECTIVES

Students will be able to:

- Identify the four classes of unintentional injuries.
- Identify risks associated with drowsy driving.
- Identify the steps in disaster planning.
- Identify elements of a crime.
- Become aware of the prevalence of acquaintance rape.
- Become aware of the prevalence of family violence.

"This above all, to refuse to be a victim."

—*Margaret Atwood*

The purpose of this chapter is to provide information to help students make informed choices on personal safety and awareness issues. Being aware of possible hazardous situations may prevent injuries from occurring and save lives.

The National Safety Council (NSC) defines an accident as "that occurrence in a sequence of events which usually produces unintended injury, death, or property damage" (Bever, 1995). Accidents are the fifth leading cause of death in the United States after heart disease, cancer, stroke, and chronic obstructive pulmonary diseases. For people between the ages of 1 and 39, unintentional injuries are the leading cause of death. In the United States in 2009, there were 128,200 deaths due to unintentional injuries and over 26,200,000 disabling injuries.

In the United States alone, we average 15 unintentional injury deaths and 4,440 medically consulted injuries every hour (NSC, 2011).

Classes of Unintentional Injuries

Motor Vehicle Safety

The leading cause of unintentional death is motor vehicle crashes. In 2009, over 35,900 individuals died in motor vehicle crashes in the United States. The 15–24 year-old age group had nearly 8,000 deaths for that year (NSC, 2011).

One of the leading factors in motor vehicle crashes is driver inattention. According to the National Highway Traffic Safety Administration (NHTSA), nearly 80 percent of crashes involve some form of driver inattention. This signifies the importance of the driving task and that the need for attention is critical (NHTSA, 2010).

> "We are taking action on a number of fronts to address the epidemic of distracted driving in America."
> –*Ray LaHood*
> *Transporation Secretary*
> *Distracted Driving Summit September, 2010*

Distracted Driving

Operating a motor vehicle is the single most dangerous activity that we do on a daily basis and yet we feel confident that we can drive and do others things at the same time.

We pride ourselves in our ability to multitask. We have been conditioned to think that we are more productive and successful if able to focus on more than one thing at a time. But can we truly multitask?

John Medina, author of *"Brain Rules"* says, "research shows that we can't multitask. We are biologically incapable of processing attention-rich inputs simultaneously." The brain focuses on ideas and concepts one after another instead of both at the same time. The brain must let go of one activity to go to another, taking several seconds. According to Professor Clifford Nass at Stanford University, the more that you multi-task, the less productive you become.

When we operate a motor vehicle, many things can be considered distractions. Any secondary activity like texting, talking on a cell phone, putting on make-up, eating and drinking, adjusting your music and even your GPS can all cause problems while driving. Taking your eyes off the road for as little as two seconds can be dangerous. We have added more distractions by using our smart phones for Facebook, Twitter and other social media.

There are 3 main types of distraction:

- Visual—taking your eyes off the road. For example, glancing down at your phone or changing songs on your CD player or iPod
- Manual—taking your hands off the wheel. Examples range from hand held cell phone use, texting, eating or changing clothes
- Cognitive—taking your mind off the task. Daydreaming or your current emotional state could play a role in your attention on the driving task.

All three types can be a serious, life-threatening practice.

Statistically, distracted driving has passed drunk driving as the number one safety concern for the driving public. Drivers on cell phones are more impaired than drivers with a .08 BAC, which is considered legally intoxicated in all states.

This is not to say that drinking and driving is not a serious problem, it brings to light, the impact of distracted driving. What about an intoxicated driver on a cell phone or texting? and the odds of being involved in an accident increases greatly.

According to NHTSA research, distraction-related fatalities represented 16 percent of overall traffic fatalities in 2009. Nearly 5,500 people were killed and 448,000 were injured in crashes involving a distracted or inattentive driver (NHTSA, 2009).

We know what distractions are out there, but what can we do to solve this problem? With nearly 5,500 fatalities in 2009 that number will only continue to grow unless we, as the driving public, make some positive changes. Legislation may work to some degree but changing our behavior is crucial in solving this problem.

U.S. Department of Transportation Secretary, Ray LaHood, cautions that researchers believe the epidemic of distracted driving is likely far greater than currently known. Police reports in many states still do not document routinely whether distraction was a factor in vehicle crashes, making it more difficult to know the full extent of the problem.

With that in mind, The Department of Transportation has hosted two Distracted Driving Summits in Washington, D.C., the most recent in September of 2010. Many states have considered passing laws prohibiting cell phone use and texting while driving. There are 30 states, and the District of Columbia that have banned text messaging for all drivers. Twelve of these laws were enacted in 2010 alone.

Changing your behavior and encouraging your friends to change may help bring an end to the senseless tragedy of distracted driving.

Drowsy Driving

Fatigue on the road can be a killer. It happens frequently on long trips, especially long night drives. There is no test to determine sleepiness and no laws regarding drowsy driving; therefore, it is difficult to attribute crashes to sleepiness. According to the NHTSA, drowsy driving accounts for approximately 100,000 accidents each year, injuring 71,000 and producing 1,550 fatalities (NHTSA, 2011). In a 2006 poll conducted by the National Sleep Foundation (NSF, 2007) reported driving a vehicle while feeling drowsy during the prior year, with 37 percent reporting that they actually dozed off while driving. It is equally as dangerous if not more dangerous to drive when you are drowsy than intoxicated. Some drivers abstain from alcohol but no one can resist the need

For more information on Distracted Driving visit there websites: enddd.org— the official U.S. Government Website for Distracted Driving distraction.gov— sponsored by the Department of Transportation (DOT) "Faces of Distracted Driving" caseyfeldman foundation.org.

The leading cause of accidental death is motor vehicle accidents.

to sleep. People are less likely to admit that they are feeling fatigued and therefore continue to drive when drowsy, leaving it up to self-regulation. Results from a recent study by the Stanford Sleep Disorders Clinic, performed by Dr. Nelson Powell, concluded that the sleepy drivers performed the same as the drunk drivers on basically all skills tested.

The NSF has created the "Drive Alert . . . Arrive Alive" campaign to help people become aware of the dangers of drowsy driving. One very important detail pointed out by this campaign is that people fall asleep more often on high-speed, long, boring, and rural highways. The more monotonous the drive, the more likely the driver will suffer some fatigue. According to the NSF, drivers who pose a greater risk for drowsy driving are those who are sleep deprived, drive long distances without breaks, drive through the night, drive alone, or those drivers with undiagnosed sleep disorders. Shift workers also pose a greater threat because they typically have non-traditional work schedules. Young people are more prone to sleep-related crashes because they typically do not get enough sleep, stay up late, and drive at night. NSF has a few warning signs to indicate that a driver may be experiencing fatigue. These include not remembering the last few miles driven, drifting from their lane, hitting rumble strips, yawning repeatedly, having difficulty focusing, and having trouble keeping the head up. The NSF also offers these tips for staying awake while driving:

- Get a good night's sleep.
- Schedule regular stops.
- Drive with a companion.
- Avoid alcohol.
- Avoid medications that may cause drowsiness.

If anti-fatigue measures do not work, of course the best solution is sleep. If no motels are in sight and you are within one to two hours of your destination, pull off the road in a safe area and take a short twentyto thirty-minute nap.

Most drowsy driving crashes involve males between the ages of 16–25 (NSF, 2008). Because of this growing problem, many colleges and universities, are providing awareness programs to try to prevent this tragedy from occurring.

In any kind of motor vehicle crash, a seat belt may save your life! The lap/shoulder safety belts reduce the risk of fatalities to front seat passengers of cars by 45 percent and for trucks by 60 percent. They also reduce the severity of injuries by 50 percent for cars and 65 percent for trucks (NSC, 2008).

Air bags combined with safety belts offer the best protection. There has been an overall 14 percent reduction in fatalities since adding air bags to vehicles (NSC, 2008). Buckle up!

Motorcycles

There are almost five million motorcycles registered in the United States. The increasing popularity with motorcycles is attributed to the initial low cost of purchase compared to automobiles, and good fuel efficiency, which is very important with the rising cost of gas. Motorcycles represent only 3 percent of registered vehicles but they represent 13 percent of the fatalities. Of the 35,900 occupant deaths in motor vehicle crashes, nearly 5,000 fatalities were motorcycle riders. Approximately 80 percent of the motor vehicle crashes result in death or serious injury. One of the main reasons motorcyclists are

Traumatic Brain Injury (TBI) can be caused by a bump, blow, or jolt to the head that disrupts normal brain function. An estimated 1.7 million people sustain a TBI annually in the U.S., killing 52,000. The leading cause of TBI deaths is motor vehicle traffic injuries, with the highest death rate among adults 20–24 years old.

killed or injured is that an estimated 33 percent of motorcycle riders are not licensed or they are improperly licensed to operate a motorcycle. Most states require an education course uniquely for motorcycles to ensure riders have the knowledge and the skill to safely ride (NSC, 2011).

Another significant factor is protection. Because there is no protection provided by the motorcycle, the rider must rely on clothing, eye protection, and of course a helmet. According to the National Safety Council, as of 2010, twenty states have mandatory helmet requirements for all motorcyclists. Another twenty-seven states require only riders less than 18 years of age to wear helmets. And there are three states with no laws involving helmet usage.

As in motor vehicle accidents, riding a motorcycle while under the influence of alcohol can decrease a rider's ability to operate the motorcycle safely. Almost 30 percent of riders killed annually are alcohol impaired. Alcohol diminishes reaction time, decision-making ability, and visual acuity. As with motor vehicles, all drivers or riders are impaired at .05 blood alcohol concentration (BAC).

Tips for Motorists and Motorcyclists

NSC offers these tips for motorists and motorcyclists:

Motorists
- Allow greater following distance behind a motorcycle.
- Be extra cautious in intersections. Most crashes occur when a motorist fails to see a motorcyclist and turns left in front of a motorcycle.
- Give a motorcycle the full lane width—never try to share a lane.

Motorcyclists
- Avoid riding in poor weather conditions.
- Position motorcycle in lane where you will be out of a motorist's blind spot.
- Use turn signals for every turn or lane change.

Bicycle Safety

According to the CDC, 500,000 people are treated in emergency rooms, resulting in 700 deaths (CDC, 2011). Wearing a helmet reduces the risk of serious head injuries by as much as 85 percent and the risk of brain injury by as much as 88 percent (NHTSA, 2007). Helmets have also been shown to reduce injuries to upper and mid-face by 65 percent.

Helmet Laws

According to the Bicycle Helmet Safety Institute, in 2007, twenty-one state laws and more than 145 local governments had enacted some form of bicycle helmet legislation, most dealing with children or adolescents.

© empipe, 2012. Shutterstock, Inc.

By wearing helmets, these bicyclists significantly reduce the risk of serious head injuries.

Bicycle Safety

According to the National Center for Injury Prevention and Control:

- Wear your helmet correctly. A helmet should fit snugly and not rock forward, backward, or side-to-side.
- Only buy a helmet if it meets or exceeds CPSC standards.
- Obey all traffic laws! Bicycles must adhere to all motor vehicle traffic laws.
- When riding at night, you must have a white front reflector or bright headlight and red rear reflector.

Home Safety

Poisoning

The leading cause of death in the home is poisoning. Poisonings account for almost 20,000 deaths annually. Children under 5 years of age are especially susceptible to household poisons, such as cleaning agents and medications. The 15–24 year old age group has a higher death rate as a result of poisons, possibly due to alcohol and drug overdoses and fatal drug interactions.

Poisoning by gases and vapors causes an average of 400 deaths each year. The primary cause of gas poisoning is carbon monoxide (CO) (odorless and colorless gas) due to incomplete combustion involving heating equipment, cooking stoves, and motor vehicle exhaust.

Hundreds of people die each year from improperly or malfunctioning fuel-burning appliances. It is important to have your heating system checked each year for any possible leaks. Carbon monoxide poisoning can also come from motor-vehicle exhaust, exhaust from a motorboat, or a generator:

- Don't use any gas-powered engines in an enclosed area.
- Don't use a gas oven to heat your home.
- Don't run the car in the garage.
- Don't sleep in an enclosed room with a gas or kerosene heater.

The symptoms of CO poisoning are severe headache, mental confusion, dizziness, and other flu-like symptoms. If you experience these symptoms, get to a place with fresh air immediately and seek medical attention.

Falls

There are nearly 30,000 deaths each year in the United States that occur due to falls, as well as almost a million medically consulted injuries. The second leading cause of death due to injuries in the home is falls, resulting in over 16,900 deaths per year. The age groups most prone to death from falls are the elderly (65 and over) and the very young (between 0 and 4 years old) (NSC, 2011). The National Safety Council estimates over eight million hospital visits were because of injuries resulting from falls.

Fires and Burns

Fires and burns account for between 2,000 and 3,000 deaths each year and are the third leading cause of unintentional death in the home (NSC, 2011).

The United States has more fire deaths each year than any other industrialized country. According to the U.S. Fire Administration, cigarette smoking is the leading cause of residential fire deaths.

Three factors can be effective in preventing injuries and fatalities from fires:

1. Take responsibility and view fire as a personal threat. We sometimes feel that fires happen to "someone else," not us.
2. Take precautions and preventative measures, such as installing smoke detectors, carbon monoxide detectors, and having fire extinguishers in the home.
3. Implement a plan of action for escaping a fire to save valuable time as well as your life.

Fire Safety 101

A Factsheet for Colleges & Universities

Every year college and university students experience a growing number of fire-related emergencies. There are several causes for these fires; however most are due to a general lack of knowledge about fire safety and prevention.

The U.S. Fire Administration (USFA) offers these tips to help reduce and prevent the loss of life and property in dormitory and university housing fires.

The Facts

In cases where fire fatalities occurred on college campuses, alcohol was a factor. There is a strong link between alcohol and fire deaths. In more than 50% of adult fire fatalities, victims were under the influence at the time of the fire. Alcohol abuse often impairs judgment and hampers evacuation efforts. Cooking is the leading cause of fire injuries on college campuses, closely followed by careless smoking and arson.

The Cause

Many factors contribute to the problem of dormitory housing fires.

- Improper use of 911 notification systems delays emergency response.
- Student apathy is prevalent. Many are unaware that fire is a risk or threat in the environment.
- Evacuation efforts are hindered since fire alarms are often ignored.
- Building evacuations are delayed due to lack of preparation and preplanning.
- Vandalized and improperly maintained smoke alarms and fire alarm systems inhibit early detection of fires.
- Misuse of cooking appliances, overloaded electrical circuits, and extension cords increase the risk of fires.

Safety Precautions

- Provide students with a program for fire safety and prevention.
- Teach students how to properly notify the fire department using the 911 system.
- Install smoke alarms in every dormitory room and every level of housing facilities.
- Maintain and regularly test smoke alarms and fire alarm systems. Replace smoke alarm batteries every semester.
- Regularly inspect rooms and buildings for fire hazards. Ask your local fire department for assistance.
- Inspect exit doors and windows and make sure they are working properly.
- Create and update detailed floor plans of buildings, and make them available to emergency personnel, resident advisors, and students.
- Conduct fire drills and practice escape routes and evacuation plans. Urge students to take each alarm seriously.
- Do not overload electrical outlets and make sure extension cords are used properly.
- Learn to properly use and maintain heating and cooking appliances.

www.usfa.fema.gov

Workplace Safety

The National Safety Council reports estimates that nearly 4,000 poeple each year die as a result of work-related fatalities, and almost 5,000,000 are injured. The Occupational Safety and Health Act was passed in 1970 to assure safe working conditions for every man and woman in the United States. The Occupational Safety and Health Administration (OSHA) is the governing body established to enforce safety rules and regulations.

The leading cause of occupational death is *motor vehicle fatalities*. According to the National Safety Council, motor vehicle accidents account for over 20 percent of the occupational deaths, which primarily involve the transportation industry; 14 percent of the deaths are due to *assaults on the job* (workplace violence), 9 percent are due to *falls*.

Occupational illnesses are conditions caused by repeated exposure to factors associated with employment, such as *repetitive strain injury* (RSI), or repeated trauma. An example of RSI, *carpal tunnel syndrome* (CTS) is inflammation in the tendons of the wrist, damaging nerves in the hand and can be caused by computer use, or any repeated use of the hands. Certain occupations pose a higher risk for CTS, such as computer technicians, surgeons, dentists, clerical workers, electricians, carpenters, and those in the manufacturing field.

Public Safety

These accidents include deaths in public places and non-motor vehicle accidents. Fatalities consist of water and air transportation accidents, railroad accidents, recreational boating and drowning fatalities, sports injuries and deaths, as well as fatalities as a result of natural disasters.

According to data from the U.S. Coast Guard, deaths associated with recreational boating average about 700 each year. Alcohol is involved in approximately 34 to 40 percent of the deaths due to boating accidents. The U.S. Coast Guard estimates that in eight out of ten boating fatalities, the victims were not wearing life jackets. Injuries associated with personal watercraft (PWC), have increased, accounting for over 1,800 deaths annually.

Water Safety Tips for College Summer Fun

While water activities are meant to be fun, you also need to be aware of possible hazards. Here are a few tips to help make your summer activities safe!!!

1. Personal Floatation Devices (PFD): State law requires all watercrafts have PFDs for everyone on board, regardless of age.
2. Weather: Tract the weather before you leave and during your time on the water. If the weather calls for storms don't take the risk. Pay attention to any weather changes and make plans accordingly.
3. No Alcohol: Alcohol and water activities are a formula for disaster. Operating a watercraft while intoxicated carries the same penalties as a DWI. Most states' alcohol laws are the same for all individuals on land or water. Consuming alcohol will also dehydrate you causing serious physical problems.
4. Be Prepared: It's important to be prepared for accidents and injuries. Be sure to have contact numbers, appropriate documentation and a first-aid kit.
5. Protect your body: Always have sunscreen, sunglasses, and hat and of course plenty of drinking water available for everyone.
6. Know the water: Make sure you are aware of your surroundings. Have a map or GPS ready in case of emergencies.

Adapted from presentexpress.com

With regard to sports injuries, data from the NSC indicate that basketball and bicycle riding account for more than half a million emergency room visits each year.

Tornadoes are the most destructive of all storms, causing almost ninety deaths each year. According to data from the National Climatic Data Center (NCDC), Texas has the greatest number of tornadoes, with 132 during an average year.

Over the last thirty-eight years, lightning has accounted for an average of eighty-nine deaths per year according to the NCDC. States with the greatest numbers of lightning deaths during these years were Florida, Texas, and North Carolina.

© jam4travel, 2012. Shutterstock, Inc.

Educate yourself about community disaster plans and procedures.

Hurricanes

National Oceanic Atmospheric Administration states: "Preventing the loss of life and minimizing the damage to property from hurricanes are responsibilities that are shared by all."

One of the most important decisions you will have to make is **"Should I Evacuate?"**

If you are asked to evacuate, you should do so without delay.

Hurricane disaster prevention includes:

- Modifying your home to strengthen it against storms
- Having the supplies on hand to weather the storm
- Use common sense in your disaster prevention

The costliest hurricane to hit landfall was Hurricane Katrina, a Category 5 storm that slammed Louisiana in August of 2005. Damages cost an estimated $91 billion.

The deadliest U.S. hurricane on record was a Category 4 storm that hit the island city of Galveston, Texas, on September 8th, 1900. Some 8,000 people lost their lives when the island was destroyed by 15 ft. waves and 130 mph winds.

Disaster Planning

You never know where you might be when a natural disaster occurs. They can occur with little warning, and you could be at home, school, or work. What will you do if basic services like water and electricity are cut off? What if communication with family and loved ones is difficult? What will you do if you are asked to evacuate your home or are required to be confined there? You need to have a plan to effectively cope with the difficulties that come when a natural disaster takes place.

FEMA, the Federal Emergency Management Agency, and the American Red Cross have created a four-step disaster planning program:

1. get informed,
2. make a plan,
3. assemble a kit,
4. maintain your plan and kit.

First, **get informed**. Be aware of high-risk hazards for your local area. Do you live in an area known to be at high risk for tornadoes, earthquakes, or hurricanes? Educate yourself about community disaster plans and ask about disaster plans and procedures for schools, places of employment and other areas that you frequent. Understand community warning systems. How will your community warn its citizens of possible risks and how will communication occur after a disaster?

Second, **make a plan.** Include the entire household in this process, especially children. Allow them to ask questions, offer input and practice this plan with them frequently. Include all caregivers who may be responsible for family members during a disaster as well. The focus of this plan is communication. If members of the household are separated during an emergency choose an out-of-town contact for everyone to call, if possible, to report their location and status. It is often easier to make a long-distance call from a disaster area than a local call. If you experience a disaster such as a fire, choose a location where all household members can meet in the immediate vicinity. A page of sample cards has been included in the notebook activities from www.ready.gov. Each member of the household should have this information handy. Next, discuss escape routes and safe places in the event of a natural disaster. Include plans for family members or guests with special needs, children, and pets to be protected during disasters.

Next, **assemble a disaster kit.** These are supplies that may be used by your household to stay safe and more comfortable, during and after a disaster. This kit should be assembled, stored in easy-to-carry containers, and reviewed at least once per year, or as your needs change. Figure 10.1 contains a list of common items.

FIGURE 10.1	
Disaster Planning	The following is a list of items recommended by FEMA and the American Red Cross that you may find helpful during and after a natural disaster. A disaster supply kit should be readily available in your home. Also consider preparing a modified version for your place of employment and vehicle.

- Three-day supply of nonperishable food and manual can opener
- Three-day supply of water (one gallon of water per person, per day)
- Portable, battery-powered radio or television and extra batteries
- Flashlight and extra batteries
- First-aid kit and manual
- Sanitation and hygiene items (hand sanitizer, moist towelettes, and toilet paper)
- Matches in waterproof container
- Whistle
- Extra clothing and blankets
- Kitchen accessories and cooking utensils
- Photocopies of identification and credit cards
- Cash and coins
- Special needs items such as prescription medications, eyeglasses, contact lens solution, and hearing aid batteries
- Items for infants, such as formula, diapers, bottles, and pacifiers
- Tools, pet supplies, a map of the local area, and other items, to meet your unique family needs

If you live in a cold climate, you must think about warmth. It is possible that you will not have heat during or after a disaster. Think about your clothing and bedding needs. Be sure to include one set of the following for each person:

- Jacket or coat
- Long pants and long-sleeved shirt
- Sturdy shoes
- Hat, mittens, and scarf
- Sleeping bag or warm blanket

Source: FEMA and the American Red Cross. Preparing for a Disaster, 2008.

Last, you must **maintain your plan.** Make sure you review your plan on a regular basis. Conduct drills to work out any foreseeable problems. Restock food supplies. Check expiration dates and replace medications, food, and water as needed. Also, check batteries in smoke detectors, flashlights, and radios.

During and after a natural disaster, the local, state, and federal governments and disaster relief agencies work to restore normal activity as soon as possible. It is your responsibility, as a citizen, to be prepared to take care of your household and loved ones until normal conditions are restored.

Personal Safety

Personal safety is something that affects our everyday lives, regardless of who we are or where we live. Crime can happen to anyone at anytime, and it is essential to take certain precautions for protection. Being aware of your surroundings and learning to avoid certain situations can reduce the likelihood of becoming a victim.

In order for a crime to take place, three elements must exist:

1. the ability of the criminal,
2. the desire of the criminal,
3. an opportunity for the crime to be committed.

As individuals, we can only control one of the above elements, the most important—opportunity. If a criminal does not have the opportunity to commit a crime, the likelihood of the crime occurring diminishes.

Despite declining crime rates over the past few years, one in eight Americans say they are more fearful of walking in their neighborhood compared to the last year. These findings from the National Crime Prevention Council Survey, sponsored by the National Crime Prevention Council (NCPC), state that 57% of Americans are more fearful of crime due to the economic downturn (NCPC, 2010).

Although this fear has prompted many individuals to become more aware of preventative steps, a substantial portion of Americans do not take simple prevention measures. Many Americans are unintentionally putting themselves at risk because they refuse to practice simple safety tips on a daily basis.

The following are a few simple safety tips and precautions to lower your risk of becoming a victim of violent crime.

Safety Tips

The National Crime Prevention Council (2003) produces an information sheet that includes tips for staying safe. They include:

Home

- Always keep doors and windows locked.
- Have adequate lighting around your home or apartment (notify manager if additional is needed).
- Do not open the door to strangers—always ask for credentials from maintenance or repair personnel.
- Do not give out any personal information over the telephone.
- Prepare records of personal items.
- Avoid being in isolated areas such as laundry rooms or parking garages by yourself.
- List your initials instead of your first name on your mailbox.
- Always have your keys ready for quick entrance into your residence.
- Have peepholes, deadbolt locks, and bars to lock sliding glass doors installed in your home or apartment.

Car

- Keep doors and windows locked.
- Always park in well-lighted areas.
- If being followed, do not go home. Go to a police station or well-populated area.
- Be aware of your surroundings at all times.

Campus

- Avoid walking alone.
- Do not leave personal possessions unattended.
- Always notice other people—make eye contact.
- Avoid taking shortcuts through campus.
- Do not walk like a victim. Walk like you are on a mission.
- Always be aware of your surroundings.
- **Trust your instincts.** If someone or something makes you feel uncomfortable, get out of the situation.
- Use well-lighted stops if taking a bus.
- Have key in hand before reaching your room or car.
- Avoid jogging or walking alone.
- Hang up immediately once you realize the nature of a harassing call.
- Call a campus escort when on campus late at night.

College Campuses

Many of the crimes on college campuses are crimes of opportunity. Theft is the most frequent crime on campus, yet it is the toughest challenge to convince students that their property can be taken. College students are typically very trusting, leaving their belongings unattended or inside vehicles in open view. Properly identifying your personal property such as backpacks, laptops, CD players, and textbooks becomes extremely important. If you consider the amount of valuables you carry with you in a backpack, including wallet, cell phones, and possibly credit cards, the need for protection against theft becomes crucial. Reducing the opportunity and using common sense is the key to most crime prevention on college campuses.

It is also important to be cautious with the amount of personal information that you make available to the public whether it is on campus or over the Internet. Social networking sites like Facebook and Twitter have become very popular, but they are not without safety concerns. With close to 1 billion active users on Facebook alone, the risk of being victimized is very real. Choose the sites you post on carefully. Two main crimes can occur by using these types of sites: identity theft and unwanted attention/stalking.

To protect yourself from identity theft choose strong passwords. Passwords that are lengthy, contain letters, numbers, and symbols and use the entire keyboard are ideal. Always type the address directly into your browser or use personal bookmarks instead of accessing the site through an email or other Web page; you might be inadvertently typing your password into a fake site. Protect your personal information: your name, birthdate, and/or social security number can be used to create numerous kinds of accounts in your name.

When you post information on the Internet, assume that it is permanent. Even if you remove it, the possibility exists that someone else has copied it to another location. Consider limiting the information you

When you post information on the Internet, assume it is permanent. Consider limiting the information you include on your profile.

include on your profile. Information that can be used to locate you, such as your address, phone number, work, or class schedule, may be found and used by someone you don't want to see. And always use the privacy settings available with any site you choose to use. The less information given out, the less likely it will be used to harm you.

Stalking

Stalking is a very common crime on college campuses across the United States, as well as the rest of society. Most stalkers are acquaintances, some with a previous connection to the target. Others can be classmates, neighbors, and co-workers. In a few cases, the stalker may be completely unknown to the target. The victim typically feels powerless, isolated, and confused. Whatever the situation, stalkers can be dangerous. It is estimated that 3.4 million people, age 18 or older, are victims of stalking each year (Department of Justice, 2006). Victims usually range in age between 19 and 39 years of age, but that does not mean it does not occur in other age groups. Approximately 1 in 4 stalking victims reported some form of cyber stalking such as email or instant messaging (DOJ, 2009)

If you know you are being stalked:

- Be very direct and tell the individual to leave you alone and never contact you again.
- Tell family, friends, co-workers that you are being stalked.
- Record everything that happens—every phone call, incident, or contact.
- Get an answering machine and keep all messages.
- Break old routines, change your normal patterns.
- Get a cell phone and keep it with you at all times.

Crime Awareness and Campus Security Act of 1990   The Clery Act was named for Jeanne Clery, a 19-year-old freshman who was raped and murdered in her dorm room at Lehigh University in 1986. Her parents were later informed that there had been thirty-eight violent crimes on this campus and the students were unaware of this problem. As a result, her parents, Connie and Howard Clery, along with other campus crime victims, convinced Congress to enact the law known as the "Crime Awareness and Campus Security Act of 1990." The law was amended in 1992 and 1998 to include rights to victims of campus sexual assault and to expand the reporting requirements of the colleges and universities. In 1998, the law was officially named the "Clery Act."

The Clery Act requires all colleges and universities to accurately report the number of campus crimes per category to the campus community and prospective students. College campuses have often been the site for criminal activity. These offenses include sex offenses, robbery, aggravated assault, burglary, arson, and motor vehicle theft. Hate crimes as well as hazing issues can be included in the reports as well as alcohol and weapons violations. Approximately 80 percent of the crimes that take place on college campuses are student-on-student, with nine out of ten felonies involving alcohol or other drugs.

As of 2002, the Clery Act also requires all states to register sex offenders, under Megan's Law, if they are students or employees of the college or university. This information is available to the campus police as well as students who request such information.

Under this law, colleges and universities can be fined for failure to report campus crimes. Omission of this information is not only illegal but it poses a threat to students' safety. The fines send a strong message for schools to take the obligation of reporting crimes and protecting students seriously.

Sexual Violence

Sexual violence, including sexual assault and rape, is a serious and frightening crime committed against women, men, and children. Sexual violence is not about sex, it is about power. It is an attempt to control a person using sex as a weapon. Rape can happen to anyone at anytime. Most rape victims are women, but that does not exclude men as victims. According to the National Crime Victimization Survey, sexual assault is the fastest growing violent crime in the United States. It occurs with increasing frequency but remains the crime least often reported to the police. It is estimated that only about 10 to 15 percent of rape cases are reported and that in one out of seven reported rapes, the male is the victim. Rape can happen to anyone at any age. Ages of reported cases range from 6 months to 90 years old, with the majority of victims under the age of 25 and the majority of their attackers also under the age of 25 (Weinberg, 1994).

Definition of Rape

The new definition, announced in January 2012 by United States Attorney General Eric Holder, is: "the penetration, no matter how slight, of the vagina or anus with any body part or object, or oral penetration by a sex organ of another person, without the consent of the victim." The new definition includes any gender of victim and perpetrator, and recognizes that rape with an object is in fact rape. This definition also accounts for rapes in which the victim is unable to give consent because of temporary or permanent mental or physical incapacity.

On college campuses, 90 percent of sexual assaults occur when the victim or attacker is under the influence of alcohol. The National Institute of Alcohol Abuse and Alcoholism (NIAAA) reported that drinking by college students contributes to an estimated 70,000 sexual assaults/date rapes each year.

What does this mean? Impairment by alcohol or other drugs places an individual in a situation where their safety could be compromised. Alcohol affects the higher learning centers of the brain, making it difficult to focus on important information. This also makes it difficult for the individual to respond to negative situations in appropriate ways. The more aware and in control of your surroundings, the less likely you will become a victim.

Most rapists plan their attack by familiarizing themselves with the victim's surroundings. In all rape cases, the attacker has the advantage from a surprise standpoint. By being aware and avoiding compromising situations, you can reduce the likelihood of becoming a victim, but this does not mean that all rapes can be prevented. Rapists commit the crime, not victims.

Studies by the Department of Justice have shown that women who used physical resistance at the beginning of the attack were two times more likely to escape rape than those who did not resist. Although choosing to resist increases your chances of injuries, you will have a higher probability of avoiding rape. All studies show that *active resistance* works in most attack situations. One study commissioned by the National Center for the Prevention and Control of Rape showed that women who are the most aggressive and use the most aggressive methods of resistance are the ones most likely to survive. Are you capable of using physical force? If so, then do it. Learning basic self-defense maneuvers can be extremely helpful in gaining self-confidence. Take advantage of anything that you can use as a weapon: pens, keys, umbrella. Punching, kicking, screaming—whatever it takes, use what you can to survive the situation. If you are inside a building, pull the fire alarm!

How you respond to the situation has a lot to do with where you are, for instance, in a mall parking lot, or in a deserted park. The best defense against an attack is to have a plan, an idea of what you would do if you were ever in a situation that called for a response. This certainly does not mean that in every situation, if you fight back you will survive. It is a good idea to have several plans to choose from. What works in one situation may not work in another—there are no guarantees!

Passive resistance could be effective in some situations. Examples of passive resistance are verbal persuasion, pleading, or submission. This sometimes can be helpful in regaining your stability and possibly giving you a chance to think through the situation and plan a defense. However, research has shown that passive resistance is not as effective as active resistance and does not seem to reduce the chance of victim injury (Bever, 1995). But the bottom line is, if it works it is successful.

Self-defense experts suggest reasons why individuals are easy targets for random violent acts. These reasons include: lack of awareness, body language, and being in the wrong place. Always be aware of your surroundings and walk like you are "on a mission"—making eye contact with everyone you pass.

Avoid being alone in an isolated area. If you feel like you are being followed, cross the street and go to a populated area. If an attacker approaches you, utilize the first rule of self-defense—run! Most people feel that they cannot escape. Even if the attacker has a weapon, if you are not under their control, then run. If you do find yourself in a violent situation, react immediately. Do not allow the attacker to take you to a second location. You have a better chance of surviving by doing whatever it takes at the original site. Do not hesitate to take action. Remember, you are responsible for your own safety, do not rely on someone else to take care of you or protect you from harm!

© Adisa, 2012, Shutterstock, Inc.

Always be aware of your surroundings and walk like you are "on a mission." Make eye contact with everyone you pass.

Acquaintance Rape

Acquaintance rape is a particularly volatile issue on college campuses. The prevalence of date rape on campus is difficult to determine because victims are even less likely to report a rape by someone that they know. Studies indicate that as many as 25% of college women will experience an attempted or completed rape while in college (CDC, 2008) and the majority of the victims knew their attacker, a classmate, friend, previous partner, or acquaintance.

Safety Tips

- When at a party or club, do not leave beverages unattended or accept a drink from someone you do not know.
- When going to a party or club, go with friends and leave with friends.
- Be aware of your surroundings at all times.
- Do not allow yourself to be isolated with someone you do not know.
- Know the level of intimacy you want in a relationship and state your limits.
- Trust your instincts—if you are uncomfortable, get out of the situation.
- Have your own transportation—if you need to end the date, end it.
- When meeting someone new, meet in a public place.

Steps to Take if Rape Occurs

- Go to a friend's house or call someone you know to come over. You do not need to be alone!
- DO NOT shower or make any attempt to clean yourself; do not change clothes or remove any physical evidence of the attack.
- Call your local Rape Crisis Center for assistance and counseling. A counselor can also accompany you to the hospital.
- Seek immediate medical attention and notify the police.

Intimate/Family Violence

Women ages 16 to 24 experience the highest per capita rates of *intimate violence*. Intimate violence is defined as physical, sexual, or psychological harm caused by a current or former spouse or partner. Every day in the U.S. more than three women are murdered by their husbands or boyfriends (Domestic Violence Statistics, 2011).

Another form of violence affecting our society is **family violence.** This includes partner violence, family violence, spouse abuse, child abuse, and battering. Family violence does not always have to be physical. Psychological abuse can be equally as harmful and can progress into physical abuse. A few examples of family violence are name calling or put downs, isolation from family and friends, withholding money, threatening or physical harm, sexual assault, disrespect, abusing trust, and harassment.

Battering focuses on control of a relationship through violence, intimidation, or psychological abuse in an attempt to create fear in the victim. The violence may not happen often, but the fear of it happening is a terrorizing factor (FBI, 1990). In most cases, victims are women; however, in a small number of cases the victims are men. In the U.S., intimate partners kill 1.5 million women each year. If you or a friend is the victim of family or intimate violence, seek help. Call the police or go to a shelter. Realize that the violence could even result in death, so action must be taken immediately. Consider using the worksheets entitled A College Student's Guide to Safety Planning included in the notebook activities at the end of this chapter.

Environmental Safety

We have spent time discussing ways to protect people. Next we will cover suggestions on protecting our environment.

Reduce, Reuse, Recycle

The Environmental Protection Agency (EPA) defines sustainability as meeting the needs of the present without compromising the ability for future generations to meet their own needs. Easy ways to live green are to reduce, reuse, and recycle.

The best way to have a positive effect on your environment is to get involved with programs through your campus or community. Simple things can make big differences. Here are some suggestions made by The Office of Sustainability at Texas A&M University:

- Bring your own bags to the grocery store. It saves paper/plastic and the bags are reusable.
- When printing, use both side of the paper. It saves money.
- Think before you print—fewer copies save paper. Also consider using recycled paper.
- Drive less. Reduce your short trips around town and combine them for one day. Or better yet, ride your bike. It saves gas and money, and you get some exercise.

- Don't use paper or Styrofoam. Use reusable plates, cups, and water bottles. Make sure you use BPA-free plastic. Exposure to bisphenol A (BPA) may cause negative health effects.
- Conserve water by spending less time in the shower or turning off the water while brushing your teeth.
- Turn off your lights and computer. Unplug your phone charger and appliances when not in use. Lower your thermostat during the winter months and raise air conditioning temperatures in the summer, especially during the day when you are not home.
- Use fluorescent light bulbs—they use 50 percent less energy and last longer. However, remember to dispose of them properly because they do contain mercury.
- Carpool when you can or use the transit system, if available.
- Recycle, recycle, recycle—the amount of garbage we create is increasing. Our landfill sites are filling up fast. Waste has a negative effect on the environment and recycling helps to reduce the need for raw materials as well as using less energy. Locally you can recycle plastics, aluminum, clear and brown glass, and newspapers. Check your local community for pick-up or deposit stations.
- Properly dispose of your used electronic devices such as cell phones and computers. A growing form of toxic waste is e-waste. With technology, e-waste now makes a significant portion of our waste. That waste contains heavy metals like mercury and lead, which can leach out of the landfills. Nearly 70 percent of all waste in our landfills comes from electronic equipment.
- Recycling your old phone keeps it and its (likely toxic) battery out of the landfill. Most phones contain metals like copper and silver. If these are recycled, it lessens the demand for mining new metals. The EPA states that recycling a million phones may reduce greenhouse gases by the same amount as taking 1,368 cars off the road for a year.
- Bringing your lunch to work or school can save money and save on the use of plastic and Styrofoam containers. If you spend about $7–8 each day on lunch, that can add up to almost $2,000 a year. Instead, make your lunch at home and use reusable containers. Bringing your coffee from home in a reusable container can save you money as well.
- Buying used goods and selling your old goods can help save the landfills and save you money. Looking online is an easy way to find great items for less money. Selling your used items such as phones, furniture, or electronics online or in a garage sale could bring you some extra cash and save the landfills. You can also donate your items to a local charity to help others and keep the landfills clear.

Reduce, reuse, recycle. Your efforts make a difference.

These are just a few ideas that you can use to make your environment a safer, greener place. Get educated! To find out how you can reduce carbon emissions or your carbon footprint, go to www.carbonfootprint.com. Visit the College Sustainability Report Card at www.greenreportcard.org to get your college or university involved in sustainability afforts.

References

Bever, D.L. *Safety—A Personal Focus* (3rd ed). St. Louis, MO: Mosby Year Book, 1995.

Centers for Disease Control and Prevention. *Bicycle Safety*, 2011.

Department of Justice. Bureau of Justice Crime and Victims Statistics. Stalking Victimization in the United States. 2006.

Driver Electronic Device Use in 2007. *Traffic Safety Facts*. National Highway Traffic Safety Administration, 2008.

Federal Bureau of Investigation (FBI). *Uniform Crime Reports*, 1990, 1991.

Federal Emergency Management Agency and American Red Cross. Preparing for Disaster. U.S Department of Homeland Security, 2008.

Grayson, Betty and Stein, Morris I. Attracting Assault: Victims' Nonverbal Cues *Journal of Communication,* Volume 31, 1981.

Glassbrenner, D. and Ye, T. Driver Cell phone Use in 2006. *Traffic Safety Facts.* National Highway Traffic Safety Administration, 2007.

Gorlick, A. *Media multitaskers pay mental price.* Stanford Report. Stanford University News, 2009.

Help Make Sustainability an Aggie Tradition. Office of Sustainability, Texas A&M University, 2008.

Medina, J. *Brain Rules.* Pear Press, 2008.

National Crime Prevention Council, *2009 National Crime Victimization Survey.* U.S. Department of Justice, Bureau of Justice Statistics.

National Highway Traffic Safety Administration, *Drowsy Driving,* 2011.

National Highway Traffic Safety Administration, Motor vehicle, 2010.

National Institute of Mental Health, National Center for the Prevention and Control of Rape. www.fullpower.org

National Oceanic Atmospheric Administration, National Weather Center, National Hurricane Center, 2012

National Safety Council: *Injury Facts, 2011 Edition,* Itasca, IL. 2011.

National Sleep Foundation. *State of the States Report.* National Highway Traffic Safety Administration, 2008.

Present Express, *Water Safety Tips for Summer Fun,* 2011.

Sawyer, R., Desmond, S., and Gabrielle, M. Sexual Communication and the College Student: Implications for Date Rape. *Health Values: The Journal of Health Behavior, Education and Promotion*, 8/31/1993.

The TerraPass. (n.d.). http://terrapass.com

Thompson, D., Rivara, F., Thompson, R. Effectiveness of bicycle safety helmets in preventing head injuries. A case-control study. *JAMA,* 1996.

Travisano, J. The Dangers of Drowsy Driving. *Current Health* 2, March 1998.

Weinberg, C. *The Complete Handbook of College Women.* New York: New York University Press. 1994.

Williams, B. K. and Knight, S. M. *Healthy for Life—Wellness and the Art of Living.* Pacific Grove, CA: Brooks/Cole Publishing Co. 1997.

U.S. Department of Justice. *Justice News,* Office of Public Affairs, 2012.

U.S Department of Transportation, *Distracted Driving Summit,* 2010.

U.S. Fire Administration, *Fire Safety 101.* Homeland Security, 2006.

Contacts

Most communities have a Rape Crisis Center, as well as centers for domestic violence. National Information Hotlines are also available.

For help contact:

Rape Abuse & Incest National Network
1-800-656-HOPE
www.rainn.org

National Coalition against Domestic
Violence
P.O. Box 34103
Washington, D.C 20043-4103
202-638-6388

National Coalition against Sexual Assault
P.O. Box 21378
Washington, D.C. 20009
202-483-7165

VOICES in Action
P.O. Box 148309
Chicago, IL 60614
312-327-1500

National Domestic Violence Hotline
1-800-799-SAFE

National Resource Center on Domestic
Violence
1-800-537-2238

Family Violence Prevention Fund
383 Rhode Island St. Suite 302
San Francisco, CA 94103-5133
endabuse.org

National Victim Center
1-800-FYI-CALL

Activities

Notebook Activities
Family Emergency Plan
Checklist of Rape Prevention Strategies
A College Student's Guide to Safety Planning

Name _____ Section_____ Date_____

 **Ready**
Prepare. Plan. Stay Informed.

Family Emergency Plan

Make sure your family has a plan in case of an emergency. Before an emergency happens, sit down together and decide how you will get in contact with each other, where you will go and what you will do in an emergency. Keep a copy of this plan in your emergency supply kit or another safe place where you can access it in the event of a disaster.

Out-of-Town Contact Name: _____ Telephone Number: _____

Email: _____

Neighborhood Meeting Place: _____ Telephone Number: _____

Regional Meeting Place: _____ Telephone Number: _____

Evacuation Location: _____ Telephone Number: _____

Fill out the following information for each family member and keep it up to date.

Name: _____ Social Security Number: _____
Date of Birth: _____ Important Medical Information: _____

Name: _____ Social Security Number: _____
Date of Birth: _____ Important Medical Information: _____

Name: _____ Social Security Number: _____
Date of Birth: _____ Important Medical Information: _____

Name: _____ Social Security Number: _____
Date of Birth: _____ Important Medical Information: _____

Name: _____ Social Security Number: _____
Date of Birth: _____ Important Medical Information: _____

Name: _____ Social Security Number: _____
Date of Birth: _____ Important Medical Information: _____

Write down where your family spends the most time: work, school and other places you frequent. Schools, daycare providers, workplaces and apartment buildings should all have site-specific emergency plans that you and your family need to know about.

Work Location One
Address: _____
Phone Number: _____
Evacuation Location: _____

School Location One
Address: _____
Phone Number: _____
Evacuation Location: _____

Work Location Two
Address: _____
Phone Number: _____
Evacuation Location: _____

School Location Two
Address: _____
Phone Number: _____
Evacuation Location: _____

Work Location Three
Address: _____
Phone Number: _____
Evacuation Location: _____

School Location Three
Address: _____
Phone Number: _____
Evacuation Location: _____

Other place you frequent
Address: _____
Phone Number: _____
Evacuation Location: _____

Other place you frequent
Address: _____
Phone Number: _____
Evacuation Location: _____

Important Information	Name	Telephone Number	Policy Number
Doctor(s):			
Other:			
Pharmacist:			
Medical Insurance:			
Homeowners/Rental Insurance:			
Veterinarian/Kennel (for pets):			

Dial 911 for Emergencies

Ready

Prepare. Plan. Stay Informed.

Family Emergency Plan

Make sure your family has a plan in case of an emergency. Fill out these cards and give one to each member of your family to make sure they know who to call and where to meet in case of an emergency.

< FOLD HERE >

ADDITIONAL IMPORTANT PHONE NUMBERS & INFORMATION:

Family Emergency Plan

EMERGENCY CONTACT NAME:
TELEPHONE:

OUT-OF-TOWN CONTACT NAME:
TELEPHONE:

NEIGHBORHOOD MEETING PLACE:
TELEPHONE:

OTHER IMPORTANT INFORMATION:

Ready

DIAL 911 FOR EMERGENCIES

ADDITIONAL IMPORTANT PHONE NUMBERS & INFORMATION:

Family Emergency Plan

EMERGENCY CONTACT NAME:
TELEPHONE:

OUT-OF-TOWN CONTACT NAME:
TELEPHONE:

NEIGHBORHOOD MEETING PLACE:
TELEPHONE:

OTHER IMPORTANT INFORMATION:

Ready

DIAL 911 FOR EMERGENCIES

< FOLD HERE >

ADDITIONAL IMPORTANT PHONE NUMBERS & INFORMATION:

Family Emergency Plan

EMERGENCY CONTACT NAME:
TELEPHONE:

OUT-OF-TOWN CONTACT NAME:
TELEPHONE:

NEIGHBORHOOD MEETING PLACE:
TELEPHONE:

OTHER IMPORTANT INFORMATION:

Ready

DIAL 911 FOR EMERGENCIES

ADDITIONAL IMPORTANT PHONE NUMBERS & INFORMATION:

Family Emergency Plan

EMERGENCY CONTACT NAME:
TELEPHONE:

OUT-OF-TOWN CONTACT NAME:
TELEPHONE:

NEIGHBORHOOD MEETING PLACE:
TELEPHONE:

OTHER IMPORTANT INFORMATION:

Ready

DIAL 911 FOR EMERGENCIES

Name _____ Section _____ Date _____

Checklist of Rape Prevention Strategies

The final test of your learning about rape is how your attitudes and beliefs affect your behavior. There are a number of things you can do to keep from being involved in a rape situation. Complete the following "Checklist of Rape Prevention Strategies" to see if you are doing everything you can to reduce your risk of involvement in a rape situation.

Circle the number that best describes how often you do each of the items below:

Never	Sometimes	Frequently	Always
1	2	3	4

For Everyone

Awareness

1 2 3 4   Think about what you really want to do with a sexual partner.

1 2 3 4   Be aware of stereotypes that prevent you from acting as you want to (such as a woman not being able to initiate sexual activity or a man not being able to say "no").

1 2 3 4   Observe how the environment is changing (such as being left at a party by your friends and having no way home).

Assertiveness

1 2 3 4   Believe and act as if you come first, without exploiting others.

1 2 3 4   Do not allow yourself to be put in vulnerable situations.

Control

1 2 3 4   Watch your use of alcohol or other substances so that you do not lose your self-control. Drug intoxication can both diminish the capacity to prevent and escape from assault as well as reduce inhibition from engaging in assaultive behavior.

1 2 3 4   Watch how others are using alcohol and other drugs and how this is affecting their self-control.

Interpersonal Relations

1 2 3 4   When dating someone for the first time, do so in a group situation or public place so that you can assess your date's behavior.

1 2 3 4   Pay attention to nonverbal cues as well as verbal cues. Do they match?

1 2 3 4   Treat others as equals. For example, share expenses so no one feels that something is "sexually owed."

Communication

1 2 3 4   Directly communicate what you are really thinking and what you want.

1 2 3 4   Ask, rather than assume, what would be most enjoyable together.

1 2 3 4   Listen to what your partner is really saying, and pay attention to the words (such as "no" means "no.").

1 2 3 4   Respect your partner's responses.

1 2 3 4   Set clear limits for acceptable behavior (such as "I would like to invite you back to my apartment to listen to music and talk. However, I do not want to do anything sexual, except kissing.").

1 2 3 4   Find out what is wanted and unwanted sexual behavior for both you and your partner.

Source: From *Exploring Our Sexuality* by Patricia Koch. Copyright © 1995 by Patricia Barthalow Koch. Reprinted by permission of the author.

Never	Sometimes	Frequently	Always
1	2	3	4

Especially for Women

Awareness

1 2 3 4   Trust your instincts when you are fearful (listen to that little voice inside you). Then act in ways to make yourself safer.

Control

1 2 3 4   Dress so you can move easily, freely, and quickly.

1 2 3 4   Yell "fire" (rather than "rape" or "help") if you need help.

1 2 3 4   Get out of a dangerous situation as soon as you sense danger.

1 2 3 4   Always have an alternative way to get home.

1 2 3 4   Take assertiveness training and self-defense courses.

1 2 3 4   Carry a device for making a loud noise, like a whistle or small air horn. Sound the noise alarm at the first sign of danger.

1 2 3 4   Avoid putting yourself in known high-risk situations, such as walking alone in dark, deserted areas or hitchhiking.

Where you live:

1 2 3 4   Have and use secure locks on all doors and windows.

1 2 3 4   Have lights in all entrances and have keys in hand when you approach your entrance.

1 2 3 4   If you live by yourself or with other women, do not use your first name on mailboxes, answering machines, or in the phonebook.

1 2 3 4   Know and avoid dangerous places (e.g., under stairs, alleys).

1 2 3 4   Know neighbors you could trust in an emergency.

1 2 3 4   Ask salespeople, repair persons, public officials, etc., for physical identification before opening the door. (Have people call ahead.)

1 2 3 4   Have an escape plan from your home.

On the street:

1 2 3 4   Walk confidently at a steady pace and be aware of your surroundings.

1 2 3 4   Keep your hands free—don't overload yourself with packages, purses, books.

1 2 3 4   Avoid dark, unlighted areas.

1 2 3 4   Walk or jog with a companion.

1 2 3 4   Walk or jog in the open, not near bushes or cars where someone can hide.

While using private transportation:

1 2 3 4   Keep your car locked and check the back seat before getting in.

1 2 3 4   Keep your car doors locked when driving.

1 2 3 4   Do not stop for anyone you do not know or does not show you official identification, like a police officer.

1 2 3 4   If your car breaks down while you're alone, attach a white cloth to the antenna and lock yourself in until a police officer arrives. If anyone else stops to help, have them call the police or garage for you.

While using public transportation:

1 2 3 4   Keep your hands free while securing purses and packages.

1 2 3 4   While sitting or standing, look aware.

1 2 3 4   If you are not sure of where you are going, ask the driver and sit near her or him.

Never	Sometimes	Frequently	Always
1	2	3	4

Communication

1 2 3 4   Practice your communication and assertiveness skills in a comfortable environment to prepare you for the times you need them to protect yourself.

1 2 3 4   Use assertive verbal confrontation if you need to (such as "I feel uncomfortable when you don't listen to me or when you touch me like that").

Interpersonal

1 2 3 4   Watch for indications that a date may hold negative, stereotyped attitudes toward women.

1 2 3 4   Watch for indications that a date may be a controlling or dominating person who may try to control your behavior.

1 2 3 4   Do not allow others to violate your personal space.

1 2 3 4   Do not assume that someone who has been nonviolent in the past will be nonviolent in the future.

1 2 3 4   Reject the activity, and let the person clearly know this, if you do not like what someone is doing to you.

1 2 3 4   Do not play games. Passivity, coyness, and submissiveness (sometimes parts of flirting) are dangerous and can support a climate of sexual aggression.

1 2 3 4   Use rape prevention strategies with everyone, since you can't tell who has the potential for rape by their appearance.

Especially for Men

Awareness

1 2 3 4   Realize that sexual relations are not "all or nothing" choices. There are many ways to give and receive pleasure. Kissing, touching, and even nudity do not mean that a person wants or expects to have genital relations.

1 2 3 4   Do not choose to involve yourself with negative influences, such as media that depict violence against women or peers who espouse negative attitudes toward women.

1 2 3 4   Ask yourself if you really want to have sexual relations with someone who does not want to have such sexual relations with you? How will you feel about your sexual behavior later, especially if the person indicated discomfort or resistance?

1 2 3 4   Consider the motivations behind your actions. Are you pursuing shared pleasure or self-gratification and power?

1 2 3 4   Consider acquaintance rape and other forms of sexual assault as crimes. An acquaintance rape happens if you have intercourse with a partner against her or his will and without consent.

1 2 3 4   Know that sexual desires are natural and spontaneous, but your actions are always within your control.

Interpersonal

1 2 3 4   Use peer pressure positively to help stop abusive behaviors which may lead to acquaintance rapes (for example, condemn rather than condone the behavior of a peer who has taken advantage of a sexual partner).

1 2 3 4   Realize that being turned down for some type of sexual interaction is not necessarily a personal rejection; it may just mean not wanting to participate in a certain act at a certain time.

1 2 3 4   Assume that "no" means "no" and do not continue. Allow your partner to take the initiative for what he or she wants.

1 2 3 4   Do not use sex for your self-gratification at the expense of others.

1 2 3 4   Do not think that you always have to initiate sexually.

1 2 3 4   Do not initiate sex if you don't want to.

1 2 3 4   Join with other men and women in taking action in eliminating negative sexual experiences, such as creating safer public environments.

Never	Sometimes	Frequently	Always
1	2	3	4

1 2 3 4   Be alert to anyone who may be suffering a verbal or physical assault. Help in any way you can, such as speaking up for someone who is being harassed at a party.

Communication

1 2 3 4   Clarify others' motivations. This will eliminate confusing friendliness with sexual invitation.

1 2 3 4   Voice your needs and feelings but realize you do not have the right to take away the freedom of choice from someone else.

1 2 3 4   Do not assume that previous permission for sexual contact applies to the current situation. ALWAYS ASK.

You should always be trying to do each of the items described on this checklist. If you are not currently using each of these as frequently as you could, explore the reasons why you are not. See if you can make the changes necessary to reduce your risk of being in a rape situation. What change will you try to make?

A COLLEGE STUDENT'S GUIDE TO SAFETY PLANNING

WHY DO I NEED A SAFETY PLAN?

Everyone deserves a relationship that is healthy, safe and supportive. If you are in a relationship that is hurting you, it is important for you to know that *the abuse is not your fault.* It is also important for you to start thinking of ways to keep yourself safe from the abuse, whether you decide to end the relationship or not. While you can't control your partner's abusive behavior, you *can* take action to keep yourself as safe as possible.

WHAT IS A SAFETY PLAN?

A safety plan is a practical guide that helps lower your risk of being hurt by your abuser. It includes information *specific to you and your life* that will help keep you safe. A good safety plan helps you think through lifestyle changes that will help keep you as safe as possible on campus, in the dorms and other places that you go on a daily basis.

HOW DO I MAKE A SAFETY PLAN?

Take some time for yourself to go through each section of this safety plan. You can complete the workbook on your own, or you can work through it with someone else that you trust.

Keep in Mind:

- In order for this safety plan to work for you, you'll need to fill in personalized answers, so you can use the information when you most need it.
- Once you complete your safety plan, be sure to keep it in an accessible but secure location. You might also consider giving a copy of your safety plan to someone that you trust.
- Getting support from someone who has experience working with college students in abusive relationships can be very useful.

MY SAFETY PLAN - PAGE 1

Staying Safe on Campus:

The safest way for me to get to class is: _____
_____.

These are places on campus where I often run into my abuser:

_____,_____

and _____. I will try and avoid those

places as much as possible or try to go when s/he won't be there.

There may be places on campus where it is impossible to avoid my

abuser. If I need to go to one of those places I can make sure a

friend can go with me. I will ask_____,

_____and/or_____.

If I feel threatened or unsafe when I am on campus, I can go to

these public areas where I feel safe (dining hall, quad, etc.):

_____and/or

_____.

I could talk to the following people if I need to rearrange my schedule or transfer dorms in order to avoid my abuser; or if I need help staying safe on campus:

Campus Police
☐ Resident Advisor
☐ Professors:_____
☐   _____

Dorm Security
☐ Dean of Students
☐ Sexual Assault Center
☐ Women's Center
☐ LGBTQ Center
☐ Counselor
☐ Other:_____
☐

If I live with or near my abuser, I will have a bag ready with these important items in case I need to leave quickly (check all that apply):

☐ Cell phone & charger

☐ Spare money

☐ Keys

☐ Driver's license or other form of ID

☐ Copy of Restraining Order

☐ Birth certificate, social security card, immigration papers and other important documents

☐ Change of clothes

☐ Medications

☐ Special photos or other valuable items

☐ If I have children— anything they may need (important papers, formula, diapers)

Staying Safe in the Dorms

I can tell these people (hall mates, roommates or RA's) about what is

going on in my relationship: _____,

_____and_____.

There will be times when my roommate is gone. If I feel unsafe during

those times, I can have people stay with me. I will ask:

_____.

The safest way for me to leave the dorms in an emergency is:

_____.

If I have to leave the dorms in an emergency, I should try to go to a

place that is public, safe and unknown by my abuser. I could go here:

_____

and/or here:_____.

I will use a code word so I can alert my family, friends, roommates and/

or hall mates to call for help without my abuser knowing about it. My

code word is: _____.

MY SAFETY PLAN - PAGE 2

Staying Safe Emotionally:

My abuser often makes me feel bad by saying this:

_____

_____.

When he/she does this, I will think of these reasons why I know my abuser is wrong:

_____,

_____ and

_____.

I will do things I enjoy, like:

_____,

_____ and

_____.

I will join clubs or organizations that interest me, like:

_____ or _____.

If I feel confused, depressed or scared, I can call the following friends or family members:

Name:_____

Phone #: _____

Name:_____

Phone #: _____

Name:_____

Phone #: _____

Name:_____

Phone #: _____

Getting Help in Your Community:

For emergencies: 911

National Dating Abuse Helpline: 1-866-331-9474

Text "loveis" to 77054

Campus police station: _____

Phone #: _____

Location: _____

Campus Health Center: _____

Phone #: _____

Location: _____

Campus Women's or LGBTQ Center: _____

Phone #: _____

Location: _____

Local Free Legal Assistance: _____

Phone #: _____

Address: _____

During an emergency, I can call the following friends, family members or residential life staff at any time of day or night:

Name:_____

Phone #: _____

Name:_____

Phone #: _____

Name:_____

Phone #: _____

Name:_____

Phone #: _____

MY SAFETY PLAN - PAGE 3

These are things I can do to help keep myself safe everyday:

- ☐ I will carry my cell phone and important telephone numbers with me at all times.
- ☐ I will keep in touch with someone I trust about where I am or what I am doing.
- ☐ I will stay out of isolated places and try to never walk around alone.
- ☐ If possible, I will alert dorm or campus security about what is happening in my relationship so that my abuser is not allowed in my building.
- ☐ I will avoid places where my abuser or his/her friends and family are likely to be.
- ☐ I will keep the doors and windows locked where I live, especially if I am alone.
- ☐ I will avoid speaking to my abuser. If it is unavoidable, I will make sure there are people around in case the situation becomes dangerous.
- ☐ I will call 911 if I feel my safety is at risk.
- ☐ I can look into getting a protective order so that I'll have legal support in keeping my abuser away.
- ☐ I can see if there are any self-defense classes available at my college or university.
- ☐ I will remember that the abuse is not my fault and that I deserve a safe and healthy relationship.

These are things I can do to help keep myself safe in my social life:

- ☐ I will ask my friends to keep their cell phones with them while they are with me in case we get separated and I need help.
- ☐ If possible, I will go to different malls, bars, banks, parties, grocery stores, movie theaters, dining halls, etc. than the ones my abuser goes to or knows about.
- ☐ I will avoid going out alone, especially at night.
- ☐ No matter where I go, I will be aware of how to leave safely in case of an emergency.
- ☐ I will leave if I feel uncomfortable in a situation, no matter what my friends are doing.
- ☐ If I plan on drinking, I will be sure to have a sober driver who is *not* my abuser.
- ☐ I will spend time with people who make me feel safe, supported and good about myself.

These are things I can do to stay safe online and with my cell phone:

- ☐ I will not say or do anything online that I wouldn't in person.
- ☐ I will set all my online profiles to be as private as they can be.
- ☐ I will save and keep track of any abusive, threatening or harassing comments, posts, or texts.
- ☐ I will never give my password to anyone.
- ☐ If the abuse and harassment does not stop, I will change my usernames, email addresses, and/or cell phone number.
- ☐ I will not answer calls from unknown, blocked or private numbers.
- ☐ I can see if my phone company can block my abuser's phone number from calling my phone.
- ☐ I will not communicate with my abuser using any type of technology if unnecessary, since any form of communication can be recorded and possibly used against me in the future.

Chapter 11
Human Diseases

© Kheng Guan Toh, 2012, Shutterstock, Inc.

OBJECTIVES

Students will be able to:

- Differentiate between communicable and non-communicable diseases.
- Discuss strategies to avoid contraction of communicable diseases and identify the symptoms and treatment for each disease.
- Know the risk factors for cancer and describe the cancer warning signs represented in the CAUTION acronym.
- Identify four cancers that affect young adults; discuss prevention and risk factors.
- Describe early detection exams and list treatment options.

- Differentiate between Type I and Type II diabetes.
- List three risk factors for Type II diabetes.

"Habits are to the soul what the veins and arteries are to the blood, the courses in which it moves."

—Horace Bushnell

The purpose of this chapter is to inform individuals regarding symptoms, methods of transmission, precautions, and treatments of communicable and noncommunicable diseases most common to the college-aged population.

Communicable Diseases

Communicable diseases are those diseases that are transmitted from person to person. These diseases can be transmitted directly by physical contact, which can include coughing or sneezing, or indirectly by contaminated water or infected insects.

HIV/AIDS (Non-Sexual Contraction)

HIV/AIDS can be contracted through blood transfusions, sharing needles, and/or the exchange of blood or breast milk from a mother to her unborn or newborn child. The groups that have been found to be at higher risk include IV drug users and those individuals who received a blood transfusion before 1985.

Tuberculosis

Tuberculosis (TB) is a communicable disease that primarily affects the lungs and was responsible for a large number of deaths and disabilities until the middle of the twentieth century. There was a sharp decline in the devastation caused by this illness from 1950 to 1980 due to the discovery of effective medications.

TB is caused primarily by the bacillus (or rod-shaped) microorganism *Mycobacterium tuberculosis*; other mycobacteria strains are responsible for some cases, particularly with coexistent HIV infection. The disease is transmitted by airborne droplets when someone with the active disease coughs, talks, or sneezes. Those at risk for contracting TB are persons who spend a lot of time, particularly indoors, with individuals who have active infectious tuberculosis.

The mycobacterium is covered with protective waxes and fatty substances, and is thus more durable and difficult to eradicate than many other infectious organisms. The bacteria lodge in the lungs, particularly the upper lobe, then migrate to the lymph nodes where an immune response occurs, mobilizing defenses which wall off the bacteria. Most individuals infected with TB are successful in "locking away" the bacillus organisms, which are then incapable of growing and multiplying. Those with 'latent' (inactive) TB are not ill and cannot infect others. However, there is an overall lifetime risk of one in ten of developing active TB later in life, particularly when immunity declines. Someone with latent TB will have a positive skin (Mantoux) test, which is a test for the presence of antibodies against the mycobacterium organism. Many physicians recommend that someone with a reactive skin test receive preventative (prophylactic) antibiotic treatment to destroy the TB bacilli and minimize the risk of developing active TB later in life. The most common prophylactic treatment is a six- to twelve-month course of the medication isoniazid.

© dragon_fang, 2012, Shutterstock, Inc.

Communicable diseases are diseases that are transmitted from person to person.

Those at greatest risk are infants, adolescents, and young adults. Common symptoms of the illness include fatigue, weight loss, lethargy, decreased appetite, low-grade fever, and night sweats. A cough generally develops slowly. Eighty-five percent of TB infections involve the lung (pulmonary tuberculosis), destroying healthy tissue in the process; however, the disease can be spread through the bloodstream to many other parts of the body including the central nervous system, bones, joints, kidneys, uterus, heart, intestines, and skin. In progressive pulmonary TB, approximately one-half of untreated individuals will die. Overall, 5 to 10 percent of patients die despite treatment due to drug-resistant disease, poor medication compliance, or improper drug therapy.

As mentioned previously, the rates of TB infection have risen over the past decade. Reasons for the increased incidence of this disease in the United States include HIV infection, which attacks the immune system and allows a latent infection to reactivate, the emergence of drug-resistant forms of mycobacteria, immigration into the United States from countries with a high prevalence of TB infection, and social conditions that foster increased risk of transmission such as poverty, drug and alcohol abuse, and homelessness.

Active TB is diagnosed with a chest X-ray, culture, and microscopic examination of sputum samples. The sputum culture not only identifies the causative organism, but also allows for determination of drug sensitivity or resistance.

Treatment for the active form of tuberculosis consists of a combination of medications due to the difficulty in destroying the organisms and the presence of drugresistant forms. The combination of choice for treatment of active disease includes the medications isoniazid, rifampin, pyrazinamide, and ethambutol or streptomycin for six to nine months (McCance and Huether, 2009). If the organism is resistant to isoniazid, then ethambutol or streptomycin is added. If HIV infection is present, a longer course of treatment is often required.

Treatment failure is usually due to irregularity in taking medications, which can foster the development of drug-resistant strains. Nationwide, 15 percent of active TB cases are resistant to one medication, and 3 percent are resistant to two medications. Therefore, it is imperative that those who are treated take their full course of medication as prescribed. It is also important to be cautious when exposed to someone with active TB while they remain contagious.

Mononucleosis

Mononucleosis, also known as "the kissing disease" because it is transmitted by saliva exchange, is primarily a self-limited (one that does not need treatment and will go away on its own) infection of young adults. The majority of cases occur in the 15 to 30 age range. This disease is most frequently caused by the Epstein-Barr virus (EBV); however, other viruses including cytomegalovirus (CMV) and the bacterium *Toxoplasma gondii* have been implicated (McCance and Huether, 2009). The virus attacks lymphocytes (cells found in blood and lymph tissues), which causes proliferation of cells in the immune system. This results in swelling of the lymph nodes, which is a prominent feature of this illness. After infection, there is an incubation period of thirty to fifty days (McCance and Huether, 2009). Initially, there are mild symptoms of headache and fatigue. This is followed by fever, lymph node enlargement (primarily those in the neck), and sore throat, which is the most common symptom and can be quite severe.

Enlargement of the spleen (splenomegaly) can occur in up to one-half of affected individuals. Rarely, this enlargement leads to the rupture of the spleen, which can be a life-threatening medical emergency. Other rare but possible complications include meningitis, encephalitis, and Bell palsy (McCance and Huether, 2009). By far, however, the most common course is a self-limiting illness with sore throat, fatigue, and fever as the principal manifestations and recovery within a few weeks.

Diagnosis is made with a blood test called the monospot agglutination test, which is specific for infection with the Epstein-Barr virus. There is also an elevation of white blood cells with a relative increase in the percentage of lymphocytes and monocytes (types of white blood cells), as well as the presence of large, irregular shaped cells called atypical lymphocytes. Up to 95 percent of infected persons have elevated liver function tests as well.

Treatment is non-specific, including bed rest, adequate hydration, and non-aspirin analgesics for pain relief. Aspirin should be avoided due to an association with Reye's syndrome, a potentially serious complication. Sore throat pain can be decreased with saltwater gargle. Participation in contact sports should be avoided for up to one month after recovery to reduce the risk of spleen rupture.

Hepatitis

Hepatitis means "inflammation of the liver." There are various causes, such as alcohol or drug-induced inflammation; however, the most common cause of hepatitis is infection with a virus. At the current time, there are six types of viruses known to cause hepatitis (A, B, C, D, E, and G). Descriptions of hepatitis have been found by Hippocrates as far back as the fifth century b.c. The first recorded cases were believed to be transmitted by the smallpox vaccine contaminated with infected human lymph tissue given to German shipyard workers in 1883.

The liver is the largest internal organ, with a weight of approximately three pounds. Essential to life, the liver performs multiple important functions, one of which is to clear various substances from the blood. These include medications and potential toxins, either ingested (i.e., alcohol) or manufactured in the body (such as ammonia). The liver also manufactures proteins necessary for bodily functions and stores sugar, fats, and vitamins.

The course of hepatitis can vary from asymptomatic infection (which is completely cleared by the immune system and unknown to the infected person) to rapid liver failure and death, or a slower process with cirrhosis and/or liver cancer. In early hepatitis there is an inflammation of the liver due to the response of the immune system in an attempt to eradicate the virus. The damaged liver produces scar tissue as it attempts to heal itself, which can lead to cirrhosis (causing the liver to shrink and harden). This makes the liver unable to perform its life-sustaining functions. The individual who is chronically infected with hepatitis B or C is at a higher risk for the development of liver cancer. Unfortunately, chronic hepatitis is often asymptomatic until irreversible liver damage has occurred.

As mentioned previously, there are six known types of viral hepatitis. Hepatitis A, B, and C are the most common and will be covered in more depth (see Table 11.1), whereas hepatitis D, E, and G are not as common and will only be briefly discussed. Hepatitis A and B are more likely to cause symptoms, whereas the B and C types are more likely to contribute to long-term health problems.

Hepatitis A

Hepatitis A poses the least serious threat to the long-term health of infected individuals. Infection is almost always acute, and the virus is generally cleared from the body by the immune system within three to four months. There is very little risk of long-term liver damage. There are no chronic carriers of hepatitis A, as there are with B and C (Crowley, 2009).

Hepatitis A is transmitted by contact with food or water that has been contaminated with infected human waste or by direct person-to-person transmission in settings such as daycare centers or institutional settings (for instance,

TABLE 11.1 ♦ Comparison of the Three Major Types of Viral Hepatitis

	Hepatitis A	Hepatitis B	Hepatitis C
Type of virus	RNA	DNA	RNA
Incubation period	2–6 weeks	6 weeks–6 months	2 weeks–6 months
Method of transmission	Fecal–oral: contaminated food or water	Blood or body fluids	Blood or body fluids
Prevention	Good hygiene and proper sanitation	Use condom if sexually active; do not share razors or toothbrushes; consider the risks if you are thinking about getting a tattoo or body piercing; do not share needles or reuse	Same as hepatitis B
Antigen-antibody test results	anti-HAV (confers immunity)	Infected persons are HbsAg positive and lack anti-HBs Immune persons lack HbsAg and have anti-HBs	HCV RNA in blood indicates virus in blood and active infection Anti-HCV denotes infection (does not confer immunity)
Signs & symptoms	Jaundice, fatigue, abdominal pain, loss of appetite, nausea, diarrhea, and fever	30 percent have no signs or symptoms Same as A and vomiting and joint pain	80 percent have no signs or symptoms Same as A and dark urine
Complications	No carriers or chronic liver disease	10 percent become chronic carriers and may develop chronic liver disease	75–80 percent become carriers and many develop chronic liver disease
Treatment	Treatment of the symptoms	Adeforir dipivoxil, alpha interferon, lamivudine, and entecavir	Interferon and ribavirin
Immunization available	Yes (age 1 and older)	Yes (first dose at birth)	No

Source: CDC, 2009. www.cdc.gov/hepatitis

group homes for mentally retarded individuals), where there is frequent close contact among clients and caretakers. After exposure, the incubation period is two to six weeks (CDC, 2009). An infected person is contagious during the ten to fourteen days prior to symptoms and during the first week of symptoms. Antibodies develop four weeks after infection (McCance and Huether, 2009).

There may be no symptoms at all, but more commonly there is a "flu-like" syndrome with fatigue, nausea, vomiting, and upper right side abdominal pain. The course of illness varies from mild symptoms lasting one to two weeks to severe symptoms that last for several months, although severe prolonged illness is rare. Less often an infected person may experience fever, darkening of the urine, and light-colored stools. Those at higher risk for contracting hepatitis A are household or sexual contacts of infected individuals, children in day care settings and their adult caretaker, patients and caretakers in institutionalized settings, as well as recent travelers to developing countries.

Diagnosis is made by testing the blood and finding elevated liver enzymes and detecting antibodies against hepatitis A. There is no specific treatment other than symptomatic, such as giving analgesics for pain and intravenous fluids in the presence of excessive vomiting to prevent dehydration. Alcohol consumption should be avoided to reduce the risk of liver damage.

A vaccine is available for this disease. The CDC recommends that persons who plan to travel to a country with poor sanitation be vaccinated approximately one month prior to travel, and repeated every four to six months if exposure continues.

Prevention consists of proper sanitation, including careful hand washing, proper sewage disposal, and effective water treatment present in developed countries. Close contacts of infected persons can help prevent infection if given immune globulin (concentrated antibodies) within two weeks of exposure (Benenson, 1995).

Hepatitis B

See Chapter 8 for more information on hepatitis B.

Hepatitis C

Hepatitis C is the most serious viral hepatitis to date, as mentioned earlier, affecting 3,200,000 Americans. There are 17,000 new cases per year in the United States (CDC, 2009) www.cdc.gov/hepatitis/statistics.htm. The disease was contracted through blood transfusions given prior to 1992 (prior to

FIGURE 11.1

Ways in Which Hepatitis A, B, and C Are Contracted

■ Frequent	▲ Common	● Uncommon/Rare

	Form of Hepatitis		
Source of Infection	**A**	**B**	**C**
Food/water	■	●	▲
Household contact	■	●	●
Needlestick injuries		▲	●
IV drug use (shared needles)	●	▲	■
Transfusions	●	■	■
Hemodialysis		▲	▲
Vaginal intercourse		■	●
Anal/oral sex	■	■	●
Mother to child at birth		■	●
Body piercing/tatooing (contaminated needles)		●	●
Within certain institutions			
Day care	▲	●	
Prison	●	▲	■
Organ transplant		●	●
Occupational exposure (e.g., medical workers)		●	▲

Source: American Liver Foundation, "Getting Hip to Hep: What You Should Know about Hepatitis A, B, and C," 2002. www.liverfoundation.org (75 Maiden Lane, Suite 603, New York, NY 10038, 1–800–GO–LIVER).

the development of techniques to detect the presence of the virus in donor blood). IV drug abuse is an important risk factor for transmission of this virus; hepatitis C transmission is very similar to that of the hepatitis B virus. The incubation period is two weeks to six months (CDC, 2009) and antibodies may not appear for several months.

Most individuals who contract the virus have no symptoms. Some will have the typical "flu-like" symptoms discussed in the previous section. Seventy-five to eighty-five percent of those infected will develop a chronic infection (www.cdc.gov/ hepatitis/Resources/Professionals/PDFs/ABCTable.pdf), which, if untreated, places the infected person at a high risk of cirrhosis, liver failure, and liver cancer.

Diagnosis is made by testing liver enzyme levels and for the presence of hepatitis C antibodies, which indicates exposure, but does not ascertain whether the infection is current. The hepatitis C virus RNA test detects the presence of the virus in the blood.

There is currently no vaccine available for hepatitis C. There is some evidence that treatment with immune globulin may prevent infection after exposure.

Hepatitis D, E, and G

Hepatitis D is a viral parasite, or incomplete virus, which is active only in the presence of a coexistent hepatitis B infection. Hepatitis E is spread through contaminated food and water, much like hepatitis A, but is not seen in the United States. Hepatitis G has been recently identified, and there will likely be additional types characterized in future years.

After infection, individuals can become contagious to others in as little as two weeks. As individuals with hepatitis are often without symptoms, it is important to be tested if exposed to the viruses. The diseases can only be correctly identified with blood tests.

A diagnosis of hepatitis is, of course, alarming. However, with advances in treatment, there can be optimism for recovery, particularly if treatment is begun early in the course of the illness. Responsibility for one's health in following through with testing and receiving treatment can reduce the menace posed to public health by these illnesses. It is also important that responsible action be taken in one's conduct with others, either with self-protection to prevent acquiring the disease or taking measures to protect the health of one's friends and family members with the precautions discussed previously.

Some of the classic symptoms associated with meningitis include high fever, severe headache, stiff neck, and a skin rash.

Meningitis

Meningitis is an inflammation of the membranes that cover the spinal cord and the brain. Meningitis is usually caused by a viral (the most common type) or bacterial infection. It is important to determine which type of infection is causing the meningitis. If the meningitis is from a viral source, typically it will be less severe and resolve on its own. The best course of action if you have contracted viral (aseptic) meningitis is bed rest, drink plenty of fluids, and take medicine to relieve fever and headaches. If the meningitis is from a bacterial source, it can result in blindness, deafness, permanent brain damage, learning disability, or even death. Most often bacterial meningitis can be treated successfully with antibiotics if caught early. Many times these individuals need to be hospitalized to receive intravenous antibiotics and to be watched closely. Some of the classic symptoms associated with all types of meningitis in anyone over the age of 2 years include high fever, severe headache, a stiff neck, and a skin rash that looks like small, purplish red spots. Other symptoms might include nausea, vomiting, discomfort looking into bright lights, confusion, and sleepiness. After close exposure to someone with meningitis, symptoms can take anywhere from two to ten days to develop, with the average being three to four days. Some of the classic symptoms listed above may be absent in individuals under the age of 2. The main symptoms to look for in newborns and small infants include: appearing slow or inactive, irritability, vomiting, loss of appetite, or not easily wakened.

Diagnosis of meningitis is typically done with a sample of spinal fluid. The spinal fluid is obtained by performing a spinal tap, in which a needle is inserted into an area in the lower back where fluid in the spinal canal is readily accessible. Then a culture is grown from the fluid to determine which type (viral or bacterial) of infection is causing the meningitis.

Meningitis is spread by direct contact through respiratory and throat secretions (for instance, coughing, sneezing, kissing, and immediate sharing of unwashed eating utensils). Fortunately, none of the bacteria that cause meningitis are as contagious as the viruses of the common cold or flu. Meningitis is not spread by casual contact or by simply breathing the air where a person with meningitis has been. There should be special concern if someone in your household or dorm, daycare, or intimate partner has contracted meningitis. In some cases a prophylactic course of antibiotics will be given to lessen the chances of contracting the illness. If an epidemic is occurring, a widespread use of vaccines may be enacted. It is important to realize that in most cases it takes the vaccine two weeks to become protective. So, it is not helpful for treatment of individuals who have already been in contact with an individual infected with meningitis.

The best ways to decrease infection rates include:

1. Covering your nose and mouth when sneezing or coughing,
2. Frequent hand washing,
3. Not sharing common eating utensils,
4. Avoiding overcrowded conditions.

The CDC recommends that college freshman living in dormitories be immunized against the meningococcal disease to reduce the risk of infection.

Common Cold

The common cold is caused by several different viruses that are spread by droplets from sneezing or coughing, or touching surfaces where the virus is present such as hands, money, or door handles. Symptoms include congestion, sneezing, sore throat, coughing, and a low-grade fever (see Table 11.2). There is no treatment for the common cold; however, the symptoms can be treated to help the infected individual feel more comfortable until the virus has run its course. Gargle with saltwater at the onset to relieve symptoms and possibly reduce the severity of the illness.

Influenza

Influenza (flu) is a viral infection of the nose, throat, bronchial tubes, and lungs. The flu is spread in a similar manner as the common cold. Symptoms include high fever, chills, headache, muscle and joint ache, coughing, and fatigue (see Table 11.2). As with the common cold, there is no treatment for the flu; however, medication can be taken to ease the symptoms.

The following reduce the risk of contracting colds and/or flu:

*   Wash hands often.
*   Keep hands away from your eyes, nose, and mouth.
*   Drink at least eight glasses of water a day.
*   Get enough rest (six to eight hours a day).
*   Use Kleenex instead of handkerchiefs.
*   Get enough vitamin C.
*   Receive a flu shot.

TABLE 11.2 ♦ Is It a Cold or the Flu?

Symptoms	Cold	Flu
Fever	Rare	Characteristic, high (102–104°F); lasts 3–4 days
Headache	Rare	Prominent
General Aches, Pains	Slight	Usual; often severe
Fatigue, Weakness	Quite mild	Can last up to 2–3 weeks
Extreme Exhaustion	Never	Early and prominent
Stuffy Nose	Common	Sometimes
Sneezing	Usual	Sometimes
Sore Throat	Common	Sometimes
Chest Discomfort, Cough	Mild to moderate; hacking cough	Common; can become severe
COMPLICATIONS	Sinus congestion or earache	Bronchitis, pneumonia; can be life-threatening
PREVENTION	None	Annual vaccination; antiviral medicines–see your doctor
TREATMENT	Only temporary relief of symptoms	Antiviral medicines–see your doctor

Source: From the National Institute of Allergy and Infectious Diseases, www.niaid.nih.gov Nov 2008

Non-Communicable Diseases

Non-communicable diseases are not transmitted person to person. These diseases can develop from many sources, some of which include genetic predisposition, behaviors such as excessive sun exposure, smoking, unhealthy eating habits, and/ or lack of exercise.

Cancer

Cancer is characterized by the spread of abnormal cells that serve no useful purpose. Tumors can be either benign, having a slow and expanding type of growth rate, remaining localized, and being well differentiated; or malignant,

© Liv friis-larsen, 2012, Shutterstock, Inc.

Reduce the risk of contracting a cold or the flu by washing your hands often.

growing rapidly, infiltrating (crowding out and replacing normal cells), metastasizing (spreading to other parts of the body via the circulatory or lymphatic system) and being poorly differentiated. There are four classifications of cancers according to the type of cell and organ of origination:

1. *Carcinoma* cancers originate in epithelium (layers of cells that cover the body and line organs and glands). These are the most common.
2. *Sarcomas* begin in the supporting or connective tissues including bones, muscles, and blood vessels.
3. *Leukemias* arise in the blood-forming tissues of bone marrow and spleen.
4. *Lymphomas* form in the lymphatic system.

Risk factors include a family history, race and culture, viruses, environmental and occupational hazards, cigarette smoking, alcohol consumption, poor dietary habits, and psychological factors that compromise the immune system. Heredity or family history is thought to account for 10 percent of all cancers with the most likely sites for inherited cancers involving the breast, brain, blood, muscles, bones, and adrenal gland (see Figure 11.2). Research has revealed a variety of internal and external agents that are believed to cause cancer. These agents are termed carcinogens and include occupational pollutants (nickel, chromate, and asbestos), chemicals in food and water, certain viruses, and radiation (including the sun).

Estimated New Cases*		Estimated Deaths	
Male	**Female**	**Male**	**Female**
Prostate 241,740 (29%)	Breast 226,870 (29%)	Lung & bronchus 87,750 (29%)	Lung & bronchus 72,590 (26%)
Lung & bronchus 116,470 (14%)	Lung & bronchus 109,690 (14%)	Prostate 28,170 (9%)	Breast 39,510 (14%)
Colon & rectum 73,420 (9%)	Colon & rectum 70,040 (9%)	Colon & rectum 26,470 (9%)	Colon & rectum 25,220 (9%)
Urinary bladder 55,600 (7%)	Uterine corpus 47,130 (6%)	Pancreas 18,850 (6%)	Pancreas 18,540 (7%)
Melanoma of the skin 44,250 (5%)	Thyroid 43,210 (5%)	Liver & intrahepatic bile duct 13,980 (5%)	Ovary 15,500 (6%)
Kidney & renal pelvis 40,250 (5%)	Melanoma of the skin 32,000 (4%)	Leukemia 13,500 (4%)	Leukemia 10,040 (4%)
Non-Hodgkin lymphoma 38,160 (4%)	Non-Hodgkin lymphoma 31,970 (4%)	Esophagus 12,040 (4%)	Non-Hodgkin lymphoma 8,620 (3%)
Oral cavity & pharynx 28,540 (3%)	Kidney & renal pelvis 24,520 (3%)	Urinary bladder 10,510 (3%)	Uterine corpus 8,010 (3%)
Leukemia 26,830 (3%)	Ovary 22,280 (3%)	Non-Hodgkin lymphoma 10,320 (3%)	Liver & intrahepatic bile duct 6,570 (2%)
Pancreas 22,090 (3%)	Pancreas 21,830 (3%)	Kidney & renal pelvis 8,650 (3%)	Brain & other nervous system 5,980 (2%)
All sites 848,170 (100%)	All sites 790,740 (100%)	All sites 301,820 (100%)	All sites 275,370 (100%)

FIGURE 11.2

Leading Sites of New Cancer Cases and Deaths—2012 Estimates

*Excludes basal and squamous cell skin cancers and in situ carcinoma except urinary bladder. © 2012, American Cancer Society, Inc., Surveillance Research.

Source: American Cancer Society. *Cancer Facts and Figures* 2012. Atlanta: American Cancer Society, Inc.

The seven warning signs of cancer are:

1. Change in bowel or bladder habits,
2. A sore that does not heal,
3. Unusual bleeding or discharge,
4. Thickening or lump in the breast, testes, or elsewhere,
5. Indigestion or difficulty swallowing,
6. Obvious change in a wart or mole,
7. Nagging cough or hoarseness.

Be certain to contact a physician if you experience any of these signs.

With any cancer, early detection is the key to treatment and survival. A common misconception is that cancer is a death sentence. However, the forms of cancer with the highest incidence and mortality rates are those directly related to lifestyle factors that can be changed or eliminated (see Table 11.3). Due to dramatic improvements in diagnosis and treatment, more cancer patients are being cured and their quality of life is greatly improved (see Tables 11.4 and 11.5. Treatment usually involves one or the combination of the following procedures:

- *Surgery*—removal of the tumor and surrounding tissue
- *Radiation*—X-rays that are aimed at the tumor to destroy or stop the growth
- *Chemotherapy*—an intravenous administration of fifty or more drugs combined to kill the cancerous cells
- *Immunotherapy*—activating the body's own immune system with interferon injections to fight the cancerous cells

Eighty to 90 percent of all cancers are thought to be caused by environmental factors that could be prevented by either avoiding certain substances or using protective substances or devices. Healthy lifestyle practices such as not smoking [30 percent of all cancer deaths are attributed to smoking (Donatelle, 2010); those smoking two or more packs a day are fifteen to twenty-five times more likely to die of cancer than nonsmokers (Hales, 2011)], exercising regularly, and avoiding sun exposure are simple yet essential ways to decrease your risk of cancer. A diet low in fat (less than 30 percent of total calories) but high in fruits, vegetables (at least five servings per day), and whole grains are the best nutritionally for reducing cancer risk. Avoid smoke-filled areas. Secondhand or environmental tobacco smoke (ETS) can increase the risk among nonsmokers. Researchers have found the risk of cancer to increase threefold with as little as three hours of exposure per day. Avoid environmental carcinogens whenever possible. Follow safety precautions if employed in or living near factories that create smoke or dust.

Skin Cancer

Overexposure to the ultraviolet (UV) rays of the sun is the primary culprit in these cases. Ninety percent occur on parts of the body not usually covered with clothes, including the face, hands, forearms, and ears. The two most common types of skin cancers are basal cell carcinoma and squamous cell carcinoma (non-melanomas). Both are usually treated successfully with surgery, especially if detected early. Subsequent tumors are likely in persons previously treated for these types of cancer. The fatality rate for these cancers is less than 1 percent.

A less prevalent but much more serious type of skin cancer is malignant melanoma, and its incidence is rising 3 to 4 percent each year (Hales, 2011). This type of cancer affected approximately 62,000 and killed approximately 10,710 Americans in 2006 (Floyd, Mimms, and Yelding-Howard, 2007). Al-

TABLE 11.3 ◆ Preventing Cancer through Diet and Lifestyle

Type	Decreases Risk	Increases Risk	Preventable by Diet
Lung	Vegetables, fruits	Smoking; some occupations	33–50%
Stomach	Vegetables, fruits; food refrigeration	Salt and salted food	66–75%
Breast	Vegetables, fruits	Obesity; alcohol	33–50%
Colon/rectum	Vegetables; physical activity	Meat; alcohol; smoking	66–75%
Mouth/throat	Vegetables, fruits; physical activity	Salted fish; alcohol; smoking	33–50%
Liver	Vegetables	Alcohol; contaminated food	33–66%
Cervix	Vegetables, fruits	Smoking	10–20%
Esophagus	Vegetables, fruits	Deficient diet; smoking; alcohol	50–75%
Prostate	Vegetables	Meat or meat fat; dairy fat	10–20%
Bladder	Vegetables, fruits	Smoking; coffee	10–20%

Here are some tips issued by a panel of cancer researchers:
- Avoid being underweight or overweight, and limit weight gain during adulthood to less than eleven pounds.
- If you don't get much exercise at work, take a one-hour brisk walk or similar exercise daily, and exercise vigorously for at least one hour a week.
- Eat eight or more servings a day of cereals and grains (such as rice, corn, breads, and pasta), legumes (such as peas), roots (such as beets, radishes, and carrots), tubers (such as potatoes), and plantains (including bananas).
- Eat five or more servings a day of a variety of other vegetables and fruits.
- Limit consumption of refined sugar.
- Limit alcoholic drinks to less than two a day for men and one a day for women.
- Limit intake of red meat to less than three ounces a day, if eaten at all.
- Limit consumption of salted foods and use of cooking and table salt. Use herbs and spices to season foods.

Sources: World Cancer Research Fund; American Institute for Cancer Research, 2003.

TABLE 11.4 ◆ Five-year Relative Survival Rates' (%) by Stage at Diagnosis, 2001–2007

	All Stages	Local	Regional	Distant		All Stages	Local	Regional	Distant
Breast (female)	89	99	84	23	Ovary	44	92	72	27
Colon & rectum	64	90	69	12	Pancreas	6	22	9	2
Esophagus	17	37	18	3	Prostate	99	100	100	29
Kidney[†]	70	91	63	11	Stomach	26	62	28	4
Larynx	61	77	42	33	Testis	95	99	96	73
Liver[‡]	14	27	9	4	Thyroid	97	100	97	56
Lung & bronchus	16	52	24	4	Urinary bladder[§]	78	71	35	5
Melanoma of the skin	91	98	61	15	Uterine cervix	69	91	57	19
Oral cavity & pharynx	61	82	56	34	Uterine corpus	82	96	67	16

*Rates are adjusted for normal life expectancy and are based on cases diagnosed in the SEER 17 areas from 2001–2007, followed through 2008.
†Includes renal pelvis. ‡Includes intrahepatic bile duct. § Rate for in situ cases is 97%.
Local: an invasive malignant cancer confined entirely to the organ of origin. **Regional:** a malignant cancer that 1) has extended beyond the limits of the organ of origin directly into surrounding organs or tissues; 2) involves regional lymph nodes by way of lymphatic system; or 3) has both regional extension and involvement of regional lymph nodes. **Distant:** a malignant cancer that has spread to parts of the body remote from the primary tumor either by direct extension or by discontinuous metastasis to distant organs, tissues, or via the lymphatic system to distant lymph nodes.
Source: Howlader N, Krapcho M, Neyman N, et al. (eds). *SEER Cancer Statistics Review, 1975–2008,* National Cancer Institute, Bethesda, MD, www .seer.cancer.gov/csr/1975_200B/, 2011.
American Cancer Society. *Cancer Facts and Figures* 2012. Atlanta: American Cancer Society, Inc.

TABLE 11.5 ♦ Trends in 5-year Relative Survival Rates* (%) by Race, U.S., 1975–2007

	All races			White			African American		
	1975–77	1987–89	2001–2007	1975–77	1987–89	2001–2007	1975–77	1987–89	2001–2007
All sites	49	56	67†	50	57	69†	39	43	59†
Brain	22	29	35†	22	28	34†	25	31	40†
Breast (female)	75	84	90†	76	85	91†	62	71	77†
Colon	51	60	65†	51	61	67†	45	53	55†
Esophagus	5	10	19†	6	11	20†	3	7	13†
Hodgkin lymphoma	72	79	86†	72	80	88†	70	72	81†
Kidney & renal pelvis	50	57	71†	50	57	71†	49	55	68†
Larynx	66	66	63†	67	67	65	59	56	52
Leukemia	34	43	57†	35	44	57†	33	36	50†
Liver & intrahepatic bile duct	3	5	15†	3	6	15†	2	3	10†
Lung & bronchus	12	13	16†	12	13	17†	11	11	13†
Melanoma of the skin	82	88	93†	82	88	93†	58‡	79‡	73‡
Myeloma	25	28	41†	25	27	42†	30	30	41†
Non-Hodgkin lymphoma	47	51	70†	47	52	71†	48	46	62†
Oral cavity & pharynx	53	54	63†	54	56	65†	36	34	45†
Ovary	36	38	44†	35	38	43†	42	34	36
Pancreas	2	4	6†	3	3	6†	2	6	4†
Prostate	68	83	100†	69	85	100†	61	72	98†
Rectum	48	58	68†	48	59	69†	45	52	61†
Stomach	15	20	27†	14	19	26†	16	19	27†
Testis	83	95	96†	83	95	97†	73‡#	88‡	86
Thyroid	92	95	97†	92	94	98†	90	92	95
Urinary bladder	73	79	80†	74	80	81†	50	63	64†
Uterine cervix	69	70	69	70	73	70	65	57	61
Uterine corpus	87	83	83†	88	84	85†	60	57	61

*Survival rates are adjusted for normal life expectancy and are based on cases diagnosed in the SEER 9 areas from 1975–77, 1987–89, and 2001 to 2007, and followed through 2008. †The difference in rates between 1975–1977 and 2001–2007 is statistically significant (p <0.05). The standard error is between 5 and 10 percentage points. #Survival rate is for cases diagnosed in 1978–1980.

Source: Howlader N, Krapcho M, Neyman N, et al. (eds). *SEER Cancer Statistics Review,* 1975–2008, National Cancer Institute, Bethesda, MD. seer.cancer.gov/csr/1975_2008/, 2011.

American Cancer Society. *Cancer Facts and Figures* 2012. Atlanta: American Cancer Society, Inc.

© Jason Stitt, 2012, Shutterstock, Inc.

Overexposure to the UV rays of the sun is the primary cause of skin cancer.

though the overall risk is 1 in 120, individuals with any of the following characteristics are at greater risk:

- Lighter natural skin color
- Blue or green eyes
- Blond or red hair
- Marked freckling on upper back
- Rough red bumps on the skin (actinic keratoses)
- Family history of melanoma
- Three or more blistering sunburns during the teenage years
- Three or more years at an outdoor summer job during the teenage years
- Living in the southern United States

A person's risk increases three to four times with one or two of the factors listed previously. With three or more, the risk is increased to twenty to twenty-five times (Marwick, 1995).

Occupational exposure to carcinogens and inherited skin disorders are risk factors as well. Malignant melanomas are highly curable if detected early; however, the chance of recurrence is high. To help prevent skin cancer: avoid

Skin Self-Exam

Skin self-exam means checking your own skin regularly for any abnormal growths or unusual changes. A skin self-exam helps find any suspicious skin problems early. The earlier skin cancer is diagnosed, the better chance you will have for a cure.

How the Test Is Performed

The National Cancer Institute (NCI) and the American Academy of Dermatology (AAD) recommend that people perform a skin self-exam once a month.

The easiest time to do the exam may be after you take a bath or shower. Women may wish to perform their skin self-exam when they do their monthly breast self-exam. Men may want to do the skin self-exam when they perform their monthly testicular self-exam.

Ideally, the room should have a full-length mirror and bright lights so that you can see your entire body.

When you are performing the skin self-exam, look for:

- New skin markings (moles, blemishes, changes in color, bumps)
- Moles that have changed in size, texture, color, or shape
- Moles or sores that continue to bleed or won't heal
- Moles with uneven edges, differences in color, or lack of even sides (symmetry)
- Any mole or growth that looks very different from other skin growths

Experts recommend that you examine your skin in the following way:

- Look closely at your entire body, both front and back, in the mirror.
- Check under your arms and on both sides of each arm.
- Examine your forearms after bending your arms at the elbows, and then look at the palms of your hands and underneath your upper arms.
- Look at the front and back of both legs.
- Look at your buttocks and between your buttocks.
- Examine your genital area.
- Look at your face, neck, back of the neck, and scalp. It is best to use both a hand mirror and full-length mirror, along with a comb, to see areas of your scalp.
- Look at your feet, including the soles and the space between your toes.
- Have a person you trust help by examining hard-to-see areas.

Considerations

Always tell your doctor if:

- You have any new or unusual sores or spots on your skin
- A mole or skin sore changes in size, color, or texture
- You have a sore that does not heal

Source: http://www.nlm.nih.gov/medlineplus/ency/article/001993.htm

the sun anytime your shadow is shorter than you are, cover up when in the sun (wear wide-brimmed hats, long sleeves, and pants), use a sunscreen with a Sun Protection Factor (SPF) of at least 15; beware of cloudy days (when burning is still possible), water (the sun's rays can reach three feet deep), and snow (which reflects sunlight). Avoid use of tanning beds or sunlamps. Observe your skin for changes in size, color, number, and thickness of moles, or pigmented growths, spots, or changes in birthmarks.

Distinguishing Benign Moles from Melanoma

To prevent melanoma, it is important to examine your skin on a regular basis, and become familiar with moles and other skin conditions in order to better identify changes. According to recent research, certain moles are at a higher risk for changing into malignant melanoma. Moles that are present at birth, and atypical moles, have a greater chance of becoming malignant. Recognizing changes in your moles, by following this ABCD Chart, is crucial in detecting malignant melanoma at its earliest stage. The warning signs are:

Normal Mole/Melanoma	Sign	Characteristic
	Asymmetry	when half of the mole does not match the other half
	Border	when the border (edges) of the mole are ragged or irregular
	Color	when the color of the mole varies throughout
	Diameter	if the mole's diameter is larger than a pencil's eraser

Photographs used by permission: National Cancer Institute.

Melanomas vary greatly in appearance. Some melanomas may show all of the ABCD characteristics, while others may only show changes in one or two characteristics. Always consult your physician for a diagnosis.

Monthly skin self-exam (SSE) can reveal cancerous changes at an early stage. Use a systematic approach. During this exam, look for abnormal growth of cells. If you notice any of these warning signs see your physician immediately.

Lung Cancer

Lung cancer is the number one cause of cancer deaths in the United States (American Cancer Society, 2004). The major cause of lung cancer is cigarette smoking, accounting for 85 percent of all lung cancer deaths, making it one of the most preventable forms of cancer. Smoking cessation decreases the death rate of lung cancer in half. Other risk factors include asbestos exposure, secondhand smoke, radiation exposure, and radon exposure. Early detection of lung cancer is difficult, resulting in only 15 percent of cases being discovered early. With early detection, there is a 43 percent chance of surviving twelve months; however, the overall five-year relative survival rate is only 16 percent. Symptoms include a nagging or persistent cough, blood in the sputum, chest pain, shortness of breath, recurring bronchitis or pneumonia, weight loss, loss of appetite, and/or anemia.

Breast Cancer

One in eight women will develop breast cancer in her lifetime (American Cancer Society, 2011). Risk factors include: age 40 years or older (see Table 11.6), family history or personal history of breast cancer, early onset of menstruation

TABLE 11.6 ◆ Probability (%) of Developing Invasive Cancers over Selected Age Intervals by Sex, U.S., 2006–2008*

		Birth to 39	40 to 59	60 to 69	70 and Older	Birth to Death
All sites[†]	Male	1.45 (1 in 69)	8.68 (1 in 12)	16.00 (1 in 6)	38.27 (1 in 3)	44.85 (1 in 2)
	Female	2.15 (1 in 46)	9.10 (1 in 11)	10.34 (1 in 10)	26.68 (1 in 4)	38.08 (1 in 3)
Urinary bladder[‡]	Male	0.02 (1 in 5,035)	0.38 (1 in 266)	0.92 (1 in 109)	3.71 (1 in 27)	3.84 (1 in 26)
	Female	0.01 (1 in 12,682)	0.12 (1 in 851)	0.25 (1 in 400)	0.98 (1 in 102)	1.15 (1 in 87)
Breast	Female	0.49 (1 in 203)	3.76 (1 in 27)	3.53 (1 in 28)	6.58 (1 in 15)	12.29 (1 in 8)
Colon & rectum	Male	0.08 (1 in 1,236)	0.92 (1 in 109)	1.44 (1 in 70)	4.32 (1 in 23)	5.27 (1 in 19)
	Female	0.08 (1 in 1,258)	0.73 (1 in 137)	1.01 (1 in 99)	3.95 (1 in 25)	4.91 (1 in 20)
Leukemia	Male	0.16 (1 in 614)	0.22 (1 in 445)	0.34 (1 in 291)	1.24 (1 in 81)	1.57 (1 in 64)
	Female	0.14 (1 in 737)	0.15 (1 in 665)	0.21 (1 in 482)	0.81 (1 in 123)	1.14 (1 in 88)
Lung & bronchus	Male	0.03 (1 in 3,631)	0.91 (1 in 109)	2.26 (1 in 44)	6.69 (1 in 15)	7.66 (1 in 13)
	Female	0.03 (1 in 3,285)	0.76 (1 in 132)	1.72 (1 in 58)	4.91 (1 in 20)	6.33 (1 in 16)
Melanoma of the skin	Male	0.15 (1 in 677)	0.63 (1 in 158)	0.75 (1 in 133)	1.94 (1 in 52)	2.80 (1 in 36)
	Female	0.27 (1 in 377)	0.56 (1 in 180)	0.39 (1 in 256)	0.82 (1 in 123)	1.83 (1 in 55)
Non-Hodgkin lymphoma	Male	0.13 (1 in 775)	0.45 (1 in 223)	0.60 (1 in 167)	1.77 (1 in 57)	2.34 (1 in 43)
	Female	0.09 (1 in 1,152)	0.32 (1 in 313)	0.44 (1 in 228)	1.41 (1 in 71)	1.94 (1 in 51)
Prostate	Male	0.01 (1 in 8,499)	2.63 (1 in 38)	6.84 (1 in 15)	12.54 (1 in 8)	16.48 (1 in 6)
Uterine cervix	Female	0.15 (1 in 650)	0.27 (1 in 373)	0.13 (1 in 771)	0.18 (1 in 549)	0.68 (1 in 147)
Uterine corpus	Female	0.07 (1 in 1,373)	0.77 (1 in 130)	0.87 (1 in 114)	1.24 (1 in 81)	2.61 (1 in 38)

*For people free of cancer at beginning of age interval. † All sites exclude basal and squamous cell skin cancers and in situ cancers except urinary bladder. ‡ Includes invasive and in situ cancer cases. §Statistic is for whites only

Source: DevCan: Probability of Developing or Dying of Cancer Software, Version 6.6.0. Statistical Research and Applications Branch, National Cancer Institute, 2011. www.srab.cancer.gov/devcan.

American Cancer Society. *Cancer Facts and Figures* 2012. Atlanta: American Cancer Society, Inc.

(before age 12), having no children, having a first child at a late age (after age 30), late menopause (after age 55), exposure to radiation, obesity, and certain types of benign breast disease (premenopausal women). Early detection is the best way to reduce the mortality rate among breast cancer patients. It is recommended by the American Cancer Society that women 20 years of age and older perform a breast self-examination once a month. Any persistent lumps, swelling, thickening or distortion of the breast, pain or tenderness of the nipple, or discharge of blood or fluid from the nipple should be reported immediately. A diagnostic X-ray, called a mammogram, can detect a tumor two or three years before it can be detected by a self-exam. The American Cancer Society recommends all women begin routine mammograms by the age of 40, and physicians recommend that women at high risk (with a family history) have mammograms every six to twelve months beginning between the ages of 25 and 35 (see Table 11.7). With early diagnosis and a localized tumor, there is an 89 percent chance of surviving five years.

TABLE 11.7 ◆ Recommended Breast Exam Schedule

Procedure	Risk	Age	Frequency
Breast Self-Exam (BSE)	Average	20 & Over	Once a Month
	High*	20 & Over	Once a Month
Clinical Breast Examination (CBE)	Average	20 to 39	Every 3 Years
	Average	40 & Over	Every Year
	High*	20 to 39	Every Year
Mammography	Average	40 & Over	Once a Year
	High*	Begin between 25 & 35	Once Every 6–12 Months

*Personal history of breast cancer or family history of premenopausal breast cancer in mother or sister.

Breast self exam

A breast self exam is when a woman examines her own breasts for changes or problems.

Many women feel that doing this is important to their health. It helps them learn how their breasts normally feel, so that if they find a lump they will know if they should call their doctor or nurse.

However, there is not agreement among experts about recommending breast self exams. It is not known for sure what role breast self exams play in finding breast cancer or saving lives.

Talk to your health care provider about whether breast self exams are right for you.

Information

If you decide to do breast self exams, make sure you do so about 3–5 days after your period starts. Your breasts are not as tender or lumpy during this time of month.

If you have gone through menopause, do your exam on the same day every month.

- First, lie on your back. It is easier to examine all breast tissue if you are lying down.
- Place your right hand behind your head. With the middle fingers of your left hand, gently yet firmly press down using small motions to examine the entire right breast.
- Next, sit or stand. Feel your armpit, because breast tissue goes into that area.
- Gently squeeze the nipple, checking for discharge. Repeat the process on the left breast.
- Use one of the patterns shown in the diagram to make sure that you are covering all of the breast tissue.

Next, stand in front of a mirror with your arms by your side.

- Look at your breasts directly and in the mirror. Look for changes in skin texture, such as dimpling, puckering, indentations, or skin that looks like an orange peel.
- Also note the shape and contour of each breast.
- Check to see if the nipple turns inward.

Do the same with your arms raised above your head.

- Most women have some lumps. Your goal is to find anything new or different. If you do, call your health care provider right away.

Source: http://www.nlm.nih.gov/medlineplus/ency/article/001993.htm

Breast self-exam (BSE) is a method utilized in an effort to promptly detect lumps located in the breast. Early detection increases survival. During this exam, one looks for masses within the soft tissue of the breast or changes in the breast appearance. Due to the varying texture, size, and sensitivity of one's breast, it is important to do the self-exam at the same time each month. The following is a guideline to determine the proper timing:

- *Women with menstrual cycles*—one week after the beginning of the menstrual period when the breasts are usually not tender
- *After menopause or hysterectomy*—choose a day that is easy to remember, such as the first day of the month.

Cervical Cancer

Cervical cancer is representative of abnormal growth and maturation of the cervical squamous epithelium. Typically there are no symptoms in the early stages (see Figure 11.3). Eventually individuals with cervical cancer will have uterine bleeding, cramps, infections, and pain in the abdominal region. Risk

Cancer Site	Population	Test or Procedure	Frequency
Breast	Women, age 20+	Breast self-examination (BSE)	It is acceptable for women to choose not to do BSE or to do BSE regularly (monthly) or irregularly. Beginning in their early 20s, women should be told about the benefits and limitations of breast self-examination (BSE). Whether a woman ever performs BSE, the importance of prompt reporting of any new breast symptoms to a health professional should be emphasized. Women who choose to do BSE should receive instruction and have their technique reviewed on the occasion of a periodic health examination.
		Clinical breast examination(CBE)	For women in their 20s and 30s, it is recommended that clinical breast examination (CBE) be part of a periodic health examination, preferably at least every three years. Asymptomatic women age 40 and older should continue to receive a clinical breast examination as part of a periodic health examination, preferably annually.
		Mammography HPV	Begin annual mammography at age 40.*
Cervix†	Women, age 21+	Pap test HPV DNA test	Cervical cancer screening should begin approximately three years after a woman begins having vaginal intercourse, but no later than 21 years of age. Screening should be done every year with conventional Pap tests or every two years using liquid-based Pap tests. At or after age 30, women who have had three normal test results in a row may undergo screening every two to three years with cervical cytology (either conventional or liquid-based Pap test) alone, or every three years with an HPV DNA test plus cervical cytology. Women 70 years of age and older who have had three or more normal Pap tests and no abnormal Pap tests in the past 10 years and women who have had a total hysterectomy may choose to stop cervical cancer screening.
Colorectal	Men and women, age 50+	Fecal occult blood test (FOBT) with at least 50% test sensitivity for cancer, or fecal immunochemical test (FIT) with at least 50% test sensitivity for cancer, or	Annual, starting at age 50. Testing at home with adherence to manufacturer's recommendation for collection techniques and number of samples is recommended. FOBT with the single stool sample collected on the clinician's fingertip during a digital rectal examination in the health care setting is not recommended. Guaiac based toilet bowl FOBT tests also are not recommended. In comparison with guaiac-based tests for the detection of occult blood, immunochemical tests are more patient-friendly, and are likely to be equal or better in sensitivity and specificity. There is no justification for repeating FOBT in response to an initial positive finding.
		Stool DNA test, or	Interval uncertain, starting at age 50
		Flexible sigmoidoscopy (FSIG), or	Every 5 years, starting at age 50. FSIG can be performed alone, or consideration can be given to combining FSIG performed every 5 years with a highly sensitive gFOBT or FIT performed annually.
		Double contrast barium enema (DCBE), or	Every 5 years, starting at age 50
		Colonoscopy	Every 10 years, starting at age 50
		CT Colonography	Every 5 years, starting at age 50
Endometrial	Women, at menopause		At the time of menopause, women at average risk should be informed about risks and symptoms of endometrial cancer and strongly encouraged to report any unexpected bleeding or spotting to their physicians.
Prostate	Men, ages 50+	Digital rectal examination (DRE) and prostate-specific antigen test (PSA)	Men who have at least a 10-year life expectancy should have an opportunity to make an informed decision with their health care provider about whether to be screened for prostate cancer, after receiving information about the potential benefits, risks, and uncertainties associated with prostate cancer screening. Prostate cancer screening should not occur without an informed decision-making process.
Cancer-related checkup	Men and women, age 20+		On the occasion of a periodic health examination, the cancer-related checkup should include examination for cancers of the thyroid, testicles, ovaries, lymph nodes, oral cavity, and skin, as well as health counseling about tobacco, sun exposure, diet and nutrition, risk factors, sexual practices, and environmental and occupational exposures.

*Beginning at age 40, annual clinical breast examination should be performed prior to mammography.

†New recommendations will be released in early 2012; please refer to cancer.org for the most current guidelines.

Note: Screening recommendations for lung cancer will be released in 2012; please refer to cancer.org for the most current information.

FIGURE 11.3

Screening Guidelines for the Early Detection of Cancer in Average-risk Asymptomatic People

American Cancer Society. *Cancer Facts and Figures* 2012. Atlanta: American Cancer Society, Inc.

factors include: first vaginal intercourse at an early age, multiple sexual partners, cigarette smoking, and infections with certain types of human papilloma viruses. See information on the Gardasil vaccine in chapter 8. The Pap smear is a screening test a physician performs in order to check for pre-cancerous cells or early cancer of the cervix. The physician obtains a sampling of tissue from inside the cervix and sends the specimen to a lab to be analyzed. Due to early detection with the Pap smear, cancer of the cervix is rare and easily treated in women who have regular exams. It is recommended that all women begin Pap tests no later than three years after first intercourse or starting at age 21, whichever comes first. This procedure should continue until an individual reaches the age of 70, at which point the physician may recommend discontinuing Pap smears. The best time to schedule a Pap smear is fourteen days after the start of a period. Do not have intercourse for twenty-four hours or any substances in the vagina for forty-eight hours before the exam.

Testicular Cancer

Although testicular cancer accounts for only 3 percent of cancers of the male genitals and urinary tract, it is one of the most common cancers in young males, with the majority of cases identified between the ages of 20 and 54 (American Cancer Society, 2007). Men with undescended testicles in childhood seem to be at greatest risk. Other risks may include: family history, inguinal hernia, testicular trauma, mumps orchitis, elevated testicular temperature, vasectomy, or exposure to electromagnetic fields. Testicular self-exams should be performed monthly to detect any enlargement or thickening of the testes. The cure rate if detected early is close to 80 percent.

How to Examine Your Genitals

1. **Roll each testicle between the thumbs and fingers of both hands.** A normal testicle is firm, smooth, egg-shaped, about 1-1/2 inches long. One testicle may be a little larger or hang lower in the scrotum. This is normal.
2. **Feel the epididymis behind the testicle on each side.** It should feel soft, rope-like and tender.
3. **Check the skin on your scrotum and penis for sores and little rough bumps.** These could be signs of STI, such as herpes, syphilis, or genital warts.
4. **If you are not circumcised, be sure you pull back the foreskin.** Check the glans and the inside of the foreskin.
5. **Look at the opening at the tip of the penis.** It should not be red or painful. A yellow or white discharge could be a sign of an STI.
6. **Feel your groin area on both sides** for any lumps or swollen glands.

It Isn't Normal:

- If you feel a lump or hard area in the testicle
- If the whole testicle feels harder than usual
- If one side of your scrotum is very swollen

These could be signs of cancer, even if there is no pain.

What if I Find Something?

Any lumps in your testicles or groin, any skin sores, bumps, or other changes in your genitals that do not seem normal should be checked right away by your health care provider.

Don't wait. Your health depends on getting care as soon as you can.

After age 50, every man should talk with his health care provider about a prostate examination.

Testicular self-exam (TSE) can detect cancer in early stages when disease is more curable. Exams should begin at age 15. Self-examination should be performed every month in order to detect any changes. The best time to perform the exam is after taking a warm bath or shower when the skin of the scrotum is relaxed.

Colon and Rectum Cancers

Colon and rectum cancers are the third leading types of cancer in men and women, claiming about 51,000 lives a year (American Cancer Society, 2011). The majority of cases occur in men and women over the age of 50. Risk factors include a family or personal history of colorectal cancer or polyps (growths) and ulcerative colitis. High fat, low-fiber diets have also been shown to increase the risk. Symptoms include bleeding from the rectum, blood in the stool, or a change in bowel habits (recurring constipation or diarrhea). Digital rectal exams, stool blood tests, and proctoscopic exams can detect early stages of colorectal cancer. It is recommended that a digital rectal exam is performed annually after age 40, a stool blood test performed every year after age 50, and a proctosigmoidoscopy performed every three to five years after age 50. Regular exercise has been shown to reduce the risk in both men and women (Payne, Hahn, and Lucas, 2008). Hormone replacement therapy in postmenopausal women may significantly lower the risk of colon cancer.

Oral Cancers

Each year, more than 34,000 new cases of cancer of the oral cavity and pharynx are diagnosed and over 6,900 deaths due to oral cancer occur. The five-year survival rate for these cancers is only about 60 percent (ACS, 2011) www .cdc.gov/OralHealth/ Topics/Cancer.htm. Oral cancer is related directly to a person's behavior. The major behavioral risk factors include cigarette, pipe, or cigar smoking, excessive alcohol use, and chewing tobacco use. Particularly vulnerable are persons who drink and smoke. Early symptoms include: a bleeding sore that will not heal, a lump or thickening, a red or white patch (lesion) that will not go away, a persistent sore throat, difficulty chewing, swallowing, or moving of the tongue or jaws. A cure is often achieved easily with early detection.

Asthma

Asthma is a respiratory disorder that involves difficulty breathing, wheezing, and/ or coughing due to the constriction of the bronchial tubes. An individual will typically notice a wheezing sound when they are trying to breathe, while coughing and/or when experiencing difficulty breathing. In some cases those who suffer from asthma can stop an attack by simply removing themselves from an irritant such as cigarette smoke. Most of the time asthma attacks require some type of medical intervention, and, in rare cases, death can result from lack of treatment. Antihistamines, corticosteroids, and bronchodilating drugs are usually successful in reducing the bronchospasm. Reducing exposure to allergens, such as air pollution, pollen, dust, secondhand smoke, animal fur, bee venom, and specific foods, as well as nonallergens such as stress or intense exercise, can help prevent further asthma attacks. In the event that one must encounter an irritant, prescription drugs are available that help prevent asthma attacks. Some individuals are more likely to have difficulties with asthma: those with a family history, presence of atopy (the predisposition to respond to environmental allergens with specific IgE antibody production), and exposure to allergens, certain viral infections, and cigarette smoke. More children than adults suffer from asthma, because many children outgrow this condition.

Diabetes

Diabetes is becoming more common in the United States. From 1980 through 2006, the number of Americans with diabetes has more than tripled (from 5.6 million to 16.8 million; see Figure 11.4) (CDC, 2008) www.cdc.gov/diabetes/ Statistics/prev/ national/figpersons.htm. Diabetes is the result of insufficient insulin production or the body's inability to utilize insulin readily produced by the pancreas. Insulin has two major functions: to move glucose from the blood to the cells of the body where it is used as energy and to convert excess glucose to glycogen, for storage as an energy reserve in the liver and the muscles for later use (Floyd et al., 2007). There are three types of diabetes, Type I, Type II, and gestational.

Type I or insulin-dependent diabetes is typically associated with childhood or adolescent onset. In this form of diabetes the pancreas does not produce insulin, and the individual requires regular injections. The signs and symptoms of Type I diabetes appear suddenly and dramatically. Symptoms include fatigue, irritability, abnormal hunger and thirst, frequent urination, and weight loss (Floyd et al., 2007). This type of diabetes is only seen in about 5 percent of all diabetics and is considered the more serious of the two forms.

Type II or non-insulin-dependent diabetes is typically associated with adult onset and obesity. In this form of the disease the pancreas produces insulin, but the cells of the body are not able to use it effectively. The onset of Type II diabetes is more gradual than Type I. Some symptoms include drowsiness, blurred vision, itching, slow healing of cuts, skin infections, and numbness of fingers or toes (Floyd et al., 2007).

Gestational diabetes is a form of glucose intolerance or insulin resistance that is typically diagnosed in some women late in pregnancy. This type of diabetes affects about 4 percent of all pregnant women in the United States each year (ADA, 2005) or www.diabetes.org/gestational-diabetes.jsp. Gestational diabetes can cause dangerously high blood sugar levels to occur in the pregnant female. This type of diabetes occurs more frequently among African Americans, Hispanic/Latino Americans, and Asians (Dabelea, Snell-Bergeon, Heartsfield, et al, 2005). (See also Figure 11.5) It is also more common among obese women and women with a family history of diabetes.

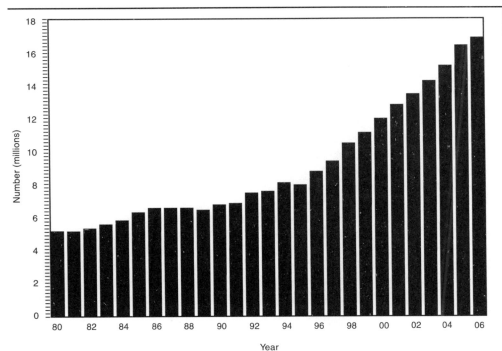

FIGURE 11.4

Number (in Millions) of Persons with Diagnosed Diabetes, United States, 1980–2006

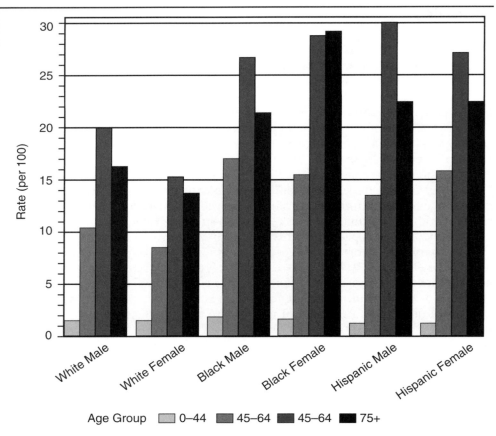

FIGURE 11.5

Age-Specific Prevalence of Diagnosed Diabetes, by Race/Ethnicity and Sex, United States, 2005

Age Group ☐ 0–44 ▨ 45–64 ▦ 45–64 ■ 75+

Gestational diabetes can be managed by eating healthy foods, exercising regularly, and in some cases, by taking medication to normalize maternal blood glucose levels to avoid complications in the mother and infant. Taking good care of yourself can help ensure a healthy pregnancy for you and a healthy start for your baby. After a pregnancy with gestational diabetes, 5 to 10 percent of women are found to have Type II diabetes. If a female has had gestational diabetes, there is a 66 percent chance that it will return in future pregnancies (www.diabetes.org/gestationaldiabetes.jsp).

If an individual suffering from diabetes is not treated, the illness can progress into a diabetic coma. If too much insulin is taken or inadequate food is eaten, an insulin reaction may occur, which, if serious, can result in a seizure (convulsions).

Patients with diabetes have a higher incidence of arteriosclerosis and the associated complications such as strokes, heart attacks, and gangrene of the lower extremities due to poor circulation, as well as degenerative effects of the small blood vessels supplying oxygen to the retina of the eye, which can lead to blindness.

The goal for those who have this condition is to balance blood sugar levels. Normal blood sugar ranges from 70 to 110 mg/dL. This can be done with insulin regimens, a structured diet, and regular exercise. With Type I diabetes, the individual usually can achieve this by monitoring the blood glucose level and adjusting the amount of insulin injected each day. In Type II diabetes, this can be accomplished with a controlled diet and regular exercise alone; in some instances oral hypoglycemic medication or insulin is required as well. The risk of developing diabetes can be reduced with regular activity, which reduces body weight and fat levels, and increases insulin sensitivity and glucose tolerance. Healthy dietary habits also decrease the fat levels as well as obesity, therefore enhancing the body's ability to transport glucose into the muscles.

From Head to Toe

Diabetes strikes nearly every part of the body. But studies show that treating diabetes aggressively can curb the damage.

BRAIN

People with diabetes are more likely to be diagnosed with dementia. Researchers don't know if the dementia is due to diabetes or to multiple mini-strokes (common in people with diabetes) that gradually impair mental function over time. If it's mini-strokes, lowering blood pressure might protect the brain.

HEART and BRAIN

The risk of heart attack or stroke is two to four times higher in people with diabetes.

Lowering high cholesterol can reduce heart attack and stroke by 20% to 50%.

Lowering high blood pressure can reduce the risk of heart attack and stroke by 33% to 50%.

FEET

Diabetes causes more than 60% of foot and leg amputations that are not caused by accidents.

Proper foot care (trim nails, check feet daily for red spots, cuts, swelling, blisters, etc.) can reduce the risk of amputation by 45% to 85%.

EYES

Diabetes is the leading cause of blindness among adults ages 20 to 74.

Every 1% reduction in A1C (from 8% to 7%, for example) lowers the risk of eye, kidney, and nerve disease by 40%.

Treating eye disease with laser therapy can reduce severe vision loss by 50% to 60%.

KIDNEYS

Diabetes is the leading cause of end-stage kidney disease.

Detecting early diabetic kidney disease (by testing urine for protein each year) and treating it can curb the loss of kidney function by 30% to 70%.

NERVES

An estimated six out of ten people with diabetes have nerve damage that can cause problems like numbness or pain in the feet or hands, carpal tunnel syndrome (in the wrist), and delayed digestion of food.

Lowering high blood pressure can reduce the risk of nerve, eye, and kidney damage by 33%.

Source: www.cdc.gov.

Image © clipart.com

Approximately 8 percent of Americans have diabetes (CDC, 2011). Diabetes is the leading cause of blindness among adults and accounts for about half of all amputations annually.

Anemia

Anemia means "without blood." It is a condition in which the quantity or quality of red blood cells is insufficient. Normal red blood cells contain hemoglobin, which carries oxygen to organs and tissues. Anemic individuals have a reduced oxygencarrying capacity. Anemias can be the result of too little iron, loss of blood (including heavy menstrual bleeding or frequent blood donations), insufficient red cell production or genetic abnormalities. Symptoms include fatigue, infection, and/or trouble healing. There are four types of anemias known:

1. *Iron-deficiency anemia*—develops with inadequate iron intake in the diet or excessive loss of iron, which can result from heavy menses. This is the most common form of anemia and can be corrected with iron supplements.
2. *Pernicious anemia*—caused by deficiency of vitamin B12, which decreases the production of red blood cells. The deficiency is due to an inability of the body to absorb B12 and is treated with vitamin B12 injections.
3. *Aplastic anemia*—stems from bone marrow failure resulting in a decreased number of red blood cells. Injury to bone marrow usually results from ingesting a toxic drug or chemical. Treatment is primarily with blood transfusions; however, the condition is most often fatal.
4. *Sickle-cell anemia*—an inherited trait caused by abnormal hemoglobins. These abnormal hemoglobins cause the red blood cells to be sickle-shaped, which impedes the flow of oxygen-carrying blood. Signs and symptoms include episodes of severe pain, swelling in hands or feet, susceptibility to infection due to a weakened immune system, and possible premature death. There is no cure for sickle-cell anemia, although the cancer drug hydroxyurea has proved to be successful in alleviating the pain. Sickle-cell anemia affects approximately 72,000 African Americans and one out of every 1,000–1,500 Latinos in the United States (Floyd et al., 2007). This type of anemia is a recessive trait-inherited condition, so there are many asymptomatic carriers without the disease. Because of this and the fact that there is no cure, the emphasis is shifting to prevention through education and genetic counseling.

Lupus

Lupus is a chronic inflammatory disease that occurs when your body's immune system attacks your own tissues and organs. There are four different types of lupus. They are: **systemic lupus erythematosus** (SLE), **cutaneous lupus erythematosus** (CLE), **drug-induced lupus,** and **neonatal lupus.**

SLE is an autoimmune disease that can affect various parts of the body including the skin, joints, heart, lungs, blood, kidneys, and brain. CLE is confined to the skin, but can evolve into SLE in approximately 10 percent of CLE cases (Lupis Foundation of America, 2008). Drug-induced lupus may develop after taking certain prescription medications. Symptoms associated with drug-induced lupus typically only last a few days to a few months. With an autoimmune disease the body cannot tell the difference between foreign substances such as viruses and bacteria and its own cells and tissues. When this happens the body begins attacking itself with auto-antibodies. This causes inflammation, pain, and damage in different parts of the body. Signs of inflammation include swelling, redness, pain, and warmth. If this inflammation is chronic, as with SLE, it can cause long-term damage. Signs and symptoms of a lupus flare include: aching all over, swollen joints, loss of appetite, recurring nose bleeds, sores on the skin, headache, nausea or vomiting, puffy eyelids, persistent fever over 100 degrees, prolonged fatigue, skin rashes, anemia, pain in the chest with deep breaths, excessive protein in urine, sensitivity to sun, hair loss, abnormal blood clotting problems, seizures, or mouth ulcers which last more than two weeks.

Lupus flares are highly variable as are the remission periods. Flare and remission periods can last a few days to a few years. Lupus affects people in varying degrees; most do not experience significant organ involvement and can lead a relatively normal life. Others have more flares and more discomfort associated with the disease and have to make changes in their previous lifestyle. More than 90 percent of people with lupus are women. Symptoms and diagnosis occur most often when women are in their child-bearing years, between the ages of 15 and 45.

In the United States, lupus is more than three times as common in African Americans as it is in Caucasians (LFA, 2008). Because diagnosis of lupus is relatively difficult, a rheumatologist is the best medical specialist to see if lupus is suspected. Because of the difficulty in diagnosing lupus, many individuals have been misdiagnosed and actually have had thyroid disease, fibromyalgia, rheumatoid arthritis, multiple sclerosis, or another disease. There is no cure for lupus, but depending upon the severity of the disease, treatment may consist of non-steroidal anti-inflammatory drugs such as ibuprofen or naproxen; corticosteroids such as prednisone or cortisone; anti-malarials such as hydroxychloroquine; or immunosuppressants for individuals who have the most severe flares of lupus.

Gastrointestinal Disorders

Ulcers, which are open sores, can develop in the lining of the stomach (gastric ulcers) or small intestine (duodenal ulcers) and are due to the corrosive effect of excessive gastric juices. Conventional theory blames lifestyle factors such as stress and diet. However, new research has identified a link between the bacterium *Helicobacter pylori* (*H. pylori*) and the formation of ulcers. One theory suggests that an infection caused by this bacterium leads to an inflammation of the stomach lining, which results in increased susceptibility of the stomach to stressors such as smoking, alcohol, high-fat diets, and/or anxiety. The most prominent symptom is a burning pain in the upper abdomen that is related to the digestive cycle. A bleeding ulcer, although not common, can be fatal. Excessive weight loss and anemia can result from an untreated ulcer. Medications that reduce stomach acid and relieve symptoms, lifestyle changes such as eating small, frequent meals, avoiding high-fat foods, cigarettes, alcohol, caffeine, and taking antacids can all reduce the effects of ulcers. One in five men and one in ten women suffer from peptic ulcers. Risk factors include: a stressful lifestyle, cigarette smoking, heavy use of alcohol, caffeine, or painkillers containing aspirin or ibuprofen, advanced age, and family history.

Irritable bowel syndrome (IBS) (spastic colon or irritable colon) is a common problem resulting from intestinal spasms. Symptoms include episodes of abdominal cramping, nausea, pain, gas, loud gurgling bowel sounds, and disturbed bowel function. No biochemical or structural abnormalities have been identified as the cause; therefore, no standard medical treatment exists for IBS. Common interventions include reducing emotional stress, eating high-fiber diets, or taking stool softeners, laxatives, and drugs to reduce intestinal spasms.

References

American Cancer Society. 2004. www.cancer.org

American Cancer Society. *Cancer Facts and Figures 2008*. Atlanta: Author. 2008.

American Diabetes Association (ADA). 2005. www.diabetes.org/gestational-diabetes.jsp

Benenson, A. *Control of Communicable Diseases in Man* (16th ed). Washington, DC: American Public Health Association. 1995.

Centers for Disease Control and Prevention (CDC). 2003. www.cdc.gov/meningitis/bacterial/faqs.htm#contagious

Centers for Disease Control and Prevention (CDC). 2005. www.cdc.gov/hepatitis

Centers for Disease Control and Prevention (CDC). 2006. www.cdc.gov/hepatitis/statistic/htm

Centers for Disease Control and Prevention (CDC). 2007. www.cdc.gov/OralHealth/ Topics/cancer.htm

Crowley, L. *An Introduction to Human Disease: Pathology and Pathophysiology Correlations* (8th ed). Boston: Jones and Bartlett Publishers, Inc. 2009.

Donatelle, R. *Access to Health* (12th ed). San Francisco: Benjamin Cummings. 2010.

Floyd, P., Mimms, S. and Yelding, C. *Personal Health: Perspectives & Lifestyles* (4th ed). Englewood, CO: Morton Publishing Co. 2007.

Hales, D. *An Invitation to Health* (15th ed). Pacific Grove, CA: Brooks/Cole Publishing Co. 2011.

Lupus Foundation of America. 2008.

Marwick, C. New light on skin cancer mechanisms. *Journal of the American Medical Association,* 274 (6). 1995.

McCance, K. and Huether, S. *Pathophysiology: The Biologic Basis for Disease in Adults and Children* (6th ed). St. Louis, MO: Mosby-Year Book, Inc. 2009.

Payne, W., Hahn, D., and Lucus, E. *Understanding Your Health* (10th ed). Boston: McGraw-Hill. 2008.

Dabelea, D., Snell-Bergeon, J. K., Heartsfield, C. L., et al. Increasing Prevalence of Gestational Diabetes Mellitus (GDM) Over Time and by Birth Cohort. *Diabetes Care* 28:579–584, 2005.

Schering Corporation. 1999. *Detection and Referral: The Primary Care Physician Guide to Chronic Viral Hepatitis*. Kenilworth, NJ. 1999.

Spence, W. "Skin Cancer: The Bare Facts." Health Edco. 1998.

www.cancer.org/docroot/CRI/content/CRI_2_2_2x_What_Causes_Testicular_Cancer_41.asp?rnav=cri

www.cdc.gov/diabetes/Statistics/prev/national/figpersons.htm

www.cdc.gov/hepatitis/HCVfac.htm#section4

www.cdc.gov/hepatitis/Resources/Professionals/PDFs/ABCTable.pdf

www.diabetes.niddk.nih.gov/dm/pubs/statistics/index.htm#allages

www.niaid.nih.gov

Contacts

American Cancer Society
800-ACS-2345
http://www.cancer.org

American Diabetes Association
800-342-2383
http://www.diabetes.org

American Institute for Cancer Research
http://www.aicr.org

American Liver Foundation
75 Maiden Lane, Suite 603
New York, NY 10038
212-668-1000
www.liverfoundation.org

Asthma and Allergy Foundation of
    America
800-7-ASTHMA
www.AAFA.org

National Cancer Institute
800-4-CANCER
www.cancer.gov

Centers for Disease Control and
    Prevention
800-232-4636
www.cdc.gov

Juvenile Diabetes Research Foundation
800-533-2873

National Headache Foundation
888-NHF-5552
www.headaches.org

National Institute of Diabetes &
    Digestive & Kidney Diseases
www.niddk.nih.gov

Activities

Notebook Activities

Current Trends Writing Assignment
Family Health Portrait (www.hhs.gov/familyhistory/)
Are You at Risk for Diabetes?
Family Tree Assignment

NOTEBOOK ACTIVITY

Current Trends Writing Assignment

What are the latest findings on a specific disease that interests you? Are there local or global implications to these findings? How does this information affect the college population and college campus?

NOTEBOOK ACTIVITY

Family Health Portrait

In order to do this project you must first research your family history. You may do an oral history or written correspondence with a family member, or you may research old records. Identify your source or sources of information. Record diseases and afflictions of all known family members through your great-grandparents. Pay particular attention to genetic disorders and the age of onset. Go to www.hhs.gov/familyhistory/ and enter your information. Once you are done, print out your Family Health Portrait. Have you inherited cardiac risk factors? Common factors to consider are family history of heart disease, diabetes, high blood pressure, high cholesterol, and some forms of cancer. What, if any, diseases are you at risk for due to your family history? What can you do now to have an impact on your long-term health for the future? How do you intend to avoid becoming "at-risk" in the future?

Please turn in your Family Health Portrait, as well as a typed (double-spaced) paragraph on how you can live your lifestyle now to best ensure you have a long and healthy life.

NOTEBOOK ACTIVITY

Are You at Risk for Diabetes?

Write in the points next to each statement that is true for you. Before each statement that is not true for you, place a zero. Then add up your total score.

1. I have been experiencing one or more of the following symptoms regularly.

   - Excessive thirst   Yes 3 _____

   - Frequent urination   Yes 3 _____

   - Extreme fatigue   Yes 1 _____

   - Unexplained weight loss   Yes 3 _____

   - Blurry vision from time to time   Yes 2 _____

2. I am over 30 years old.   Yes 1 _____

3. I am more than 20 percent overweight. (See next page.)   Yes 2 _____

4. I am a woman who has had more than one baby weighing over nine pounds at birth.   Yes 2 _____

5. I am of Native American descent.   Yes 1 _____

6. I am of Hispanic or African American descent.   Yes 1 _____

7. I have a parent with diabetes.   Yes 1 _____

8. I have a brother or sister with diabetes.   Yes 2 _____

                                                        Total _____

Scoring 3–5 points
You probably are at low risk for diabetes. Do not just forget about it, though, especially if you are 30, overweight, or of African American, Hispanic, or Native American descent.

Scoring over 5 points
You may be at high risk for diabetes. You may even have diabetes already.

What to do about it
See your doctor promptly. Find out if you have diabetes. Even if you do not have diabetes, know the symptoms. If you experience any of them in the future, you should see your doctor immediately.

Note: This test is meant to educate and make you aware of the serious risks of diabetes. Only a medical doctor can determine if you do have diabetes.
Source: American Diabetes Association.

At-Risk Weight Chart

*Weight in pounds without clothing and without shoes.

Height in Feet/Inches	Women	Men
4'9"	134	
4'10"	137	
4'11"	140	
5'0"	143	
5'1"	146	157
5'2"	150	160
5'3"	154	162
5'4"	157	165
5'5"	161	168
5'6"	164	172
5'7"	168	172
5'8"	172	179
5'9"	175	182
5'10"	178	186
5'11"	182	190
6'0"	194	
6'1"	199	
6'2"	203	
6'3"	209	

This chart shows weights that are 20 percent heavier than what is recommended for men and women with a medium frame. If your weight is at or above the amount listed for your height, you may be at risk for diabetes.

Name _____ Section _____ Date _____

Family Tree Assignment

Assignment MUST BE TYPED and include all info below if you want credit

In order to do this project you must first research your family history. You may do an oral history or written correspondence with a family member or you may research old records. Identify your sources of information. Record diseases and afflictions of all known family members through your great-grandparents. Pay particular attention to genetic disorders and the age of onset. Have you inherited cardiac risk factors? Common factors to consider are family history of heart disease, diabetes, high blood pressure, high cholesterol, and some forms of cancer. What, if any, diseases are you at risk for due to your family history: What can you do now to have an impact on your long-term health for the future? How do you intend to avoid becoming "at risk" in the future? Please type (double-spaced) your detailed family history in the first paragraph. In the second paragraph relate how you can live your lifestyle now to best ensure you have a long and healthy life. You can also include a drawing of your family tree if this enhances the project, but it is not necessary.

Ask about all kinds of diseases: cardiovascular diseases (arteriosclerosis, atherosclerosis, peripheral vascular disease, hypertension, heart attack, stroke, etc.). Obesity, cancer, diabetes, low back pain, osteoporosis, mental health disorders (depression, bi-polar, schizophrenia, panic disorders, general anxiety disorders, etc.). Report all diseases in your family. The more you know of your family history the better.

If you are adopted and you have no idea who both biological parents are: you can still benefit from doing this assignment. Lifestyle is a huge factor in several of the diseases that will be covered in class.

Chapter 12
Complementary and Alternative Medicine

© Luna Vandoorne, 2012. Shutterstock, Inc.

OBJECTIVES

Students will be able to:

- Identify components of holistic self-care.
- Define key terms related to complementary and alternative medicine (CAM).
- Become familiar with the therapies contained in each major CAM domain.
- Identify pros and cons associated with each major CAM practice.
- Identify benefits of mindfulness in everyday life.
- Participate in a self-guided relaxation/meditation practice.

"The doctor of the future will give no medicine, but will interest his patients in the care of the human frame, in diet, and in the cause and prevention of disease."

—Thomas Edison

Introduction

by Amy V. Nowak, Ph.D. TAMU

As an adult, making informed healthcare decisions is key to achieving higher levels of health and wellness. To become an informed healthcare consumer, it is important to be aware of the many choices available to you in healthcare today. Learning about each form of healthcare, as well as its risks and benefits, will allow you to make the best choices that meet the needs of your health situation.

Americans value choice in any venue and healthcare is no different. When buying a car, you want a quality vehicle to meet your needs, a company that can give you a good product, and a salesperson that you trust, and who is dedicated to helping you meet your goals. The same goes for healthcare. You want to find a healthcare option that fits with your healthcare needs, a treatment which will be effective, and a healthcare provider whom you trust and who is dedicated to helping you. With healthcare, you have the option of choosing one or a combination of healthcare approaches and providers to best meet your needs.

There are two main camps of healthcare today. You are probably very familiar with what is called conventional medicine. When you go to a conventional clinic or hospital, doctors and nurses work to diagnose an illness and then treat the symptoms with medication, surgery, or radiation. The roots of conventional medicine date back to the mid-1800's with the discovery of the germ and its relationship to illness. While this is the main form of healthcare used in the United States and similar developed nations around the world, more and more people are turning to other types of healthcare that do not fit in the mainstream of conventional medicine.

The other main category of medicine is a group of traditional systems and practices, which are currently called complementary and alternative medicine (CAM). The terms complementary and alternative are actually designations of how traditional medical practices, some of which developed thousands of years ago, are used in relation to conventional care. Systems and practices are considered **complementary** when used in conjunction with conventional care and **alternative** when used instead of conventional care. The emphasis in CAM is holistic, in the sense that its purpose is to treat the whole person and support the body's natural ability to heal itself. The increasing use of CAM is expected to continue as people seek out options in healthcare to best meet their needs.

Medicine has come a long way since the days of the snake-oil salesmen of the early nineteenth century. In the 1800's, homeopaths, midwives, naturopaths, and an assortment of lay healers used herbs and nostrums to combat illness. Thanks to the wonders of modern conventional and emergency medicine, many of the ill and injured can survive what fifty years ago would have meant certain death. This is surely being played out in the modern landscape of the war-torn Middle East. Due to improved body armor, field medical procedures, and medevac capabilities, wounded soldiers are surviving what they would not have survived in the Vietnam War or World War II. Conventional medicine can work mini-miracles in acute trauma care, the treatment of bacterial infections and life-threatening diseases. Life saving antibiotics and other drugs have revolutionized the medical field. What conventional medicine has failed to do is prevent the lifestyle-related hypokinetic diseases that plague Western society. Conventional (also called Western, allopathic, or biomedical) medicine developed from the evidence-based scientific method. Traditionally, alternative medicine (also called natural, unconventional, or unorthodox in the past) has been based on anecdotal evidence, word of mouth, testimonials, or even the placebo effect. Scientists in the bio-medical research community are recognizing that more and more Americans are choosing complementary and alternative medicine (hereafter referred to as CAM), and therefore funding to test the safety and efficacy of CAM approaches is increasing. *Part of the attraction of the CAM modalities may be their identification with prevention rather than cure, and consequently CAM has come to be identified with wellness and self-care.*

© Hannamariah, 2012, Shutterstock, Inc.

Alternative practitioners emphasize a wholesome diet rich in organic fruits, vegetables, nuts, seeds, fiber, pure water, and organically raised meat products.

Today, alternative medicine is also called holistic, complementary, or integrative. Refer back to the wellness dimensions from Chapter 1; a holistic practitioner considers the physical, emotional, mental, social, occupational, environmental, and spiritual factors associated with the individual as a "whole person." "Practitioners of alternative medicine approach healing from a holistic perspective where the primary goal is the creation and maintenance of optimum health in body, mind, and spirit. In addition to the comprehensive care they provide to achieve that goal, they also serve as teachers, instructing their patients in effective methods of selfcare. Such methods not only assist patients in their journey back to wellness, but also help them prevent disease from occurring in the first place "(Goldberg, 2002).

Alternative practitioners emphasize **holistic self-care.** A wholesome **diet** minimizing intake of processed food with foods rich in organic fruits and vegetables, nuts, seeds, fiber, pure water, and organically raised meat products is recommended. **Exercise** is critical to maintaining physical health. Adequate **sleep** is necessary to allow the regenerative processes in the body to work. Keeping the **environment** at home and work healthy may mean adding indoor plants, air filters, humidifiers, and avoiding toxic chemicals and secondhand smoke. Peace of mind and contentment are part of **good mental health.** Spiritual health is also considered an important part of self-care. **Spiritual health** can be gained through prayer, meditation, or even giving of yourself through volunteerism. *In alternative or holistic care, the patient takes an active role and is responsible for looking at all aspects or his/her health.*

How many Americans are using CAM? According to a 2007 National Health Interview Study (NHIS) four out of ten adults use some form of CAM therapy on a regular basis. Twelve percent of children (ages 0–18 years) use CAM (see Figure 12.1). Native Alaskan and American Indians were the most likely to use some form of CAM, followed by white adults. Caucasian college-educated women in a higher income bracket use CAM more than other segments of the

FIGURE 12.1

CAM Use by U.S. Adults and Children

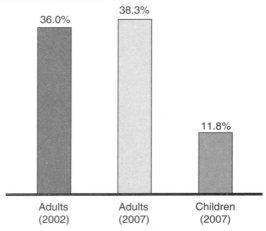

Source: National Institute of Health.

population. However, CAM is practiced by all types of people across racial, cultural, and socioeconomic lines (see Figure 12.2). The most commonly used CAM therapies are non–vitamin, non–mineral, natural products (for instance, fish oil, echinacea, DHA, glucosamine, and ginseng), deep breathing, meditation, yoga, massage, chiropractic care, and diet-based therapies (see Figure 12.3). Chiropractic is used the most by patients with back pain.

Note: The 2007 NHIS did not include folk medicine practices (i.e., covering a wart with a penny and then burying it) or religious healing, as in prayer for oneself or for others. The 2002 NHIS did include prayer in its survey.

Figure 12.4 shows several accepted and widely used treatments that are rooted in CAM. Indeed, even exercise prescribed as a healing modality was once considered "alternative." "In an age of M.R.I. scans and spinal fusion surgery, a treatment as low tech as exercise can seem to some patients rudimentary or even dangerously illogical" (Ryzik, 2005). Cardiovascular exercise helps with increased circulation and flexibility, and core muscle strength focuses on supporting the spine which can help prevent future pain. Perhaps in the future many more CAM modalities will become mainstream (see Table 12.1).

FIGURE 12.2

CAM Use by Race/ Ethnicity among Adults 2007

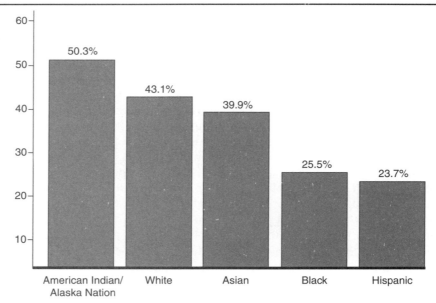

Source: National Institute of Health.

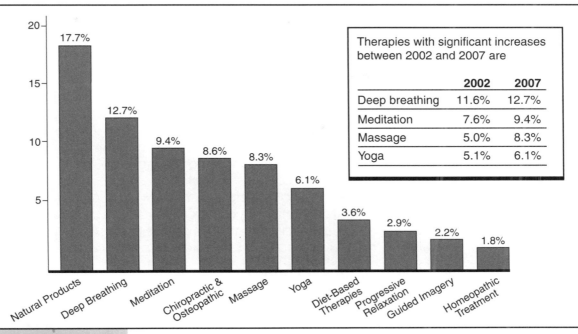

FIGURE 12.3

Ten Most Common CAM Therapies among Adults 2007

Source: Center for Disease Control

Alternative Healthcare Systems

Alternative healthcare systems are holistic "whole person" systems. Whole person systems refer to treating more than just a patient's symptoms. The CAM practitioner often interviews the patient in an attempt to determine the patient's history, eating habits, lifestyle choices, and so on. Some patients report that they appreciate the fact that their practitioner often regards self-care, positive lifestyle habits, behaviors, quality of life, and the combined role of the mind, body, and spirituality in health, disease, and healing as being very important (WHCCAMP, 2002). Typically the CAM practitioner works out of a small facility and spends a fair amount of time with their patient, which

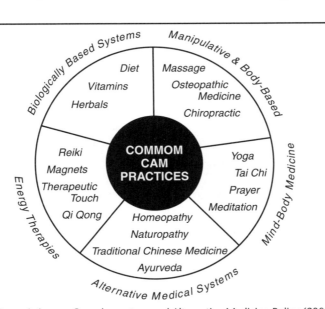

FIGURE 12.4

CAM Domains and Their Related Pratices

Source: White House Commission on Complementary and Alternative Medicine Policy (2008)

Essential Oils

by Mike Hanik, M.S. TAMU

Essential oils are the natural, aromatic, volatile liquids found in shrubs, flowers, roots, trees, bushes, and seeds. Essential oils are also capable of readily changing from liquid to vapor at normal temperatures and pressures. Each essential oil may consist of hundreds of different and unique chemical compounds that defend plants against insects, environmental conditions, and disease. They also help plants grow, live, and adapt to its environment. Essential oils are extracted from aromatic plant sources by steam distillation. This allows the essential oils to be highly concentrated. It often takes an entire plant to produce a single drop of essential oil.

Essential oils often have a pleasant aroma and their chemical makeup may provide many health benefits. This is why essential oils have been used throughout history by many cultures for medicinal and therapeutic purposes. Recently there has been a renewed interest in studying the many benefits of essential oils.

Peppermint oil has been shown to have a calming and numbing effect. It has been used to treat headaches, skin irritations, anxiety associated with depression, nausea, and diarrhea. In test tube experiments, peppermint kills some types of bacteria, viruses, and fungus suggesting it may have antibacterial, antiviral, and antifungal properties.

Another common essential oil is lavender oil. Research has confirmed that lavender produces calming, soothing, and sedative effects when its scent is inhaled. Lavender oil may also help alleviate insomnia, anxiety, and fatigue.

Prior to using essential oils it is important to learn about the chemistry and safety of the oils. In order to experience the benefits of essential oils, high quality of pure essential oils must be used. A person will not experience the benefits of essential oils if they use diluted, adulterated, or synthetic oils.

It is important to research the companies that supply the essential oils. Learn how the company selects, grows and harvests its plants. Where the plant is grown, the quality of the soil, and time of day that the plant is harvested can all impact the quality and makeup of the essential oil. The distillation process is also important in making high quality essential oils. In order to get the best quality essential oils, proper temperature and pressure, length of time, equipment, and batch size must be closely monitored throughout the distillation process. Like any other product, it is important to fully research and understand essential oils in order to make an informed decision.

TABLE 12.1 ♦ Currently Used CAM Modalities
CAM Modalities Now in Mainstream Medicine
Codeine for pain
Digitalis for heart failure
Quinine for malaria
Aspirin for fever
Behavioral therapy for headache
Hypnosis for smoking cessation
Exercise for diabetes
Support groups for breast cancer
Low-fat, low-cholesterol diets

may be more attractive to the patient than the short fifteen-minute appointment most people get with their busy conventional doctor. Included in the Alternative Healthcare System domain of CAM is ayurvedic medicine, homeopathic medicine, Native American medicine, and traditional Chinese medicine (including acupuncture and Chinese herbal medicine). Interestingly, the CAM therapies with the most acceptance by the medical community are some of the most infrequently used by patients—hypnotherapy, acupuncture, and biofeedback.

Ayurveda is thought to be the oldest medical system known. In Hindu mythology Ayurveda is considered the medicine of the gods. In Sanskrit, ayurveda is "knowledge of life," with life being defined as mind, body, and spiritual awareness. "Ayurveda is based on the belief that the natural state of the body is one of balance. We become ill when this balance is disrupted, with specific conditions or symptoms indicating a particular disease or imbalance. Ayurveda emphasizes strengthening and purifying the whole person, whereas in conventional medicine, the focus is on a set of symptoms or an isolated region of the body" (Alternative Medicine Foundation, 2005).

Ayurvedic teaching states that every living thing in the universe is made of these five elements: earth, water, fire, air, and space. The elements combine to determine a dosha, or metabolic type. A person's personality and character determine which of three doshas they are: Vata, Pitta, or Kapha. The practitioner can determine which dosha a patient is, then prescribe botanics, exercise, yoga, and scash or massage therapy according to the person's particular dosha type. Ayurvedic practitioners mainly diagnose by observation and by touch. Caution with botanicals is advised as a 2008 study determined that a type of ayurveda that uses Rasa shastra (herbal medicines mixed with minerals and metals) may be cause for concern. Twenty-one percent of the medicines tested (obtained from the Internet) had unsafe levels of lead, arsenic, and mercury (Saper, Phillips, Sehgal, et al., 2008).

Homeopathy is based on a three pronged theory that *like cures like*, treatment is very individualized, and less is more. Homeopathic practitioners give very diluted forms of the substance that causes the symptoms of the disease in healthy people to the ill in the hopes that it will help support the body's natural healing power. The World Health Organization (WHO) has cited homeopathy as one of the systems of traditional medicine that should be integrated worldwide with conventional medicine in order to provide adequate global care in the twenty-first century (Goldberg, 2002). Homeopaths use low cost herbals, chemicals, and minerals.

Naturopathy is based on the motto "Vis Medicatrix Naturae," which is Latin for *helping nature heal*. Naturopaths emphasize restoring health rather than curing disease. Naturopaths utilize many different healing "tools" found in nature, such as magnets, water, heat, crystals, the sun, herbal medicine, manipulation, light therapy, electrical currents, and more. Naturopaths argue

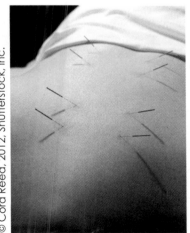

Acupuncture is an ancient medical art using the insertion of very fine needles into the body.

that Americans should return to a more natural and to a simpler way of life. Some naturopaths contend that we should go so far as to cease fluoridation of water and eliminate the addition of preservatives to food. There are three naturopathic training schools in the United States and one in Canada. Although these schools have a four year program emphasizing humanistic medicine, the naturopath is not an M.D.

Traditional oriental medicine (TOM) is a comprehensive system that dates back to the Stone Age. Also called traditional Chinese medicine (TCM), it includes acupuncture, acupressure, herbal medicine (discussed under Biological-Based Therapies), oriental massage, and qi gong (discussed under Energy Therapies). **Acupuncture** is an ancient medical art using the insertion of very fine needles on the body in order to affect physiological functioning in the body. The needles are placed on the body at points that correspond to twelve meridians throughout the body. Manipulation of the needles, electrical stimulation, heat, and burning herbs (moxibustion) can be used in acupuncture. Before making a diagnosis, the practitioner talks with, and asks questions about, the patient. Typically the acupuncturist will check the pulse and the tongue of the patient to help diagnose the problem. A reputable acupuncturist will use disposable needles or sterilize reusable needles in an autoclave. With the millions of people treated with acupuncture, there have been relatively few complications reported to the U.S. Food and Drug Administration (FDA). Acupuncturists have a Master of Traditional Oriental Medicine and are required to be state-licensed.

All TOM recognizes an energy force that flows through the body called qi (pronounced chi). Qi consists of the spiritual, physical, mental, and emotional aspects of life. Yin and yang are the vital forces of life that run throughout the twelve meridians within the body. Stimulation of points on the meridians is thought to activate the qi, which restores the body's equilibrium and allows the free flow of qi. The body is considered a flowing, self-healing system. Pain and discomfort can be the result of stagnation of energy which needs to be brought back into balance. Patients may experience calm and peacefulness as well as rejuvenation when their qi has been restored.

U.S. medical doctors became more interested in acupuncture in 1971 when James Reston, a well respected New York Times columnist, had to undergo emergency surgery while in China. Doctors there eased his post-surgery pain with acupuncture. There have been numerous studies done in the United States on the effectiveness of acupuncture. In December 2004 results of the largest randomized, controlled phase III clinical trial of acupuncture ever conducted were published in the *Annals of Internal Medicine*. The study was conducted on 570 patients with osteoarthritis of the knee. The results showed

Can acupuncture give the athlete an edge in competition? It is possible that acupuncture treatment can be a positive adjunct to training, just like massage or physical therapy. Needles placed at sites of inflammation may reduce time out of training due to injury or swelling of tissue. There is little research, but Whitfield Reaves (2008) has used pre-performance needling and found personal benefit. Ear (auricular) acupuncture has been used during an athlete's competition, with small "tacks" kept in the ear. Acupuncture points don't work for everyone, but perhaps some sports acupuncture can make your next run a little more enjoyable.

that "acupuncture reduces pain and functional impairment of osteoarthritis of the knee" (NIH, 2004). Dr. Brian M. Berman, M.D. of the University of Maryland School of Medicine directed the study and concluded that acupuncture is an effective complement to conventional arthritis treatment. According to a CDC 2002 survey, 2.1 million Americans have used acupuncture.

Acupressure is similar to acupuncture, but without the needles. The practitioner applies pressure to critical points along the meridian lines to balance yin and yang. There are different pressure points corresponding to specific parts of the body. The pressure releases muscular tension and promotes circulation of blood and qi to promote healing. Gradual steady penetrating pressure for up to three minutes is common (Gach, 1990). Simple acupressure techniques can be practiced on oneself. For example, between the forefinger and thumb is an acupressure point for headaches. **Shiatsu** is a type of acupressure massage using fingers, elbows, fists, and so on to apply pressure to restore the flow of energy in the body.

Manipulative and Body-Based Therapies

Manipulative and body-based therapies in CAM use movement or manipulation of part of the body (see Figure 12.5).

Chiropractic is a medical treatment defined as the science of spinal manipulation. Chiropractic is the most commonly used form of CAM in the United States with 18 million Americans visiting the chiropractor each year. A June 2005 Consumer Reports Survey of 34,000 readers reported that of those interviewed with back pain, more went to the chiropractor than used prescription drugs. Practiced in earnest in the United States since 1895, chiropractic can trace its roots back to Galen and Hippocrates who laid their hands on patients for manipulation. Chiropractic is considered to be the oldest indigenous CAM practices in the United States (NIH Lecture Series, 2002). Chiropractic has been seen in the past to be in competition with conventional medical treatment. Early in the last century, state medical boards used their power to restrict chiropractic practice. The chiropractors successfully brought an antitrust suit against the American Medical Association for allegedly trying to eliminate chiropractic practice in the United States. Today the medical

> "When qi gathers, the physical body is formed, when qi disperses, the body passes on."
>
> –Ancient Chinese Proverb

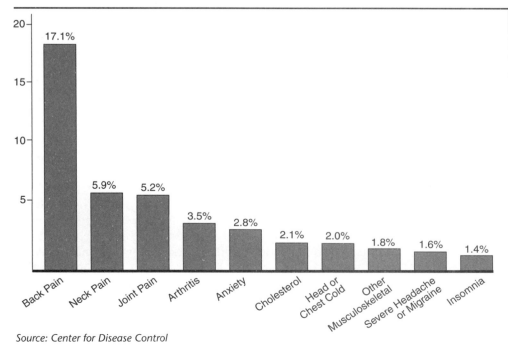

FIGURE 12.5

Diseases/Conditions for Which CAM Is utilized in the U.S.

Source: Center for Disease Control

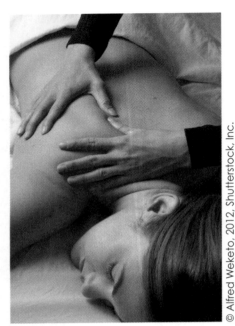

© Alfred Weketo, 2012, Shutterstock, Inc.

Massage involves manipulation of muscle and connective tissue to enhance function and promote relaxation and well-being.

doctors and the doctors of chiropractic enjoy a better working relationship. Chiropractors train for up to six years with in-depth courses in anatomy, physiology, nutrition, and pathology. They also have clinical training.

Chiropractors manipulate the spine, often with high-velocity, low-amplitude spinal adjustments, to align the spine in order to let energy flow through the nervous system. It is unclear exactly how chiropractic works, however scientific evidence supports the use of chiropractic to treat acute or chronic back pain (NIH Lecture Series, 2002). Safety is always a concern, and the apparent risk for lumbar vertebrae adjustment is one in 1 million. Back and head complaints are the most common reason patients visit the physician or chiropractor, which results in $100 billion annually in lost productivity.

Many Americans suffer from neck pain. A recent study looked at the effectiveness of spinal manipulation, home exercise and medication to reduce acute neck pain. The spinal manipulation group received adjustments and mobilization exercises for the spine. The home exercise group received detailed instructions for gentle exercises for the neck and shoulders to be done 6 to 8 times per day. The third group received non-steroidal anti-inflammatory drugs (NSAIDS) as well as acetaminophen. Narcotic medications were an option for those who could not tolerate the NSAIDS. Both the exercises and the spinal manipulations groups were equal in improvement with participant rated pain. At 12 weeks, 82% of the exercise and manipulation groups experienced a 50% reduction in pain. Of the medication group, 69% noted improvements of at least 50% reduction in pain. The findings were similar at 26 and 52 weeks. "Additionally, the spinal manipulation group reported greater global improvement, participant satisfaction and function than the medication group" (NCCAM, 2012). The results from this study suggest that movement-based therapies can be effective in chronic pain management, especially before invasive techniques like surgery are considered. The *Clinical Journal of Pain* also reported results from a 2009 study that chronic neck pain patients experienced benefits from therapeutic massage (NCCAM, 2009).

Massage involves manipulation of muscle and connective tissue to enhance function of those tissues and to promote relaxation and well-being. Massage is growing in popularity as the use and acceptance of massage therapy increases. Many Fortune 500 companies are including massage as a benefit for their employees. Even small companies that offer on-site fifteen-minute massage are seeing the benefit in lower employee absenteeism due to headache, fatigue, and back pain (AMTA, 2005). Deep tissue, Swedish, myofascial release, petressage (kneading), sports massage, and trigger point therapy are just a few of the popular types of massage today.

Reflexology is based on the fact that the feet and hands represent a microcosm of the body and that specific parts of the foot and hand correspond or "reflex" to other parts of the body. Working with the feet has been used in many ancient medical practices; however William Fitzgerald developed modern reflexology in the early 1900's in England.

Craniosacral therapy has its origins in the 1800's with Andrew Still M.D. The current form of craniosacral therapy was developed by osteopathic physician John E. Upledger at Michigan State University as a therapy that uses gentle touch to evaluate the physiological functioning of the craniosacral system. The craniosacral system is comprised of the membranes and the cerebrospinal fluid that surrounds and protects the spinal cord. Imbalance in the cerebral and spinal systems may cause sensory or motor dysfunction (IAHE, 2005). As relaxing as a massage, this therapy is typically used by people experiencing chronic pain who have not found relief with other therapies.

Biological-Based Therapies

Biological-based therapies use substances found in nature such as food, vitamins, minerals, herbal products, animal-derived products, probiotics, amino acids, whole diets, and functional foods. Some biological-based therapies are evidenced-based. For example, the FDA now fortifies some foods with folic acid to deter potential neural tube defects in developing fetuses. There are other biological-based therapies that are as of yet unproven. An example is the use of shark cartilage as a treatment for cancer. The consumer should be informed and use common sense and do a little research before spending money and making important decisions regarding healthcare. Drugs are monitored by the FDA, but biological-based systems are measured for truth in advertising by the Federal Trade Commission (FTC). The following biological-based therapies are just a few of the options for consumers today.

Macrobiotics is more than a diet, it is a discipline based on a philosophy of balance in accordance with the universe. It involves managing or changing diet to enhance health or for spiritual benefit. Macrobiotics is characterized by excluding meat and concentrating heavily on whole grains. Besides modifying diet, basic macrobiotic practices emphasize an active life, a positive mental outlook, and regularly eating small portions. There are numerous testimonials from cancer patients that have recovered from a stage IV cancer diagnosis using the macrobiotic diet. The National Cancer Institute has funded a clinical study to determine the effects of a macrobiotic diet on cancer therapy (www .clinicaltrials.gov/ct/gui/c/alb/show/ NCT00010829). As you recall, evidence-based science needs clinical trials to provide scientific evidence in order for a therapy or treatment to have wide acceptance.

Herbals and dietary supplements are a hot trend in the industry, making manufacturers four billion dollars richer each year. Herbal therapy has been around for several thousand years. It is likely the oldest and most widely used therapy with roots in traditional Oriental medicine and the ayurvedic tradition. Herbs are substances derived from trees, flowers, plants, seaweed, and lichen. Herbs are prepared in several different forms: tinctures which contain grain alcohol for preservation, freeze-dried extracts, and standardized extracts. Herbs are contained in some manufactured drugs; drugs can also contain a synthetic copy of the herb. *Many plant extracts can be very beneficial, however it is prudent to remember that herbs are drugs and should be consumed only as prescribed.* Even if the consumer is using the herbal remedy correctly, there may be an adverse interaction with food, over-the-counter drugs (OTC), vitamins and minerals, or prescriptions drugs. Recent studies done by NCCAM (NIH, 2002) found that St. John's wort reduces the action of a common AIDS drug called Indinavir (see Figure 12.6). St. John's wort, commonly used for mild to moderate depression, clears 50 percent of all pharmaceutical drugs from the human body (Markowitz et al., 2003).

An herbalist is a practitioner who bases most of his therapy on the medicinal qualities of plant and herbs. Herbs are prescribed so much in some parts of Europe that they might not even be considered alternative. There are volumes of testimonials, lots of anecdotal evidence, and many cultural traditions supporting herbal therapy. Gingko biloboa is purported to help with memory. St. John's wort helps with depression (some studies support this, some refute it). Saw palmetto helps manage an enlarged prostate. Butterbur, bee pollen, and stinging nettle may help with allergy symptoms. Evening primrose oil helps to manage PMS. The list is endless! When working with an experienced herbalist it is important to try and regulate the quality of the product you are getting. Using caution, especially when self-prescribing, is important because: safety is assumed, not

> "Let thy food be thy medicine and thy medicine be thy food."
> —Hippocrates (460–377 B.C.)

> "No illness which can be treated by the diet should be treated by any other means."
> –Moses Maimonides (1135–1204)

© Brian Chase, 2012, Shutterstock, Inc.

Many plant extracts can be beneficial, however it is prudent to remember that herbs are drugs and should be consumed only as prescribed.

FIGURE 12.6

Biologically Based Systems: St. John's Wort Lowers Blood Levels of HIV Protease Inhibitor Indinavir

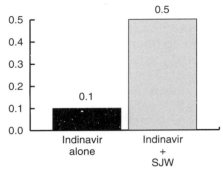

Note: HIV Inhibition threshold = 0.1. Indinavir Level (ug/ml)

proven; products are not standardized; products can be contaminated; you may have an allergic reaction, some herbs or certain amounts of the herb can be toxic, and the herbs can interact with drugs. Purity, standardization, and quality of the herbs can be an issue in consistency and the amount of the herb in the product. Another reason to use caution is that sometimes we get the sense that if a little works, perhaps a little more will work better. Toxic levels of drugs and herbs can be dangerous. If your friend takes 200 mg of a drug or herb, then you might do the same with disastrous consequences. You may be a nonresponder for that substance and get no result, or you may tolerate the substance and need a larger amount. Another issue is the amount of product actually contained in the packaging. See Figure 12.7 on ginseng.

An example of an unsafe drug is ephedra, derived from the Chinese herb Ma Huang. Traditionally Ma Huang has been used in China to treat asthma and other ailments associated with respiration. Ephedra was confirmed to be a factor in the death of Orioles pitching prospect Steve Belcher in February of 2003. Steve was taking ephedra to give him energy and to assist him with weight loss. The facts that Steve used ephedra, it was hot, and he was exercising combined to cause his death. The FDA has since banned the use of ephedra. If you are wondering about the safety of a particular herb, a very informative website that contains warnings and safety information is the USFDA Center for Food Safety and Applied Nutrition's Dietary Supplements: Warnings and Safety Information (www.cfsan.fda.gov/~dms/ds-warn.html).

Did You Know?

National Consumers League Food and Drug Interaction Brochure

NCL is your consumer healthcare advocate.

Medicines are powerful. The drugs your physician prescribes to you can help your health. A drug's effectiveness can be rendered ineffective or enhanced by food, drink, herbs (botanicals), and other drugs in your diet. Log on to this Web site, write, or call the NCL to obtain this important food and drug interaction brochure.

www.nclnet.org

National Consumers League (nonprofit membership organization)

1701 K Street, NW, Suite 1200

Washington DC 20006 (202) 835-3323

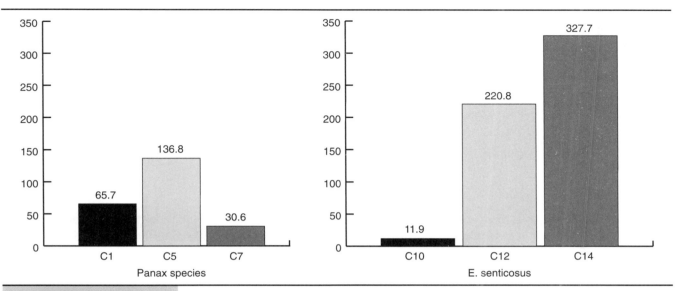

FIGURE 12.7

Variability in Commercial Ginseng Products
Adapted from Harkey, *American Journal of Clinical Nutrition*, 2001.

Functional foods are foods that contain compounds like phytochemicals that are beneficial beyond basic nutrition, especially when eaten on a regular basis as part of a varied diet. This is a relatively new classification of foods and the specific benefits are still being determined. It is possible that functional foods act synergistically with other foods and antioxidants. See Table 12.2 for examples of functional foods and potential benefits. Isoflavones in soy products, omega-3 fatty acids in cold water fish, essential fatty acids and fiber in ground flaxseed, and probiotic yeasts found in some yogurts are examples of other functional foods. If you eat a wholesome diet with plenty of fruits and vegetables and whole grains, then most likely you are getting functional foods in your diet (Corbin et al., 2009).

Vitamins and minerals are two of the six essential components for life in the human diet. As with herbs, a little is good but more is not always better. Use caution when megadosing on vitamins and minerals to avoid toxicity and health risks. As always, it is good to consult your physician or an educated CAM practitioner. We will not discuss the particulars of vitamins and minerals here; however, remember that often the best way to get vitamins and minerals is through a daily balanced diet. For those that have chronically deficient diets, a multivitamin and mineral supplement is most likely a good recommendation. For evidence-based information on herbal and supple ments, log onto *HerbMed* for herbal information or to *Medline Plus* for other supplement information; the address is found at the back of the chapter in the list of resources.

"The revolution we call mind-body medicine was based on this simple discovery: Wherever thought goes, a chemical goes with it. This insight has turned into a powerful tool that allows us to understand, for example, why recent widows are twice as likely to develop breast cancer, and why the chronically depressed are four times more likely to get sick. In both cases, distressed mental states get converted into the bio-chemicals that create disease."
—Deepak Chopra, M.D. (1993)

TABLE 12.2 ♦ Examples of Functional Foods and Potential Benefits

Carotenoids	Potential Benefits
Beta-carotene: found in carrots, pumpkin, sweet potato, cantaloupe	May bolster cellular antioxidant defenses
Lutein, zeaxanthin: found in kale, collards, spinach, corn, eggs, citrus	May contribute to healthy vision
Lycopene: Found in tomatoes, watermelon, red/pink grapefruit	May contribute to prostate health
Flavonoids	**Potential Benefits**
Anthocyanins: found in berries, cherries, red grapes *Flavanones*: found in citrus foods *Flavonols*: found in onions, apples, tea, broccoli	May bolster antioxidant defenses; maintain brain function and heart health
Isothiocyanates	**Potential Benefits**
Proanthocyanidins: found in cranberries, cocoa, apples, strawberries, grapes, peanuts	May contribute to maintenance of urinary tract health and heart health
Sulforaphane: found in cauliflower, broccoli, brussels sprouts, cabbage, kale, horseradish	May enhance detoxification of undesirable compounds; bolsters cellular antioxidant defenses
Phenolic Acids	**Potential Benefits**
Caffeic/ferulic acids: found in apples, pears, citrus fruits, some vegetables, coffee	May bolster cellular antioxidant defenses; may contribute to maintenance of healthy vision
Sulfides/Thioles	**Potential Benefits**
Sulfides: found in garlic, onions, leeks, scallions *Dithiolthiones*: found in cruciferous vegetables	May enhance detoxification of undesirable compounds; may contribute to maintenance of heart health and healthy immune function

Source: From *Concepts of Physical Fitness*, 15th Edition, by Charles Corbin et al. Copyright © 2009 by McGraw-Hill Companies. Reprinted by permission of The McGraw-Hill Companies, Inc.

There are numerous meditative techniques. Almost all techniques involve focus on breathing.

Mind-Body Medicine

Mind-body medicine taps into the connection between the physical body and the very powerful mind. Mind-body therapies are designed to enhance the mind's capacity to influence the body. Creative therapy involving dance, art, and music, as well as prayer and mental healing, are considered to be in the mind-body category.

Meditation is a way to deal with the effects of chronic stress. The person meditating is able to let go by focusing primarily on taking time (twenty minutes is great) to relax, shutting out external stimuli. There are numerous meditative techniques, and there really is no "right" way to meditate. Almost all techniques involve focus on breathing. The most important factor is to commit the time to just do nothing. This can be a challenge in our busy lives today. Try simply to find a quiet place, eliminate distractions, close your eyes, repeat a word or phrase that is meaningful for you, and say that word over and over with each exhalation. Allow yourself to just let go. "For 30 years, research has told us that meditation works beautifully as an antidote to stress," says Daniel Goleman, author of *Destructive Emotions* (2003). More and more conventional

Meditation Exercise

The most important thing is to allow yourself to do nothing.

Easy steps to meditation:

1. Eliminate distractions.

Turn off the cell phone, decide not to answer the door, let family or friends know you are unavailable for the next ten or fifteen minutes. Go to the bathroom, get a drink of water, and generally take care of any physical distractions that might arise. You might find it helpful to set a timer.

2. Just sit.

Get comfortable—consider sitting on a folded blanket to allow for less stress on the knees. Take a deep breath and allow your spine to extend and your ribs to lift. Maintain a tall posture as you soften your shoulders. Dim lights, a candle, incense, and appropriate music are nice but not necessary.

3. Let go.

Practice silence. Close your eyes and quietly observe the thoughts that come to your mind. Acknowledge them and then let them go. Let go of the outside stimuli so you can focus inward.

4. Listen.

Listen to the sounds of life in and around you. Become receptive to the sounds that are obvious, but also to the sounds that you normally don't hear because your attention is elsewhere. Hear without judgment; just observe. Notice your awareness of the present as it deepens.

5. Use your senses.

Cultivate an awareness of the present moment through sensations. Be attentive to where your body is connecting to the earth. What do you feel? Softness, hardness, coolness, warmth, pressure, and ease. How does your body change with each inhalation and exhalation? Settle into the present moment using your breath and your senses. Begin to focus on your inner self.

6. Simply breathe.

Attend to your breath. Try not to change your breath, just observe it how it is. Use all of your senses to increase awareness of how your body responds to your breath. Relax into your breath. Follow the rhythm of your breath with each inhalation and exhalation. When your mind wanders, just refocus and come back to the breath.

7. Mantra.

Saying a simple word, a phrase, a prayer, or anything meaningful to you over and over again as a mantra can coax you into a contemplative state. Repeat the mantra softly and slowly in an undulating rhythm with your breath, like riding a wave.

8. Practice kindness.

In your quiet state, consider someone who might be in need of some understanding and goodwill. Focus on this person. "In your mind's eye, send this person love, happiness, and well-being. Soften your skin, open the floodgates of your heart, and let gentle goodwill pour forth."

With consistent practice, meditation can make a difference in your life.

Adapted from Meditation 101 by Claudia Cummins, **Yoga Journal.** www.yogajournal.com/practice, 2009

health professionals are recommending meditation as a way to deal with chronic stress as well as chronic pain. Experiencing the calming effect of meditation, if only for ten minutes each day, creates a period of physical relief that can enhance immune function. Over time, the benefits of meditation can have a cumulative effect, improving the well-being of the meditator (Heistand, 2005). With practice, it can calm the body and quiet the mind. The benefits are numerous. Try committing to the above Meditation Exercise technique daily for one week to see if it has a positive effect on your life.

Meditation practice can alter brain activity. Andrew Newberg is a University of Pennsylvania neurologist who has studied changes in brain activity during meditation. Using radioactive dye with functional brain imaging, Newberg demonstrated that the brains of Tibetan Buddhist monks blocked

Beginning Your Own Spiritual Journey

Whether a person's quest for spiritual health takes the form of a love for nature, a weekly visit to a place of religious worship, or some other guise, it is clear that spirituality benefits overall health. While it is possible to achieve spiritual health in many ways, the following ideas have helped a number of people on their spiritual path:

Relaxation and Meditation

"There is no greater source of strength and power for me in my life now than going still, being quiet, and recognizing what real power is," says Oprah Winfrey on the segment of her daily television show called "Remembering Your Spirit." Many people take the time to sit quietly and to meditate; for example, more than five million people worldwide practice transcendental meditation, one popular relaxation technique.

Time in Nature

For Henry David Thoreau, who fled civilization to live on Walden Pond, nature was the temple of God and the perennial source of life. A powerfully spiritual moment—and one we have all experienced—is the instant we are confronted with earth's perfection and are filled with awe. The scientist Carl Sagan wrote about his time-in-nature experience: "The wind whips through the canyons of the American Southwest, and there is no one to hear it but us." The crisp, clean smell of the woods after rainfall, the soothing rhythm of crickets on a summer night, the beauty of freshly fallen snow—these experiences inspire unspeakable awe and humility because of the small but rich part that we, as individuals, play in the larger scheme of the universe.

Intimacy with Others

Loving selflessly is part of spiritual experience. Living life with passion and allowing ourselves to "feel" may be the greatest element of the spiritual journey. Experiencing emotion through a poignant musical passage, feeling the grief of a lost love, and surrendering to love's beauty are all part of human spirituality. By giving, sharing, and loving, we become whole and experience all that we are capable of feeling.

Spiritual Readings

Ranging from inspirational self-help books available at the local bookstore to traditional religious works, the written word has provided insight and guidance throughout human history, during its times of joy and darkest moments. For some it's the Bible; for others, it may be the Quran; and for still others, it may be a contemporary book such as *Spiritual Healing: Scientific Validation of a Healing Revolution* by Daniel J. Benor, M.D. (Vision Publications, 2001). To find books that will foster your personal growth and healing, listen to what others recommend and then search for whatever will move you or speak to you.

Prayer

Prayer may be the oldest spiritual practice and the most popular one in America. Almost all world religions include a form of prayer. Says George Lucas, who plays on religious themes such as good and evil in his blockbuster *Star Wars* series, "Religion is basically a container for faith. And faith is a very important part of what allows us to remain stable, remain balanced." The mental and emotional release, along with a sense of connection to a transcendent dimension, may be at the heart of prayer's effectiveness.

From *Psychology Today* (September/October 1999), 48; The Transcendental Meditation Program (see http://www.tm.org).

out information from the part of the brain that orients the body in space and time. The monks focused their energy inward, while blocking out any external stimuli (Pure Insight, 2005).

Previous studies have determined that meditation has a positive influence on symptoms of stress and anxiety. Another more recent study used brain imaging to look at specifically which regions of the brain were affected by mindfulness meditation. In the study conducted by researchers from University of Massachusetts Medical School and the Bender Institute of Neuroimaging in Germany, the meditation group had increases in gray matter concentration in the left hippocampus. The hippocampus is an area of the brain involved in learning, memory, and emotional control. This is one of the first studies to actually look at what is going on in the brain during meditation.

Applied psycho-neuro-immunology is based on research into psycho-neuroendocrino-immunolgy, the science of how our experiences are encoded neurologically and about how this affects our immune and hormonal systems. How our bodies' encounter, adapt, and react to stress directly affects our immune system. This approach treats the whole body. Our minds can keep us in a dark hole of hopelessness and helplessness with a condition like depression, which can cause a breakdown of our immune system. The reverse can be true as well. "The profound power of the mind that causes this rundown and eventual loss of resistance can also naturally be used positively to tune-up and boost the immune system to maximum level: to repel viruses, bacterium and other micro-organisms and to speed up healing" (AAAPNI).

Prayer and Spirituality—*Newsweek* recently did a cover story on the growth of spirituality in America today (Adler, 2005). The article greatly contrasts with the cover story of a 1966 *Time* article entitled "Is God Dead?" Spirituality is experiencing resurgence among Americans: 55 percent of Americans consider themselves spiritual and religious, and 24 percent consider themselves spiritual but not religious. Young people especially seem to be searching for greater meaning in a rigorous form of faith and prayer. Wanting more than what traditional religious services offer, they want to experience God in their daily lives. Many are drawing on the influence of Eastern religions to enhance their traditional doctrines. Meditations, centering prayer, silent contemplation, as well as disciplines like yoga, are often used in addition to traditional church services (Adler, 2005).

More than half of the medical schools in the country now offer an elective course on "Spirituality and Medicine." Questions abound about the role of prayer in healing the sick. Eighty-four percent of Americans polled believe praying for the sick can improve their chance of recovery (Kalb, 2004). Anecdotal evidence says prayer works. Science demands concrete evidence; however, prayer is hard to measure.

Yoga is a mind/body/spiritual discipline that is rooted in the ancient Hindu religion traced back 5,000 years. Yoga has become popular in the United States in the last several decades. According to the *New York Times*, 16 million Americans currently practice yoga. There are many different styles of yoga—gentle, meditative, powerful, and relaxing yoga to name of few. Movement in yoga can be rigorous and intense, or gentle and calming. Physicians are recognizing the benefits that a yoga practice can have on strengthening the physical body and quieting the mind. In addition to the many physical benefits, the practice of yoga with emphasis on breathing can be a great stress management tool. Movement, breathing, chanting, and sound are a prelude to meditation and conscious relaxation that regular yoga practice can provide. Conscious relaxation gives our minds a break from the daily chatter and unending stimuli to which we are continuously exposed.

Guided imagery is a concept that has been used successfully with people suffering from post-traumatic stress disorder. Psychologist Kathleen Reyntjiens, Ph.D., reports that imagery was an integral part of her recovery efforts with those recently traumatized by Hurricane Katrina. "As our previous

> "Yoga is the stilling of the restlessness of the mind."
>
> —Yoga Sutras

Evidence is mounting that spending time with a loved pet has emotional, psychological, and physiological benefits.

research with imagery has indicated, these simple self-regulation techniques—especially imagery and conscious breathing—are helping to minimize distress, anxiety, hypervigilance, anger, sadness, and insomnia, and allow all of us to be more effective, efficient, kind and caring neighbors in our survival and clean-up efforts" (Naparstek, 2005).

Mindfulness is a concept that includes strategies and activities that help us be more in the present moment. This helps us connect more intently with ourselves, others, and with nature. Peacefulness can be the result of being mindful throughout the day. Mindfulness is often thought of in conjunction with spirituality.

Feldenkrais method is "a form of somatic education that uses gentle movement and directed attention to improve movement and enhance human functioning. Through this method, you can increase your ease and range of motion, improve your flexibility and coordination, and rediscover your innate capacity for graceful, efficient movement" (The North American Feldenkrais Guild). Feldenkrais is excellent for dancers, athletes, and others, as well as those limited by neuromuscular pain or neurological dysfunction. Moshe Feldenkrais, an Israeli engineer, developed this technique.

Somatic movement re-educates the neuromuscular system toward greater health and well-being. Through hands-on movement work by the somatics practitioner, "people can learn to manage stress, relieve back pain, breathe more freely, heal from trauma to the neuromuscular system, and speed recuperation after illness or surgery" (Brockport, 2005). The Feldenkrais method is a type of somatic movement education. Meditation, visualization, craniosacral therapy, and myofascial release techniques are often practiced by the somatic movement practitioner.

Animal-assisted therapy is the use of companion animals to help people with special needs. Evidence is mounting that spending time with a loved pet not only has emotional and psychological benefits, but physiological benefits as well. The act of petting and caring for a loved animal can reduce blood pressure and heart rate and improve survival rates from heart disease (Arkow, www.animal therapy). Close to half of the psychologists responding to a survey indicated prescribing a pet to combat loneliness or depression. According to Phil Arkow, instructor of the Animal Assisted Therapy course at Camden County College in Blackwood, New Jersey, elderly people who have pets visit physicians 16 percent less than those who do not; dog owners in particular make 21 percent fewer visits. "A pet is an island of sanity in what appears to be an insane world. Friendship retains its traditional values and securities in one's relationship with one's pet. Whether a dog, cat, bird, fish, turtle, or what have you, one can rely upon the fact that one's pet will always remain a faithful, intimate, non-competitive friend—regardless of the good or ill fortune life brings us" (Dr. Boris Levinson, child psychologist).

Energy Therapies

Energy therapies engage the use of energy fields that surround the body and penetrate the body. The science behind energy fields has yet to be proven.

Qi gong combines movement, meditation, and regulation of breathing to enhance the flow of vital energy (qi), improve blood circulation, and enhance immune function (Donatelle, 2004). Qi gong literally means the skill of attracting vital energy. Those that practice qi gong call it a "self-healing art" that uses visualization and imagery with movement and meditation.

Reiki (pronounced ray-key) is a type of energy work that utilizes touch and visualization. Reiki is based on ancient Tibetan teachings and is said to date back thousands of years. Today reiki is practiced using the Eastern concept of the five chakras in the body, as well as using the organs and glands from Western anatomy.

Therapeutic touch is purported to induce the relaxation response, alleviate pain, and to speed the healing process. In therapeutic touch, the patient is not actually touched. In one study people were wounded on their arms. The control group had conventional therapy, while the other group experienced therapeutic touch. The entire second group experienced quicker healing (Wirth, 1990).

Bioenergy practitioners use psychotherapy, grounding exercise, and deep breathing to assist in releasing muscular tension, pain, and illness. Pain and illness are thought to be caused by suppressed emotions and behaviors (AMFI, 2005).

Ultimately the responsibility lies with the patient to secure quality health care. As time goes on, more CAM modalities will be studied and the results will help guide consumers to which therapies are best for each individual person.

Mindfulness in Everyday Life

Being mindful means focusing attention on what you're experiencing from moment to moment. It's a daunting challenge in a hectic world, but science has begun to establish that it's a worthwhile habit to cultivate. You can start by getting a sense of how much time you spend not being mindful. See if you recognize any of these statements from a questionnaire developed at the University of Rochester:

- I find it difficult to stay focused on what's happening in the present.
- I snack without paying much attention to what I'm eating.
- It seems I'm "running on automatic" without much awareness of what I'm doing.
- I rush through activities without being really attentive to them.
- I tend to walk quickly to get where I'm going without paying attention to what I experience along the way.
- I find myself listening to someone with one ear and doing something else at the same time.
- I tend not to notice physical tension or discomfort until they really grab my attention.

If these sound familiar, there's plenty of room for increasing mindfulness in your daily life. Take note of times when your thoughts are creating stress or distracting you from the present moment. The Mind/Body Medical Institute suggests that you slow down as you go about everyday activities, doing one thing at a time and bringing your full awareness to both the activity and your experience of it. Here are some tips for integrating mindfulness:

- Make something that occurs several times during the day, such as answering the phone or buckling your seat belt a reminder to return to the present—that is, think about what you're doing and observe yourself doing it.
- Pay attention to your breathing or your environment when you stop at red lights.
- Before you go to sleep, and when you awaken, take some "mindful" breaths. Instead of allowing your mind to wander over the day's concerns, direct your attention to your breathing. Feel its effects on your nostrils, lungs and abdomen. Try to think of nothing else.
- If the present moment involves stress—perhaps you're about to speak in public or undergo a medical test—observe your thoughts and emotions and how they affect your body.
- Find a task you usually do impatiently or unconsciously (standing in line or brushing your teeth, for example) and do it mindfully.

Being mindful doesn't mean you'll never "multitask," but you can make multitasking a conscious choice. It doesn't mean you'll never be in a hurry, but at least you will be aware that you are rushing. Although upsetting thoughts or emotions won't disappear, you will have more insight into them and become aware of your choices in responding to them.

From *Harvard Women's Watch*, Vol. 11, #6, February 2004.

There are many more CAM therapies than are mentioned in this chapter. Conventional physicians and those they work closely with want the same things as most CAM practitioners—for patients to have good health and wellness. "The effectiveness of the healthcare delivery system in the future will depend upon its ability to make use of all approaches and modalities that provide a sound basis for promoting optimal health. People with better health habits have been shown to survive longer and to postpone and shorten disability" (WHCCAMP, 2002). Certainly many CAM practices will be useful in contributing to the nation's health goals. The modern patient is more informed and involved in his or her own health. Most likely the marriage of essential conventional practices with complementary and alternative therapeutics will be the way of the future.

Using the Internet for Credible Medical Information

You may find the Internet a valuable resource for researching potential CAM therapies. Using a typical search engine could net you thousands, if not more, hits. This information is intended as a resource to help you sift through the "junk mail" of sorts and to determine what is actual credible information.

Distinguish between different sorts of Web resources:

Information sites—have a domain ending .edu (education), .gov (government), .org (nonprofit organization), .net (technical services)—typically very reliable.

Advice and referral sites—look for the credentials, reputation, or experience to see if the source is credible.

Activist sites—typically promoting a particular cause rather than providing information.

Chat groups—can be unreliable but also a valuable extension of your community; a great way to connect with others sharing the same experience, such as a rare disease.

Individual testimonials—interesting but not always reliable or authoritative.

Commercial sites—the majority of Web sites are commercial and typically set up to sell products, therefore the information is usually biased.

TIP: You can avoid commercial Web sites by including "NOT .com" in your search string.

Other questions to consider:
Who is the group providing the Web site? How is the Web site funded?
How is the information selected and presented? What are the qualifications of the author?
Does the site follow ethical practices? (The Web site should be current; check their privacy policy if they ask information from you.)

Reference: The Alternative Medicine Foundation

References

Acupuncture Relieves Pain and Improves Function in Knee. *Osteoarthritis NIH News,* December 20, 2004 press release.

Adler, J. In Search of the Spiritual. *Newsweek,* August 29, 2005. Alternative Medicine Foundation www.amfoundation.org

American Massage Therapy Association. www.amtamassage.org Phone (847) 864-0123

Arkow, P. *Animal Assisted Therapy: A Premise and a Promise*. http://www .animaltherapy. net/Premise%20%26%20Promise.html

Association for the Advancement of Applied Psychoneuroimmunology. http://hometown.aol.com/AAAPNI

Barnes, P. M., Bloom, B., and Nahin, R. *CDC National Health Statistics Report #12*. Complementary and Alternative Medicine Use Among Adults and Children: United States, 2007. December 10, 2008.

Chopra, D. *Ageless Body, Ageless Mind*. Harmony Books. 1993.

ClinicalTrials.gov; US National Library of Medicine, US National Institute of Health. www. clinicaltrials.gov/ct/gui/c/alb/show/NCT00010829

Corbin, C. et al. *Concepts of Physical Fitness* (15th ed). Dubuque, IA: McGraw Hill. 2009.

International Alliance of Healthcare Educators (IAHE). Craniosacral Therapy/ Somatoemotional Release: Education for better patient care. 2005. http:// www.iahe.come/ html/therapies.cst.jsp

Donatelle, R. J. *Access to Health* (8th ed). Pearson/Benjamin Cummings. 2004. Feldenkrais Educational Foundation of North America (FEFNA) 3611 SW Hood Ave. Suite 100 Portland, OR 97239, USA http://www.feldenkrais.com

Gach, M. R., *Acupressure's Potent Points*. Bantam Books. 1990.

Goldberg, B. *Alternative Medicine, The Definitive Guide* (2nd ed). Berkeley, CA: Celestial Arts. 2002.

Goleman, D. *Destructive Emotion: A Scientific Dialogue with the Dalai Lama*. 2003. Alternative Medicine Foundation Information. How to Assess Credibility on the Web. 2009. www.amfoundation.org/assess.htm

Information on Clinical Trials being conducted; www.clinicaltrials.gov/ct/ gui/c/alb/show/NCT00010829

Kalb, C. Faith and Healing, *Newsweek*, November 10, 2004.

Markowitz, J. et al. Effect of St John's Wort on Drug Metabolism by Induction of Cytochrome P450 3A4 Enzyme. *JAMA*, (290),1500–1503. 2003. Naparstek, B. *Health Journeys*. 2005.

National Institutes of Health. NCCAM Online Continuing Education Lecture Series, Manipulative and Body-Based Therapies: Chiropractic and Spinal Manipulation. 2002. http://nccam.org/main.php

Psych-Neuro-Immunology http://hometown.aol.com/AAAPNI/

Pure Insight. 2005. http://pureinsight.org/PI/index/html

Saper, R. B., Phillips, R. S., Sehgal, A., et al. Lead, mercury, and arsenic in U.S. and Indian-manufactured Ayurvedic medicines sold via the Internet. *Journal of the American Medical Association*, 300(8):915–923. 2008.

Somatic Movement Studies http://www.brockport.edu/~dance/somatics/ techniques.htm, 2005.

Reaves, W. Acupuncture and the Athlete, *ACSM Fit Society*, Fall 2008.

Ryzik, M. Z. Exercising That Back Pain Away. *New York Times*, September 15, 2005. Wirth, D. P. The Effects of Non-Contact Therapeutic Touch on the Healing Rate of Full Thickness Dermal Wounds. *Subtle Energies*, Vol. 1, No. 1, 1990.

USFDA Center for Food Safety and Applied Nutrition's Dietary Supplements: Warnings and Safety Information. www.cfsan.fda.gov/~dms/ds-warn.html

White House Commission on Complementary and Alternative Medicine Policy (WHCCAMP). Final Report. 2002. *(electronic version)*

Contacts

Acupuncture and Oriental Medicine Alliance

www.acupuncturealliance.org

Alternative Medicine: Health Care Information Resources

http://hsl.mcmaster.ca/tomflem/altmed .html This is an extremely thorough resource of alternative medicine for the informed consumer.

Alternative Medicine Foundation

www.amfoundation.org

American Massage Therapy Association

www.amtamassage.org

Phone (847) 864-0123

American Yoga Association

www.americanyogaassociation.org

The Art of Living Foundation www .artofliving.org Information on the science of the breath and it's healing qualities. Worldwide organization.

Center for Mindfulness in Medicine, Health Care, and Society; University of Massachusetts Medical School

www.umassmed.edu/cfm

Complementary and Alternative Medicine: From Promises to Proof. NIH

Craniosacral Therapy Association of North America

FDA/Center for Food Safety and Applied Nutrition

http://www.cfsan.fda.gov/~dms/ds-warn .html Warnings and safety information regarding dietary supplements.

Heistand, C. http://www.orgsites.com/ca/ acco/_pgg4.php3 very thorough site using CAM with cancer patients.

HerbMed http://www.herbmed.org Evidence-based herbal resource http://nccam.nih.gov/news/images/ campractice.htm (CAM category picture)

Medline Plus http://medlineplus.gov/ An excellent resource that is a service of the U.S. Library of Congress and the National Institute of Health.

MedWatch The FDA Safety Information and Adverse Event Reporting Program

http://www.fda.gov/medwatch

Mind/Body Medical Institute www. mindbody.harvard.edu

Movement Educators www. movementeducators.com This site features a free Mindful Movement Lesson in the Fledenkrais method.

National Institute of Ayurvedic Medicine (NIAM)

www.niam.com

National Association of Chiropractic Medicine (NACM)

www.chiromed.org

National Institutes for Health National Center for Complementary and Alternative Medicine (NCCAM)

http://nccam.org/main.php

Nutrition Science News

http://exchange.healthwell.com/ nutritionsciencenews/ information and research on natural medicine

Psych-Neuro-Immunology

http://hometown.aol.com/AAAPNI/

Psycho-Neuro-Immunolgy

http://www.alpha-cs.co.za/ PsychoNeuroImm.htm source of CD's to listen to harness the power of the mind to help health and well-being.

Qigong Association of America

http://www.qi.org/

Resources for Body, Mind and Spirit

www.healthjourneys.com Bellaruth Naparstek's very informative site. Ms. Napastek is a guided imagery pioneer and creator of desktopspa.com, (800) 800–8661.

Shiatsu: Japanese Massage

http://www.rianvisser.nl/shiatsu/e_index. htm This site includes a "do-in" link where you can learn specific exercises.

Somatic Movement Studies

http://www.brockport.edu/~dance/ somatics/techniques.htm

Core movement patterning, Somatic Release and Contact Unwinding-educational/therapeutic techniques developed in East-West Somatics.

Tips for the Savvy Supplement User: Making Informend Decisions and Evaluating Information

http://www,cfsan.fda.gov/~dms/ds-savvy. html Dietary supplement info

University of Michigan Integrative Medicine

http://www.med.umich.edu/umim/

Source of the Healing Foods Pyramid.

USFDA Center for Food Safety and Applied Nutrition's Dietary Supplements: Warnings and Safety Information.

www.cfsan.fda.gov/~dms/ds-warn.html

White House Commission on Complementary and Alternative Medicine Policy, March 2002.

WHO Guidelines on Developing Consumer Information on Proper Use of Traditional, Complementary and Alternative Medicine.

Yoga Journal Periodical and online at www.yogajournal.com Excellent resource for all things related to yoga, relaxation, stress management and meditation.

Recommended Books For Further Reading

Ageless Body, Timeless Mind. By Deepak Chopra (Harmony Books, 1993)

Awakening the Spine. By Vanda Scaravelli (HarperCollins Publishers, 1991)

Peace Is Every Step: The Path of Mindfulness in Everyday Life. By Thich Nhat Hanh (Bantam Books, 1992)

Relax and Renew By Judith Lasater (Rodmell Press, 1995)

Wherever You Go There You Are: Mindfulness Meditation in Everyday Life. By Jon Kabat-Zinn (Hyperion, 1995)

The Spectrum: A Scientifically Proven Program to Feel Better, Live Longer, Lose Weight, and Gain Health. By Dean Ornish (Ballantine Books, 2007)

Name _____ Section_____ Date_____

Name _____ Section _____

College Health Risk Assessment Assignment

Body Mass Index

Go to http://www.cdc.gov/healthyweight/assessing/bmi/index.html. Calculate your BMI and write it here: _____ . Are you in underweight, normal, or overweight? _____

Do you agree with this assessment?

What behaviors do you engage in that have resulted in your current BMI?

Are you satisfied with this BMI? If not, how will you change It?

Alcohol and Tobacco

Go to https://interwork.sdsu.edu/echug2/?id=TAMU&hfs=true. Complete the e-CHUG interactive survey about alcohol and tobacco use. View your results and answer the following questions:

1. How many cheeseburgers did you eat last month?

2. How many questions did you answer correctly about Alcohol and Your Body?

3. With your highest reported BAC of _____, it would take you _____ hours for your BAC to return to zero.

4. What does the biphasic response curve show?

5. Based on your family risk, your of developing future alcohol dependence is_____.

6. In your lifetime, you have smoked _____ cigarettes.

7. You rated the importance of making a change in your personal use of alcohol as _____ .

Note: If you have trouble accessing this website, just search for e-CHUG online. Several universities offer the same survey and you should be able to find one that works with your browser.

Sexuality

How do the media (music, television, movies, & magazines) influence the attitudes and beliefs that young adults have about relationships and sexuality?

Who or what influences your decisions about relationships and sexuality?

Safety

Go to http://collegestudentsafety.com/cosaar.html. Choose one article and write a brief summary.

Article Title: _____

Summary:

Glossary

Abortion—any expulsion from the uterus of a fetus before it is able to survive.

Abstinence—refraining from something, e.g., certain foods, alcoholic beverages, or sexual intercourse.

Abuse—to mistreat or insult.

Accident—that occurrence in a sequence of events that produces unintended injury, death, or property damage.

Acquired immune deficiency syndrome—a reliably diagnosed disease that is at least moderately indicative of an underlying cellular immune deficiency, for example Kaposi's sarcoma in a patient aged less than sixty years or opportunistic infection where there is no known underlying cause of cellular immune deficiency nor any other cause of reduced resistance reported to be associated with the disease.

Activity nervosa—a condition where the individual suffers from an ever-present compulsion to exercise, regardless of illness or injury.

Acupuncture—traditional Chinese practice of inserting fine needles through the skin at specific points especially to cure disease or relieve pain (as in surgery).

Adenosine triphosphate (ATP)—high energy compound formed from oxidation of fat and carbohydrate and used as an energy supply.

Adoption—to take legally into one's own family and raise as one's own child.

Aerobic—means "in the presence of oxygen," and is used synonymously with cardiovascular.

Alcohol poisoning—an overdose of alcohol, which may lead to death.

Alcoholism—a chronic progressive disease that includes a strong need to drink alcohol despite the negative consequences.

Alimentary—pertaining to food.

Alternative healthcare systems—personalized holistic "whole person" healthcare emphasizing patient interview, history, eating habits, lifestyle choices, and so on.

Alveoli—tiny air sacs in the lungs through whose walls gases such as oxygen and carbon dioxide diffuse in and out of blood.

Amino acids—organic compounds containing carbon, hydrogen, nitrogen, and oxygen. They are the building blocks of protein.

Amphetamines—drugs that stimulate the nervous system.

Anaerobic—occurring in the absence of oxygen.

Anemia—a condition in which the blood is low in red cells or in hemoglobin, resulting in paleness and weakness.

Angina pectoris—insufficient blood flow to the heart muscle that results in severe chest and arm pain.

Anorexia nervosa—a state of starvation and emaciation usually resulting from severe dieting and excessive exercise.

Antibiotic—any of certain substances, such as penicillin or streptomycin, produced by various microorganisms and capable of destroying or weakening bacteria.

Antioxidants—compounds that come to the aid of every cell in the body facing an ongoing barrage of damage resulting from daily oxygen exposure, environmental pollution, chemicals and pesticides, additives in processed foods, stress hormones, and sun radiation.

Anus—the opening located just behind the perineum at the lower end of the alimentary canal that allows for elimination of solid waste.

Aorta—the large artery that receives blood from the left ventricle and distributes it to the body.

Arrhythmia—an irregularity in the rhythm of the heartbeat that often precedes a heart attack.

Arteriosclerosis—hardening of the arteries.

Asthma—a respiratory disorder that involves difficulty breathing, wheezing, and/or coughing due to the constriction of the bronchial tubes.

Asymptomatic—without symptoms.

Atherosclerosis—long-term buildup of fatty deposits and other substances such as cholesterol, cellular waste products, calcium, and fibrin on the interior walls of arteries.

Atria—the two upper chambers of the heart in which blood collects before passing to the ventricles.

BAC (Blood Alcohol Concentration)—the ratio of alcohol measured in the blood to total blood volume.

Bacteria—microorganisms that have no chlorophyll and multiply by simple division: some bacteria cause diseases, but others are necessary for fermentation.

Barbiturates—depressants used to induce sleep and relaxation.

Benign—non-invasive, non-cancerous (of a growth). Describes a condition or illness that is not serious and does not usually have harmful consequences.

Binge drinking—consuming five or more alcoholic beverages in one sitting for men, four for women.

Bingeing—consuming an excessive amount of food in a short period of time.

Blackout—individual has amnesia about events after drinking, though there was no loss of consciousness.

Blood pressure—the force exerted by the blood on the walls of the blood vessels; 120/80 is considered average.

Body composition—measures percentage of body fat in relation to the percentage of lean body mass (muscle, bone, and internal organs).

Breast—the mammary gland.

Bulimia nervosa—a process of bingeing and purging.

Caffeine—mild stimulant found in cola, coffee, chocolate.

Camaraderie—loyalty and warm, friendly feeling among companions.

Cancer—a disease characterized by the spread of abnormal cells that serve no useful purpose.

Carbohydrates—the body's main source of fuel. Between 55–60 percent of an individual's diet should be composed of carbohydrates.

Carbon Monoxide—odorless, tasteless gas that is highly toxic and contains carcinogens.

Carcinoma—any of several kinds of epithelial cancer.

Cardiovascular—pertaining to the heart and blood vessels.

Cardiovascular endurance—the ability of the body to perform prolonged, large-muscle, dynamic exercise at moderate-to-high levels of intensity. In order for this process to occur, the heart, lungs, and blood vessels must deliver oxygen to working muscles and the body's metabolic system must use oxygen to process fuels for sustained activity.

Cardiovascular exercise—when performed within certain guidelines, develops higher levels of cardiovascular endurance by improving the efficiency and strength of the cardiovascular system. Cardiovascular exercise uses large muscle groups in a continuous, rhythmic nature for an extended period of time.

Cervix—the neck of the uterus.

Cesarean section—delivery of the fetus through an abdominal incision.

Chemotherapy—use of a specific chemical agent to arrest the progress of, or eradicate, disease in the body without causing irreversible injury to healthy tissues.

Chiropractic—a health care approach that focuses on the relationship between the body's structure—mainly the spine—and its functioning.

Chlamydia—a sexually transmitted infection caused by a bacteria-like intracellular parasite called chlamydia trachomati, which can infect humans and birds.

Cholesterol—a crystalline substance of a fatty nature found in the brain, nerves, liver, blood, and bile. It is not easily soluble and may crystallize in the gallbladder and along arterial walls.

Clitoral hood—consists of inner lips, which join to form a soft fold of skin, or hood, covering and connecting to the clitoris.

Clitoris—a small erectile organ of the female genitalia.

Cocaine—psychoactive substance found in the leaves of the coca plant; stimulant.

Codeine—narcotic commonly found in cough suppressant.

Coercion—to restrain by force.

Cold—viral infection of the respiratory tract, causing congestion, sneezing, sore throat, coughing, and a low-grade fever.

Colon—the large bowel extending from the cecum to the rectum.

Coma—deep, prolonged unconsciousness caused by injury or disease.

Communicable—transmissible directly or indirectly from one person to another.

Communication—giving or exchanging information or messages.

Compatible—getting along or going well together.

Complex carbohydrates—provide the body with a steady source of energy for hours. The best sources of complex carbohydrates are breads, cereals, pastas, and grains.

Compromise—a settlement in which each side makes concessions.

Concede—to admit as true, valid, or certain.

Conception—the creation of a state of pregnancy; impregnation of the ovum by the sperm.

Condom (female)—a sheath, made of latex, placed into the vagina before sexual intercourse. Condoms help protect both partners against sexually transmitted infection.

Condom (male)—a rubber sheath used as a male contraceptive. Condoms help protect both partners against sexually transmitted infection.

Conviction—a strong belief.

Coronary arteries—two arteries branching from the aorta that provide blood to the heart muscle.

Cowper's glands—responsible for depositing a lubricant fluid in the semen to help with sperm motility.

Culture—a growth of bacteria or plant in a prepared substance.

Cyber—Internet.

Depo-Provera—a hormone shot injected into the arm or buttocks every twelve weeks.

Depressants—category of drugs that depress the nervous system.

Depression—a hollow or low place.

Diabetes—the result of insufficient insulin production or the body's inability to utilize insulin readily produced by the pancreas.

Diaphragm—a rubber cap that encircles the cervix to act as a contraceptive. It should be used with a spermicidal jelly or cream.

Diastolic blood pressure—the lowest arterial pressure attained during the heart cycle.

Dietary fiber (roughage or bulk)—a type of complex carbohydrate that is present mainly in leaves, roots, skins, and seeds. Dietary fiber is the part of the plant that is not digested in the small intestine, and it helps decrease the risk of cardiovascular disease, cancer, and may lower an individual's risk of coronary heart disease.

Disease—any deviation from or interruption of the normal structure and function of any part of the body. It is manifested by a characteristic set of signs and symptoms and in most instances the origin, route of transmission, and prognosis is known.

Distress—negative stress. It is a physically and mentally damaging response to the demands placed upon the body.

Divorce—to dissolve the marriage with one's spouse.

Duration—the length of time in which an activity or exercise is performed. Duration is generally expressed in minutes.

Economic—the management of income and expenditures.

Ecstasy—a drug that is chemically similar to mescaline and methamphetamines.

Ejaculation—the sudden emission of semen from the erect penis at the moment of male orgasm.

Emotion—any specific feeling, as love, hate, fear, anger, and so on.

Epidemic—a disease spreading rapidly among many people in a community.

Epididymis—a small, oblong body attached to the posterior surface of the testes. Mature sperm are stored in the epididymis until they are released during ejaculation.

Epithelium—cellular tissue covering external body surfaces or lining internal surfaces.

Essential amino acid—amino acids that the body cannot produce; thus, they must be supplied through an individual's diet.

Estrogen—a generic term referring to ovarian hormones.

Ethyl alcohol—a colorless liquid that depresses the nervous system. Made by the fermentation process and found in alcoholic beverages.

ETS (Environmental Tobacco Smoke)—second-hand smoke inhaled by the non-smoker.

Eustress—a positive stress that produces a state of well-being.

Exercise—a subcategory of physical activity that is planned, structured, repetitive, and purposive in the sense that the improvement or maintenance of one or more components of physical fitness is the objective. "Exercise" and "exercise training" frequently are used interchangeably and generally refer to physical activity performed during leisure time with the primary purpose of improving or maintaining physical fitness, physical performance, or health.

Exercise prescription—individualization of an exercise program on the basis of the exercise duration, frequency, intensity, and mode.

Exercise stress test—a test that involves analysis of the changes in electrical activity from the heart from an electrocardiogram taken during exercise.

Extravagant—going beyond the reasonable limits; wasteful or spending too much.

Fallopian tubes—tubes extending from beside the ovaries to the uterus that transport developed ovum. Fertilization usually takes place within the fallopian tubes.

Fat-soluble vitamins—vitamins transported by the body's fat cells and by the liver. They include vitamins A, E, D, and K.

Fats—the body's primary source of energy. Fat has many essential functions, including: providing the body with stored energy, insulating the body to preserve body heat, contributing to cellular structure, and protecting vital organs by absorbing shock.

Fear of obesity—an over-concern with thinness.

Fertilization—the impregnation of an ovum by a sperm.

Fetal Alcohol Syndrome—a group of physical and behavioral defects in a newborn caused by the mother's alcohol use during pregnancy.

Fibrin—insoluble blood protein formed in blood clots.

Flexibility—a health- and performance-related component of physical fitness that is the range of motion possible at a joint. Flexibility is specific to each joint and depends on a number of specific variables, including but not limited to the tightness of specific ligaments and tendons. Flexibility exercises enhance the ability of a joint to move through its full range of motion.

Foreskin—the prepuce or skin covering the glans penis.

Frequency—the number of times an exercise or activity is performed. Frequency is generally expressed in sessions, episodes, or bouts per week.

Gastrointestinal—pertaining to the stomach and intestine.

GHB (Gamma Hydroxybutrate)—a fast acting, powerful drug that depresses the nervous system.

Glucose—a simple sugar that circulates in the blood and can be used by cells to fuel ATP production.

Glycogen—a complex carbohydrate stored principally in the liver and skeletal muscles that is the major fuel source during most forms of intense exercise.

Gonorrhea—a sexually transmitted infection caused by the bacteria called Neisseria gonorrhea.

Hallucinogens—drugs that affect perception, sensation, and awareness.

Hazard—conditions or set of conditions that have the potential to produce injury and/or property damage.

Health—a state of complete physical, mental, and social well-being and not merely the absence of disease or infirmity.

Healthy—having good health.

Heart attack—when an artery that provides the heart muscle with oxygen becomes blocked or flow is decreased.

Hepatitis—inflammation of the liver in response to toxins or infective agents.

Heroin—a very strong narcotic.

Herpes—a lifelong, viral, sexually transmitted infection that can cause small blisters on the skin and mucous membranes.

High-density lipoprotein—a plasma protein relatively high in protein, low in cholesterol. HDL helps eliminate cholesterol from the body.

Honest—truthful and trustworthy.

Human chorionic gonadotropin (HCG)—a hormone produced by the placenta during pregnancy.

Human immunodeficiency virus (HIV)—a retrovirus that infects human T cells causes acquired immune deficiency syndrome.

Human papilloma viruses (HPV)—viruses that cause genital warts, some of which have a high correlation with cervical cancer.

Hymen—the thin mucous membrane that closes part or sometimes all of the opening of the vagina.

Hypertension—abnormally high blood pressure.

Hypokinetic—too little activity.

Immunotherapy—any treatment used to produce immunity.

Implantation—the insertion of living cells or solid materials into the tissues, e.g., implantation of the fertilized ovum into the endometrium.

Infection—the successful invasion, establishment, and growth of microorganisms in the tissues of the host.

Infidelity—unfaithfulness especially in marriage.

Influenza—an acute, contagious viral disease, characterized by inflammation of the respiratory tract, fever, and muscular pain.

Inhalants—chemicals that produce vapors having psychoactive effects.

Insoluble fiber—dietary fiber that does not dissolve easily in water; therefore, it cannot be digested by the body.

Insomnia—abnormal inability to sleep.

Intensity—refers to how much work is being performed or the magnitude of the effort required to perform an activity or exercise.

Intimate—very close or familiar.

Intimidate—to make afraid as with threats.

Intoxication—a transient state of physical and mental disruption due to the presence of a toxic substance such as alcohol.

Intrauterine device—a small plastic device that is inserted into the uterus to impede conception or prevent implantation of a fertilized egg.

Intravenous—directly into a vein.

Irrevocably—that which cannot be undone.

Irritable bowel syndrome—unusual motility of both small and large bowel which produces discomfort and intermittent pain, for which no organic cause can be found.

Ischemia—reduced blood flow.

Isolation—to set apart from others.

Jealous—resentfully suspicious of rivalry.

Labia majora—two longitudinal folds of skin that extend on both sides of the vulva and serve as protection for the inner parts of the vulva.

Labia minora—the delicate inner folds of skin that enclose the urethral opening and the vagina.

Lactic acid—a metabolic acid resulting from the metabolism of glucose and glycogen. Accumulation will produce fatigue.

Lactovegetarians—individuals who eat dairy products, fruits, and vegetables but do not consume any other animal products (meat, poultry, fish, or eggs).

Legume—a pod, such as that of a pea or bean that splits into two halves with the seeds attached to one of the halves.

Leukemia—a disease characterized by an abnormal increase in the number of leukocytes.

Leukoplakia—pre-cancerous condition that produces thick, rough, white patches on the gums, tongue, and inner cheek.

Lice—plural form of louse. Small, wingless parasite found on humans and some animals.

Lifestyle activities—term frequently used to encompass activities that a person carries out in the course of daily life and that can contribute to sizeable energy expenditure. Examples include taking the stairs instead of using the elevator, walking to do errands instead of driving, getting off a bus one stop early, or parking farther away than usual to walk to a destination.

Love—a passionate affection of one person for another.

Low-density lipoproteins—major cholesterol carriers that bind to receptors in various tissues, including the liver, muscle, and arteries. High levels of LDL are likely to lead to atherosclerosis.

Loyal—faithful to one's friends and ideals.

LSD (Lysergic Acid Diethylamide)—a hallucinogenic drug that distorts reality.

Lung—either of the two spongelike breathing organs in the thorax of vertebrates.

Lymphoma—any of a group of diseases resulting from the proliferation of malignant lymphoid cells.

Macrominerals—the seven minerals the body needs in relatively large quantities (100 mg or more each day).

Macronutrients—provide energy in the form of calories. They include carbohydrates, fats, and proteins.

Malignant—cancerous; a growth that tends to spread into nearby normal tissue and travel to other parts of the body.

Marijuana—from the cannabis sativa plant where the leaves and stems are dried and rolled into cigarettes.

Marriage—a close union.

Maximal oxygen consumption (VO$_2$ Max)—the highest rate of oxygen consumption an individual is capable of during maximum physical effort. Measured in ml/kg/min.

Meditation—a conscious mental process using certain techniques—such as focusing attention or maintaining a specific posture—to suspend the stream of thoughts and relax the body and mind.

Melanoma—a tumor arising from the pigment-producing cells of the deeper layers in the skin.

Meninges—the three membranes that envelop the brain and spinal cord.

Meningitis—inflammation of the meninges.

Menstruation—the flow of blood from the uterus once a month in the female. It commences about the age of thirteen years and ceases at about forty-five years of age.

MET—refers to metabolic equivalent, and one MET is the rate of energy expenditure while sitting at rest. It is taken by convention to be an oxygen uptake of 3.5 milliliters per kilogram of body weight per minute. Physical activities frequently are classified by their intensity using the MET as a reference.

Metabolism—the sum of all the vital processes by which food energy and nutrients are made available to and used by the body.

Microminerals—minerals that are essential to healthy living. They are needed in small quantities (less than 100 mg per day).

Micronutrients—regulate many bodily functions such as metabolism, growth, and development. They include vitamins and minerals.

Microorganisms—a microscopic cell. Often synonymous with bacterium but includes virus, protozoan, rickettsia, fungus, alga, and lichen.

Minerals—inorganic substances that are critical to many enzyme functions in the body.

Moderate-intensity physical activity—On an absolute scale, physical activity that is done at 3.0 to 5.9 times the intensity of rest. On a scale relative to an individual's personal capacity, moderate-intensity physical activity is usually a 5 or 6 on a scale of 0 to 10.

Mononucleosis—a self-limiting viral infection causing a sore throat, fatigue, fever, and possible spleen enlargement.

Monounsaturated fats—fats found in foods such as olives, peanuts, and canola oil, peanut oil, and olive oil.

Mons pubis—the soft fatty tissue covering the pubic symphysis on the female genitalia.

Morbidity—the state of poor health, the degree or severity of a health condition.

Morphine—a narcotic used for quick pain relief.

Mortality rate—a measure of the number of deaths in a given population.

Muscle-strengthening activity (strength training, resistance training, or muscular strength and endurance exercises)—physical activity, including exercise that increases skeletal muscle strength, power, endurance, and mass.

Myocardial infarction (MI)—heart attack.

Narcotics—drugs used to relieve pain.

Nicotine—a highly addictive compound that is extremely poisonous.

Non-essential amino acids—amino acids that are manufactured in the body if food proteins in a person's diet provide enough nitrogen.

Obesity—the deposition of excessive fat around the body, particularly in the subcutaneous tissue.

Occlusion—the closure of an opening, especially of ducts or blood vessels.

Occupational illness—conditions caused by repeated exposure associated with employment.

Opium—the base substance for all narcotics.

Oral contraceptive (the pill)—a prescription medication containing the hormones estrogen and/or progestin.

Oral—pertaining to the mouth.

Osteoporosis—a disease characterized by a loss of bone density.

Ovary—female reproductive gland where eggs are produced and released usually once a month.

Over-training—a condition caused by training too much or too intensely.

Overweight—weighing in excess of the normal for one's age, height, and build; *overweight* adults typically have a body mass index of 25 to 30.

Ovolactovegetarians—a type of vegetarian who eats eggs as well as dairy products, fruits, and vegetables, but does not consume meat, poultry, and/or fish.

Parasite—one who lives at others' expense without making any useful return.

Parent—a person in relation to his or her offspring; a mother or father.

Partner—someone with whom you spend a lot of time and possibly the rest of your life.

PCP (Phencyclidine hydrochloride)—a hallucinogenic drug that blocks pain and produces numbness.

Penis—the male organ through which semen and urine pass. It has three main sections: the root, shaft, and glans penis.

Perineum—the smooth skin located between the labia minora and the anus.

Peripheral vascular disease—any abnormal condition arising in the blood vessels outside the heart, the main one being atherosclerosis, which can lead to thrombosis and occlusion of the vessel resulting in gangrene.

Pernicious—causing great injury or destruction.

Physical activity—any bodily movement produced by the contraction of skeletal muscle that increases energy expenditure above a basal level. In these Guidelines, physical activity generally refers to the subset of physical activity that enhances health.

Physical fitness—the ability to carry out daily tasks with vigor and alertness, without undue fatigue, and with ample energy to enjoy leisure-time pursuits and respond to emergencies. Physical fitness includes a number of components consisting of cardiorespiratory endurance (aerobic power), skeletal muscle endurance, skeletal muscle strength, skeletal muscle power, flexibility, balance, speed of movement, reaction time, and body composition

Polyunsaturated fats—fats found in margarine, pecans, corn oil, cottonseed oil, sunflower oil, and soybean oil.

Praise—to communicate worth or value.

Pregnancy—being with child, e.g., gestation from last menstrual period to delivery, normally 40 weeks or 280 days.

Probiotics—live microorganisms (in most cases, bacteria) that are similar to beneficial microorganisms found in the human gut. They are also called "friendly bacteria" or "good bacteria."

Progression—the process of increasing the intensity, duration, frequency, or amount of activity or exercise as the body adapts to a given activity pattern.

Prophylactic—preventive or protective; esp., preventing disease.

Prostate—a small gland at the base of the male bladder and surrounding the urethra.

Protein—essential "building blocks" of the body. They are needed for the growth, maintenance, and repair of all body tissues.

Psychoactive—mind-altering.

Psychoactive drugs—any agent that has the ability to alter moods, behavior, and perception.

Pubic—in the region of the genitals.

Pulmonary circulation—the part of the circulatory system that moves blood between the heart and lungs.

Purging—self-induced vomiting or elimination of food.

Ratings of perceived exertion—a system of monitoring exercise intensity based on assigning a number to the subjective perception of target intensity.

Rectum—the lowest or last segment of the large intestine.

Relationship—connection by blood or marriage.

Repetitions—the number of times a person lifts a weight in muscle-strengthening activities. Repetitions are analogous to duration in aerobic activity.

Respiratory system—deals with gaseous exchange. Comprises the nose, nasopharynx, larynx, trachea, bronchi, and lungs.

Reye's syndrome—consists of cerebral edema without cellular infiltration. Presents with vomiting, lethargy, confusion, rapid heartbeat, and respiration. May progress into a coma. There is an association with aspirin administration and viral infections.

Risk—the probability that a hazard will be activated and produce injury and/or property damage.

Rohypnol—a drug prescribed for sleep disorders; potent tranquilizer; "date rape drug."

Sacrifice—to give up one thing for the sake of another.

Sarcoma—a malignant growth of the connective tissue including muscles and bones.

Saturated fats—fats found primarily in animal products such as meats, lard, cream, butter, cheese, and whole milk.

Scabies—a highly contagious, itching skin disease caused by a mite that burrows under the skin to lay its eggs.

Scrotum—the pouch in the male that contains the testes.

Secretion—a fluid or substance formed or concentrated in a gland and passed into the alimentary tract, the blood, or to the exterior.

Self-esteem—belief in oneself.

Self-worth—the value placed upon oneself.

Semen—the fluid secreted from the testicles and accessory male organs, e.g., prostate.

Semivegetarian—a person who eats fruits, vegetables, dairy products, eggs, and a small selection of poultry, fish, and other seafood. These individuals do not consume any beef or pork.

Sexually transmitted infection—an infection (bacterial, parasitic, or viral) that is transmitted during vaginal, oral, or anal sexual activity, or in some cases by simply touching an infected area.

Sickle-cell anemia—an inherited chronic anemia found chiefly among African Americans, in which red blood cells become sickle-shaped due to defective hemoglobin.

Simple carbohydrates—sugars that have little nutritive value beyond their energy content.

Soluble fiber—dietary fiber that dissolves in water.

Sperm—an abbreviated form of the word spermatozoon or spermatozoa.

Spermicide—an agent that kills spermatozoa.

Sterilization—an operation performed on the female (tubal ligation) or male (vasectomy) to permanently prevent conception.

Strength—a health and performance component of physical fitness that is the ability of a muscle or muscle group to exert force.

Stress—the nonspecific response to demands placed on the body. "Nonspecific response" alludes to the production of the same physiological reaction regardless of the type of stress placed on the body.

Stroke volume—the amount of blood pumped with each heartbeat.

Stroke—the vessels that supply the brain with nutrients become damaged or occluded and the brain tissue dies.

Symphysis—joint of the pubic bones in the female.

Symptom—any circumstance or condition that indicates the existence, as of a particular disease.

Synthesize—the combining together of parts to form a whole.

Syphilis—a serious bacterial infection caused by the spirochete Treponema pallidum. This sexually transmitted infection can have three stages and be fatal.

Systemic circulation—the part of the circulatory system that moves blood between the heart and the rest of the body.

Systolic blood pressure—the highest arterial blood pressure attained during the heart cycle.

Tar—by product of burning tobacco; dark sticky substance which contains carcinogens.

Target heart rate zone—the range of heart rates that should be reached and maintained during cardiovascular endurance exercise to obtain training effects.

Testes—the reproductive glands inside the scrotum, which are also referred to as testicles. Sperm and hormone production are the two main functions of the testes.

THC (Tetrahydrocannabinol)—the active ingredient in marijuana.

Threat—an expression of intention to hurt, destroy, or punish.

Thrifty—not wasteful.

Thrombosis—the intravascular formation of a blood clot.

Tolerance—a condition in which an individual adapts to the amount of drug consumed to experience the same effects, e.g., alcohol use, and so on.

Triglyceride—an ester derived from glycerol, the chief component of fats and oils.

Trust—a firm belief in the honesty, reliability of another.

Tuberculosis—an infectious disease characterized by the formation of tubercles in body tissue; primarily affecting the lungs.

Ulcer—an open sore on the skin or some mucous membrane, discharging pus.

Unsaturated fats—fats derived primarily from plant products.

Urethra—the passage from the bladder through which urine is excreted.

Uterus—the hollow, pear-shaped muscular organ into which the ovum is received from the fallopian tubes and where it is retained during fetal development. When a female is not pregnant, it is about the size of a fist.

Vaccine—any preparation used to produce immunity to a specific disease.

Vagina—a sheath; the canal from the cervix to the vulva.

Values—beliefs or standards.

Vas deferens—a long tube through which sperm travel during ejaculation.

Vegans—true vegetarians. Their diets contain absolutely no meat, chicken, fish, eggs, or milk products.

Venae cavae—the large veins through which blood is returned to the right atrium of the heart.

Ventricles—the two lower chambers of the heart from which blood flows through arteries to the lungs and other parts of the body.

Vigorous-intensity physical activity—on an absolute scale, physical activity that is done at 6.0 or more times the intensity of rest. On a scale relative to an individual's personal capacity, vigorous-intensity physical activity is usually a 7 or 8 on a scale of 0 to 10.

Viral—involving, or caused by a virus.

Virus—tiny, infective agents that can multiply in plants and animals, causing various diseases.

Vitamins—organic substances that are necessary for normal body metabolism, growth, and development.

Vulva—the external female genitalia.

Water-soluble vitamins—vitamins not stored in the body for a significant amount of time. Amounts that are consumed and not used relatively quickly by the body are excreted through urine and sweat. Examples include the B vitamins and vitamin C.

Wellness—a process of making informed choices that will lead one, over a period of time, to a healthy lifestyle that should result in a sense of well-being.

Note: Page numbers followed by "f" indicate figures; those followed by "t" indicate tables.

A

"ABCS" of heart disease and stroke prevention, 113
Abdominal wall, 77
Abortion, 292
  choosing, 291–292
  medication, 290
Abstinence, 282
Abusive relationships, 254
  phases of, 254
  signs of, 254t, 267
Acquaintance rape, 387–388
Acquired Immune Deficiency Syndrome (AIDS), 305
  cases by age, 307t
  cases by top ten states/ dependent areas, 307t
  cases by transmission category, 306t
  cure for, 305
ACS. *See* American Cancer Society (ACS)
ACSM. *See* American College of Sports Medicine (ACSM)
Actinic keratosis, 415
Action, in SCM, 6, 9f
Active resistance, 386–387
Activity. *See* Physical activity
Activity index, calculating, 95
Activity nervosa, 42–43
Activity Pyramid, 65f
Acupressure, 447
Acupuncture, 446–447
Acupuncturists, 446
Acute fulminant hepatitis, 314
Acute muscle soreness, 80
Adaptation, in fitness training, 72
Adderall, 355
Addictive behavior questionnaire, 367–368
ADHD (attention-deficit/ hyperactivity disorders), 355, 356
Adoption, 291

Advertising Council's Innocent Victims, 334
Aerobic exercise, 63–68
  vs. anaerobic exercise, 67–68
  benefits of, 64–67
  defined, 63, 67
  guideline for adults under 65, 73
  interval training and, 68
Affection, in relationships, 261
African Americans
  CVD risk in, 116
  diabetes and, 423, 424f
  hypertension risk in, 122
  lupus in, 427
  obesity in, 129f
  osteoporosis and, 137
  sickle-cell anemia in, 426
  stroke risk in, 126–127
Agape, 248
Age
  AIDS cases by, 307t
  biological age, 140
  CVD and, 128
  nutrients for individuals over 50, 156
  obesity and, 129f
  osteoporosis and, 138
  real age, 141
  syphilis and, 302f, 303f
Aging, 139–140
  creativity and, 141
  physical activity *vs.* inactivity in older men, 140t
  staying mentally vigorous, essentials for, 140
AHA. *See* American Heart Association (AHA)
AIDS. *See* Acquired Immune Deficiency Syndrome (AIDS)
Air pollution, outside activities and, 89
Alcoholic cirrhosis, 339

Alcoholic hepatitis, 339
Alcoholic pellagra, 339
Alcoholism, 338
Alcohol poisoning, 336–337, 378
Alcohol screening self-assessment, 369–370
Alcohol use and abuse, 330–341
  beverage types, 330
  binge drinking, 336
  blood alcohol concentration, 331–333
  boating accidents and, 380
  chronic effects of, 338–340
  college drinking, 334, 335–336
  crimes on college campuses and, 385
  defined, 330–331
  detectable amount of, 340
  drinking and driving, 333, 334–335
  drinking problems, 337–338
  ethyl, 330
  fire fatalities on college campuses and, 379
  information on, resources for, 340
  laws relating to, 334, 340–341
  motorcycle accidents and, 377
  physiological effects of, 331
  sexual assaults on college campuses and, 386
  societal problems associated with, 333–340
Alcohol Use Disorders Identification Test (AUDIT), 370
Allergens, outside activities and, 90
Alternative healthcare systems, 443, 445–447
  ayurveda, 445
  defined, 443
  homeopathy, 445
  naturopathy, 445–446
  TOM, 446–447

Alternative medicine, 440. *See also* Complementary and alternative medicine (CAM)
AMA (American Medical Association), 447
Amenorrhea in Female Athlete Triad, 42, 43, 43f
American Association of Cereal Chemists, 172
American Cancer Society (ACS)
  breast self-examination, 418, 419
  early cancer detection guidelines, 420f
  exercise to prevent cancer, 133, 134
  Guidelines on Nutrition and Physical Activity for Cancer Prevention, 112
  mammograms, 418
  new cancer cases and deaths, leading sites of, 412f
  skin self-examination, 416
  smokeless tobacco users, 344
  smoking cessation, 345
American College of Sports Medicine (ACSM), 61, 64, 112
  bone preservation, exercise prescriptions for, 139
  Exercise and Hypertension, 122
  Exercise Is Medicine, 112
  inactivity as cardiac risk factor, 64
  osteoporosis prevention guidelines, 138
  physical activity guidelines, 61, 73
  resistance training progression, 75
American Heart Association (AHA)
  2020 Health Impact Goal, 112
  blood pressure categories defined by, 121, 122f
  Heart Attack Symptoms and Warning Signs, 123, 124
  hypertension as cardiac risk factor, 127
  inactivity as cardiac risk factor, 63–64, 111
  Metrics of Cardiovascular Health, 114, 114f
  physical activity guidelines, 61, 73
  smoking cessation, 345, 346f
  sodium recommendations, 193
  waist-to-hip ratio, 118

American Medical Association (AMA), 447
American Red Cross, 381, 382
American Stroke Association (ASA), 112, 126
Amphetamines, 350
Amputations, diabetes and, 425
Anabolic androgenic steroids, 353–354
Anaerobic exercise, 67–68
Anal canal, 271
Anemia, 425–426
Aneurysm, 119, 126
Angel dust, 352
Angina pectoris, 66
Animal-assisted therapy, 456
Annals of Internal Medicine, 446–447
Anorexia nervosa, 41
Anterior muscles, 78f
Anthocyanins, 168t
Antioxidants, 163, 166, 166t
Anxiolytic (anti-anxiety) drugs, 355
Aplastic anemia, 426
Appetite suppressants, 220
Applied psycho-neuro-immunology, 455
Arguing, rules for, 251
Arteriosclerosis, 119–120, 121f, 424
ASA (American Stroke Association), 112, 126
Assaults on the job, 380
Asthma, 422
Atherosclerosis, 66, 119–120, 120f, 341
Athletic shoes. *See* Footwear
Attention-deficit/hyperactivity disorders (ADHD), 355, 356
Atypical lymphocytes, 406
AUDIT (Alcohol Use Disorders Identification Test), 370
Ayurveda, 445

B
BAC. *See* Blood alcohol concentration (BAC)
Back muscles, 77
Bacteria, beneficial, 169t
Bacterial STIs, 293–303
  chlamydia, 293
  gonorrhea, 293, 296
  pelvic inflammatory disease, 293, 296, 299
  syphilis, 299, 301, 304f

Ballistic stretching exercises, 83–84
Bariatric surgery, 211
Barrier methods of pregnancy prevention, 283–285
  diaphragm and Femcap, 284
  male condom, 283–284
  over-the-counter contraceptives for women, 284–285
Basal cell carcinomas, 413
Battering, 388
Bee pollen, 449
Behavior change
  decisions, factors influencing, 7f
  goal setting and, 8–9
  stages of, 5–6
Behavior modification planning
  good stress managers, characteristics of, 35f
  time killers, common, 33f
Beta-carotene, 168t
Beta glucan, 168t
Bicycle Helmet Safety Institute, 377
Bicycle safety, 377–378
Bifidobacteria, 169t
Binge drinking, 336
Binge-eating disorder, 42, 44
Bioenergy, 457
Biological age, 140
Biological-based therapies, 449–452
  functional foods, 451
  herbals and dietary supplements, 449–451
  macrobiotics, 449
  vitamins and minerals, 451
Biotin, 164t, 170t
Bipolar disorder, 37
Birth control. *See* Pregnancy prevention
Bisexual, 274
Blackout, 338
Blindness, diabetes and, 425
Blood. *See also* Circulation
  composition of, 149
  flow to heart, 66–67, 66f
  route of, during gas transport, 66–67, 66f
Blood alcohol concentration (BAC), 331–333
  calculating, 332
  defined, 331
  elimination process, 333f
  factors influencing, 332
  intoxication, 333
  tolerance, 333

Blood sugar levels, diabetes and, 424
BMI. *See* Body Mass Index (BMI)
Boating accidents, 380
Body composition, 213
Body image, 40, 41. *See also* Eating disorders
Body Mass Index (BMI), 212–213
  calculator, 229
  health risk measured by, 117
  obesity defined by, 213, 214
  table, 212t
Body shape, associated risks and, 130f
Bone mineral density, 76
Brain attack, 123. *See also* Stroke
Breast cancer, 417, 418
Breastfeeding women, nutrients for, 156
Breast self-exam (BSE), 418, 418t, 419, 420f
Bruise, 85t
BSE (breast self-exam), 418, 418t, 419, 420f
Bulimia nervosa, 42
Burn-out, 80
Burns, 378–379
Butterbur, 449

C
Caffeic acid, 169t
Caffeine, 348–349
  in beverages, 348, 349t
  defined, 348
  excessive consumption of, 349, 350
  pregnancy and, 349
  reducing consumption of, 349
Calcium
  facts about, 166t
  in foods, examples of, 169t
  intake, 136, 137–138
  in milk/dairy, 182
Calories, Nutrition Facts Label
  death decreased by expenditure increase, 111f
  fat, upper limit on, 159t
  fat calories in food, percentage of, 160t
  needs, determining, 213
  severe restriction of, 217, 218
  for weight loss, 216–217
  in weight management, balancing, 155, 209f
CAM. *See* Complementary and alternative medicine (CAM)
Cancer, 133–134, 411–422

alcohol use and abuse and, 339–340
breast, 417, 418
causes of, 413
cervical, 419, 421
cigarette smoking and, 342–343, 343f, 359–360
classifications of, 411–412
colon and rectum, 422
five-year survival rate, by race, 415t
five-year survival rate, by stage at diagnosis, 414t
HPV and, 308–309
lung, 417
macrobiotics and, 449
new cancer cases and deaths, leading sites of, 413f
oral, 422
physical activity and, 133–134, 134t
preventing, through diet and lifestyle, 413t
prevention of, 133
probability of developing, 418t
reducing, goal in, 11
risk factors for, 133, 412
screening guidelines for early detection of, 420f
skin, 413, 415–417
smokeless tobacco and, 342, 344
testicular, 421–422
treatment, 413
warning signs of, 413
Cancer-related checkup, 420f
Cannabinoids, 347–348
Carbohydrates, 157–158
  complex, 157
  dietary fiber, 157–158
  fat intake and, 159
  on Nutrition Facts Label, 193f
  simple, 158
Carbon monoxide, 341–342
  poisoning, 378
Carcinomas, 412
Cardiorespiratory endurance, 99
Cardiovascular disease (CVD), 112–119, 127–133
  "ABCS" of prevention, 113, 116
  cholesterol levels and, 113, 116, 120, 121f, 127
  cigarette smoking and, 121, 127, 342–343
  deaths attributed to, 116f
  diabetes and, 424
  positive attitude in cardiac rehabilitation, 124

risk factors for, 114–116, 127–128
risk for, measuring, 117–119
self-assessment of, 145
triglyceride levels and, 116, 119, 120, 121f, 128
waist-to-hip ratio and, 117f, 118, 128, 135
in women *vs.* men, 115
in women who smoke and use oral contraceptives, 122, 285, 286, 287
Cardiovascular endurance, 63
Cardiovascular fitness, 63–75
  aerobic exercise and, 63–68
  Cooper's 1.5-Mile Run and, assessing with, 105
  defined, 63
  evaluating, 73–75
  exercise prescription for, 68–71 (*See also* FITT exercise regimen)
  exercise session for, components of, 71–72
  exercise to improve, 113, 114f
  heart disease I.Q. quiz, 103–104
  heart rate and, measuring, 68, 69f
  importance of, 63
  7 Metrics of Cardiovascular Health, 114, 114f
  target heart rate range and, 63, 68–70, 69f, 71, 97
  training principles in, 72–73
Carotenoids, 166t, 168t, 452t
Carpal tunnel syndrome, 380
CDC. *See* Centers for Disease Control and Prevention (CDC)
Centers for Disease Control and Prevention (CDC)
  "ABCS" of heart disease and stroke prevention, 113
  acupuncture use, 447
  bicycle safety, 377
  Guidelines for Treatment of Sexually Transmitted Infections, 281
  hepatitis vaccination recommendations, 314, 408
  HIV/AIDS identified by, 305
  inactivity as cardiac risk factor, 64
  lifestyle affecting longevity of life, 109, 110–111, 112
  meningitis vaccination recommendations, 410

Centers for Disease Control and
    Prevention (cont.)
  smokeless tobacco use, 342
  smoking cessation, 345–346
  Youth Risk Behavior Survey,
    2007, 275
Cerebral embolism, 126, 127
Cerebral hemorrhage, 126, 127
Cervarix vaccine, 308
Cervical cancer, 308, 309, 310f,
    419, 421
Cervical infections, 311t
Chemotherapy, as cancer
    treatment, 413
Chewing tobacco. See Smokeless
    tobacco
Childhood obesity, 129–132
Chiropractic care, 442, 447–448
Chlamydia, 293
  rates by region, 295f
  rates by state, 295f
  reported cases and rates by
    state, 294t
  transmission and symptoms of,
    293, 310t
  treatment of, 293
Cholesterol
  in fats, 158, 159
  HDL, 113, 121f
  LDL, 113, 116, 120, 121f
  levels, CVD and, 116, 120,
    121f, 127
  on Nutrition Facts Label, 193f
  in oils, 186
ChooseMyPlate, 188–191
Chronic bronchitis, 342
Chronic obstructive pulmonary
    diseases (COPD), 342
Cigarette smoking. See also
    Smoking cessation; Tobacco
  cancer and, 342–343, 343f,
    359–360, 413, 417
  CVD and, 121, 127, 342–343
  fire deaths caused by, 379
  life expectancy of smokers
    and, 343
  nicotine addiction
    questionnaire, 361
  osteoporosis and, 138
  physical effects of, 342–343,
    343f, 359–360
  vs. water pipe smoking, 344,
    344f
  "Why Do You Smoke?" test,
    363–364
Cigar smoking, 343
Circulation
  acupressure to improve, 447

collateral, 65, 67, 120, 123
  in diabetes, 424
  exercise used to improve, 65,
    67, 120, 123, 442
  in peripheral vascular
    disease, 120
  qi gong to improve, 456
Circulatory system, 66, 66f
Circumcision, 272
CLA (conjugated linoleic
    acid), 168t
Clery Act, 385
Clinical weight loss
    programs, 220
Clitoral hood, 270
Clitoris, 270
Clove cigarettes, 343
Club drugs, 351–352
  MDMA (ecstasy), 351
  Rohypnol (roofies), 351–352
  2C-B, 351
Cocaine, 350
Codeine, 354
Collateral circulation, 65, 67,
    120, 123
College campuses
  fire-related emergencies
    and, 379
  personal safety tips for, 384
  safety awareness and, 384–385
  sexual violence and, 386
  stalking and, 385
  water safety tips and, 380
College students
  alcohol use and abuse by, 334,
    335–336
  energy drinks and, caffeine
    in, 349
  parental relationship stages
    and, 239–241
  peer relationships and, 241–244
College Student's Guide to
    Personal Safety Planning,
    388, 399–402
Colon and rectum cancer,
    420f, 422
Common cold, 410, 411t
Communicable diseases, 404–411
  common cold, 410, 411t
  hepatitis, 406–409
  HIV/AIDS (non-sexual
    contraction), 404
  influenza, 410–411, 411t
  meningitis, 409–410
  mononucleosis, 405–406
  tuberculosis, 404–405
Communication
  gender differences, 238–239

left-brain vs. right brain
    dominance, 238, 238t
  open, 236–237
  readiness for sexual activity
    and, 275
  in relationships, 236–239
  strength of, self-test for, 261
  styles of, 237, 238–239
Complementary and alternative
    medicine (CAM), 439–461
  alternative healthcare systems
    in, 443, 445–447
  biological-based therapies in,
    449–452
  commonly used, 442, 443f
  energy therapies in, 456–458
  Internet for information
    on, 458
  introduction, 440
  mainstream, 442, 445t
  manipulative and body-based
    therapies in, 447–448, 449
  mind-body medicine in,
    452–456
  NHIS Study on Americans
    using, 441–442, 442f
  treatments rooted in,
    442, 443f
Complementary medicine, 440.
    See also Complementary
    and alternative medicine
    (CAM)
Complex carbohydrates, 157
Compression as cause of stroke,
    126, 127
Compromise, in
    relationships, 239
Condoms, 283–284
  advantages of using, 284
  effectiveness of, 283
  problems with using, 283–284
  reasons for using, 276
  right way of using, 283f
  STIs and, 283
Condyloma (genital warts), 306,
    308, 308f
Conjugated linoleic acid
    (CLA), 168t
Contemplation, in SCM, 6, 9f
Contraceptive implant, 289
Contraceptive patch, 286–288
Cooldown and stretch, in exercise
    session, 72
Cooper's 1.5-Mile Run, 105
COPD (chronic obstructive
    pulmonary diseases), 342
Core musculature, 76–77
Corona, 272

Coronary artery disease, 120, 123
Coronary collateral circulation, 120, 123
Corpus cavernosa, 272
Corpus spongiosum, 272
Cowper's glands, 273
Crabs, 314
Craniosacral therapy, 448
Creeping obesity, 214
Crime Awareness and Campus Security Act of 1990, 385
Curl-up Test, 101
Cutaneous lupus erythematosus, 426
CVD. *See* Cardiovascular disease (CVD)
Cytomegalovirus, 405

D

Daily values on Nutrition Facts Label, 191–192, 193f
Dairy products. *See* Milk/dairy
Date rape, 250, 352
Dating, 247–251
    arguing and, rules for, 251
    date rape and, 250, 352
    jealousy and, 250
    love and, 247–249
    safe sex activities in, rating, 250
    things to do in, 249
Death
    caloric expenditure and, 111f
    due to CVD, 116f, 118f
    leading causes of, 10f
Dehydration, 89, 171–172
Delayed-onset muscle soreness, 80
Department of Health and Human Services (DHHS)
    Dietary Guidelines for Americans, 112, 154
    health benefits of physical activity, 62f
    Million Hearts Initiative, 112
    physical activity guidelines for Americans, 62f
Depo-Provera, 288
Depressants, 355
Depression
    antidepressants for, 37
    eating disorders and, 39, 43, 44
    exercise and, 37
    stress and, 36–37
    suicide and, 38
DHHS. *See* Department of Health and Human Services (DHHS)
Diabetes, 134–135, 423–425

age-specific prevalence of, by race/ethnicity and sex, 423, 424f
    amputations and, 425
    At-Risk Weight Chart, 436
    blindness and, 425
    blood sugar levels and, 424
    body parts affected by, 425
    CVD and, 128
    defined, 134
    exercise and, 128, 134–135
    gestational, 423, 424
    number of persons diagnosed with, 423f
    prevention of, 128, 134
    risk factors for, 134, 435–436
    Type I, 423, 424
    Type II, 423, 424
Diamond, Marian, 140
Diaphragm and Femcap, 284
Diastolic blood pressure, 65, 121, 121f
Diet. *See* Nutrition
Dietary fiber, 157–158, 157t
    functional and total, 168t
    insoluble, 158, 168t
    on Nutrition Facts Label, 193f
    soluble, 157, 168t
    sources of, 157t
Dietary Guidelines for Americans, 112, 154–156
    balancing calories to manage weight, 155
    building healthy eating patterns, 156
    foods and food components to reduce, 155
    foods and nutrients to increase, 155–156
Dietary supplements, 218, 219, 449–451
Dieting, weight loss and, 216, 217–218
    fad diets, 216, 223, 224
    reasons to give up dieting, 218
    severe calorie restrictions, 217, 218
    yo-yo dieting, 216
Disaster kit, 382
Disaster planning, 381–383, 382f
Disease, 403–437
    communicable, 404–411
    non-communicable, 411–427
    preventing, 9
Dislocations, 85t
Disordered eating in Female Athlete Triad, 42, 43f

Dissociative drugs, 352
Distress, 30
Dopamine, 351
Dowager's hump, 138
Drinking and driving, 333, 334–335
    effects on driving, 334t
    getting arrested for, 334, 340–341
    stopping an intoxicated individual from driving, 334, 335
Drinking problems, 337–338. *See also* Alcohol use and abuse
"Drive Alert . . . Arrive Alive" campaign, 376
Driving under the influence (DUI), 340. *See also* Drinking and driving
Driving while intoxicated (DWI), 340. *See also* Drinking and driving
Drownings, 380
Drug Abuse Warning Network, 352
Drug-induced lupus, 426
Drug Induced Rape Prevention and Punishment Act of 1996, 352
Drug misuse and abuse, 329–371. *See also* Alcohol use and abuse
    anabolic androgenic steroids, 353–354
    cannabinoids, 347–348
    club drugs, 351–352
    dissociative drugs, 352
    hallucinogens, 352–353
    inhalants, 353
    introduction to, 330
    opioids, 348
    prescription drugs, 354–357
    stimulants, 348–352
    tobacco, 341
DUI (driving under the influence), 340
DWI (driving while intoxicated), 340

E

Ear (auricular) acupuncture, 446
Early Childhood Obesity Prevention Policies (IOM), 61
Eating disorders, 39–46
    action for, course of, 45, 46
    activity nervosa, 42–43
    anorexia nervosa, 41

Eating disorders (cont.)
   binge-eating disorder, 42, 44
   body image and, 40, 41
   bulimia nervosa, 42
   causes of, 43, 44, 46
   depression and, 39, 43, 44
   fear of obesity, 42
   forbidden foods, 53–54
   osteoporosis and, 138
   risk factors for, 39f, 41, 43
   sneaking food, 55
   stress and, 39
Eating out. *See* Fast foods/eating
      out
Ecstasy (MDMA), 351
Eggs, from fertilization to
      implantation, 278,
      278f, 279f
Ejaculation, 273
Emergency contraception (EC)
      pills, 290–291
Emotional dimension of wellness,
      2f, 3
Emphysema, 342
Endometrial cycle, 278, 279
Energy drinks, 219–220
Energy therapies, 456–458
   bioenergy, 457
   qi gong, 446, 456
   reiki, 456
   therapeutic touch, 457
Environment
   cancer and, 414
   exercise and, 87–88
   holistic self-care and, 441
   safety in, 388–389
   wellness and, 2f, 4
Environmental Protection Agency
      (EPA), 388
Environmental tobacco
      smoke, 345
EPA (Environmental Protection
      Agency), 388
Ephedra, 450
Epididymis, 272–273
Epstein-Barr virus, 405, 406
Eros, 248
Essential amino acids,
      159, 161
Essential fatty acids, 451
Essential nutrients, 156–172
   antioxidants, 163, 166
   carbohydrates, 157–158
   fats, 158–160
   functional foods, 167–171
   minerals, 163
   organic foods, 167
   protein, 159, 161

   vitamins, 163, 164–166, 167
   water, 171–172
Essential oils, 444
Estimated Energy Requirements
      (IOM), 214t
Ethyl alcohol, 330
Etonogestrel, 289
Eugenol, 343
Eustress, 30
Evening primrose oil, 449
Excitement, in female sexual
      response, 272
Exercise. *See also* Aerobic exercise;
      Physical activity
   activity index, calculating, 95
   aging and, 140–141
   anaerobic, 67–68
   CAM and, 441
   cancer and, 133–134, 134t
   collateral circulation and, 65,
      67, 120, 123, 442
   CVD and (*See* Cardiovascular
      fitness)
   depression and, 37
   diabetes and, 128, 134–135
   environmental conditions and,
      87–88
   fatigue in strenuous, 67
   footwear for, 85–87
   hypertension and, 122, 127
   hyponatremia and, 88–89
   illness and, 89
   injuries and, 84–85
   low back pain and, 136
   myocardial infarction and, 122
   not starting, risk of, 90
   osteoporosis and, 139
   outside activities, concerns for,
      89–90
   problems related to, reference
      guide for, 85t
   pulmonary ventilation and, 67
   Safety of Exercise Participation:
      PAR-Q and You, 93
   stretching, 83–84
   stroke and, 126
Exercise and Hypertension
      (ACSM), 122
Exercise Is Medicine (ACSM), 112
Exercise prescription
   for cardiovascular fitness,
      68–71
   for muscular fitness, 77, 80
   Exercise session, 71–72activity,
      71–72
   cooldown and stretch, 72
   pre-stretch, 71
   warm-up, 71

Explosion phase, in abusive
      relationship, 254

F
Fad diets, 216, 223, 224
Fallopian tube, 271–272, 290
Falls
   in home, 378
   in workplace, 380
Family Emergency Plan, 393–394
Family Health Portrait
      activity, 433
Family tree assignment, 437
Family violence, 388
Fast foods/eating out, 225, 231
   sensible choices in, 162
   super-sized meals and, 222, 224
   tips for, 225, 226
Fatigue, in strenuous exercise, 67
Fats, 158–160. *See also* Oils
   calories in, upper limit on, 159t
   fat calories in food, percentage
      of, 160t
   Food Guide Pyramid and,
      187–188
   monosaturated, 159
   on Nutrition Facts Label, 193f
   polyunsaturated, 159
   saturated, 158
   sensible choices for good
      health, 162
   solids, examples of, 191
   trans, 158
   unsaturated, 158–159
Fat-soluable vitamins, 163, 164t
Fatty acids, 158, 168t, 194
FDA. *See* Food and Drug
      Administration (FDA)
Federal Emergency Management
      Agency (FEMA), 381, 382
Federal Trade Commission
      (FTC), 449
Feldenkrais method, 456
FEMA (Federal Emergency
      Management Agency),
      381, 382
Female Athlete Triad, 42–43, 43f
Female sexual anatomy, 270–272,
      270f
Female sexual response, phases
      of, 272
Femcap, 284
Fertility awareness-based methods
      (FAMs), 282–283
Ferulic acid, 169t
Fetal alcohol syndrome, 340
Fetus, prenatal development of,
      279–281, 280f

Fiber. *See* Dietary fiber
Fight-or-flight response, 65
Fires, 378–379
Fitness, 59–105. *See also* Physical
   activity
   cardiovascular, 63–75
   digital technology used in, 138
   muscular, 75–84
Fitness training principles, 72–73
   individual differences, 72, 73
   overload and adaptation, 72
   reversibility, 73
   specificity, 72
FITT exercise regimen, 68–71
   frequency, 68
   intensity, 68, 70
   time, 70
   type, 70–71
FiveFingers shoe, 86–87
Five-year survival rate
   by race, 415t
   by stage at diagnosis, 414t
Flavonoids, 166t, 168–169t, 452t
Flexibility
   defined, 83
   functional strength training
      for, 83
   importance of, 63
   loss of, 82–83
   stretching exercises, 83–84
   training, 73
Flu, 410–411, 411t
Flunitrazepam, 351
Fluoride, 166t
Folate, 164t
Food and Drug Administration
      (FDA)
   acupuncture complications, 446
   biological-based therapies, 449
   Center for Food Safety and
      Applied Nutrition, 450
   ephedra banned by, 450
   HPV vaccines approved by, 308
   nicotine regulations, 341
   prescription drug
      guidelines, 357
   Ritalin abuse, 355
   trans fat values, 158, 192
   weight loss products, approved/
      banned, 220, 223
Food Guide Pyramid,
      172–188, 173f
   daily activity and, 187
   fats and, 187–188
   fruits, 180–182
   grains, 172, 174–176
   milk/dairy, 182–183
   oils, 186–187

protein/meats and beans,
      184–185
   RDA based on 2,000-calorie
      diet, 161f
   vegetables, 177–179
Food shopping, healthy, 224
Footwear
   buying guide, 86
   cross trainers, 85
   exercise and, 85–87
   minimalist running shoe, 86–87
   running shoes, 85, 86
Foreskin, 272
Formation, 136
Fractures, 85t
Frenulum, 272
Frequency
   in FITT exercise regimen, 68
   in weight training, 77
Friendships, 244–246
Fructo-oligosaccharides, 169t
Fruits, 180–182
FTC (Federal Trade
      Commission), 449
Functional foods, 167–171
   in biological-based
      therapies, 451
   defined, 167
   examples and benefits of,
      168–171t, 452t
Functional movement, 76–77
Functional strength, 83
Fundus, 271

G
Gamma hydroxybutyrate (GHB),
      352
Gardasil vaccine, 308
Gas transport, route of blood
      during, 66–67, 66f
Gastronintestinal
      disorders, 427
Gay, 274
Gender
   communication differences,
      238–239
   CVD and, 115, 128
   diabetes and, 423, 424f
   gonorrhea and, 298f, 299f
   obesity and, 129f
   probability of developing
      cancer, 418t
Genital herpes, 304–305
   initial visits to physicians'
      offices, 304f
   transmission and symptoms of,
      304, 310t
   treatment of, 305

Genital warts (condyloma), 306,
      308, 308f
Gestational diabetes, 423, 424
GHB, 352
GHB (gamma
      hydroxybutyrate), 352
Gingko biloboa, 449
Ginseng, 450, 451f
Girls on the Run, 132
Glans penis, 272
Globesity, 129
Gluts, 77
Glycogen, 67–68, 76
Goal setting, behavior change
      and, 8–9
Gonorrhea, 293, 296
   rates by age among
      men 15-44, 299f
   rates by age among women 15-
      44, 298f
   rates by region, 298f
   rates by sex, 298f
   rates by state, 302f
   reported cases and rates by
      state, 297t
   transmission and symptoms of,
      294, 296, 312t
   treatment of, 296
Grains, 172, 174–176
   examples of, 168t
   ounce equivalent of, 174–175
   RDA of, 174
   serving size, 176
   of wheat, composition
      of, 176f
Green living, tips for,
      388–389
Group projects, 242–243
Guided imagery, 455–456
*Guidelines on Nutrition and Physical
      Activity for Cancer Prevention*
      (ACS), 112

H
Hallucinogens, 352–353
'Halo' effect, 211
Harvard Alumni Study, 117, 127
Hashish, 347
HDL cholesterol, 113, 121f
Health
   factors influencing, 11–12
   fitness related to, 63
   Healthy People 2020 and, 11–13
   indicators, 11
   Physical Activity and Health
      report, 36, 64, 64f, 109,
      110, 112, 114, 128
Healthy Eating Pyramid, 194f

Healthy habits, 224–226
  building healthy plate, 224 (*See also* MyPlate)
  fast foods/eating out, 225, 226, 231
  fitness *vs.* fatness, 225
  healthy food shopping, 224–225
  healthy weight gain, 224
Healthy People 2020, 11–13
Healthy plate, building, 224. *See also* MyPlate
Healthy relationships, 236–239, 261
  communication in, 236–237, 238–239, 261
  compromise in, 239
  positive self-worth and, 236
  spelling, 237
  ten commandments of, 244
  trust in, 239
Heart attack. *See* Myocardial infarction
Heart Attack Symptoms and Warning Signs (AHA), 123, 124
Heart disease I.Q. quiz, 103–104
Heart rate
  measuring, 68, 69f
  recovery, 75
  target range, 63, 68–70, 69f, 71
Heat, exercising in, 87–88
Heat and humidity chart, 88f
Heat cramps, 85t, 87
Heat exhaustion, 85t, 87
Heat stroke, 85t, 87
Helicobacter pylori (H. pylori), 427
Helmet laws, 377–378
Hepatitis, 406–409
  A, 406, 407–408
  B (*See* Hepatitis B)
  C, 408–409
  comparison of major types of, 407t
  contracting, 408t
  course of, 406
  D, E, and G, 409
  risk assessment, 327
Hepatitis B, 313–314
  diagnosing, 309, 312
  incubation period, 312, 313
  transmission and symptoms of, 309, 312t, 407t
  treatment, 407t
  treatment of, 313–314
Hepatotoxic trauma, 339
Herbalist, 449–450
Herbal medicine, 446

Herbals, 449–451
Heredity, CVD and, 128
Heroin, 348
Herpes simplex virus (HSV). *See* Genital herpes
Heterosexual, 274
High blood pressure. *See* Hypertension
High-density-lipoproteins (HDL), 113, 121f
Hip muscles, 77
Hippocampus, 455
Hispanic/Latinos
  diabetes and, 423, 424f
Hispanics/Latinos
  CVD risk in, 116
  hypertension risk in, 122
  obesity in, 129f
HIV/AIDS, 305. *See also* Acquired Immune Deficiency Syndrome (AIDS)
  non-sexual contraction of, 404
  St. John's wort and, 449, 450f
  transmission and symptoms of, 305, 312t
  treatment of, 305
Holistic self-care, 441
Holmes and Rahe Life Events Scale, 34
Homeopathy, 445
Home safety, 378–379
  falls, 378
  fires and burns, 378–379
  poisoning, 378
Homophobia, 274
Homosexual, 274
Honeymoon phase, in abusive relationship, 254
Hormonal methods of pregnancy prevention, 285–290
  contraceptive implant, 289
  contraceptive patch, 286–288
  CVD in women who smoke and, 122, 285, 286, 287
  Depo-Provera, 288
  emergency contraception pills, 290–291
  intrauterine device, 288–289
  oral contraceptive pills, 285–286
  sterilization, 290
  STIs and, prevention of, 289t
  vaginal ring, 286
HPV. *See* Human Papilloma Viruses (HPV)
Human Immunodeficiency Virus (HIV). *See* HIV/AIDS

Human Papilloma Viruses (HPV), 306, 308–309
  genital warts and, 306, 308, 308f
  screening and cancer, 308–309
  transmission and symptoms of, 307, 310t
  treatment of, 309
  vaccine, 308
Hurricanes, 381
Hydrocodone, 354
Hydrosalpinx, 293
Hymen, 271
Hypertension, 120–122
  categories defined by AMA, 122f
  complications of, 120
  CVD and, 127
  diastolic blood pressure, 65, 121, 121f
  exercise used to improve, 122, 127
  risk factors for, 122
  as "silent killer," 120
  stroke and, 126
  systolic blood pressure, 65, 121, 121f
  teen sleep patterns and, 120
Hypokinetic, defined, 110
Hypokinetic conditions, 90, 110–152
  aging, 139–140
  arteriosclerosis, 119–120, 121f
  cancer, 133–134
  CVD, 112–119, 127–133
  diabetes, 134–135
  heart attack, 122–123, 124–125
  hypertension, 120–122
  low back pain, 135–136
  metabolic syndrome, 135
  osteoporosis, 136–139
  peripheral vascular disease, 120
  prevention of, 140–141
  stroke, 123, 126–127
Hyponatremia, 88–89

I

Illness, exercise and, 89
Immunoglobulins, 309
Immunotherapy, as cancer treatment, 413
Inactivity. *See* Physical inactivity
Inactivity physiology, 64
Indinavir, 449, 450f
Individual differences, in fitness training, 72, 73
Influenza, 410–411, 411t
Inhalants, 353

Injuries, exercise and, 84–85
Insoluble fiber, 158, 168t
Institute of Medicine (IOM)
   daily physical activity
         recommendations, 61
   Early Childhood Obesity
         Prevention Policies, 61
   estimated calorie
         requirements, 214t
   estimated energy
         requirements, 214t
Insulin, diabetes and, 423, 424
Intellectual dimension of
      wellness, 2f, 3
Intensity
   in FITT exercise regimen, 68, 70
   in weight training, 77
Internet
   for CAM information, 458
   relationships, 245–246
Interval training, 68
Intimate violence, 388
Intoxication, 333
Intoxication assault, 340
Intoxication manslaughter, 340
Intrauterine device, 288–289
Inulin, 169t
Iodine, 166t
IOM. *See* Institute of Medicine
      (IOM)
Iron, 166t
Iron-deficiency anemia, 426
Irritable bowel syndrome
      (IBS), 427
Isoflavones, 451
Isothiocyanates, 169t, 452t

J
Jealousy, dating and, 250
Joint sprains, 85t
Journals, 8

K
Karvonen formula, 70, 97
Ketamine hydrochloride (Special
      K or K), 352
K-hole, 352
Kinsey Scale of Sexual Behavior,
      274, 275f
Kissing disease, 405–406
Korsakoff's syndrome, 340
Kyphosis, 138

L
Labia majora, 270
Labia minora, 270
Lactobacilli, 169t
Lactovegetarians, 194

Latex cup (diaphragm), 284
Lats, 77
LDL cholesterol, 113, 116,
      120, 121f
Left-brain *vs.* right brain
      dominance, 238, 238t
Leptin, 218
Lesbian, 274
Let's Move! Campaign, 108
Leukemias, 412
Leukoplakia, 342
Life expectancy, 109–111, 109f
Lifestyle
   cancer prevention and,
         413t, 414
Lifestyle activity, 110
   benefits of healthy,
         111–112
   hypokinetic conditions affected
         by, 110
   life expectancy affected by,
         110–111
   vs. weight, significance in,
         117–118
Lightning, 89, 381
Liver disease, 338–339
Load, in weight training, 77
Long slow distance training, 70
Love
   dating and, 247–249
   defining, 247, 252
   models of, 247, 248
   styles of, 248
Low back pain, 135–136
   exercise and, 136
   healthy back test, 147–148
   prevention of, 136
   risk factors for, 135–136
Low-carbohydrate high-protein,
      220, 221–222
Low-density lipoproteins (LDL),
      113, 116, 120, 121f,
      158, 163
Low responder to exercise
      stimulus, 72
LSD (lysergic acid
      diethylamide), 353
Ludus, 248
Lung cancer, 417
Lupus, 426–427
Lutein, 168t
Lycopene, 168t
Lymphomas, 412
Lysergic acid diethylamide
      (LSD), 353

M
Macrobiotics, 449

Macrominerals, 163
Macronutrients, 154
Magnesium, 166t, 169t
Ma Huang, 450
Maintenance, in SCM, 6, 9f
Male sexual anatomy,
      272–274, 273f
Malnutrition, alcohol use and
      abuse and, 339
Mammograms, 418
Mania, 248
Manipulative and body-based
      therapies, 447–448, 449
   chiropractic, 447–448
   craniosacral therapy, 448
   massage, 448
   reflexology, 448
Mantoux test, 404
Marijuana, 347–348
Marriage, 252–253
   contemplating, 252–253
   happy, characteristics of, 253
   successful, tips for, 253
Massage, 448
Mate, qualities of
      perfect, 257
Maximum oxygen uptake, 74
MDMA (ecstasy), 351
Meats and beans. *See* Protein/
      meats and beans
Medication abortion, 290
Meditation, 452–455
Megan's Law, 385
Melanomas, 413, 415, 417
   "ABCD rule" in checking for,
         416, 417
   non-, 413
Men
   aging and physical activity *vs.*
         inactivity in older, 140t
   CVD in, *vs.* women, 115
   gonorrhea in, 299f
   myocardial infarction
         symptoms in, *vs.*
         women, 123
   syphilis in, 303f
Meningitis, 409–410
Menstrual cycle, 277–278, 277f
Mental health, 441
Mental health disorders, 36–46
   depression, 36–37
   eating disorders, 39–46
   far-reaching "ripple effect"
         of, 36
   suicidal behavior, 38–39
   types of, 36
Metabolic syndrome, 135
Metabolism boosters, 220

Methamphetamines, 350–351
Microminerals, 163
Micronutrients, 154
Milk/dairy, 182
    RDA of, 182
    sensible choices for good
        health, 162
    serving size, 183
Mind/Body Medical Institute, 457
Mind-body medicine, 452–456
    animal-assisted therapy, 456
    applied psycho-neuro-
        immunology, 455
    Feldenkrais method, 456
    guided imagery, 455–456
    meditation, 452–455
    mindfulness, 456
    prayer and spirituality, 455
    somatic movement, 456
    yoga, 455
Mindfulness, 456, 457
Minerals
    in biological-based
        therapies, 451
    excess amounts of, effect
        of, 167t
    facts about, 166t
    functional, 169t
    macrominerals, 163
    microminerals, 163
    on Nutrition Facts Label, 193f
Minimalist running shoe, 86–87
Mini-pills, 285–286
Minor in possession (MIP), 340
MIP (minor in possession), 340
Moderate activities, 62
Moles, 416, 417
Mononucleosis, 405–406
Monosaturated fats, 159
Monospot agglutination
    test, 406
Monounsaturated fatty
    acids, 168t
Mons pubis, 270
Morning after pill, 290–291
Morphine, 354
Motorcycle safety, 376–377
Motor vehicle safety, 374–377
    distracted driving, 374–375
    drowsy driving, 375–376
    tips for, 377
    in workplace, 380
Muscle cramps, 85t
Muscles
    anterior, 78f
    core musculature, 76–77
    endurance of, 75, 101
    of inspiration, 67

posterior, 79f
soreness of, 80, 85t
strength of, 75
Muscular fitness, 75–84. *See also*
    Weight training
    benefits of, 76
    components of, 75
    core musculature and, 76–77
    current level of, assessing, 101
    exercise prescription for, 77, 80
    functional movement, 76–77
    importance of, 63
    muscle soreness, 80
    over-training, 80
    reasons for working muscles, 75
Mycobacterium, 404
Myocardial infarction, 66,
    122–123, 124–125
    exercise and, 122
    Heart Attack Symptoms and
        Warning Signs (AHA),
        123, 124
    narrowed or blocked arteries
        resulting in, 122, 123f
    reduction in risk for, 125f
    symptoms of, in women *vs.*
        men, 123
    women who smoke and use
        hormonal contraceptive
        methods, 122
MyPlate, 188–191

N

NASPE (National Sports
    and Physical
    Education),61
National Cancer Institute,
    342, 449
National Center for Chronic
    Disease Prevention and
    Control, 345–346
National Center for Injury
    Prevention and
    Control, 378
National Center for the
    Prevention and Control of
    Rape, 386–387
National Climatic Data Center
    (NCDC), 381
National Consumers League
    Food and Drug Interaction
    Brochure, 450
National Crime Prevention
    Council (NCPC), 383
National Crime Victimization
    Survey, 386
National Health Interview Study
    (NHIS), 441–442, 442f

National Heart, Lung, and
    Blood Institute Obesity
    Guidelines, 224
National Highway Traffic Safety
    Administration (NHTSA),
    374, 375
National Institute of Alcohol
    Abuse and Alcoholism
    (NIAAA)
    alcohol-related unintentional
        injuries and, 335–336
    drinking by college students
        and, 386
    drinking problems and, 337
National Institutes for Health
    National Center for
    Complementary and
    Alternative Medicine
    (NCCAM), 449
National Oceanic Atmospheric
    Administration, 381
National Safety Council (NSC)
    accident defined by, 374
    falls and, 378
    helmet requirements for
        motorcyclists, 377
    sports injuries and, 381
    tips for motorists and motor
        cyclists, 377
    work-related fatalities
        and, 380
National Sleep Foundation (NSF),
    375, 376
National Sports and Physical
    Education (NASPE), 61
Natural disasters, 380
    hurricanes, 381
    lightning, 381
    planning for, 381–383, 382f
    tornadoes, 381
Natural methods of pregnancy
    prevention, 282–283
    abstinence, 282
    fertility awareness-based
        methods, 282–283
    withdrawal method, 282
Naturopathy, 445–446
NCCAM (National Institutes for
    Health National Center
    for Complementary and
    Alternative Medicine), 449
NCDC (National Climatic Data
    Center), 381
NCPC (National Crime
    Prevention Council), 383
Neonatal lupus, 426
NHIS (National Health Interview
    Study), 441–442, 442f

NHTSA (National Highway Traffic Safety Administration), 374, 375
NIAAA. *See* National Institute of Alcohol Abuse and Alcoholism (NIAAA)
Niacin, 164t
Nicotine. *See also* Cigarette smoking; Smoking cessation
    addiction questionnaire, 361
    defined, 341
Night exercise, 90
Nonclinical weight loss programs, 220
Non-communicable diseases, 411–427
    anemia, 425–426
    asthma, 422
    cancer, 411–422
    diabetes, 423–425
    gastronintestinal disorders, 427
    lupus, 426–427
Non-essential amino acids, 159
Non-melanomas, 413
Non-steroidal anti-inflammatory drugs (NSAIDS), 448
Nootropics, 356
NSAIDS (non-steroidal anti-inflammatory drugs), 448
NSC. *See* National Safety Council (NSC)
NSF (National Sleep Foundation), 375, 376
Nutrients
    Dietary Guidelines recommendations, 155–156
    essential (*See* Essential nutrients)
    for specific population groups, 156
Nutrition, 153–206. *See also Dietary Guidelines for Americans*
    cancer prevention and, 413, 414t
    dietary analysis project and, 197–200
    dietary supplements and, 218, 219
    energy drinks, 219–220
    essential nutrients, 156–172
    Food Guide Pyramid, 172–188
    for good health, 162
    Healthy Eating Pyramid, 194f
    holistic self-care and, 441

issues in, other, 188–195
    MyPlate, 188–191
    Nutrition Facts Label, 191–194, 193f
    vegetarianism, 194–195
Nutrition bars, 219–220
Nutrition Facts Label, 191–194

O
Obesity
    activity used to help, 214, 215
    in adults, percentage of, 208f
    causes of, 132, 209–210
    childhood, 129–132
    creeping, 214
    CVD and, 128–129
    defined, 213, 214
    fat distribution and, 129, 130f, 212–213
    fear of, 42
    focus on, *vs.* fitness, 133
    health risks of, 128
    medical costs associated with, 215f
    prevalence by race, ethnicity, sex, and age, 129f
    prevention, 214
    psychological response to, 132
    waist measurement as indicator of health risks, 213
    weight loss `halo' effect, 211
Occlusion, 119, 120
Occupational dimension of wellness, 2f, 3
Occupational illnesses, 380
Occupational Safety and Health Act, 380
Occupational Safety and Health Administration (OSHA), 380
Office of Sustainability, Texas A&M University, 388
Oils, 186–187
    cholesterol in, 186
    composition of, 159t
    counting, 187
    essential, 444
    examples of, 191
    RDA of, 186
Omega-3 fatty acids, 168t, 194, 451
Open container, 340
Opioids, 348, 354–355
    codeine, 354
    heroin, 348
    hydrocodone, 354
    morphine, 354
    oxycodone, 355

Opium, 348
Oral cancer, 422
Oral contraceptive pills, 285–286
    emergency contraception pills, 290–291
    mini-pills, 285–286
    the pill, 285
Organic foods, 167
Orgasm, in female sexual response, 272
Oriental massage, 446
Osteoporosis, 136–139
    amenorrhea and, 138
    bone loss during spaceflight, 137
    calcium intake and, 136, 137–138
    defined, 136
    exercise and, 139
    in Female Athlete Triad, 42, 43f
    formation, 136
    prevention of, 138
    resporption, 136
    risk factors for, 136, 137–138, 151
    as "silent disease," 136
Ovarian cycle, 278, 278f
Ovaries, 272
Overload, in fitness training, 72
Over-the-counter contraceptives for women, 284–285
Over-training, 80
Overweight. *See also* Obesity
    causes of, 209–210
    defined, 213
Ovolactovegetarians, 194
Oxycodone, 355

P
Pantothenic acid, 164t
Parasitic STIs, 314–315
    pubic lice, 314
    scabies, 314
    trichomoniasis, 314–315
Parental relationship stages, 239–241
    after college (extended visit), 241
    before college, 240
    during college, 240–241
Parenthood, 291
Passive resistance, 386–387
PCP (phencyclidine hydrochloride), 352
Peer relationships, 241–244
    group projects, 242–243
    roommates, 243–244

Pelvic inflammatory disease (PID), 293, 296, 299
  chlamydia and, 293
  gonorrhea and, 296
  transmission and symptoms of, 299, 310t
  treatment of, 299
Pelvis floor muscles, 77
Penis, 272, 274
Perineum, 271
Peripheral vascular disease, 120
Pernicious anemia, 426
Personal fitness. *See* Fitness
Personal safety, 383–384
  on campus, tips for, 384
  in car, tips for, 384
  elements for a crime to take place, 383
  at home, tips for, 383
Phencyclidine hydrochloride (PCP), 352
Phenolic acids, 169t, 452t
Phosphorus, 166t
Physical activity, 61–63. *See also* Exercise
  aging and, 140–141, 140t
  benefits of, 62f
  CVD and, 116f
  in exercise session, 71–72
  Food Guide Pyramid and, 187
  guidelines, 62f
  importance of, 61–63
  I.Q. quiz, 103–104
  as key to healthy lifestyle, 111–112
  life expectancy and, 109–111, 109f
  moderate, 62
  popular forms of, 210f
  program, components of, 73
  stroke prevented by, 127
  vigorous, 62–63
  for weight loss, 216, 217t
Physical Activity and Health: A Report of the Surgeon General. See Surgeon General's Report
Physical dimension of wellness, 2f, 3
Physical inactivity
  as cardiac risk factor, 63–64, 111, 114, 128
  CVD risk and, 114, 128
  vs. physical activity in older men, 140t
Physiological adaptations, 76
PID. *See* Pelvic inflammatory disease (PID)
The pill, 285

Pipe smoking, 343
Plant stanols/sterols, 169t
Plateau, in female sexual response, 272
PMS (premenstrual syndrome), 278, 350, 449
PNF (proprioceptive neuromuscular facilitation), 84
Poisoning, 378
Polydextrose, 169t
Polyneuritis, 339
Polyols, 169t
Polyunsaturated fats, 159
Polyunsaturated fatty acids, 168t
Portion size, 40
Posterior muscles, 79f
Potassium, 166t, 169t
Pragma, 248
Prayer and spirituality, 455
Prebiotics, 169t
Precontemplation, in SCM, 6, 9f
Pregnancy, 279–291
  caffeine use during, 349
  nutrients for, 156
  STIs and, 281
  trimesters of, 279–281, 280f
Pregnancy prevention, 282–291
  barrier methods, 283–285
  hormonal methods, 285–290
  natural methods, 282–283
Premenstrual syndrome (PMS), 278, 350, 449
Prenatal development of fetus, 279–281, 280f
Preparation, in SCM, 6, 9f
Prepared foods, sensible choices of, 162
Prescription drugs, 329–371, 354–357
  danger from, 355
  depressants, 355
  ethical considerations of illicit use of, 356
  FDA guidelines on how to use, 357
  opioid pain relievers, 354–355
  stimulants, 355
Prescription nootropics, 356
Pre-stretch, in exercise session, 71
Primary prevention, 9
Probiotics, 169t, 451
Proprioceptive neuromuscular facilitation (PNF), 84
Prostate cancer, screening guidelines for detecting, 420f

Protein/meats and beans, 159, 161, 184–185
  essential amino acids, 159, 161
  non-essential amino acids, 159
  on Nutrition Facts Label, 193f
  ounce equivalent in, 185
  RDA of, 184
  sensible choices for good health, 162
  soy, 170t
Psychedelics. *See* Hallucinogens
Psychological abuse, 388
Pubic lice, 314
Public safety, 380–381
Pulmonary ventilation, 67
Push-up Test, 101

Q
Qi, 446, 447
Qi gong, 446, 456
Quickening, 281

R
Race/ethnicity. *See also* African Americans; Hispanics/Latinos
  CAM and, 441–442
  diabetes and, 423, 424f
  lupus and, 427
  obesity and, 129f
Radiation, as cancer treatment, 413
Rape
  acquaintance, 387–388
  on college campuses, 386
  definition of, 386
  prevention strategies, 387, 395–398
  resisting, 386–387
  safety tips, 387
  statistics, 386
  steps to take if rape occurs, 388
Rating of perceived exertion scale (RPE), 68, 70, 70t
Real age test, 141
Recovery, in weight training, 77
Recovery heart rate, 75
Rectum and colon cancer, 420f, 422
Reflexology, 448
Reiki, 456
Relationship report card, 263–265
Relationships, 235–267
  abusive, 254, 254t, 267
  affection in, 261
  communication in, 261
  dating and, 247–251
  ending, 251–252

friendships, 244–246
healthy, 236–239, 261
Internet, 245–246
loving, elements of, 252
marriage and, 252–253
perfect mate, qualities of, 257
stages of, 247–253
successful, tips for, 248
types of, 239–244
unhealthy, 253–254
Relationship types, 239–244
parental relationship stages, 239–241
peer relationships, 241–244
Repetition, in weight training, 77
Repetition-maximum, in weight training, 77
Repetitive strain injury, 380
Reproduction, 277–292
abortion, 292
adoption, 291
eggs, from fertilization to implantation, 278, 278f, 279f
endometrial cycle, 278, 279
menstrual cycle, 277–278, 277f
ovarian cycle, 278, 278f
parenthood, 291
pregnancy, 279–291
Resolution, in female sexual response, 272
Resorption, 136
Respiratory system, 67
Restaurant foods. See Fast foods/ eating out
Reversibility, in fitness training, 73
Reward systems, 8
Riboflavin, 164t
RICE, 84
Ritalin, 355
Rockport one-mile walk test, 74, 74t
Rohypnol (roofies), 351–352
Roofies (Rohypnol), 351–352
Roommates, 243–244
RPE (rating of perceived exertion scale), 68, 70, 70t

S

Safety awareness, 373–402
bicycle safety, 377–378
college campuses, 384–385
environmental safety, 388–389
Family Emergency Plan, 393–394
home safety, 378–379
motorcycle safety, 376–377

motor vehicle safety, 374–377
natural disasters, 380
personal safety, 383–384
public safety, 380–381
sexual violence, 386–388
sports injuries, 380, 381
unintentional injuries, classes of, 374–377
water safety, 380
workplace safety, 380
St. John's wort, 449, 450f
Sarcomas, 412
Saturated fats, 158
Saw palmetto, 449
Scabies, 314
Schizophrenia, 37
Scrotum, 272
Secondary prevention, 9
Secondhand smoke, 345
Selenium, 166t, 169t
Self-talk
defined, 35
negative vs. positive, 35–36
stress reduced by, 35–36
Self-worth, positive, 236
Seminal vesicle, 273
Seminiferous tubules, 272
Semivegetarians, 194
Serving size, 192, 193f
Set, in weight training, 77
Set-point theory, 212
7 Metrics of Cardiovascular Health, 114, 114f
Sex
offenders, registering, 385
rules about sexual health, 247
safe sex activities, rating, 250
Sexual arousal
female response to, 270, 272
male response to, 273, 274
Sexuality, 269–327
female sexual anatomy, 270–272
hepatitis risk assessment, 327
male sexual anatomy, 272–274
readiness for sexual activity, 275–276
reproduction, 277–292
sexual orientation, 274–275
STIs, 292–316
Sexually transmitted infections (STIs), 292–316
attitudes about, 325–326
bacterial, 293–303
common, 310–312t, 313t
condoms and, 283
hepatitis risk assessment, 327

parasitic, 314–315
pregnancy and, 281
prevention of, 315–316
rates for contracting, 301f
risk, levels of, 293
risk sheet, 296f
viral, 304–309, 313–314
Sexual orientation, 274–275
Sexual violence, 386–388. See also Rape
Shape Up America!, 138
Shiatsu, 447
Shin splints, 85t
Sickle-cell anemia, 426
Side stitch, 85t
Silicone cup (Femcap), 284
Simple carbohydrates, 158
Skill-related fitness, 63
Skin cancer, 413, 415–417
basal cell carcinoma, 413
malignant melanoma, 413, 415, 417
moles, distinguishing from melanoma, 417
preventing, 417
risk factors for, 415
squamous cell carcinoma, 413
Sun Protection Factor, 417
Skin self-exam (SSE), 416, 417
SLE (systemic lupus erythematosus), 426
Sleep
holistic self-care and, 441
hypertension in teens and, 120
National Sleep Foundation (NSF), 375, 376
Stanford Sleep Disorders Clinic, 376
Smokeless tobacco, 342–344
cancer and, 342, 344
forms of, 342
leukoplakia and, 342
Smoking cessation, 345–347
"Do You Want to Quit?" test, 365
effects of, 345, 346f
lung cancer and, 417
programs for, 121
six-point program, 371
steps in, 345, 346
Snuff, 342. See also Smokeless tobacco
Social dimension of wellness, 2f, 3
Sodium, 166, 166t, 193f
Soluble fiber, 157, 168t
Somatic movement, 456
Soy protein, 170t

Special K or K (ketamine hydrochloride), 352
Specificity, in fitness training, 72
Sperm, 273–274
SPF (Sun Protection Factor), 417
Spinal manipulation. *See* Chiropractic care
Spiritual health
   holistic self-care and, 441
   prayer and, 455
   wellness and, 2f, 3
Sports injuries, 380, 381
Squamous cell carcinomas, 413
SSE (skin self-exam), 416, 417
Stages of Change Model (SCM), 5–6, 9f
Stalking, 385
Stand2Learn, 131
Stanford Sleep Disorders Clinic, 376
Stanol/sterol esters, 169t
Static stretching exercises, 84
Sterilization, 290
Stimulants, 348–352
   amphetamines, 350
   caffeine, 348–349
   cocaine, 350
   GHB, 352
   methamphetamines, 350–351
   prescription drugs, 355
Stinging nettle, 449
STIs. *See* Sexually transmitted infections (STIs)
Storge, 248
Strength training, 73
Stress, 29–58. *See also* Mental health disorders
   CVD and, 128
   defined, 30
   distress, 30
   eustress, 30
   heart and, 65
   managers, characteristics of good, 35f
   manifestation of, 31–32
   self-talk to reduce, 35–36
   Stress Journal, 51
   Student Stress Scale, 34–35, 34f
   Time Budget Sheet, 49
   wellness and, 29–35
Stressors
   in college students, 32–33, 32f
   managing, 31–35, 31f
   reconizing, 32, 35
Stretching exercises, 83–84
   ballistic, 83–84
   PNF, 84
   static, 84

Stroke, 123, 126–127
   "ABCS" of prevention, 113
   in African Americans, 126–127
   causes of, 126–127, 127f
   exercise and, 126
   ischemic, 126
   symptoms/warning signs of, 126
Stroke volume, 65
Student Stress Scale, 34–35, 34f
Substance Abuse and Mental Health Services Administration (SAMHSA), 350
Sugar alcohols, 169t
Suicidal behavior, 38–39
Sulfides/thiols, 170t, 452t
Sulforaphane, 169t
Sun Protection Factor (SPF), 416
Super-sized meals, 222, 224
Support groups, 8–9
Surgeon General's Report
   activity recommendations, 61, 64, 109–110, 112
   caffeine intake during pregnancy, 349
   childhood obesity as epidemic, 130
   cigarette smoking, 127, 341
   family health problems, record of, 128
   Healthy People, 11, 13
   Healthy People 2020 and, 11–12
   inactivity as cardiac risk factor, 64, 114, 128
   mental health disorders, 36
   Physical Activity and Health, 36, 64, 64f, 109, 110, 112, 114, 128
   Shape Up America!, 138
Surgery, as cancer treatment, 413
Sustainability, 388–389
Syphilis, 299, 301, 304f
   rates by age among men 15–44, 303f
   rates by age among women 15–44, 302f
   rates by state, 303f
   reported cases and rates by state, 300t
   stages of, 299, 301
   transmission and symptoms of, 299, 301, 312t
   treatment of, 301
Systemic lupus erythematosus (SLE), 426
Systolic blood pressure, 65, 121, 121f

T
Talk test, 68, 70
Tar, 341
Target heart rate range, 63, 68–70, 69f
TB (tuberculosis), 404–405
Tendinitis, 85t
Tension phase, in abusive relationship, 254
Tertiary prevention, 9
Testes, 272
Testicles, 272
Testicular cancer, 421–422
Testicular self-exam (TSE), 421–422
Tetrahydrocannabinol (THC), 347
Texas A&M University
   bone loss during spaceflight, 137
   Health Science Center, 131
   Office of Sustainability, 388–389
Therapeutic touch, 457
Thiamin, 164t
Thrombosis, 126, 127, 345
Time, in FITT exercise regimen, 70
Time killers, common, 33f
Tobacco, 341–347. *See also* Cigarette smoking
   clove cigarettes, 343
   components, 341–342
   environmental tobacco smoke, 345
   pipe and cigar smoking, 343
   resources for more information on, 347
   smokeless, 342–344
   types of use, 342–344
Tolerance, 333
TOM. *See* Traditional oriental medicine (TOM)
Tornadoes, 381
Toxoplasma gondii, 405
Traditional oriental medicine (TOM), 446–447
   acupressure, 447
   acupuncture, 446–447
   defined, 446
   shiatsu, 447
Trans fats, 158, 192
Trichomoniasis, 314–315
Triglyceride levels, 116, 119, 120, 121f, 128
Trimesters of pregnancy, 279–281, 280f
Trust, in relationships, 239
TSE (testicular self-exam), 421–422

Tubal ligation, 290
Tuberculosis (TB), 404–405
2C-B, 351
Type, in FITT exercise regimen, 70–71
Type I diabetes, 423, 424
Type II diabetes, 423, 424

U

Ulcers, 427
Ultraviolet (UV) rays, 413
Unhealthy relationships, 253–254
  abusive, 254, 254t, 267
  signs of, 253–254
Uniform Crime Report (FBI), 333
Unintentional injuries, classes of, 374–377. *See also* Safety awareness
U.S. Coast Guard, 380
U.S. Department of Agriculture (USDA)
  Dietary Guidelines for Americans, 112, 154
  Food Guide Pyramid, 172, 173f
U.S. Fire Administration, 379
Unsaturated fats, 158–159
Urethra, 270–271
USFDA Center for Food Safety and Applied Nutrition, 450
Uterine cancer, screening guidelines for detecting, 420f
UV (ultraviolet) rays, 413

V

Vagina, 271
Vaginal ring, 286
Vas deferens, 273, 290
Vasectomy, 290
Vegans, 194
Vegetables, 177–179
  cup equivalent of, 178–179
  RDA of, 177
Vegetarianism, 194–195
Vigorous activities, 62–63
Viral STIs, 304–309, 313–314
  genital herpes, 304–305
  hepatitis B, 309, 312, 313–314
  HIV/AIDS, 305
  HPV, 306, 308–309
Vision, alcohol use and abuse and, 331
Vitamins, 163, 164–166, 167
  A, 164t, 166t, 170t, 177
  B1, 170t
  B2, 170t

B3, 170t
B5, 170t
B6, 164t, 170t
B9, 170t
B12, 164t, 170t, 182, 426
in biological-based therapies, 451
C, 164t, 166t, 171t, 177, 180
D, 164t, 171t
E, 163, 164t, 166t, 167, 171t
excess amounts of, effect of, 165t
facts about, 164t
fat-soluable, 163, 164t
in fruits, 180
functional, 170–171t
K, 164t
megadoses of, adverse effects of, 219
on Nutrition Facts Label, 193f
in vegetables, 177
water-soluable, 163, 164t
VO₂ Max, 74
Vulva, 270

W

Waist measurement as indicator of health risks, 213
Waist-to-hip ratio, 117f, 118, 128, 135
Warm-up, in exercise session, 71
Water, 171–172
  dehydration and, 89, 171–172
Water intoxication, 88–89
Water pipes, 343, 344
Water safety, 380
Water-soluable vitamins, 163, 164t
Weight gain, healthy, 224
Weight loss
  bariatric surgery and, 211
  behavior modification and, 216
  countdown to, 216t
  dieting and, 216, 217–218
  `halo' effect, 211
  leptin and, 218
  physical activity needed for, 216, 217t
  questionnaire, 223
  recommended, 215–216
  successful, guidelines and tips for, 219, 221
  walking combined with cutting calories and, 216t
Weight loss products/ programs, 220
  appetite suppressants, 220

clinical/nonclinical, 220
low-carbohydrate high-protein, 220, 221–222
metabolism boosters, 220
Weight management, 207–233.
    See also Healthy habits
  body composition and, 213
  caloric balance and, 209f
  healthy body weight and, 212–213
  physical activity in, 213, 214
  super-sized meals and, 222, 224
Weight training. *See also* Muscular fitness
  beginning, guidelines for, 81f
  definitions used in, 77
  vs. functional movement, 76
  muscular endurance increased by, 75
  myths, 80, 82
Wellness
  defined, 2
  dimensions of, 2–4, 2f
  factors influencing, 4, 5f
  financial, 4
  profile, 5, 6
  stress and, 29–35
Wernickes disease, 340
WHO. *See* World Health Organization (WHO)
Whole person systems, 443. *See also* Alternative healthcare systems
Wicking, 87
Withdrawal method, 282
Women
  capable of becoming pregnant, nutrients for, 156
  CVD in who smoke and use hormonal contraceptives, 122, 285, 286, 287
  gonorrhea in, 298f
  myocardial infarction in, *vs.* men, 123
  over-the-counter contraceptives for, 284–285
  pregnant or breastfeeding, nutrients for, 156
  syphilis in, 302f
Workplace safety, 380
Workplace violence, 380
World Health Organization (WHO)
  Alcohol Use Disorders Identification Test, 370
  health defined by, 2
  homeopathy, 445

World Health Organization (cont.)
  obesity classified as disease, 111, 128–129, 210
  survey of legal and illegal drug use, 330
  waterpipe smoking, 344

Y
Yeast, 169t
Yin and yang, 446, 447
Yoga, 455
Yo-yo dieting, 216

Z
Zeaxanthin, 168t
Zero Tolerance Law, 340
Zinc, 166t